THE SHOCHET

A Memoir of Jewish Life in Ukraine and Crimea

Pinkhes-Dov Goldenshteyn

Touro University Press Books

Series Editors
MICHAEL A. SHMIDMAN, PhD (Touro University, New York)
SIMCHA FISHBANE, PhD (Touro University, New York)

THE SHOCHET

A Memoir of Jewish Life in Ukraine and Crimea

Pinkhes-Dov Goldenshteyn

Volume Two

Presented and Translated by Michoel Rotenfeld

LC record available at https://lccn.loc.gov/2023024382
LC ebook record available at https://lccn.loc.gov/2023024383

Published by Touro University Press and Academic Studies Press.
Typeset, printed and distributed by Academic Studies Press.

ISBN 9798887196121 (hardback)
ISBN 9798887196138 (paperback)
ISBN 9798887196152 (epub)

Touro University Press
Michael A. Shmidman and Simcha Fishbane, Editors
3 Times Square, Room 654,
New York, NY 10036
press@touro.edu

Book design by Kryon Publishing Services
Cover design by Ivan Grave.

On the cover: Issachar Ber Ryback, Reznik (1917)
(Source: Wikimedia Commons)

Academic Studies Press
1007 Chestnut St.
Newton, MA 02464, USA
press@academicstudiespress.com
www.academicstudiespress.com

FIGURE 11. A portrait of Pinkhes-Dov Goldenshteyn by his relative, the painter Salomon Bernstein. See Appendix A6 (pp. 746–750) for more details about Bernstein. (Courtesy of Shifra Bernfeld of Petakh-Tikva.)

Contents

Map of Crimea and Southern Ukraine

- The place names used on the map are those used in the text. When differing from its current name, its current name follows in parenthesis.
- For more details about each location see Glossary 3: Geographic Locations in Eastern Europe (pp. 890–899).

PART III

My Forty Years as a *Shoykhet* and Moving to Palestine, 1873–1929

Here in the third part is a description of my life as a *shoykhet*, cantor, and *moyel* in Bakhchisaray, where I resided from 5639 until 5674.[1] At that point, I emigrated from Bakhchisaray to *Erets-Isruel*, hoping to have a peaceful life there.

My life in *Erets-Isruel* is depicted in a separate section—in an addendum to Part III—where I tell of the suffering, the deathly fear, and the exile that I endured there.

Pinkhes Goldenshteyn
(The *Shoykhet* of Bakhchisaray)

---

1 From 1879 until 1913. A *shoykhet* is a kosher slaughterer. Though the word *shoykhet* has been spelled in the text according to the academic standards of transliterating Yiddish words (see "A Note About the Translation," p. xi), the popular spelling of *shochet* has been used in the title.

CHAPTER 22

As the *Shoykhet* of Slobodze, 1873–1875

The Poor Terms of My Contract • Leyb-Yoyls Brings Another *Shoykhet* to Slobodze • Bringing Back the Tolner Rebbe's Certification • The Tolner Rebbe's Response and Letter • Being Harassed by Itsye Kon • Being Harassed by the Influential Slovske • Having to Walk to Kópenke and Tshobritsh • Crossing the Icy Dniester River by Boat • My Encounter with a Wolf • Establishing New Conditions for Use of My Services • The Townsmen Take Me to Rabbinical Court • Carrying Out the Rabbinical Ruling

First, I want to describe the work that the *shoykhet* had to do in Slobodze every day. Even if he were an angel, he would not have been able to meet everyone's demands, particularly the demands of the coarse individuals who knew me since childhood, as mentioned earlier.

The village was extremely long—it stretched out over four to five *versts*, and the thirty Jewish families there were spread out over its entire length.[1] The *shoykhet* had to live in the village center so that no one would be unfairly farther or closer than the other. The village did not have a butcher shop, so whoever purchased a calf or a lamb had it slaughtered at his home.[2] The *shoykhet* had to walk to the customers' homes to do the slaughtering. In the summer, the *shoykhet* was particularly busy when the young lambs came of age and everyone was buying them. The owners would use the forequarters of the animal for

---

1 The author writes on p. 412 below that Slobodze was over six to seven *versts* long, and he writes later on p. 440 that it was seven to eight *versts* long.

2 The purchaser would then sell to others the meat he could not use for himself.

themselves and would sell the hindquarters for next to nothing because all they needed were the hides and the kosher forequarters.[3]

Since you now know all of this, I will draw your attention to something else. They wrote my contract as follows: Each household was obligated to pay me a weekly stipend, everyone according to his means, ranging from ten to twenty *kopeks* a week—meaning that some would pay ten, others fifteen, and still others twenty *kopeks*, which was the most anyone paid. In return, the *shoykhet* had to slaughter poultry at no charge for everyone and would receive three *kopeks* for each lamb slaughtered, twenty *kopeks* for a young sheep, and thirty *kopeks* for a cow, whether it turned out to be kosher or *treyf*. This "exemplary" contract added up to an income of three and a half rubles a week, apart from the income from the additional slaughtering fees, which was calculated to be two and a half rubles a week. That meant that the *shoykhet* earned a total of six rubles a week, apart from other sources of income: tips for *kapores*, gifts for Purim and Hanukah, payment on the eve of Yom Kippur for leading the services on the High Holidays, and another two rubles a week for reading the Torah. Undoubtedly this would have been a good place for a young man who had suffered as much as I had, and I should have considered myself lucky.

I did not compose the terms of the contract; these were the terms that had been used from time immemorial, so these same terms were used for me without any innovations. I did not like the contract because I understood that it was not a good idea that the *shoykhet* had to collect his wages from each household separately—making the rounds week after week trying to claim his stipend. But I had to agree because those were the terms set previously, and I understood that I would not be able to do any better if I did not accept the first point in the contract regarding the weekly stipend. I assumed that since the previous *shokhtim* had made a living, I would certainly be able to do so as well. I did not have time to ask how they had managed because, living as I was in great want, I thanked God for the little that I now had. Regarding the future, God is a Father and He would certainly not abandon me. So I remained the *shoykhet* there.

I arrived in Slobodze in Adar of 5632 [*sic*].[4] My infant son Srul-Burekhl was by then already three months old.[5] They treated me nicely since I was their

3 Jewish law prohibits the eating of a kosher ruminant animal's sciatic nerve and certain fats found in the hindquarters. See Genesis 32:33 and *Shulkhan Arukh* (*Yoreh Deah* 65). Since they are labor intensive to remove, Jews generally sell the hindquarters to non-Jews and eat only the forequarters.

4 The author did not arrive in Slobodze in *Adar* of 5632 (February-March 1872), but rather in *Adar* of 5633 (March 1873), as is evident from the sequence of events until this point.

5 Srul-Burekhl is a diminutive form of Isruel-Burekh.

new *shoykhet* and they enjoyed the way I led the services, read from the Torah, and read the *Megilla* on Purim.[6] I particularly remember Purim that year and the generous gifts of food they gave me and how everyone willingly gave me their weekly stipend exactly as specified on the list I was given.[7] Though it turned out to be quite embarrassing going around collecting it like a pauper, at least the effort was not in vain. Nonetheless, I was asked to slaughter very few lambs and only once a week would someone request that I slaughter a calf. Everyone simply continued to have me slaughter chickens and geese, thereby sparing them from having to pay a single *kopek* more than the ten to fifteen *kopeks* which I collected as my stipend.

I thought that they would continue to pay their stipends on time. What I did not know was that they were only paying their weekly stipends now, when they had a lot of poultry to slaughter; they did not have to pay anything extra to have fowl slaughtered. I also did not know that the *shokhtim* in Slobodze had never licked honey there, something which I only discovered at this point.

My landlord, Reb Itskhok Kon, and his family had very much befriended me, and they appeared to me to be good people.[8] I did not realize that he and his family were the first to badmouth each *shoykhet*, and that one needed to guard oneself against them and not benefit from their good neighborliness because their compassion was actually cruelty. At first, I warmly accepted their goodwill and thought more highly of them than of anyone else in the village, including the wealthy and influential Mendl Slovske. Even though Slovske's weekly stipend was larger than anyone else's, I valued the Kon family more than him. These particular two families were the heads of the village, and everyone else would sing to their tunes. As I quickly learned, if one was ever searching for impudent people, one could find among these villagers the best and the finest, the likes of whom could not even be found in the large cities. So if the head of one of these two families began to wage war against the *shoykhet*, agitators would immediately appear from all sides and spew all sorts of slander, resulting in a commotion surrounding the *shoykhet*. The *shoykhet* would have trouble from all sides, and he would be shamed and disgraced by each and every impudent person. "Why?" you might ask. There was no reason. That was just how it had to be, for no reason at all. I only became aware of all of this—that the *shoykhet*'s peace and quiet was solely dependent on those two families—after a

---

6 March 13, 1873.

7 On Purim, every Jew is obliged to send to at least one other person two gifts of food and those who send many such gifts are to be praised (*Kitsur Shulkhan Arukh* 142:1–4).

8 Spelled כהן (pronounced Kohen in Modern Hebrew) in the original, this surname was likely pronounced in that area as Kon (Kohn).

short while, and, once I learned this, I devoted all of my energy to accommodate them, as you will read further on.

Reb Kon played a pious Hasidic role, though he was coarse.[9] Looking at him, you would see what appeared to be a Hasid through and through, and he would even run to the *mikveh* periodically.[10] He had no children but he had a wife who was a devoted follower of the Tolner Rebbe, and she was also very coarse.[11] His mother-in-law, Ester, and her other son-in-law, Leyb-Yoyls, were also part of the family.[12] This Leyb-Yoyls was a renowned Talmudic scholar with an impressive breadth of knowledge; he was a devout Tolner Hasid as well—one of the Tolner Rebbe's closest Hasidim. His elderly mother-in-law was very proud of him, and the Kon family mirrored her opinion. Reb Itsye Kon's household was considered the preeminent Hasidic house in the village, and the Tolner *minyan* was also held at his house. Everyone would go to pray at his house on *Shobes* and *Yontef.* After the morning services, he would provide alcoholic beverages for *Kiddush*, and a bite to eat. Therefore, all who prayed there sided with him, particularly since he supported the *minyan* at his own expense and had his own Torah scroll. Naturally, the *shoykhet* had to pray at Kon's *minyan* on *Shobes*, even though there was another *minyan* at the other end of the village (though it had fewer people, and they were even coarser than those at Kon's *minyan*).

The other *minyan* was at the house of the wealthy Mendl Slovske, who had a wife who was a devout follower of the Savráner Rebbe.[13] In fact, because of her, Slovske considered himself a Savraner Hasid. Not only was Slovske an extremely coarse person, but he was conceited and vain. He would also supply his crowd with good drink and feed them all so that they would come to pray at his house, which he did only out of envy of the Kon family. The rivalry between Slovske and Kon was the root of all the strife regarding the *shokhtim* in Slobodze, since the *shoykhet* could in no way, shape, or form satisfy both of

---

9 Since the title Reb in Yiddish normally precedes a personal name and not a surname as done here, perhaps the author writes "Reb Kon" in sarcasm.

10 In many Hasidic communities, the men go to the *mikveh* before morning prayers almost on a daily basis. See Wertheim (1992:102–105) on the significance of the *mikveh* in Hasidic life.

11 A "devoted follower" is the translation of the word *Khside*, the feminine form of Hasid, in the original Yiddish. Though not used in the Yiddish vernacular, *Khside* is occasionally used in written Yiddish. Nonetheless, among today's Hasidim, a Hasidic woman is often called a *Khsideste* (חסידטע).

12 Leyb-Yoyls indicates that Leyb was the son-in-law of a man named Yoyl, as indicated on p. 408. In ch. 24, p. 488, the author indicates that Leyb's surname was Fishman.

13 The Savraner Rebbe, Rabbi Duvid Giterman (died 1912), was the brother of the Chechelniker Rebbe, Rabbi Moyshe Giterman (ca. 1838–1870), mentioned in ch. 7, p. 157. He was also a second cousin to the Bendérer Rebbe, Rabbi Itskhok "Itsikl" Vertheym (ca. 1848–1911), mentioned in ch. 21, p. 370 (Assaf, 1974:82).

them. It did not matter what the *shoykhet* did: if he went to Kon's *minyan*, then Slovske's *minyan* would become incensed; if he went to Slovske's *minyan*, then Kon's *minyan* would become infuriated. But the wrath of Kon's *minyan* was more dangerous than Slovske's. Kon's side was more powerful since it included the very learned Leyb-Yoyls, mentioned above, who could report the *shoykhet* to the Rebbe in Tolne, and the *shoykhet* would then be finished—forever, God forbid. For that reason, the previous *shokhtim* had prayed only at Kon's house and preferred to suffer at the hands of Slovske's side, knowing that they would not suffer much from Slovske himself because he was a busy person occupied with his business matters. On the other hand, Reb Kon was the exact opposite of Slovske. Kon was constantly at home and had plenty of time to hear slander and gossip. When someone would come to incite him against the *shoykhet*, he could be found relaxing at home along with his wife, Sheyndele, and his elderly mother-in-law. And those three could incite their Talmudic scholar, the Hasid, the said Reb Leyb, to cause a commotion reaching the higher and lower heavenly spheres at the *minyan*, and thereby bring about the *shoykhet*'s downfall.

Naturally, the previous *shokhtim* had all been terrified of the wrath of the Kon family, so they always attended their *minyan*, sang their song, and flattered them. Once I realized all this through hearsay, intuition, and my own observations, I decided to go the way of compromise with both families by attending one *Shobes* at Kon's and the next at Slovske's. I also did the same regarding *Yontef*. This pleased everyone except myself because I had to walk so far, resulting in my not having any rest on *Shobes* and *Yontef*. But I did this for the sake of peace. I became friends with the Hasid, Reb Leyb-Yoyls, so that he would not have anything against me. I did not mind his telling me that he wanted to test me in the laws of *sh'khita* to see if I knew them, and I allowed him to test me. He then said that we should study together the laws of *sh'khita* and *treyfes*, because he wanted to learn them with a *shoykhet* so that he could better understand their practical aspects.[14] I did not mind studying with him, although he insisted that the sessions take place at his home. I should have refused to study with him there, since it did not befit me and was not befitting for the community.[15] Nonetheless, I agreed because I saw that his true intention in asking me to study in his home was just a ruse to give him the opportunity to stir up a quarrel against me, the new *shoykhet*, for he had assumed that

---

14 *Treyfes* denotes animals that have been slaughtered and then discovered to be *treyf*, meaning halakhically unfit for consumption due to certain irregularities in the animal's internal organs.

15 Perhaps it was not befitting for the community because it was not honorable for someone in his position to be subjected to an individual's demands.

I would definitely refuse him. So I decided to agree and yield for the sake of peace, and peace lasted until after *Shvues.*[16]

After *Shvues*, Reb Leyb's true intentions became apparent: he desired that I too should become a Tolner Hasid. "Why shouldn't you become a Tolner Hasid?" he asked me. "It's an embarrassment for us to have a *Chabadnik* as a *shoykhet.* How can such a thing go on here? You should know that if you don't take my advice, you'll regret it." Naturally, I laughed at his words and said, "What type of an embarrassment is it that I'm not a Tolner Hasid? Does the concept of *sh'khita* depend on being a certain type of Hasid? Is a very learned, religious, God-fearing *shoykhet* who is not a Tolner Hasid unfit to be a *shoykhet,* God forbid?! And if the *shoykhet* is not a learner, not a God-fearing person, and not an expert in *sh'khita* but he has the one worthy quality of being a Tolner Hasid, then is he fine and good?! God forbid! Are you, Reb Leyb, so misguided as to think that way?"

He replied, "I don't want to argue with you. But I'm telling you that if you don't become a Tolner Hasid, you'll regret it."

From that day onwards, our friendship ended. When I would come to study with him as we had agreed upon, I began to notice that my presence was no longer tolerated in his house. So I stopped going to him, and he did not even ask me why I stopped coming.

Little by little, I noticed hatred spewing from the family of Itskhok Kon, Leyb-Yoyls's brother-in-law. Just like Leyb was called Yoyls, referring to his late father-in-law Yoyl, Itskhok was called Itsye-Yoyls. When the Kon family began to hate me too, I knew that a new life was now starting for me as a *shoykhet.* In such a situation, one would have had to begin using flattery and deception, and I knew that it would not be good for me if I did not do so. But by nature I am not a flatterer, God forbid. I hate lies with a passion. And I won't be two-faced even if it would cost me my life. Consequently, they became greatly incensed. I spoke frankly and told them that there was no way that they could cause me to do any of these three things: flatter, lie, or be two-faced. And in case they would wrong me, I have an almighty God in whom I place my trust. God would help me if I remained truthful. Even if I suffered, it would not bother me, as long as my conscience was pure. I would not be anyone's insincere follower, just like I am not an insincere Jew, God forbid, and I will always say the truth without flattery.

Itsye-Yoyls's household then began to torment me. They began by seeking out my faults, and then advanced to finding transgressions as well. Since I was their neighbor, they were able to find my faults easily, and they found some

---

16 June 1–2, 1873.

minor transgressions too, which they spread throughout the village in order to undo me and oust me from my position. In the meantime, both women in the Kon house—Itsye-Yoyls's wife and mother-in-law—provoked and agitated the village's Jewish populace against me. My greatest sin was that I was not a Tolner Hasid and did not believe in the Tolner Rebbe and in his miracles.[17] Another transgression was my not going to the *mikveh* at least once a week, which was a sign that I was a *misnaged,* God forbid. Yet another sin: who ever heard of a half-year passing without the *shoykhet* traveling to a Hasidic Rebbe or at the very least sending a *pidyen* to his Rebbe? But listen closely for more: who ever heard of a *shoykhet* holding his baby in his hands when he prayed or studied Torah? Since we were neighbors, they were able to observe me as I took my crying baby in my arms while I was praying or studying. This would happen when my wife was not home, and I had to calm my child down. But to them this was certainly a sin—for obviously the baby could not keep himself clean.[18] They found additional transgressions and faults in me: I was not compliant enough, I would never give in to anyone, and everything had to be done my way. Another one of my faults was that, unlike the other *shokhtim,* I never went to anyone's house to spend time with them and relate stories of the miracles performed by the Rebbe; instead, I was always at home with my wife. In addition, I did not drink, and a Hasidic Jew needed to drink a little liquor. In short, I was full of faults and transgressions, which were discussed and amplified in the *minyan* at Kon's house.

At first, they spoke about me quietly so that I would not hear, but they later let loose and gossiped all over the village. From mouth to mouth, the talk about me became exaggerated and barbed, until a few impudent people began to attack me by showing off their knowledge of all my sins. Of course, they had gotten drunk at Itsye-Yoyls's, who—to fan the flames of hate—did not spare the refreshments even during the week, and especially not after prayer services

---

17 It is common for Hasidim (particularly in the past) not to think highly of Rebbes other than their own. Pinkhas Minkovsky, "Mi-sefer khayai," *Reshumot* 1 (1918): 97–122; 2 (1922): 125–158; 4 (1926): 123–144; 5 (1927): 145–160; 6 (1930): 71–100. Mekler (1931:197–199) relates that the Tolner Rebbe (Rabbi Duvid Tversky) and the Sadigorer Rebbe (Rabbi Avrum-Yankev Fridman) once exchanged stories in which each praised the other's Hasidim for displaying devotion to their own Rebbe while showing a complete lack of interest in other Rebbes. Chabad Hasidim, in particular, were known for showing relatively little interest in the miracle stories of even their own Rebbes, for they were much more interested in studying their Rebbes' Hasidic discourses. As was said regarding the second Rebbe of Chabad, Rabbi Dov-Ber of Lubavitch (1773–1827), "Miracles were rolling around him but no one wanted to pick them up" (Rabbi Y. Y. Schneersohn, *Igrot-Kodesh,* 2:376).

18 According to Jewish law, one may not study Torah or pray in the presence of excrement, including that of an infant (*Kitsur Shulkhan Arukh* 5:1–5).

at his *minyan* on *Shobes* and *Yontef*. When I noticed the behavior of his family, the first thing I did was to move out of his residence and rent another place in the village, from a Walachian.[19] I now did not have to constantly look at them and they could not as easily send brazen people to yell at me, and they would be unable to track my every move.

It became so bad that I could not even speak with my wife at home, because they crept about my windows at night to hear and see the goings-on. You can imagine the size of my home—it consisted of only one room which served as an entrance hall, hallway, parlor, dining room, bedroom, and kitchen, too; so it was impossible to conceal even one word from them. I would pour out my heart to my wife at home, and the next day everyone would know what I had said. At first, I did not know how it happened, but afterward I learned that they were constantly standing about outside our windows where they heard everything that was said. Consequently, I moved my residence away from their prying eyes.

This fanned the flames, and they now grew even angrier, so I stopped going to their *minyan* and began going to Slovske's—or, better said, to the *potshtar*'s, meaning the mail keeper, as some called him. I would go there every *Shobes*. The mail keeper was Itsye-Yoyls's competitor, and they were sworn enemies. Naturally, he was happy with this turn of events and greatly reveled in it.

When Itsye-Yoyls saw that I had left his *minyan*, he became even more furious. Especially enraged was his brother-in-law Leyb-Yoyls, the Talmudic scholar, even though he was actually pleased that I no longer came to his *minyan* because he could now lead the services and also read the Torah. He was well-off and did not perform these functions for the extra income that they provided as I did. He carried them out because of the honor they brought his brother-in-law Itsye, his sister-in-law, and his mother-in-law. And now everyone learned that he truly possessed all these excellent qualities: he was a Hasid and he granted the congregation the honor of his leading the services. So you can imagine that my absence did not bother him at all and also provided him with good material which would serve him in his agitations against me among the local Jews. Since their *minyan* had always been the primary *minyan*, and since the *shoykhet* had always attended their *minyan*, it was obvious that the *shoykhet* was causing them to lose their influence. The *shoykhet* was not listening to them and was going to the mail keeper's *minyan*. How could they allow that? Well, since the *shoykhet* was causing them to lose control of the village, they would cause him to lose his position.

---

19 A Walachian means a Romanian. The United Principalities of Moldavia and Walachia, which were autonomous but still vassals of the Ottoman Empire, were only officially named Romania in 1866. See also ch. 10, p. 184, footnote 11.

In short, things were heating up and they were making a big to-do regarding the *shoykhet.* The slander about me was now reaching the city of Tiraspol too, but the Tiraspolers made little of it—they knew me and they knew them. In town, their slander actually had the opposite of its intended effect: the Tiraspolers put them to shame and rebuked them for treating me badly. They went on to explain to them that Slobodze had gotten hold of a fine *shoykhet* but did not know how to appreciate him. Nonetheless, the effect of their words on those Slobodzer scoundrels only lasted until their return home, where they promptly forgot the good words of the Tiraspolers and continued to carry out the agitators' schemes. I was constantly tormented like this. I was poor and was persecuted from all sides. You can now understand the life—the bad luck—that I had in Slobodze. There was absolutely no difference between my previous life and my current one, except that now I did not have to wander around anymore and be separated from my wife and child. We lived and suffered together, sat at our own table, and were even able to give a hungry person something to eat. Yes, I struggled to earn my daily bread, but I accepted these difficulties with love. It was better than being separated from my family and better than eating at my in-laws'. If God wanted to, He could turn those who hated me for no reason into friends. This is how we would console ourselves.

Meanwhile, the summer ended and the High Holidays were approaching.[20] They began campaigning against permitting the *shoykhet* to lead the services on Rosh Hashanah and Yom Kippur. They would seek to hire someone else to do so in order to hurt me financially. At that time, I had never led the High Holiday services anywhere, so I made little of it because I was afraid of leading those services. In short, they could not find anyone to hire because they would only pay a total of thirty rubles, so Leyb-Yoyls led *Shakhris* at no charge and, by force of circumstance, they had to resort to me to lead *Musaf* and only paid me twenty rubles, thinking that they were being overly generous.[21] I was such a success during the High Holidays that some changed their minds about me, but it did not last long before they were persuaded once again to continue persecuting me.

I lived like this in Slobodze for a year, during which I did not have a life. I worked extremely hard with superhuman strength. I had no rest, neither by day nor by night, and on top of that I suffered harassment from enemies who hated me for no reason. The only things keeping me going were my wife's devotion

20 Rosh Hashanah occurred on September 22–23, 1873.

21 *Shakhris* is the morning prayers. *Musaf* is an additional prayer recited in the morning, directly after *Shakhris* on *Shabes* and most Jewish holidays.

and my dedication to my child, without which I would have run to wherever my eyes would have led me as long as I no longer had to look at such wicked people.

You will find it puzzling why I had so much work in such a small village that I had to work day and night, so I will explain it to you. The actual *sh'khita* work was only for an hour a day at the most, but that would have been the case if one was slaughtering the animals in a slaughterhouse or in a courtyard. But *sh'khita* there was neither at a set time nor a set place. In Slobodze, if someone wanted to have an animal slaughtered and sell off the meat like a butcher, he would buy a lamb and then send for the *shoykhet* to come to his house. Do not forget that the village was six to seven *versts* long and that the Jewish houses were spread out along the entire length of the village. So when someone at one end of the village sent for me to slaughter, I had to go. As soon as I had left home, someone else from the other end of the village would send for me to do some slaughtering for him, but, naturally, a while would pass by before I would return home from the first place. If the second person had no patience, he would keep running over to my home to find out if I had returned yet—and would sometimes actually be cursing too. Upon my return from my first job, my wife would tell me that another person had already been at the house three times in search of me. In such a case, I did not even sit down to rest for a minute but ran over to his house. I would then find that they had slaughtered the lamb themselves, to be sold to non-Jews.[22] So, as it turned out, I had gone there for naught, which I resented. If I was fortunate to find a live lamb and slaughter it, I would still have to keep justifying my delay. If the slaughtered animal turned out to be kosher, the owner would become softer and speak like a *mentsh*.[23] But if, as luck would have it, the animal was found to be *treyf*, the owner would then become really angry due to the loss of sales, which was all the fault of the *shoykhet* for whom he had to wait so long. Then his wife would come out to help him, "You, my husband, don't deserve such treatment. You also help pay the *shoykhet*'s salary just like that other person, so why did the *shoykhet* first go to that other person? You saw how late he came to us, and then he goes and makes the animal *treyf*."[24] If you think that it ended there, you are wrong! Upon returning home from the second person, my wife told me that so-and-so had come over twice in search of me and had angrily said, "How is it that the *shoykhet* was near my house earlier

22 They had slaughtered it not according to Jewish law, rendering the meat non-kosher.

23 The author means that after the animal was slaughtered, its lungs were inspected. If they were found to be healthy as prescribed by Jewish law, the animal was deemed to be kosher.

24 The wife unfairly blamed the author for "making the animal *treyf*" though he had simply declared it unfit for kosher consumption upon discovering an abnormality or the like in one of the animal's organs after it was slaughtered.

and did not bother coming over to ask me if I needed any animals slaughtered?" Upon hearing this, I had to run over to this third person at the other end of the village and justify myself by explaining that had I known, I certainly would have put my honor aside and have asked him. But whenever I went to one end of the village, did I need to ask all the Jewish households there if they needed any animals slaughtered? With this third person, matters would end as it did with the second: if the animal was found to be kosher, my troubles were minor—but if it was found to be *treyf*, my troubles were major. A half a day could pass like this, and I would have slaughtered not more than three or four lambs. In the late afternoon, similar requests for *sh'khita* would once again begin coming and could last until midnight—again with my only having slaughtered three or four lambs.

And do not forget that if this was a Thursday, I still had to go around collecting my weekly stipend, which one would pay, another would let it remain as a debt, and yet another would be in the midst of quarreling with his wife and would let out his entire rage on the *shoykhet*'s head. Or perhaps I would approach someone who was about to travel to town to buy some liquor. He would heap curses upon me and say, "Now you're asking for money?" as if I was obliged to know that he was traveling at that moment to buy some liquor and could certainly not pay me. Or upon arriving at an inn, I would find drunken non-Jews fighting while the Jewish tenant innkeeper, his wife, and children were screaming and crying out of fear. I would then have to run away. So these debts remained uncollected from week to week, and, consequently, I was only able to collect my money from half of those on my list while the debts of the other half remained uncollected.

When there was peace between me and the community, all of this was still bearable, but when strife developed, each person considered himself to be a somebody. One person would say that the *shoykhet* should not treat him so rudely by demanding payment of his weekly stipend. Yet another considered himself all-important because he had been harassing the *shoykhet*, so the *shoykhet* should certainly not dare to demand payment from him because in any case he did not want him as the *shoykhet* there. He claimed, "It's fine if he slaughters without asking for payment, but he is no *shoykhet* of mine if he asks for any money."

From all of this, you can now understand my life there and how happy I was. I earned about three rubles a week, on which I, my wife, and child needed to subsist while having to work so bitterly hard, suffer so greatly, and endure so much persecution from all sides. I think that from this brief description you can now have some idea of the type of people there were in Slobodze. I do not know if another person could have lasted. But I—the unfortunate orphan that I was—was accustomed to suffering and living in want since childhood, as you know. So I could continue to bear and endure everything while still living, repaying my previous debts, providing clothes for my family, and buying some more furniture for our home—chairs, a table, a small bed, and so on—so that our home would be presentable and so that my enemies would say about me that I had become rich and was living among them like a count. It also enraged them that my wife was beautiful, a gracious hostess, an efficient housekeeper, and an able housewife, the likes of which they were not accustomed to. They were used to seeing beautiful and efficient housekeepers being married to the well-to-do but were surprised that a *shoykhet* had such a wife. So when my wife gave the tailor some material to sew her a dress in honor of Pesach—which I think was the first dress for which I had the honor of paying from my earnings since we married—they thought she most likely was having a stylish dress made, which must cost at least ten or twelve rubles, including the tailoring.[25]

Now listen well to what those murderous boors shamelessly did, right in the middle of baking *matses*.[26] In Slobodze, it was customary for all the Jewish men to gather in a house to bake *matses* for Pesach, and everyone helped out. During the baking, they evidently began to talk about the *shoykhet,* and they began to speak about my wife having given the tailor material to sew a stylish dress for herself. Of course, this produced an outcry in all the heavenly spheres, especially since the *matses* were being baked in Itsye-Yoyls's house.[27] Someone said that it was impossible, while another swore that it was true and that he was going to show it to the women during the *matse* baking. Everyone was greatly interested in seeing what type of a modern woman the *shoykhet*'s wife was, and what type of lowly *shoykhet* they had. Some yelled out that he should run over to the tailor's and bring back the dress for all to see. As soon as this was said, it was as good as done. They ran off to the "glorious" village tailor and brought the dress back with them.[28] Everyone looked at it and wickedly made fun of

---

25 Pesach started the night of April 1, 1874.

26 On Pesach, Jews are required to eat *matses,* special unleavened flat bread, as stated in Exodus 12:8, 12:17–18, and elsewhere.

27 Since Jewish communities expected their *shokhtim* and their families to be the pillars of religious piety, a *shoykhet*'s wife concerned with the latest fashions was considered to have breached these norms. Nonetheless, in this case, it may have been that Freyde's dress was perfectly proper, but that her accusers were merely faultfinding. In fact, the author never writes that his wife actually asked for a modern or stylish dress to be made for herself; these claims only appear in his accusers' charges against her.

28 The author is being sarcastic about the improbable idea that a village tailor would have even known how to make a dress of the latest style, something that only a city tailor might have known.

it. During the excitement, one of them grabbed the dress, put it on, and began to dance, and the whole group began to dance with him. You can just imagine the joy they had during the *matse* baking while savoring the victory they had achieved. And if you think that it was a teenager or a young married man who had tried on the dress, the answer is no—it was a forty-year-old man by the name of Khayem Varnitse.[29] So, as you can well imagine, my wife was never able to wear that dress. How could she possibly have worn it? Do you think she enjoyed *Yontef*? Certainly not. She did not even want to pick up the dress from the tailor. She spent the entire Pesach crying over our having been punished by God so severely and mercilessly. This is what they did to her, though it hit me just as hard. Nonetheless, they had meant to hurt her only out of envy for her beauty and excellent housekeeping, as described above. But this was yet minor compared to what they would still do to me.

I will now relate another one of their cruelties. I wanted to have twenty *funt* of *shmure matses* baked for me.[30] The wheat and the milling cost me four rubles, apart from the tremendous amount of work involved, as you can imagine.[31] I went to those baking the *matses* and asked them to bake my twenty *funt* of flour into *matses*. We settled on a price of two rubles, which I paid in advance because otherwise they would not do it. I stipulated that they should roll the *matses* thin and follow my detailed instructions carefully.[32] You cannot imagine how they sabotaged me—like murderers. They took revenge on me in quite a nasty manner, meaning that those who rolled the dough made it thick and they took it out of the oven when it was still raw. I cried, pleaded with them, and screamed, but they just laughed like cold murderers. So I took home my raw, half-baked *shmure matses*, which I could not even use as non-*shmure matses*, for they had made my half-*pud* of *matses* unusable for Pesach and had charged me

29 This surname is also spelled Varantsa in Russian-language sources. See, for example, Beider, (2008:1:928).

30 *Shmure matses* literally means "guarded *matses*" and refers to round, handmade *matses* made from grain that has been closely guarded from any contact with moisture from the moment of harvesting. This is done in order to ensure that no fermentation or leavening occurs.

31 To ensure that the wheat has never come into contact with moisture until the mixing of the flour, extreme precautions are taken. See *Shulkhan Arukh* (*Orakh Khayim* 453:4). See the following reminiscences of the process: Rabbi Y. Y. Schneersohn (*Likkutei Dibburim*, 1:255–259), Meiselman (1995:133–141), and Sacks (1969:73–75).

32 There are many possible stringencies that can be implemented in the baking of *shmure matses*, among them ensuring that the *matses* are rolled thin so that their centers will be thoroughly baked; this practice avoids any vestiges of raw dough which would render the *matses* unfit for Pesach. See *Shulkhan Arukh* (*Orakh Khayim* 461).

two rubles to do so.[33] Instead of being able to earn some extra money for Pesach by selling *shmure matses* in Tiraspol, I had lost the entire six rubles and suffered much heartache and sorrow. And I could not even oppose them because the perpetrators were the greatest ruffians of the village and belonged to the families who were Kon's henchmen. I suffered like this for an entire year, but it is impossible to describe everything in detail.

My first year ended, and the harassment increased. It reached the point that Leyb-Yoyls got hold of a young married *shoykhet*, a Tolner Hasid, who was seeking a position as *shoykhet*. Leyb-Yoyls took him and brought him to Slobodze to his brother-in-law Itsye-Yoyls. Both brothers-in-law took this *shoykhet* in and worked toward dismissing me and appointing him as the local *shoykhet*. Without putting up any resistance whatsoever, everyone aligned themselves with the new *shoykhet* and began using him. What did it matter to them that I was suffering? They certainly had no mercy, especially for a *shoykhet*. What was a mere *shoykhet*, after all? Was he a human being? You may ask, "Isn't it forbidden? Doesn't the Torah forbid it?" So how could they steal my livelihood?[34] But they justified themselves by saying if it was forbidden then Leyb-Yoyls—who was a Hasid, a religious Jew, and a scholar—would not be doing it; since he was doing it, it was certainly permitted. The only one who stood up for me was the mail keeper, Mendl Slovske, who induced his *minyan* to continually raise an outcry on my behalf. He did not do this out of compassion for me but to spite Itsye-Yoyls and his *minyan*.

Meanwhile, you can imagine how thrilled I was from all of this. I realized that things were bad, so I traveled to Tiraspol and made a commotion in the Tolner *kloyz*. They sent for Leyb-Yoyls and reprimanded him. He justified his actions by saying that he did not mean to destroy my livelihood, God forbid; he only meant to assist me, to give me a chance to have the merit of coming under the wing of the *tsadik*, the leader of the generation, and become a Tolner Hasid. He did not think it was fitting for the village where he lived to have someone who was not a Tolner Hasid living there. Consequently, if I would just travel to Tolne and bring back certification papers from the Rebbe, he would become my best friend. And just like I was being persecuted from all sides now, upon my return from Tolne—as a Tolner Hasid—the situation would reverse itself,

---

33 A half a *pud* is 20 *funt*, which is equivalent to approximately 18.1 lb. Some people are particular to use *shmure matses*, which are more expensive than non-*shmure-matses* (i.e., regular *matses*), only for the Pesach *Seder* and use regular *matses* for the rest of Pesach.

34 Depriving a person of his livelihood by unfairly encroaching on his territory is an unfair business practice forbidden by Jewish law. See Greenwald (1955:105–109) for instances of this issue among *shokhtim* as cited in *halakhic* works.

things would then go well for me, and there would be peace and quiet. When the Tolner Hasidim heard that Leyb-Yoyls's entire intention was only to convert me and bring me under the wing of the holy Rebbe, they had absolutely nothing to say except to order me to run over to the Rebbe in Tolne.

I swallowed my pride and went to see Leyb-Yoyls at his house, and asked him, "How can you ask me to do this when I do not have enough money to support myself and I definitely do not have enough money to cover traveling expenses to the Rebbe?" He replied, "Whoever doesn't have enough money to travel to the Rebbe must go on foot, but he has to be at the Rebbe's court, particularly a *shoykhet*. I have nothing against you, but you need to bring certification papers from the Rebbe." I said, "How can I possibly do that? What will my family live off of while I'm gone?" He answered, "I don't care to know about your problems. That's your business—your worry." I saw that arguments or pleas would not help. He had absolutely no compassion. I returned home with a broken heart. We shed many a tear over our bitter luck. We decided that I had to do it; I had to try to obtain some money to cover the expense of traveling to Tolne.[35]

I traveled to Tiraspol and borrowed fifteen rubles to be repaid with interest.[36] Since, at present, I did have a source of income and people also considered me to be well-off, I was able to obtain fifteen rubles on credit. I returned home and left six rubles with my wife to support herself during the two weeks I would be gone, and I kept nine rubles for traveling expenses. I said my goodbyes and set off for Tolne in the month of *Shvat*.[37] I arrived in Tolne quite early on a Tuesday morning and actually went in to see the Rebbe that very day without having to pay the *gabbai* even one *kopek*. Though the Rebbe's door was besieged by numerous people and the door was guarded by a strong and sturdy *gabbai*, I, nonetheless, quickly made it into the Rebbe's room. The *gabbai* was very angry at me for doing such a thing, but he could do nothing about it.

If you are interested to know how I was able to enter to see the Rebbe without it costing me a *kopek*, I will tell you. It was quite simple. I noticed that a crowd of perhaps 100 men was standing around waiting to be allowed in to meet with the Rebbe. I spoke with a few of them, and they told me that they had

35 Rabbi Duvid Tversky (1808–1882) of Tolne—son of the famed Hasidic Rebbe, Rabbi Mordkhe (1770–1837) of Tshernobl, Ukraine (now Chernobyl), was one of the most influential Hasidic Rebbes in the Ukraine with thousands of Hasidim. He wrote the following works: *Birkat David*, *Kehilat David al ha-Torah*, and *Magen David*.

36 The author certainly borrowed this money in accordance with Jewish law. Although paying interest to another Jew is forbidden, there are ways this can be done according to Jewish law, as explained by Cohen (1984:187–188).

37 January-February 1874.

FIGURE 12. The Tolner Rebbe, Rabbi Duvid Tversky (1808–1882), was one of the most influential Hasidic Rebbes in the Ukraine. He supported Pinkhes-Dov Goldenshteyn in his struggle with a corrupt local community leader.

been standing there for two days and nights and could not make their way in to see the Rebbe. The *gabbai* let in whoever he wanted. Those who gave him a nice sum of money were obviously allowed to enter, while the poor could stand there for three to four days and nights since fresh, new people were constantly arriving. I went and stood in a corner near the wall that held the door to the Rebbe's room. I stood there as if I had no interest in entering to see the Rebbe, so those who were standing near the door were not paying attention to me. When the *gabbai* unlocked the door in order to let in some people, I noticed that he had managed to let in only one person and needed to let in another. I pushed myself through quickly and swiftly so that all the people standing there did not have a chance to stop me. Even the *gabbai* with his iron hands did not have a chance to catch me, because he had not expected to do battle on that side. He only succeeded in yelling out, "Get out of there. Come back." But I ignored his screaming since by the time I heard him I was already well inside. He was forbidden from stepping away from the door, while I was not obliged to listen to his order. In short, that was how I came to be standing in a room now only one door away from the Rebbe.

The door to the Rebbe's room stood half-open, which enabled me to see the Rebbe as he was sitting. Standing next to the Rebbe were a man and woman who were having a private audience with him. When they would leave, others would enter from the room in which I was waiting. Not many people were waiting in this room, but I had no patience and tried to figure out a way to enter to see the Rebbe immediately after that couple would leave. Being impatient, I decided to enter the Rebbe's room without the permission of the *gabbaim*, for next to the open door stood another *gabbai* waiting to receive his *kopeks* before admitting people to enter. But this *gabbai* was tall and skinny with a pair of long arms, so I placed myself directly behind his back. When I noticed the Rebbe bidding farewell to the couple—as the couple began to take leave and while the *gabbai* was preparing two others to enter in their place—I gave a push and snuck in from behind his back. I was now standing before the Rebbe. The *gabbai* did not even have a chance to ask, "Who's that? What's going on? What? Entering on his own?!" I understood that the *gabbai* was extremely displeased, but he could not yell at me. He could only give me a stern look.

I approached the Rebbe's chair, gave him my hand, and greeted him. He asked me who I was, and I told him in short and showed him my contract with the Jewish community of Slobodze, which Leyb-Yoyls had also signed. I told him that I had been the *shoykhet* there for a year now and that Leyb-Yoyls was persecuting me for not being a Tolner Hasid. He wanted me to become a Tolner Hasid and to obtain certification papers from the Rebbe, after which there would be peace. Meanwhile, Leyb-Yoyls had brought in a *shoykhet* who was encroaching on my territory and was actually a Tolner Hasid. I added that I was a Lubavitcher Hasid. He asked me where I had learned *sh'khita*. I showed him my certification papers that I had from the *shokhtim* in Tiraspol and Bendér, from whom I had learned *sh'khita*. The Rebbe told me that he would give me certification papers tomorrow and that I should travel home safely.[38] I left feeling happy. At my lodgings, everyone was astonished. "How's it possible? He just arrived and already had a chance to meet the Rebbe. A rare privilege, a rare privilege. We're waiting here since before *Shobes* and we haven't yet met with the Rebbe."

The next day, I went to the Rebbe's court and asked for the Rebbe's scribe. When I found him, I asked him if the Rebbe had told him to write anything for me. He replied that he had not received anything yet but that he would shortly be at the Rebbe's court regarding other matters and perhaps he would hear something from the Rebbe then. I waited a few hours, and he finally came to me and said, "The Rebbe told me to write for you a really fine letter of certification. Young man, you impressed the Rebbe as a fine *shoykhet*." I said, "Reb Yermye (that was what they called him), please, Reb Yermye, write it down right away because I can't spend a lot of time here. I left my family without anything to eat and without money, and I also don't have money to continue staying here." He said that even though he had a lot of work, he would nevertheless make sure that my papers would be ready to be signed, and he asked me to return in the evening. I returned and that very evening I received my certification from the Rebbe where he wrote that even "a stringent soul may eat from his *sh'khita*," meaning that even a *Giter-Yid* could eat from my *sh'khita*.[39]

Since it was already the eve of *Shobes* and it was too late to leave town, I spent *Shobes* at the Rebbe's court.[40] The first thing early Sunday morning, I left Tolne for Uman. From Uman, I went to Khashtshevote, where my sister Súre lived. I figured that I would use the opportunity to visit her. We were both

---

38 Kahana (1973:416–420) cites cases recorded in halakhic works where Hasidic Rebbes interfered in the appointment of *shokhtim* of nearby towns. He also cites a similar case to this one involving the Tolner Rebbe in which another Hasidic Rebbe refused to allow a community to dismiss their *shoykhet*.

39 Meaning that even a Hasidic Rebbe could eat from the author's *sh'khita*. The Tolner Rebbe's exact words in Hebrew: נפש היפה תאכל מזבחו.

40 From the author's description of the course of events since his arrival in Tolne on Tuesday, it seems that it was only Wednesday night, yet he states here that it was already "the eve of *Shobes*," implying that it was Thursday night.

overjoyed since we had not seen each other in a while.[41] I spent approximately two days with her.

I then came up with a clever plan to use regarding Slovske, the mail keeper. When he would see that Leyb-Yoyls had succeeded in having me obtain a letter of certification from Tolne, he would persist in demanding that I bring certification papers from his Rebbe, and he was a Savraner Hasid. In truth, he would not be doing this out of devotion to the Savraner Rebbe but rather because of his rivalry with Leyb-Yoyls, to show that he was more influential. *Nu*, what would I do then? Slovske would hurt me more than Leyb-Yoyls, because Leyb-Yoyls had some self-respect while Slovske did not have any at all when his power and honor were at stake. Since I was already away from home on this arduous journey, it would be best for me now to put an end to such exhaustive trips by traveling to Savrán, to the Rebbe there. I prepared a letter to the Savraner Rebbe as if it was from Slovske. It stated that he was sending a *shoykhet* to meet privately with the Rebbe to obtain a letter of certification, after which Slovske would then support the *shoykhet* and make sure that he would earn a livelihood in Slobodze. I wrote the letter without fear. I was not afraid that the Rebbe with his divine inspiration would realize that I had written it myself, because I figured he would be so proud that *shokhtim* from the ends of the world were being sent to him to be examined. I entered to see the Rebbe with this letter, and he told me to write the letter of certification and he would sign it. I left there with my goal accomplished and thereby brought home two certification documents from two rabbis—*Gite-Yidn*—within two weeks.

Naturally, I only exhibited the letter of certification from the Tolner Rebbe and kept the one from the Savraner Rebbe hidden, thinking that its time would certainly come. In the meantime, we will discuss the impact that the Tolner certification had on the Jews of Slobodze, particularly on Leyb-Yoyls. When I returned home and related that I had brought back certification from the Rebbe, no one could believe that it was true. After all, Leyb-Yoyls had explained to them that obtaining slaughtering certification would not come easy even for a Tolner Hasid. Someone who was not a Tolner Hasid and had never before been to see the Rebbe would have to wait around a few months until he obtained certification. So they believed that I was surely trying to deceive them. When I heard this, I went with a few people to Leyb-Yoyls to show him the Rebbe's letter of certification. He would not even look at it and said that it was forged. "I'll teach

---

41 The author and his sister Sure had last seen each other a little over a year before in December 1872 (ch. 21, p. 373).

you not to show a falsified letter of certification," and he traveled off that very day to the Rebbe in Tolne as if his very life depended on the matter.

I now clearly saw his duplicity for what it was. His intention had been to destroy my source of livelihood, but he had camouflaged it with piety and Hasidism, saying that all would go well for me if I would only bring a letter of certification from the Rebbe. This was said to look good in the eyes of the people, but in his heart he had not expected me to receive a letter of certification from the Rebbe so quickly. He figured that while I was waiting in Tolne, he would send a note to the Rebbe containing all types of slander against me, thereby preventing me from obtaining the Rebbe's certification. All of his actions would then be justified. After all, if the Rebbe would not give Pinye-Ber certification, then he was no *shoykhet.* But seeing that his entire plan had been foiled, Leyb-Yoyls's needed desperately to prevail, so he personally ran to the Rebbe with the hope of convincing him to believe all the evil that he had fabricated about me. After all, he was one of the Rebbe's close Hasidim, a fine Talmudic scholar, and was able to afford to give the Rebbe a very nice *pidyen.*[42]

Meanwhile, I had that other *shoykhet* in the village encroaching upon my slaughtering rights. But what could I do? I just had to struggle along solely with the support of the mail keeper's cronies who were also a bunch of ruffians. They did not support me out of a sense of compassion or common decency. No, God forbid! What did they know of compassion, particularly for a *shoykhet*?! They were simply siding with me to spite Itsye-Yoyls and Leyb-Yoyls. Since the two brothers-in-law were saying "no," they had to say "yes."

Eight days later, I received word from the Tolner *kloyz* in Tiraspol that I should come. They needed me urgently regarding something concerning my own benefit. I walked to Tiraspol immediately. I entered the *kloyz* where the Tolner Rebbe's closest Hasidim told me about the downfall that Leyb-Yoyls had suffered at the Rebbe's court.

When Leyb-Yoyls arrived in Tolne, these Tiraspolers were already there. Upon seeing him, they understood that he had come because of the *shoykhet* and went right to the Rebbe to wait until Leyb-Yoyls came for a private audience with the Rebbe. When Leyb-Yoyls entered to see the Rebbe, they also went in and heard the Rebbe ask him, "Well, Leyb, how are you doing? Did you send away your *shoykhet*?"

"Which *shoykhet*?" Leyb asked.

"The one that you brought into your village to force Pinye-Ber out," the Rebbe said.

42 Meaning that Leyb-Yoyls was able to give the Rebbe a very nice sum of money.

Frightened, Leyb answered, "I? I brought him? The community brought him."

"But you're the Talmudic scholar, the exemplary Jew, and the Hasid in your village. You could have stopped it and told them that it was forbidden. In truth, how could you have allowed such a thing to happen?"

He replied that he had actually made a compromise—that the *shoykhet* should obtain certification papers from the Rebbe and, once he would obtain them, they would send away the other *shoykhet*.

The Rebbe said, "He received certification papers from me. So why did you come here?"

"I didn't believe that he had received the certification papers so quickly. I figured that he was deceiving us."

"God forbid," answered the Rebbe. "What do you mean he deceived you? He received certification papers from me. Actually, I liked him. We have some esteemed Hasidim from Tiraspol right here. Let's ask them." The Rebbe turned to them and asked, "Do you know him?"

"Yes, we know him, and how! He's lived among us in Tiraspol since he was a child. He's a very pious young man and had very religious parents from a fine lineage. We've never heard anything bad about him."

"You hear?" said the Rebbe. "So what do you have against him?"

"Yes, Rebbe, but he's become 'light.'"[43] He meant that the *shoykhet* had become lax in his religious observance.

"Light?" the Rebbe asked. "It can't be. I just saw him, and he was a bit heavy, *kenehore*." The Tolner Rebbe, of blessed memory, liked to make witty remarks to get his point across.[44] "So," said the Rebbe, "I responded humorously, but I'm interested to know what type of laxity you noticed in him."

"A lot. A lot . . ."

"Pick one thing from all that you saw," he said.

"The *shoykhet* and his wife carried a bed together out of their house."

"So what type of laxity is that?"

"Yes, Rebbe. His wife was then in the days when she was supposed to be separated from her husband."[45]

---

43 *Kal* in the original literally means "light" in Hebrew but is used here as in the sense of frivolous.

44 In his memoirs, Minkovsky (1918:114) writes, "Reb Duvidl used to spice his conversations with riddles and enjoyed jokes . . ." Mekler (1931:120–121) also comments that the Tolner Rebbe "liked to make witty remarks, which were often sharp and amusing" and then provides a couple of examples.

45 Jewish law requires a husband and wife to keep some distance from one another during parts of her menses (*Kitsur Shulkhan Arukh* 153:4–15). At these times, they are not only

"So tell me, are you the guardian over people's personal lives? Did you see it yourself?"

"My wife saw them, and she knew about it . . ."

"But don't you know that Jewish law states that women aren't acceptable as witnesses,[46] especially since your wife can't personally testify to all of these details? It appears that you're just vying for power."

"No, Rebbe. I'm not vying for power. The villagers don't want him as their *shoykhet*."

"You just stand aside, and everything will be good. You're the driving force in this conflict."

"But Rebbe, can I eat from his *sh'khita*?" he asked, ignoring the entire conversation.

The Rebbe replied, "Yes. Why not? As long as you have meat to eat," and with these words the Rebbe rose from his chair and Leyb-Yoyls had to step aside.

"Here we've repeated for you word-for-word what the Rebbe said to Leyb-Yoyls," concluded the Tiraspolers. And they also told me that I should have no fear, "God will help you, and he'll receive his due from God because the Rebbe's words will certainly come true—he'll be reduced to poverty. Even if he would want to eat from your *sh'khita*, he won't be able to afford it.[47] We called you over to relate this so that you should know of the downfall that Leyb-Yoyls suffered at the Rebbe's court. Upon his return home, he certainly won't tell anyone or will tell lies. So you should know that if he continues to keep the other *shoykhet*, don't keep quiet but write about it to the Rebbe."

I thanked them for their friendship and gave praise to the Master of the World for bestowing on me such bountiful kindness. I then returned home to my village. Upon my arrival, I encountered Leyb-Yoyls himself. It was obvious that he had accomplished nothing in Tolne, yet the other *shoykhet* had not been dismissed. Leyb-Yoyls's thirst for power was so strong that he could in no way break it, and he kept thinking to himself that perhaps—just perhaps—he would be able to prevail. He had already shown that he was not a true Hasid but was just donning a false Hasidic mask since it served his purposes. If he had been a true Hasid and believed in his Rebbe's words, he should have dropped that other *shoykhet* immediately and made peace with me. He was not aware that I already knew everything, and I intentionally did not mention this to anyone so that I would hear all the lies that he would tell.

---

prohibited from touching but are also prohibited from carrying an object together, like the bed mentioned above.

46 *Shulkhan Arukh* (*Khoshen Mishpat* 35:14).

47 The Tolner Rebbe's stipulation, "As long as you have meat to eat," was viewed as foreshadowing Leyb-Yoyls's descent into poverty.

Everyone asked him if he could prove that I had brought falsified certification papers, to which he replied, "No, he did actually receive them from the Rebbe but the Rebbe does not know what he's up to." With this statement, he simply put his foot in his mouth. "How could it be," asked the simple villagers, "that the holy Rebbe does not know yet what you know? Eh, Leyb, that's really not befitting for you to say." When they saw that he could not prove anything, they began to somewhat distance themselves from him and he lost his prominent standing. But since the crowd continued to be supplied with good food and drink, Leyb's instigations began anew.

I realized that Leyb-Yoyls was not abandoning his contentiousness and that the other *shoykhet* was not being dismissed, so I followed the advice of those prominent individuals of Tiraspoler and wrote the Rebbe everything that had happened. Eight days later, I received a letter from the Rebbe which I was to give over to Leyb and keep a copy for myself. That letter was written with fire.

The Rebbe wrote the following: He had already given me a letter of certification stating that even "a stringent soul may eat from his *sh'khita*" and had also declared this a second time when Leyb came to him, explicitly telling him that Pinye-Ber was a kosher *shoykhet* and one could eat from his *sh'khita*. Despite all of this, Leyb was still vying for power and keeping that nefarious *shoykhet*. Leyb should reconsider what he was doing and with whom he was playing because he was playing with fire. The Rebbe also wrote in the letter that he was going to write to the Tiraspoler rabbis that they should forbid the encroaching *shoykhet* from slaughtering anything and that any utensils used by those who would eat his meat from this day onwards would be considered *treyf*.[48]

Right after the letter was received, the strife in the village was silenced. Leyb-Yoyls was simply afraid to set foot in Tiraspol because all of Tiraspol was talking about him and what had transpired in Tolne, since those important Tiraspolers who had witnessed it had told everyone. I also publicized my copy of the Rebbe's letter to him. This served to break the hearts of Leyb and his brother-in-law. They dismissed the other *shoykhet* who had been in the village for two months, and made peace with me, thank God. I was now able to be calm. My former enemies began to hold me in very high esteem. We began to live a new life—just like when we had first started out there. Itsye-Yoyls and I would sometimes discuss among ourselves what had transpired during that period of strife, and I would point out to him the difference between us, namely,

48 Though Tiraspol had only one rabbi, "the Tiraspoler rabbis" includes those who served as rabbinical judges.

that despite his persecution of me, I had done him many favors without his knowledge.

But do not think, my loved ones, that this calm period in my life endured—it only lasted about a month. The strife resumed in the way I had anticipated months earlier, but I had already "prepared the cure before the appearance of the malady."[49] When the mail keeper noticed that I was now at peace with the Kon family—meaning with Itsye-Yoyls and his brother-in-law Leyb-Yoyls—and that I now went to pray at their *minyan,* he sent his ruffians to persecute me with every type of harassment and indignity. For example, they would send false messengers to call me over to do some slaughtering at one end of the village, yet upon my arrival it would turn out that no one had sent for me. Upon returning home, I would then find an order for me to go to the other end of the village, to which I went right away, but ultimately it would also turn out to be for naught. Afterward, I no longer wanted to go anywhere to do any slaughtering until the person himself came to me, which caused an uproar, and then new fights began. Naturally, my weekly stipends suffered. They began to give me less in cash and would just allow their debts to increase. Even the wealthy mail keeper, Slovske, stopped paying.

I began to suffer greatly, and my distress grew from day to day. I lived solely off the weekly stipends of Itsye-Yoyl's *minyan.* I could do nothing about this situation because Slovske's anger at my attending Kon's *minyan* was merely an excuse—the real reason for his anger was due to his rivalry with the Kon family. So I had to suffer as all the previous *shokhtim* in Slobodze had suffered. In Tiraspol, a saying used to circulate about the village of Slobodze that it was the place where the souls of *shokhtim* became purified, similar to how souls are purified in the River Dinur. As soon as *shokhtim* traverse the Dinur River, meaning, step foot in Slobodze, they become purified and are elevated to higher levels.[50] My one consolation was that the people of Tiraspol knew of my troubles in Slobodze and would comfort me and help me rally my strength.

Now listen well to the scandal that occurred between the mail keeper and me—but first I must describe an incident that happened. One of my neighbors was an impoverished young family man named Shulem Fuks, who seemingly could not have had anything against me. He had no lambs to slaughter, and he never paid me a weekly stipend. I performed a *bris* on his son without

---

49 Based on the Talmudic saying, "God provides the cure before the malady" (Talmud, *Megilla* 13b).

50 According to the *Zohar* (1:201a, *Mikets*), after the soul leaves its earthly station, it proceeds through many levels of spiritual purification from wrongdoing, the final level being the River Dinur (literally meaning "fire"), from which the soul emerges completely purified.

charging him a *kopek*. One would think that such a person would not have anything against the *shoykhet*. When *Simchas Torah* came along,[51] the influential Itsye Kon along with his cohorts went through the village wishing everyone "*Git Yontef*."[52] They actually thought very highly of the obligation to rejoice on *Yontef*, believing that they must definitely be joyful and make others joyous.[53] Kon and his bunch came to my house to wish me "*Git Yontef*." After sitting around for about a half hour, they got up to leave and dragged me along with them. I did not really have any desire to go along because drinking did not interest me and walking along with the likes of them certainly held no attraction for me. Nonetheless, because Kon himself had asked me along and was showing me respect, I could not refuse them since they would suspect that I was embarrassed to join their group. In truth, their suspicions would certainly have been justified. Nonetheless, my heart told me, "Don't go. Something's bound to happen." In short, I went with them.

We left my house and set out along the street to the house of someone else from the *minyan*. Naturally, everyone was happy. But of course! They were with Kon, the *shoykhet*, and Leyb-Yoyls as well. We went a little ways and saw a large group, singing happily, coming toward us. That was Slovske with his cohorts. Seeing them, we stood off to the side of the street to leave it open for them to pass peacefully. When they noticed us, they became overjoyed and headed toward us, shouting "Hurrah" and "*Git Yontef*." Naturally, our group answered with voices filled with good cheer, "*Git Yontef. A git Yontef*," and everyone began to sing. It seemed so joyous and wonderful to see Jews singing in the middle of the street. All the non-Jews were sitting around observing how those remarkable Jews were still joyous despite all of their hardships and persecutions. I stood from afar and looked at the scene, trying to figure out how I could slip away from them because their celebration did not appeal to me at all. As I stood there thinking, someone came from behind me and lifted his hand up and gave me a hard slap on the cheek. I looked around and noticed who the arrogant scoundrel was. It was the young married man, Shulem Fuks. He had been afraid to approach me face to face and was even afraid to remain standing behind me, so he ran away. At that moment, everyone began slapping each other right and left. The screams of the wives of the beaten and wounded reached the heavens. I did not see who did the hitting, who was hit, or who the agitator was among them, because I immediately left for home as soon as I had been slapped. I only

---

51 October 4, 1874.

52 Meaning "Good Holiday."

53 *Kitsur Shulkhan Arukh* (103:1–14, 138:7).

heard the screaming and saw how the non-Jews had to tear them apart from each other.[54]

The next day, one could see wagons loaded with wounded and beaten Slobodzer men, all bandaged up. Some had their heads bandaged, others their noses or eyes, yet others their feet, and so on. In brief, they looked like cripples returning from a war. All were traveling to the doctors to have papers issued which they could use to sue in court. You yourself can imagine what a heavenly disgrace this was. The entire city of Tiraspol resounded with the news. Everyone was in court, except for me. Though I had received the first smack and knew who had started the fight because everyone else had been drunk while I had been sober and lucid, I had slipped away immediately and did not want to take anyone to a court of justice. We have an almighty God, and I would rather that He judge instead of the Justice of the Peace. I said, "May God pay him back a slap for a slap," which is actually what happened, as I am certain that you will find out upon reading the section of my work describing the "reward" with which God repaid each of my enemies.[55] There you will also see how God repaid that Shulem Fuks, though he apologized to me. That was the only slap that I received from a Jew in my life. I say from a Jew because on three occasions I was hit by non-Jews, but this had yet to come and will be described further on.[56]

Nu, since you now know the episode of my *Simchas Torah* slap, I will tell you about the scandal that occurred between the mail keeper and me. The mail keeper decided to get a hold of me and break my bones—as befitting a mail keeper in those times. *Nu,* why shouldn't the wealthy Slovske thoroughly trounce this *shoykhet* who was badmouthing him by saying that he owed him money and was not paying him? True, Slovske was not paying the *shoykhet,* but

---

54 Katsovitsh (1919:198–199) describes a similarly violent scene on *Simchas Torah* in a small town near Poltava, Ukraine, in about 1880, though that fight occurred between *maskilim* and traditionalists. Botoshansky (1942:1:147, 236) describes how, out of jealousy, some impoverished, coarse Jews accosted a wealthier Jew on *Simchas Torah* in 1903 in the author's hometown of Kiliya, Bessarabia (now in Ukraine), and that on *Simchas Torah* in 1907 in Petrovca, Moldova, the two sides of an old communal conflict fell into a vicious fight, though they all danced in harmony the next morning. Such communal fights apparently occurred on *Simchas Torah* because it is the one Jewish holiday where many Jews freely imbibe and the entire Jewish community is out and about together, whether outside or in synagogue. This periodically resulted in communal tension becoming unleashed. On the other hand, on Purim, the other Jewish holiday when alcohol is freely imbibed, Jews usually do so in their own homes in the afternoon.

55 In ch. 29, pp. 570–572, the author describes the fates of his enemies, but only of his later enemies in Bakhchisaray.

56 The author only records one incident in ch. 23, pp. 452–454, where a non-Jewish nobleman hit him.

he ought to know the reason why. But that the *shoykhet* should be so brazen as to tell others that the mail keeper owed him for ten weeks and was not paying him—such insolence warranted that the *shoykhet* be thoroughly beaten.

Meanwhile, I had no idea that he harbored such ill feelings toward me. When I would come to him to ask him, ostensibly, if he needed a chicken slaughtered, I would incidentally ask for what was owed me. I would then also alert him to the fact that the longer he delayed the greater his debt would grow, and that I was poor and could not wait any longer, and so on. At such times, I noticed that he would become very angry and would say, "I'll pay one lump sum soon enough. I mean it seriously." Why would he speak in such anger, I wondered. I could not understand it at first but the question was soon answered for me when I realized that the mail keeper felt that the whole business was beneath his dignity.

In short, I kept on waiting like that until the eve of Pesach.[57] That morning, I woke up quite early and ran over to the mail keeper's so that I would be sure to find him at home because I needed the money for *Yontef*. I entered his house, and he was there. He said, "I've been waiting for you. It's really good that you came," and he called out, "Leye! Tell them to give the *shoykhet* the chickens that you need slaughtered for *Yontef*." I slaughtered the chickens, wished him a "*Git Yontef*," and expected that at any moment I would be paid the money owed to me. No one was in the house except for me and him. I noticed that he was squirming and turning colors, but how was I to know the reason? He said with apprehension—I could barely hear him, "Certainly you want to be paid," which obviously bothered him. I answered, "As you can understand, Reb Mendl." He ostensibly groped in his pockets, and said, while standing up from his chair, "Come. I'll give you your money."

He left the main part of the house along with me, and we entered the foyer. Upon entering the foyer, he rushed and locked the door that led outside and shut the door to the kitchen tightly so that no one could enter. The only door remaining was the door to the house from which we had just entered. He shut that door too and locked it with a key. He did all of this in the blink of an eye. I noticed what was happening. His eyes were seething like a bandit's, but I flashed a smile and said, "*Nu*, Reb Mendl? Are you ready? I know what you have in mind, but you've come to the wrong postal station."[58] He proceeded with his designs and lifted his hands to strike me. I naturally did not let him lower his fist and shoved him hard toward the corner so that his soul almost left him. I

57 April 19, 1875.

58 Mendl Slovske was the mail keeper.

was then able to grab both his arms so that he could not move, and I pushed him into the corner, saying loudly, "You murderer! You bandit! You still want to strike me? May you be struck down by God and by man! You call yourself a Jew? A *goy* like you needs a *shoykhet*? You murderer! I'll soon rip you to pieces." I then pressed him against the wall until he began to scream. "Let me go, Reb Pinye-Ber. I was just kidding but you're attacking me in earnest." I replied, "You meant it seriously but you made a mistake. You didn't meet up with the right postal station." I then unlocked the door and left for home.

In the village a rumor circulated that I had pummeled the mail keeper. With my actions, everyone had their revenge because he had beaten up a few of the villagers in the past. But with me he had his true comeuppance. He was sick that entire Pesach and was ashamed to show his face in the village and especially in Tiraspol, because his enemies had circulated news of the incident and had even added dozens of lies to embellish the story. In short, any way you looked at it, it was good and fine in more ways than one. If this would only happen to all enemies of the Jews! What a heavenly disgrace it was that a Jew wanted to seize and beat a *shoykhet*. And when did he do it? On the eve of *Yontef* of all times—when the *shoykhet* came to slaughter his chickens for *Yontef* and to wish him a "*Git Yontef*." But anything was possible among the inhabitants of Slobodze—anything could be believed about them. From this episode, you can understand how all of those other debasing incidents could have occurred there.

The commotion blew over, Pesach passed, and it was already, thank God, *Shvues*.[59] It was then that the mail keeper took to the task of removing me as the *shoykhet* with whatever power he had. He made up his mind to prevail no matter what the cost. The first thing was to have me harassed as much as possible, and nothing could deter him from his desire to cause me harm. I was able to surmount everything only because God created me with a quick wit; I was able to understand my enemies and know how to protect myself from them. God, in His tremendous kindness, stood by me and made sure that my enemies would never have a chance to take their revenge. When the mail keeper saw that there was nothing he could do to me, he began to demand that I bring him certification papers from his Rebbe, from Savran, and he would then stand aside. He contended that since Leyb-Yoyls had succeeded in having the *shoykhet* travel to Tolne and bring certification papers, he wanted the *shoykhet* to travel to Savran and procure certification there as well.

Upon hearing this, I said that I would bring him certification papers from Savran if he would guarantee our agreement with a handshake. He would not

59 June 9–10, 1875.

shake hands on the agreement, but he gave his word in front of everyone that he would be back on my side as soon as I traveled to the Rebbe in Savran and returned with certification papers. I said that I would not insist that he shake hands on the agreement since I anyway knew for sure that he would violate the handshake and not keep our agreement even if I showed him certification papers from his Rebbe. Nonetheless, I wanted him to give his word in front of everyone that he would leave me and my family alone and stop making our lives miserable if I would bring certification from the Rebbe in Savran. Slovske said that he agreed though the *shoykhet* had sinned against him, which he would never forget. I asked him, "How did I sin against you? Was it when you wanted to hit me, and I prevented you from doing so?" Everyone was surprised when I said this to him straight to his face, because a rumor had been circulating in Slobodze that the *shoykhet* had smacked someone without provocation. He had no reply and agreed that we would make peace when I would bring back certification papers from the Savraner Rebbe. "Good," I said, "I'll bring you the certification document right away," and I removed the certification document from my pocket and showed it to them. All were amazed and did not believe that it was the Rebbe's signature. So I had to tell them the story of how I received the certification, which you already know from earlier, and peace was made between us. But despite this, I had to be very careful because I already knew with whom I was dealing. I knew that our peace was for appearance sake only and that they would be searching for the slightest opportunity to do me wrong.

When Itsye-Yoyls heard that there was peace between me and the mail keeper, he began to harass me, saying that I was not a true Tolner Hasid as I had traveled to two Rebbes at the same time. Since I hate flattery, I told him the truth, "I'm not a Tolner Hasid, and I'm certainly not a Savraner Hasid. I'm simply a proper and pious *shoykhet*. Even the Tolner Rebbe himself was not interested whether I was or was not his Hasid—all that mattered to him was that I was a proper *shoykhet*. You won't change me. This is what I am, and this is how I'll stay." My reply impressed him, and peace finally reigned between me and Itsye-Yoyls's *minyan* and between me and the mail keeper's *minyan*. The peace was obviously only on the surface, so I was careful not to afford them the opportunity to do me wrong. I pretended not to hear and not to know any of the gossip that was said about me or told to me about them. A small period of time passed by quietly like this, causing outsiders to think that I had it very good and that I was then living a happy life.

That is how I languished and suffered during the two and a half years I was in Slobodze, particularly during the quarrelsome period when the weekly stipends were not being paid on time. Certainly you are curious to know how I survived that period of strife, so here are the details. There is a saying that it is good to walk on foot next to a heavily loaded wagon, which is also how it was with me.[60] I was living in that village and suffering, but it was still much better than my previous situation, when I was wandering around without a livelihood. The reason Slobodze was better is because people would lend me money when they saw that I had a steady job. In addition, my position made it possible for various side jobs to come my way, like leading the services on the High Holy Days and slaughtering chickens for *kapores*, when people would give me tips. I survived that way and slowly paid off the debts I owed from my days as a wheat merchant, as you may recall.

Now listen and I will tell you about the corrupt character of a certain fellow. You probably remember that I owed Shaye Ternofske fifty rubles and that I gave him my last bit of silver without my wife's knowledge so that he would be certain that I would repay him.[61] When God helped me by providing me with a position as a *shoykhet*, I began to slowly pay off my debt by giving him a few rubles every month, which I am sure he had not expected. Upon bringing him the last two rubles, I said to him, "Here are the last two rubles that I owe you. Now, give me back my few pieces of silver." He pretended not to know what I was talking about and took the two rubles.

I told him, "Reb Shaye, give me my few pieces of silver."

He replied coldly, "When you bring me another five rubles, I'll surrender your silver to you."

I asked him, "What five rubles? Do I owe you another five rubles?"

He replied, "I waited so long for payment. What about interest?"

I went numb. I had not expected him to be so depraved. I berated him thoroughly and said, "Just like I paid you the fifty rubles, even though in all fairness you didn't have it coming to you, I'll also pay you these five rubles. But you won't own any more than that for the rest of your life." I left angry and irritated. From that moment on, I avoided him like an offensive stench and paid him the five rubles through someone else.[62] I do not know whether he truly

---

60 Furman (1968:149) explains this Yiddish saying as follows: it is better to walk on foot next to a full wagon as opposed to traveling on board an empty one, thereby advising one to stay in close proximity to a successful merchant, because one can always earn something by just being around him. Similarly, Goldenshteyn earned very little (walking on foot), but since he had a steady job (a full wagon) people would lend him money and his position also allowed him to earn extra income.

61 This incident occurred over six years earlier, in April 1869 (ch. 19, p. 322).

62 The Torah (Exodus 22:24, Leviticus 25:36–37, and Deuteronomy 23:20–21) prohibits one Jew from charging or receiving interest from another, unless the loan is conducted in a specified manner, e.g., as a partner in a business. The author would have been permitted to repay

reconsidered or if his wife persuaded him to do so, but he reduced the amount of interest to three rubles. But for me he had lost the status of a *mentsh.*

I did not repay just this loan but also many other debts which I had accumulated. For example, I repaid the twenty rubles that I had borrowed to pay for the "wonderful" rights to slaughter in Slobodze and the fifteen rubles that I had borrowed to travel to Tolne.[63] Perhaps you think that I was now debt free, but if you think so, you are mistaken. I was now even deeper in debt, but it was easier for me to repay my debts because I had a steady job. Yet I would never have sunk into such great debt if it were not for all the guests who visited me. They cost me no small amount, which was simply beyond my means.

One guest was Shaye-Ksiel, the *shoykhet* of Peresetshine, who came on the behalf of my late brother Isruel's widow. He asked me to assist him in paying for the wedding of Freydele, my brother's daughter, whom he was marrying off.[64] This episode cost me much health. I had no money and could not borrow any, and he demanded that I should at least repay him for his traveling expenses to Slobodze. Believe it or not, I was not even able to give him that much. So I hired a wagon and traveled with him to Tiraspol to see if I could possibly obtain on credit a piece of linen with which some blouses could be made for Freydele. But I was not able to do even that. I was filled with shame. I was disgraced before him; perhaps he thought that I was that stingy, God forbid. I was also upset that I had to spend a silver ruble, which I did not have, for the wagon ride into Tiraspol. A little later, when my position became more secure, I was able to borrow as much as I wanted because my enemies publicized that I was wealthy and then some.

My sister Sure then came with my sister Tsipe's ten-year-old son Duvidl.[65] Her visit cost me several rubles. She stayed with me for three or four weeks,

---

the five rubles only if he intended the money to be payment for the silver and not the interest (*Kitsur Shulkhan Arukh* 65–66; Reisman, 1995:408–418).

63 In ch. 21, p. 366, the author described how he pawned his wife's pearls for twenty rubles, with which he paid the previous *shoykhet*'s moving expenses.

64 The JewishGen Romania Database (www.jewishgen.org/databases/Romania) includes the transcription of an 1875 special list of Jewish males in Peresetshine under the age of eighteen. This list mentions two sons of a Kisil-Shaye Fleyshman, who is probably identical with Shaye-Ksiel. Kisil is a variant of Ksiel. Note that Jews in previous generations were often not particular regarding the order of their personal names. Based on the next footnote, this incident happened either in 1873, the year that the author arrived in Slobodze, or the following year.

65 Since Sure Vaynberg had taken in and raised her nephew Duvid, who was born 1864 (ch. 18, p. 305), this incident happened about 1874. Though Duvid is not mentioned again, the author writes in a letter from the 2nd of *Adar* II 5689 (March 14, 1929) that he was residing in Kishinev. The author's letter, dated the 21st of Tamuz 5686 (July 3, 1926), states that

and I gave her some money for her expenses and purchased some new clothes for my nephew. After Sure left, other guests began to visit, such as my in-laws. Every one of their visits cost me because they expected to be reimbursed for their expenses in supporting us during those hard years when we had no money.

My sister Ite also began visiting to find out what her brother was doing and how he lived. Upon seeing my "wealth," she could not bear to impose upon me. But I was eager to keep her dear son Itsele with me and to teach him Torah.[66] She liked my plan, though she could not live without him. Nonetheless, she thought that she would become used to being away from him as it would be to his benefit, since he was growing up without a father. She stayed on with him for a short while until he became accustomed to us and then she left. A week later, he began to miss his mother, so I sent him back. When I went to Tiraspol a week later, my sister cried to me that she could not put up with her son. I asked her, "Will he stay with me?" "Yes," she replied, "now he wants to be with you." "At your home," Itsele added, "there's food to eat." I took him back to my home. He stayed with me the entire week, and I studied Torah with him.

Shobes came. After finishing the daytime meal, we went to sleep and Itsele went outside. When we awoke from our sleep, he was not in the house. He had been gone from the house for a couple of hours by then and had not yet returned. I went around asking people about him in all the places where I figured he might be, but "there was no voice and no one answered."[67] No one had seen him, and I did not find him at anyone's home. I was now becoming distraught. What could this mean? What became of him?

It was night already and he had not returned. I ran to the Dniester River. Perhaps he went to bathe there with the local boys. Upon reaching the river, I could not see or hear a thing. I asked the non-Jewish men who were catching fish and the non-Jewish women who were carrying water from the river if they had seen a little boy. I described his appearance to them. "No," they replied.

Meanwhile, it had become late. I ran back. Perhaps he returned and I would find him at home. I came home and he was not there. In the meantime, I was told that there was a fire at the other end of the village. I went there and asked the children if they had seen him. They replied, "No." I thought to myself, if God would perform a miracle by letting me find him upon returning home again, I

---

the impoverished Duvid had a wife named Beyle, whose hand was lame as a result of an injury suffered in a pogrom, and that they had children, and grandchildren. (The pogroms in Kishinev occurred in 1903 and 1905.) See Appendix B3 (pp. 774–807) for full translations of those letters.

66 Itsele (born 1862) was about twelve years old at the time.

67 Kings I 18:26.

would know that God was bestowing miracles upon me and that my suffering was due to His love for me.[68] I returned home, and the child was not there. What should I tell you? How I was able to survive the night, I have no idea. It must be that I am stronger than iron, for how else could I have endured that night? Our home was full of sobbing. My wife and I cried the entire night. How would I explain to my sister the disappearance of her child—her only son—when she had no hope of ever having another son who would be able to say *Kaddish* for her?[69] And how would I be able to bear seeing her grief. I felt horrible.

Around midday, a Slobodzer resident returned from Tiraspol and brought me the news that that delightful child, Itsikl, was in Tiraspol. Out of joy, I grabbed him and began to hug and kiss him. But afterward, I became skeptical. I thought that perhaps he had just wanted to comfort me and ease my pain. So I put my two feet on the ground and walked into town to see for myself. I came into town and saw my Itsele happy and lively. You can imagine how happy I was; out of joy, I began to dance. My sister asked me what I was doing, so I told her how frightened I had been since yesterday. She told me that on *Shobes* during the day, he suddenly turned up in Tiraspol. She asked him, "What's going on Itsele? How did you arrive here on *Shobes* of all days?" He replied with a lame excuse; he did not want to stay with his uncle since he was bored there. He did not tell her that he had left without telling anyone. I immediately went to tell my wife the news that Itsele was in Tiraspol.

***

It's now time to return to the story of my life over the course of the next year, and the final chapter of my suffering in Slobodze. But before we begin, I ask you to have patience and listen to a few words about how "refined" the residents of Slobodze were. One of the people there was called Reb Shmiel Slobodzer,[70] who was so "well learned" that he said upon once finding a *Korben Minkhe*

---

68 According to the Talmud (Brakhot 5a–5b), God may bring suffering upon a person either as a punishment for his sins or as a method of improving his character. The latter type of suffering is called "suffering of love," for it comes upon those whom God loves in order to refine their character. The author felt that if nothing tragic actually occurred to his nephew and he returned safely, then the suffering he experienced must have been "suffering of love," i.e., simply to refine him.

69 The *Kaddish* is a special prayer for the deceased, recited preferably by their sons (*Kitsur Shulkhan Arukh* 26:1).

70 Slobodzer, meaning "from Slobodze," was not his surname but a nickname used by those outside of Slobodze.

sidur containing various Jewish laws in Yiddish, "Believe me, if I had had such a prayer book in my youth, I would have been able to rule on *halakhic* matters."[71] Though he used to pray the entire day and would constantly be grumbling, he could not correctly pronounce even one word of the Hebrew prayers. When counting *Sfira*, he would stick a small piece of wax in his prayer book next to that day's *Sfira* to keep track of the day, but his mischievous grandchildren or some other kids would later move the wax.[72] So when he came the next night to the *minyan* to pray and would hear that they were counting a different day of the *Sfira* than the one he had marked, he would make a commotion, "How can it be! Scoundrels! No one knows where we're up to in counting *Sfira*!" It seemed to him that everything he did was holy. *Nu*, what do you say about the learned residents of Slobodze? Reb Shmiel's son-in-law was also a "well-learned person." A *shoykhet* was of no significance to him—hire him, dismiss him, who cares?

I once went over to the elderly Reb Shmiel on the eve of Yom Kippur to slaughter his *kapores* chicken for him. He began to recite the *Bney Odom* prayer with difficulty—and maybe he is still at it. He was staring at the *Bney Odom* prayer—and the rooster was staring along with him.[73] In short, I had to help him through it. He eventually succeeded in worming his way through the *Bney Odom*. Then began a new challenge for him—finding on the very same page the prayer "This is my exchange,"[74] which is said afterward, but he could not find it.

---

71 A *Korben Minkhe sidur* is a prayer book which is usually used by women and includes the Yiddish translation of many prayers, Yiddish-language supplications, and instructions in Yiddish for many of the laws pertaining to running a Jewish household. Hence, reading such a prayer book hardly made anyone a learned rabbi.

72 Jews are obligated to verbally count the forty-nine days between the second day of Pesach (the anniversary of Moses leading the Jews out of Egypt) and *Shvues*, when the Jewish people received the Torah at Mt. Sinai. This is called in Yiddish *tseyln sfire*, i.e., counting the *Sfira*, and is also called "counting the *Omer*." On each of these forty-nine days, a special Hebrew blessing is recited, followed by the number of days of the *Sfira* to be counted (*Kitsur Shulkhan Arukh* 120:1–11). Prayer books include the specific wording for the counting of each of the forty-nine days of the *Sfira*. It is to such a list that Reb Shmiel affixed a piece of wax to mark his place.

73 *Bney Odom* is a prayer recited during *kapores* and is generally recited while the person is holding a live chicken. It is quite common for the chicken to be glancing in the direction of the prayer book while the person is saying *Bney Odom*. This is the source of the Yiddish expression, "*Kukn vi a hon in Bney Odom*" which means, "Looking at the *Bney Odom* prayer like a rooster," which refers to someone looking at a text without having a glimmer of understanding of its contents. The author is joking here that Shmiel's understanding of this prayer was similar to that of the rooster's.

74 On the eve of Yom Kippur, each of the three times one recites the *Ze khalifosi* prayer ("This is my exchange, this is my [symbolic] substitute, this is my [symbolic] atonement; this rooster will go to its death, and I will go to a long life of peace"), one circles the *kapores* chicken over one's own head.

In the prayer book were instructions printed in small letters, and he was curious to know what was written there. He mistakenly began to recite as a prayer the instructions "For someone who will *shlog kapores* for someone else. . . ."[75] He caught himself and said, "You know what? Hey! Here's the prayer for someone who is *shlogn kapores* for another person." He then skipped that section. He then came across the instructions for two people to *shlog kapores* together, "Two people who *shlogn kapores* together! I don't need that. I need the prayer that starts with the words, 'This is *my* exchange,'" He finally grew tired of searching for the right prayer and said in anger, "The *shoykhet* should read it for me. All of this is written for the *shoykhet* but not for the layman."[76] I gave a chuckle and said, "True enough, Reb Shmiel, the *shoykhet* himself should *shlog kapores* with you [that is, should flail you about],[77] because without the *shoykhet,* you don't even *toyg af kapores* [that is, you're useless]."[78] How do you like this "Torah scholar"? And in Slobodze were many such "scholars," and they were my rulers and bread-givers.

We will now continue with my account of how I lived during my final year in Slobodze. Once the turmoil of the persecutions I had endured had quieted down, I began to look around to see if it was so worthwhile to continue suffering there or perhaps it was advisable to abandon the place. Since I had a reputation in the entire district as a good *shoykhet,* I could easily obtain another position. I would just need to seek one out. So I decided to try to make a new and better arrangement for myself with the community of Slobodze. If I could accomplish this, then good—Slobodze would then become a place of income for a *shoykhet,* and I would be able to live there calmly like a *mentsh.* But if I would not be able to carry out my new arrangement, then it would not be the place for me and I would abandon Slobodze and seek out a new place. Since I

---

75 *Shlogn kapores* literally means "to waive the *kapores*" and involves taking a live chicken in the right hand and moving it in a circular motion around the head three times while reciting certain prayers. Many prayer books, as well as the one Reb Shmiel was using, include instructions on the correct conjugation of the Hebrew words of the *Ze khalifosi* prayer depending on the circumstances, e.g., for someone *shlogn kapores* for someone else; for two people *shlogn kapores* with one chicken; a person *shlogn kapores* for himself, etc.

76 In actuality, these instructions are considered to be quite simple and are certainly geared toward the layman.

77 The Yiddish expression "*shlogn kapores* with someone" is a humorous way of saying "to thrash someone about."

78 The Yiddish expression "*toygn af kapores*" literally means "being fit for *kapores*" (fit only for circling around one's head like a chicken used for *kapores*) and is used figuratively regarding anyone or anything that is "good for nothing." In saying "you don't even *toyg af kapores,*" the author is making a pun meaning, "you aren't even 'fit for *kapores*,'" since he can't even *shlog kapores* without the *shoykhet*'s help.

knew that carrying out my plan would not be easy, as it would cause new strife and leave me without an income, I secured myself another source of income so that I would be able to endure the fight for a while.

In order to carry out my plan, I first obtained a part-time position in two villages in the area. One village, called Tshobritsh, was three *versts* from Slobodze and had twelve Jewish families living there. The second, called Kópenke, was on the other side of the Dniester River, three or four *versts* from Slobodze, and had eight Jewish families living there. I arranged with these two villages that I would come twice a week to slaughter chickens, sheep, and cows. I would also perform any circumcisions that were needed and would receive supplementary income from any of their celebrations that would require my services.[79] This totaled five rubles a week. I began to go to those villages regularly and my positions there became firmly established.

The residents of Slobodze began to have complaints against me that I was not there when they needed me. I thought to myself, "Just wait a little longer and you'll even have more complaints against me." In brief, I informed them that I was absolving all previous debts due me and from now on I would not be accepting weekly stipends. Whoever wanted a chicken slaughtered should know that he had to pay me five *kopeks* in advance to have it slaughtered, ten *kopeks* for a goose, the same for a turkey, fifteen *kopeks* for a lamb, and sixty *kopeks* for a cow, apart from the small pieces of meat which were traditionally given to the *shoykhet*.[80] You can imagine the commotion this caused in the village, though I had little to fear. I let them know that I was no longer afraid of them. I was no longer their *shoykhet*. I was now a *shoykhet* in Kopenke and Tshobritsh, but not their *shoykhet*. I found it useful to live in their village, but they were not obligated to use my services. They were welcome to drag themselves to wherever they wanted to have their animals slaughtered or they could bring another *shoykhet* to Slobodze if they wanted.

I stopped walking to everyone's house to do the slaughtering. If anyone needed anything slaughtered, they would have to come to me. I did not have the devilish strength to walk so much—and especially for naught. No more feudal servitude. I was not going to remain an eternal slave.

I approached those Slobodzers who had animals slaughtered only once every two or three weeks,[81] and I clarified my plan as follows, "Why should you

---

79 Such supplementary income could include payment for singing at a wedding ceremony, tips for performing circumcisions, and similar services.

80 The author leaves out that he charged twenty-five *kopeks* to slaughter a young sheep, as mentioned on p. 439 below.

81 The original states "once or twice a week," which is a mistake as made clear below.

have to pay a weekly stipend when you don't make use of the *shoykhet* every week. As it turns out, you make use of the *shoykhet* only once every two or three weeks, so it ends up costing you thirty *kopeks* to have one chicken slaughtered.[82] My new arrangement is better for you because slaughtering a chicken now only costs you five *kopeks*. Those who have a lot of animals to slaughter should do the worrying. With my new arrangement, you won't be in debt to the *shoykhet*. In that way, he won't have anything against you, and you won't have anything against him. It will only be bad for those few who use the *shoykhet* often. It will now cost them more than they had to pay until now." I reasoned with them like this and drove home my point so that every thick-skulled one of them agreed to the new arrangement, even though they were originally against it. They had been afraid that I was removing their control over me and was altering the order of the world since time immemorial—all the way back to Slobodze's very beginnings. But now that they heard that I was excusing their previous debts and reducing their slaughtering costs to five *kopeks* every three weeks, they were convinced and were actually saying, "This is truly wonderful." Everyone is interested in saving money. You can imagine that it did not take a tremendous amount of effort to win them over, and they all joined me in my plan.

Even those who made much use of the *shoykhet* joined my ranks. They figured that they could have twenty young sheep slaughtered a year, and that would only cost them twenty times twenty-five *kopeks* for the year.[83] Since I was no longer asking for my weekly stipend, the new arrangement would cost them less than the old system.

The only ones who were reluctant to go along with my plan were ten to twelve villagers who made steady use of the *shoykhet* throughout the year because they were constantly selling meat as butchers. They raised a ruckus. Previously they had been quite powerful because all had stood by them, but everyone immediately withdrew their support once I explained my new arrangement (which you already know). I had little to fear from these ten to twelve villagers, because I knew that they could not force me to slaughter anything. After all, I had no contract with them stating that I had to slaughter anything for them. They also could not force me to leave Slobodze nor could they bring in another *shoykhet* because no one in Slobodze would be willing to pay a new

82 Those paying the lowest weekly stipend of ten *kopeks* would end up spending thirty *kopeks* every three weeks.

83 Hence, under the new system, twenty young sheep would cost 500 *kopeks* to slaughter, while under the old system it would have cost a minimum of 900 *kopeks*. In the original Yiddish, the author mistakenly writes "twenty-five *gildn*" (equal to 375 *kopeks*) instead of "twenty-five *kopeks*."

shoykhet a weekly stipend. I knew this quite well, and I knew that they would simply yell until they tired of it, which is exactly what happened. They shouted until they grew tired, and, ultimately, they had to apologize and begin paying for each animal separately.

I insisted that they pay me in advance for any slaughtering done so that I would not need to have any further dealings with them in case the animal was found to be *treyf* or the person did not have any cash on hand. So I set the rule that I would slaughter only after I had received my payment. I was overjoyed when I realized that I had some hard cash. I would finish the work week and bring home four to five rubles. I no longer needed to run around collecting debts and begging, "Give me at least something."

Thank God, things calmed down. Everyone became accustomed to the new arrangement, and everyone admitted that it was very good and that they had a *shoykhet* with something of a Talmudic mind. The only ones not satisfied were those who constantly sold meat as butchers. They were bitter because it was costing them so much, and they felt that they were supporting the *shoykhet* for the entire village. I pointed out to them that they were making a mistake since they were in fact earning well and had no need to complain that it was costing them so much. In short, eventually they also calmed down and peace and tranquility returned.

It was then that I looked back and realized how deep in the ground I had been and how lowly they had treated me as a *shoykhet*. I began to look around to see what items I was lacking in my house and bought some furniture. When one walked into my house now, it was as if one was entering one of the homes of the finest residents of the village. When my sister Ite came to visit, she was delighted that her brother had such a clean and beautiful home and that at last he was making quite a fine living. It might appear to you that I was now doing quite well and that things could not have been better. But if you think so then you are mistaken—Pinye-Ber could not have things go that well for him. Things could not improve so quickly for him—and maybe things would never be good for him, God forbid.

You probably remember from my narrative that I had to walk to two villages to do some slaughtering twice a week. Just consider that I had to walk the entire length of Slobodze—seven to eight *versts*—twice in the course of each day, besides walking to those two villages, each of which was four to five *versts* long.[84] You now understand that I had a good bit of work set out for myself,

84 Though the author had stopped going to private individuals, he was still going to the ten to twelve villagers who sold meat as butchers, as related in the next paragraph.

meaning that I worked over and above my capacity and it would be impossible for me to last long working this way, particularly during the winter in the cold and in the snow when the days were short and I had to walk at night. From all this, you can imagine that my situation was far from perfect. I began to think about my health; the way I was neglecting myself and ruining my health which could even cause me to die. As it was, two mishaps had already occurred to me practically causing me to lose my life, which I will relate later. So I decided to carry out yet another plan. If I was able to put this plan into effect, I would finally be able to say that I was doing well and could consider myself lucky. If not, in order to free myself from all the walking I had to do, I would at long last have to leave Slobodze with all of its "good fortunte". It would have been impossible to go on like that for long, particularly when my life was imperiled a few times. Meanwhile, I could not leave my *sh'khita* positions in the two villages because without them I would not be able to carry out my new plan in Slobodze, just like I was not able to carry out my prior plan without them, as you already know.

I had established the paying of *sh'khita* money instead of a weekly stipend and everyone was satisfied apart from those twelve villagers who made constant use of the *shoykhet* since they were selling meat as butchers. They were quite displeased, but they paid me and were accustoming themselves to that arrangement. When my second plan would be implemented, Slobodze would be a place where a *shoykhet* could earn his livelihood in a reasonable manner. I introduced my second plan by notifying all of the butchers that I would no longer be walking to each butcher's house separately to do my slaughtering. Instead, there would be set times for *sh'khita* and set places. This meant that everyone needed to bring their lambs to be slaughtered at one end of the village and I would go there once a day. Similarly at the other end of the village, they should fix a set time in the morning or in the late afternoon (it would be their choice) and bring to that location whatever animals needed to be slaughtered. Otherwise, they would need to bring the animal to me at my home, meaning that if they had something else for me to slaughter after the set time, they would have to bring it to me. This is what I informed them.

You can well imagine the uproar this caused. Now steaming mad, they said, "What else will you come up with? How can you do this?" but I had made up my mind once and for all. Whichever way it would work out would be good for me. If they went along with my plan, I would have found myself a reasonable place of income and I could stop working in the neighboring villages. If they brought the animals to me, I would slaughter them, and if they did not, I would not go to them either. If my plan failed and they would not be satisfied with my availability in their area once a day, it would be clear that Slobodze was not a place for me to earn a living. I would wrest myself from them, because by this time I was already sick of running all over to slaughter their various animals. I was also sick of constantly holding those two villages over them like a strap. Additionally, I had placed my life in peril more than once going to those places, particularly Kopenke, which was four *versts* away, on the other side of the Dniester River. More than once, the Dniester overflowed and the current became strong, making it dangerous to cross by boat. I once barely made it across with my life. Those who were standing on a nearby mountain thought that I had sunk under the ice together with the boat, but I had actually been saved by a miracle. So you can imagine the danger involved in walking in the direction of that village. The actual road to Kopenke went through a forest, after which were gardens. In the summer the road was tolerable but walking on that road in the winter was frightening, I was playing with my life. I will now tell you about an extremely terrifying experience I had. It actually occurred a short time before I came out with my second plan. One could say that this scare led me to end the wretched existence I was living in Slobodze, thereby certainly rescuing me just in time, as you will learn below. But for now, I will tell you about the scare that I had walking to Kopenke.

At the end of the month of *Heshvan,* I needed to be in Tiraspol. So on Sunday, in the late afternoon, I walked to Tiraspol, which was a total of twelve *versts* away, and I slept there.[85] Quite early on Monday morning after praying, when I was ready to return home, I realized that I would need to leave for Kopenke shortly after arriving home. But if I had any work to do in Slobodze, I would not be able to arrive in Kopenke in time because the day was short. So it seemed like a better idea to go home via Kopenke, since the distance from Tiraspol directly to Kopenke was the same twelve *versts* as from Tiraspol to Slobodze. The only difference was that in going to Kopenke I would need to cross the Dniester by boat.

I finished praying in Tiraspol and at 10 o'clock I crossed the Dniester by boat and continued on my way toward Kopenke. The road went through a village called Kitskón, which was located on the top of a mountain where a convent was located. From the village of Kitskon, one still had to walk another eight *versts* to Kopenke. Four *versts* from Kitskon, one entered a small forest. Beyond the forest there were gardens that stretched on until one reached Kopenke. I left

85 November 28, 1875 was the last Sunday in *Heshvan,* 5636. The year is 1875 since this incident took place a month or two before the author's daughter, Khone-Reyzele, was born, which took place between December 1875 and January 1876 (see later on p. 446).

Kitskon and began to descend the mountain. I could see the small forest, and then I heard the sound of dogs howling in the woods. I did not pay attention to the howling and kept walking along the way with gusto. I figured that shepherds were grazing their sheep and their dogs were barking. I then noticed something running low to the ground out of the forest, but I was not sure if it was a calf or a dog because of its distance from me. I continued on my way and came closer to the thing, and the thing came closer to me as it was running toward me. I noticed that it was a dog. I began to worry that perhaps it was a mad dog. If so, what would I do? I did not have a stick in my hand and there were no stones to be found. Meanwhile, the dog came closer. I saw that it was a large dog. It suddenly dawned on me that perhaps it was actually a wolf. *Oy*! I was seized by terror. What should a person do in such a situation? How could one save oneself from a wolf? I had no stick, no stones—only God to come to my aid. Only the one, beloved God could have mercy on me and save me from the wolf's sharp fangs. I began to consider turning back but realized that would be useless since the wolf would catch up with me anyway. Since I could no longer flee at that point, I had to continue on. Whatever God would hand out would be how it would be. I continued walking in extreme terror for I thought that at any moment the wolf could pounce on me, eat my flesh, and finish me off. "A fine end," I thought to myself.

Meanwhile, I noticed that the wolf had crossed the road from the right side to the left. As the wolf strayed off the road to the left, I deviated off the road to the right. When I noticed what was happening, I felt relieved because God had shown me that He would help me and that the wolf was afraid of me—because God had decreed it to be so. On the other hand, I thought that perhaps that was the nature of the wolf so that he would have an easier time catching his prey. In the meantime, the wolf emerged across from me. It was truly a large, frightening, and ferocious wolf. Out of fright, I did not know what to do. I placed my hand in my breast pocket near my slaughtering knife. I remained standing and yelled out, "Master of the Universe, have mercy on me and save me in the merit of my poor wife and child." The wolf stopped in its tracks, looked me over from head to toe and seemed to be wondering, "Why are you shouting? Am I bothering you? Go your way and stop yelling." It suddenly dawned on me, "Why am I standing before my Angel of Death?" I started to run and then looked behind me to see if the wolf was chasing me. I saw that the wolf was standing in its place for some time while it kept looking at me, as if he was saying, "I had to let such a tasty morsel go because God decrees it to be so. What a pity!"

In short, I reached Kopenke, thank God, and by nightfall had reached my wife and child. I told them the miracles that God had performed for me. My wife cried a lot and made me swear that I would stop walking through those dangerous areas, "If you can work it out so that you can earn a living here, then fine. If not, see to it that you find yourself another position—anything, just as long as your life will be safe. Make sure you safeguard your life so that I shouldn't be left a young widow with children, God forbid. Srul-Burekhl, may he live and be well, is already four years old [*sic*] and soon I'll be a mother of two children.[86] Have pity on us and save your life before it's too late."

After all of this, I took measures to end all that walking by trying to implement my plan (which you already know) of having set times for slaughtering at the two ends of the village or else having them bring me their animals to be slaughtered at my home. But I realized that this was impossible to implement even if they had not been opposed to it, because the butchers in my village did not purchase cows or sheep wholesale at the marketplace ready to be slaughtered. Here it was not like that. As it happened, they purchased them individually. One day a butcher had an animal that needed to be slaughtered and the next day he did not. In the morning, he did not have an animal to be slaughtered but by late in the day he had purchased one. So when the *shoykhet* came at the designated time, he might not have had anything to slaughter though he would have something to slaughter a little later.[87] This was especially the case regarding those butchers who slaughtered only once in a blue moon; they certainly could not know when they would obtain an animal at a good price. Since the butcher would only be earning twenty *kopeks*, why would he pay a non-Jew thirty *kopeks* to bring the animal by cart over to the *shoykhet*? How could that have been worthwhile? I finally realized that I would not be able to succeed in this endeavor and would have to leave this place for another. I—as well as the residents of Slobodze—suffered greatly for three or four weeks.

Now that I had decided to leave Slobodze, I wanted to successfully obtain compensation for the exclusive slaughtering rights in Slobodze. I did not want to leave the position open for another *shoykhet* to come there without paying for these rights. Meanwhile, I continued to insist that I would not go to their houses but that they should bring the animals to me at my home. I did this intentionally to agitate them—to have them rise up against me and say that I was being unjust, which would then bring the entire matter to its ultimate conclusion. I made sure to incite the worst ruffians of the village, who actually ran

---

86 Srul-Burekhl was actually almost three years old, since he was born in January 1873 (ch. 21, p. 381) and this incident took place a month or two before the author's daughter, Khone-Reyzele, was born between December 1875 and January 1876 (see later on p. 446).

87 Once they purchased a lamb, they evidently needed to have it slaughtered right away, possibly to recover their money promptly, to eat it immediately, or for some other reason.

to bring another *shoykhet*. Meanwhile, I ran and brought the rabbi of Tiraspol, Rabbi Lerner, and the Tiraspoler *shokhtim* Reb Shloyme and Reb Zolmen and asked them to rule according to Jewish law how much I was entitled to receive for relinquishing the slaughtering rights.[88] I asked them not to make any compromises for the sake of peace, because I would only agree to remain if I would not have to keep walking to everyone's houses day and night. It so happened that one night as I was returning from slaughtering some animals, some scoundrels from the village surrounded me and wanted to beat me up. I was compelled to take my slaughtering knife out of its case and show them that I would defend myself with knife in hand—regardless of who was standing there—which would certainly cause them to be injured, whereupon they all scattered. Therefore, I could not remain living in such a place where my life was not safe. And so it was that the *shokhtim* and the rabbi found me to be in the right; if they did not agree to bring the animals to my house, they would need to placate me by paying me for the slaughtering rights—otherwise they would not be able to dismiss me.[89] They ruled that they must give me fifty rubles for the slaughtering rights in order to be freed from being their *shoykhet*.

I immediately agreed to the ruling and countersigned a statement agreeing that Slobodze would remain free for the taking upon my receipt of fifty rubles for the slaughtering rights. They would be able to bring in whichever *shoykhet* they wanted, and I would have no claim to those rights from that day onward. But the Slobodzers wanted to procrastinate and said that they currently had no money and would only be able to pay in two weeks. Their intention was that if I did not agree to wait two more weeks, they would be able to continue with their machinations against me and not pay me a thing. Others figured that I might reconsider my position and give in to them if they delayed payment for two weeks, while still others were delaying payment because they actually did not want to let me go. In any event, I was willing to wait two weeks for the money and warned that if they did not pay up, I would remain there as a *shoykhet* and my stipulation of having them bring their animals to me would remain in effect, as mentioned earlier.

88 Rabbi Yisruel-Avrúm Lerner (1839/1840–1915) was the rabbi of Tiraspol. He was first appointed to be the rabbi of Balyn, Ukraine, in 1865, after which he was appointed as the rabbi of Tiraspol (Gotlib, 1912:83). He wrote two rabbinical works, *Kuntres Bet Yisrael* (Warsaw, 1912) and *Shmot Bnei Yisrael* (Poltava, 1913). The author brought the rabbi and two *shokhtim* to form a three-man rabbinical court.

89 This rabbinical ruling is interesting considering that the author did not officially pay for the slaughtering rights upon his arrival in Slobodze, though he gave twenty rubles to the previous *shoykhet* for his moving expenses (ch. 21, p. 385–386).

During the course of those two weeks, my wife gave birth to a little girl during the week of the Torah portion of *Vayishlakh* in *Teyves* 5635 [*sic*], and I named her Khone-Reyzele.[90] After services, I invited everyone over to my house for some honey cake and liquor—not as their *shoykhet* but simply as a resident of the village since I had already renounced Slobodze with all of its "good fortune." I then left my wife and children with the elderly midwife whom I had brought for the childbirth and traveled off to a certain *shteytl* where I had heard they needed a *shoykhet.*

I arrived in the *shteytl,* which was located in the administrative district of Tiraspol and was called Buzinove. It lies close to Baronev—they are not even a *verst* apart from one another—and just a small stream separates them. Baronev is in the administrative district of Odessa, while Buzinove is in the administrative district of Tiraspol. Baronev was a large *shteytl*—there were two *shokhtim* there and a rabbi who was a powerful kosher-meat tax farmer as was sometimes found among Jews. On the other hand, Buzinove was a very small *shteytl* of thirty Jewish families who were poor to boot.[91] Upon my arrival in Buzinove, the people became enthusiastic over me and did not want to let me leave. They wanted to write a contract with me stating that I would receive fifty rubles a year for leading the services during the High Holidays and that I would not be obligated to lead the services the rest of the year—only when I wanted to. My salary would be five *kopeks* for slaughtering a chicken, ten *kopeks* for a goose, two rubles for a cow or a calf, and one ruble for a lamb. They offered me such generous terms because they liked me. Based on the *sh'khita* payments, it seemed to me that I would be able to earn a nice living there. Even if they slaughtered only two calves a week, I would have earned four rubles. If you added the slaughtering of chickens and lambs and the payment for leading the services, I would be earning a total of six rubles a week, which was equal to my salary in Slobodze, and I would not have to do all that walking. In Buzinove, the only walking that I would have to do was from my house to the butcher in the neighboring courtyard and then home again. And they had a beautiful *shul,* which was also not far away. I liked the people there for they seemed honest. In

90 The year was 5636 (December 1875)—not 5635 (December 1874)—which can be calculated by working backward from his move to Bakhchisaray in March 1879 (ch. 23, p. 462). Hence, Khone-Reyzele was born during the week of the Torah portion of *Vayishlakh* in 5636 (December 5–11, 1875), which was in *Kislev*—not in *Teyves,* as the author writes. Nonetheless, she could have been born in *Teyves* if the author meant to write that she was born during the week of the Torah portion of *Vayigash* or *Vayekhi,* which occurred at the end of December 1875 and early January 1876.

91 For more about kosher-meat tax farmers, see ch. 23, p. 470.

short, I agreed to become their *shoykhet*, wishing it would go well, and I traveled home to bring my family there.

CHAPTER 23

The Nobleman's Attack and Moving to the Crimea, 1876–1880

Departing Slobodze • Arriving in Buzinove as Its *Shoykhet* • My Life in Buzinove • Much Honor Yet Little Earnings • Becoming a Marriage Broker • The Nobleman's Attack • Leaving My *Sh'khita* Position in Buzinove and Selling the Slaughtering Rights • Traveling in Search of a Position as a *Shoykhet* • Obtaining a Position But Needing to Raise Money for the Slaughtering Rights • Raising a Little Money and Becoming the *Shoykhet* in Bakhchisaray • The Horrible Suffering I Endured in the Community-Owned Residence[1] • Persecution at the Hands of the Main Instigators • The Harassment Increases—Only Six Rubles a Week instead of Eight • My Encounter with Simkhe Mayster

I still had to wait about eight days to move to Buzinove because my wife did not want to move before the baby was a month old.[2] After a month had passed, I loaded all my household possessions onto two wagons—along with a third wagon for us to ride in. If you remember, when I arrived in Slobodze, even one wagon was too much.[3]

---

1 This content entry and the subsequent ones are mistakenly printed at the beginning of ch. 25 in the original.

2 The author arrived in Buzinove in January or February 1876 when his daughter, Khone-Reyzele, was a month old. See ch. 22, p. 446, footnote 90.

3 See ch. 21, p. 386.

When the residents of Slobodze saw that I was serious about leaving, they had regrets and began to try to reconcile with me so that we would stay. They mainly tried to convince my wife, but they did not know that she had been the primary force behind our moving. They were even willing to give me fifty rubles just to remain there. My wife and I were both of the same opinion: "no" and "no." In short, we bade farewell to everyone and thankfully left with our lives. That very same day, we arrived in Buzinove. In having moved from a small village to a more developed town, we had at last arrived, thank God, in a place that was certainly more pleasant and satisfying in all respects.[4]

When I arrived in the *shteytl* of Buzinove as their *shoykhet*, my son Srul-Burekhl was four years old [sic] and Khone-Reyzele was a month old, and I was as if newly born.[5] I sat at home and rested for I no longer needed to walk anywhere. There was little to slaughter and the sole butcher in town had me slaughter only one or two animals a week. Each household would have a chicken slaughtered for *Shobes*, but they would bring the chicken to me at my home. At the beginning, I very much liked Buzinove as I was able to rest after all the walking I had been doing. But after having rested, it began to sicken me that I had been so hasty in moving to this wasteland. True, the people there treated me honorably and were appreciative of getting hold of a good *shoykhet*, but what use was this to me if my earnings were not enough? My situation became worse with the beginning of Great Lent when the sole butcher with his sole eye (he was blind in one eye) stopped having anything slaughtered.[6] I then ended up using fifty rubles of my own savings by Pesach.[7] Bad! I had been duped once again into taking a position in the wrong place. If I had not been in a rush and had searched more, I could have certainly landed a good place, but—as they say—nothing good happens from haste. But I also could not blame myself, since I had wanted to save myself by escaping from that hellhole. After all, they

4 Though Slobodze and Buzinove both had only about thirty Jewish families, Buzinove was larger and more developed. For example, Buzinove had its own synagogue whereas private homes were used for prayer in Slobodze.

5 Srul-Burekhl was three years old, not four. See also ch. 22, p. 444, where he is again mistakenly referred to as being four years old.

6 Great Lent, or Great Fast, is the most important fasting season in the church year in Eastern Christianity (including the Russian Orthodox Church). As in the Western Christian Church, the Eastern Great Lent covers the forty days before Easter, yet they differ in theology, practice, and timing. In 1876, Great Lent lasted from February 27 until April 15 (or February 15–April 3 per Old Style dating). Since the non-Jews refrained from eating meat, poultry, fish, and their derivatives during Great Lent, the butcher stopped having cattle and sheep slaughtered since he was not able to sell off the unwanted hindquarters, as explained in ch. 22, p. 404, footnote 3.

7 April 8–16, 1876.

surely would have tried to convince us to remain in Slobodze, and we would certainly have stayed. So this way, I was at least out of Slobodze. Yet how I would support myself remained a question. At least in Buzinove I was treated honorably and was not constantly placing my life in danger. If God decreed it, I would not remain there long.

A few months after my arrival there, I began to feel so ill that I had to remain lying down. I had to get to a doctor, and, by chance, a doctor came to Buzinove. So I asked him to examine me, which he did. He said, "Nothing's wrong with you. You're quite healthy. But you must walk and stop staying put. You were used to walking a lot and then you suddenly stopped and began resting, which is having a bad effect on you. In short, you must walk a lot every day and then you'll become completely well." I understood that he was right. I began to take walks over to Baronev as well as taking idle walks, and I quickly recovered, thank God.

I had no slaughtering to do and I wanted to walk, but I had nowhere to go. So I began to broker marriages between the Jewish families of Buzinove and Baronev and those in the large cities. I now had something to do, and I took many extra walks with high hopes of eventually earning something. I was able to take leave of the *shteytl* because when I was not there, my butcher would call over a *shoykhet* from Baronev; I would take half of the *sh'khita* money of whatever he slaughtered. This way, the residents of Buzinove had no complaints against me that they were suffering from the lack of a *shoykhet*. They knew well that a *shoykhet* earned little there and that he had to seek out other means of making a living. So no one opposed my making a new life for myself consisting of both marriage brokering and slaughtering animals and fowl. I could always find a wagon traveling from Buzinovke to Rozdelnye, which was thirty-five *versts* away, and to Odessa, which was fifty *versts* away.[8] But I had to walk on foot to Tiraspol, Bender, and Kishinev, since traveling there was expensive and, in that business, I needed to make multiple trips. So walking to those places enabled me to go often; otherwise, I would not have seen results.

To make a long story short, I acquired the reputation of being an extremely reputable marriage broker. Because I was flying all over the place, people thought that I was earning who knows how much. But I knew the truth: *melomdim*, marriage brokers, and especially *shokhtim*—particularly in such a wasteland—were all on the same level. By now, I had worked as a *melomed*, a marriage broker, and a *shoykhet*, and each had only enabled me to struggle along on four rubles

---

8 Note that Buzinove is referred to here as Buzinovke. A similar example is Donetsk, Ukraine, which before 1924 was called both Yuzovo and Yuzovka.

a week. The only bit of luck I had was that everything was inexpensive, which enabled my wife and two children to get by—and clothe themselves too—on those four rubles a week. I suffered like this in Buzinove for three years. I had no difficulties at all from the residents there for they treated me honorably, as I wrote earlier.

I will now describe my family life—what occurred to me, my wife, and children—during those three years. You already know a bit, so I will now relate the rest. In 5637 I traveled to Tiraspol regarding marriage brokering.[9] The evening that I left, my children were happy and healthy. I played with my little daughter Khone-Reyzele while holding her in my arms. Upon returning home three days later, I found my wife sitting *shivah*.

"What happened?" I asked. "Did you receive bad news from your parents, God forbid?"

She replied, "Khone-Reyzele died just yesterday."

"When did she have time to get sick? I just left her happy and healthy."

"She contracted diphtheria and died of the fever in less than twenty-four hours."

You can imagine how I cried and wailed. But of what use was that? I was not easily consoled because it seemed to me that I would have been able to save her had I been home. She died on the 11th of *Shvat*.[10] She had been all of two years old. But I had to console myself because my wife was pregnant, so I took comfort that God would quickly return my loss by giving me a child who would live a long and good life. And that is what happened. After the tragedy that occurred on the 11th of *Shvat* 5637, God returned my loss two months later. My wife gave birth to a daughter whom I named Nekhamele.[11] May she truly be an eternal comfort.[12]

My Srul-Burekhl was by then already a fine boy. He was handsome and could recite *Kiddush* with a pleasant melody. Everybody used to give him a *kopek* to hear him recite it. When someone would stop him in the middle of the street to ask him, "Srulikl, here's a *kopek*. Make *Kiddush* for me," he would unassumingly stand up straight and recite it loudly, so that it was a delight to listen to. He was loved by the entire *shteytl*—especially by the women, who would bless

---

9 Referring to January 1877, as indicated below.

10 January 25, 1877.

11 Nekhame was born in *Nisan* of 5637 (March 1877). This date corresponds to the birth date of February 11, 1877 that Nekhame (under the name Nechama Brockman) used on her 1928 petition for US Citizenship (#176698) to the US District Court for the Eastern District of New York.

12 Nekhame means "comfort" in Hebrew.

the local children that they should be like him. This caused us much pleasure. So we were pleased to see that our son was growing up to be a pious boy with sincerity and without deceit.

I must relate something else that happened to me in Buzinove which resounded throughout the entire region. It actually occurred during the winter, a short while after I had been struck by the tragedy of my daughter's death. During that time, I had to travel somewhere regarding marriage brokering. Since it was freezing and snowing outside, I dressed warmly and left my house with the thought of walking over to Baronev to hire a wagon. Just as I was leaving the *shteytl* and entering the open country, I heard a wagon approaching from behind me. I did not pay attention to it and went along my way. Upon hearing the approach of the wagon close behind me, I walked to the side of the road so that it could have clear passage without hindrance and so that I could also walk freely. Because it was so cold and the passing wagon was of little interest to me, I did not even allow myself to look back to see who was traveling in the wagon. But when I walked off the road and the wagon moved ahead of me, I noticed that it was an expensive carriage with three horses harnessed to it. A coachman sat on the coachbox and a big, fat nobleman was arrogantly stretched out inside. I noticed all of this at a glance and made nothing of it. I just continued walking my way more quickly to reach Baronev sooner.

Suddenly, I heard the nobleman shout to the coachman in Russian, "Stop!" He then grabbed the whip from the coachman's hands, jumped off the carriage, and headed right toward me, saying in Russian, "You *Zhid*.[13] You aren't taking off your hat? You see that a nobleman is driving by, and you aren't removing your hat." I actually had with me a good walking stick, which I raised before him and said, "If you strike me with that whip, I'll pound you over the head with this stick." He did not back down and lashed me with it and raised his hand to whip me again. I took my stick in both of my hands and, while holding on to each end, flung it over his head and squeezed him against me, holding the stick against the entire breadth of his shoulders. I had him fettered where he could not move a limb. Whenever he wished to move, the stick would squeeze his back. He could not move his arms because I had them firmly locked within my own. He was quite fat and beefy, but I was also no lightweight. Whenever he tried to tear himself away from me, I would give him a jab in his back with the stick and knee him right in his stomach so that he danced back and forth as if he was reciting *Boi ve'shulem*.[14] He shouted "Let me go, *Zhid*!" And I replied, "I'll continue holding

---

13 In the Russian language, *zhid* is a pejorative term for Jew.

14 *Boi ve'shulem* (*Boi ve-shalom* in Modern Hebrew) are the opening words to the last stanza of the Friday-night Hebrew prayer *Lekhó Doydi* (*Lekha Dodi*) which ushers in the Sabbath.

you until witnesses come along and see what's happening. You won't be able to tear yourself from my hands unless I myself let you go." He tried to tear himself away and screamed because it hurt him. I said, "Stop struggling, stay still, and you won't be hurt. The stick won't scrape you then and my knee won't jab into you." I noticed that the non-Jews of Buzinove remained in their little huts and were watching what was happening, but no one came over to separate us. The non-Jews coming from Baronev did the same; they stood there and looked at what was happening, but no one approached us because no one wanted to testify to such an episode.

After holding him like that for perhaps a half hour, he began to plead for me to let him go, "*Zhidovchik*, I won't do anything to you."[15] I replied, "Let the carriage move over here, and I'll let you go. But be sure not to use your whip again or else you'll suffer the consequences." And that is what happened. He told the coachman to move the carriage close to us and I let him go. He then grabbed the whip, lashed me again with it, and wanted to climb onto the carriage, but I did not let him sit down. At that point, I firmly took him into my grip and told him, "Now you'll be with me until others eventually come along. If not, you'll burst here under my arms." I spat in his face and said, "See what your arrogance has brought you—that a rotten *Zhid* has spat on you."

He yelled for the coachman to climb down and help him to free himself from this *Zhid*. The coachman said that he could not leave the horses otherwise they would flee. I also asked the coachman to come down from the carriage. I would have then climbed onto it, driven straight to the Justice of the Peace, and let the coachman and the nobleman chase after me. But the coachman did not want to come down, so the nobleman remained pinned under my arms until it began to turn dark. By then I was tired of holding such a big boar and he was pleading and swearing to me that he would now be fine and good. Meanwhile, a young non-Jew, one of his hired hands, suddenly appeared. Upon seeing him, the nobleman began to say in a tearful voice, "My child, see what this *Zhid* is doing to me. Save me, Oleksiy."[16] I said, "Good, Oleksiy, that you came. Be a witness that I'm letting him go but you are not to mix in at all," and I let him loose.

The nobleman regained his confidence, and murder burned strongly within him. He desecrated his oath and began to strike me so hard that the whip flew out of his hand. Naturally, I would not let anyone spit in my porridge and

---

The author is humorously comparing the nobleman's being thrust back and forth to a Jew's reciting *Boi ve'shulem* since he turns about for this stanza and bows side to side.

15 *Zhidovchik* is an endearing form of the word *zhid*, meaning "Jew."

16 Oleksiy is the Ukrainian form of Aleksei.

threw him to the ground.[17] He stood up and grabbed hold of me. I fell down with him but naturally ended up on top of him. Oleksiy could not tolerate this and began to mix in. He rolled me off the nobleman, which enabled the nobleman to get on top of me. Imagine fighting with such a wild boar for some two hours, in our heavy winter coats—and that wild boar was now on top of me. I certainly no longer had the strength to throw him off me. When I would try to hurl him off, his Oleksiy would prevent me from doing so and would help the nobleman stay on top of me while he kept pounding me in the head.

I cannot remember now how I was able to get out from under his hands nor do I know how I had the strength to make it home. I was confused from the blows I had received to my head. Upon entering my house, I lay down and cried over my bad luck, over my encounter with Esau.[18] I personally had wrestled with Esau—and not with his angel as Jacob, our forefather, did.[19] Looking at me, my wife and child cried and asked, "What's the matter with you? What happened to you?" In tears I told them all the details, which you already know.

Meanwhile, some people entered my house and said, "Do you know who that nobleman is?"

"No! How should I know?"

They replied that the nobleman was actually the landowner of our *shteytl*.

"Let him be whoever he is," I said, "but attacking people on the road? If I live to see morning, I'll go to a lawyer and file a complaint against that nobleman. I won't excuse his behavior. I have witnesses—the coachman and Oleksiy."

In short, I woke up quite early and heard the church bell ringing like it did when a non-Jew died. I started out toward Baronev to file my complaint and noticed that the *shteytl* was in an uproar and everyone was running toward the nobleman's courtyard.

"What's going on?" I asked.

They then told me that the nobleman had shot himself that day.

"Shot dead?" I asked.

"Yes," they said. "They even rang the church bell."

"*Nu*," I said, "'So shall they perish.'[20] He received his just reward from God Himself."

---

17 "Not letting anyone spit in one's porridge" is a Yiddish expression denoting "not standing for any bullying."

18 In Yiddish, a brutal non-Jew is sometimes referred to as Esau.

19 Rashi's commentary on Genesis 32:25 explains that the man with whom Jacob wrestled was Esau's angel.

20 *Ken yovdu* in the original. This Hebrew expression is based on *Judges* 5:31 and is traditionally said upon hearing of the death of, or misfortune befalling, a rabid antisemite.

Naturally, I then remained at home. When God wills it, His punishment is swift. This was a tremendous sanctification of God's name.[21] All the non-Jews would say when they would see me pass by, "Do you see that Jew? When our nobleman wronged him, he was immediately punished by God, though nothing ever happened to him no matter much how much he beat us." The nobleman was a Pole, a wicked Haman, who used to cause the non-Jews much trouble and beat them murderously.[22] When one of them failed to remove his hat for him, he would beat and break his bones for not doing so. Everyone hated him, which is why no one ran over to help him when I was fighting him. All knew that I was right, and they had their revenge in seeing him suffer in my grasp. Upon later hearing all of this, I understood why the coachman had not wanted to come down from the coachbox, though he could have if he had wanted to. Pointing at me, everyone said, "The nobleman beat that *Zhidovchik*, and God immediately struck him down. It probably happened because that *Zhidovchik* is pious." Everybody was saying that God stands by the Jews and that Jews have a God in Heaven. The reason that he shot himself has to be understood the following way: He could not bear the disgrace of having had such a debasing encounter with a *Zhid*. And with what type of a *Zhid*? A fanatical one with *peyes*. And that contemptible Jew had humiliated him so! Without a doubt all of this caused him to shoot himself.

You are certainly wondering why there was no resulting lawsuit. Of course, I did not press charges because I was satisfied with the divine decision that the nobleman ended up being the victim.[23] And out of honor for the deceased, it was not befitting for the nobleman's family to press charges, for the truth would come out in court that he had shot himself. Instead, they wiped his name clean in order to bury him honorably either by saying that he had shot himself by accident or that he had lost his mind. In sum, although I am providing a natural explanation for these events, everyone said that his death had been miraculous, and the entire region was talking about this episode.

I remained in that *shteytl* for three years. I never heard a harsh word from the Jews there. On the contrary, they liked me and appreciated me—and I felt the same toward them. It was difficult for me to part from them because I was fond of them. The only problem was that I did not earn much there, which was

21 Rashi's commentary on Leviticus 10:3 explains the Jewish concept that God's name becomes sanctified when Godliness becomes apparent in the natural world, particularly when an evil person is being punished.

22 Most landowners in the Ukraine were Polish (Subtelny, 1988:215).

23 The original states, "I was satisfied with the divine decision that the nobleman was the atonement for all of us," meaning that if a calamity had to occur, it was better that it happened to him than to anyone else.

not their fault since they paid according to their means. I even grew accustomed to living that sort of life—supplementing my income with my earnings from marriage brokering—and I lived quite nicely, and some people were busy speculating how much money I made. But I did not like such a life, because marriage brokering was no way to earn a living for a *shoykhet* who is forbidden to utter any lies.[24] Since brokering marriages was very difficult without lying, it took me a long time until I was able to finalize a match and I needed to run around and travel quite a bit. So when a ruble finally fell to my lot from marriage brokering, it had already been spent long before. So I began to think of ways of wresting myself from there before long. My wife also agreed to my plan to search for someone to purchase the slaughtering rights from me and then moving my wife to Baronev while I searched for a new position as a *shoykhet.* If I had not first sold the slaughtering rights, I would not have been able to obtain even a *kopek* for them later. And that's what I did. I found a *shoykhet* by the name of Reb Nokhmen from the Bulgarian village of Katarzhi.[25] A fine *shoykhet* who led the services with a pleasing voice, he gave me fifty rubles for the slaughtering rights. With the consent of the villagers, I prepared a document transferring the rights to him. I then immediately rented a place in Baronev and moved my family there. Since many Jewish families in Baronev supported themselves by selling dairy products, I purchased two cows with those fifty rubles, and they became our household's only means of support. So I earned three rubles a week from them. Once that was arranged, I was free. I could now think about leaving in search of a new position.

But I had many matches which I still hoped to wrap up, and, according to my calculations, a few rubles would fall to my lot from them. Now that I was no longer tied down to a slaughtering position, it would be easier for me to devote time to them. So I hired a *melomed* to teach my Srul-Burekhl and traveled off to Odessa for marriage-brokering purposes. That was on *Rosh-Khoydesh Sivan* 5678,[26] and I figured that I would certainly find a slaughtering position by *Yontef.*[27] If not, I decided that I would then take my family to Perkón, where my wife's parents, sister, brothers, and relatives lived, so that she would not be

---

24 A *shoykhet* was expected to be a God-fearing, honest person (Berman, 1941:85).

25 At the end of the eighteenth and beginning of the nineteenth century, ethnic Bulgarians, Albanians, Germans, Greeks, and others settled in the Ukraine where they often established their own agricultural colonies and villages. Once established, Jews often moved into these settlements (Olson, 1994:28, 119, 256–257, 272).

26 June 2, 1878.

27 *Yontef* refers here to *Shvues,* which occurred on June 7–8, 1878.

lonely. Her parents, together with my wife and children, could then make use of the two cows until God would have compassion on us and provide me a good place of employment. And that is what happened. Before *Yontef*, I brought my family to Perkon, while I myself led the services in Slobodze. The Slobodzers nearly strained every nerve in their bodies trying to convince me to be their *shoykhet* again, which I would in no way consider. No position, God forbid, was better than my returning to be their *shoykhet*. I earned about fifty rubles for leading the services there on the High Holidays, and I earned some twenty-five rubles from selling *esroygim*.[28] I also earned a little money both from marriage brokering and from slaughtering. When I passed through a village that did not have a *shoykhet*, I would do some slaughtering for them.

I bought a few new articles of clothing for my wife and child and paid the debts that she had incurred. Though she was living with her parents, I made sure that she would not have to ask them for anything. I was by then no longer the Pinye-Ber of before; I was then, thank God, able to seek out a means to support my family. Therefore, she was now treated honorably, particularly since they knew that she would not be staying there long, God forbid. They knew well that I would not rest until I found a place of employment.

Right after *Sukes*,[29] I traveled off to Odessa. I spent a couple of weeks there, during which I heard that in the Crimea—in Yevpatoriya-Kozlov—was a fine opening for a *shoykhet*, so I traveled there.[30] But finding no available position, I was put up by the *shoykhet*, Gavriel.[31] I led the services, which people really liked. Once people found out that I was a *shoykhet*, they wanted me to remain there as their *shoykhet*. I said, "How can I stay here when you have two *shokhtim*?" They thought it would be proper for me to forcibly step in, but I could not justify such an action, even though a *shoykhet* did just that several years later. In short, I stayed there a couple of days. They gave me a few rubles for leading the services, the *shokhtim* gave me a few rubles for my travel expenses, and I traveled off to Simferopol.

Arriving in Simferopol, I saw that there was no available position for me, but I ran into the kosher-meat tax farmer of Bakhchisaray who told me that

---

28 *Esroygim* is plural of *esreg*.

29 *Sukes* ended on October 19, 1878.

30 Yevpatoriya (often spelled Eupatoria in English) is also called Kozlov, a Russified version of its Crimean Tatar name, Kezlev. Yevpatoriya is the spiritual center for Crimean Karaites until today. For more about the Karaites, see ch. 25, p. 509, footnote 25.

31 "Gavriel Segal, the *shoykhet* . . . of Yevpatoriya" is listed among the pre-subscribers to the tenth volume of Rabbi Khayim Khizkiyahu Medini's *Sdei Khemed* (1901:197). He was also among the rabbis and *shokhtim* to whom Rabbi Medini sent letters in 1899 stating that he had arrived in Hebron (Rabbi Medini, 2006:1:212).

they had a contentious *shoykhet* with whom the *shteytl* was constantly at odds.[32] They had brought him to rabbinical court and had received a ruling from three rabbis that he would have to be paid 500 rubles for the slaughtering rights if they wanted him to leave.

"*Nu*," I said, "How can I approach them when I don't have any money? So I have no reason to go there."

"*Nu*," he said, "Young man, I have the kosher-meat tax for another year so I can arrange for you to slaughter there for a year."[33]

I replied, "What does it matter if you or the town's residents want to use me as your *shoykhet*. If I don't have the money to purchase the slaughtering rights, I would be forbidden to remain there as the *shoykhet*."

He told me how the *shoykhet* there had it out for him and was causing him harm. "So I am not allowed to save myself?" He explained to me that I could save him by traveling with him to Bakhchisaray. "Once the *shoykhet* sees that I've brought along another *shoykhet*, he'll get scared, and I'll be able to have my way with him regarding everything and will be saved."

"If so, in order to help save you, I'll travel there with you, but I want to be paid 30 rubles in cash now for a month's stay so that you won't be able to take advantage of me by withholding or delaying payment. I'll stay up to a month, but if you don't come to an outcome by then, I'll leave. And if you make peace with him even after one day, I'll also leave."

He was agreeable to my conditions and paid me the thirty rubles. I traveled to Bakhchisaray to spend *Shobes* there.[34] Upon my arrival, I made my way

---

32 Later on p. 465, the kosher-meat tax farmer (sometimes simply referred to as the tax farmer) is identified as Benyumin Kizilshteyn and the nature of his position is explained.

33 Though Benyumin says that he holds the kosher-meat tax only for one more year, the next auction for the kosher-meat tax, held every four years, was to be held at the end of 1881, shortly before the author's contract ended (see ch. 25, p. 504, footnote 2). In addition, though Benyumin only offered him one year of work, the community heads made a three-year contract with the author.

34 In 1873, only some fifteen Jewish families lived in Bakhchisaray, out of a total population of more than 12,000, almost all of whom were Muslim Crimean Tatars who spoke Crimean Tatar, a Turkic language (Deinard, 1873). In the late 1870s, some twenty Jewish families resided in Bakhchisaray, out of a total population of 14,000, and the synagogue had recently been rebuilt. The synagogue had originally been built by the Krymchaks, an indigenous Rabbinite Jewish community of the Crimean Peninsula, but it fell into the hands of non-Jews after their departure in the 1820s (Deinard, 1879:1:104). In 1896, approximately forty Jewish families lived in Bakhchisaray, while in 1909 there were some sixty Jewish families (Hadas, 1896; Keren, 1981:171). The author's son Raphael Goldenstein (1916:53) mentions that since there were no more than twenty-five Krymchaks in Bakhchisaray, they worshiped in the same synagogue and were buried in the same cemetery as the Ashkenazim. During the Soviet period, the number of Jews remained stable, numbering 228 souls in 1939.

FIGURE 13. The Khan bath (similar to a Turkish bath) in Bakhchisaray, Crimea, an area in Tsarist Russia populated by Muslim Tatars who spoke their native Turkic language and rarely spoke Russian. This postcard, postmarked October 20, 1912 (Old Style dating), was sent by Pinkhes-Dov Goldenshteyn's son Shloyme to his brother Raphael in Cincinnati, with the note, "You probably remember this place." (Courtesy of Virginia "Ginny" Starr of Grass Valley, California.)

straight to the main *gabbai,* because it was not fitting for me to approach the *shoykhet* for lodging. The main *gabbai* did not run an inn, but who would turn away a fellow Jew—particularly when this *gabbai* was considered to be one of the pious Jews of Bakhchisaray? He was called S. Mayster.[35] It's true that he was a simple glazier yet a pious Jew, which is the reason I trusted him so much.

In the first half of July 1943, the Germans murdered over 1,000 Jews from Bakhchisaray and the surrounding area (Slutsky & Feldman, 1972). For details regarding the Karaite population of Bakhchisaray, see ch. 29, p. 573, footnote 14.

35 The author refers to Simkhe's surname sometimes as Mayster and at other times as Maynster. (In Yiddish, the word for a "master craftsman" is either *mayster* or *maynster.*) Since the list of Bakhchisaray donors to the Jewish Colonial Trust appearing in *Ha-Melits* (November 22, 1900, p. 4) refers to a member of the family as Mayster, that spelling has been used throughout this translation for consistency.

As mentioned in ch. 1, p. 90, footnote 8, Jews living in traditional communities in Tsarist Russia before the First World War generally used surnames only for official purposes and not among themselves. Nonetheless, the author's work makes it clear that Ashkenazi Jews in the Crimea were using surnames among themselves already by the late 1870s. In general, the less traditional elements of Jewish society were the ones to move to the Crimea, which only began to be settled in substantial numbers after the Crimean War of 1853–1855. For more about the Jews of the Crimea, see the Introduction, pp. 16–17.

I found it difficult to believe that this pious Jew had deceit within him and was a man of evil counsel, as you will later discover.

When he noticed me, Mayster was overjoyed. After hearing that I was a *shoykhet* and was seeking a position, he said, "You have a ready place right here. Our *shoykhet* is only here until another *shoykhet* comes and pays him 500 rubles for the slaughtering rights." I replied, "I already heard about it and there is nothing to talk about. I have no money. I only want to remain here for *Shobes,* earn some money for my travel expenses, and then continue on my way."

When I finished leading the services on *Shobes,* everyone was very pleased with me and wanted me to remain there as their *shoykhet.* But I told them that their words were wasted. In passing, I found out how the *shoykhet* had wronged the tax farmer and how he had caused him harm. They paid me several rubles for leading the services on *Shobes.* I was ready to leave the next day, but I, of course, had to wait for the kosher-meat tax farmer.

The kosher-meat tax farmer came around and found me at Mayster's and talked openly right in front of him. Mayster testified that everything he said was true. "If so," I thought to myself, "I can help him in order to help save the hard-earned money of my fellow Jews." The tax farmer and I walked over to a hotel on the pretext that he was hiring me as the *shoykhet* for the entire remaining period of time that he held the concession to the kosher-meat tax. This made the desired impression on the entire *shteytl* and everyone actually danced for joy. "We will soon be rid of our *shoykhet.*" But only the tax farmer and I knew that this was merely a ruse to threaten the *shoykhet.* The *shoykhet* saw that it was going badly for him; the tax farmer had another *shoykhet* to whom the entire *shteytl* was agreeable. He was now afraid that when his contract ended, he would not be able to obtain even a single *kopek* for the slaughtering rights. Therefore, he began to try to smooth things over with the tax farmer and actually, on that same day, they settled matters between themselves and I left that very night. But before leaving, the *gabbaim* and others there said that I should make sure to raise the funds and should unquestionably accept the position because the *shoykhet,* in any event, would no longer be there.[36] "In any case, leave us your address." I left them my address and amicably bade them farewell and traveled off. Meanwhile, I had—thank God—earned some forty rubles in three weeks.

---

36 In Bakhchisaray, the author uses the term *gabbaim* to denote the officials of the Jewish community, which include a main *gabbai* (referred to in the original simply as "the *gabbai*"), the treasurer, and additional *gabbaim.*

I wanted to set out for the Caucasus but I was dissuaded from doing so.[37] Instead, I was advised to return to the Crimea to make sure that I concentrated all of my efforts on securing that position in Bakhchisaray. I had seen other Jewish communities during my travels in the Crimea, and Bakhchisaray had impressed me as a pious *shteytl*, and I wanted to be the *shoykhet* there. The ten rubles a week that they paid as salary together with the side income would total fifty rubles a month, I would be a lucky man if I could obtain that position. Therefore, it would be wrong to let such an opportunity slip by. Such a position does not come up frequently. With this idea in mind, I traveled back to Perkon with fifty rubles. I found my family healthy and told them everything that had happened to me. Meanwhile, I received a letter from Bakhchisaray that I should obtain some money and return to them as soon as possible.

Firstly, I sold my best cow for fifty rubles, though she was worth more. But I was in a rush to raise money as soon as possible before another *shoykhet* came along because I knew what measly luck I had. I now had 100 rubles. So I began to plead and implore my relatives and friends to save me and help me stay alive. I did not want, God forbid, charity or donations but interest-free loans for a small amount of time until God would help me retain the position. I succeeded in borrowing ten rubles from some, fifteen rubles from others, and even twenty-five rubles from a few. I took one person's last ten rubles; the poor thing had no other money, but his compassion for me was very great. I promised him that I would send him the first of my earnings. I understood that everyone who lent me money had no expectation of receiving their money back, but they lent it to me so that I would later not be able to say that I had forever remained a pauper because of them. But I had no such thoughts. On the contrary, I meant to repay each person with tremendous gratitude. In short, during the two weeks that I worked on this, I raised 125 rubles. Together with my 100 rubles, I now had 225.[38] I wanted to at least somehow scrape together 300 rubles.

---

37 Boats traveled regularly from Odessa, stopping in Feodosiya and Kerch in the Crimea, across the Strait of Kerch and through the Black Sea to Batoumi, Georgia, which is at the foot of the Lesser Caucasus Mountains. The Caucasus is a mountainous region between the Black and Caspian Seas including Azerbaijan, Georgia, and Armenia. Beginning in the 1860s, the Imperial Russian government permitted some Ashkenazi Jews to move outside of the Pale of Settlement, to which Jews were restricted, and to live there. By 1897, over 43,000 Ashkenazi Jews lived in that region (Slutsky, 1972).

38 Since the author wrote earlier that he returned from the Crimea with fifty rubles, he evidently had fifty rubles saved from the seventy-five rubles he had made by leading the services during the High Holidays and selling *esroygim*.

I beseeched my wife's uncle, the wealthiest person in her entire family. He lived in Ternifke, which was near Perkon, and was called Yankev the Blind. That wealthy and coarse person scoffed, "Ha, ha, ha, is it money you want? I should lend you some?" With tears in my eyes, I told him my situation, which he knew quite well, and how I now had the fortunate opportunity to obtain a good position which would hopefully enable me to graciously repay the loan, and so on.

He said to his nasal-voiced wife, Aunt Rifke, "Do you hear? Pinye-Ber is asking for us to loan him money!"

She replied, "Lend him a ruble."

"No," he said. "He's asking for 100 rubles, or at least 75."

"So much—75 rubles? How does he have the gall to ask for it? And on what basis should we give it to you?" she asked in her nasal-toned voice.

I stayed with them for twenty-four hours and pleaded, spoke, and cried, but it did not help. They would not give me anything more than the one ruble that my aunt had mentioned. "You can repay it or not repay it, but no more than a ruble."

I finally gave up in disgust. Without even saying goodbye, I left. "Never mind! You'll see how God will help me without you. Evidently you're not worthy enough to have a portion in this *mitzvah* to help save an entire family. But when you'll need me, I'll treat you differently. You'll then know how a person needs to treat others. You'll see what an almighty God we have." With these words, I traveled home to Perkon.

Arriving in Perkon, I left my wife fifteen rubles for expenses and traveled off alone with 210 rubles to Bakhchisaray for the purpose of taking the position there. I arrived there on the eve of the *Shobes* before *Rosh-Khoydesh Adar.*[39] A celebration broke out in the *shteytl:* "The *shoykhet* came to stay! He's apparently brought money along, otherwise he wouldn't have come." I led the services that *Shobes* and sang the prayer to bless the new month, which very much pleased everyone.[40] They were excited over the manner in which I led the services because they had only had Lithuanian cantors and had never heard a Polish Jew lead prayers before.[41] In short, they wanted to hold a meeting on Saturday night, after *Shobes,* about accepting me as their *shoykhet.*

---

39 February 21, 1879.

40 During the morning prayer services of the *Shabes* preceding the beginning of each Hebrew month (*Rosh-Khoydesh*), after the reading of the *Haftorah,* a special prayer is recited blessing the incoming month. This prayer is normally recited with cantorial embellishments.

41 In this part of Tsarist Russia, a speaker of Southeastern (Ukrainian) Yiddish dialect (see the Introduction to the Glossaries, p. 856) was referred to as a Polish Jew. Evidently, most of the Jews of Bakhchisaray originated in Bessarabia and nearby provinces in the Ukraine and wanted a cantor who pronounced the Hebrew words of the prayers the same way they did.

I had my work cut out for me that night. Upon arriving at the meeting on Saturday night, the townspeople asked me, "*Nu*! Did you bring money?" I replied that I had 200 rubles and if they wanted me as their *shoykhet* they should lend me the remaining 300 rubles so that I could pay the *shoykhet* for the slaughtering rights there. They said, "If our community had any money, we'd lend it to you. There's no one who can lend you money since there are no wealthy people here. We're practically all artisans who have our own debts to repay, so your request is difficult for us." I suggested to them that they do this together to make it easy since a community is made up of more than one person. "I don't mean that one of you should loan me money, but that all of you together should do so. This way it will be easy for you and I'll repay you from my salary." Everyone liked this suggestion, and they quickly composed a list among themselves and the 300 rubles was raised.

"*Nu*," they said to me, "now you can be sure that you'll be our *shoykhet*." Some townspeople even suggested that I should start slaughtering right away and that they should begin paying me my salary. I explained to them that, "Until the current *shoykhet* holds the money for the slaughtering rights in his hand, until he issues a document stating that he no longer holds any claim to the slaughtering rights, and until I draw up a contract with you that you accept me as your *shoykhet* with full slaughtering rights, I'm not your *shoykhet*." Everyone shouted out that I was in the right. They then wanted to end the meeting, which I stopped in order to say a few words. I asked them, "Though we agreed how to raise the money, tomorrow each of you will get involved in his own business. But who's going to do something about this? Nothing gets done by itself. We have to appoint two people to collect the money according to the list that was prepared and then pay the current *shoykhet* and bring this to a conclusion." In short, they appointed an elderly townsperson by the name of Reb Duvid Kizilshteyn and his son Reb Shulem to act on this matter and bring it to a conclusion.[42] With that, everyone left the meeting.

The next day, I gave my 200 rubles to Reb Shulem Kizilshteyn, and he began to go around collecting the rest of the money. But the total was not collected so quickly because some postponed giving money until the next day while others completely refused to give anything. About ten days passed by before all the money was in Reb Shulem Kizilshteyn's hands. I finally lived to see them

---

The author's son Refuel, aka Raphael Goldenstein (1916:53), writes that, by the early 1900s, the Jewish community of Bakhchisaray was "made up of Lithuanian and Polish Jews"; regarding Lithuania, see ch. 15, p. 241, footnote 13.

42 The 1859 revision list (poll-tax census) of Kishinev lists Duvid Kizelshteyn (born ca. 1824) and his son Shulem (born ca. 1844).

collect all the money in hard cash, but they then had to speak with the current *shoykhet* himself. The *shoykhet* said that upon receiving the money, he would leave that very day to find himself another position because he was not going to go against the ruling of the rabbis, especially since he had already inquired about a certain position but was not going to travel there without the money. They gave the *shoykhet* the 500 rubles for the slaughtering rights and he issued a document stating that from that day forward he had absolutely no claim to the slaughtering rights and was not the *shoykhet* in Bakhchisaray, which practically closed the matter. The only part missing was the contract that the townspeople needed to draw up with me. The main part was done. *Nu,* should it have been difficult to draw up a contract when everyone was in agreement? That was how it should have been if no one's selfish interests had been involved. Mixed into the process were those who had caused strife with that other *shoykhet* and were now causing discord in hiring a new *shoykhet.* And these were the very people in the *shteytl* whom I had trusted to be pious and had thought were careful to choose a devout *shoykhet.* I now recognized them to be frauds and quarrel mongers who acted only out of self-interest. There is a saying that people use: You don't know someone until you've done business with him. Only once I began to do business with them did I know them for who they really were. I can truthfully tell you that if had I realized who they were earlier—before giving them my bloody 200 rubles—I would have left in disgust. But instead, I suffered and witnessed their crimes against justice and humanity for their own personal gain. As things went on, I became even more acquainted with their corruptness, but I could not change my predicament for the better and I have remained stuck here until today, *Rosh-Khoydesh Tamuz* 5669, a period of thirty-one years.[43]

So you certainly must be interested to know all the schemes that I overcame and all the battles that I won until, thankfully, God helped me prevail over them. But first, I must introduce to you the rabble rousers who waged the wars against the *shoykhet.*

The main instigators were the *gabbaim* of the *shul* and the assistant crown rabbi.[44] No one else from the community was responsible for causing the

---

43 June 19–20, 1909. The author is approximating his thirty years and four months in Bakhchisaray.

44 Beginning in the 1830s, the Tsarist Russian government began to compel every substantial Jewish community to appoint a crown rabbi (*rabiner* in Yiddish), most of whom were irreligious and had little traditional Jewish education. Hence, Jewish communities had a double rabbinate consisting of an authentic, traditionally educated rabbi (*ruv*) who served as the community's spiritual leader, and a crown rabbi (*rabiner*) who, as a government official, who was in charge of documenting Jewish births, marriages, and deaths and delivered addresses in Russian on various occasions but who had no real religious jurisdiction. In the Ukraine,

contention. They were dragged into it unwillingly and did not even know what they were being dragged into. They followed because, after all, the *gabbaim* told them to do so. When I came to Bakhchisaray, the *gabbaim* were Reb Simkhe Mayster and his brother-in-law Reb Yankev Medvedye.[45] The assistant crown rabbi was the elderly Duvid Kizilshteyn, whom you know from earlier. They also had another brother-in-law, who was Reb Duvid's brother, by the name of Benyumin. He was the kosher-meat tax farmer to whom I had to go to get paid. Now that you know all of this I will begin to relate the next part of my story.

You certainly remember that we decided that they had to draw up a contract with me in Hebrew in the usual style and manner as is customary throughout all Jewish communities. It was to include all the conditions included in the contract of the previous *shoykhet*. Everyone agreed on the following: a salary of ten rubles a week, two *funt* of meat a day, the spleen and intestines of every kosher animal,[46] the house in the synagogue courtyard where all the *shokhtim* had lived was to be mine at no charge, and I would receive 100 rubles for leading the services on the High Holidays, apart from income that I would earn from weddings and for performing circumcisions.[47] Everyone signed except for the kosher-meat tax farmer and the *gabbaim*, who did not want to sign. "Why? Don't you want to sign the contract?"

"The contract has to be rewritten," said the main *gabbai*, S. Mayster.

"What's the matter?"

"Well," Mayster said and pointed to his brother-in-law, Medvedye, "Tell him, Reb Yankev, why you don't like the contract."

"We'll tell you tomorrow how to write the contract," said Yankev Medvedye.

---

the office of crown rabbi was often reduced to an absurdity as it was usually filled by those entirely ignorant of Judaism though often well-educated secularly (Freeze, 2002:95–130; Shochat, 1975). Having such a small Jewish community, Bakhchisaray had only an assistant government rabbi (see Friedlander, 2013:13); since they could not afford both a rabbi and a *shoykhet*, they had only a *khazn-shoykhet* (combination cantor and *shoykhet* (see the Introduction, pp. 26–27). Often the *shoykhet* served as the rabbi of such a small Jewish community, as both Deinard (1879:1:104) and Hadas (1896) note regarding the *shoykhet* of Bakhchisaray, though Hadas was specifically referring to the author. This does not mean that the *shoykhet* made halakhic decisions, but it simply means that he was considered the authority regarding Jewish religious matters.

45 Simkhe Mayster was apparently the main *gabbai* and the treasurer (see ch. 25, p. 504 below).

46 The *shoykhet*'s compensation often included a bonus consisting of "the tongue, the spleen, or the large intestines," which was determined by the custom of the town (Berman, 1941:63–64).

47 The custom to pay a gratuity to the synagogue functionaries at weddings was known as *rakhash*, an acronym of the first Hebrew letters of the words rabbi, *khazn* (cantor), and *shames* (sexton). The author, being the cantor, would have received a portion of this gratuity (Rivkind, 1959:108).

Meanwhile, Reb Duvid and Reb Benyumin also did not sign in deference to Mayster and Medvedye. And I could not be considered employed without their signatures because they were the government-authorized directors of spiritual matters there.

The next day, they decided to undertake the following plan: Since they were simple people who did not understand Hebrew, they needed the contract written in a language that they could understand. Since they had already been burned by their previous *shokhtim* they decided that the contract should be written in Russian. Did you ever hear of such a thing—writing a *shoykhet*'s terms and conditions in Russian? It seemed comical to me, but what should I have done? I kept quiet and agreed to their demand. Meanwhile, the day ended, and I thought that all that remained to be done was to have the terms and conditions written in Russian the next day.

I returned the next day, dragged everyone together, and was looking forward to see this matter being brought to a close. But they came up with another change: They did not want the contract to mention any perpetual slaughtering rights because they did not want to be stuck with a *shoykhet* if he would not work out. I felt sick. "How's this possible? Why didn't you tell me before? I wouldn't have given away my 200 rubles and wouldn't have wasted all this time." The day ended, and I also agreed to this demand.

I had a notary prepare a document and gave it to them to sign, but they rejected another point. What was the matter? Since they had already been burned by their previous *shoykhet,* they wanted to write the contract for a period of three years, without perpetual slaughtering rights. And they would have the following choice at the end of the three years: if they wanted to keep me—fine; if not, I would have no claim and they would return my money as a gift, meaning that the contract would not make any mention of my having put up 200 rubles of my own money. I then spent the next few days in anguish until I consented to this too.

I thought that I was then finished with them but no. I came to them and told them, "Write it however you want as long as we bring this to an end and you stop tormenting me."

They replied, "Why do you say that we're tormenting you? We're only taking precautions. After getting burned on hot soup, you blow the next time even if it's cold."

I said, "But this must be brought to a close. How long will you continue to take precautions? Figure out once and for all what you want."

"We'll tell you the final points tomorrow. If you agree to them, we'll sign the contract and bring it to a close."

I waited impatiently until the next morning. I came the next day with Reb Duvid and found a written contract with the following points: 1) They were hiring me as the *shoykhet* for three years. After three years, they had the following choice: if they wanted to keep me, fine; if not, I would have no claim and they would then give me a gift of 200 rubles, as mentioned earlier. 2) The salary for my leading the services on the High Holidays and the entire year would only be 75 rubles and not 100 rubles as the previous *shoykhet* had received. 3) The salary for slaughtering would be as follows: the kosher-meat tax farmer would give me six rubles a week the first year and eight rubles the next two years. In addition, the butcher would give me two *funt* of meat a day and the house in the courtyard of the *shul* would belong to me without charge. What should I tell you, my loved ones? Upon hearing these savage points, I practically froze in my tracks. When the community got wind of this, everyone was beside himself and said that it was inhumane. After all, how can one utter from one's lips that a *shoykhet* can live on six rubles a week? A shoemaker's apprentice earns more than that.

They tried to justify themselves to the community as follows: "Since the *shoykhet* borrowed 300 rubles from us, he needs to repay it by having it deducted from his salary. His reduced salary reflects a 200-ruble deduction during his first year [by paying him 6 rubles a week instead of 10]; a 100-ruble deduction during his second year [by paying him 8 rubles a week instead of 10]; and an extra 100-ruble deduction during his third year—50 for us and 50 toward the 200 rubles we'll have to compensate him if we decide not to keep him.[48] If he stays, his salary will then be as planned—10 rubles a week. At that point, we won't mix in."

In short, cruel "justifications" and inhumane demands. Everyone resented it, but no one could do anything to help. I cried and bemoaned my fate. I had gotten myself into this fix and could not back out. If I could have taken back my 200 rubles, I would have run away and not looked back. You can imagine how I resented having to agree to these points. In brief, I figured that the worst point was my being paid six rubles a week the first year, but the other points did not bother me. Their taking precautions so that I should not have the perpetual slaughtering rights would not help them at all because the slaughtering rights would be mine once I repaid them the 300 rubles I owed them. After three years, I would not listen to them anyway and would also not need any terms and conditions. I was only bothered by the six rubles a week during the

48 The original mistakenly states that there was a 150-ruble deduction instead of a 100-ruble deduction in the author's third year there.

first year, which only added up to a difference of 100 rubles a year since I would have consented to eight rubles (instead of ten), using two rubles a week to pay my debts.[49] So it boiled down to only a difference of 100 rubles. Even if I would have raised a furor and gotten back my 200 rubles, I would anyway have soon had to repay those back home who had lent me money and start looking for a new position. And who knew if I would find one with a better salary? Since it was not in my best interest to leave there, I had to give in, and God would help me. In short, I signed two copies of the contract. The community kept one and I kept the other. The *gabbaim* were ecstatic—simply overjoyed—especially the main *gabbai*, Mayster, who felt like he had conquered Brod because he had been responsible for all of their deviousness.[50]

The *shoykhet* left right after Purim for a new *sh'khita* position, while his family stayed until after Pesach.[51] I began to slaughter and was meanwhile without my family.[52] I would sleep at either Reb Duvid Kizilshteyn's or his son Shulem's house. Only after *Rosh-Khoydesh Iyar* did I bring my small family which consisted of my wife and our two small children—my seven-year-old son Srul-Burekhl and my two-year-old daughter Nekhamele.[53] Meanwhile, I rented a place to live until the house in the synagogue courtyard would become vacant. A few weeks later, the previous *shoykhet*'s family left and my family and I moved into that cold house, which was given to us at no charge. In leaving Perkon, my relatives helped me out with several rubles because otherwise I would certainly not have been able to have them join me there so quickly since it cost a nice few rubles. In short, I was now a resident of Bakhchisaray. Though poor, I liked it there, if only to be on my own and together with my wife and children.

A week after my family arrived in Bakhchisaray, I learned that one could not live there on six rubles a week. My wife went to the street for the first time and returned home furious and in tears. "For Heaven's sake, you bandit! What did you do? How could you have done such foolishness? How can we live on six rubles a week? We're going to starve from hunger with these exorbitant prices! Everything here costs two or three times more than back home.

---

49 A standard year in the Hebrew calendar has fifty weeks.

50 Brod (now Brody, Ukraine) was a large Jewish commercial center in eastern Galicia from the mid-eighteenth century until the early 1880s.

51 Purim was on March 9, 1879, and Pesach was April 8–15, 1879.

52 The author's account relates that he began working in Bakhchisaray in March 1879, which is confirmed by a letter from the Rabbi Khayim Khizkiyahu Medini dated the 16th of *Heshvan* 5640 (November 2, 1879), in which he writes that the author had been at his position for eight months (Rabbi Medini, 2006,1:11). A translation of the letter appears in Appendix C1 (pp. 808–810).

53 *Rosh-Khoydesh Iyar* was April 23–24, 1879. Nekhame was a little over one year old.

Who can survive here? How can we survive on your small salary?" This was her pronouncement, which she expressed with bitter tears. I understood that everything she said was correct, but how could I improve our lot now? I comforted her by saying that God would certainly not abandon us, which she had to admit was true. So we began to lead our lives in Bakhchisaray on six rubles a week including paying back our debts—the 200 rubles which I had borrowed from common, poor people who had lent me their last few rubles. How could I not return their money to them? You can now understand how we lived that first year, particularly during the period right after we arrived. We lacked everything, needed everything, and had no money.

I only stayed in my rented quarters for a month. Afterward, I moved into the house in the synagogue courtyard which at least did not cost me anything. At that time, I considered myself lucky to have it, though after a year I ran from that "good fortune," as you will later learn why.[54]

The house consisted of two halves. Past the entrance was a door to the right which opened to a room half-occupied by a large oven while the rest served as a dining room, bedroom, children's room, and anything else you wanted to call it. The left side of the small house, meaning the other half, also consisted of one room, which had a heating stove to warm the room in the winter. This room could have been called a study or a bedroom—call it what you want so long as there was another room so that the *shoykhet* could live comfortably like a count. But do not think that I was able to occupy both halves. I had to make do with only the half with the large oven, but in any case I did not have many possessions. In short, we began to accustom ourselves to our current cramped lifestyle.

The community was very satisfied with me, and I also had no problems with them. Yet as much as I appeared to be doing well, it continued to smolder around me. In a corner lay coals which people thought had completely gone out, but they were actually still glowing inside. When a gentle wind blew on them, they began to ignite, and they turned into an inferno that burned everything around them. The fire spread over the entire city and the smoke caused the entire area to become darkened with fumes and soot. The air remained stuffy for a long time afterward until God finally had compassion on me and began to clean the air by extinguishing the fire and destroying the embers. Only then was there sunshine, calmness, and quiet, with streams of fresh air all around, as will be related in my narrative in detail.

54 Later on p. 477, the author writes that he lived in that house for two and half years.

Of course, the extinguished coals that were glowing inside and the wind that fanned them and made them into a hellish fire were none other than the *gabbaim*, meaning the community leaders, together with Benyumin.[55] At the head of them all was Simkhe Mayster, who never stopped thinking up new ways to bury the *shoykhet* under the pretext of benefiting the community and helping his poor brother-in-law Benyumin, the so-called kosher-meat tax farmer.[56] Benyumin did not earn the title of kosher-meat tax farmer by leasing or buying the rights to collect this tax from city hall, as was normally done. He was simply referred to by this title because he sat in the kosher butcher shop demanding the meat tax from every kid and ordering the *shoykhet* around like the bygone noblemen did their serfs.[57] In Bakhchisaray, the right to collect the kosher-meat tax was not allowed to be leased or auctioned off to a particular individual but was given over to the Jewish community to manage.[58] They then had to provide an accounting to the Municipal Board of Revenue and Expenditures. So the community appointed Medvedye and Mayster to provide this accounting, which was always shown to be balanced or in excess because they reported the *shoykhet*'s salary as costing them ten or twelve rubles a week instead of the six rubles per week that they were actually paying.[59] Of course, the difference was given to Benyumin as his allotment.

Although I seem to have elaborated on this unnecessarily, you will see that these details are not pointless. They will clarify for you the political maneuverings which infuriated the community and set such a raging enmity against me, an unfortunate *shoykhet* whose lot had cast me to a place in the Crimea which

---

55 In his Yiddish memoirs, Rabbi Levi Glicman (1934:56) describes in similarly dramatic terms the communal strife that embroiled his father, the head *shoykhet* of Breslov (Bratslav, Ukraine), "[T]he spark of envy began to be fanned. At first, it became just a small fire but it then developed into a hellish fire—a seven-headed, poisonous, blazing snake."

56 A kosher-meat tax farmer (*bal-takse* in Yiddish) bought the rights to collect taxes levied on both the slaughtering and sale of kosher meat, some of which was sent to finance Jewish communal institutions, though the tax farmers tended to abuse the taxpayers. This kosher meat tax was called the "box tax" (*korobka* in Russian and *takse* in Yiddish), and the funds raised had little oversight and were frequently embezzled by government officials or used by the government against the Jews (Berman, 1941:183, 193–202; Rivkind, 1959:112, 217; I. Schneersohn, 1968:215, 217–218; Urussov, 1908:33–34).

57 It was common for Jewish parents to send a chicken with one of their children to the *shoykhet* to have it slaughtered.

58 The kosher-meat tax was auctioned off every four years. But if no one made a bid on it, it remained in the hands of the Jewish community, meaning the municipality chose two or three Jewish townsmen to run it (see ch. 26, p. 536).

59 The wording in the original in ambiguous as to whether both Medvedye and Mayster or merely Mayster was to provide the accounting. Later it is implied that Mayster was the main *gabbai* and the treasurer.

had such "benefactors" as its community leaders. They had already chased two *shokhtim* away from there and ruined their two families, and now I had become their victim. This is the reason that I elaborated a bit, so that you can understand everything exactly. You will now be able to understand on your own accord every last vicious act of those "well-meaning" individuals—even those details which I am unable to set down in writing.

Now that I have given you the background, I can resume my narrative. I was now a resident of Bakhchisaray. Though we lived in want, our lives were seemingly calm. Upon arriving there, I imagined how I would live a tranquil life now, but as Rashi comments, "Jacob wanted to settle down in tranquility, and then the trouble of Joseph and his brothers' hatred toward him was thrust upon him."[60] Upon me was thrust the hatred of the community leaders, who at first tried to disguise themselves as being well meaning by making Benyumin out to be the culprit. But they proved to be Benyumin's accomplices whenever he was not capable of doing the dirty work himself.

Two months after I settled there, a quarrel erupted when everyone realized that Benyumin was paying the *shoykhet* six rubles a week but was not repaying the four rubles to the community. He was paying nothing at all and was either taking it for himself or was splitting it with the *gabbaim*. The community began to yell, "How's this possible? If he's not repaying the money borrowed from us, he should at least give the four rubles to the *shoykhet*." Those who had lent money yelled that they should be repaid otherwise the *shoykhet* should not slaughter anything. They had no other leverage to use. Well, if they were quarreling, why should I bear the brunt of it? I continued to slaughter every day and pretended to know nothing about it. Meanwhile, Thursday came along and I had to pick up my weekly wages. Reb Benyumin said to me, "Never mind. You can wait to pick it up next week. I don't have any money now." I said, "How can I wait? I have to pay back the money I borrowed for the entire week!" He replied, "That's not my concern." When I saw that no arguments were helping, I returned home feeling miserable and cried quite a lot over my bitter luck. The next week, I again had to borrow some money and barely survived to see Thursday, when I demanded my pay for two weeks. He said, "Go to the community. Let them pay you. I don't have any money." His political motive was as follows: Since the community was demanding that he pay me ten rubles a week, he was showing them that he was not legally obligated to pay me anything because he, personally, had no contract with anyone stating that

60 Rashi's commentary on Genesis 37:2.

he must pay and maintain a *shoykhet*.[61] So he sent me to the community for my salary to show them that even the six rubles that he was paying me was an act of generosity on his part. As you can imagine, after such a reply my eyes darkened out of sadness to such an extent that I could not find my way home. And with what was I returning home? Once the community learned of his reply, they became enraged at the kosher-meat tax farmer, Benyumin, and told me not to slaughter anything under any circumstances. I had no other choice but to do what they said.

Benyumin called me over to slaughter, but I did not go. "Pay me my salary for those two weeks," I said. He began to curse and swear at me with such repulsive and nefarious words—the likes of which I had never heard in my life. I stood there and did not answer him. I just shed tears over my bitter luck. I considered the circumstances of our unfortunate rabbis, cantors, *shokhtim*, and so on, who were thrown at the mercy of such people and had to endure so much only to die of hunger. Better to be a manual laborer than to have one of these spiritual occupations. He continued cursing me while I remained silent. In the end, he said, "You won't go slaughter anything, but you're going to have to!" and he left and had me summoned to city hall.

I entered city hall, and their lawyer was sitting there.

The mayor said to me, "They're complaining that you aren't slaughtering and that you're causing the city to be without any kosher meat for the Sabbath."

I replied, "I'd slaughter even now but they need to pay me what's owed me for two weeks. I don't want to work for nothing."

The lawyer said, "You must go slaughter. Your wages have nothing to do with this. If you're owed money, then demand to be paid. But why is the city to blame? There are sick people and the Sabbath is coming. They must have meat."

I replied, "I'm not obligated to supply meat. I'm merely a laborer who works on my own accord. When I'm paid, I work; when I'm not paid, I don't. Regarding the sick, let them send me their chickens and slaughtering fees and I'll slaughter them right away."

The mayor shrugged his shoulders thereby indicating that there was nothing to be accomplished here as my arguments were legitimate.

The lawyer said, "How can he say that he's not obligated to slaughter? He has a contract with us stating that he has to do so and that we're not allowed to hire anyone else to slaughter."

"So let him show his contract," said the mayor.

---

61 Benyumin was evidently not obligated to pay the *shoykhet* since he was not actually the kosher meat tax farmer.

I immediately realized that it would not be in my best interest to show my contract, so I told the mayor, "I don't have any contract with them. If you need an indication that I'm right then have him produce his copy because two copies are always made when signing a contact." With these words, I left city hall and the lawyer left right afterward.

Outside, we found the *gabbaim*, Medvedye and Mayster, and the kosher-meat tax farmer, Benyumin, standing and waiting for an answer. When the lawyer saw them, he yelled out, "Listen, gentlemen! You've made a big mistake regarding this *shoykhet* whom you take to be naïve. No, he's a sly one. He's smarter than all of us and a better attorney than I am. You won't be able to have your way with him at all." I heard all of this when he was shouting it to them. Afterward, he left with the *gabbaim* to confer among themselves, and I went home.

Late at night, I was handed payment for those two weeks so that I would go to work early the next day, Friday morning, and slaughter, meaning that I had prevailed. But along with my victory came hatred toward me from the community leaders. A bitter disagreement ensued, which grew over time until it reached heavenly proportions. The strife ignited in full bloom when my first year came to an end when I was supposed to begin receiving eight rubles a week, but Benyumin did not want to give me more than six. I did not want to take anything less than eight and actually could not take anything less because I had endured so much the previous year in trying to live off of six rubles while also paying off my debts. That first year, I paid back the 200 rubles that I owed the twelve people back home. For leading the services on the High Holidays, I received 100 rubles.[62] And throughout the rest of the year I earned another 100 rubles on the side from performing circumcisions, from tips given to me for naming newborn girls, and on Purim and Hanukah.[63] Yet I did not enjoy any of that side income because I used it to pay my debts. You can understand how well I lived that year, especially with the persecution that I also had to endure, as you will learn from my subsequent narrative. So I had to hold my own and insist upon eight rubles a week, otherwise I would not be able to support myself.

---

62 Rosh Hashanah and Yom Kippur were on September 18–19, 1879, and September 27, 1879, respectively. Earlier it states that the author's contract specified that he would be paid seventy-five rubles for leading the services on the High Holidays. In ch. 25, p. 506, the author writes that he always earned only seventy-five rubles for leading the services in Bakhchisaray for the entire year, including the High Holy Days.

63 A special Hebrew prayer naming a newborn Jewish girl is recited in synagogue during the reading of the Torah. On Purim, the community members each used to give money to the one who chanted the *Megilla*. Wealthier members of each community used to give Hanukah *gelt* (gift money given on Hanukah) to the rabbi, *shokhtim*, and others serving the community's spiritual needs (Rivkind, 1959:103–104,146–147).

In short, I was not guilty of causing the contention, which you yourselves can see as well.

Listen to how cruel they could be. It happened precisely on the 21st of Adar 5640.[64] God had blessed me with a son whom I had named Itskhok-Yosef, may his light shine.[65] I had to hire a Jewish woman to attend my wife from the childbirth until after the *bris*. In my house was also a *melomed* whom I had engaged to teach my son Srulikl. For the sake of my son, I had to board the *melomed* at our house where he taught him and two other children, that is, I had a *kheyder* in my home. Imagine! All of this was in the half of the house, which was half taken up by the oven while the other half was cold, bare, and unfit to sleep in. And it was at that time that the following episode occurred. Among everyone else, three poor people attended my son's *bris*. I celebrated the *bris* with an elaborate meal and served the poor nicely. They could not have had it any better. After the *bris*, everyone left, including the poor who said their good-byes and left satisfied. Shortly before nightfall, I noticed that one of the poor people was returning with a small sack. It seemed to me that he had been sent to me to spend the night, which turned out to be true. He came into my house, threw down his sack, and sat himself down.

I said, "Mister, what do you want? You already left, so why did you return?"

He replied, "I want to spend the night here."

I said to him nicely, "*Nu*, tell me yourself if you can spend the night in this room. A woman who recently gave birth and an attendant are already staying here. Also a midwife is supposed to be coming over to spend the night. There's a *melomed* in the house, as well as myself and two children. I have nowhere to put myself. Now, tell me yourself how can I possibly accommodate you?"

He impudently answered, "I don't care what becomes of you as long as there's place for me. After all, it's my house more than yours. It's a community-owned residence for the poor and you've taken it for yourself."

Upon hearing his reply, I felt heavy-hearted and noticed that he was still inebriated from the *bris*. I amicably said to him, "Mister, if so then take your bundle and leave now before I . . ."

He began to yell loudly, "You're telling me to leave? I'll show you who's going to leave sooner." And he lifted up his stick with which he wanted to hit

---

64 March 4, 1880.

65 In ch. 24, p. 485, the author writes that Itskhok-Yosef was born on the 20th of *Adar* 5640, i.e., March 3, 1880, the day before this incident occurred. Since Ashkenazi Jews do not generally name after the living, this means that the author's father-in-law, Shulem-Itskhok Hershkovitsh, had died beforehand. He was last mentioned as being alive in 1878 (ch. 23, p. 457). This son is later referred to by the nickname Yosl.

me over the head, saying, "I'm soon going to split your head." A member of the community who had missed the *bris* was sitting in my house, and he saw everything. He grabbed the stick from the poor drunkard and flung him into the courtyard. At that moment, I was quite shaken up, not because of the stick and not because of his shouting, but on account of my wife who had recently given birth. Upon seeing what happened, she thought that he had split my head because he had raised the stick close to her bed. After all, the entire house was only six ells long.[66] She gave a shrill shriek. We tried to calm her down and soon brought over the midwife. Only then did I go out to the courtyard to see what had happened to that poor person. Meanwhile, that community member had brought the police. Once the poor person noticed the police, he suddenly became sober and began to plead with us to forgive me, "I'm not to blame. Don't hand me over to the clutches of the vicious police." I said, "Tell me who put you up to this?" He pointed to the *gabbai*'s house and said, "I went over there for a donation, and they told me to spend the night at the *shoykhet*'s and to not leave there under any circumstances.[67] For this, they paid me a nice sum of money," and he continued to plead, "Have pity!" I replied, "Why didn't you have pity on us before creating such an outrage?" In short, I provided the police with generous glasses of liquor and told that poor man to go straight to the train station, thereby ridding myself of him.

Just consider to what means their cruelty had led them. They stopped at no evil as long as it would harm the *shoykhet*. That episode cost me and especially my wife much health. It took us a long time to uproot that fright from her. We tried various means to help her eradicate that fear, including spiritual remedies,[68] medicines, and, in case it was caused by an evil eye, removing it by special means.[69] Ultimately, God had compassion on this impoverished mother, and she became completely well.

Regarding their cruelty, I will mention one more injustice into which they dragged practically the entire community without anyone being able to protest.

---

66 Various countries have different lengths for an ell, i.e., *eyl*(*n*) in Yiddish. The Old Russian ell is equal to approximately 1.38 ft. Hence, six ells would be 8.3 ft.

67 Likely referring to the main *gabbai*, who was Simkhe Mayster.

68 *Segula* in the original. A *segula* is a spiritual remedy traditionally understood to lead to an improvement in one's fortune. For instance, being honored to be *kvater* (the one honored with carrying the baby into the room to undergo a *bris*) is a *segula* for having children of one's own. A *segula* often involves reciting certain chapters of Psalms on a daily basis or being scrupulous in the performance of a certain *mitzvah*. Among a list of spiritual remedies for ridding oneself of fright, Lifshits (2008:202–203) mentions giving charity and being careful in reciting the appropriate blessings before and after eating.

69 Most Yiddish-speaking Hasidic communities have individuals who are recognized as being proficient in removing an evil eye.

You know that in my house there was a large oven. All of a sudden, on *Rosh-Khoydesh Nisan*,[70] some community members came to me and said, "Listen up, *shoykhet*. Either you bake *matses* or give us access to the oven so that we can bake *matses*."

I said, "'What's the connection between *shmita* and Mt. Sinai?'[71] What does baking *matses* have to do with a *shoykhet*? My father wasn't a baker, and I'm also not one. When you said that you yourselves would bake, who then are you?"

"Whoever wants can bake," they said. "Move out of here into the other side of the house, and we'll start baking *matses*."

Upon hearing their plans, I became petrified. "How's this possible? Where will we stay? Isn't there an oven somewhere else that you can use? Is this the only one?"

They replied, "This is a community oven. We don't need to find another one elsewhere, especially when the *gabbaim* told us to use this one. So we've decided to use this one. But we're giving you a choice. If you want to, you can bake the *matses*. Take on the contract and earn yourself some money for Pesach because you're going to suffer anyway from all the commotion."

My wife and I began to argue, "Fellow Jews! Have some compassion! How can I do this? I myself can't bake *matses*, and if others do it here, we'll suffer from all the noise and commotion and my wife, children, and I will then be cast into the adjacent small room, which is cold and wet." We argued and pleaded like this. It appeared that they were receptive to our words and then they left. Nonetheless, the next day, a wagon filled with wood drove over and dumped its load into the courtyard. Outside, fresh wet snow was falling, and everything weighed heavily on my heart.

In short, they helped me move my bed linens to the adjacent room—the cold, wet one—and my unfortunate family and I were now relegated there. With tearful eyes and embittered hearts, we gazed speechlessly at each other, while our eyes spoke for themselves, "Where in the world are we living? Among people or wild animals?" So we suffered and endured that living hell—no, better call it the seven gates of hell because the *matse* baking lasted seven days and every day was for us a separate hell in itself, and the *gabbaim* delighted in hearing of our anguish.

---

70 March 13, 1880. Since *Rosh-Khoydesh Kislev*, which is two weeks before Pesach, fell on *Shabes* that year when it would not have been appropriate to make plans for baking and other forbidden forms of work, perhaps they came on Saturday night after the conclusion of *Shabes*.

71 Rashi's question on Leviticus 25:1, "Why is Mt. Sinai mentioned specifically in connection with the laws of the sabbatical year (*shmita*)?" became a Yiddish folk expression used when questioning the relevance of two unrelated matters.

In brief, God helped us survive that living hell, and we returned to our residence in the large room where the oven was. We then began to prepare for the *Yontef* of Pesach.[72] With the approach of Pesach the next year, I did not repeat the same foolishness again but decided to bake the *matses* myself since I would anyway have had to suffer during those seven days of baking. And that is what I did, and everyone was satisfied except for the community leaders. They did not like it and were fuming over my having earned so much. "Thirty rubles! How's it possible? He's now become so rich!" Some said, "What does it matter to us what he earned? He did not ask for any more money than last year, and he and his wife slaved away for seven days and suffered from all the noise and commotion."

Eventually, I left the community-owned residence along with the community oven, the baking of *matses*, and all its "good fortune." I rented a place in town, allowing me to serve the community only as its *shoykhet*. I had lived in that community-owned house for two and half years where I endured plenty, but I have only related the main episodes. I cannot begin to describe all of the trivial ways in which they tormented me that I had to endure.

It is now time to return to the continuation of our story, namely, what happened to my salary during my second year there. I was supposed to begin receiving eight rubles a week, but Benyumin did not want to give it to me, which resulted in the infernal fire of strife that broke loose. Everyone asked me not to cause any problems and to simply accept six rubles a week, but I would in no way hear of it. Once, at dusk, I ran into Simkhe Mayster, the man of evil counsel. He stopped me, "Reb Pinye-Ber, wait. I want to talk with you about something that's for your own good." I replied, "Certainly, I want to hear what you have to say, especially when it's for my own benefit." He looked around to see if anyone was nearby and began to contend that I should not make any problems, that I should stop harassing him, and that I should accept six rubles a week without causing a ruckus. When he saw that his words were having no effect, he began to make a confession to me.

72 March 27 to April 3, 1880.

CHAPTER 24

Corruption in Bakhchisaray and Ungrateful Relatives, 1880–1889

Simkhe Mayster's Confession • Traveling to Karasubazar • Receiving Certification in Slaughtering from the *Khakham* Medini • The Letter from the *Khakham* Medini to the Jewish Community of Bakhchisaray

Listen to the confession of Simkhe Mayster:

"Reb Pinye-Ber, listen to what I have to tell you! There was a *shoykhet* here in Bakhchisaray for 30 years.[1] He was a good *shoykhet* and a Talmudic scholar with fine children—one of them even married the child of Rabbi Khaym-Leyb Khaymovitsh, the rabbi of Kakhovka—yet we put an end to his being the *shoykhet* here.[2] Do you think it was because he used to drink liquor? No! In the Crimea, that completely doesn't matter to us. Crimean Jews are not so particular regarding such trivialities. After all, you see that after all our accusations he's still a *shoykhet* in the Crimea—in the larger city of Armyansky Bazar. They treat him honorably there and they disregard our having had his meat prohibited here with the help of rabbis and 'witnesses' who 'testified' that he slaughtered while drunk, that he allowed his son—who did not know the slightest thing

1 According to the author's account here, Bakhchisaray had an Ashkenazi Jewish community at least since the 1840s, although a large influx of Ashkenazi Jews only started to arrive in the Crimea after the end of the Crimean War in 1856 (Keren, 1981:36,52).

2 More formally known as Rabbi Khaym-Yehude Khaymovitsh (ca. 1826–1897), he was the author of the *halakhic* work, *Khok la-Khadash* (Lvov, 1906).

about *sh'khita*—to slaughter, and many more such matters.[3] Do you know why this happened? Not because of his sins! Though you don't know him, you've heard that we still consider him an honorable *shoykhet* and he certainly could have continued on here. But do you know why he's no longer here or what we had against him? We just wanted Benyumin to be able to put some bread on his table, but that *shoykhet* did not want that. He yelled that we were robbing him and that Benyumin was taking away his livelihood. So we—meaning Medvedye and his brothers-in-law who wanted Benyumin to have an income—had no other choice but to arrange all sorts of means to get rid of him."

"The new *shoykhet* that we hired afterward was also a respectable *shoykhet*. You, of course, know him. He's truly a fine person, a Talmudic scholar, and a skilled *shoykhet*, who is now a *shoykhet* in a reputable city by the name of Yuzeve in the province of Yekaterinoslav. What do you think we had against him? Was it because he did business dealings, swindled people, and sat in the coffeehouses?[4] We considered that to be nothing—particularly when there was not so much *sh'khita* work that had to be done. Being a fighter, he filed a complaint against us—he really had no choice. After all, he had to save himself in order not to be bereft of income. But we prevailed and received a ruling from three rabbis that we could hire a new *shoykhet* if we gave him 500 rubles for his exclusive slaughtering rights. So he had no points of rebuttal, and we hired you. Do you know why we did all of this? We wanted our brother-in-law Benyumin to have some income which that *shoykhet* didn't want. So, we then hired someone else, which is how we've come to you, Pinye-Ber."

"By now you understand yourself with whom you're dealing and against whom you need to wage war. We want Benyumin to be able to put some bread on his table—and you too. So I'm telling you, take six rubles a week and don't make any problems. The community does not need to know. Whose business is it how much you're paid? Let them think that you make eight rubles a week while you know that you earn six. If you agree to this, then you can remain here as the *shoykhet* for as long as you live. What would we then have against you? As a matter of fact, you're a fine Jew with a lot of virtues. If you'd take six rubles, then there would be enough remaining for Benyumin to put some bread on his table. And if we're satisfied with you, then the entire community will be satisfied

3 Jewish law forbids *shokhtim* to slaughter while intoxicated. See *Shulkhan Arukh* (*Yoreh Deah* 1:8) and Greenwald (1945:38–39).

4 Thanks to Prof. Yitzkhok Niborski for identifying the word קאַפּעניעס, in the original, as referring to the Yiddish word *kofeynes*, denoting coffeehouses or taverns. The author's son Refuel (Raphael) Goldenstein (1916:46) notes the widespread use of coffeehouses in the Crimea, "Here in the coffee house, Krimchak, Karaite, and Tatar meet on common ground."

with you because they heed our every word. Whatever we say goes. If you consent to accepting six rubles, it will be good for you and for us. But if you insist on eight rubles a week, then dig in your heels. You may actually succeed in earning that amount for a while, but don't expect to remain here as the *shoykhet* for long. And good luck in trying to stay here the following year—or even better luck trying to stay the entire three years—but don't expect to remain here longer. But I think that we'd be able to get rid of you quickly if we seriously set our minds to it. You still don't know us. But don't cry later that we've ruined you. You've been forewarned, and I've told you the truth—as Heaven is my witness." His confession ends here.

Nu, what do you say about that? What could I answer him? Hearing the truth from the culprit himself made me feel quite miserable. I said, "I can't consent to anything not written in the contract—nothing short of receiving six rubles a week the first year and eight rubles the second year. I can't take anything less because it's impossible to live on eight rubles especially with the exorbitant prices here. I'm not, God forbid, changing or make any innovations in the contract, so you won't be able to claim that my changes are the cause of the strife. I'm only fighting your desire to enslave me. If your Benyumin needs income, let him work. He'll then earn his own income instead of leeching off the hard work of *shokhtim*—refined Jews—to support that most crude boor. No, Reb Simkhe! If I'd find out today that I was without a job, I still couldn't agree to subject and lower myself to the status of a slave. I've a wife and small children, and I must work hard for them but not for someone else. God lives, and He'll certainly enable me to prevail . . ."

"*Nu*," he said. "Remember, Pinye-Ber! You'll regret this later."

"What do I have to regret here? I've nothing to lose. If I manage to get paid eight rubles a week, I'll have nothing to regret. And if not, I won't be able to support myself anyway because I can't live off of six rubles a week. So there's nothing to regret." With these words, we parted.

Returning home, my wife noticed that I was upset and asked me, "What's wrong? Who did you run into now?" and other such questions. I asked her to allow me to calm down. She understood that something terrible had happened to me and waited impatiently until I began to tell her everything that you already know. Naturally, she agreed with my response to him. Drenched in tears, she ran over to the children, who were already asleep, and said, "My darling children. *Oy*, my precious ones. Why doesn't God at least help us in your merit, my sinless souls? Why doesn't He want your parents to be able to provide you with enough bread to eat your fill? *Oy*, Master of the Universe! Help us in the merit of my children!" All of this was said loudly while weeping so that the children awoke and also began to cry. Of course, there's no question that I was also crying—I had already been in tears since I began walking home.

No matter how much I thought about the matter, there was just no other alternative except to insist on one thing—eight rubles a week as we had agreed upon in the contract. For the time being, as long as the contract was valid, they needed to fulfill the terms written there. If they wouldn't, then they would have to see me in rabbinical court. The world is not lawless, God forbid. In brief, we decided to fight as long as possible. I said, "If I don't succeed, then nothing will have been lost. But if I do succeed, all will be good and I won't want for anything." This happened on Wednesday. On Thursday, Benyumin told me to go slaughter, and I told him to give me eight rubles. He cursed me and did not want to give me the money. As I left, I told him that I would not slaughter until he gave me eight rubles a week.

Benyumin ran to his community leaders, and I complained to the community. Everyone said that I was in the right. I prevailed upon some of them to support me, and out of compassion they laid themselves on the line and waged an open war for me, though they knew that they were risking losing the honor of being called up for *Maftir* or for the sixth *aliya*.[5] But at the time, they did not take the loss of these honors into account but championed my cause. "We also have a say in communal affairs, and we say that the *shoykhet* shouldn't slaughter until he's given eight rubles a week." In short, their efforts helped and I was given eight rubles, and I went to slaughter. So, I began to receive eight rubles a week, but the head instigators' anger seethed and they sought new ways to dispose of me.

All of a sudden one morning I found out from someone that the community leaders had worked out a plan which was as follows: "In hiring Pinye-Ber, we took a stranger as a *shoykhet*. He says he's a *shoykhet*, but who really knows who he is? Let him travel to the *shokhtim* in Simferopol to be certified in slaughtering. Also, let him travel to Karasubazar to the *Khakham*,[6] Rabbi Khizkiyahu

5 The *Maftir* is the last *aliya* (the honor of being called to the Torah) during the reading of the Torah on *Shabes*, holidays, and some other occasions. The person called up for *Maftir* also reads the *Haftorah* (the weekly selection from the Biblical book of Prophets) or has someone read it in his stead. Receiving this *aliya* is considered a special honor and is reserved for prominent people or those observing a *yortsayt*, bar-mitzvah, wedding, etc. The sixth *aliya* on *Shabes*—out of a total of seven—is also a most prestigious honor among many Hasidim and communities that follow the Kabbalah (Wertheim, 1992:226).

6 *Khakham* literally means "wise man" in Hebrew and is a title for rabbis among *Sephardic* Jews.

FIGURE 14. The great Sephardic sage Rabbi Khayim-Khizkiyahu Medini (1833–1904), better known by the name of his monumental work *Sdei Khemed*, was the rabbi in Karasubazar, Crimea. According to his son, Pinkhes-Dov Goldenshteyn was a friend and admirer of Rabbi Medini. See Appendix C2 (pp. 811–813) for details.

Medini,[7] and obtain his certification so that we can know that he's actually a good *shoykhet*." How do you like that plan? They did not mention my salary at all but were suddenly interested in only one thing—that their *shoykhet* should have certification from the *shokhtim* in Simferopol. Receiving certification from just the rabbi was not good enough because he was close by and traveling to him would cost me too little money. They wanted to waste my time and money so that my current salary of eight rubles would be squandered unnecessarily. They did not want me to derive any benefit from my salary increase.

Nu, what could I reply to such a request? I asked them, "Why on earth were you quiet about this matter until now?" to which they replied, "It was truly wrong of us, but we just realized that it could happen that anyone could represent himself as a *shoykhet*." Naturally, I had to agree to their demands.[8] In short, I traveled to Karasubazar and met with the *Khakham* who gave me certification papers. Apart from the certification papers, he also wrote a letter to my community describing the full extent to which I pleased him and requesting them to treat me honorably.[9] How did it happen that he should write my community

---

7 Rabbi Khayim Khizkiyahu Medini (1833–1904), better known by the name of his monumental work *Sdei Khemed*, was born in Jerusalem where his father was the head of the Sephardic rabbinical court. Upon his father's death in 1853, he traveled to Constantinople, Turkey (now Istanbul), where he earned some money as a private tutor. Since he knew Turkish, he was asked to become the rabbi in the Crimea of the Krymchaks, an indigenous Rabbinite Jewish community of the Crimean Peninsula, who spoke their own dialect of Crimean Tatar, a Turkic language. Towards the end of 1866, he accepted and then moved to Karasubazar in the Crimea, establishing a yeshiva and raising the level of the Krymchaks' observance. Though many sources refer to him simply as Rabbi Khizkiyahu Medini, he added the name Khayim when ill in 1878. In 1899, he returned to Jerusalem, where he lived for two years before relocating to Hebron, where he died. His monumental work, *Sdei Khemed*, is a multi-volume encyclopedia of rabbinical responsa, which was one of the primary indexing resources for responsa until the development of modern resources in the mid-twentieth century and is still widely used. For a comprehensive biography of Rabbi Medini, see Hirshler (2001). In both his thesis on the Krymchaks (1916:77–78) and in his Hebrew-language article about Rabbi Medini in *Ha-Toren* (1925:18), the author's son Refuel (Raphael Goldenstein) mentions Rabbi Medini's 1899 departure for Jerusalem, as described to him by his father who participated in the event. See Appendix C2 (pp. 811–813) for his full description of this event and for the translations of two additional episodes which Raphael heard from his father regarding Rabbi Medini. [Perhaps the only book or article regarding the Krymchaks to cite Raphael's thesis is Blady (2000:115–130), who mistakenly refers to him as Goldstein. Significantly, Blady notes the Krymchak customs mentioned by Raphael that are apparently not mentioned elsewhere.]

8 By the eighteenth century, Jewish communities began to insist that their *shokhtim* "receive, irrespective of any license acquired elsewhere, a *kabala* [i.e., certification] from a local rabbi" (Berman, 1941, 92).

9 Though not mentioned by the author, Rabbi Medini also wrote the community leaders of Bakhchisaray a letter some four months earlier on the 16th of *Heshvan* 5640 (November

FIGURE 15. An 1879 Hebrew letter from the great Sephardic sage Rabbi Khayim-Khizkiyahu Medini, defending Pinkhes-Dov Goldenshteyn. For a translation of the letter, see Appendix C1 (pp. 808–810). (By permission of the Klau Library—Hebrew Union College—Jewish Institute of Religion in Cincinnati.)

a letter? Two days after my departure, the *shokhtim* in Simferopol received a dispatch that I was not agreeable to the community and that they wanted to drive me off altogether. This very dispatch, which they thought would be used to harm me, turned out to be to my benefit as it only served to convince the *shokhtim* how corrupt the community leaders in Bakhchisaray were.[10]

I returned home happy that I had succeeded, thank God. The community leaders, though, had not expected such a downfall. They had believed that I would be away for five or six weeks during which they would hire another *shoykhet*. They had thought that by the time I returned it would be too late for me to regain my position. Now they were quiet because they had absolutely nothing to say. The members of the community who were uninterested in the strife were delighted with the *Khakham*'s letter of strong praise for me and they began to revere me. Those interested in the strife ground their teeth. They remained outwardly quiet while they secretly searched for ways of getting rid of me. And the more they reflected on the foolishness of their scheme, the greater was their embarrassment. Now they were forced to live with me in peace, though in their hearts they wished otherwise. So they sought out new plans for disposing of me as quickly as possible.

Let me leave this subject for a while to tell you about my private life at home and about my children whom God had granted us during our few years in Bakhchisaray. You of course know that I came to Bakhchisaray in 5640 [*sic*] with my little son, Srul-Burekhl, a boy of six or seven, and my little daughter Nekhamele, who was two.[11] Two years after arriving in Bakhchisaray, my son Yosefl was born on the 20th of *Adar*.[12] I was then still living in the *shul* courtyard (may this never happen to you), which is already familiar to you from the episode involving the poor person I encountered shortly after Yosl's birth.[13]

2, 1879) regarding a previous attempt to oust the author and replace him with a *shoykhet* named Shmuel. Rabbi Medini warned them not to commit such a serious crime. This letter is apparently the singular piece of outside evidence extant that corroborates the unwarranted persecution that the author suffered. See Appendix C1 (pp. 808–810) for a translation of the entire letter.

10 Afterward, Rabbi Medini was made aware of this telegram and felt compelled to write to the Jewish community of Bakhchisaray.

11 The author settled in Bakhchisaray in 5639 (1879), as explicitly written in the preface to Part III (p. 401), made clear in ch. 23, p. 462, and as mentioned in Rabbi Medini's 1879 letter (see Appendix C1 (pp. 808–810). Nekhame was a little over one year old at the time, not two.

12 As the author writes in ch. 23, p. 473, his son Itskhok-Yosef (nicknamed "Yosefl" here) was born in 5640 (March 3, 1880) which was the beginning of his second year in Bakhchisaray—not two years after his arrival.

13 Yosl, Yosele, and Yosefl are all Yiddish diminutives of Yosef.

Now was the year 5642, my fifth year [*sic*] in Bakhchisaray.[14] God granted me another son, Yankele (may he live and be well)—I should really refer to him by his proper name, Yankev—who was born on the 20th of *Shvat*.[15] The older children were growing up, little ones were being added to the family, the prices were exorbitant, and my eight rubles a week was now not enough for us to live on. But I held nothing against anyone, God forbid, as long as they would at least let me live in peace. I worked exceedingly hard while my wife stood in the kitchen and cooked for wayfarers and boarders. Everyone knew that anyone needing a meal was able to go to the *shoykhet*'s wife, where he could get lunch and dinner. Some would spend the night while others would pay monthly for room and board. My wife, poor thing, undertook more than she could in order to be a true helpmate to me. So a lot of income came our way over the course of the year thereby enabling us to make ends meet and even to send our oldest son Srul-Burekhl to study in Poland to make him a proper Jew.[16]

My wife took Srul-Burekhl and brought him to my sister Sure who lived in Khashtshevote in the province of Podolia. Srul-Burekhl was then eleven years old [*sic*].[17] My wife also took along the baby Yankele, who was then three months old. She left with both children shortly after Pesach of 5643 [*sic*] while the other two children, Nekhamele and Yosl, remained at home with me.[18] Nekhamele was then six years old and Yosl was three.[19] By the time their mother returned, I had suffered enough from them. The noise they made used to reach to the very heavens. I once found them standing in the attic of the shed. The children had gone up the stairs leading to the attic where they kept yanking at the attic door.

---

14 The year 5642 was the author's fourth year in Bakhchisaray—not his fifth.

15 February 9, 1882. The date according to the Julian calendar was January 28, 1882, which was the date of birth that Yankl (under the name Jacob Goldeen) used on his draft registration cards from the First World War (Vancouver, Washington, September 12, 1918) and the Second World War (Portland, Oregon, 1941). He was generally called in Yiddish by the diminutives Yankl and Yankele.

16 As mentioned in the next paragraph, Isruel-Burekh was sent to Khashtshevote in the province of Podolia, which was also referred to as Poland in Yiddish. See ch. 3, p. 111, footnote 13.

17 In 1882, Isruel was only nine years old—not eleven. If this discrepancy seems too large to be possible, consider that the author writes on p. 489 below that Isruel was sixteen or seventeen upon his return home after six years of study, thereby implying that Isruel could have been sent away as young as ten, which is only a one-year discrepancy. Later, the author also sent his son Refuel at the age of nine to study in Khashtshevote (ch. 27, p. 546). Since there were basically no yeshivas in the Crimea, he sent his sons to his sister in Khashtshevote, which had a yeshiva.

18 As mentioned in footnote 15 above, the year is 5642 (1882)—not 5643 (1883)—since the author's son Yankl is now three months old and was born in February 1882. So the author's wife left after Pesach ended on April 11, 1882.

19 Nekhame was then only five years old, and Yosl was two.

The girl started it all, and the boy just followed her lead. I came exactly at the moment when they succeeded in ripping the door open and I nearly died from shock—they had almost killed themselves, God forbid. I thanked God for sending me there at that precise moment, thereby saving them.

As much as I suffered from the two children staying with me, my wife suffered even more from the other two. When God brought them safely to Khashtshevote, she had to remain there eight days until Srul-Burekhl became accustomed to his new environment and to the foods they ate there. Of course, her bidding him farewell, leaving him, and being separated from her son are impossible to describe. She might have spent several more days there but the baby became ill and there was no proper doctor there. So she decided to travel to Bender, and the baby arrived there half-dead. During that time, she prayed and pleaded with God. She had risked so much only for His sake. All she wanted was to make her son into a good Jew who studied His holy Torah, so why was this happening to her? In short, God heard her prayers and the baby recovered, thank God. We underwent all of this—I am not even including the large expense this incurred—because we wanted our son to be a pious Jew. I was certainly in no position to send my son away to study, but we both worked hard and sent whatever money was asked of us on his behalf.

My son grew accustomed to his new environment thanks to my sister's devoted care. He lacked nothing except his home. The delight we received from reading the nice notes he wrote us kept us going. As time passed, he made more progress in his studies and he remained there for three years. He was now studying the Talmud and *Tanakh*.[20] But since Khashtshevote was a fanatical *shteytl* and I did not want him to grow up to be an impractical person and a fanatic, I decided to bring him to Tiraspol, where I also had relatives. Even though the city of Tiraspol was Jewish, it was a commercial and an intellectual city. There were good *melomdim* there, and the secular-studies teachers and the local children his age were also respectable. In short, I had my son brought to Tiraspol. I managed to do all of this shortly before control of that miserable kosher-meat tax was removed from my enemies, which proved to be the antidote to my problems.[21]

---

20 This term generally refers to the study of the Prophets and the Writings, the second and third sections of the Bible.

21 In the fall of 1885, Isruel was brought to Tiraspol after staying three years in Khashtshevote. The author later confirms that Isruel was in Tiraspol for three years on p. 488 and again on p. 502 in writing that Isruel had been away from home for a total of six years (three years in Khashtshevote and three years in Tiraspol). Since Isruel was brought to Tiraspol shortly before control of the kosher-meat tax was removed from the author's enemies, as mentioned here, this corresponds to the author's preventing the

Bringing my Srulikl from Khashtshevote to Tiraspol cost me plenty—both blood and money. And I could not send him until I found someone going there to send him with, which is a journey of 200 *versts*. After all, a boy of thirteen could not travel there alone and in no way could either my wife or I travel there. But God helped and we accomplished this when someone from Khashtshevote took him straight to Tiraspol and delivered him into the care of my relatives—my niece Ester-Khaye (the daughter of my sister Ite, of blessed memory) and her husband Yankev Kaushaner.[22] I paid them for his room and board, which—as you understand—I arranged via the mail. In the same manner, I hired a *melomed* and a teacher, to teach him secular subjects. He made good progress in all subjects and acquired a fine name for himself in Tiraspol. All of his friends boasted about him, and we enjoyed the notes he wrote immensely.

Our greatest hope was for God to help our Srulikl return home from Tiraspol as a *mentsh*. The younger children would then have him as a good example to emulate and would endeavor to be Jews and *mentshn* like their brother.[23] A year after his arrival in Tiraspol, I transferred him to a more advanced *melomed* who taught Talmud—to Leyb-Yoyls of Slobodze, who was the same Leyb Fishman who had persecuted me when I lived in Slobodze, as you may remember from my description of him. God had now turned the tables; he had become a *melomed* in Tiraspol, and I was now his employer. My son studied with him, and I made a point of paying him well. His being reduced to a *melomed* was only a portion of his punishment for his machinations, but you will find a description of God's true punishment inflicted upon him and his family in a separate chapter where the fates of all of my enemies will be depicted.[24] That separate chapter will teach you the lesson that everything is repaid. God waits long and pays well. Nothing is overlooked. At times, He delays that payment because He is waiting for repentance—perhaps the person will regret his actions and repent.

In brief, Reb Leyb-Yoyls was teaching my son, and it was costing me a good amount of money. I kept him in Tiraspol more than three years and brought him home in a fortunate and propitious time as a young man of

---

kosher-meat tax consignment from falling into the hands of his enemies in late 1885 as mentioned in ch. 26, p. 524

22 This is the author's first reference to the passing of his sister Ite. Because he last mentions her in 1874 (ch. 22, p. 440), she must have died between 1874 and 1886. Ester-Khaye's husband, Yankev Apatshevsky, was called Kaushaner since he was from the city of Kaushán (aka Kovishón). See Appendix D2 (pp. 820–821) for a genealogical chart of the extended Teplitsky family.

23 *Mentshn* is the plural of *mentsh*.

24 In ch. 29, pp. 570–572, the author describes only the fate of his enemies in Bakhchisaray.

sixteen or seventeen.[25] He was handsome as gold, had a refined Jewish face, could write in Yiddish, Russian, and a little bit of German. Most importantly, he had a good knowledge of *Tanakh* and Hebrew grammar and he could study the Talmud well. We certainly delighted in seeing what he had become. As it states, "The mother of the sons rejoices. Praise God."[26] In truth, we praised God for allowing us to live to see such a precious child grow up to be a pious Jew—and soft-spoken too. All of our friends were pleased, but our enemies could not stand it and sought even more aggressive ways to persecute me. Pointing at my Srulikl, they would say, "Look at what a wealthy person can do with his son. Why can't we do that? Because we don't have the means! We'd also be able turn our sons into rabbis, but how can we do that? He's as rich as Korach, so he can do it."[27] Out of envy, they began to persecute me even more so that I would not have money to educate my children.

In short, Srulikl was now at home. The question arose, "What should I now do with him?" Should I teach him *sh'khita*? It was still too early. He was quite young for that. Should I continue to study the Talmud with him myself? I did not have any time. Should he study the Talmud by himself? No, he still needed guidance because he might think he understood it when he really did not.[28] My head was spinning as I racked my brains in trying to come up with a plan for him. Since I had two growing boys who were already beginning to study the Talmud, why not hire a learned *melomed* to teach or study with all three sons.[29] He would serve as a *melomed* for the younger two and as the study partner for the older one. And that's what I did. I found a pious Jew, a brilliant Torah scholar, whom I hired for four rubles a week—in addition to room, board, washing his clothes, tobacco, and money for the public baths—all at my expense. And they needed a separate room to be used during the day for study and at night for sleeping. I kept this *melomed* for a year until my Srulikl turned eighteen, at which point I began to teach him *sh'khita*.[30] He grasped well the manual skills involved and

---

25 As mentioned in ch. 24, p. 486 above, Isruel was sent away to study in April 1882. He returned home in April 1888 at the age of 15, after being away for six years, as related later on p. 502.

26 Psalms 113:9.

27 "As rich as Korach" is a Yiddish expression denoting someone tremendously wealthy. The Talmud (Sanhedrin 110a) states that the Biblical Korach, who incited the people against Moses, was so wealthy that the keys of his treasure stores alone were a load for 300 white mules.

28 The study of Talmud is quite complex. Hence, it is common for one who is not well trained in its intricacies to misinterpret and convince himself that he has understood the subject matter properly.

29 Isruel returned home in 1888, and the author's two growing boys were Yosl, aged eight, and Yankele, aged six.

30 Isruel turned eighteen in December 1890.

diligently learned the laws of *sh'khita*. In a period of over a year, he completed learning the skill of *sh'khita*. Thank God, I accomplished the task of training him as a *shoykhet*, and he then obtained fine certificates of slaughtering from the *shokhtim* in Simferopol, Sevastopol, and Melitopol, and also from the rabbis in those cities.[31]

We must now leave my Srulikl's story until later and relate to you what happened at our home during our second year in Bakhchisaray, namely which guests began to come and what I endured from them.[32] This was apart from the harassment I withstood from my enemies, but I will speak about them later. For the time being, we will discuss the guests.

One morning, I opened the gate and found two unexpected—yet important—guests standing at the door. Do you know who they were? My mother-in-law, Dvoyre, and her daughter, a girl of fifteen—my wife's sister. I ran into the house shouting the news, "Freyde! Do you know who's come to visit? Your mother and your sister Tsipe." Naturally, a commotion erupted among the children, and meanwhile the arriving guests entered our home. Everyone kissed, spoke, and cried—each one louder than the other. Questions and astonishment were not lacking—we were interested in thoroughly knowing what had happened to both of them and why they had come so unexpectedly, which was justified with one answer, "Over time, you'll know everything. Meanwhile, we're tired from our travels." I agreed that they should first rest well from their journey, so she ended up resting up at my home for some four or five weeks and returned home—naturally only once I reimbursed her for her travel expenses. She left her daughter with me on the following pretext, "Let her stay with you. Around you, she'll mature and will certainly ease her sister's housework load."

A month had not yet passed since my mother-in-law's departure when we received a short letter that I should send Tsipe home because a groom-to-be was waiting for her. She also wrote me his name. I actually knew him and knew that he was suffering from an illness, God forbid—epilepsy.[33] Upon hearing this, I became quite agitated. After all, how could one think of finding a match for such a young girl of fifteen who could not even converse with others yet?

31 In 1891, the rabbi in Simferopol was Rabbi Bole-Binyomin Demant, as mentioned in ch. 26, p. 526, footnote 19. The rabbi of Sevastopol was Rabbi Shmuel-Yerukhem Yunovitsh. In 1887 or shortly afterward, Rabbi Yunovitsh left Uman, where he had been the rabbi of the Lithuanian Jews, for Sevastopol (Rabbi Medini, 2006:1:89).

32 The author arrived in Bakhchisaray in March 1879; hence, his second year began in March 1880. Since he writes on p. 491 below that his mother-in-law, Dvoyre, visited during the winter, she evidently visited during the winter of 1880–1881.

33 The author merely notes the Hebrew initials "ח.נ.," which apparently stand for *khole nofel*, meaning epilepsy.

And what type of a match was found for her? One that would cause her eternal unhappiness. I wrote my mother-in-law a letter and explained to her how inhumanely she was treating her own daughter behind her back.

A telegram in Russian arrived to the "engaged Tsipe" with congratulations. Upon hearing the news, Tsipe was overjoyed that she was now a bride-to-be. "How can you be so happy? Fool! Where did your mother sell you? Why don't you have any patience to wait for a better, healthier groom and not take a groom with such an illness, God forbid?" She did not want to hear about it. She only knew that she was now engaged and wanted to travel home. Meanwhile, a letter came from her mother telling her to return home for the writing of the engagement contract and that she herself would have to come for her if I would not send her home. I saw that things were bad; her mother would come, which would cost me even more money. Without any other choice, I had to send her home, pay for her travel expenses, and also buy her a dress and a piece of calico for blouses—and she left. All of this cost me forty rubles in cash, apart from all the extra household expenses that they cost me. With my poverty, I missed their presence like a hole in the head. This happened during the winter between Hanukah and Purim.[34]

Between Purim and Pesach,[35] I received a short letter from my wife's wealthy uncle, Reb Yankev Royzman, who was called "Yankev the Blind" from Ternifke. If you remember, I related how "graciously" he treated me when I was trying to obtain the position of *shoykhet* in Bakhchisaray and asked him to lend me money, which he refused to do.[36] That lout was now writing me a letter, which went as follows, "Pinye-Ber, perhaps you can do me a favor by arranging for my son Shimshen to be called for military conscription in Bakhchisaray, that is, have his place of conscription transferred from Tiraspol to you in Bakhchisaray."[37] Anyone else in my position would have immediately pointed out his past injustices, and cursed him out as well. But being that I like to do

34 Hanukah ended on December 3, 1880, and Purim occurred on March 15, 1881.

35 Pesach started the night of April 13, 1881.

36 See ch. 23, p. 462. Yankev was first mentioned in ch. 18, p. 299.

37 In 1874, Tsarist Russia radically reformed its conscription policy by creating a lottery-based uniform conscription system for both Jews and non-Jews. Recruits served in the military for six years, which was later reduced to four. Despite the reforms, the Jews were deathly afraid of being conscripted because of the extreme difficulty of keeping even the most basic precepts of Judaism, such as eating kosher or the observance of *Shabes*, in the army, let alone the myriad of other religious obligations incumbent upon traditional Jews (Braver, 1966:68–69). In addition, Jewish recruits were abused, treated like enemies of the state, and had no hope of advancement; thus, throughout their entire military service they remained surrounded by abusive, illiterate, base peasants, while the literate non-Jews of a higher class were quickly advanced (Slutsky, 1975:6–9; I. Schneersohn, 1968:186–188, 407–411).

everything rationally, I saw that refusing to do his son a favor would not be proper. Why was the son to blame for his father's failure to be a *mentsh*? Why not let Reb Yankev see that such an insignificant, poor Pinye-Ber could also be useful to the world and could be of benefit to his son and to him as well. Let him then be ashamed and learn a lesson. Though I did not yet know if transferring him would be helpful, I would certainly be moving in the right direction if I worked at it. But If I did not try to help him and he would report to the conscription board in Tiraspol, he would be as good as conscripted. At least if he was transferred here, where so few Jews lived, he might stand a chance.[38]

I wrote my uncle a friendly letter and did not even hint to our previous encounter so that he should not feel ashamed. I told him what the local authorities recommended that he do: prepare the paperwork, send it on time along with the required fees, and have his son come so that they could see him. In short, his son came exactly in time for Pesach. Granted, he did bring a jug of wine for the four cups,[39] but he continued to eat and drink on account of that wine until the transfer was ready in May.[40] He saw how much money I gave the authorities and then traveled home to his father, who then sent me the cost of the transfer. But his father apparently thought that I would be insulted if he paid me for my efforts and for his son's lodgings, so he sent me nothing for them. I figured that he would certainly pay me when he would report to the conscription board in October.[41]

But listen, dear readers, to what transpired when he reported to the conscription board, and you will then come to know his unseemly treatment of me and how his coarse and indecent character paled in comparison to his stinginess. Nonetheless, I treated him in the most refined and polite manner so that he should see and know what a *mentsh* is and what kind of person earns the right to be called a *mentsh*. I am writing all of this deliberately and in great detail in order that you, dear readers, should take it as a lesson on how to be a *mentsh* and how to conduct yourselves with others in order to be worthy of being called a *mentsh*.

---

38 Apparently, fewer Jews were conscripted in the Crimea at that time due to their much smaller population there. In 1897, the province of Taurida (which included the Crimea) had the second lowest percentage of Jews (4.2%) of any other province in the Imperial Russian Pale of Settlement, to which Jews were restricted (Lestschinsky, 1897:42).

39 Every adult Jew is obligated to drink four cups of wine at each Pesach *Seder* (*Kitsur Shulkhan Arukh* 119:1)

40 May 1881.

41 October 1881.

In October 5641 [*sic*][42] my uncle, Yankev the Blind, came from Ternifke with his oldest son Shimshen to appear before the conscription board. He arrived on a Wednesday, and conscription began the next Monday. My uncle asked me about the recruits who were reporting that year to the conscription board. I made it clear to him that there were a total of five Jews, two who had exemptions and three who did not.[43] His son was of the latter group. I knew four of them but did not know one of the three who had no exemptions.

As we were speaking, two guests entered. As you may remember, at that time I was still living in the community-owned house in the synagogue courtyard.

"Good morning, my fellow Jews. Does the *shoykhet* live here?"

"Yes," I replied.

"*Oy*! Thank God! We were barely able to find our way to a fellow Jew. We walked from the train station through the entire city without coming across a single Jew—only Tatars. And when we asked them where the Jews live, we couldn't understand their answers."[44]

"No matter, as long as you were able to find your way to the *shoykhet.* Sit down my dear Jews." I then asked, "Where are you from and where are you traveling to?"

The older of the two replied while pointing to the younger one, "I've brought my son-in-law here for conscription, though none of our ancestors ever lived here. It has already cost me over 200 rubles to have his recruitment transferred here, and I still don't know if my efforts will accomplish anything."

I asked him the name of his son-in-law, which he told me. I then realized that he was the one I had not known out of the three recruits without exemptions. He appeared to be healthy, but I did not like the appearance of one of his eyes. It looked like it was covered by a cataract, which may have been temporarily induced—it was common for the Polish Jews to do such handiwork to avoid

42 Based on the chronology of events until now, it is 5642 (October 1881)—not 5641 (October 1880).

43 Three classes of military exemptions existed. The first and highest class of exemption was for an only son who was the sole wage-earner for his family. The second level was for the only wage-earning son (though other sons were in the family) who assisted his father in supporting his family. And the third was for a brother of a soldier who had fallen in combat. When there was a shortage of recruits without exemptions, even those with first-class exemptions were conscripted (Dubnow, 1918:201; Polonsky, 2010:430; Slutsky, 1975:6).

44 Bakhchisaray's population was primarily comprised of Crimean Tatars who spoke the Crimean Tatar language, which is a Turkic language, and almost no Russian.

recruitment.[45] As it now turned out, only two out of the three without exemptions were fit for duty since this out-of-towner was certainly unfit. After all, who here would inform the authorities, God forbid, that the cataract was induced? This was not Poland. Of the remaining two, my relative was naturally a robust Bessarabian young man—nurtured on wine and *mamaliga*—looking fit enough to be a royal guardsman.[46]

When my Uncle Yankev saw before him the woeful sight, he began to take stock of the situation and groaned, "Oh no! What should I do? My son is as good as conscripted." Out of distress, he attacked his son with vehement curses and yelled at him, "Why are you so healthy? Why didn't you do something to yourself several weeks ago like everyone else did?" He then wanted to force his son to take the contents of a flask that a *feldsher* had given him to use at a time of need. At that point, I really gave him a piece of my mind, telling him that not only did he lack even the slightest bit of trust in God but on top of that he wanted to ruin his son's life. "Who knows what type of illness such a medicine could bring about? It would be better for the Tsar to have a healthy soldier and for you to have a healthy son." He replied, "It would be better for me to bury him than have him become a soldier." Of course, this last remark was sheer nonsense, said in the heat of the moment. He actually wanted to save him.

We said all of this on the other side of the house so that our guests should not hear us. Upon returning to the other room, we now no longer found the guests there, but my wife told me that they did want to lodge and also eat with us, because they were afraid of being served *treyf* elsewhere. After my wife agreed that they should stay with us, they went into the street to take care of various matters. I asked her, "Where will you put them?" to which she replied, "In the cold half of the house, which we'll heat up well at night. During the day, we'll manage somehow. What else does one do with strangers?" "You're right, my wife, but nevertheless where will you seat everyone? You have your uncle and his son, this fellow and his son-in-law, and me and the children. Everything will be on your head and in such a small room. Are you sure that you can handle all of this?" She gave a smile and said, "I've known for a long time that you

---

45 In the effort to avoid military conscription in Tsarist Russia, Jewish recruits sometimes tried to make themselves unfit for service by cutting off one or more fingers or by attempting to temporarily blind an eye, which often unintentionally resulted in permanent blindness (Slutsky, 1975:15–16). The author calls this recruit a Polish Jew since he was from Bolte in Podolia (as mentioned in ch. 25, p. 515) and Podolia was referred to as Poland in Yiddish (see ch. 3, p. 111, footnote 13).

46 *Mamaliga* was a staple food in Bessarabia (most of which is currently part of Moldova) and Romania. It consists of cornmeal made into a thick, solidified porridge. Bessarabian Jews were known to love wine (Rozhanski, 1981:8).

appreciate my capabilities but ask me if my mother appreciates my abilities?" which was a bit of sarcasm regarding my mother-in-law's behavior toward us. I answered, "Your mother is not worthy of having a daughter like you."

While I was speaking with my wife, Uncle Yankev was sitting in a corner of our house along with his son and was asking him to take the medicine which would immediately begin to turn him yellow—thereby giving him the appearance of someone ill—and would make his eyes run. His son in no way wanted to take it, despite his father's torment. While wiping his tears from his blind eye, Uncle Yankev turned to me and asked in a tearful voice reminiscent of the chant used for *kines*, "Tell me, Pinye-Ber, what should I do with him? He wants to be a soldier!" I calmed him down. "Your son's right. Whether he'll be conscripted is still in doubt. God can still extricate him. But from your medicine, he'll certainly become ill. Uncle, think about what you want to do!" And with the following words, I addressed his son, "Listen, Shimshen! Being that he's your father, you must obey everything he says—but not this! It's very good that you don't want to take that medicine." Shimshen solidly agreed not take the prescription, while my uncle wrung his hands and cried. I said, "Don't grieve. Trust in God and don't lose your faith." Meanwhile, the two guests returned, became acquainted with my uncle and his son, and found out that they both had sons who would be drawing numbers in the military lottery.[47] Naturally, they eyed one another uncomfortably like two roosters and guarded their words in each other's presence.

In the afternoon, my uncle called me over to the side and said to me as follows, "Do you know, Pinye-Ber, what I've decided? Perhaps it would be good to approach the doctors who'll be examining the recruits during the conscription process." I replied, "That probably wouldn't be unreasonable—as long as there would be money. It could likely cost some 200 rubles." He said, "I'm not sparing any expense to save my son." I explained that this kind of remedy is much more suitable than the previous type he wanted to give his son, because the doctors can do someone a favor if they so desire. I added, "One of the doctors in Simferopol is a Jew whom I know well and the other is a non-Jew whom I don't know. But we only have to talk with the Jewish one since he is in alliance with the other. I know of many cases of recruits who were exempted by them. But if you want to do something like this, then leave for Simferopol today, this Thursday night, because conscription begins on Monday and the doctors along

47 "Since the number of men of military age greatly exceeds the required number of recruits, the Russian law provides that lots be drawn by the conscripts to determine the order in which they are to present themselves for examination to the recruiting officers" (Dubnow, 1918:2:201).

with the authorities will be leaving Simferopol to come here on Sunday, which will then be too late." My uncle asked me to accompany him there. I agreed since I could not bear to watch his pain, though it was not easy for me to go away for *Shobes*. I still had a lot of work to do in preparing the meat for *Shobes* and had to ask permission from the main *gabbai* to release me from leading the services and reading the Torah on *Shobes*. I also had to gain the consent of the kosher-meat tax farmer, who would not agree unless I took along a sack of sheep-tail fat to sell in Simferopol. Though I knew that sack of fat would cause me plenty of anguish in running around trying to sell it, I agreed to sell it—as long as I could accompany my uncle to the doctor to do whatever possible to save his son and show him who is a *mentsh* and what it meant to be a *mentsh*...

After finishing slaughtering the chickens on Friday morning, I rented a carriage and took along my uncle and his son—and the kosher-meat tax farmer's sack of fat—and headed off toward Simferopol. We arrived there at noon. I washed up right away and went over to the doctor, leaving my uncle and his son in the street.[48] The doctor welcomed me nicely and listened closely to what I had to say. He replied, "Why did you come here so late? You know that there are only three days left until conscription begins. The authorities can now easily track anyone entering my house. But for your sake, I'll advise you what to do. You should bring over the young man immediately, and I'll examine him. For the time being, until I see him, I can't say anything. Just come in the evening through this entrance at the appointed time." I left and related everything to my uncle, who wrung his hands and said, "What can be done? He's just so very healthy." My uncle waited impatiently until the appointed hour. His son and I went in to see the doctor. Near the entrance, my uncle handed me 200 rubles, saying, "*Nu*, give the doctor this money—as long as he exempts my son." He himself remained outside, walking around in the street while praying wholeheartedly to God.

In examining my nephew—that *mamaliga*—the doctor said, "No, my friend, he's completely healthy![49] I can't help him at all. He'll certainly be recruited." When my pleas did not help, I pushed the 200 rubles into his hand. The doctor then said, "No, my friend, I certainly want to earn this money, but I can't. I can only promise you this: If I can, I'll try to mislead them regarding his

---

48 The author presumably washed up after travelling on the dusty road.

49 Rozhanski (1981:8) writes that the main characteristic of the ethnic identity of Romanian and Bessarabian Jews "is their earthiness: their love of nature, the body, wine, and song. Their nickname '*mamaliga*' [i.e., a cornmeal mush, which constitutes much of their diet] is possibly, like every nickname, slightly humorous, coarse, and exaggerated, but in every exaggeration lies some truth..."

eyesight. I'll then be able to return him home for you to continue to raise, and we can then talk about money."

I unhappily went outside where I found my uncle in tears. He asked me, "*Nu*, what happened? Did the doctor take the money?" "No," I replied, "meanwhile he did not take it," and I told him what you already know. He then castigated his son again for being so healthy and barraged him with all types of curses, which he did not stop doing until we reached our lodgings. The young man cried and did not respond to his father's torments at all but let out his distress in eating dinner—he ate enough for his father too—and followed it with a glass of wine. Every spoon of soup that the son ate was accompanied by another of his father's curses. Yet by that time, the young man was as accustomed to my uncle's tune as he was to the tune of *Kol Mekadesh*.[50] They continued in this manner throughout Friday evening and *Shobes* day.

Late *Shobes* afternoon, my uncle said to me, "Let's try to go to the Christian doctor. I'm willing to pay 300 rubles—as long as my son is exempted." I agreed and after *Havdalah* we left for the home of the Christian doctor, where they told us that he had just left for such and such a pharmacy.[51] We went to that pharmacy, where they told us that he had just left to such and such a sick person. We went there, but by now we were falling off our feet because driving around in a wagon was not suitable in such circumstances. In short, we arrived there, and they responded that he had been there but had just left, and they did not know where he went. I came out and told my uncle what they had said. He replied, "Let's go to his home again." I stopped and said, "Listen, Uncle! If you want to go, then go alone. I'm not walking any further! I have a rule: If I want to do something and it goes smoothly, then fine. But if not, that means I don't need to do it and I stop doing it. The same thing is happening to you. We've done everything possible, and it's just not going. The first doctor did not want to take any money, and we've been looking for the other one already for three hours and we can't find him. It's certainly God's Will." I then handed him the 300 rubles and said, "Have pity on your money that you're looking to bury, and God will help you without these doctors. That's how it appears to me." Naturally, he took back the money—but with tears—and he reluctantly returned with me to our lodgings, which we had to leave in two hours in order to return home.

Only then did I remember the bag of fat that still remained unsold. How would I be able to find a customer in the middle of the night? Daybreak would

50 *Kol Mekadesh* is one of the popular *zmires* chanted during the Friday-night Sabbath meal.

51 *Havdalah*, literally meaning "separation" in Hebrew, is the prayer said over wine, made after nightfall at the conclusion of Shabes and Jewish holidays. It marks the end of every holy day and the transition to the regular days of the week.

not be for a while, and I had to find a way to sell it. Nonetheless, I did find a customer who bought it for a low price, though even then I had to loan him the money. Though I later suffered a loss from the transaction, at least I was rid of that bag of fat. I could now return home, and I thanked God that I had found that purchaser. On the way back, my uncle groaned and wrung his hands while I felt happy that I had saved him 300 rubles. My heart told me that his son would not be conscripted and that he would be able to keep his money—and that is what happened.

On Monday, all the Jews drew high numbers, so they were not needed to fill the quota of conscripts, and they remained free.[52] Not one of them was even called over to substantiate any information about himself. You can imagine how much I teased my uncle afterward. Nonetheless, my uncle was impatient and eager to receive the red ticket so that he could return home that very day, a Wednesday.[53] I ran into the office and asked the secretary for it, and he immediately gave me the ticket, saying, "You'll certainly make it worth my while since I would have only issued the ticket in a few days from now—and nothing smaller than a five-ruble tip." I promised him a tip and actually expected that my uncle would surely give it, for this would certainly be his responsibility.

Now listen to how my uncle treated me in the end. It is actually because of his lack of compassion that I am describing this episode at such great length so that you can understand what type of a person he was. I related all that I endured from him and his son (let alone the costs involved in hosting them) and especially how I saved him 300 rubles. (I could have easily done him the greatest favor by lying and fabricating a tale of how the doctor had taken the money). And now hear the way this contemptible person treated me when I brought him the red ticket. I told him that it would only be proper to give the secretary five rubles, to which he snapped back at me, "Five rubles? I'll give him nothing! He won't take thirty or forty *kopeks*?" I explained to him that the secretary could have tied him up here until Sunday when he would have had to give him the five rubles himself, and that he released the ticket early only on my behalf! My uncle maintained his position and would not give more than a half a ruble. Of no help was my pointing out that he would be turning

52 Melamed (1922:1:276–278), from a village near Hulyaypole, Ukraine, relates in his memoirs that in 1883 a total of 200 men from the area were summoned to appear before the conscription board. Only those who had drawn lots numbering one to 135 were conscripted into the military while the rest who had drawn high numbers, including Melamed who had drawn 185, were exempted. As Dubnow (1918:2:208) writes, "When the quota is completed, the remaining conscripts, i.e., those who, having drawn a high number, have not yet been examined, are declared exempt from military services."

53 A red ticket denoted military exemption.

this non-Jew against other Jews who would need his assistance and that he was making a mockery out of me in front of this official. Through this secretary, I had been able to do many favors for my fellow Jews, but how could I show my face in front of him again? "I'm begging you, Uncle, do me this favor and accommodate this official. If not, I'll have to pay him myself because I can't tell him that you only gave me fifty *kopeks* to give him. Why, he wouldn't believe me. And even if he would, he'd say, 'Who told you to give him the red ticket? You should've sent him to me to pay me directly!'" In short, my begging and explaining was of no use, and he left leaving me a small pittance for all of my effort—and certainly nothing for room and board. Apart from my remaining in debt after they left, I also remained an object of ridicule in the eyes of the secretary. After my uncle left, I had to give the secretary three rubles of my own money, and I am pretty sure that the official did not trust me. He did not tell me so, but I could see that in his heart he thought that I was not a trustworthy Jew. "I thought that this rabbi was a truthful person, but in the end he also appears to be a swindler."[54] With his stinginess, my uncle had brought shame to the Jewish people. He then left, and we never heard from him again—or better said, by then I no longer wanted to hear from him again.

Recently, on *Rosh-Khoydesh Av* 5674 [*sic*],[55] I ran into his son Shimshen in Tiraspol, who told me all that happened to his father and to his family. This will be related in a separate chapter where I will describe all the retributions that came upon all the wicked people I knew to show them that God pays a person back according to each and every deed—whether good or bad.[56]

Soon after the departure of my blind uncle, Yankev of Ternifke, I received a letter from my Uncle Duvid-Leyb of Perkon,[57] relating that his son Mordkhele needed to report for military conscription that coming year. He wrote that "since Uncle Yankev stopped his son from being conscripted, which was all due to you, Pinye-Ber," he also wanted me to have his son's place of conscription transferred to Bakhchisaray, which would hopefully result in a happy outcome for his son, that is, exemption. He also noted that he was sure that I would not

54 Non-Jews often consider every Jewish functionary to be a rabbi.

55 Corresponding to July 24, 1914, which is not possible since the author had already left for the Land of Israel in November 1913, as noted in the beginning of ch. 30, p. 605. Perhaps the typesetter mistook the year 5672 (1912) for 5674 (1914), which could look similar in the author's handwriting.

56 In ch. 29, pp. 570–572, the author describes the fates of his enemies in Bakhchisaray but does not mention his Uncle Yankev. (Metrical records from Bender show that a Shimshen, the son of Yankev Royzman, age twenty-nine, divorced in 1890.)

57 Duvid-Leyb was clearly the uncle of the author's wife, since he lived in the same village, Perkon, as Freyde's parents.

refuse him. How was I supposed to respond to such a letter? Certainly I could not refuse him, and I wrote him asking him to prepare all the paperwork. I knew the procedures, but a new regulation was added that the recruit had to reside in his place of recruitment for the preceding six months. So I wrote him that Mordkhele should already come in December.[58] After he stayed in my home for six months, it was now closer to the time of his conscription,[59] so I found him some work so that he could earn some money for himself, which is what happened. He earned twenty rubles a month, so he now had money to live on. He presented himself for conscription quietly and calmly and was, thank God, exempted. During that time, he became like my own child. As Mordkhele was departing, my Nekhamele burst into tears, crying that she also wanted to go with him to Perkon to see her grandmother. She was then six years old. Mordkhe also insisted that she come and said to us, "Let me take her along. She'll be our dear guest and we'll arrange for her to be taught there." We then gave her to him to take along. Our daughter stayed there until after Pesach, during which time she visited with all of the relatives.[60] From our wealthy Ternifker relatives our daughter did not receive one gift—not even a *groshn*—apart from a kiss and a compliment, "Freyde's little daughter is a beautiful little girl." Our nasal-voiced aunt said in her nasal tone, "Just look, Yankl, I would never have believed that she's a *shoykhet*'s daughter.[61] She's dressed as beautifully as a little aristocrat—how can they indulge a child like that?" Their wickedness is indescribable.

You would think that my expenses were finally reduced because I now had no guests—but unfortunately that did not last long. One morning, my Nekhamele suddenly ran in all out of breath, "*Mome, Tote,* I'm here—and Grandmother's here too." And in walked my dear, faithful mother-in-law.

"How did you come here so suddenly? You always come unexpectedly! Why didn't you write that you're coming?"

"Eh, children, why do I need to write? As soon as I thought about visiting you, I up and left!"

"But why on earth did it bother you that Nekhamele was there. Who asked you to bring her home?"

"Who, then, should I have asked? I wanted to visit you, so I also took her along! What are you going to do about it?"

Her words sounded to me like she was perturbed by my question.

---

58 December 1881.

59 The time of Mordkhele's conscription was October–November 1882.

60 Pesach lasted from April 21 to April 29, 1883.

61 Yankl is a Yiddish diminutive form of the name Yankev. This uncle and aunt of the author's wife were Yankev "the blind" Royzman and his wife, Rifke, mentioned on pp. 491–499.

After my mother-in-law stayed with us for six weeks, I gave her ten rubles for her travel expenses, and she went home, though not happily. She thought that I had by then become a rich man in the Crimea and would be able to give her enough money to open a store, where she could carry on as she used to. She had no patience to remain at home and be a homemaker like all other women. So she became dejected and returned home. Her stay cost me a nice amount of money and cost even more in health—mostly her daughter's—because during her entire stay she constantly criticized and lectured my wife, as usual. But this was too much for my refined wife to bear, and she did not want to tell me about her suffering. So she kept it to herself until she was free of her.

After my mother-in-law's departure, a completely unexpected guest arrived from Bender.[62] Since my wife's uncle Velvl's son, Arn-Khayem, had to report for conscription, he came to hide out at our home and ended up staying eight months.[63] I worked hard and supported him. Perhaps you know why? What did I owe him? Just because his mother was my mother-in-law's sister—my wife's aunt—was I then obligated to support her son with us, though I had never benefited from them in any way? To make a long story short, as it turned out, I had problems with him and he did not listen to me, but neither my wife nor I had the nerve to ask him to leave. Finally, God had compassion on us, and he left on his own accord. We were now rid of this guest too.

Two months later, I received a letter from Tiraspol from my nephew Itsl, my sister Ite's one and only son. He asked me if he should bring potatoes to the Crimea because he heard that they were selling there for a high price, which was actually true. I wrote him back providing him with the going price and asked him, should he decide to come, to bring along my Srulikl from Tiraspol since it was already *Rosh-Khoydesh Nisan*.[64] In brief, God helped me to have very dear guests that Pesach.[65]

---

62 As is clear from the rest of the chapter, the author does not mean that the next guest came shortly after his mother-in-law's departure but rather is simply mentioning the next guest to arrive, who came about a year and a half afterward.

63 Both sisters of the author's mother-in-law, Rukhl-Leye (ch. 14, p. 232) and Blime (ch. 18, p. 309), married men named Velvl. Since Rukhl-Leye is mentioned in 1865 as having a son named Khayem (ch. 14, p. 232) and since Khayem would have been too old to be conscripted here in 1887, Arn-Khayem was most likely Blime's son. Arn-Khayem arrived in Bakhchisaray in May 1887, as calculated backward from the date of the author's son Isruel's return home in March 1888 (see p. 502 below).

64 March 13, 1888. It was two weeks before Pesach.

65 March 27–April 3, 1888.

Itsl, my sister's son,[66] whom I had not seen in ages, brought along his brother-in-law, Yankev Kaushaner (Ester-Khaye's husband, with whom my Srulikl was boarding) and the most beloved of my guests, my son Srulikl. The joy at my home was indescribable. You yourself can imagine the delight we had at seeing such guests, especially my son whom I had not seen in six years.[67] Never mind the difficulty in covering the expenses of such a *Yontef*—in spite of it we still had tremendous pleasure.[68] We cheerfully procured everything so that nothing was lacking on *Yontef*, and we spent the *Yontef* together quite joyously. My nephew Itsele brought a wagon full of potatoes and earned a profit from it, and I reimbursed Ester-Khaye's husband for his expenses.[69] Right after *Yontef*,[70] they both left happy and satisfied. But I did not imagine then that I would be seeing my nephew, Itsele, for the last time. From that moment on, I never saw him again. A few years later, he left for America and remained there his entire life.[71]

---

66 The last time the author mentions seeing his sister Ite's son, Itsl Goldshteyn, was when he was approximately twelve in about 1874 (ch. 22, pp. 434–435).

67 Isruel returned home in March 1888, since he left home six years earlier in April 1882, as mentioned above on p. 486.

68 Pesach is the most expensive of Jewish holidays, with the added expense of enough wine for four cups of wine for each person on both *Seder* nights and hand-made *shmure matses*.

69 The expenses were likely for the author's son Isruel's room and board.

70 Pesach ended that year on April 23, 1889.

71 Itsl Goldshteyn (under the name Isaac Goldstein), with his wife, Khaye, and two children (Avrúm and Ite), left from the port of Hamburg, Germany, aboard the steamship *Gellert* and arrived in New York City on December 24, 1889. He died in Portland, Oregon, in 1907. See Appendix A3 (pp. 726–729) for more details.

CHAPTER 25

The Threat of Banishment from Tsarist Russia, 1881–1884

Using a Non-Jew, a Greek, as a Front to Assume Control of the Kosher-Meat Tax • Grabbing the *Gabbai* by the Lapels • Foreign Subjects Ordered to Leave Russia • The Great Suffering Caused by the Decree • Writing a Petition to the Minister of Interior • Admitting to the Government Official How I Became a Romanian Subject • The Government Official's Advice • Friends in Bolte Send My Father's Entry in the Poll-Tax Census with the Corresponding Household Number • Receiving a Temporary Document Allowing Me to Remain in Russia • My Enemies' Horrible Denunciations • The Government Official Hides Their Denunciations Under the Tablecloth and Does Not Submit Them • Becoming a Russian Subject and Receiving My Official Russian Internal Passport

It's now time to return to the subject of my enemies, who did not stop scheming against me and persecuting me (though God always protected me from them) the entire time. We left off where they were bound by the kosher-meat tax [*sic*] and had no other option but to keep me as their only *shoykhet*; they could neither push me out nor bring in another *shoykhet* until four [*sic*] years had ended.[1]

---

1 The author seems to be confusing the Jewish community's four-year kosher-meat tax consignment ending in November 1881 (see p. 504 below) and his three-year *sh'khita* contract ending in March 1882 (ch. 23, p. 467), since both ended within months apart from each other. It seems likely that it should state, "We left off where they were bound by my contract and had no other option but to keep me as their only *shoykhet*. They could neither push me out nor bring in another *shoykhet* until three years had ended."

Meanwhile, they did not cease their efforts to destroy, as much as possible, all my sources of income.

Shortly before the four years of the kosher-meat tax consignment ended, we had to make an estimate of how much was collected.[2] In the report, I emphasized several points that were useful for me and damaging to them. In November, right before the new year began, an auction was held for the kosher-meat tax, so I used a non-Jew—a member of the city council—as a front to submit an official bid for me in his name. My enemies did not expect this at all and thought that the submission had come from me, against whom they had prepared two weapons. The first was how could a *shoykhet* hold the kosher-meat tax himself?[3] Their second weapon was their knowing that I was a Romanian subject, which would have immediately invalidated me from being the kosher-meat tax farmer and would, by default, leave it in their hands.[4] So they were shocked upon learning that the kosher-meat tax had been won by a wealthy non-Jew, a Greek, who had bought the kosher-meat tax for the *shoykhet*.[5] Their protests were to no avail. The kosher-meat tax had been yanked out of their hands by this Greek, who then authorized me to handle it for him for the entire four years.

That was how I did away with that Benyumin and his clan. They would now have to wait an entire four years for another opportunity. Benyumin now also had to start looking for a means to put some bread on his table. I also quickly dismissed the *gabbai*, Simkhe Mayster, as the treasurer, and Galkin, the lawyer, was appointed in his place [*sic*].[6] For me, it did not matter which one of them filled the position, though it did serve as a bit of a defeat for Simkhe and had the added benefit of my no longer having to look him in the face when reading from the Torah on *Shobes*. The lawyer did not attend *shul* often on *Shobes*,

---

2 The kosher-meat tax consignment ended right before the new elections of the *gabbaim* of Bakhchisaray, which was held every four years. Since the next election apparently occurred at the end of 1885 (see p. 506), this election occurred at the end of 1881.

3 Since the duties of the kosher-meat tax farmer included preventing the slaughtering of any animals when the tax was not paid, *shokhtim* were generally invalidated from filling this position (Berman, 1941:195).

4 In the original Yiddish, here and below, the author describes himself as a Moldavian rather than a Romanian subject. The United Principalities of Moldavia and Walachia was only officially named Romania in 1866, and Romania gained its independence from the Ottoman Empire in 1877. In ch. 15, pp. 237–239, the author describes how he crossed the border from Tsarist Russia to Romania in 1865 to obtain a Romanian passport.

5 As an ethnic Greek born in Tsarist Russia, he was fully eligible to buy the kosher-meat tax. Greeks lived in the Crimea for centuries.

6 Though Simkhe Mayster was apparently dismissed from being both the main *gabbai* and the treasurer, Galkin only replaced him as the main *gabbai* while Yankev Medvedye replaced him as the treasurer (see on p. 506 below).

so I rarely had to see him. Though the lawyer was not as heartless as Mayster, he was also a bad person. Someone else was also appointed as the crown rabbi,[7] meaning that Reb Duvid Kizilshteyn was also removed from his position, which was taken over by Reb Itskhok-Nute Nutkovitsh, who was a quiet, fine, and pious person—though a clod. It was impossible to accomplish much with him. He would never do anyone a good turn, but neither would he do anything bad. In short, I remained in the same circumstances with the same mortal enemies all around me. I had no support from anyone and had to continually wage both internal and external battles. The former refers to my personal struggle to support my household. Covering all my expenses, under such circumstances, was no simple matter since my every effort to supplement my salary was undermined. My external battle was fighting for my income as a *shoykhet* and rescuing myself at every moment from new misfortunes and afflictions set upon me by my enemies. I forgot to mention that all the previous *gabbaim* were removed except for Medvedye, who was now the *gabbai* [assigned to be the treasurer] instead of Simkhe.[8] Medvedye was Simkhe and Benyumin's brother-in-law, the main instigators among my enemies, as you already know. You can just imagine the type of virtue that I could expect from such community leaders.

Their first attempt to torment me was instigated by the new treasurer and the new main *gabbai*.[9] I worked hard for an entire year leading the services and reading the Torah. During Rosh Hashanah and Yom Kippur, I led everything in between *Adon Olam* and *Anim Zmires*,[10] which includes the morning prayer services, the reading of the Torah during which I made a thousand *Mishebeyrakhs* (dozens for each person),[11] and *Musaf*. I did not spare any effort in making all these *Mishebeyrakhs*, as long as it brought in more money for the *shul*.[12] I was

---

7 Whenever the author refers to the crown rabbi of Bakhchisaray, he is actually referring to the assistant crown rabbi since Bakhchisaray was too small a community for a crown rabbi. (For more about crown rabbis, see ch. 23, p. 464, footnote 44.) The crown rabbi was elected by the Jewish community for a period of three years. His term in Bakhchisaray coincided with the appointment of new community leaders and the end of the three-year consignment of the kosher-meat tax.

8 Further on, Yankev Medvedye is twice referred to as the treasurer.

9 Referring to Yankev Medvedye and Galkin, respectively.

10 *Adon Olam* (meaning "Eternal Lord") are the first two words of a prayer recited at the beginning of morning services. *Anim Zmires* is part of the liturgy that comes at the end of the *Shabes* and *Yontef* prayers.

11 Each person called to the Torah is given the opportunity to have blessings (beginning with the Hebrew words *Mishebeyrakh*, literally, "He [i.e., God] who blessed . . .") recited on his behalf and on behalf of his family members and friends. The reciting of this blessing is called in Yiddish "making a *Mishebeyrakh*."

12 Traditionally, each *Mishebeyrakh* (see previous footnote) is accompanied by a pledge to donate to the synagogue or some other charitable cause.

also the *shofar* blower and led *Minkhe* and *Marev*. I led all the prayers since I was the only one who could do so. No one was able to relieve me beginning with *Kol Nidre* all the way to "Next Year in Jerusalem."[13] I am writing everything in detail so that you should have a feeling for how bitterly hard my life was. For my services for the entire year, including the High Holy Days, I earned a total of 75 rubles. Until my arrival, they had paid 100 rubles but only paid me 75, which remained law forever more. Though the congregation quite often wanted my wages to be supplemented by as much as 25 rubles, the community leaders would not allow it.

Listen to how cruel they were to me in that year of 5645 [*sic*], the year that Medvedye became the treasurer.[14] During the High Holy Days that year, the congregation was exceptionally pleased with my leading of the services. Even the lawyer Galkin told me, "Well done"—not to mention the rest of the congregation. They all said that I deserved to be paid the entire 100 rubles. So I figured that after such a favorable reception I would be paid the entire 100 rubles and that certainly my usual 75 rubles would be given to me if not on the eve of Yom Kippur by the collection plates, then certainly on the night after Yom Kippur ended.[15]

Listen to the settlement that I ultimately received for leading the services. When I was not paid even on the night following Yom Kippur, I ran to the house of the main *gabbai*, but he had left town.[16] I then ran to the treasurer, and exclaimed, "Give me money!" He replied, "I have no money, and without the main *gabbai*, I won't be able to pay you anyway." I then asked, "What's going to be? I must have money! I've waited an entire year for this! I borrowed against this payment, and my creditors have waited until now. How will I answer them now? They don't let me pass through the street!" In short, my crying and pleading was to no avail. I had to wait until *Sukes* when the main *gabbai* would return. On the eve of *Sukes*, I set out for the main *gabbai*'s house but ran into him in the street.

---

13 *Kol Nidre* is a declaration recited in synagogue before the evening service as Yom Kippur begins. "Next Year in Jerusalem" is recited by many communities at the end of the Yom Kippur services.

14 The author apparently meant to write 5642 (late 1881)—not 5645 (late 1884)—which is when Yankev Medvedye became the treasurer, as mentioned on p. 505 above. In the 1885 elections, Moyshe Kalk became the treasurer (ch. 26, p. 524).

15 On the afternoon of the eve of Yom Kippur, separate collection plates for various charitable causes are traditionally set out in synagogue and all members of the congregations make donations.

16 Apparently referring to Galkin.

I said, "Reb Yankev! It seems to me that it's already time to pay me my money!"

"Why the rush?" he replied.

I answered, "I'm poor and am being harassed from all directions."

He answered me nonchalantly, "*Nu*, why should it matter to me that you're being harassed?" and walked off without another word.

I felt so disheartened. I stopped him, grabbed him by the lapels, and told him, "Stay put, you bandit. You need to pay me immediately! I'm not letting you leave. I can't run after you anymore!" I continued to yell at him like that until everyone on the street had gathered around us. Everyone was on my side. He soon went into a store with me and paid me—of course only the 75 rubles. He had intentionally aggravated me so that he would have a pretext for finding me undeserving of a bonus and to make me glad to be receive at least 75 rubles. My enemies also used this incident to prove that the *shoykhet* did not deserve to be paid any more. After all, he had stopped a *gabbai* in middle of the street and disgraced him by saying, "Give me money! If not, I'll beat you up, and so on!"[17] Out of hate, Medvedye naturally used the opportunity to boast that I deserved to be despised by him. But what had led me to accost him? *That* he was not telling anyone!

Though, my beloved children, you certainly know of my poverty and my suffering, I did not even tell you ninety percent of it yet. Therefore, I will not delay and will relate everything in detail. Though I know that you will not have any pleasure from the details and that they will certainly cause your hearts grief and pain, yet on the other hand you will be proud of your parents' struggle, suffering, and bitter toil to do all that they could so long as they did not have to resort, God forbid, to any handouts. They also accepted everything with love—as long they could raise their children to be Torah-observant Jews and respectable people. Despite the hard work and the torment from our enemies, we did not let anything stop us.

I will start by presenting you with my daily schedule of everything I had to do with regard to *sh'khita* and the other ways I earned income. At the crack of dawn, I had to get up and prepare the slaughtering knives. As soon as it became light, I prayed the morning services and then ran to the slaughterhouse, which was not only a distance of two *versts* away but was on a bad road at that. I write "ran" because I had to go there as quickly as possible so as not to miss

---

17 Note that his enemies' exaggerated version of the incident adds that he threatened to beat up the *gabbai*.

the *sh'khita* because it started at the crack of dawn.[18] Since I did not want to go there before praying, I had to race to the slaughterhouse. Upon my arrival there, I had plenty of work to do with the Spanish sheep and cattle, which took me two to three hours.[19] I then returned home to drink a cup of tea and afterward went to the butcher shop. If the slaughtered meat arrived in town when I did, then I had to forfeit the tea and go straight to the butcher shop. I had to remain in the butcher shop until noon and usually did not remain idle. I removed the forbidden sinews and fats from the meat and also removed the kosher fat so that it could then be sold that day.[20] I also supervised to make sure that, God forbid, the kosher meat would not become interchanged with nonkosher meat because there was no Jewish butcher, so I had to mark every piece of meat. Without me there, no one was allowed to buy any kosher meat. When I returned home at noon, it could happen that I would have to return up to three times for late customers who wanted kosher meat. I had to go because if I didn't, the customer might have bought some nonkosher meat and said, "The *shoykhet*'s to blame."

After having a bite to eat at noon, I then had to collect the kosher fat from the various butchers and bring it all to one place, my butcher shop,[21] because I used to slaughter sheep for several nonkosher butchers, who compensated me with the sheep's fatty tails. I would only take the tails of those sheep found to be kosher.[22] In the fall, I was able to slaughter a lot of sheep in exchange for their tail fats like this. Nonetheless, obtaining the fat was hard work: slaughtering, examining the lungs, removing the tails, carrying them away, removing any forbidden matter, and then selling them. And when no customers could be found, I had to go off to Sevastopol or Simferopol to search for customers there, which had to be done the same day. For example, if I set off for Simferopol on a Tuesday morning, I then had to return home that same Tuesday night. Disregarding my exhaustion from the hard work and not having slept the previous night, I nevertheless had to prepare the slaughtering knives before the crack of dawn, pray,

---

18 The slaughterhouse did not belong to the author, and he was not in charge of the appointed time for kosher slaughtering.

19 Spanish sheep (Merinos) were first introduced to the Ukraine in 1803 (*Report of the Commissioner of Patents for the Year 1855: Agriculture*, 1856:44).

20 Jewish law prohibits the eating of certain sinews and fat of cattle, sheep, and goats. Their removal, called *treybern* in Yiddish, demands expertise. See *Shulkhan Arukh* (*Yoreh Deah* 64 & 65).

21 This is a reference to the butcher shop in which the author worked until noon.

22 The author also slaughtered sheep for Crimean Tatars, as mentioned later in this paragraph. As adherents of Islam, Crimean Tatars require religious slaughter of their animals. Jewish slaughtering practices are similar enough to render animals fitting for most Muslims (Berman, 1941:231–233).

and then go to the slaughterhouse as usual. Many times, I would have to go to the slaughterhouse twice in one day: at dusk when a Tatar had the urge to slaughter an ox, or during the day when the kosher meat ran out at the butcher shop. One thing you should know is that *sh'khita* is quite difficult work. Do not forget that slaughtering fowl also takes time and effort. And when a *bris*, wedding, or engagement party occurred in town, I had more slaughtering to do and also had to find the time to do everything else. On *Shobes*, I also had no rest for I had to lead *Shakhris* and *Musaf* and read from the Torah—everything by myself.

My dear wife also had her fair share of work to do. Since she had no help in the house because we could not afford it, she took care of all the housework by herself. By then, we had four children apart from Srulikl, the oldest, since another child by the name of Shulem had been born.[23] She had to clothe, wash, and attend to the children, as well as put up with their whims. She also had to cook for all of us, accommodate visiting relatives and other guests who came once in a while, and wash the floor—everything by herself. You need to understand just how bitterly hard she worked. When I had to go to Simferopol to sell fat, she had to cover for me at the butcher shop where she would supervise and remove the forbidden veins and fats from the meat. Being able to rely on her for this was of tremendous help to me, as the Talmud states, "If he is worthy, his wife will become his helpmate."[24] Thanks to her assistance, I was able to travel off to earn money by selling kosher fat. That is also how I was able to tear myself away from home in the summers and go all the way to Chufut-Kale, a Karaite cemetery four *versts* away, to cut and engrave tombstones.[25] I was only able to

---

23 Shloymele is mistakenly mentioned in the original as being the child's name, even though he was not born until 1889 (ch. 27, p. 549). The author is actually referring here to his son Shulem, whose birth in 1884 is mentioned in ch. 27, p. 539.

24 See ch. 18, p. 298, footnote 24.

25 Karaites are a Jewish sect that broke off from rabbinic Judaism in the eighth century by rejecting the Talmudic-rabbinic tradition. Though they still exist today, they only number some 30,000, with most residing in Israel. Chufut-Kale (pronounced Tshufut-Kale), meaning "the Jews' Fortress" in the Tatar language, was an age-old Karaite town, now in ruins, on the top of an impressive mountain near Bakhchisaray. The Karaite settlement probably started there in the fourteenth century with the conquest of the town by the Tatars. Rabbinic Jews also lived there for a period of time until the eighteenth century. Though Chufut-Kale was all but deserted during the Crimean War (1853–1856), the controversial Karaite author Avraam Firkovich (1786–1874) continued to live out his last days there. In a nearby valley lies the large and impressive Karaite cemetery, called the Valley of Jehoshaphat, originally consisting of some 5,000 Hebrew tombstones, some dating back to the fourteenth century. The cemetery was used until recently by the few remaining Karaites in the Crimea (Fedorchuk & Shapira, 2011; Gammer, 2011:88). In a letter from July 15, 1930 (see Appendix B3, p. 801), the author implies that his going to Chufut-Kale in the mountains to engrave tombstones was some of the hardest work he had ever performed.

FIGURE 16. Karaites hired Pinkhes-Dov Goldenshteyn to engrave tombstones for them in their cemetery in Chufut-Kale, which is located in the mountains near Bakhchisaray, Crimea and dates back to the fourteenth century. This photograph shows tombstones there dating from the late nineteenth century, when Goldenshteyn was engraving them.

earn additional income like this because of my wife's assistance in the butcher shop, which she did in addition to all of her work at home. Nothing was too difficult for us as long as we would not have to resort (God forbid) to any handouts, would be saved from my enemies, and would be able to properly educate our beloved children, as described in detail earlier.[26]

I worked bitterly hard in the summers. Right after returning from the slaughterhouse, I would stay for an hour or so at the butcher shop. Afterward, I would have my dear wife cover for me at the butcher shop until noon, while I would take a piece of bread and leave straight for Chufut-Kale (as mentioned above) where I would work until evening. Returning home exhausted, I would eat and then go to sleep. Quite early in the morning, I would once again run over to the slaughterhouse and then again go off to Chufut-Kale to continue engraving tombstones. The bitterer the work, so much sweeter was the reward. With these extra funds, God helped me pay my children's *melomdim*. Apart

26 In ch. 23, p. 474, the author writes that he hired and boarded a *melamed* in his home to teach his children. In ch. 24, p. 486, he describes the great efforts entailed in sending Isruel away to study to "make him a proper Jew."

from Srulikl, I had by then Yosl and Yankele, for whom I had to hire *melomdim* to teach them Torah. And Nekhamele also attended classes in secular subjects apart from her being taught Torah subjects by a *melomed*. My enemies knew all of this and were burning with envy, "Look at the kind of children he's raising—all handsome, clever, and educated. How do you like how he finds ways of earning money in every way he can? He has it better than all of us!" True, I did have it better than all of them since God had blessed me with a good wife and dear children. One look at them and I would forget all my troubles and would accept all the hardship with love.

All of a sudden, all of my enemies regained their hope in doing away with me. A circular arrived stating that all foreign subjects had to return to their native countries, and, if not, they must become Russian subjects.[27] Their lawyer had read about the decree before the circular reached Bakhchisaray. He informed them about it, and they danced for joy. When the circular arrived in Bakhchisaray, they made sure to immediately inform me that I had to leave Russia. You can just imagine how happy I was to hear such news. After all, how could I afford to move with my wife and small children in such poverty? And where would we go? The chief of police told me to petition to become a Russian subject.[28]

I submitted such a petition right away to the Minister of Interior stating that I was requesting to become a subject of Russia, yet I was not happy.[29] Unexpectedly, my heart froze as if it was telling me, "You won't be able to rid

---

27 Although the author was born in Tsarist Russia, he lived in Russia as a Romanian subject. (He describes obtaining his third and final Romanian passport in ch. 18, p. 288.) As explained on p. 512, footnote 30 below, Jews were generally excluded from becoming naturalized as Russian subjects. From the author's account on p. 517 below, this decree on foreign subjects occurred in 1884, though various Tsarist Russian provinces enforced the laws of expelling foreign Jews at different times, e.g., the foreign Jews of the provinces of Podolia and Volhynia were expelled in 1885 ("Expulsion of Foreign Jews in Russia," 1885). Errera (1894:39–40) states that there were 150,000 Romanians, Turks, and Austro-Hungarians residing in Tsarist Russia, many of them Jews like Pinye-Ber who were born in Tsarist Russia but held foreign passports. A similar decree was issued in 1886–1887, when Rabbi Khizkiyahu Medini (ch. 24, p. 483, footnote 7), a Turkish citizen, was saved from expulsion through the intervention of several notables (Farfel, 1912:86). Errera (1894:38–42) also relates that 2,000 foreign Jews were ultimately expelled en masse in 1891 and 1892 from Odessa alone, though large numbers were like Goldenshteyn in that they were Russian born despite holding Romanian or Turkish passports. Errera goes on to describe the tremendous suffering these exiles endured, with a third of them dying from the cold and starvation.

28 "Most individuals [in Tsarist Russia] turned to the centuries-old custom of writing petitions to resolve their legal predicaments" (Avrutin, 2010:81).

29 On becoming a Russian subject, the applicant would be issued a Russian internal passport, which was a form of identification document used for movement within Tsarist Russia. Though the original only states "Minister," I have written "Minister of Interior" for clarity's

yourself of this matter easily. You'll suffer more than enough because of it!" In short, I submitted my petition and then lived with hope and dread. Perhaps, God forbid, they would refuse me, which is exactly what happened. Three months later, I received a reply from the Minister stating, "Except Jews," meaning that, yes, one could become a Russian subject, but this only applied to non-Jews and not to Jews.[30] So I had to leave Russia. *Nu*, what should I do now? I cried and wailed. Upon seeing me cry, my children also cried, and then looking at my children, I cried even harder. All my neighbors came running over, thinking that we were mourning a death in the family, God forbid. Several such days passed by until I realized that crying and depression would be of no use. I needed to obtain some advice on how to protect myself from my enemies' schemes.

Several days later I was called in to see the police. I went there and was given a paper to sign stating that I would liquidate all my possessions and leave the country, that is, leave for Romania, within three months. I again became very worried, but my wife consoled me, "Don't worry. God will help us in the merit of our children. Don't worry, be happy, and seek some good advice."

I traveled off to Simferopol to ask the advice of people experienced in such matters. I was advised to submit a petition admitting that I was a Russian subject since birth, that I had been using a foreign passport to avoid military conscription, and that I now wanted to return to being a Russian subject. I liked their advice. I conferred with the secretary of the city counsel of Bakhchisaray who was my friend, and he advised me as follows, "Go to Simferopol to a certain prominent nobleman who is my dear friend and a very good person.[31] He likes to do favors for others. He's a government official who works for the Governor General of the province.[32] Go directly to him at his home—not at his office. Tell him the truth and ask his advice. Whatever he tells you to do, you should do."

The next day, he gave me a letter for the nobleman, and I travelled off to Simferopol. Upon my arrival, I went to see him. He welcomed me cordially, which made it apparent that he was a good person. I gave him the secretary's letter, which he read while he shook his head back and forth in sorrow. Finally,

---

sake since that ministry generally dealt with internal passports in Tsarist Russia (Avrutin, 2010:92–93).

30 Jews could become Russian subjects only if they apostatized to Christianity, which only a negligible number of Jews chose to do (Errera, 1894:40).

31 The original states, "Go to Tiraspol," which is clearly a mistake, as indicated in the next paragraph.

32 This government official is later described as working for the provincial office of the Treasury (ch. 26, p. 519). Here it states that he works for the Governor General of the province, which is referring to the province of Taurida.

he said, "I already know everything that you desire. I can do the greatest favor for you. I have a lot of sympathy for you. I see, and it's obvious, that you are pious and a poor family man. I understand that you were born a Russian (subject). When you prove it with facts, you'll be saved. But you must tell me the entire truth about how you obtained your Romanian passport. If I know the truth, I can advise you, but if you hide the truth from me, my advice won't be effective and will harm you, God forbid." I swore to do so and then told him the entire truth, which you already know. He then said, "Now listen to my advice. You should obtain a copy of your birth record and make sure that you also obtain a transcript of your father's entry in the poll-tax census of the town where he was registered as a taxpayer.[33] After obtaining these documents, you should come to see me again at my home. I'll then tell you what you need to do further." I thanked him sincerely and returned home.

My enemies were in joyous celebration. They were counting the minutes, wishing that the months would pass and I would already be expelled. They could then say, "Our hands have not shed this blood."[34] But they did not know that God was with me, as it states, "And God seeks the pursued."[35] But what was I supposed to do now? Where would I obtain a copy of my birth record? Where would I obtain a transcript of my father's entry in the poll-tax census? I would not be able to provide them with these documents unless I went to Tiraspol! How could I afford to travel there? Who would cover for me? How would my wife and children support themselves? These were my worries at the time, but there was not a lot of time for me to spend thinking about them. I borrowed some money and went into debt over my head. I asked a *shoykhet* from Simferopol by the name of Reb Yankev Bukhshtab to cover for me until I returned, which he did out of pity for me. And I traveled off.

Upon arriving in Tiraspol, I learned that no record of my birth existed because it was not common to register births in those times, particularly for such fanatical parents as my own.[36] I also learned that though my parents lived

33 In Tsarist Russia, a series of poll-tax censuses (*revizskie skazki*, literally "revision lists") were taken between 1772 and 1858 for the purpose of establishing a direct capitation tax. Each census was a revision of the previous one (hence its name). Such census records generally listed all family members and their ages (Avrutin, 2010:22–24). Since this nobleman is described in ch. 26, p. 519, as working for the provincial office of the Treasury, which received a copy of each poll-tax census, perhaps his position made him knowledgeable in such matters (Freeze, 1999:10).

34 Deuteronomy 21:7.

35 Ecclesiastes 3:15. This verse means that God is on the side of the one being pursued.daniel

36 Many Jews were very wary of government innovations like the registration of Jewish births which the Tsarist Russian government began to enforce in 1835 and implemented with taxation and military conscription in mind (Braver, 1955:42; Freeze, 1999:8–9).

in Tiraspol, they were registered as taxpayers elsewhere, though no one knew where and I had no one to ask. Now go find out where! I went to the crown rabbi of Tiraspol and promised to give him three rubles merely for conducting a search of the metrical records, whether or not he would find anything. And if he would find anything, I would pay him separately for each record however much he asked. And that was my first step on my fortuitous road out of my predicament.

The next day, I went to the crown rabbi who told me that he was only able to find the somber record of my mother's death. I said, "*Nu*, good. Give it to me." He then asked, "What are you going to use it for?" I replied, "What's it matter to you? I'm paying you whatever it costs!" I paid him and he gave me a transcript of her death record, which opened my eyes to where I needed to go further. On the record was written the name of Ester-Khaye's husband. I found out that my father, of blessed memory, Itskhok Goldenshteyn, the son of Khayem, was registered as a resident of Bolte. In short, I now had to travel to Bolte to search for my father's entry in the poll-tax census.

The crown rabbi also explained to me that I could draw up my own delayed birth record by obtaining the signatures of older residents who had received honors at my *bris* and who knew that I was born on such and such date in such and such year to Itskhok Goldenshteyn, a registered resident of Bolte.[37] After having them sign it, I would then need it to be signed by the municipality and by the police. Once I did that, it would be just like a proper birth record. What do you think of the crown rabbi's suggestion? Nothing else had helped so far, so I began to arrange for my own record of birth. I actually found some residents who had been at my *bris*—I even found my *kvater*—and they all signed.[38] At the police station and at the municipality, I had no difficulties—they also signed right away.[39] So everything went smoothly, thank God. After being in Tiraspol for three days, I was finished with the paperwork. I then went to Bolte to obtain the other papers, namely my father's entry in the poll-tax census.

I arrived at the municipal offices of Bolte and asked them to search for such and such a name in the archives. In brief, they searched the archives but found no record of such a townsman. Meanwhile, an elderly man by the name

---

37 Such honors at a *bris* include being the *kvater*, as explained in the next footnote.

38 A *kvater* refers to the man honored with carrying the baby into the room to undergo a *bris*.

39 In 1848, a law was passed in Tsarist Russia allowing three respected Jews to verify the age and name of a person without a birth record. Since so many individuals subsequently took advantage of this statute to avoid conscription by obtaining false identity documents, it was repealed in 1881. Nonetheless, in 1883, "the state determined that individuals could obtain legal proof of their dates of birth in a court of law" (Avrutin, 2101:57). Though the author did not go to a court of law in 1884, he did have it signed by the municipality and the police.

of Reb Yekhezkel entered and the Jewish clerk searching the records asked him, "Actually, since you were once the head of a nearby village, perhaps you remember the name of this person who was a registered townsman here in Bolte?" He then gave a chuckle and said, "Why are you only searching for someone from the city of Bolte? You'll need to search the records of the entire region because, at one time, if someone lived in any of the *shteytlekh* in the region of Bolte, he would have been recorded as a registered taxpayer of Bolte. And searching all of those records would take a month." How could I remain there for so long, even excluding all the money such a search would cost me?! But just listen to the divine providence that occurred.

If you recall, two Jews from Bolte once stayed with me; a father-in-law had brought his son-in-law to Bakhchisaray for registration in the military.[40] I asked around and found them, and they treated me like a dignified guest. They advised me to travel home right away, and they would take care of the matter. I returned home dejected. When my enemies noticed from my appearance that I had not been delivered from my misery, they rejoiced and counted the minutes until my deadline to leave the country.

Three weeks later, I received a letter from my friends in Bolte that they had found the necessary document, and they sent me an official transcript of the entry of my father's family in the poll-tax census with the corresponding household number.[41] I was overjoyed and immediately set off to the nobleman in Simferopol. From my appearance, the nobleman realized that I had not come emptyhanded. I showed him all the documents, which he liked.

He then said, "Now you're saved. First, you need to submit to the Governor General a petition accompanied by these documents. Do the same with your children's birth records."

I said, "My children were recorded as being Romanian subjects."[42]

"It doesn't matter as long as their births were registered. I'll write you the wording of the petition, but you should have someone copy it over neatly. You'll

---

40 See ch. 24, p. 493.

41 The author's friends found out that his father was listed in the poll-tax census of nearby Kódeme (Kodyma); see p. 154. These censuses have no indexes, so knowing the household number was crucial. Some Kodeme censuses were stored in the Kamyanets-Podilskyy archives until 2003 when a fire erupted there. The surviving records were transferred to the Khmelnytskyy archives; no inventory has yet been made.

42 The only one of the author's children whose birth record has been located and occurred before this event took place in 1884 is that of his son Isruel-Burekh which was recorded in 1871 in Bender (see ch. 21, p. 381). It does not refer to the author as a Romanian citizen but rather as a resident of Tiraspol. Perhaps the author means that on the birth records of his children born in Bakhchisaray (before 1884), he is referred to as a Romanian citizen; but those could not be located.

need to hand it to the Governor General, or you can send it by mail. You do know that this is going to cost you money?!"

"I know that it's worth a lot though I don't know if I am in a position to compensate you fully."

He said, "Give me whatever you can! I'm not going to bargain with you."

I replied that I could give him fifty rubles, and it remained at that. I gave him fifty rubles, but he did me favors worth more than a thousand. May he live a long life, if he is still alive.

Back in Bakhchisaray, I prepared all the paperwork, wrote the petition, and then returned to Simferopol. I entered the provincial administrative offices where I was directed to a certain person. At first, I did not recognize him, but as he began to speak with me, I recognized him by his voice as the nobleman. He took my papers, looked them over to see if all was in order, and then took them to another room where he spent a long time. He then wrote me a note with a number on it and gave it to me and said, "Take this. You're going to show this when they try to bother you in three months. You need to guard it safely. This is your temporary document allowing you to remain in Russia. Now you can go home."

On the day that those three months were up, it was undoubtedly my enemies who had the police sent over to make sure that I was ready to leave the country. Of course, I showed them the note that I had. The police chief said to me, "What a guy! You'll be able to exonerate yourself. You did well! You submitted a petition to the Governor General. You'll soon be confirmed as a Russian subject and will be able to stay." That was how my enemies learned the secret that I had submitted a petition to the Governor General to become a Russian subject, because until then they had known absolutely nothing. Upon realizing how far they were from accomplishing their goal, a fire ignited within them. In short, they then set out with abandon to prevent me from being permitted to become a Russian subject.

They submitted three separate denunciations of me.[43] The first one notified the Governor General that Pinkhes Goldenshteyn, a Romanian subject who wanted to become a Russian subject, was the same person whose request had been refused by the Ministry of Interior and was now requesting it behind the Minister's back from the Governor General! How could the Governor General now grant his request? The second stated that, "This Pinkhes Goldenshteyn indicates that he was born in Russia. As a result of his admission, we have learned that he is a fugitive recruit who evaded military duty."

---

43 Denunciation of a fellow Jew to the non-Jewish government is considered by Jewish law to be a crime of the most severe order. See *Shulkhan Arukh* (*Khoshen Mishpat* 388).

Their third denunciation stated that on *Shobes* someone had brought Goldenshteyn a document with the forged signatures of the Jewish residents of Bakhchisaray stating that they had accepted him as an official resident of Bakhchisaray.[44] They wrote that no one had actually signed it out of fear of being associated with a declaration accepting a runaway soldier as an official resident. They also asked for an investigation of this declaration to be made as demanded by law. They could not resist and sent their precious Benyumin to deliver it to the appropriate government offices right on *Shobes*. They considered this third denunciation to be such an important *mitzvah* that the laws of *Shobes* had to be annulled on its behalf.[45] Such was the extent of those murderers' burning desire to prevail.

After making such indictments against me, they now certainly assumed that not only would I be expelled from Russia but that I would be exiled to Siberia! Yet the nobleman held all these denouncements under his tablecloth so that they would never reach the Governor General. Consider for a moment the nobleman's kindness; though not Jewish, he had compassion for me and utterly destroyed their allegations.

Precisely on *Hoyshane-Rabe* of 5645, the 21st of *Tishre*, I was truly written and sealed for a good year, which I had eagerly anticipated and impatiently awaited.[46] It was on that day that I received my Russian internal passport, and I, my wife, and children (under the names we had used until then) became Russian subjects and official residents of Bakhchisaray.[47] No details were altered so that my enemies would not have any fodder for any new denunciations. But I

44 The author had asked the residents of Bakhchisaray to sign a document accepting him as an official resident of Bakhchisaray, which everyone signed sometime during the week. He evidently needed such a document as a preliminary step in becoming a Russian subject, as mentioned below. Afterward, the heads of the community attempted to unjustly invalidate this document by lying that the signatures had been forged.

45 Jewish law generally only permits the laws of *Shabes* to be annulled to save a human life. See *Shulkhan Arukh* (*Orakh Khayim* 329:1). Certainly, there was no way to justify Benyumin's transgression of the prohibition of carrying on *Shabes* to deliver the denunciation.

46 October 10, 1884 was *Hoyshane-Rabe*, literally meaning "Great Supplication," which is the seventh day of the Jewish holiday of *Sukes*. Though the Jewish people and the world are judged by God for the coming year on Rosh Hashanah and the judgment is sealed ten days later on Yom Kippur, yet a person may still repent and effect a change in the verdict until *Hoyshane-Rabe*, when the final verdict is delivered, according to the *Zohar* (*Vayekhi* 120a; *Truma* 142a).

47 The author writes that he and his family members were registered "under the names we had used until then" because in Tsarist Russia even slight alterations in the transliteration of Jewish names could later result in great difficulties (Avrutin, 2010:66–67, 147–153, 161–162). A Russian internal passport was evidently issued to him as proof that he was now a Russian subject and an official resident of Bakhchisaray.

did succeed in changing one fact that I knew my enemies would never be able to detect, since they did not know my age until now. When I drew up my delayed birth record in Tiraspol, I took the chance and made myself ten years older than I actually was. I figured that it would eventually help my Srulikl when he would report for military conscription.[48] Since my falsified year of birth would then make me elderly, he could claim to be in the first class of military exemptions.[49] I thought that though I was sweating and suffering now, making my year of birth earlier than it actually was would at least spare us from suffering when my Srulikl had to report for conscription. And this later saved him from serving in the military and saved the rest of us from a lot of new difficulties, as will be described later in my story.

Meanwhile, we had all become official residents of Bakhchisaray. The municipality had noted us in their books and then had immediately issued me a Russian internal passport. All of this was done on *Hoyshane-Rabe*, as mentioned earlier. You can understand how joyous our *Simchas Torah* was.[50] On *Simchas Torah*—and *Shmini Atseres* as well[51]—practically the entire city, not just Jews but also Christians, flew and ran over to my house to congratulate me. No one, thank God, walked away unsatisfied.[52] But my enemies' joy of *Yontef*—and after *Yontef*—was disturbed.

For a while, they went around dazed until they found a new means of hurting me. Though I thought that they would now refrain from further attacks, they ultimately gathered new strength and began once again to do their dirty work.

---

48 The author was about thirty-six and Isruel was only eleven years old at this time. When Isruel reported for conscription in 1892 (ch. 27, p. 543), the author's falsified year of birth made him appear to be fifty-four.

49 The first and highest class of military exemption was for an only son who was the sole wage-earner for his family. Regarding the other classes of military exemptions, see ch. 24, p. 493, footnote 43.

50 October 12, 1884. *Shmini Atseres,* meaning the "Eighth (day) of Assembly," is the Jewish holiday immediately following the seven days of *Sukes.* Outside of the Land of Israel, *Shmini Atseres* is celebrated for two days. The second day is called *Simchas Torah,* meaning "Rejoicing with the Torah," and is an extremely joyous holiday.

51 October 12–13, 1884.

52 In other words, the author had enough liquor to dispense liberally to everyone.

CHAPTER 26

Persecution in Bakhchisaray, 1884–1889

The Nobleman and His Family Visit Us · The Wickedness of the Shoemaker and His Wife · The Court Case Regarding the Piece of Meat · Being Falsely Accused of Stealing Animal Fat · The Old *Melomed*'s Encroachment on My Exclusive Slaughtering Rights · Hiring Another to Lead the High Holidays to Spite Me · My Agony Over the *Esreg*

Before we begin relating the tale of my enemies' wicked deeds, I must tell you the good deeds of that righteous gentile, the nobleman who rescued me. Apparently pleased at having saved an entire family, he desired to meet the beneficiaries of his kindness, become acquainted with those he had saved, and see if we were at least grateful for the kindness he had bestowed upon us.

Suddenly, one fine Sunday shortly before Hanukah, a carriage packed full of people arrived in front of our house.[1]

The secretary of the city council of Bakhchisaray entered and said, "I've brought you some guests."[2]

I asked him, "Who are the guests?"

"The department head, meaning the nobleman from the provincial office of the Treasury, has come with his family to acquaint themselves with you and your family."

He had not concluded his words when the nobleman, his wife, and three small children entered. He had two girls and a boy. Naturally, I greeted him very warmly and welcomed him in. He embraced and kissed me and

1 Hanukah began the night of December 12, 1884.

2 As mentioned in ch. 25, p. 512, the secretary was the author's friend and had originally recommended him to meet with the nobleman.

FIGURE 17. Construction of the Khan's Palace in Bakhchisaray began in the sixteenth century and was the main residence of a succession of Crimean-Tatar Khans (rulers). The Khans' political rule of the area lasted until 1783, when Tsarist Russia annexed the region from the Ottoman Empire. The walled palace compound contains a mosque, a harem, living quarters, gardens, and a cemetery. Already under the Tsar, it was open to the public. In 1884, the nobleman who helped save Goldenshteyn from being expelled from Tsarist Russia visited him in his home. Afterwards, the nobleman and his family toured the Khan's Palace, taking along Goldenshteyn's seven-year-old daughter, Nekhame.

introduced himself to my wife, and then introduced his wife and children as well. Nekhamele was a very pretty child, and they really enjoyed her—and Yosele and Yankele too. They said, "You have very beautiful children" and could not stop complimenting them.

Of course, the nobleman's wife already knew who I was from before, but only from afar. But now she gave me her hand,[3] congratulated me on my liberation, and said, "I'm so glad that my husband was able to rescue such a wonderful family." We spent the time pleasantly, and I invited them to eat lunch with us. They accepted my invitation but asked me to allow them to tour the Palace until lunch.[4] Of course I allowed them to go. They went off and took my Nekhamele

3 Even according to Maimonides, who rules that physical contact between a man and a woman other than his wife is forbidden by the Torah, touching when not done out of affection or passion is permissible, though other authorities differ. (See *Shulkhan Arukh* [*Yoreh Deah* 157:1] and Shakh §10.) Since this incident involves the wife of a prominent government official, perhaps lenient conduct was justifiable.

4 The building of the Khan's Palace in Bakhchisaray began in the sixteenth century and was the main residence to a succession of Crimean-Tatar Khans (rulers). The Khans' political rule of the area lasted until 1783, when Tsarist Russia annexed the region from the Ottoman Empire. The walled palace compound contains a mosque, a harem, living quarters, gardens,

along. They socialized with us pleasantly until evening. The secretary brought a violin since the nobleman was a talented player, and we danced. They travelled home very pleased.

With this I finish my tale of registering myself as a Russian subject and becoming an official resident of Bakhchisaray.

Nonetheless, the evil deeds brought about by my enemies were far from over. They were constantly seeking new schemes by which they could torment me. Now listen to the following scheme which they plotted. Next door to the lawyer lived a couple, a shoemaker and his wife, true scoundrels who were instigated to constantly harass me. He was one of the real troublemakers in town and was forever busy with community affairs. The *gabbaim* always gave him an *aliya*, which he liked. They also used him regularly for their vile dealings because of his vulgar mouth. He knew how to be abusive, and everyone stayed away from him. So it should come as no surprise that his wife was no better than him. She was proud of her brazenness, and she would pick a fight with some woman or another on a daily basis. So these two respectable citizens were indispensable to the lawyer and the *gabbaim* and became their instruments to endlessly torture the *shoykhet* and his family. Since I know you will be very interested in all the details, I will summarize it for you instead of being lazy and omitting it.

When the shoemaker would see me in the street, he would attack me in his drunkenness and begin to curse me without any provocation, simply because he was in the mood. On *Shobes* in *shul*, he would arrive early and wait for me at the door. As soon as I would enter, he would begin heaping curses on me, of course for no reason whatsoever. I would swallow his abuse, not responding with even one word. When I had to lead the services and read from the Torah, he always seized the opportunity to curse me before the services began. During the reading of the Torah, the *gabbaim* always directed me to call up the shoemaker since he certainly deserved to be called up for the honored reading of the sixth *aliya*! I understood that this was done to spite me, to unravel my nerves. Nevertheless, I controlled my instincts, which did not want to follow the direction of the *gabbaim*, since I would have preferred not calling him up to the Torah altogether. The lawyer and the *gabbaim* smiled, and the shoemaker also smiled. In other words, together they well understood that the motive here was to aggravate the *shoykhet*. In any event, I read the appropriate section in the Torah and then immediately called up another person for the next *aliya* without reciting a *Mishebeyrakh* for the shoemaker, though the custom was to recite

---

and a cemetery. Already under the Tsar, it was open to the public, though permission from the provincial governor was needed to spend the night there (Golovinskiy, 1894:238–241).

one for each person called up to the Torah. The *gabbaim* then instructed me to recite a *Mishebeyrakh* for him, to which I responded, "Why don't you recite one for him yourselves? I can't recite it for him."[5] I then asked the next person to say the blessings over the Torah so that we could proceed with the reading of the Torah. The *gabbaim* wanted to stop the Torah reading until I would recite a *Mishebeyrakh* for their darling, but I told them that under no circumstance would I do it, and I threatened to step down from the *bimah*. So they had no choice but to back down.[6] I accomplished my objective, but you can only imagine how they were fuming at me for my maneuver. The shoemaker now really felt justified, "What's this! A *shoykhet* should make such a laughingstock out of me, and, above all, not follow the instructions of the *gabbaim*! I'll get even with him! I'll teach him a lesson!"

Afterward, the shoemaker's dear wife began to seek me out daily. I would avoid her and guard myself from that mouth of hers, yet the time eventually came when Satan's plan succeeded. One morning, I walked into the butcher shop and noticed that she was already there. She began to make use of that mouth of hers, pretending to be speaking to others while really insulting me. I immediately wanted to flee but could not since I needed to bring home some meat for lunch. So I asked the butcher to cut me off a piece of meat, and I showed him which cut I wanted. While the piece of meat was on the scale, the shoemaker's wife ran over and said, "Give me that meat." Naturally, he gave me the piece of meat, which she then grabbed and tried to wrench from my hands. Had I let her take it, Satan would not have succeeded in his plan. Yet, against my nature, I refused to give it up, a result of my being so upset at her gall. Here we were standing in a shop full of meat, and she wanted the exact piece of meat I was taking. In any case, I refused to let go. I took the meat and wanted to leave as quickly as possible. But listen to what now happened. I was holding the meat, and she was trying to snatch it away from me while blocking my way out of the shop. You can understand that she was not going to be able to tear it away from me, yet the situation was bad since I had no way to leave. In the butcher shop was a thin wall made out of boards. So I pushed out one of the boards and exited through the newly-formed narrow doorway. She ran around the back and managed to grab onto my clothes in an attempt to stop me. But do you think she could have possibly restrained me? On the contrary, she wound up lying on the ground. Exactly what happened, I had no idea and was not interested in the

---

5 The author could not bear reciting the blessings of the *Misheybeyrakh* for the likes of the shoemaker and his family.

6 The author was the only one in the community who knew how to read from the Torah, as mentioned in ch. 25, p. 509.

slightest as long as I was out of there. I ran home as if from a fire and bemoaned my bad luck that even a gossiping meddler should prevail over me.

The next day, I heard that they had filed a claim against me in court. Suddenly a police officer arrived at my house and summoned me to appear at court at 10:00 in the morning. I arrived punctually at 10:00 in time to see them leaving full of glee at having already arranged for me to be sentenced to three months imprisonment. How exciting, a real joy—they had caught the Leviathan in a net. May it only happen to my enemies. They had successfully conspired for my case to be the first to be heard that day and made sure there would be no delays. The idea was for me to be convicted behind my back before my arrival, because a defendant was not allowed to make any counterclaims if he did not arrive on time. The accusation was entirely contrary to the facts, which you already know from my account. You cannot imagine how much suffering and heartache I endured and how much money I spent travelling around to fight the verdict. Finally God had compassion on me and I was freed from the judgment.

But do not think that my enemies let me rest for long. They quickly found another means of tormenting me, which would cost me money and affect my health. They came up with a case against me that showed promise of having me arrested for a number of months. It happened as follows. Benyumin brought sixty *funt* of animal fat into the butcher shop for me to *treyber*.[7] After doing so, only fifty-five *funt* remained. Unexpectedly, Benyumin submitted a lawsuit against me in the magistrate's court.[8] According to the law, since he had brought me sixty *funt* of fat to *treyber*, and, after doing so, it turned out that only fifty-five *funt* remained, the court should demand payment for the missing five *funt* of fat and I should be prosecuted for stealing. Benyumin added that in the likely case that the theft was by means of false scales, I should be prosecuted for deceit, which was not a matter of simply being jailed but meant being incarcerated in prison—and not merely for one month.[9] You can now imagine how viciously their petition had been written. But, thankfully, God swiftly saved me from that allegation too. After my prior experience, I was by now aware of their underhanded practices, and this time I prevented the case from being tried in

7 To *treyber* denotes the expert removal of certain sinews and fat of cattle, sheep, and goats, the eating of which is prohibited by Jewish law. See *Shulkhan Arukh* (*Yoreh Deah* 64 & 65).

8 The magistrate's court (*mirovoi sud* in Russian) was for smaller criminal and civil cases. It first appeared in Russia in 1864 and was abolished in 1889 (Burbank, 2004:320).

9 Apparently, fat is discarded during the *treybern* process and, in this case, five pounds of fat were lost.

my absence. I brought along witnesses to testify and prove the truth of my position. And God helped me.

It is now time that we return to the next part of our general narrative. In the meantime, the Greek's four-year concession of the kosher-meat tax quickly passed and a new auction was soon to be held.[10] I now had the new headache of preventing the kosher-meat tax consignment from falling into the hands of my enemies.[11] So I initially made sure that the election of the *gabbaim* would be held on time. I then accomplished my first objective, which was for new *gabbaim* to be elected. Those elected were people who had never believed they would hold positions in town. One of them was a shoemaker by the name of Yosef Grinblat, who was elected as the main *gabbai*. Another one was a furrier named Moyshe Kalk, who was elected treasurer. Both were first-rate scoundrels and wine drinkers. The third one elected to round out the trio was a fellow named Y. Reyzner.[12] He happened to be from a fine family and was himself not a coarse person, but he had become addicted to liquor. They all had no problem keeping up with the corruptness of their predecessors, and the previous community leaders were afraid to start up with them, because they knew that if they did, they would be put in their place without delay.

My second objective was that a new estimate be made on the new kosher-meat tax and that this estimate should be delivered to the Governor General.[13] I wanted it arranged directly with the Governor General so that it would not be worthwhile for the new *gabbaim* to involve themselves with the kosher-meat tax. I was able to arrange and confirm all of this.

Now listen to the crime that they pulled off, which happened as follows. Two years after Reb Leyb Volberg became in charge of the kosher meat tax, an elderly Jew, a *melomed*, arrived in town shortly after Pesach.[14] I even helped him set up a *kheyder* by obtaining permission for him to teach several children in the women's section of the *shul*. Right after *Shvues*,[15] I found out that this old

10 The author had his son Isruel brought from Khashtshevote to Tiraspol in the fall of 1885 (ch. 24, p. 487). This event occurred right before the author's enemies were discharged from controlling the kosher-meat tax, referred to here. The dating of many of the events in this chapter are based on the date of this passage.

11 As mentioned later on p. 538, the author somehow obtained the rights to the kosher meat tax, though after two years the contract was put in Leyb Volberg's name.

12 Reyzner was elected as one of the *gabbaim*. Apparently, at the same time, Leyb Volberg was elected as the assistant crown rabbi (see p. 529 below).

13 The previous estimate was based on the kosher-meat tax collected during the preceding four years (ch. 25, p. 504).

14 Calculated backward from the next election occurring at the end of 1889, this incident apparently occurred after Pesach ended on April 23, 1889.

15 June 5–6, 1889.

melomed was also a *shoykhet* and that he was slaughtering chickens in the synagogue courtyard. I approached him to clarify the issue, which he did not deny.

He said, "It's true, I've slaughtered some chickens here and will continue to do so for anyone else who brings them here."

I asked him, "Who permitted you to encroach on my slaughtering rights, which is forbidden by the Torah?! If you are truly a *shoykhet*, then the Torah doesn't permit you to slaughter. And if you're a transgressor, a wicked person, I'll deal with you through the authorities."

The old *melomed* did not back down and said, "All of this is my business. If you can prohibit me through the authorities, then go ahead. Who's stopping you?"

In the meantime, I looked around and I saw a couple of troublemakers running toward me. They looked like they were ready to tear me apart if I would touch that old Ashmedai.[16] I was lucky that I controlled myself, but I left agitated and ran straight to Reb Leyb, who I thought would immediately forbid him from slaughtering as demanded by Russian law. After all, Reb Leyb had the right to do so since the contract for the kosher-meat tax was in his name. Besides, being also the crown rabbi, he could send a notice directly to the city council which could prohibit that old *melomed* from slaughtering.[17] The bottom line was that when I told him the whole story he just laughed at me and said, "Why are you yelling like this? What did he do to you that was so terrible? So he slaughtered a chicken or two! Are you now ruined?" And then he smirked and commented coolly, "Nothing's going to become of it. Just go home and calm down." I explained to him how harmful it was; it was not the two chickens that bothered me but that slaughtering here would become a free-for-all. There was a possibility that he would then begin to slaughter at the slaughterhouse, which would then slaughter my entire livelihood! He just laughed at me and said, "Why do you worry so much? Nothing is going to become of it!" while smiling with revenge and great satisfaction, though he could not openly express his delight about the incident in front of me.[18] I realized his attitude immediately and walked away totally dejected.

How was this possible? I had been through so many battles and taken so many precautions. After everything was said and done, such an unexpected

16 Ashmedai is described in the Talmud (Gitin 68a) as being the king of the demons.

17 The author calls Leyb Volberg the crown rabbi which he uses as shorthand for his actual title of assistant crown rabbi, as mentioned in ch. 23, p. 464, footnote 44. In fact, Volberg is referred to as the "assistant rabbi" in the list of Bakhchisaray donors to the Jewish Colonial Trust appearing in *Ha-Melits* (November 22, 1900, p. 4).

18 Evidently, all the officials of the Jewish community despised the author since he was preventing them from embezzling the kosher-meat-tax funds.

outrage was being perpetrated against me, and I had no way of safeguarding myself! What then would I do if that old *melomed* actually began slaughtering in the slaughterhouse? I could bring a ruling from the rabbi in Simferopol prohibiting the meat he slaughtered, but would that old *melomed* and his buddies really care about a rabbinical ruling? [19] In the meantime, I needed to come up with a plan. New headaches were now beginning, and they awakened within me past woes, as if my heart was telling me that this would become a source of great aggravation. I wrote a letter to the rabbi of Simferopol, and he replied, "We are aware of this fellow who has already been banned from slaughtering for a long time. It's forbidden to eat from the meat he has slaughtered." The rabbi offered to send his ruling to the community of Bakhchisaray, but he was uncertain if they would follow the ruling. The rabbi added, "But since you are in charge of the kosher-meat tax, you should have the ability to prevent the *melamed* from slaughtering through the secular legal authorities." I spat at the idea and said, "All hope is not lost. God will help me. Just as He delivered me from all my previous troubles, so will He save me from my present predicament." [20]

In the interim, I heard that people in town were murmuring, and I saw that they were avoiding me. Suddenly, one bright morning as I entered the slaughterhouse, I encountered some guests, two young scoundrels: a tailor by the name of Hersh Akerman, and a furrier by the name of Berl Nutkovitsh. The two of them had come to guard the old *melomed* so that he would be able to slaughter in the slaughterhouse. They were there to protect him from my harassment. I cannot describe my feelings. My heart just froze looking at the scene. I have no idea where I drew the strength to refrain from breaking the bones of all three of them to prevent them from ever reappearing at the slaughterhouse. I did not succumb to that tempting urge. My powerful resolve conquered it, and I did not utter even the slightest comment and tolerated the incident patiently. Although my health suffered by having to watch their destruction of my source of livelihood, God gave me the strength to stay calm. At last, I finished my work at the slaughterhouse and returned home.

While I was walking back into town from the slaughterhouse and also when sitting in the butcher shop, I observed that the community was divided

---

19 Probably referring to Rabbi Bole-Binyomin Demant, who was born ca. 1839 in Lithuania. He first held two rabbinical positions in Lithuania and in 1883 became the rabbi of Simferopol, where he served in that capacity until his death in December 1893. His son, Rabbi Yosef-Bentsion Demant, was the rabbi of Yalta and author of a number of rabbinical works (Eisenstadt, 1902:10–11; Gotlib, 1912:90–91; Melamed, 1922:258).

20 The author was frustrated by Rabbi Demant's advice to turn to the secular authorities. Since Leyb Volberg was both the assistant crown rabbi and in control of the kosher-meat tax, he would be able to thwart any appeal made to the municipality.

into two factions. Though half of the community continued purchasing their meat at my shop, the other half did not. I understood that those who did not enter my shop belonged to the *melomed*'s faction.

Upon concluding my work at the shop, I hurried over to Reb Leyb Volberg and asked him, "Why are you silent?"

He responded, "What can I do?"

I said, "What do you mean, 'What can I do?' Just don't allow him to slaughter! You have the right to prohibit him from slaughtering."

He said, "What should I do with those scoundrels? They wanted to break my bones, so I had to permit him to slaughter." His reply was said so coldly and with such a wry smile that you could have thought he was relating some joke and that we were not dealing with the bleeding of my very livelihood from me. My blood was being spilled, and he was acting totally indifferent as if he had nothing to do with the matter.

Realizing that harsh words would only make matters worse, I began to plead with him, "How could you have done that? You permitted that *shoykhet* to slaughter, but the kosher-meat tax that he takes for each chicken belongs to me! He should be paying me the tax. Reb Leyb, you know how much I have to pay the city council in taxes."

He replied, "Yes, you're right," as if I had not been up until now. "But don't worry. Even though you may think I'm not loyal to you, I made sure to take the necessary precautions."

I then asked him, "What are you referring to?"

He repeated himself and said, "I arranged for you to receive your full share of the tax. By law, you should only be receiving one *kopek* for each *funt* of meat. Yet since you sit in the butcher shop and *treyber* the meat, you take two *kopeks* for each *funt*. So we decided that the old *melomed* should also take two *kopeks* for each *funt* of meat that he sells in his butcher shop but that he should keep one *kopek* for himself and give the other to you for the tax." He finished with a statement tainted in irony, "See, you won't be losing a thing!" He pretended to be unaware that one *kopek* barely covered the amount due the city council and that my profit was the remaining *kopek*. How could I survive with such an arrangement? That *melomed* would be taking one *kopek* for himself but he would not be giving me the other *kopek*, which he was obligated to give me in full. He would steal as much as he wanted for himself.

Volberg seemed totally oblivious to my plight and said, "*Nu*, why are you silent? Are you still dissatisfied?"

I responded, "I'm definitely not satisfied! And you are certainly my assassin, my ruin! My tears, those of my desperate wife, and those of my children shall not flow in vain. Whereas my enemies' numerous attempts to destroy me have failed, you, my dear supposed friend, have succeeded in such a fine and exalted manner. They were justified in picking you as the rabbi because you really are an excellent arbitrator and have done a fine job at that! I wish such misfortune upon you and upon all my enemies! Don't think, Reb Leybenyu, that God will forgive you for this.[21] No, such murderous deeds are not forgiven! Don't think I'm doomed and will succumb, God forbid. No, I've stumbled into a troublesome situation, but, with God's help, I'll prevail!"

The part of the community that was backing and supposed to be paying the old *melomed* was not composed of the most generous individuals. In addition, the bodyguards who were supposed to protect him did not want to do so unless they were paid. Slowly, the bodyguards lost interest in accompanying the old *melomed* and then ceased to go altogether. The *melomed*'s situation deteriorated to the point that he was left without any support. And one dark night at some unearthly hour, he left. He did not live out the year and died that winter.

The above circumstances dragged on for four months, though to me it seemed like four years. My suffering during those four months was so great that it would have knocked many a man off his feet even if the suffering had been spread over four years. Just consider all that I had to endure, even apart from my income being reduced by half. Since I was not able to concentrate on my various earnings, I ended up letting many of my sources of side income slack off and the coarser elements in town took advantage of my situation. In addition to my financial problems, I suffered abuse from every tailor's assistant, shoemaker, and so on. Everybody figured that they would be looked upon favorably and would generate a good name for themselves by getting even with the *shoykhet*. They figured they would receive a respectable *aliya* on *Shobes* in *shul* as their reward for abusing the *shoykhet*. My situation was similar to the position of the Jewish people since it is customary for anyone who abuses and pains the Jewish people to be elevated to a high position in the government.[22] Likewise, a *shoykhet* in Bakhchisaray was considered fair game by every lowlife. By harming the *shoykhet*, he could thus earn a good name for himself, be considered a fine person, and receive the best *aliya* and a thank you from the *gabbaim*.

---

21 Leybenyu is a diminutive form of Leyb Volberg's name.

22 Talmud (Gitin 56b) states, "Whoever persecutes the Jews becomes a leader."

Now I do not want you to be mistaken and think that I am referring to the old *gabbaim*, those enemies of mine, Medvedye, Mayster, and Galkin.[23] No my dear readers, I do not mean them! I mean the brand new *gabbaim*: a shoemaker named Grinblat who was a proficient drunkard; a furrier named Nutkovitsh who was an even bigger drunk;[24] and a third who eclipsed the other two, namely Mr. Reyzner. In addition, the "goodhearted" Mr. Volberg was elected crown rabbi; you already know all about him from the description of my most recent episode. It is these very *gabbaim* I am referring to and they are the ones who really made my life miserable. As soon as they were elected, I realized that life would not be good with them around and that they would be even worse than the previous *gabbaim.*

There were times when I would run into the *shul,* open the ark, and lean inside as I cried and pleaded with the holy Torah scrolls to intercede on our behalf since we had no more strength to endure all this suffering. It was not such an issue for me since I would leave for work and forget my situation for a while, because, by nature, I was not a worrier. But, when I would enter my house, I would often feel helpless seeing the suffering of my unfortunate wife and children. And why did we have to suffer? For what sin? I used to want to hide from my wife and children. As soon as I arrived home, I would sink into a pillow pretending to be taking a nap, so that my wife and children should not notice the tears pouring down my face. Nonetheless, my wife understood me very well and would then do the same herself. When we would tire of crying, we would sit and comfort one another. Such scenes were common in our home, yet God always helped us.

But as soon as we were done with one problem, another would arise. For example, after the departure of the old *melomed,* the slaughterer, I started to think about the upcoming High Holidays when I would earn seventy-five rubles for leading the services.[25] I was also counting on my earnings from slaughtering *kapores,* from the charity plates, and from selling of *esroygim.*[26] I figured that my total earnings for the season would be about 100 rubles, which would have helped me pay off a bit of my debt and given me some money for the winter's firewood. Instead, we were faced with a new calamity. When my enemies

23 The word טענות ("complaints") is mistakenly printed in the original Yiddish instead of the word טעות (mistake), as in the phrase "be mistaken."

24 Nutkovitsh's first name was Berl, as mentioned above on p. 526.

25 Referring to the High Holidays of 1889. Rosh Hashanah occurred on September 26–27, 1889 and Yom Kippur on October 5, 1889, as calculated backward from the date of the next election of the *gabbaim* held in late 1889 (see p. 536, footnote 38 below).

26 Evidently among the collection plates set out for various charities on the eve of Yom Kippur (see ch. 25, p. 506), a plate was also set out to collect tips for the *shoykhet.*

realized that I had been freed from that old slaughterer, they began to devise a new plan to harm me. They reckoned that seventy-five rubles was too steep a price to pay someone for leading the High Holiday services. I would have led *Shakhris* and *Musaf*, read the Torah, and blown the *shofar*, for just seventy-five rubles. They figured they could find someone with some experience for a lot less, which would be doubly advantageous to them. Firstly, they would have some extra money to spend on liquor, and, secondly, they would have hurt the *shoykhet* and caused him a monetary loss. In addition, their plan would certainly give the previous *gabbaim* great pleasure. In truth, all these trials and tribulations originated with the previous *gabbaim*, because the current ones did not have the brains to come up with such plans.

In any event, I was being attacked from all sides. With the new *gabbaim*, those drunkards, my situation was really difficult, since I was not even able to discuss anything with them, which they understood quite well and then tortured me even more. The whole bunch of them would walk into the *shul*, and one of them would proceed to lead the services, which they knew would really bother me. They knew it would wrench my heart to see an ignoramus who could not read properly, was not that religious, and was a drunkard to boot approach the lectern to lead the services. Sometime later, the shoemaker, who was now the main *gabbai*, decided that he himself would lead the services from now on, thereby showing everyone that he could serve as the cantor throughout the year.[27] Since he was the main *gabbai*, he thought that he had the right and was entitled to do as he pleased. This showed that they did not need me to lead the services throughout the year and that they could hire a poor Jew for the High Holidays for whatever they could get away with. You may ask, what would happen if that poor Jew could not lead the services very well? Well, at least they would have saved themselves some money! And how would the *shoykhet* manage without this extra income? That did not concern them at all. Upon noticing that I was crying and that my wife and children were weeping loudly, they then became convinced that they had attained their objective. While reveling in delight, they added, "He should know who he's dealing with and how to behave as *shoykhet* in Bakhchisaray!"

Even though the previous *gabbaim* could not tolerate the situation out of sheer decency and could have done something about it if they had wanted to, they nonetheless refused. Their reasoning was as follows, "If he thinks that we were mean to him, then let him see that there are worse people than us! Though

---

27 Referring to Yosef Grinblat, as mentioned above on p. 529.

we can't stomach these drunkards, we're not going to interfere. Let him know and see the difference between us and them."

Let us now return to our previous discussion. For the High Holidays, they found a Jew, a *melomed,* in Simferopol who agreed to lead the services for fifty rubles. Being overjoyed with the success of their plan, they even drank a bit of liquor in honor of the occasion. The *melomed* they hired quickly and monotonously recited *Slikhes.*[28] All that could be said was that he had at least recited it. Yet, they thought it was worthwhile as long as the *shoykhet* had suffered a loss and had now realized what Bakhchisaray was all about. I accepted it all with love and resolved to pray sincerely and plead before God on Rosh Hashanah and Yom Kippur. Certainly, God would then have compassion upon me from now on and save me from my bitter enemies. I understood that from this point onwards God's attribute of mercy would dominate and such calamities would cease to come upon me because the *gabbaim* had already reached the pinnacle of wickedness.

Rosh Hashanah turned out to be a double *Simchas Torah* for my enemies: they had a good laugh at how the *melomed* led the services, and they delighted in the pain and embarrassment I felt as I stood in the corner and continually cried. I would have even left the *shul,* but there was nowhere else to pray. In short, I had to stand there and endure my shame. That was also the situation as *Yom Kippur* services began, but during *Kol Nidre* the *melomed* began to gag horribly and was not able to continue. Nonetheless, with some loud, laughable sounds emanating from his throat, he barely managed to drag on to the end of the services.

In *shul,* a clamorous commotion broke out. "How could such scandals be allowed to occur and make a mockery of the entire congregation? How could they have brought such a worthless and lame cantor to lead the services when we already had a fine one of our own? Ours isn't even expensive, especially when you consider that the fellow they hired was being paid fifty rubles plus room and board, which adds up to close to eighty rubles! So how much did they really save?" These arguments were made by those on the sidelines who usually did not involve themselves in communal affairs out for fear of losing the privilege of being called up for *Maftir*.

Sparks were flying in the women's section, while not a single word of defense could be heard from the *gabbaim*'s own wives, who were even more

28 *Slikhes* (*Slikhot* in Modern Hebrew) literary means "pardons" and are penitential prayers recited early in the morning on the days preceding Rosh Hashanah and afterward until Yom Kippur. Here the hired cantor was apparently leading the recitation of *Slikhes* on the day before Rosh Hashana.

FIGURE 18. Pinkhes-Dov Goldenshteyn's book stamp (1.75"W x 2.75"H) stating his name and place of residence, Bakhchisaray, in both Hebrew and Cyrillic letters. In Russian, his name appears as "Pinkhus Itskovich Goldenshteyn." Metrical records from Tsarist Russian frequently used the spelling of Pinkhus. Itskovich denotes "the son of Itsko," i.e., Itskhok.

silent than their husbands. The women did not know if it was the High Holidays or *Simchas Torah.*[29] To make a long story short, no one was satisfied with the services and everyone regretted the decision to hire someone else.

On *Yom Kippur* morning, the *melomed* completely refused to lead the prayers. Since there was no one who could lead the services, they decided to ask me, and I understood that this was not the appropriate time to force them into pleading with me to do so. Though I knew that I would never be compensated for my efforts, I also knew that if I did not do it they would have felt that they were once again in the right. As I went over to the lectern to lead the services, I sensed that everyone was breathing a sigh of relief. They now sensed that it was *Yom Kippur,* a time to plead before God. They finally saw the difference between me and others in leading the services and no longer envied me as before. Though they used to say, "How's it possible? For three days' work, he demands such a clump of money—as much as seventy-five rubles! No way!" Instead they said

29 The High Holy Days are characterized by a certain seriousness, in contrast to *Simchas Torah,* which is a noisy holiday filled with loud singing.

from then on, "His services are worth 200 rubles, not a mere seventy-five." Since I did not refuse them when they were stuck without a cantor, they realized that I was a *mentsh* and ceased doing battle with me for a short while.

But, my dear reader, do not think that their silence lasted long. Suddenly, one Friday night during *Kabules Shobes,* the treasurer, the drunkard Kalk, and his entire gang walked into the *shul* intoxicated. Kalk began to shout at me for not having waited for him. You may possibly think that it was still quite early, but, no, I am telling you that it was actually late and I was about to start *Marev.* That drunk ran over to the lectern and tried to drag me away by force. Just imagine the insolence of it all. *Nu,* do you really think he was able to drag me away? Naturally, I did not allow it, unless he had wanted to drag me and the lectern off together. But there was no way that he could have mustered enough strength for that, unless his cronies would have helped him, which they did not. On the contrary, they pulled him away and took him with them, certainly straight to the tavern. How do you like that pretty scene?

I had to bear all of this and hope that God would deliver me from all my troubles. You are probably wondering how it is possible that a *shul* full of people allowed this to go on. I will clarify the matter for you. Actually, they were upset, but nobody wanted to stick up for the *shoykhet* because they were afraid of being berated by those scoundrels. I can prove to you that they were upset, for the police commissioner approached me the very next morning and asked, "What happened in your synagogue yesterday?" I pretended to know nothing of the matter, so he said, "Tell me, what are you afraid of? I know that Moyshe Kalk affronted you yesterday! But if you don't press charges, I can't do anything about it. I'd really like to punish them for their actions, so tell me what happened!" So I told him what had occurred and added, "But I forgive them. I don't want to press charges." He responded, "If you want to forgive him, that's his good luck, but he's not going to get away with the scandal he caused in the synagogue yesterday! If you don't press charges, then I'll take him to court as required by law and then you'll have to testify!" It was obvious that the townsmen had reported the incident to him, and, consequently, Reb Moyshe Kalk received his just reward. The police commissioner prepared a written record of the incident and summoned witnesses including me. Kalk was sentenced to jail for only two weeks, thanks to me, since I had played down his culpability in my testimony. Nonetheless, that was a sufficient lesson to alter the outlook of those drunken *gabbaim.*

This was nothing in comparison to the persecution I suffered at the hands of the drunken community leaders. They always found some new material to use in their schemes against me, for example, the following incident with the *esreg* and the injustice done to me by that old *melomed* working as a *shoykhet*. There are people in the area who still remember the foolishness of their persecutions.

Every year, I used to order a box of some ten to twelve *esroygim*. You can imagine the "tremendous profit" that I earned from selling these *esroygim*, yet my intention was to guarantee that at least one fine *esreg* would be available in town, and I always made sure that this fine *esreg* remained in my possession. In the year that the following incident occurred, I ordered *esroygim* as usual but only eight since they were very expensive that season. Since my fine *esreg* was worth six rubles and was too expensive for me to keep, I commented that I would be willing to sell it if someone was interested in buying it. This bit of information reached the ears of our Reb Simkhele,[30] and he approached me right on the eve of *Yontef* with an offer to buy my *esreg*.[31] Now even though I had said earlier that I would be willing to sell it, I no longer felt like selling it; it was as if my heart was urging me not to. Simkhe kept insisting, saying, "You're poor. Wouldn't it be better for you to save your money to pay your children's *melamdim*?" In short, due to my tight financial situation and Simkhele's lengthy talk, I became agreeable to sell it to him but on the condition that I would still retain partial ownership, meaning that I would be able to recite the blessing on that *esreg* every day of *Sukes* but would perform the wavings of the four species during *Hallel* using the community's *esreg*.[32] How was I to know that this entire agreement was intended to make a mockery of me? I accepted the five rubles that Reb Simkhe gave me for the *esreg*, and he departed joyfully. As soon as he left my house, I immediately regretted having sold it to him; I did not know why, but my heart began to pound inside me.

The following morning,[33] I rose early, immersed myself in the *mikveh*, and began walking over to *Simkhe*'s to say the blessing over the *esreg*. As I walked, I kept thinking that my suspicions that he would do me wrong were really groundless. In fact, he then handed me the *esreg* and let me make the blessings over it, as we had agreed. But listen to what occurred afterward. As I walked

---

30 Referring to Simkhe Mayster.

31 The eve of *Sukes* occurred on October 9, 1889.

32 The taking of the four species (the *esreg*, aka citron, and the branches of the palm, willow, and myrtle) is a Biblical commandment incumbent upon Jews (Leviticus 23:40). It involves holding them together on each day of *Sukes* and gently waving them in a prescribed manner, particularly during *Hallel* (*Kitsur Shulkhan Arukh* 137:1–4). *Hallel* is a prayer generally consisting of Psalms 113–118, which are said as a unit on most Jewish holidays. Due to the rarity of the *esreg* in Europe in previous generations, Jewish communities usually purchased one or more communal *esroygim* to be used by its members during *Sukes*.

33 This was the morning of the first day of *Sukes*, October 10, 1889.

into *shul* for morning prayers, I noticed that everyone was huddled into several small whispering groups. As I approached, they fell silent, and I understood that I was the topic of conversation. A couple of them could not control themselves and asked me, "Where's your *esreg*?" I responded, "I don't have my own this year but own one jointly with Simkhe." "Really?" one of them replied. In short, I began to lead the services and continued until the *Shimenesre*. Now, it was time to recite *Hallel*, and nobody was handing me an *esreg*. They asked me, "What's the matter? Where's your *esreg*? So I responded, "I'm the cantor for the community, so I deserve to use the community's *esreg*!" They said, "No you don't! If you were willing to sell your *esreg*, then you don't deserve one." What a wonderful piece of deduction.

I thought that if I just stepped away from the lectern and stopped leading the prayers, they would then be forced to hand me an *esreg*, but that is exactly what they were waiting for.[34] As soon as I stepped away from the lectern, the drunken main *gabbai*, Yosef the shoemaker,[35] walked over to the lectern to lead the remaining prayers. Of course, the virtuous Simkhele did not say to me, "For the sake of peace, take the *esreg*, and I'll pray without waving the four species" or "Take the *esreg* and I'll use the community *esreg*," because his real intention in buying the *esreg* was not for the sake of a *mitzvah* but was rather for the sake of strife. You can just imagine my pain and embarrassment. So I did not attempt to lead the services the entire *Sukes*. On *Hoyshane-Rabe*, I stood as a mourner on listening to the shoemaker lead the *Hoyshanes* prayers with his crude, cobbler tune, but I had no other choice since there was no other *shul*.[36] My wife and I shed rivers of tears over this foolishness perpetrated against me.

Fervor over the incident did not die down that entire year. It only weakened when I did not have a box of *esroygim* delivered the next year and they had to buy them from Simferopol for a much higher price than they were used to paying me. To top it off, the *esroygim* were horrible and unfit for use. After all, what did drunks know about *esroygim*?[37] That was when they finally realized that I had been in the right, which resulted in the situation quieting down for some time. After all, they had become bored of talking about the same issue for

---

34 The author was hoping to force them into handing him an *esreg* since no one else was qualified to lead the services.

35 The surname of Yosef the shoemaker was Grinblat, as mentioned on p. 529 above.

36 *Hoyshane-Rabe* was on October 16, 1889. *Hoyshanes* (*Hoshanot* in Modern Hebrew) are a series of prayers recited on each day of *Sukes* following the *Hallel* prayer, where the leader holds the four species and encircles the *bimah* as the congregations follows him (*Kitsur Shulkhan Arukh* 137:11).

37 Jewish law requires certain qualifications in order for the *esreg* to be fit for use in fulfilling the *mitzvah*.

such a long time and needed to find a new one. Actually, it was not long before God granted them a fresh diversion. The town livened up once again because another battle was being waged with the *shoykhet,* of which you will soon learn the details.

Shortly after the incident of the *esreg,* my four years of holding the kosher-meat tax, which caused me much unhappiness, came to an end. It was now time for the new auction of the kosher-meat tax consignment to be held.[38] I decided not to bid on it and not to lease it. If it had no takers, it would then fall to the administration of some of the Jewish townsmen, meaning that that the city council would appoint two or three Jewish men to administer the tax. They would then be required to pay the *shoykhet* and deliver the leftover funds to the city council. I figured this would be a better arrangement for me, but, as it turned out, it caused me much heartache, pain, and endless humiliation. How was I supposed to know that they would appoint my worst enemies to supervise the kosher-meat tax? The city council meant no harm and had the best of intentions, but, after all, they were not Jewish, so what would they know? They only knew that the "synagogue elder" must certainly be a fine person because the Jewish community had chosen him, which was proof enough that he must have been the most qualified candidate.[39] They made the same calculation regarding the treasurer.

Now just imagine, my dear friends, the following: The three members of the synagogue board went to the city council and asked to be appointed as the administrators of the kosher-meat tax committee. When the city council replied that they needed an additional member so that there would be four administrators, these three fellows recommended one of their cronies, a real scoundrel by the name of Hersh Akerman. You are already familiar with the fellow, since he was one of the bodyguards who used to escort the old *shoykhet* to the slaughterhouse, and it was this fellow whom they registered as the fourth member. This was all done on *Shobes* without my knowledge.

Saturday night after *Havdalah,* the door opened and the likeness of a human being entered. I say "the likeness," for Hersh Akerman was no human being. He said, "*A gite vokh,* Reb Pinye-Ber!"[40]

---

38 The new auction of the kosher-meat tax consignment was held at the end of 1889, since this auction and the election of new *gabbaim* was held every four years and the previous one had apparently been held at the end of 1885.

39 "Synagogue elder" is the translation of the Russian words *starosta sinagogi,* which was used by the city council to refer to the *gabbai,* probably the main *gabbai.*

40 "*A gite vokh*" means, "A good week." This is the traditional greeting said after *Shabes* ends on Saturday night, which marks the beginning of the Jewish week.

I responded, "Why are you suddenly wishing me, '*A gite vokh*'?"

"Yes," he said, "Do you know why? I've come so that you can hand over your slaughtering knives!"

I said, "The slaughtering knives? What are you talking about? Do you slaughter animals that you need slaughtering knives? You can also slaughter people without knives—you do it with your malicious tongue!"

He said, "Are you going to argue with me? I came to talk to you nicely and inform you that I was appointed an administrator of the kosher-meat tax and that you're forbidden to slaughter without my knowledge. In short, from now on, the knives will be in my custody, and when you need them for slaughtering, you must come to me to pick them up. I'll then either accompany you in person or send someone to accompany you to the slaughterhouse. Now do you understand?"

I replied sarcastically, "I understand you very well, and if you don't leave immediately, I'll throw you out." And, indeed, I began to shout at him, "Out of here! You drunk! You murderer! You came to confiscate my knives? I'll split your skull!"

My friend, Reb Hershele, quickly hurried out the door into the courtyard where one of his friends awaited him. I promptly chased the two of them out of the courtyard.[41]

An hour later, a policeman arrived and summoned me to the mayor. I entered the mayor's office where I met my old friends, the members of the synagogue board.

The mayor asked me, "Why did you throw him out of your courtyard?"

I responded, "Because he wanted to rob me of my tools upon which my livelihood depends." I then explained, "These tools do not belong to the community and the administrator cannot prohibit me from slaughtering without him or from slaughtering where I want to. He just has to be informed when I do some slaughtering so that he can then collect the tax. If I was caught cheating, he'd have the right to take measures against me, but as of now I've done nothing wrong. And you know, to avoid dealing with such administrators, I may just think about staying home and letting him find another *shoykhet*. After all, what right does he have to come to me and demand my knives?" To make a long story short, the mayor understood the truth of my words and told them to leave. He then told me not to slaughter anywhere without their knowledge. In short, the following day I did not set off to the slaughterhouse without one of them accompanying me.

---

41 Hershele is the diminutive of Hersh.

Afterward, Akerman used to be with me in the slaughterhouse where he kept an eye on how many animals were deemed kosher and how many were deemed *treyf*. In town, I had different drunken townsmen watching my every move. In short, I suffered throughout that entire month while they did not hand over any money to the municipality nor pay me my wages. So what was I supposed to do? Actually, I was able to do something about it, but it required a battle.

At the butcher shop, they used to order me around like a servant, which eventually led to my throwing one of them from inside the butcher shop all the way outdoors into the mud. He was so embarrassed that he never returned to the shop. Then the rest of those henchmen filed a suit against me, which is actually what I wanted to happen. Once summoned, I was able to prove that the supervisors had collected the tax for the entire month and had squandered it away on drink. I said, "If they aren't paying my wages and they aren't submitting any money to the municipality, what type of administrators are they? I'll hand over to the municipality as much as you decide as long as you release me from their hands. If not, I won't be going to the slaughterhouse anymore. Do as you see fit."

The bottom line was that the city council put an end to their administrative careers and appointed me in their stead. They did assign me an assistant, someone with whom I was already familiar, Mr. Volberg, the crown rabbi. In any event, I said good riddance to those four. As for Volberg, he was tolerable. He was certainly no instigator. And I was, after all, in charge, especially after I submitted to the provincial administrative offices a request that the kosher-meat tax remain under my care for a specified price, and the kosher-meat tax ended up in my possession since the city council knew me to be an honest person.[42] Regarding those drunkards, the city council demanded forty rubles from them, which gave them more than enough to talk about for a long time, so much so that they could not enjoy the *treyf* wine that they had purchased using the kosher-meat tax funds. From that point on, the kosher-meat tax remained in my possession without any further harassment from anyone.[43] Everyone knew that the kosher-meat tax had to remain under my control, which is how it remained for a good number of years with no one even dreaming of trying to appropriate it from me.

Since the persecutions has quieted down, we can now begin to think about my personal life and see how the lives of my wife and children were progressing and what needed to be done for them.

---

42 Evidently, the provincial administrative offices accepted the city council's favorable opinion of the author.

43 The harassment apparently ended in 1895. See ch. 29, p. 569, footnote 1.

CHAPTER 27

Raising My Children and My Wife's Death, 1884–1897

My Son, Shulemke, Becomes Ill • The Doctor's Mistake • My Son Withers Away • Isruel-Burekh Becomes a *Shoykhet* in Simferopol • Isruel-Burekh Becomes Engaged and His Mother Is Greatly Aggravated over the Match • Isruel-Burekh Marries • Yosele and Yankele Become Artisans • Refúel Is Taken to Khashtshevote to Study Torah • My Wife Becomes Deathly Ill • Traveling to Visit My Wife, Only to Find Her No Longer among the Living • Nekhame Marries

You already know from before that God blessed me with children. I brought Isruel-Burekh and Nekhamele to Bakhchisaray as small children. While I was being persecuted there, God blessed me with more, including a Itskhok-Yosele and a Yankele, may they live long.[1] I was also blessed with a little boy named Shulem and a son named Refulikl. You are already familiar with Yosele and Yankele because I have discussed them more than once. But since I have not spoken until now about the other two children, Shuleml and Refulikl, I will do so now.

On the 14th of *Teyves* 5644, my son Shulem was born.[2] He was a very beautiful child, and his cleverness, his beautiful eyes, his way of expressing himself, and his beautiful little voice—at which all marveled—are impossible to describe. Nonetheless, he did not have long to live. Since I did not have any *shulem* outside,[3] I thought that God would grant me my Shulem that I had at home. But it was not destined for me, so God also took away that Shulem.

1 Yosele is a diminutive form of Yosef.

2 January 12, 1884.

3 *Shulem* (pronounced *shalom* in Modern Hebrew) means "peace."

Shulem used to love to run after his older siblings to *kheyder*. Once, upon returning from *kheyder*, Shulem complained that his foot hurt him. His mother and I examined him thoroughly but could not see anything the matter, so he continued to play. The next day, as I approached our house from the street, I found Shulem lying on a stone outside next to the door.

I asked him, "What's the matter, Shulem?"

"Nothing, *Tote*."

"What are you doing here?"

He replied, "My foot hurts me."

I told him to stand up. He wanted to stand, but the poor thing could not.

He said, while crying, "*Oy*, my foot!"

I grabbed him in my arms and ran with him into the house and then ran with him to the doctor. The doctor gave him an ointment. The next day, we saw that our son had taken a turn for the worse. He now had a fever, and his little foot was red and swollen. I again ran to the doctor, but he was not home. I ran to a woman doctor, but she did not want to come over since the other doctor was already treating him. Meanwhile, he was becoming worse. We both stood next to his bed and cried, not knowing what to do. I kept running over to the doctor's to find out if he had returned. He did not return until the third day. Upon entering our house, he grabbed his head and ripped the prescription label off the bottle of ointment. I immediately understood that he had made a grave mistake. When I tried to take the label from him, he would not let me. In short, he now prescribed new medicines, but it was already too late.

The swelling spread over my child's entire body, and I saw that he was dying. I was even able to anticipate when his last minutes would be according to the rate that the swelling was spreading up toward his neck. When I saw that his neck was becoming swollen, I knew that my son was being choked. And that is what happened. He spoke until the swelling reached his neck, and then his pure soul left his body. He still managed to communicate with us through his eyes as he looked at us all. He appeared to be contemplating his poor parents and their tragic situation. His eyes conveyed his love for his parents and the heartbreak he felt at having to leave them.

Two hours earlier when he was yet able to speak, he asked to see the baby Refuel whom he loved dearly. We brought the baby to him, and he looked adoringly at him until he was overcome in his final moments and forgot about everything.

He was sick a total of five days. He had lived for all of three and a half years. He passed away on the 21st of *Tamuz* 5647.[4] Our tragedy practically knocked

---

4 July 13, 1887.

us off our feet, and for quite a while we could not be calmed or consoled. Who knows if we would have managed to survive had God not provided the cure before the wound.

Seven months earlier, the angel Refuel had been dispatched to heal our wounds—may he continue to be with us forever.[5] God granted him to us on Tuesday, the 21st of *Teyves* 5646, and we called him "the angel."[6] May God grant him a long life. He was named for my father, of blessed memory, whose name was Itskhok-Refúel. Nonetheless, since I already had a son named Itskhok, I was only able to give him one of my father's names, so he was named Refuel.[7] From birth, he was as handsome as an angel, so we called him "Refuel the angel." He was our great consolation and the healer of the wounds that we had suffered seven months after his birth. Just as Refulikl's pleasant features shone, so did he grow to be quite a clever and happy child.[8] He caused us to completely forget our loss. A year and a half later, God blessed me with a beautiful girl whom I named after my sister Rukhl-Tsipe, of blessed memory, but I only gave her the name Rukhl. She removed even more of the pain of our loss. My daughter was born on the 27th of *Heshvan* 5648.[9] A year and ten months later, God completely replenished my loss by blessing me with a baby boy whom I named Shloyme. He was born on the 10th of *Elul* 5649.[10] With our newly born Shloymele, our consolation was complete, since Shloyme also means "peace." These three children gladdened our hearts.

At this point I would like to describe each of my children individually including our efforts on behalf of each one of them until maturation, the profession that each studied, and the course in life each followed until the present day.

I will begin with my oldest son Isruel-Burekh, may he be well. If your memory serves you, you already know quite a bit about him, so I will now complete his story. I had taught him the laws of *sh'khita,* and he received certification from a number of *shokhtim* and rabbis, having impressed them all with his skill. But what would we do about his future? Trying to find him a suitable

---

5 Refuel (Raphael in English) means "God heals" in Hebrew. This is the name of the angel who brings healing.

6 December 29, 1885.

7 The complete name of the author's son Yosl was Itskhok-Yosef, as mentioned on p. 539 above.

8 Refulikl is the diminutive of Refuel.

9 November 14, 1887.

10 September 6, 1889. Shloyme's birth record from Bakhchisaray indicates in Russian that "Shlyome Goldenshteyn" (Shulem Goldshteyn in the Hebrew section) was born on August 1, 1889 (August 13, 1889 per New Style dating) and the 16th of *Av* according to the Hebrew calendar. Beginning in February 1918, the Gregorian calendar (New Style dating) replaced the Julian calendar (Old Style dating) in Russia. In Tsarist Russia, officials often made little effort to record births precisely. The author is noted on the birth record as being the *moyel.*

FIGURE 19. Pinkhes-Dov Goldenshteyn's oldest son, Isruel (1873–1946), served as a *shoykhet*, cantor, and *moyel* in Feodosiya, Crimea, for some forty years—until he emigrated to France in 1935. Note that his *peyes* are tied above his temples. This photograph was taken in March 1910. (Courtesy of Lisa Unterberg Delafontaine of Rye Brook, New York.)

wife was not an option, since he had not yet appeared before the conscription board.[11] So I kept him at my side; he was a very good worker and saved me much work.[12] Since he naturally needed a bit of an income to cover some necessities, I allowed him the proceeds of selling the forbidden fats removed from the slaughtered animals.[13] This brought him approximately four rubles a month, so he had a bit of spending money while we took care of his basic needs. He stayed with us under this arrangement until the time came for him to appear before the conscription board, and he was released from conscription.[14] My enemies even attempted, unsuccessfully, to prompt the authorities to conscript him, but God delivered me from this calamity.

Shortly after being exempted from conscription, Isruel accepted a position as *shoykhet* in one of the towns outside of Simferopol along the railway line. His salary was fifteen rubles a month plus room and board, which was raised to twenty rubles after some time. This was sufficient for him to cover his expenses and buy his own clothes. My expenses dropped then, but that did not last long. People started to suggest suitable matches for him, so it was necessary for him to travel to meet the proposed parties. His salary was now no longer sufficient, particularly after he became engaged and had to buy clothes for the wedding. So I had to pitch in. I borrowed over 200 rubles, since I had to purchase clothes for myself, my wife, and my daughter Nekhamele. He received a dowry totaling 200 rubles, which only sufficed to pay for the wedding expenses and to buy some gifts for the bride-to-be. So the additional costs fell on my shoulders. I was left with a debt of 200 rubles, but at least we were fortunate to have married off our dear son.[15]

---

11 The author did not want to marry off Isruel at that point only for him to be conscripted later and separated from his family for six years, as was compulsory at the time.

12 Isruel's January 1906 certification of his brother Refuel as a *shoykhet* (see Appendix C3, p. 816) indicates that he had been a *shoykhet* for seventeen years, i.e., since about 1889.

13 The original refers to the removed fats as *treybitshkes*, from the Yiddish word *treybern*. The translator has not found this word documented elsewhere.

14 Though actually born January 7, 1873, Isruel's birth was officially recorded as occurring on December 14, 1871 (December 26, 1871 per New Style dating) as mentioned in ch. 21, p. 381. Based on his birth record, he would have had to appear before the conscription board in October-November 1892 (Slutsky, 1975:6).

15 Isruel married Gitl (ca. 1875–1968), who was the daughter of Mordkhe Aginsky. One of the volumes of Rabbi Khayim Khizkiyahu Medini's *Sdei Khemed* (1896:[5]) lists Mordkhe among its pre-subscribers and mentions that he was a *shoykhet* in Feodosiya. The metrical records of Feodosiya indicate that they were married on September 9, 1894 (September 21, 1894 per New Style dating) and that Gitl was nineteen years old. However, according to a letter written by Isruel on August 28, 1939 (see Appendix B3, p. 807), they were actually married a week earlier—on the 13th of *Elul* (September 14, 1894 per New Style dating). Isruel's memory was presumably more accurate than the marriage record, since people gave

With bitter hearts, we wept plenty over the fate of our son. He had married into a family full of sick people: the mother was paralyzed and had been bedridden for a number of years; one of her sisters suffered from consumption; and one of her brothers looked more dead than alive. The bride-to-be, so thin and pale, was apparently not too healthy either. The father appeared to be the strong one among them. When the mother of the groom-to-be took a look at this robust bunch, she started to wring her hands in despair, but there was nothing she could do. She remained as helpless as she had been when she first learned of the ill health of the bride-to-be. After her son's engagement, when she learned that the bride-to-be was ill (she was not yet aware of all the sickness in the family), she was anguished and appealed to her son, "They say that with a healthy head you should not crawl into a sickbed.'" He refused to listen, but she kept belaboring the point, day in and day out. Finally, one day when I was present, she became insistent that he break the engagement. When she realized that he would not listen under any circumstances, she started to beat her hands against her chest and with a thundering shout said "*Oy*, I've lost my child, my Srulikl," and she fell down in a dead faint.

I calmed her down and explained to her that one cannot interfere like that when it comes to a match. I said, "Don't you realize it's God's will. He wants to marry only this girl. She's certainly his predestined spouse, and one shouldn't tamper with something predestined. Those who prevent the predestined are swept away, God forbid. So protect your life if it's dear to you." After I admonished her like that, she did not say one word and never spoke to our son about the matter again. In any event, the marriage took place, thank God, and both he and his wife are alive and well. May they both live together to a ripe old age. By marrying, though, he had actually ruined his mother's health. Her beating her chest before the wedding had affected her heart and she became ill, though she had been a healthy woman until then. Later I will discuss her illness in general and her bitter end.

After returning from the wedding and being in debt, we began to think about the future of our two older boys, Yosele and Yankele. Yosele was already fourteen years old and Yankele was twelve. They were two fine children who could read and write.[16] Of course, they obviously had a firm knowledge of *Tanakh*, and they were even able to study the Talmud independently. But what

---

little thought at that time to the exactness of government records. Since his oldest child was born in 1899 in Feodosiya, Isruel was apparently working as one of at least two *shokhtim* in Feodosiya, in addition to being a cantor, by that time.

16 The author is referring to their being able to read and write Russian. They would have known how to read and write Yiddish at an early age.

type of trades would they learn? We were not able to support them as students. After all, we had our daughter Nekhame, may she live and be well, who was maturing, and it was time to start thinking about a match for her.[17] So we decided that our sons would each learn a trade, which is what we arranged. We apprenticed Yosele to a cabinetmaker in Simferopol for three years. He would be provided with food, but his clothing remained my responsibility. Yosele was a quick learner, and the artisans were greatly impressed with his wonderful work. A year later, we apprenticed Yankele to a tinsmith, but his employer treated him badly and he suffered quite a bit.[18] I then apprenticed him to someone who was more respectable and an artisan of a higher caliber. He promised him sixty rubles for his third year of work. All was going well.

We shed plenty of tears before making the decision to turn our children, who would have made fine Torah scholars, into artisans.[19] I know that you will ask, "As long as you were going to turn them into artisans, why did you choose such coarse trades?" I preferred these because those in the finer crafts, such as jewelers and watchmakers, had to also work on *Shobes*, but cabinetmakers and tinsmiths never worked on *Shobes*. In addition, carpentry and metalwork can be developed into commercial enterprises. A cabinetmaker can become the owner of a furniture warehouse, meaning that he can hire other cabinetmakers to do the work and then sell ready-made furniture. A tinsmith can do the same thing; he can open a store selling all types of metal utensils and avoid doing physical labor. With God's help, their lives actually worked out that way; the plans we had in mind for them came to fruition and they attained commercial independence and a degree of prosperity.

So let us now turn to our son Refulikl. We had already worked out a plan for Yosele, but what were we to do with Refulikl? We realized that he could develop into more than an artisan. An apprenticeship in a craft was clearly not for him, which was obvious to anyone who observed his behavior, his manner of playing with friends, and his joyful nature. We loved him greatly. He liked to make jokes and to be lively. It was a delight to listen to the novel language that he developed at a very young age. All small children speak in a manner unique

17 In Europe, Jewish parents were particularly concerned with marrying off daughters because they had to pay a dowry to the groom and for the wedding expenses.

18 Yankele's apprenticeship was in Melitopol, as mentioned later on p. 555.

19 The author discusses his sisters' refusal to apprentice him to an artisan in ch. 9, p. 179. Among many learned and middleclass families, having an artisan in the family was a source of embarrassment. Elset (1920:5) writes that Jews in Eastern Europe did not generally respect artisans because they were held to be economically weak. For this reason, Goldenshteyn emphasizes below how his sons could eventually utilize these skilled trades to develop themselves commercially.

to children, but they usually only have a few words that are completely different than those of their parents. But the angel Refuel developed his own vocabulary for everything. Isruel-Burekh became fascinated and made a list of Refuel's entire lexicon, which included over 100 words. In short, we decided that when he grew up a little, we would have him educated to be a learned and pious Jew. Even though Nekhamele was already eighteen years old, we figured that God would certainly help us financially.[20] Meanwhile, our expenses for Refulikl were minimal, and our two older single sons were now costing us very little as well. So God would have to help us. The situation was bad, but we were used to it. We just had to make sure that Refulikl would not be turned into an artisan as well. Having settled the issue, we arranged for Refulikl to be sent to my sister Sure in Khashtshevote in Poland, where my son Isruel had spent his early years. We decided that I would travel with him there, so I asked my son Isruel to stand in for me during my absence. Refuel's mother wept bitterly over him, but her determination to turn her son into a God-fearing Jew gave her the strength to resist the need to be near her son.[21]

Shortly after the week following Pesach, I took my son and traveled with him to Khashtshevote. But do not think that the parting of mother and child, their bidding each other farewell, went smoothly. No! Parting was so difficult for them that I thought that he and I would have to remain at home, for even a stone would have melted listening to his mother's weeping. It was impossible to tear her away from him at all, as if she had a premonition that she would never lay eyes upon him again. He wept plenty too. On Sunday of the week of the Torah portion of *Shmini* [*sic*] of 5655,[22] he and I left straight for the ship at Sevastopol. By Monday, we were already in Odessa, where we spent the day. During the day, I was walking in the street with my son when he noticed some beautiful toys for sale. I bought him a toy horse for fifteen *kopeks*. He enjoyed it immensely and played all kinds of games with it. He was extremely happy all day, especially when we traveled by horse and wagon, when he asked to be seated next to the driver. When the horses did not want to pull the wagon uphill, he pulled out his toy horse and handed it to the driver to harness to the wagon to make it easier to pull. We had a good laugh from his joke, and he meanwhile

---

20 Being that Nekhame was eighteen, the year was 1895. The author was concerned about being able to pay for Nekhame's dowry and wedding and for Refuel's yeshiva education out of town.

21 Refuel was sent to Khashtshevote since there were basically no yeshivas in the Crimea.

22 The Torah portion of *Shmini* comprises Leviticus 9:1 to 11:47. Since Sunday of the Torah portion of *Shmini* (April 14, 1895) was in the middle of Pesach when yeshivas were not in session, the author and Refuel likely left the following week—on Sunday, April 21, 1895, of the Torah portion of *Tazriya-Metsora* (Leviticus 12:1 to 15:33).

became distracted and forgot about his home and his mother. On Wednesday night, we arrived in Khashtshevote, and, after spending *Shobes* there with the child, I returned home.

Parting with my son was also extremely difficult for me. My heart was really touched when he kept pleading "*Tote*! Take me home with you." I convinced him that I would be back in a week to take him home, and I also gave him a nice bit of money. He calmed down and asked that his mother return with me. Of course, I promised him that I would do so, and so we parted. My sister, my brother-in-law, and my son just stood there as I traveled off.

Upon returning home, I told my wife everything, including the manner in which I parted from the child. We were both sorry it had to be that way, but we comforted ourselves in knowing that at least he would grow up to be a learned Jew. True, we had turned two of our sons into artisans, but the other two would be Torah scholars.[23] Half would pursue earthly occupations, and the other half would pursue heavenly occupations.[24] We must now suspend our account of Refuel and continue with the story of my family life.

In *Av* 5651, our daughter Ite was born.[25] She was named after my sister Ite. She passed away as a baby, living only until *Nisan* 5652.[26] In the year 5653, God replaced our loss with a newborn daughter, whom we named Miriam.[27] Nonetheless, He took her away from me. She lived only four months.

In *Nisan* 5655, we had a son whom we named Khayem after my grandfather.[28] This child, Khayeml, also did not live for more than four months.[29] From the time of his birth, his mother was very ill and began to feel that she was nearing the end of her days. Once, she called me to her bed and said, "My dear Pinye-Ber, listen to what I'm going to tell you, but don't panic! You know that

---

23 Referring to the author's sons Isruel-Burekh and Refuel.

24 A reference to the Talmud (Beitsa 15b) where it states that one should divide one's time on the holidays: half of one's time should be dedicated to heavenly pursuits (i.e., prayer and Torah study) and the other half to worldly pursuits (i.e., eating, drinking, etc.).

25 According to Ite's birth record, she was born on July 24, 1891 (August 5, 1891 per New Style dating) and the first day of *Rosh-Khoydesh Av*, according to the Hebrew calendar.

26 April 1892.

27 There is a discrepancy in Miriam's birth record. It states that she was born on March 28, 1893 (April 9, 1893 per New Style dating) but gives the date according to the Hebrew calendar as the 20th of *Nisan* (April 6, 1893 per New Style dating). Her surname is misspelled as Goldshteyn in Russian but is spelled correctly in the Hebrew section.

28 According to Khayem's birth record, he was born on March 28, 1895 (April 5, 1895 per New Style dating) and the 11th of *Nisan* according to the Hebrew calendar. His surname is misspelled as Goldshteyn, and the author is listed as being the *moyel*.

29 Khayeml is the diminutive of Khayem.

I won't live much longer!" So I told her, "Stop that foolish talk! How can you permit yourself to utter such words? After all, you're a mother of young children!" She replied, "That doesn't frighten me. I know you're a devoted father and that you'll protect them after my death just as you did when I was alive. Only one thing frightens me—the welfare of our Rukhl. If Rukhele will end up with a stepmother . . ."[30] At this point, her tears made it impossiblefor her to continue, and I began to weep and cry out, "What do you want from me? Why are you destroying my life with your depressing talk?!" You can imagine the numerous tears that I shed upon hearing her talk in such a manner.

In the middle of the winter of the year 5656, my wife became seriously ill.[31] We consulted doctors frequently, and she tried all sorts of medications. She was constantly rallying herself. Whenever her condition would ease up, she would drag herself about. She asked me to take her to the hospital in Simferopol, but I did not do it. I preserved her life by keeping her at home, and she and I continued to persist like this until *Shvues*.[32] At that point, I could no longer stand up to everyone's entreaties to provide her with medical attention, so I said that I would try to bring a doctor from Simferopol; if he could not help her then I would take her to the hospital there.[33] To make a long story short, I brought a doctor, which cost me a nice sum of money, but as it turned out he did not help at all. In the middle of the month of *Sivan*,[34] I rented a wagon and brought her to the Jewish hospital in Simferopol, where they realized that her condition was extremely serious. After she spent two days there, they transferred her to a non-Jewish hospital, because they thought that it was necessary to operate. The operation was performed there and actually went well. When I spoke to my wife after the surgery, she seemed pleased and optimistic. I returned home and sent Nekhamele to be with her. After spending three days with her mother, Nekhamele came home satisfied with her mother's progress. I then paid another visit to my wife. After she updated me on her situation, I left feeling once again pleased and optimistic.

Two days later, I traveled back to see how she was doing, but I was too late. She had passed away before my arrival and was already lying in the morgue. You

---

30 Rukhele is the diminutive of Rukhl.

31 Winter 1895–1896.

32 May 18–19, 1896.

33 Doctors from bigger cities were considered to be much better than the small-town doctors available locally.

34 The end of May 1896.

can imagine my reaction to such terribly shocking news. I kept wondering how it was possible for such a fine soul, such a righteous woman, to die so alone like that. Was it not enough that she departed the world at such a young age and left little orphans behind? Did she also have to die in a non-Jewish hospital with no relatives at her side? Not even I, her faithful husband, was next to her during her last moments. This distressed me immensely, and I wept and mourned bitterly. But, after all, how would that be of any use?! I sent word to my children to come to Simferopol. I had her eulogized by the rabbi,[35] and on Wednesday, the 6th of *Tamuz*,[36] she was laid to rest.[37] "May her soul be bound up in the bond of eternal life."[38]

My Refulikl and Yankele were unfortunately not at their mother's funeral.[39] I sent them telegrams notifying them to say *Kaddish* for their young, devoted mother.

My wife's illness and her death threw me off my feet. I had spent every last *kopek* and remained impoverished and forlorn, with six small children. I still had a daughter whom I now had to marry off. The only one out of the house was Isruel-Burekh, whom my wife had yet managed to marry off. I felt so downtrodden. You can surely understand how dire my situation was.

Three months after her mother's death, people began suggesting suitable matches for Nekhamele, and every one of them was asking for a dowry. Now, even though I had no money, I could not let anyone know. I could not promise a large dowry, but I had to promise something. In any event, with good fortune, one of the many matches came to fruition, and I was obligated to promise 500

---

35 The rabbi of Simferopol was Rabbi Bentsion Kretshmer (aka Kretsmer), who was born in 1870. His maternal uncles were the renowned Talmudic scholars, Rabbi Betsalel ha-Kohen (1820–1878) and Rabbi Shloyme ha-Kohen (1828–1905) of Vilna. In 1895, Kretshmer married the daughter of the late rabbi of Simferopol, Rabbi Bole-Binyomin Demant (ca. 1839–1893) mentioned in ch. 26, p. 490, footnote 31, and then assumed his position (Gotlib, 1912:137; *ha-Melits*, September 5, 1895, p. 4).

36 June 17, 1896. Freyde's Simferopol death record incorrectly states that she died on June 6 (June 18 per New Style dating), which would have been the day after her burial. This error and the one made in the date of her son Isruel's marriage (see p. 543, footnote 15 above) testify to the general lack of accuracy found in Jewish metrical records in Tsarist Russia. Her death record indicates that she died of a small abscess near her kidneys and correctly notes that she was forty-four years old.

37 A 2004 visit to the large, almost barren Jewish cemetery in Simferopol yielded only a few tombstones. Freyde's tombstone was not present.

38 Samuel I 25:29.

39 Refuel was studying in Khashtshevote, and Yankele was in Melitopol.

[*sic*] rubles as the dowry, which had to be paid in full by the wedding date.[40] I postponed the wedding by six months.[41]

Now I had the formidable task of raising this large dowry, outfitting the bride with wedding clothes, and covering the wedding expenses, while I literally did not have even a *kopek* to my name. But if God wills it, anything can happen, and everything falls into place when one trusts in God. And that is precisely what happened. God helped me and took care of everything. Some good people had pity on me and gave me an interest-free loan and were prepared to wait for repayment for a long time. The shops gave me credit and even insisted that I take as much as I needed; they were not afraid because they knew me to be honest. God helped me in another way too; people started to ask me at that time to serve as a *moyel* in Sevastopol. I became quite well-known in that capacity and earned a tidy sum performing circumcisions. This was a new source of income that enabled me to pay off my debts after Nekhamele's wedding.

In any event, God helped me, and I paid the dowry of 500 [*sic*] rubles at the wedding. I spent 600 rubles on clothing, and the wedding expenses were an additional 200 rubles.

We made a magnificent wedding. I brought musicians from Simferopol.[42] After the wedding, I remained 1200 rubles in debt, and, in addition, still owed the groom 100 rubles as part of the dowry.

---

40 The engagement contract indicates that Nekhame became engaged to Menakhem-Mendl Brakhtman (later Brockman in America) of Feodosiya on Saturday night, the 7th of *Shvat* 5657 (January 10, 1897) in Bakhchisaray (see Appendix B1, p. 761). Though the author mentions twice in this chapter (pp. 549, 550) that the dowry was 500 rubles, the engagement contract stipulates that a dowry of 400 rubles had to be paid five days before the wedding.

41 The author originally wrote in the engagement contract (see Appendix B1, pp. 758–761), dated the 7th of *Shvat* 5657 (January 10, 1897), that the wedding was to be held five months later, on the 11th of *Sivan* 5657 (June 11, 1897). Nonetheless, the *ksube* (Jewish marriage contract) indicates that the wedding was actually held six months later, on the 4th of *Tamuz* 5657 (July 4, 1897). Both the original engagement contract (*tenaim*) and the *ksube* are in the possession of Nekhame's granddaughter Cynthia (Brockman) Unterberg.

42 The original *ksube* states that the wedding was held in Bakhchisaray. It is traditional for the wedding to be held in the bride's hometown.

CHAPTER 28

Remarrying and My Children's Departure from Russia, 1896–1910

A New Mother for My Children • My Wife Helps Me Work and Repay My Debts • Yosele Travels Off to America • The Sad News of My Sister Sure's Death • Refulikl Travels Off to the Yeshiva and Is Sent Back Home Ill • Refulikl Travels Off to America and Studies for His Doctorate in Theology • Rukhele Travels to Paris to Study in a University • Shloymele Becomes a Pharmacist

After my Nekhamele's wedding, I no longer had anyone at home to mind the children. So I let others suggest marriage prospects to me so that I could marry upon Nekhamele's departure. Once I realized that I would not be able to find the right woman among the Jews of the Crimea, I decided that I would have to travel to Tiraspol or Bender, meaning that I would return home where they knew me and I knew them. Since I did not find the right person there, God steered me on the correct path and I found the right woman in Odessa. You might think that she appealed to me due to her beauty or wealth, but I am telling you no. Actually, among the prospective matches there were young, beautiful, and rich women who had up to 6,000 rubles in cash. Though my wife had no money and was not beautiful in appearance, she was beautiful in her acts of loving kindness and was good natured. Since I needed a mother for my children, I could not limit myself to women who would be financially sensible options, though I was heavily in debt. I firmly decided to marry only for the children's welfare and not my own. As I am writing my story now, it is already seventeen years since we married,[1] so I can say that a stepmother like her is a rarity.[2] From the day that she met them, my children no longer felt like orphans. She simply treated them as a devoted mother would, and they loved her as a mother. Even now that they are grown, they treat her lovingly as they would their own mother.

Upon first coming to my house, she noticed that all my earnings were being used to pay off my debts, and I did not allow myself to live as I should. Observing this, she began laboring alongside me, went beyond her abilities, and helped repay my debts. Another woman would have protested, but she consoled my bitter heart saying that she would work hard and earn money to help pay off everything as quickly as possible. And that is what she did for three years, until all our debts were paid up. And it was not only debts we had to pay off. Do not forget that I had to pay for Refulikl's expenses in Poland, which also cost a tidy sum. And then there were the household expenses which ended up totaling somewhere between sixty and seventy rubles a month no matter how frugally we lived. We never would have managed solely on my income as *shoykhet* in Bakhchisaray; our income was supplemented nicely, when God willed it, by my earnings from performing circumcisions. Finally, when I became free of all debt, I began to think of myself and my wife. We purchased some new clothes and spruced up the house as it had been entirely neglected, and we began to breathe

---

1 The author's marriage record, held in the State Archives of Odesa Oblast (DOAA), indicates that they married on July 1, 1897 (July 13, 1897 per New Style dating), which was only nine days after his daughter Nekhame's wedding. Hence, it is unlikely that he began to seek a wife in various cities only after Nekhame's wedding, and he probably even started to do so before Nekhame's engagement in June 1897. After all, the author writes on p. 556 below that he visited his son Refuel in Khashtshevote before his wife Freyde's first *yortsayt* in early July 1897, and Odessa is on the way to Khashtshevote. It is interesting to note the haste in which he remarried after Nekhame left home, since she had served as the caregiver for her younger siblings since Freyde's death. Though the author writes here that it has been seventeen years since his remarriage, implying that he was writing these lines in 1914 when he was already in the Land of Israel, he suggests twice later in this chapter (p. 560, footnote 35; p. 564, footnote 53) that he wrote this chapter in 1913 while still in Bakhchisaray; hence he had actually been married sixteen years at this point.

2 Feyge-Rashe was born ca. 1854 in Lithuania. After her mother's death when she was a girl, her father Yitskhok-Dovid Yudelevitsh moved to Odessa where he married Hadassah (nicknamed Udye), apparently leaving Feyge with relatives in Lithuania. Feyge married her first husband Moyshe-Avrom Krezberg (aka Kreyzberg) in about 1873. Their only child Duvid was born that same year in Odessa, and her husband died in 1884. According to a personal interview in 2001 with the author's granddaughter Aliza (Goldenshteyn) Bernfeld, Feyge was called *Mime* Feyge (meaning Aunt Feyge in Yiddish) by the author's older children, which is the common appellation for a stepmother in Yiddish, and simply *Mame* (Mama) by his younger children. For more details about Feyge and her family, see the Appendix A4 (pp. 730–732).

a little easier. In addition, I no longer had any enemies. God had stuffed up the mouths of all my enemies, those who had persecuted me until now, and He gradually began paying them back.

Now I will briefly describe how I needed to support each of my children in order to set them on their feet. There is nothing more to write about Srul-Burekhl and Nekhamale, for they were no longer dependent on me or my support. But I must write something about all that I had to do for the five remaining younger children and how I could not even think about my own situation.

Regarding Yosele, you already know that I apprenticed him to a cabinetmaker for three years. Meanwhile, his three years of apprenticeship ended. A year after his mother's death, he began to earn a small salary, which was better than nothing. I needed to supplement his income by helping him purchase new clothes for *Yontef* and pay for his trips home. I had to go as far as buying him tools, thereby finally turning him into a self-sufficient cabinetmaker. He opened a workshop in Bakhchisaray, and I supported him and maintained him with everything he needed so that he could make something of himself. That was until he had to appear before the conscription board.[3] He was conscripted and sent to serve in Kiev for three years. His appearance at the conscription board and his years in the military cost me a lot of money, besides the anguish it caused me.[4] During his three years of service, I used to send him ten rubles monthly, plus care packages.[5] Eight months before his military service was to end, they wanted to send him to the Far East, to the Russo-Japanese War, so he deserted the army.[6] His desertion and subsequent immigration to America cost me more than 300 rubles, apart from the pain and suffering. From then on, he no longer cost me anything and did not need my support. Upon his arrival in America, he went straight to my nephew, my sister Ite's son Itsye, whom you may remember. There he met Itsye's attractive and eligible daughter. They found favor in each other's eyes and soon married. They live amicably together and are, thank God, wealthy.[7]

---

3 Yosl was conscripted into the Russian army in late 1901, as made clear below.

4 Clearly, the author unsuccessfully tried to bribe officials to exempt his son from military service, as he did with all of his sons.

5 The packages may have consisted of kosher food, which was likely difficult to obtain in the military.

6 The Russo-Japanese War (February 8, 1904–September 5, 1905) was won by Japan and gave Japan power over Korea and Manchuria. See Appendix A2, p. 704, for details regarding Yosl's escape from Tsarist Russia.

7 The manifest of the steamship *Ivernia*, which embarked from Liverpool, England, states that "Joseph Goldenstein" arrived in Boston on February 24, 1905. He joined his first cousin Isaac (Itsl) Goldstein in Portland, Oregon, and married his daughter Ite (Edith) on August 27, 1905. For more about Itsl Goldstein, see Appendix A3, pp. 726–729. In America, Yosl first went by the name of Joseph Goldstein but changed his surname to Goldeen in 1911.

FIGURE 20. A photograph of Pinkhes-Dov Goldenshteyn's son, Yosl (later Joseph Goldeen), while serving in the Tsarist-Russian military in 1904 in Kiev. Courtesy of Lisa Unterberg Delafontaine of Rye Brook, New York.

Here we will leave Yosl and begin discussing Yankl.

You certainly remember that Yankl was apprenticed to a tinsmith in Melitopol. He too finished his apprenticeship a year after his mother's death and came home and began to work here in Bakhchisaray. He had no work here, so he traveled to Simferopol and then left for Sevastopol, where he accepted a position with a fine artisan who did all types of metalwork.[8] He received very low wages, practically those of an apprentice boy, but he was satisfied as long as he was attaining a thorough mastery of his craft. Meanwhile, four or five years passed, and I supplied him with whatever he lacked. Nonetheless, Yankele tried not to impose on me unless he had to, and I never refused him. I continued to help him until it was time for him to become engaged and marry so that he could set up his own workshop and purchase good tools.

When Yankl reported to the military conscription board, it also cost me some money and anguish.[9] After all, how could I have predicted that he would be rejected? He then married, thank God.[10] A year after his marriage, I realized that he would not be able to support a family with his workshop. He was working very hard and barely earning an income. And working in Sevastopol was dangerous because of the military maneuvers being carried out there at that time; Sevastopol was then like an erupting volcano.[11] Out of fear for my son's and daughter-in-law's lives, I encouraged them to immigrate to America to join Yosele in Portland, and they took a liking to the idea. But the lack of money was

---

8 In 1829 the Tsarist government prohibited Jews from residing in Sevastopol, which had become the chief Russian naval base on the Black Sea, and the Jews already living there were forced to leave by 1834. Beginning in 1859, various categories of Jews, including merchants registered in the guilds and artisans, were permitted to live there. By 1897, 3,910 Jews (out of a total population of 52,838) lived in Sevastopol.

9 Born in January 1882, Yankl would likely have reported to the conscription board at age twenty-one in October–November 1903.

10 Yankl married Khine Tarlo, known in Russian as Fanya, on January 7, 1906 (December 25, 1905 per Old Style dating), according to the metrical records of Feodosiya. She and her relatives later spelled their surname as Tarlow in America.

11 Sevastopol was the site of origin of the mutiny of the Black Sea Fleet of 1905, which was part of the failed Russian Revolution of 1905. Pyotr Schmidt, who was lieutenant commander of a destroyer in the Imperial Russian Navy, gave some impassioned revolutionary speeches in October 1905 in Sevastopol that led to his arrest. Protests resulted and the authorities were forced to release him. The unrest continued and spread to more than 2,000 soldiers, port workers, and seamen stationed on shore. In November 1905, the insurgents were joined by the crews of the cruiser *Ochakov* and the battleship *Panteleimon* (formerly known as the *Potemkin*, which was made famous by its crew's rebellion in June 1905 in the midst of the Russo-Japanese War). They started a mutiny of the Black Sea Fleet and appointed Schmidt as their commander. Government forces quickly defeated them and captured Schmidt, who was executed in March 1906.

an issue, so I gave them 300 rubles and, thank God, they traveled to Portland, where they are earning a fine living.[12]

Here we will leave Yankele's story and begin relating Refuel's.

You know that Refulikl was in Khashtshevote with my sister Sure when his mother died. A year after his mother's death and before both Nekhamele's wedding and my own remarriage, I was in Khashtshevote and I saw my dear son Refulikl.[13] At that time he understood little of his situation. He was used to being there and did not miss home. Upon leaving, I left him several *kopeks* as a parting gift. He was happy and proud of his father, but he did not comprehend that he had lost such a devoted mother. I remember that my sister Sure cried profusely upon my departure as if she sensed that she would be seeing me for the last time. Her heavy weeping was unusual, and looking at her, I also had to cry.

A year and three months later, I received the sad news that my sister Sure, the only one of my four sisters I still had left, had died.[14] You can imagine how I wailed. But how would crying and mourning help? You have to console yourself and forgot that which the earth covers over. You have to think about the living and care for them. The dead cannot be brought back to life.

My concern now was what I should do with Refulikl. Bring him home? What would I do with him? He had cost me so much. Would all my efforts go to waste?[15] Meanwhile I decided to put him under the care of my nephew, Duvidl.[16] I had Duvidl study with him and that way the tuition would not fall to an unknown *melomed*. Refulikl could already comprehend a Talmudic text, but I knew that studying long-term under Duvidl would not be good for his advancement since Duvidl had a convoluted method of study. So I sought every pretense to remove my son from his hands. Meanwhile, I heard that in Uman

---

12 The passenger manifest of the steamship *Umbria*, which embarked from Liverpool, indicates that "Jacob and Chiene Goldenstein," residents of Simferopol, arrived in New York City on August 5, 1906. They joined his brother Yosl in Portland, Oregon. Yankl first went by the name of Jacob Goldstein but later changed his surname to Goldeen, as his brother Yosl had, and in the late 1920s started informally using the name James. In the United States, his wife Fanya became known as Fannie.

13 The author's wife Freyde's first *yortsayt* was in early July 1897, Nekhame married on July 4, 1897, and the author remarried on July 13, 1897. Apparently, the author visited Refuel in June 1897. Since the author was in the area of Tiraspol, Bender, and Odessa seeking out a suitable second wife, as mentioned on p. 551 above, he evidently took the opportunity to visit Refuel in Khashtshevote.

14 Sure Vaynberg died in September or October 1898.

15 The author means that, if he brought Refuel back to Bakhchisaray, which was devoid of religious Jewish youth his age, he would abandon his Talmudic studies.

16 Duvidl was son of the author's sister Tsipe and was last mentioned in ch. 22, p. 433.

there was a yeshiva where they studied properly, so I decided to send Duvidl some money right after Pesach to take Refulikl to Uman and bring him to the yeshiva.[17] I also decided not to pay heed to the costs involved since it was worthwhile for him to be in a large city where he would see all types of people. He would not only be seeing fanatical Jews but instead would have the opportunity to see Jews involved in commerce as well. Through this, he would not grow up a fool. And that is what I did; I sent him to Uman.

After Pesach, I sent Duvidl what I owed him along with twenty rubles to cover both the expenses of taking Refulikl to Uman and the tuition to be paid to the directors of the yeshiva. Duvidl brought him to Uman and enrolled him in the yeshiva there. He arrived there on *Rosh-Khoydesh Iyar* 5658.[18] I had asked Duvidl to tell the directors who my son was so that they would be sure to treat him warmly and protect him from adversity.[19] Duvidl took it upon himself to regularly travel to Uman to see how my son was doing. Also, my son began to think for himself, because he had already turned thirteen and could write and complain to me on his own.

He was there for a year, and the poor boy suffered there a lot. Though I used to send them money for his upkeep, they treated him abusively. In *Nisan* 5649, I brought him home.[20] He had grown up nicely to become a typical Polish-Jewish fanatic—and how! He did not want to acknowledge Nekhamele as his sister because she did not cover her hair.[21] He also did not want to acknowledge Yosl and Yankl as his brothers because they shaved with razors.[22] He delighted only in me—and in our house. "*Oy*, my house!" He ran around the yard and was overjoyed: "I'm walking here in my father's yard!" The unfortunate soul was so glad to be in his own home, but his brothers could not tolerate him and he could not tolerate them. He called them heretics, and they called him a Polish-Jewish idiot or accused him of acting holier-than-thou.

---

17 Pesach ended on April 14, 1898.

18 The first day of *Rosh-Khoydesh Iyar* was on Friday, April 22, 1898.

19 The author wanted the directors of the yeshiva to know that Refuel had lost his mother.

20 Refuel was returning home for Pesach (March 26–April 2, 1899), which starts in the middle of the month of *Nisan*.

21 Jewish law requires married women to cover their hair (Ketubot 72a). Nonetheless, at the turn of the nineteenth century, when contact with general society became more frequent, many young Orthodox women stopped covering their hair, embarrassed by their kerchiefs and crude *sheytlekh* (wigs).

22 The Torah (Leviticus 19:27) forbids Jews from shaving their beards with a straight razor. Before the advent of certain halachically permissible electric razors, which enabled one to shave with scissor action, Jews who wanted to remove their beards without transgressing this Biblical prohibition generally used a sulphuric compound in the form of a powder, which served as a depilatory.

He highly regarded his stepmother, whom he was meeting for the first time. She promptly showed him maternal affection, which he reciprocated with his friendship. We both sympathized with him greatly over the hardships he had endured in the yeshiva in Uman and over his having to return to the yeshiva after Pesach to resume his unsettled life of suffering. After all, we could not let him stay in the Crimea. If he did not return to the yeshiva we would lose everything we had invested in him until now and everything would have been a waste. In short, *Yontef* passed quickly and we began to contemplate sending him back. We thought that he would not have any desire to return to such an itinerant lifestyle, particularly since our home was so dear to him. Yet, since he was so religious and Judaism was more important to him than all else, he set his mind on returning. So, on *Rosh-Khoydesh Iyar*[23] we sent him with a Jewish person we knew who was traveling directly to Uman. This time, however, he would not be learning in the yeshiva but with a *melomed*. He did so and studied there for a year. I told him to go to Duvidl in Khashtshevote for Pesach,[24] then return to Uman, and from there leave immediately for Mir where there was a large yeshiva.[25] I had agreed with the visiting fundraiser for the Mirer yeshiva that I would send my son there, and he heartily assured me that he would accept him and keep an eye on him.[26] I had already provided Refuel with enough funds for his expenses.

In brief, on *Rosh-Khoydesh Iyar* 5660[27] my son left for the yeshiva in Mir, where he was accepted as a student. He used to write me nice letters from there. But my son could no longer endure such an itinerant lifestyle, which had a bad effect on his young body, and he began to feel ill. Unexpectedly, I received a letter from the yeshiva that my son was not healthy. The fundraiser also passed through town and gave me a report that my son's health was weak. He had

---

23 April 10–11, 1899.

24 April 14–21, 1900.

25 The renowned Lithuanian-style yeshiva in Mir, Belarus, was founded in 1815. Leadership of the yeshiva was transferred ca. 1900 from Rabbi Avróm Tiktinsky (1854–1931) to Rabbi Elye-Borukh Kamay (1840–1917). After relocating during the First World War and then a number of times during the Second World War, it evolved into several yeshivas, primarily in Jerusalem and Brooklyn (Mirsky, 1956:87–132).

26 Melamed (1922:2:82) mentions that in 1893 the brother of the Mirer yeshiva's fundraiser was Rabbi Yankev-Moyshe Holyand, the rabbi of the Jewish agricultural colony of Mezherich (Ferter Numer in Yiddish) in which Melamed was raised. Since Mezherich (47°37' N, 36°25' E) is located close to the Crimea, perhaps the author and Melamed are referring to the same fundraiser. Rabbi Holyand's surname is known from his obituary, which appeared in *Ha-Melits* (July 14, 1895, p. 2).

27 April 29–30, 1900.

studied there a total of two years, and they sent him home to me in 5662.[28] My son returned home a skeleton—only skin and bones—with no flesh on him. He was a tall, slender young man and as pale as flax. I was thankful that they had pity on him by sending him home to me while he was still alive and while there was still hope to save him. I ran with him straight to the doctor, who immediately told me that it was Refuel's luck that he had come straight home because, if not, he would shortly have contracted consumption. The doctor prescribed lots of fresh air and plenty of milk, which I arranged for him until God helped me and he began to regain color in his face. In this way, he gradually regained his health completely. I have only my wife to thank for this, for it was she who put him on his feet as if he were her own child.

Upon completely recuperating, he began to contend that he wanted to travel to Odessa to learn Russian and secular subjects.[29]

I said with fright, "How can it be? You've cost me so much money which I invested so that you'd grow up to be a pious and religious Jew. And in the end you want to become a heretic?![30]

He replied, "Then what type of a profession can I go into? I look like an idiot to everybody. I don't know a word of Russian, neither spoken nor written! Tell me yourself, *Tote*, how do I appear to the world?

"What on earth do you want?"

"Meanwhile, I want to learn Russian!"

"So you can study with your sister Rukhl. She'll teach you Russian, and you'll teach her Hebrew. That way you'll both learn a language, you Russian and she Hebrew."

He did not want to listen to my suggestion and wanted to leave for Odessa, so I scolded him. I was so overwrought that I burst into tears. He could not bear my pain and had to agree to my suggestion that he would teach Hebrew to Rukhl and she would teach him Russian since she had completed three years

---

28 1902. His entry in *Who's Who in American Jewry, 1926* (1927:207) under the name "Raphael Goldenstein" confirms that Refuel studied in the yeshiva in Uman until 1900, but it differs from the author's account in stating that Refuel studied in Mir until 1903 rather than 1902.

29 By the 1880s, the Jewish community of Odessa was one of the largest in Tsarist Russia and was largely secular with numerous non-religious educational institutions.

30 At that time, the study of secular subjects generally went hand-in-hand with the abandonment of Jewish beliefs and observance. Already by the mid- to late 1890s, the underground dissemination of secular studies and literature of the Jewish Enlightenment movement (Haskalah) was widespread in the yeshiva in Mir, as well as in most Lithuanian-style yeshivas (Etkes & Tikochinski, 2004:218; Rolnick, 1954:72). In a letter from 1972, Refuel's widow, Claire, writes that upon leaving the yeshiva in Mir, he had become a *maskil*, i.e, a follower of the Haskalah (Claire V. Goldenstein Silver letter, June 27, 1972, SC-4028, American Jewish Archives, Cincinnati, Ohio).

of *gimnaziia.*[31] The rest of the time I would study with him the laws of *sh'khita.* My plan now appealed to him, and he began to study Russian with Rukhl, she began to study Hebrew with him, and he diligently took to studying the laws of *sh'khita.* After a short while, he left my tutelage as a fine *shoykhet.* His adeptness at sharpening the slaughtering knife and his *sh'khita* were to be admired. Wherever he went, the rabbis and *shokhtim* gave him certification papers permitting him to slaughter. So my plan was accomplished but, unfortunately, not completely.

Refuel's training as a *shoykhet* lasted two years, and by that time he was already eighteen. He received his certification papers in the months of *Kislev, Teyves,* and *Shvat* of 5664.[32] That same year, after Pesach,[33] the *shoykhet* of Dzhankoi asked me to send my son to cover for him for a month because he had to travel to Lithuania.[34] I sent him there, where he spent an entire month. All the townsmen were delighted with him and wanted to take him as their *shoykhet,* but he decided that he would abandon me and travel to America. He explained to me that immigrating to America would be the best plan for him. There he would obtain the best of positions and would no longer mask his appearance since the *shokhtim* in America dress European style while here in Russia they must masquerade themselves and pretend to be fanatics.[35] I dissuaded him from emigrating, but he then came to me with the argument that I must let him leave, for otherwise I was placing his life in danger.[36] I saw that he was not speaking out

---

31 In Tsarist Russia, a *gimnaziia* was a state-run school generally equivalent to high school and junior college but often including the middle school years. Since the author writes on p. 561 below that Rukhl had finished an additional four grades in 1906 by the age of eighteen, by 1902, at the age of fourteen, she evidently completed the three earlier grades mentioned here.

32 Mid-November 1903 until mid-February 1904. Refuel actually turned eighteen (as mentioned in the previous sentence) in December 1903. At the Klau Library—Hebrew Union College in Cincinnati are two documents certifying Refuel as a *shoykhet*: one dated *Kislev* 5665 (December 1904) from Rabbi Shmuel-Yerukhem Yunovitsh, the rabbi of Sevastopol, who certified his older brother Isruel (ch. 24, p. 490, footnote 31) and the other dated *Teyves* 5666 (January 1906) from his brother Isruel. See Appendix C3 (pp. 814–816) for full translations.

33 Pesach ended that year on April 7, 1904.

34 In 1898, Meyer Fridzaytshik was the *shoykhet* in Dzhankoi, Crimea (*Ha-Melits,* no. 235, November 7, 1898, p. 6). Perhaps he was still the *shoykhet* there in 1904. In Yiddish, Lithuania can also refer to Belarus, northeastern Poland, northern Ukraine, Latvia, or Estonia (see ch. 15, p. 241, footnote 13).

35 *Shokhtim* in Eastern Europe were expected to be the most religious and traditional members of their communities and to have full, untrimmed beards and wear long jackets. See Melamed (1922:1:271–272) who offered to return his slaughtering certification after trimming his beard and donning a short jacket. Note that the author writes "here in Russia"; for indications that he wrote this chapter in 1913 while still in Bakhchisaray before moving to the Land of Israel, see p. 552, footnote 1, and p. 564, footnote 53.

36 The nature of the danger is unclear.

of delirium, so I had a passport made for him, gave him 200 rubles for expenses, and sent him off to America.[37]

Upon arriving in America, he began studying secular subjects.[38] He became well-known throughout America.[39] His photograph was even printed in the periodicals, which he sent me so that I could see it.[40] Afterward, he enrolled in a university to obtain his Doctor of Theology degree and similarly enrolled in the rabbinical seminary to become a *rabiner*.[41] That is what became of my son the *shoykhet* and former yeshiva student. May God help him successfully complete both university divisions, and may God always protect him with success and blessings. May he meet with success wherever he turns.

---

37 "Raphael Goldstein" arrived in New York City on February 15, 1906 on the steamship *Majestic*, which departed from Liverpool, England. He went to live with his brother Yosl (Joseph) in Portland, Oregon. In America, Refuel first went by the name Raphael Goldstein, the same surname used by Yosl. When Yosl changed his name to Goldeen in 1911, their brother Yankl (Jacob) followed suit, but Raphael reverted to Goldenstein.

38 Upon arriving in Portland, Refuel first worked as a clerk until he attained proficiency in English and then attended the Allen Preparatory School from 1909–11.

39 By the time this chapter was written in 1913 (see p. 564, footnote 53 below), Refuel's only known published article was his translation of Count Leo Tolstoy's 1891 essay in praise of the Jewish people entitled "What is a Jew?" (Tolstoy, 1911), which was published a few months after Tolstoy's death. It has been widely reprinted, often without giving credit to its translator.

40 The only known photograph of Refuel published by the time this chapter was written in 1913 appears in "A School for Poor Foreigners" (1907), which describes the night school founded by the National Council of Jewish Women—Portland Section and includes a description of their prized student "Raphael Goldstein" who had become conversant in English in less than a year. For details, see Appendix A2, p. 709.

41 In September 1911, Refuel (Raphael) simultaneously enrolled in the Hebrew Union College (HUC) in Cincinnati, Ohio and in the University of Cincinnati, where he majored in philosophy and minored in German. He was certainly not the first former yeshiva student to enroll there; Masliansky (1924:224) writes that when he visited HUC ca. 1895 he was told that they had some ten students who once studied in the yeshivas in Telzh (now Telsiai, Lithuania) and Volozhin (now Valozhyn, Belarus). Refuel obtained his Bachelor of Arts degree in June 1915 and was conferred with the degree of rabbi in June 1916. The author was apparently under the impression that Refuel was studying to be something like a *rabiner*, which in Tsarist Russia denoted a crown rabbi whose job was to record Jewish vital records and deliver addresses in Russian on various occasions but who lacked any real religious jurisdiction (see ch. 23, p. 464, footnote 44). Though most crown rabbis were not observant of Jewish tradition, some were, and it was certainly not a contradiction for them to have been so. Hebrew Union College, which Refuel attended, was under Reform auspices. It produced no graduates who were traditionalists based on their belief that the Torah was merely divinely inspired and was not God's word. Since the Reform movement had no presence in Tsarist Russia, it is unlikely that the author realized the extent of Reform Judaism's departure from tradition.

FIGURE 21. Pinkhes-Dov Goldenshteyn's three sons and wives in Portland, Oregon, circa 1907. Standing (from left to right): Yosl (Joseph Goldeen) and Yankl (Jacob "James" Goldeen). Sitting: Yosl's wife (and cousin) Edith; Refuel (Raphael Goldenstein); and Yankl's wife Fannie. (Courtesy of Shifra Bernfeld of Petakh-Tikva.)

Regarding my Rukhl, the following occurred. After Refuel's emigration, she traveled to Simferopol where she passed the examinations for four grades, then obtained a certificate of completion, and returned home.[42] I assumed that this put an end to her education, for four grades was enough for a girl from a middle-class family. She rested up until the High Holidays and did nothing.[43] Suddenly, on the second day of *Sukes*,[44] a telegram arrived from Nekhame stating that one of us should come since two of her children had come down with

42 Though the lower grades of *gimnaziia* did not have quotas for Jews, the upper grades did and Rukhl was evidently not admitted. Hence, she completed the course work for the next four grades at home, as an external student, and then presented herself for examination at the age of eighteen in Simferopol after Refuel's emigration in 1906 (Dubnow, 1920:3:29–31,159). At about this time, she started to use the Russian name of Raisa and was generally known by the nickname of Raya.

43 Rosh Hashanah was on September 20–21, 1906, and Yom Kippur was on September 29, 1906.

44 October 5, 1906.

scarlet fever.[45] So Rukhele went there, ran the household, and remained there until the children recuperated.

While in Feodosiya, Rukhl's desire to study was reignited. Since she wanted to graduate from the *gimnaziia* as an external student, she did not want to return home because she knew that I would not allow her to continue her studies.[46] So she remained in Feodosiya the entire winter. When I informed her that I wanted her to return home for Pesach,[47] she told me that she was preparing for her examination and could not afford to spend her time traveling. She asked me to pay her expenses for at least her last two months there. Since I knew that, in any case, I would not be able to have any effect on her, I promised to support her and agreed to pay for her tutors and for whatever else she needed for her examination. Thank God, she passed her exams but returned home suffering greatly from exhaustion like Refulikl had as you may remember. I myself then suffered much from worrying about her until she regained her former strength. She then began to think about studying further, which I in no way wanted to agree to, for what would be the practical outcome of her studying further? I explained to her in a nice way that it could harm her health; I was afraid to take a heavy-handed approach for it might have made matters worse. But she was steadfast in her decision to travel off to study, so I had to agree.

She soon arranged to be accepted at the Petersburg Polytechnical University and she needed to pay the 150-ruble annual tuition in advance. I sent the 150 rubles, and a month later she left to start school.[48] She traveled through Yekaterinoslav, where she stopped off to meet up with my wife's son and daughter-in-law.[49] She planned to spend three days there until all of the female students would assemble and travel together to Petersburg. And that is when my Rukhele became ill and felt quite sick. She quickly went to an acclaimed doctor who listened to her and questioned her, and then told her to travel home. He said that she had always lived in the warm Crimean climate and had become ill in Yekaterinoslav due to the climate change, so how could she travel further

45 Nekhame Brakhtman resided in Feodosiya. By that time, all of her five children had been born and ranged from two to eight years of age.

46 As an external student, Rukhl was not allowed to attend the *gimnaziia*; instead, she studied and was tutored at home and was allowed to take an examination at the *gimnaziia* to pass each grade. Since Rukhl had only completed seven grades out of eight or nine grades in *gimnaziia*, she still had to pass one or two more grades to obtain her diploma. A diploma was necessary for admittance to university.

47 March 30–April 6, 1907.

48 Referring to the Petersburg Polytechnical Institute, which opened for students in 1902. After numerous name changes, it is now called the St. Petersburg State Polytechnical University.

49 Feyge's son was Duvid Kreyzberg who was married to Klara.

north to Petersburg? So he told her that she should travel home! When he saw that words alone would not deter her, he proved his point by telling her the facts about his own daughter: she had not listened to him and went to Petersburg where she died, even though much money was spent trying to cure her. And that was due to the effect that the bad weather had on her. "With you, it will be the same." Naturally, after hearing such words from an acclaimed doctor, she gave in and returned home.

After much effort and pleading, I managed to retrieve the tuition of 150 rubles from their hands. Rukhl now remained at home. This unexpected turn of events pleased me, as I thought that she would not want to study further. But she had her own ideas well entrenched in her mind and did not want to hear of any marriage prospects, which I thought was the most practical idea. She thought it would be more practical to continue studying, if not in Petersburg then in some city abroad where the climate is warm like in the Crimea and where there were no restrictions, no quotas on Jews. In short, she pestered me so much that I had to agree to let her travel to Paris. But since it would cost a lot of money, which I felt was beyond my capabilities, I stipulated that I would support her for one year only and that she had to earn her own way afterward. But I deceived myself because I ended up supporting her for three years straight. She studied in Paris at the Law Faculty, which was expensive to attend.[50] She herself worked very hard in school. Though she was not yet finished, I very much wanted to see her and sent her enough money for her travel expenses. So she returned home for three months upon completing her third year.[51]

During her fourth year, I was not able to help her finish her studies at the Faculty, so her brothers in America sent her living expenses.[52] Also, her younger

---

50 The Paris Law Faculty was one of four faculties comprising the University of Paris; it ceased to exist in 1970.

51 In a postcard postmarked October 20, 1912 in Sevastopol, Rukhl's brother Shloyme writes to their brother Refuel (Raphael) in Cincinnati that Rukhl had already left Tsarist Russia for Paris. (This postcard is among Raphael's papers held by his daughter-in-law Virginia "Ginny" Starr of Grass Valley, California.) Being that Rukhl visited the author in 1912 after three years in France, she evidently first arrived in Paris in 1909. Upon her arrival in Paris, her stepmother Feyge's relative, Salomon Bernstein, help her settle down, according to Rukhl's niece Aliza Bernfeld as heard from her father Shloyme. While in law school, Rukhl met a non-Jew named Pierre Blondin (1891–1948) with whom Rukhl had a son named Boris Blondin on August 21, 1911. Pierre's parents refused to allow him to marry her because she was Jewish. Perhaps Pierre cared for Boris during Rukhl's trip home to Bakhchisaray in 1912. See Appendix A2 (pp. 718–720) for more details regarding Rukhl and Appendix A6 (pp. 746–750) for details regarding Bernstein.

52 Referring to Rukhl's brothers Yosl and Yankl in Portland, Oregon, who were known there as Joseph and Jacob Goldeen.

FIGURE 22. Pinkhes-Dov Goldenshteyn's daughter Rukhl (Raya) Oulianoff (1887–1966) with her son Boris Blondin (1911–2000) in Beynat, France circa 1934. (Courtesy of Shifra Bernfeld of Petakh-Tikva.)

brother Shloymele supported her somewhat, and she will complete her studies and attain her goal this year.[53]

Now all there remains for me to relate is about my youngest child, Shloymele. From childhood, he suffered many bouts of illness. Starting at four years of age, he began to suffer from toothaches. He used to fall ill every month,

53 "This year" is evidently referring to 1913 when the author was still living in Bakhchisaray and before he moved to the Land of Israel. Rukhl never completed her fourth year of law school.

and we endured much from him. When he turned six, he began to grow like all other children. He became healthy and did well in his studies. At seven years of age, he sadly lost his mother. His crying and lamenting for his mother was astonishing. To think that such a small child should understand so well the great tragedy that had befallen him. When his stepmother arrived, he was the first to take a liking to her. She came to love him, and he also loved her. But don't imagine that my second wife had no anguish from him.

On a *Shobes* in the middle of winter, in the month of *Shvat*,[54] after eating the *Shobes* daytime meal, he started to leave the courtyard. I asked him, "Where are you going?" He answered, "I'm going to bring a friend over to play with me. I'm coming right back." And he left. I remained lying down and fell asleep. From my slumber, I seemed to hear the door opening and closing. I opened my eyes and noticed that my Rukhele was walking around the parlor and speaking quietly. I entered the parlor and saw that Shloymele was lying on the sofa, and she was placing wet towels on him. I ran over out of fright and asked what was going on over there. He answered, "Nothing, *Tote.* I fell, so Rukhele is putting cold water on it." I glanced at him and saw that he was horribly pale, that his pants were ripped over his knee, and a piece of his flesh was ripped out. He asked to leave the room to urinate. How frightened I was to see that his urine was not clear but was a thick, dark-red blood. I gave a shout to run for the doctor. Upon the doctor's arrival, he examined him and said that he had received a severe blow when falling on some stones. In brief, he said that we should put ice in the area of his kidneys and on his head, not give him anything to eat, and not move him from his position for three days.

We did not think that he would live, but when a person has years and it is destined for him to live, then everything needed to save his life occurs at the right time. For example, if I had not examined him thoroughly, I would not have known the danger of his illness. Furthermore, if we had not found the doctor at home, a lot of time would have passed until his arrival and every minute was precious. In addition, ice is unobtainable in Bakhchisaray, but it "just happened" that ice was then available.

Like a devoted mother, my wife saved him. Particularly after his recovery, she attended to him when we had to improve his health and strengthen him with good food. The doctors told me that since he was a young child, he would heal. We just needed to make sure that he did not lift anything heavy and did not work hard until he turned thirty. So we did not apprentice him to an artisan. We had him tutored as an external student until he passed the

54 *Shvat* usually occurs in January or February.

examination for four grades of *gimnaziia*.[55] Later, we arranged for him to be an apprentice in a pharmacy and afterward an assistant pharmacist. At that time, he had to appear before the conscription board.[56] He appeared before the board and was conscripted into the military. I certainly cried that such a precious child had to serve in the military, particularly since he was not supposed to do any hard work. On top of that, I could not do anything except pray to God to help me and assist me in rescuing him from the clutches of the antisemitic Russian military. And that is what happened. God showed me a way to rescue him. It cost me more than 300 rubles, but he was discharged, thank God, and never even had to look at a barracks.[57] He returned to his work in the pharmacy and works as an assistant pharmacist until today.[58] Meanwhile, he is completing his third year as an assistant and needs to enroll in a university to study pharmacy. He will then be able to think about marriage after having reached his professional goal in life.

Now that I have precisely described everything regarding my children and the events in their lives, I can return to the continuation of my general life story, which will interest my children and the casual reader.

As you may remember, I already promised you a long time ago to relate the fates of my enemies, how each of them was punished. I will now fulfill this promise, and you will learn their fates in the next chapter.

---

55 For more regarding external students, see p. 563, footnote 46 above.

56 Born in September 1889, Shloyme would have reported to the conscription board in October-November 1909.

57 Nonetheless, Shloyme was later conscripted into the Tsar's army during the First World War where he served as a paramedic, as related by his daughter Aliza Bernfeld in a personal interview in 2001. See Appendix A2, p. 721, for details.

58 When the author wrote this chapter in 1913 (see p. 564, footnote 53 above), Shloyme was working in Simferopol, as indicated by two Russian-language postcards, postmarked January 29, 1913 and November 24, 1913, written by Shloyme to his brother Refuel (Raphael). They are among Raphael's papers held by his daughter-in-law Virginia "Ginny" Starr of Grass Valley, California.

FIGURE 23. Pinkhes-Dov Goldenshteyn and his son Shloyme in 1913 in Simferopol, Crimea, where Shloyme was working as an assistant pharmacist. (Courtesy of Shifra Bernfeld of Petakh-Tikva.)

CHAPTER 29

Preparing to Leave for Palestine, 1910–1914

Selling My Exclusive Slaughtering Rights and Moving to *Erets-Isruel* • The Bitter Fates of My Enemies • Purchasing the Karaite's House for the Jewish Community of Bakhchisaray • Visiting the Apostate Kizilshteyn • Relating an Episode in the Life of the Baal Shem Tov to the Apostate • The Apostate's Return to Righteousness • The Apostate's Purchase of the House from Me to Be Remodeled as a *Mikveh* • He Dies as a Jew

Eighteen years already passed since the harassment against me has come to an end.[1] During this time, I successfully set up all my children with professions and supported them throughout their years of study, as you already know from the story of my life until now. Old age had also begun to creep up on me, and I had to start thinking of how to provide for myself in my later years. I needed to try to find a place that could support a *shoykhet* who could no longer work very hard. After all, Bakhchisaray is the type of city that can provide a *shoykhet* with his morsel of bread only as long as he can work hard. When he can no longer do so, he has nothing because no pension can be expected or had. So I had to take care of and provide for myself in time. I decided to leave Bakhchisaray, sell my exclusive slaughtering rights to an appropriate *shoykhet*, and then travel to the Holy Land, where I would spend my last few years, however many I was destined to have.

For three years I searched for a *shoykhet* to take my place. Finally I found one and sold the slaughtering rights to him for 600 rubles. After thirty-five years

1 The author is evidently referring to the eighteen years prior to 1913 when he arrived in the Land of Israel (see the next footnote). Hence, the harassment finally ended in 1895.

of service, I left Bakhchisaray and came, thank God, to *Erets-Isruel,* for which my heart had always yearned.[2] Thank God, I merited settling in Petakh-Tikva. This section of my autobiography that you are reading is currently being written in Petakh-Tikva, with praise to the Almighty for granting me educated, upright children from whom I derive much pleasure.[3] May it not be disturbed, God forbid. They support me honorably in my old age so that I lack nothing except to serve and praise God for his kindnesses. More than everything else, I am grateful that He has granted me the ability to live in *Erets-Isruel.*

***

Now I will write in detail the fates of all those who persecuted and harassed me. You will see that nothing is forgotten or ignored by God.[4]

First of all, I want to write about S. Mayster, the "religious Jew," who ostensibly assumed the role of a pious Jew and acted as if all of his actions were motivated by the fear of God. He played the greatest part in my persecution, as you already know. God punished him by taking his child, who was only a few years of age. Afterward, a single son of eighteen was also taken from him, then a single daughter of nineteen, and a short time later his wife. Yet, he did not repent at all. He did not have any pleasure from his children, only pain and heartache. He had only one daughter left, and she did not live too badly in Feodosiya. She wanted her father to have some pleasure from her, so she asked him to come enjoy some time with her and her family. And that was the cause of his demise. He left Bakhchisaray, for which he had done so much during his lifetime, only to die elsewhere. He lay in bed a total of three days. According to what I was told, before he died he expressed his remorse and repented for having caused me pain. If it is true, I forgive him.

Regarding his brother-in-law, Medvedye, his wife died leaving him with orphans to take care of. A few years later he himself died.

That Akerman ended up in Feodosiya, where he died and left behind an impoverished widow and spoiled children. His son apostatized to Christianity.

---

2 The author arrived in the Land of Israel on November 30, 1913, after serving for thirty-four years as the *shoykhet* of Bakhchisaray, as mentioned in ch. 30, p. 605.

3 Based on this statement, this is first chapter that the author is writing in the Land of Israel, with the exception of the section regarding the fate of his enemies, as noted on p. 571, footnote 6 below.

4 See the Introduction, pp. 63–66, for a discussion about the author's belief in God's vengeance against his enemies.

Grinblat the tailor also ended up moving to various cities in his search of a livelihood and wound up in the city of Yalta.[5] There his daughter went astray, and his sons were also unrespectable. He lived in great poverty until he died without having derived any pleasure from his children.

Moyshe Kalk was taken to Perekop for a visit. There he desired to bathe in the sea and drowned. His wife was left here a poverty-stricken widow with small children.[6] She turned to me for help, and I supported her and her children as much as possible. His widow was barely able to scrimp by, and she and her children finally had to leave for another city since it was impossible for her to survive here. A nice ending for him . . .

One of their followers was Yerakhmiel Brotsky, the tailor.[7] He and his elderly wife did not live to see even one of their children marry. Three daughters and two sons remained unmarried. One daughter died at the age of thirty, and the remaining two daughters, ages thirty-eight and forty, are still single. The oldest son, who is about fifty, found a non-Jew to be his "bed warmer,"[8] and the other son, aged forty-three, is still unmarried and lives with his parents. The elderly father died now in 5673,[9] and his elderly widow is still alive.

My enemy Reyzner ended up in another city where he died and left behind a young widow and young children. And no remnants remain of many of my other enemies, though it is difficult for me to enumerate them. None of my enemies remained unscathed, except one who had the privilege of continuing to reside in Bakhchisaray.

I will now relate to you about their leader, Reb Leybenyu, the crown rabbi, and the punishment that he incurred.[10] He had a total of four daughters and only one son. One daughter, who was eighteen and unmarried, died after a

---

5 No tailor named Grinblat is mentioned earlier, though a shoemaker named Yosef Grinblat is first mentioned in ch. 32, p. 524.

6 "Here" refers to Bakhchisaray, though on p. 570 above the author writes that he is in in Petakh-Tikva. While still in Bakhchisaray in 1913, the author wrote this long-promised section about his enemies, referred to in his "In Lieu of a Preface" (p. 85), in ch. 22 (p. 428), and twice in ch. 26 (p. 488 and p. 499), though the rest of the chapter was written in Petakh-Tikva. See also footnote 9 below.

7 Unlike the author's other enemies mentioned in this chapter, Brotsky was not mentioned in earlier chapters.

8 *Soykhenes* (*sokhenet* in Modern Hebrew) in the original. Rabbi David Altshuler's classic Biblical commentary, *Metsudat Tsion*, translates this Hebrew word appearing in Kings I 1:2 as a "bed warmer."

9 The Hebrew year of 5673 refers to the period between September 1912 and September 1913, when the author was still residing in Bakhchisaray. This is another indication that the author wrote this section about his enemies while still in Bakhchisaray.

10 Referring to Leyb Volberg.

long illness, may God protect us. He married off his other three daughters, but he had little pleasure from them. His only son also became ill and died, may Heaven protect us. He subsequently sunk into a deep depression and had to be guarded from taking his own life. He used to travel around from one daughter to the other. Eventually, he sold his house and moved out of Bakhchisaray permanently. So, until he dies, he will be away from his hometown.

It appears to me that I have now discussed the punishments from God that were received by my enemies. It is now time to return to my narrative of how I left for *Erets-Isruel*, what I merited to do before leaving Bakhchisaray, and what I accomplished for my community so that they should have an eternal remembrance of me for generations to come. Despite my inability to accomplish this with my own money, it was a great merit for me that I was able to achieve much through my intercession, even though the actual donation was given by someone else. From this episode you will see that one only needs to have a true desire to do good in order for God to help out; things will then be done as one had wished, even though one may not have any riches except a rich desire to do good.

Since I first moved to Bakhchisaray, I had always been distressed that it lacked a good *mikveh*. The *mikveh* had been built in the old style; one had to walk thirty steps downward to reach the water.[11] The *mikveh* itself was old and was about to give way. I always complained to the *gabbaim* and community members that we needed to fix the *mikveh* or build a new one, but I could in no way prevail upon them to do this. So their wives gradually stopped going to the *mikveh* simply because they were afraid that it would cave in. Some women would travel to the *mikveh* in Simferopol or Sevastopol, but they eventually stopped traveling there since one trip to the *mikveh* ended up costing them more than a ruble. Because the situation greatly bothered me, I worked with all my strength to have the *mikveh* repaired and ran to the *gabbaim* and to the community members to impress upon them the importance of the matter.

---

11 A *mikveh* is a pool of rain or well water of at least 200 gallons that is used by married Jewish women to attain ritual purity on a monthly basis. See *Shulkhan Arukh* (*Yoreh Deah* 201:1). Since older *mikvehs* generally used either spring or ground water, it was often necessary to construct steps that descended deep into the ground to reach the water table. With the advent of technology, *mikvehs* were designed using newer methods, including pressure pumps, enabling *mikvehs* to be built closer to ground level (Reiss 1995:25–26,38). The author's son Refuel, aka Raphael Goldenstein (1916:55), writes that the original *mikveh* in Bakhchisaray adjoined the synagogue in the same courtyard, as per Krymchak rule. The synagogue had originally been built by Krymchaks (Deinard, 1879:1:104).

Meanwhile, the Jewish community began to build a *gimnaziia*.[12] Someone had donated both a parcel of land worth 800 rubles to build it on and 800 rubles toward its construction. Taking him as an example, other townsmen also made donations toward this cause. When I approached them to request funds for the repair of the *mikveh*, they replied that presently they could not donate toward this cause but would build a new *mikveh* when the *gimnaziia* was completed.[13]

Upon completion of the *gimnaziia*, I went to them again. They told me that they had debts to repay. Once they were paid off, they would make sure that a *mikveh* was built.

It disturbed me greatly that even the religious wives had stopped using the *mikveh* and had stopped traveling to the out-of-town *mikvehs*. But I could not do anything more. All of a sudden, I heard that a Karaite had turned up; he had inherited a house next to the *shul*.[14] Only a wall separated his house from the *shul* and in his yard was a large, deep well of water, and the house had stores and apartments facing the street.[15] When I heard that this Karaite was seeking someone to purchase his house, I had a glimmer of hope that help might have arrived for the *mikveh*. I quickly ran to the *gabbaim* and to the community members with the suggestion that they should not pass up this opportunity and buy it from him to build a new *mikveh* there. They laughed at me and said, "He's not the only inheritor. That property has a lot of inheritors. In fact, he's not an

---

12 The Jewish community was building its own privately funded Jewish *gimnaziia*, which would not have been sponsored by the state and obviously would not have had any Jewish quotas.

Though not mentioned by the author, the building which housed Bakhchisaray's only synagogue collapsed in 1896, thereby causing its thirty-two Jewish families to hold prayer services in private houses. Only in August 1900 was an impressive stone synagogue completed with funds donated and raised by Tsvi Koltin from former residents both near and far (Keren, 1981:89; Rabinovits, 1900).

13 Their unwillingness to prioritize the building of a functional *mikveh* over the *gimnaziia* testifies to their low level of Jewish observance. As Rabbi Yisrael Meir Kagan (1839–1933), known by the name of his magnum opus as the *Khafets Khayim*, writes that a Jewish community's obligation to build a *mikveh* takes precedence over building a synagogue or purchasing a Torah scroll (Draper, 2016:247). Jewish law even requires a Jewish community to sell its Torah scrolls or synagogue to raise funds for the construction of a *mikveh* (Rabbi M. Feinstein, 1963:82).

14 During the Crimean War (1853–1856), some eighty Karaite families abandoned nearby Chufut-Kale (see ch. 25, p. 509, footnote 25) and settled in Bakhchisaray. In 1872, they finished the construction of an ornate stone synagogue for themselves (Deinard, 1873). By the late 1870s, approximately seventy Karaite families lived in Bakhchisaray. On a visit to Bakhchisaray in 2004, the translator saw this former Karaite synagogue, which is on Sevastopol Street, in a state of abandonment and dilapidation; it had been purchased by Crimean Tatars to be renovated as a mosque.

15 The exact setup is vague. Perhaps the house was actually a building that housed stores and apartments.

inheritor at all; his wife is, and she is only one of a number of inheritors. So how can he sell it and how can anyone buy it from him? You see yourself that no one is buying it from him!" A nice argument. I was barely able to prevail upon them to go over to the notary, a Jew from our community,[16] to have him call the Karaite over so that we could understand exactly what he was selling and find out how he had acquired the power of attorney to sell it.

The Karaite came and showed that he had power of attorney from his wife, the inheritor of the property. He said that although there were other inheritors, he had assumed the responsibility of coming to terms with them, and it was not necessary for the purchaser to have any dealings with them. He suggested that we settle on a price and give him a down payment. He would then give a promissory note, which would be submitted to the circuit court where the house would be sold for the amount that was still owed, and the Karaite would eventually be paid the balance. After he finished talking, the notary expressed his opinion that it could be done but the money that would be given could be at risk. Naturally, the *gabbaim* were hesitant to go ahead with the deal and wanted to leave, but I would in no way allow them to do so until they finished speaking with the Karaite. My arguments in favor of it caused them to lose their patience. They said to me, "Good. Buy it if you think you can. If you believe that divine providence is at play, then hand over your own money and let it be yours! If it goes well, we'll reimburse you." In fact, I decided to do just that, and I soon concluded the transaction with the Karaite. I gave him the down payment of 200 rubles and received from him a promissory note. I later handed it over to a lawyer, agreeing to pay 110 rubles for his services as soon as I received the receipt of the bill of sale from the circuit court. I also drew up an agreement with the Karaite stating that I had purchased the house from him for 1,000 rubles, that he had received 200 rubles as a down payment, and that I would have to pay him the balance within three months. Naturally, everyone ridiculed me and said that the poor *shoykhet* had fixed himself good and could say goodbye to his money. But I was not worried. The only aspect that bothered me was that the entire episode was taking so long.

A year quickly passed and "we heard nothing and no one was responding."[17] The court had not yet put the property up for sale and everyone made fun of me.[18] But that did not bother me because I trusted in the Almighty that I would

---

16 A notary named Markov appears in a list of Bakhchisaray donors to the Jewish Colonial Trust appearing in *Ha-Melits* (November 22, 1900, p. 4).

17 Kings I 18:26.

18 Though the Russian word for "auction" is used in the original, the author is clearly discussing a government sale, since he wrote earlier that he would be the sole buyer (as opposed to the

not come to any harm, God forbid, because I was only an emissary carrying out this *mitzvah*.[19] Also, I had not done it for my own benefit: I had not purchased the house to earn a profit, but only for the sake of the *mitzvah*. Since I had risked my money only for the sake of the *mitzvah*, I would certainly be successful. And that is what happened. The house ended up becoming mine, and I paid the Karaite 700 rubles. Since I had no more money left, I wanted the *gabbaim* to pay me the remaining 300 rubles, which they also did not want to give me.[20] But God helped me out also regarding this, because right then I received in the mail the 300 rubles I needed from the new *shoykhet* for the slaughtering rights.[21] I went straight from the post office to the Karaite to pay him those 300 rubles, and he gave me a document stating that from that day forward he had no claims against me forever more.

Now I needed to start thinking about how I would recuperate my money. I had to travel to *Erets-Isruel*, and I knew quite well that the balance the *gabbaim* had in the community coffers was no more than 200 rubles. And even if they collected contributions from the community members to repay me the 1,150 rubles,[22] wouldn't they still need additional funds with which to build the *mikveh*?[23] I was certain that if I left the country they would not build the *mikveh*. After all, I knew those *gabbaim*. I was afraid that my dream of a new *mikveh* would not be implemented. So I considered a new plan where I would travel around the region and collect contributions. The *gabbaim* laughed at me for suggesting such an idea, but I did not lose heart. I set out on my way and collected a total of ten rubles. I saw from the experience that this plan was not going to work.

I then considered approaching a wealthy Jew named Heftman in Sevastopol who was born in Bakhchisaray.[24] So I took along the two leaders

---

sole bidder) from the court.

19 "Persons sent to perform a *mitzvah* will come to no harm" (Talmud, Pesakhim 8b).

20 The sale price of the house was 1,000 rubles, as stated on p. 574 above. The author paid the Karaite 200 rubles earlier and evidently paid him an additional 500 rubles at this time, so he still owed the Karaite 300 rubles.

21 The author writes on p. 569 above that he was selling the slaughtering rights for 600 rubles. The 300 rubles that he received here from the new *shoykhet* was only part of the total 600 rubles he was to receive.

22 On p. 574 above, the author wrote that he had agreed to pay a down payment of 200 rubles, a 110-ruble lawyer's fee, and 800 rubles afterward, which totals 1,110 rubles—not 1,150 rubles as stated here. Perhaps the 40-ruble difference was for other minor fees that the author did not specify.

23 That is, the community would need additional funds to remodel the house to accommodate a *mikveh*.

24 The Tsarist Russian business directory, *Vsia Rossiia* (1895:593) lists a Pinkhus (son of Yosef) Geftman, a bread subcontractor, as a resident of Sevastopol. Geftman is the Russian pronunciation of Heftman.

of the community and we traveled there. But he did not give me what I had expected. I thought that he would either pay for all the costs involved in building the *mikveh,* which would then be named for him, or pay for rebuilding the courtyard, which we would name for him. That is what I thought, but he thought differently. He gave us a contribution of 100 rubles and his son gave 25. My pleas were of no help; he would not give more. He promised to give more money only if we really needed it once the construction was underway. Since we could do no better than that, we returned home.

The community leaders ridiculed me, "*Nu,* Pinye-Ber, so Heftman has already donated most of the money. Isn't that so?" I replied, "Don't laugh. Meanwhile, he made a nice contribution. If we would only come across several more donors like him, we could already build the *mikveh.* But where can we find them?"

Sometime later, I identified another wealthy man. He lived in Feodosiya and was also born in Bakhchisaray, so I decided to turn to him.[25] I suggested to the community leaders what I wanted to do, and they burst out laughing, "What? You want to turn to that *meshumed* and drag us along? [26] The things you manage to think of! Knock that idea out of your head! He won't help you at all! Go there by yourself and you'll see what he's about!" So, I set off alone to meet with him, and I accomplished even more than I expected. It would now be fitting to elaborate a bit about what happened and relate how it went with him, who he was, and what type of a person he was. I am doing this as an eternal remembrance of Reb Nusn-Nute, the son of Reb Arn Kizilshteyn of Feodosiya.

You know already that he was a native of Bakhchisaray and from a respectable family. He had family spread throughout many cities in the Crimea, including Sevastopol, Simferopol, Melitopol, Feodosiya, and, of course, Bakhchisaray, where practically all of the elders of his family—his older brothers and his sisters—were the finest and most influential community members. It was from this family that this very affluent resident of Feodosiya originated, and I later made him Bakhchisaray's benefactor.

He was an apostate and a usurer, who lived with his wife, who had also apostatized.[27] Of course, his family was ashamed of him. Whenever a conflict ensued between a member of his family and someone else, his relative was immediately bombarded with the words, "Your brother, the apostate." Years

25 This wealthy man, Nute Kizilshteyn, was actually originally from Kishinev. For more details, see p. 594, footnote 65 below.

26 A *meshumed* denotes a Jew who has apostatized, i.e., renounced Judaism for Christianity.

27 Kizilshteyn had no progeny, as is made clear below.

earlier,[28] I unexpectedly heard that the apostate had sent a letter to the Jewish community of Bakhchisaray to ask if they would accept a Torah scroll which he wanted to donate to their *shul*. Since his older brother was the crown rabbi, another brother was the head of the community, and a nephew was the *gabbai*, he thought that his offer would certainly not be declined.[29] A meeting was soon held and a few voted to accept the Torah scroll only if he would donate money along with it, but I disagreed. I felt we should not push him away by demanding money but that we should do quite the opposite—bring him closer to Judaism. Since his heart was drawing him to do a good thing, we had to accept the Torah scroll and draw him closer. Yet his family forbade the community from accepting the Torah scroll. They resented the apostate's suddenly making himself vocal and were upset that he was being spoken about on every street. Wherever you went, you heard people speaking about the apostate, who he was, and what a sullied family the Kizilshteyns were. This caused resentment among the Kizilshteyns.[30] So the apostate withdrew his offer to his birthplace and to his family and approached the Jewish community of Karasubazar. There the *Khakham*, of righteous memory, gave instructions that his Torah scroll should be accepted.[31] Apparently, he agreed with my opinion, meaning that accepting it could lead to his return to Judaism. After all, he agreed to accept the Torah scroll from the apostate with the stipulation that he should first immerse in a *mikveh*, which he hoped would bring him back to Judaism.[32] Of course, the apostate promised him that he would do so, and, in fact, from that time onward he began to make himself heard by making large donations to various Jewish communities, but he always excluded his hated hometown of Bakhchisaray. Time flew by and twenty-three years elapsed.[33] All of his brothers died, as did

---

28 Footnote 33 below explains that the events described apparently occurred in 1890.

29 The 1859 revision list (poll-tax census) of Kishinev shows that Nute (referred to as Nutke Kizelshteyn) was one of six siblings, including a brother named Duvid, who the author tells us was the assistant crown rabbi upon his arrival in Bakhchisaray in 1879 (ch. 23, p. 465). Perhaps the other brother, referred to as the head of the community, is Benyumin, who the author tells us was the kosher-meat tax farmer (ch. 23, p. 470). Nute's nephew is likely referring to Duvid's son Shulem, who is also mentioned in ch. 23, p. 463.

30 Another factor which may have contributed to the refusal of Kizilshteyn's relatives to accept his donation was the rumor that he was involved in unorthodox business practices (Keren 1981:128).

31 Referring to Rabbi Khayim Khizkiyahu Medini (1833–1904). For more about this renowned sage, see ch. 23, p. 483, footnote 7.

32 When an apostate wants to revert to Judaism, he must first immerse in a *mikveh*. See gloss of Rabbi Moshe Iserles (1530–1572), known as the Ramó, on *Shulkhan Arukh* (*Yoreh Deah* 268:12).

33 Since the author makes it clear that he first met the wealthy Kizilshteyn in 1913, the episode involving Rabbi Medini apparently occurred twenty-three years earlier in 1890.

all of his opponents. Over time, things quieted down and the entire episode was forgotten.

I now thought about the matter and inquired about this person. I was told that he was stingy and chased the poor out of his home. There were times when he did good, but you had to catch him at the right time, and just try to guess when he was having one of his good moments. I considered doing as follows: I would first write him a nice letter, send it by registered mail, and request a reply. Since "we heard nothing and no one was responding," I became weary waiting for his response.[34] I then found out from someone that he was still angry at everyone from Bakhchisaray. Since I understood that I would not be able to accomplish anything at all with my letter, I decided to travel to see him.

I arrived in Feodosiya before *Shobes*. I took my son along and went to see him, only to find out that he was asleep.[35] Since it was Friday and was becoming a bit late,[36] I postponed meeting him until Saturday night after *Shobes*. In short, I took along my son and son-in-law after *Havdalah* and we went to see him.[37] Though he did not know me, he knew my son and son-in-law well, so I assumed that he would welcome us as proper guests. We arrived at his house and knocked on the front door. No one opened it. We knocked on the rear door, but no one opened that one either. We saw that the parlor was lit up and Kizilshteyn himself was sitting next to a table. My son-in-law said, "What are we, tramps who have to knock on the back door? Let's go back to the front. We'll ring the bell as long as it takes until someone will open the door." We rang the bell for quite a while until someone opened the door. I think that if I had gone alone, I would never have been allowed in. But since my son and son-in-law were friendly with him, we were allowed inside since it was an embarrassment not to open for them. As we started to walk toward him, we heard him yell in Russian from the parlor, "Guests aren't welcome!" I stood by the threshold of the parlor and greeted him. I said that I had brought regards from his relatives in Bakhchisaray. He gave a shout, "Shut the door! Don't let him enter. I don't accept any guests! Leave! All of you!" And he picked himself up and withdrew deeper into the rooms of the house. Imagine how embarrassed we were. My son and son-in-law shouted, "An apostate remains an apostate!" My son said, "I asked you, *Tote*, not to go to him. I told you that you wouldn't accomplish anything at all. He's a bad person, but you didn't believe me. Now you see to whom you came. Our own embarrassment doesn't bother us, but how can we be silent at your embarrassment!" My

34 Kings I 18:26.

35 Referring to the author's son Isruel-Burekh, the only one of his sons living in Feodosiya.

36 *Shabes* would soon be starting.

37 Referring to the author's son-in-law Mendl Brakhtman who resided in Feodosiya.

son and son-in-law screamed and yelled, their voices were heard throughout the courtyard, and all the neighbors knew what was happening.

By daybreak, the entire city knew of the incident involving Kizilshteyn's expulsion of the Bakhchisarayer *shoykhet* from his home in disgrace, and all the *shoykhet* wanted was a donation for Kizilshteyn's former community. It was not enough that he did not give a donation, but he even chased them out of his home. Already that day, everyone in the entire region knew of the incident. Upon returning home to Bakhchisaray, I was teased and ridiculed whenever I encountered anyone. The newspapers also described the "welcome" I had in Feodosiya. Nonetheless, I did not lose heart, and I did not give up on him. My heart told me that I would ultimately be able to influence him, but it would take patience and work. Of course, if I could have obtained funds for my community in another manner elsewhere, I would not have undertaken to do such a thing because it was as difficult as extracting blood from a "stone," especially when it came to a Kizilshteyn—meaning a "flint stone." But I had no other option and could do no better, though I could sell the house and yield a profit whenever I wanted. I could have sold it for 2,000 rubles, but how could I think about making large profits? Even if I had been given 3,000 rubles for it, I would not have sold it because I had purchased it for the sake of performing a *mitzvah* for the community, as you already know.

Before leaving for Feodosiya where I planned to spend some three months with my children until I left for *Erets-Isruel*,[38] I gave my community a final warning that they had until *Sukes* to raise the funds and reimburse me for the money I had laid out for the house.[39] I warned them that if they did not return my money, I would have to sell the house. I asked them to guarantee that I would have my money by then. I told them that I was agreeable to waiting so that the house would become theirs because I was not interested in making a profit; the *mitzvah* was more precious to me than money. Of course, they all agreed wholeheartedly and promised to raise the money by *Sukes*. But this was a false promise on their part because they had no money then and would have no money by *Sukes*. For how would they be able to raise such an amount of money? And what money would they use later to build the *mikveh*, particularly since I had been the driving force in the entire fundraising campaign and I was leaving them? Just as their promise was false, the warning that I gave them (as mentioned above) was also false, meaning that it was only for appearance's sake. I wanted

---

38 Since the author arrived in the Land of Israel on November 30, 1913 (ch. 30, p. 605), he left Tsarist Russia in late October or early November. Hence, he arrived in Feodosiya three months earlier, in late July or early August.

39 October 16–24, 1913.

them to be afraid and begin thinking that perhaps the *shoykhet* would really sell, thereby prompting them to make every effort to raise the money. Nonetheless, I had firmly decided not to sell under any circumstances and to try in any way possible to raise those funds on my own.

I decided to go to the apostate once again, putting aside my honor and only having the *mitzvah* in mind. It would not be easy to convince such a sinful person to return to righteousness and merit this great *mitzvah*. So I had to accept any difficulties in this matter with love, and I prayed to God that He should not allow Kizilshteyn's sins to prevent him from performing the *mitzvah* in its entirety. I went to the wealthy Kizilshteyn and knocked on his door. One of his domestics soon came out and asked me who I was and what I needed. I replied, "I need to speak with Kizilshteyn himself. I'm the Bakhchisarayer *shoykhet*." He left and returned shortly, allowing me to enter. Kizilshteyn walked toward me so that I would not walk too deeply into the interior of the house, and he remained standing in front of me in the first room.

He asked me, "What do you want from me? Why are you bothering me with your letter and your coming here? You're pestering me for nothing. You won't accomplish anything here with me! Leave me in peace!"

I quickly replied, "Be calm, Kizilshteyn. I didn't come here to pester you, God forbid! I don't want to entangle you in any business dealings. I only want to make your acquaintance. Since I was the *shoykhet* in your place of birth for thirty-five years, I know your entire family even better than you do, and I've heard a lot about you, but I've never met you. So I wanted to meet you now and personally introduce myself. Once we become acquainted, I have something good to tell you."

He looked me over with a cold glare and said, "If so, come over to the table in the parlor and we'll spend some time together."

I answered, "We both have as much time to spend together as you'll permit because I've recently been freed of my position."

"How so?" he asked.

"Yes," I said to him. "I've already moved out of Bakhchisaray and am moving to *Erets-Isruel*. I have children here in Feodosiya, so I came here to bid them farewell. Since I was here anyway, I decided that I'd come meet you and introduce myself, though you . . ." Before I could finish my sentence, he blurted out, "Though I chased you away."

"Yes, yes," I said. "Though you chased me out of your home, I, nonetheless, wanted to show you that Jews don't bear hatred for such nonsense. We know that no one is in complete control of himself, and everything is caused by divine providence. That's how it was destined to be, and you're not to blame. It had to be that way. If you'd permit me, my dear sir, I'd like to tell you a story of the Baal

Shem,[40] which will explain your wrongdoing against me, and so on." He then wholeheartedly asked me to tell him the story and promised to hear it through until its end, though it was long. After all, we had plenty of time. I will relate it here in short, though I told it to him at greater length.

In this story,[41] it happened that the Baal Shem Tov, shortly before his demise, blessed one of his close disciples whom he loved very much that he should be healthy and that he should support himself and his family only through relating stories that he knew about the Baal Shem Tov.[42] How do you

---

40 Rabbi Israel Baal Shem Tov (literally "Master of the Good Name") is also referred to simply as the Baal Shem ("Master of the Name"). A Baal Shem was a rabbi known to perform miracles and heal the sick.

41 This story of the Baal Shem Tov was first published in *Adat Tsadikim* (Lvov, 1865:20–23), which is a collection of Hasidic stories published anonymously by Michael Levi Frumkin (1845–1904). He then reprinted it in 1869 under his own name. Frumkin subsequently changed his surname to Rodkinson. In recent years, there has been some renewed interested in Rodkinson, who later became a controversial figure (see Heller, 2004; Meir, 2016). The minor differences between the author's version and the version in *Adat Tsadikim* are indicated in footnotes. It is unknown whether the author's rendition derives in some way from the version in *Adat Tsadikim* (whether he read it or heard it from others who had read it) or if he heard it from a completely independent source.

In 1907, Rabbi Naftoli Hertz Ehrmann (1907:170–189), under the pseudonym of Judaeus, wrote a historical novel about Rabbi Seckel Loeb Wormser (1768–1847), known as the Baal Shem of Michelstadt (a town in Germany), and included in it a reworked version of this story with Rabbi Wormser in place of the Baal Shem Tov. In fact, many Orthodox-Jewish English readers had known the plot of this story from the English translation of Ehrmann's work, *The Baal Shem of Michelstadt* (1973:133–151). In the published Talmudic commentaries of Rabbi Seckel Loeb Wormser (1983:13), the preface asserts that the stories that Ehrmann relates were actual events in the life of Rabbi Wormser. Nonetheless, Ehrmann (1907:iii) explicitly writes that his book is a work of historical fiction. Ehrmann was not a historian, and his only other published historical work is also clearly historical fiction.

42 The version in *Adat Tsadikim* (1865:20) states that the name of this disciple of the Baal Shem Tov was Yankev and that he was also his *meshores* (personal attendant). It also states that the Baal Shem Tov promised Yankev that he would eventually become rich by relating stories about him, but in the interim he earned a handsome income from relating these stories.

Though the Baal Shem Tov passed away in 1760, the 1764 census of Polish Jewry mentions five people in Mezhbizh identified as "of the Baal Shem," among them a Jankiel Ayzykowicz, i.e., Yankl son of Ayzik. Rosman (1996:110,135,163,167) suggests that Jankiel was referred as such because he was the Baal Shem Tov's "servant or personal assistant" and identifies him as Yekl of Mezhbizh, a disciple of the Baal Shem Tov. Yekl is mentioned several times in *Shivkhei ha-Baal Shem Tov* (Praises of the Baal Shem Tov), the first printed collection (1815) of stories about the Baal Shem Tov (Carelbach, 1990:62,207,237,295). Nonetheless, it seems more logical to suggest that Jankiel mentioned in the 1764 census was one and the same as Yankev the *meshores* mentioned in *Adat Tsadikim* and in *Shivkhei ha-Baal Shem Tov* (Carlebach, 1990:210).

Rosman mistransliterates the name Yekl (a nickname for Yankev) as either "Yakil" or "Yokel," because he did not realize that it is written in *Shivkhei ha-Baal Shem Tov* in Yiddish—not in Hebrew. Though *Shivkhei ha-Baal Shem Tov* was first published in Hebrew, place

like such a means of earning a living? Certainly, he was quite upset but what else could he do? After all, the Rebbe had given him this blessing, and he was not able to speak with the Rebbe about it again since he passed away shortly afterward.[43] In brief, he lived a horrible and impoverished life, wandering from city to city so that he could relate stories of the Baal Shem Tov. He was constantly on the road to new places where his old stories could find new ears that had never heard them before. It always puzzled him why the Baal Shem Tov, who had been so fond of him, had blessed him with such a very difficult means of earning a living. But since he himself was a religious Jew and a fervent Hasid, he believed that it was not for naught and was certainly for his own good.

He continued earning a living like this for some two or three years, until he came to a city where he heard that in a certain country lived a man of means who liked to hear stories of the Baal Shem Tov and who paid a *rendl* for every episode he heard.[44] Upon hearing this news, he felt a glimmer of hope that he would be saved from poverty, and through this wealthy man he would earn a large sum of money which would suffice for his entire life. He just could not believe that it was true, but if it was, he would be saved from poverty; based on the number of stories that he knew, he would be able to earn 500 *rendlekh*.[45] He started to make a lot of inquiries about the wealthy man and he eventually found someone traveling from that city who confirmed the story. He quickly wrote a letter to his wife and children stating that he was making a long trip that could last up to a year because he had to stop in every city along the way to earn enough to cover his expenses, but his trip home should be much quicker after his success there. He also told them of the purpose of his trip, which we are already familiar with.

In sum, he arrived at the city of residence of the wealthy man where he found that everything he had been told was true. In addition, he heard that the wealthy man was a religious, good Jew and maintained a *bes-medresh* in his courtyard where Jews, whom he supported at his own expense, studied Torah. Hearing about all of this caused him great joy. He walked into the wealthy man's courtyard and went straight to the *bes-medresh*. He set down his bag and sat down to rest. Immediately, some people came over, greeted him warmly and asked him where he came from. He answered their questions and told them the purpose of his visit. They were astonished that someone so impoverished

---

names and Yiddish personal names are written in Yiddish, which was stan¬dard practice in Hebrew works printed in Eastern Europe before the Second World War and is still common practice in many Hasidic works.

43 "The Rebbe" refers to the Baal Shem Tov.

44 The version in *Adat Tsadikim* (1865:20) states that the wealthy man lived in Italy. A *rendl* is a ducat, i.e., a gold coin.

45 Plural of *rendl*.

had within himself the strength to endure such a long and perilous journey. Meanwhile, one of them asked him if he had a lot of stories to tell, because he wanted to know how much money the guest was about to earn. How stunned they were upon hearing their strange guest say, "I have at least 500 stories to tell!" "How's that possible?!" they exclaimed. "He's about to earn a fortune!" Envy burned within the first inquirer, who said, "That can't be true. He must be a swindler!" The guest answered innocently, "There's no swindle here, God forbid. It's just that I was with the Baal Shem Tov, of blessed memory, for so many years that I saw and heard my fill . . ."

Luckily, the conversation did not last long since one of them glanced out of the window and noticed that the wealthy man was walking toward the *bes-medresh* to pray. The *bes-medresh* suddenly became silent as everyone sat down at his place, and all rose in his honor when he entered. The guest also rose, and he studied the wealthy man as if he were slightly familiar. The wealthy man stood still and also studied the guest as if he were somewhat familiar. The wealthy man then greeted him and asked, "Where are you from?" The guest replied that he was from Poland and that he was not only a student of the Baal Shem Tov but had been one of his close adherents, and he told him the reason for his visit.[46] That envious inquirer could not control himself and said to the wealthy man, "He says that he has at least 500 stories to relate."[47] Upon hearing that, the wealthy man slapped one hand against the other joyfully and said, "Very good. I've been looking forward to finding such a person for a long time. He'll give me a detailed account of all he knows, and I'll reward him handsomely since I'll now be spared the bother of waiting months and years until someone comes and relates some more stories to me. So, my friend, consider yourself a guest in my house. I'll give you your own private room and you'll eat at my table, which is how you'll stay with me until you finish telling me all of your stories." And that's what happened.

After praying, an attendant came from the wealthy man's house, took the guest's bag, and led him to a beautiful room. All of his clothes were taken, and he was brought fresh, white garments and linen. His own clothes would be returned to him once they were washed. At mealtimes, he was brought food and drink. Similarly, he was brought Jewish books to study. Yet, he became impatient; every minute seemed like a day while waiting to meet the wealthy man.

---

46 As stated later, the guest was from Mezhbizh in Podolia Province (now Medzhybizh, Ukraine) where the Baal Shem Tov lived. Jews used to refer to Podolia also as Poland (see ch. 3, p. 111, footnote 13).

47 The author's account mentions this envious first inquirer, who is not mentioned in the version in *Adat Tsadikim* (1865:20–21).

Three days passed this way, and the wealthy man had neither shown himself nor summoned the guest to see him.

On the fourth day, the wealthy man came by and told his guest that he had not been able to find time to listen to his stories as he was occupied with his business affairs, but he would be free on *Shabes*. He had come to alleviate his guest's astonishment at having been left for three days without being summoned. He now let him know that he would like to hear a story at the Friday-night *Shabes* meal and asked him to prepare a nice story. The guest was very happy and began to prepare a story to relate. He was so excited that he was barely able to survive until Friday. Sitting at the table on Friday night with the entire household and unfamiliar guests, the wealthy man asked him to tell a story. But how terrified and horrible he felt when he wanted to begin speaking: from all of the stories that he knew, he could not recall even a single one. He began to scratch his head and rub his hands together in anguish. The wealthy man noticed his plight and comforted him saying, "Fear or excitement can cause a person to become confused, and one can forget what he wanted to say. But it's all right. Don't torment yourself over it. *Shabes* is yet long. You'll remember the story yet and tell it to us. It can be either tomorrow at the midday meal or at *Shaleshides* in the late afternoon."[48] The guest became even more aggravated as a couple of people began whispering and chuckling among themselves, calling him a swindler who was trying to deceive the wealthy man just so as to have a nice place to stay for a while. At that, everyone left the table, and the guest returned to his room in a state of anguish and feeling deeply embarrassed.

At the table the next day, the wealthy man asked him, "*Nu*? Did you remember anything yet?" "No!" he replied. "To my great distress, I still can't remember a thing!" Everyone laughed, "How's it possible that you can't even remember one story out of all those that you know?" But the wealthy man continued to console the guest, saying that he would remember at *Shaleshides*. Yet, at *Shaleshides*, the same scenario repeated itself. The wealthy man consoled him further while the others mocked him. The envious inquirer was also in attendance at *Shaleshides*, and he was beaming with joy at the guest's downfall. In brief, he mocked the guest and made biting jokes aimed at him, thereby causing others to laugh at him. The guest endured the jokes begrudgingly while taking comfort in the wealthy man's reassurance that he would eventually remember a story of the Baal Shem Tov. But even after *Havdalah*, he still could not remember anything and the wealthy man bade him farewell for the entire

48 *Shaleshides* is the third and last meal on *Shabes* eaten in the late afternoon after *Minkhe* on Saturday.

week, saying that he could not see him until the next *Shabes,* by which time he would certainly recall some episode in the life of the Baal Shem Tov.

The second *Shabes* came and went just as the first *Shabes,* and after *Havdalah,* once again the wealthy man consoled him and bade him farewell until the third *Shabes*. The third *Shabes* came and passed like the first two, and by then everyone was laughing at the guest. One person thought him to be a liar, another assumed he was mad, while a third concluded that he was a swindler. His only consolation was that the wealthy man was not laughing at him; on the contrary, he treated him with great honor. But everything has a limit. By the third *Shabes,* the wealthy man himself had fallen into despair, thinking, "Who knows what's happened to him?" After *Havdalah,* the wealthy man told the guest to leave for home on Tuesday.[49] Though the wealthy man was quite preoccupied with his business affairs, he would be at home on Tuesday and would oblige the guest by listening to him if he recalled anything before leaving. The unfortunate guest sat and bemoaned his bad luck. He did not understand what was happening to him or in what way he had sinned against the Baal Shem Tov which was causing him to now be punished like this. Not only had he suffered greatly in traveling to the wealthy man, but he would now have to endure another year on the road only to return home empty-handed to his impoverished wife and children. Such thoughts consumed him until Tuesday, by which time he had failed to recall anything. The wealthy man gave him a generous donation and bade him farewell.

As soon as the guest left the house, he recalled a story and quickly ran back. The wealthy man was still standing near the window and was gazing regretfully at the guest who was leaving with little more than the disgrace he had suffered at the hands of the entire household. Upon noticing his guest hastily returning, the wealthy man ran toward him and asked, "What's happening? What did you forget?"

The guest yelled, "No, no, my merciful master, I actually remembered a story! I want to tell it to you. So please hear me out so that I would have at least earned something while I was with you!"

"Yes, yes," said the wealthy man. "Good. Come inside upstairs and we'll hear your story!"

The guest entered the house, put down his bag, and accompanied the wealthy man into a room where he began to tell the story that he remembered:

---

49 In the version in *Adat Tsadikim* (1865:21) the guest decides on his own to leave on Saturday night, and the wealthy man asks him to stay at least until Tuesday.

Once on a Saturday night after *Shabes* and *Havdalah,* the Rebbe called for the horses to be harnessed.[50] He gathered together his disciples, including myself, and told us to be seated on the wagon. The Rebbe sat down in the first seat, and we sat around him as we were accustomed to do. He told Oleksiy to drive the horses hard and to travel quickly. We soon realized that he was going to utilize his gift of miraculously shortening the route because of the urgency of the journey, and that is what happened. With the rise of the morning star, we arrived at a big city which was very beautiful, large, and wealthy.[51] I don't know the name of the city to this day, but I do know that the city was in a far-off country, hundreds of miles from Poland. In short, the horses stopped next to a gate.[52] The Rebbe asked for the gate to be knocked upon so that it should be opened, but no one answered. The Rebbe asked for it to be knocked upon again, and we were asked by one of the inhabitants, "Who's there? What could Jews need now at such an awful time when we're all in danger?" But we pleaded with them until they opened the gate. After driving the wagon into the courtyard, we quickly entered the house. The members of the household were amazed that we had come there. They looked us over from head to toe. They asked us from where we had come, and how astonished they were when they heard that we were from Poland!

"Were you on the road a long time?"

"Only since right after *Havdalah,*" we answered.

They suspected us of lying, God forbid. They said, "So go to sleep. It has to be so quiet that no one can be heard talking. If not, we'll all be in danger!"

"What's going on?"

They replied, "Tonight is the night before the first day of Easter, the day in which they celebrate the resurrection of the founder of their religion.[53] For that reason, no Jew should appear

50 *Adat Tsadikim* (1865:22) states that this story of the Baal Shem Tov occurred some 10 years beforehand, ca. 1753, some seven years before the Baal Shem Tov's death.

51 Oleksiy is the Ukrainian form of Aleksei. Bruder (193-?:1) writes that city to which the Baal Shem Tov traveled was Ger (Góra Kalwaria), Poland.

52 See Nigal (1994:33–49) for a discussion of this phenomenon in Jewish sources.

53 "Tonight" is early Sunday morning, since they arrived just before sunrise. In both the author's version and in the version in *Adat Tsadikim* (1865:21) Easter is referred to as "their Pesach" since Easter uses much of Pesach's symbolism and occurs at the same time of the year. In

on the street. Jews are not safe from being attacked even in their own homes, particularly since the cardinal treats the Jews atrociously. Not only does the cardinal preach the entire night about the evils of the Jews, but a podium is set up in middle of the street where he stands and thunders against the Jews before an angry crowd of some 100,000 gentiles. After such a speech, the masses are apt to attack the Jews, murdering them all, and plundering their homes and stores, and so on." All of this was related tearfully by an elderly Jew of the household. He warned us to lay deathly quiet and still, each person in his own place.

Suddenly the Rebbe, the Baal Shem Tov, called me over and said, "Go over to the cardinal and tell him that he should come to me." Despite the entire household's sadness and fear, they broke out laughing and said, "How can you possibly commit such madness?! This has to be the idea of a lunatic." Yet I knew with whom I was speaking and who was sending me. I understood that this was a holy mission and said that I was prepared to go but did not know the way to the cardinal nor did I know his language. The Baal Shem Tov replied, "Take my cane in your hand. Go immediately and speak the language you know."

A cry arose in the house, "How can it be?! Where are you sending him? We're all doomed! If we let you leave, the wrath of the masses will pour out on all the Jews! We won't let you out of the house under any circumstances!" But the Baal Shem Tov calmed them. He told them that it would not cause them any harm, and, on the contrary, it would be of great benefit to the Jews.

I took the Rebbe's cane and immediately left the house; the cane carried me through the air.[54] I was soon near the cardinal. He was sitting on his armchair and was preparing to deliver his venomous speech. At first, he was quite frightened when he noticed that a stranger, especially a Jew, was in his room. I greeted him and told him that the Baal Shem Tov was summon-

---

addition, the word for Easter in many languages is derived from the Hebrew word Pesach, e.g., *Pascha* in Latin, *Paskha* in Russian. The story refers to the "first day of Easter" since Easter Sunday starts both an eight-day period often called the Octave of Easter and a fifty-day period called Eastertide.

54 The version in *Adat Tsadikim* (1865:22) makes no mention of a cane or of him being carried through the air.

ing him and was asking him to come immediately. I spoke to him in common Yiddish, and he wondered how I had been let through the large crowd awaiting him outside and how none of his attendants had noticed or stopped this wretched Jew's entry or notified him that such a contemptible person was requesting entry. For these reasons, the cardinal understood that it was the Baal Shem Tov who had sent for him and who had made it possible for his messenger to enter unnoticed.

After contemplating this for a while, the cardinal answered me, "Go tell your Rebbe that I can't come now. In short, he should forgive me that I can't fulfill his request immediately because I need to deliver a speech to the crowd that is awaiting me but tell him that I'll join him in four hours." I returned quickly to the house. When they noticed that I had returned safely, they realized who the Rebbe was and they were much more relaxed. They now considered the Rebbe to be holy and capable of accomplishing wonders and held him in high esteem. Upon my relating the cardinal's message to the Rebbe, he told me to immediately return and tell him that he should come right away or else the consequences would be grave. This time, they did not cause a commotion; they remained quietly seated and just marveled at how the Rebbe's mission was being carried out. I left immediately to go to the cardinal a second time.

When I arrived, the cardinal was standing on the podium surrounded by various priests, bishops, and important government figures. Around the podium stood a crowd of tens of thousands of people who had come to hear his speech. It had already been publicized a month in advance together with the topics he would be addressing in his speech on the first day of Easter. Upon noticing me, the cardinal began to feel ill and had to sit himself down in an armchair. I related the Rebbe's words, and he said, "Can't you see for yourself what's going on here! How can I leave?"

I replied, "You can leave here if you want to. Going to the Rebbe won't last long. Postpone your speech for ten minutes, and another priest can speak in the meantime."

He replied, "How can I leave? They'll see where I'm going!"

I said, "Grasp onto the cane that I'm holding, and no one will notice you. I'll also bring you back like that." The cardinal

> agreed, and we soon arrived at the house where the Rebbe was. The Rebbe quickly took him into a separate room where they spent several minutes together. The Rebbe then told me to escort him back to his place, which I did, and I then returned speedily to the Baal Shem Tov. The Rebbe promptly requested that the horses be harnessed, and we rode off. By nightfall, we were at the Rebbe's house in Mezhbizh."

The guest concluded, "That's all I know of the story. Until today, I don't know what happened later to the cardinal, whether he delivered his speech, and whether Jews were harmed as a result of his speech. I don't know the name of the cardinal, the name of the city, the name of the country that it was in, under what circumstances he was forced to listen to the Rebbe and had to go to him, or what the Rebbe told him in those few minutes. I only know half a story, and I can't tell you the rest because I don't know!"

"I've waited so long to hear this story but have not merited to do so until this very day!" exclaimed the wealthy man jubilantly. "And now that I've merited hearing this story from you, you can remain here forever. I'll send for your family who can come here at my expense, and I'll support you forever. And if you don't like this suggestion, I can make you wealthy so that you'll be able to make a living at home in Poland.[55] Now I'll tell you the other half of the story, the half that you don't know."

> I was born a Jew in Poland. I left my parents and set out on a bad course in life and became an apostate. The Jesuits taught me and implanted in me a hatred toward my Jewish brothers. I became a rabid enemy of the Jews, and I rose higher and higher within the Church hierarchy until I became a cardinal. To make a long story short, I was sleeping in my bedroom one night when an elderly Jew appeared to me in my dream and said to me, "You *meshumed*! Stand up and come with me right away!" I was quite startled and woke up. I crossed myself and fell back asleep. But the elderly man reappeared and called me once again. I now awoke with a scream, which my attendants heard. They quickly came over in fright and asked, "What's the matter?" I calmed them, and they left. I began to contemplate what was happen-

55 The author writes "*makhn a lebn*" (making a living), an English expression translated into Yiddish, which he also uses twice at the very end of ch. 34. He probably learned this expression from his children's letters from America.

> ing to me. Who was that elderly man? What does a *meshumed* mean? And where was he calling me to go? I was lying down and thinking when the elderly man approached again. He began to repeat what he had said earlier and then threw himself on me. I began to scream in terror, and my attendants ran in with the same question, "What's the matter?" I did not sleep the remainder of the night. During the day, I kept thinking about my dream of the previous night and tried to contemplate all its details. Since I had slept so little, I lay down to sleep during the day. As soon as I dozed off, I noticed that the elderly man was entering alongside a distinguished-looking Jew. The elderly Jew pointed at me and said, "There! That's my 'precious' grandson, the *meshumed*, who causes me to suffer so much disgrace!" The other person replied, "It's not so bad. He can repair everything. He can return to being a Jew and can still do much good for other Jews."

Upon hearing these words, the repentant wealthy man of Feodosiya suddenly interrupted and said, "*Oy*! It also happened to me that way! I returned to being a Jew through a dream!" Noticing that I had hit the mark with my story, I did not let him interrupt me and said to him, "It would be better for you to listen to this story. Afterward, you can tell me about yourself." He agreed and said to me, "*Nu*, continue."

> My elderly grandfather said to the other person, "Rebbe, help me return him to righteousness. If not, I'll choke him and be completely rid of him." The other person responded, "That's no accomplishment! His death won't be of use to you. But if he continues to live and returns to Judaism, he could do much good. Since he's quite wealthy, he can give a lot of charity and do many acts of loving kindness, thereby still bringing you much honor in the World of Truth."[56] As they were speaking, they turned to me and said, "We've decided that you have to choose. You have one of two options: either you depart this world now or you return to being a Jew now!" I said that I'd think about it. My grandfather didn't consent to my postponement, but the other person, whom he called Rebbe, did and said to me, "Let it be as you say. We're giving you a period of a month, and then we need

---

56 Referring to the "World to Come," the spiritual world following death.

a proper answer—yes or no!" I asked who the Rebbe was and whether he was a relative, a member of our family. My grandfather replied, "No, he's the holy Baal Shem of Mezhbizh.[57] He's a friend of all Jews and wants all sinful Jews to repent. I was close to him when I was alive. With his help, I attained a high spiritual level in the World to Come. I asked him to come with me to help me save you from your apostasy because I suffer greatly in the other world from your transgressions. If not for you, I would have reached the highest level there." Upon completing those words, they left and I fell fast asleep.

Upon awaking, I remembered everything. Those two personages stood vividly in front of my eyes, and the dream did not leave my thoughts wherever I went. I thought about it. What should I choose—life or death? Should I die as a *goy* or return to being a Jew and live? Two weeks passed with these thoughts in my mind, and I could not come to a decision. I had sunk so deeply into spiritual impurity that death seemed more agreeable than a return to Judaism. That's how strongly I loathed the Jews. Additionally, I didn't really believe that my life could be harmed, God forbid. I thought that the dream would remain a dream, and I began to rejoice, write, and prepare for Easter so that I could deliver a profound and powerful speech full of hatred and poison against the Jews, which was always my greatest pleasure. But how frightened I was when my elderly grandfather angrily entered the room in the middle of the day and said to me, "You're still thinking about what you should do? You sinful *meshumed*! I'm going to soon bring you to your end!" When I saw him, I fainted. My attendants quickly ran in, revived me, and then left. But my elderly grandfather would not give up. He kept yelling that he was going to finish me off. So I promised him that I would return to Judaism because it was better to be a Jew than to depart from this world. But I asked him to at least leave me be until the first day of Easter, meaning until I delivered my speech; I very much wanted to poison the masses with hatred toward

57 The version in *Adat Tsadikim* (1865:23) states that the cardinal's holy ancestors asked the Baal Shem Tov to save his soul, which was lofty, and the Baal Shem Tov alone then appeared to him in a dream on a daily basis.

> the Jews before I left them and abandoned them forever.[58] But he did not want to consent to my request and said, "I'll send my Rebbe, the Baal Shem Tov, to you. Whatever he decides will be." I replied, "Good, send him. He appears to be a good person, and he'll certainly allow me to deliver my last speech, which took me so much effort to prepare."[59]
>
> Then the Baal Shem Tov came to our city and sent you to fetch me. Upon coming with you to the Baal Shem Tov, he told me that under no circumstances was I to deliver my hateful speech. I was to leave the podium and postpone delivery of the speech for another designated occasion. Over time, I was to sell off my possessions and flee to a distant country where I was to become an observant Jew. He drew up a course of repentance and instructed me what to do with my wealth and how to conduct myself for the rest of my life. He promised me that he would pray to God for my repentance to be accepted. He told me, "God will give you a sign when it has been accepted. When someone will come and tell you your own story, you will know that your repentance has been accepted." That's why when you first came here, I recognized you slightly and was waiting for you to tell me my story. Upon seeing that you could not relate anything at all, I understood that the situation was not so simple and that my sins were causing your loss of memory. I understood that I needed to intensify my efforts to repent and give more charity. During the past three weeks that you spent with me, I continually increased my efforts to completely repent until now when you related the first half of my story. I know now that my repentance has been accepted."

With that ended the story which I told the wealthy, former apostate of Feodosiya. I then said to him, "That's why I don't hold anything against you for the disrespect that you showed me because the time had not yet come for your repentance to be accepted. I understood that you weren't to be blamed for your actions; they were the result of the transgression in which you were

---

58 The version in *Adat Tsadikim* (1865:23) notes that the cardinal very much wanted to incite the masses to murder a Jew.

59 The version in *Adat Tsadikim* (1865:23) mentions the cardinal's dream briefly, which only occurred the night before he was to deliver his speech. In his dream, the cardinal's ancestors plead with the Baal Shem Tov to return the cardinal to Judaism and beseech the cardinal to return to the fold. He agrees but, in the morning, found his evil inclination to be too overpowering. At that point, the Baal Shem Tov arrives in town and sends for him.

steeped in the past. Apparently, you've been purified through the many *mitzvahs* that you have been doing lately. I just heard that you recently paid for the costs of building a new synagogue for the Krymchaks, which is costing you several thousand rubles.[60] Also, you've donated a house to be used as a *Talmud Torah*.[61] All of this has helped your repentance to be accepted."

He replied, "I'm asking you to come over more often because it's a pleasure to spend time with you." At that point, I said goodbye and left satisfied with my first visit to him, though I had not yet presented my request to him and did not know how he would respond to my request. But meanwhile I left satisfied, noticing how strongly my story had affected him. With my story I had hit the nail on the head in identifying how he had returned to Judaism. All of this gave me hope that I would be able to succeed with my request.

Eight days later, I went to see him again, and he welcomed me warmly. The first discussion between us concerned the story of his life, which he related at great length. Since not all of it is of interest, I will relate the parts that will interest the reader.

He became an apostate out of love; he fell in love with a Jewish woman who had apostatized, and she would not consider marrying him unless he did so as well. Since he had been wayward from the time he was a small child and had left home at the age of fifteen or sixteen, apostatizing did not matter to him in the slightest. He related further that his return to Judaism came about through a dream. When his apostatized wife died, he had the greatest regret over his apostasy since she was buried in a non-Jewish cemetery.[62] That experience awoke in him a fear of having to be buried there, so he began to seek a means of returning to Judaism.[63] Meanwhile, he began to reacquaint himself with Jews and to make donations to Jewish institutions.[64] He had spent fifty-seven years

---

60 The Krymchaks are an indigenous Rabbinite Jewish community of the Crimean Peninsula who used to speak their own dialect of Crimean Tatar, a Turkic language. There were two Krymchak synagogues in Feodosiya (Goldenstein 1911:6:55; Keren 1981:50, 211). Perhaps Kizilshteyn funded the building of the second, being that he resided in Feodosiya.

61 In Eastern Europe, a *Talmud Torah* denoted a traditional Jewish elementary school but differed from the privately funded *kheyder* in that it consisted of several grades, was financed by the community, and usually served the children of the poor.

62 Kizilshteyn had also already purchased a plot for himself in the non-Jewish cemetery ("Inyane ha-Yehudim," 1914). Jewish law prescribes that Jews be buried in their own burial grounds.

63 In Tsarist Russia, a Jew who had apostatized to the Russian Orthodox Church was strictly forbidden from reverting back to Judaism and was punishable under the criminal law code (Avrutin, 2010:123; Stanislawski, 1987:189).

64 One of the methods of repentance in Judaism is donating charity according to one's abilities (Maimonides, *Mishne Torah*, Laws of Repentance 2:4).

practicing a non-Jewish religion, until the appearance of a notice stating that an apostate was permitted to return to Judaism.[65] As soon as he spotted the notice, he quickly submitted a petition requesting permission to return to his previous religion. It cost him quite a sizable sum of money and a lot of effort until he received the authorization to do so, and he reverted to Judaism publicly here in Feodosiya, the very place where he had been known until then as an apostate.[66] Nonetheless, he was still enraged at Bakhchisaray, and he was even angrier at his own brothers and family since they did not want to accept the Torah scroll that he had wanted to donate. So from that time onwards he did not want to hear about them, and he distanced himself from them just as they had distanced themselves from him. That was also the reason that he did not declare them as inheritors in his will, and so on. At that, he became quite agitated, and I had to stop him and calm him down by diverting the conversation. This time, I also had to leave without presenting my request which I left for another opportunity.

Two weeks later, I came to him on a Saturday night, after *Shobes*, and I remained there until after midnight. While there, I found an opportune time to broach the subject that I needed to speak to him about. I explained to him that his family's crime against him was not as great as he thought; after all, his family had suffered much disgrace on his account at the hands of his numerous enemies. So it would be only fair to take good care of his family so that everyone would know and believe that he was now really a Jew who was repenting. They would realize that he was seeking to do *mitzvahs* and was giving large charitable donations. Hence, he should see to it to build a new *mikveh* in Bakhchisaray, which would bring honor to his late parents and family members, who had endured great indignities during their lifetimes through him and were still suffering. He became quiet upon hearing my final words.

I said, "Reb Nute, answer me! Is my idea good?"

---

65 A Law of Religious Toleration was passed in Tsarist Russia on April 17, 1905 and included a provision permitting Jews who had apostatized to Christianity to return to Judaism (Stanislawski, 1987:189). The 1859 revision list (poll-tax census) of Kishinev notes that his father "Aron Kizelshteyn" died in 1855 and that Nutke (diminutive for Nute) apostatized from Judaism to Christianity in 1857. The author writes that Nute has lived "fifty-seven years" as a Christian, from 1857 to 1914, yet the author had already moved to the Land of Israel by 1914 and a few inferences in this chapter make it clear that this chapter was written in 1913. Hence, either the year 1857 or the period of "fifty-seven years" is off by one year.

66 Avrutin (2010:124) indicates that a relatively small number (684) of apostatized Jews reverted to Judaism between 1905 until 1912. He attributes these small numbers to their reluctance to lose the privileges that motivated them to apostatize in the first place, such as the right to live outside of the Pale of Settlement and professional and education opportunities. Perhaps the difficulty and expense involved in reverting to Judaism, as mentioned here, were also contributing factors.

He replied, "Yes, your idea is good, but I need to decide whether I want to do it."

I said, "Certainly you have to think about it! For me, it's enough that you're thinking it over, but when can I come back for an answer?"

"In three days."

I thanked him and parted from him amicably.

When I returned three days later to hear his answer, he approached me with the following reply, "Yes! I can purchase the house that you bought to serve as a new *mikveh*. Since you have a ready deed, I'll make the payment in the presence of the notary, have the deed transferred to my name, and donate the house to the Jewish community of Bakhchisaray for them to rebuild as a *mikveh* with their own money, since the house and the lot won't be costing them a thing."

I told him, "Of course, there will be witnesses who'll both sign before the notary that the deed has been transferred to your name and also attest to my receipt of the money. I very much want that those same witnesses should also hear the conditions under which I am selling you my house."

He consented to everything I said, and at a propitious hour we went by carriage to the notary. I was absolutely delighted. I left him sitting at the notary's while I ran to find two witnesses. I brought the rabbi of the city and the *gabbai* of the *shul* in Feodosiya, and the matter was finalized.[67] He and I, as well as the two witnesses, signed our names, and he paid me the money owed me down to the very last coin, meaning 1,125 rubles. Even though I had calculated that I was owed 1,150 rubles, he bargained the price down by 25 rubles.

I was extremely pleased that the matter had finally been completed. All of Feodosiya resounded with my accomplishment. The rabbi and the *gabbai*, as well as everyone else, were amazed. "How's it possible?" they asked. "How were you able to bring this about? We live here, and we couldn't convince him to do anything. While you're at it, persuade him to donate something to us as well since he holds you in such high regard and you're so proficient in such matters!" "Yes," I said, "hopefully God will enable me to influence him to do much more!" We bade each other farewell, and everyone went home.

That same evening, I went over to his house and found him overjoyed at what he had accomplished that day. He asked me, "Did I do a *mitzvah* today?"

I said, "And what a great *mitzvah*! But, Reb Nusn-Nute, you're not finished with that single *mitzvah*. You still have to perform a lot of other *mitzvahs*! After all, you have the potential to do them; you just need a desire to do them."

---

67 Rabbi Dov-Ber Abelson (1870s–1941) served as the rabbi of Feodosiya from at least 1902 until the Nazis murdered him along with the rest of the Jews of Feodosiya in 1941 (Keren, 1981:219, 362; Eisenstadt, 1901:9; Abelson, 1985:16).

That subject led us to discuss his last will and testament. To convince me of the accuracy of his description of its contents, he retrieved his will and read to me all of its clauses. When he finished reading it, he asked me, "*Nu*? How do you like it?"

I replied, "Of course, you'll accomplish much good with it. You've donated your large courtyard as a home for the aged,[68] and you've also donated the remaining part of your estate to serve as its pharmacy and as lodging for its attendants.[69] You've also bequeathed a certain sum of the money in your bank accounts for this home for the aged. You've also provided the Jewish burial society with a large amount of money. But why did you appoint strangers and wealthy people as its trustees when they have little interest in you or in your soul? And even worse, how could you have named the non-Jewish city mayor as a trustee? He'll stain your glory!"

My words left him feeling a bit embarrassed, and he said, "*Nu*! Why not let me hear your ideas!"

I responded, "You can still fix up everything because you're still alive, thank God, though it might cost you some 100 rubles to redo you will. First of all, you should take out the mayor and replace him with a Jew. As for the Jews you included, you should replace them with others who'll be more useful!" He asked, "Who do you have in mind when you say 'others who'll be more useful'?" I said, "Appoint members of your own family to be the trustees, and also add two trustworthy people who aren't related. For example, you need to have six trustees, so make four of them family members and the other two unrelated. They should be paid a monthly salary so that they should always make sure that your fund won't fall to ruin and that your wishes will be implemented exactly as specified in the will. That way they won't let each other steal from it and they will want everything to be arranged properly so that they may continue receiving these needed salaries. That's what you should do. Do as I say, Reb Nute!"

He yelled, "I'll do as you say! I love you as my own father!" With that, he embraced me and gave me a kiss. Naturally, I responded with a kiss. And so we grew to be extremely close friends. He rewrote and revised his will exactly as I

68 Referring to the several buildings in Kizilshteyn's large courtyard (Keren, 1981:128).

69 Kizilshteyn's house and property on Lazaretnaia Street were bequeathed to the Jewish community to establish a Jewish hospital—not a Jewish home for the aged as the author recalls. In the years after the revolution of February 1917, Kizilshteyn's residence housed most Jewish communal institutions in Feodosiya such as a Hebrew and Yiddish library, a soup kitchen, public baths, and a café where literary and musical programs were held. The meeting hall there was used by the Jewish community council, the Jewish scouts, and other Jewish youth groups. In addition, a *shoykhet* was set up in one of the corners of the courtyard ("Inyane ha-Yehudim," 1914; Keren, 1981:138,203–204).

had advised. I will now relate how I also influenced him to include in his new will a donation to the city of his birth, which would serve as an eternal remembrance to him. He was leaving the Jewish community of Feodosiya a valuable estate worth 80,000 rubles and money in the bank totaling 170,000 rubles. At that, I asked him why his own birthplace of Bakhchisaray, which was such a poor Jewish community, should be so disgraced.

He asked, "What do you want from me with your Bakhchisaray?"

I responded, "Everything that I do is only for the benefit of you and your family. After all, you can see that I am not deriving any personal gain from your will. I only want you to merit many *mitzvahs*."

He asked, "But will you be my witness in the World to Come?"

"Yes!" I then said, "If you believe that there's a World to Come, then prepare nourishment for it."

He then signed over a house worth 7,000 or 8,000 rubles to the Jewish community of Bakhchisaray. He asked me, "*Nu*? Still not enough?"

"No!" I replied. "How's it possible that you gave Feodosiya so much money but none to Bakhchisaray?"

"What do you mean 'none'? I just paid you cash for the house, and it will be going to the Jewish community of Bakhchisaray. Secondly, I don't have any more cash. But since my wife's jewelry is here and it's worth some 2,000 rubles, I'll write in my will that it should go to Bakhchisaray and the money from its sale should be used to purchase a Torah scroll, a crown, and other holy objects.[70] *Nu*, are you now satisfied?"

"No," I said. "I want the eight-branched silver candelabrum that you have. You should immediately donate it to the *shul* in Bakhchisaray." With that, I embraced him and gave him a kiss, and he also responded with a kiss.

He said, "How remarkable that you're only thinking about providing for your former community!"

I replied, "I have to think about them because for thirty-five years they provided me with a livelihood. And you have to make amends with the city of your birth, the place where your parents lived, rejoiced, worried, suffered losses, and so on."

With those words, he took the candelabrum and gave it to me, saying, "Take the candelabrum for the *shul*. But let it remain here until tomorrow because I

70 A silver crown is often made to fit over the upper ends of the rollers when the Torah scroll is closed. "Other holy objects" could include a decorative silver breastplate adorning the front of the Torah scroll and a silver pointer used by the reader of the Torah scroll.

want to give it to the goldsmith to inscribe with my name, the date, and that I am donating it to the *shul* in Bakhchisaray. On top of that, I'll even donate half a *pud* of candles."[71] And that's what happened. It was engraved with those words, and his nephew delivered it to the *shul* in Bakhchisaray. Thank God, I achieved all of this; it was much more than I could have ever imagined.

A day before the notary finished preparing the document, I had to leave for *Erets-Isruel*.[72] I had no choice; if I would have delayed my trip for a day, I would have missed my ship and my passport for travel abroad would have also expired. Nonetheless, I had enough time to see to it that Bakhchisaray's spiritual administration completed everything according to my wishes.

Since I saw that my leaving for *Erets-Isruel* made a strong impression upon him, I wanted to bring him here to *Erets-Isruel*, especially since he had asked me to write him from *Erets-Isruel*. Indeed, I did write him. In return, he sent me a letter stating that my wishes regarding all the clauses of his will had been fulfilled, except that the house that he signed over to Bakhchisaray's Jewish community was sold for 7,800 rubles. They received 800 rubles of it in cash, and the remainder would yield 500 rubles annually, which would belong to the Jewish community of Bakhchisaray. I immediately responded with a letter of thanks, and I also described for him life in *Erets-Isruel*. I did not receive a letter in return, which puzzled me. But his silence was soon solved; I was informed that he had died one morning having made a good name for himself and having left a remembrance for generations to come.[73]

---

71 Half a *pud* is equivalent to slightly less than twenty pounds.

72 The author left shortly after *Sukes*, which ended on October 24, 1913, and arrived in the Land of Israel on November 30, 1913 (ch. 30, p. 605).

73 Nusn-Nute Kizilshteyn's Feodosiya death record states that he died on April 15 (April 2 per Old Style dating), 1914, corresponding to the 19th of *Nisan* and that he was seventy-nine years of age, i.e., born ca. 1835. Nonetheless, the 1848 revision list (poll-tax census) of Kishinev explicitly states that Nute was born in 1837, and the 1859 revision list of Kishinev states that Nutke was seventeen in 1854, i.e., born in 1837. His death record notes that he was formerly known as Vasily Ivanovich Kizilshteyn, which was the Russian name he had adopted upon apostatizing. An article in *Ha-Zeman* ("Inyane ha-Yehudim," 1914), and reprinted in Keren (1981:128), states, "In Feodosiya, the wealthy Kizilshteyn left all his possessions, valued at 200,000 rubles, to its Jewish community for the purpose of establishing a [Jewish] hospital and for other charitable purposes. Earlier, Kizilshteyn had accepted the religion of the Russian Orthodox Church and had made donations to their churches. Afterward, he returned to the religion of his ancestors. Although he had prepared a grave for himself in the Christian cemetery, Kizilshteyn was buried in the Jewish cemetery." Since the ruble was worth about $0.50 in 1914, 200,000 rubles in 1914 is equivalent to $3,131,660 in 2024. Tragically, all of his charitable funds, estate, and donations were certainly confiscated by the Soviet authorities only a few short years later.

With that ends the story of Reb Nusn-Nute Kizilshteyn, of blessed memory.

In Petakh-Tikva, I received a letter from the Jewish community of Bakhchisaray in which they thanked me for all of my efforts and informed me that everything had been done in accordance with my wishes and theirs.[74]

74 On a visit to Bakhchisaray in 2004, the translator heard from an elderly Crimean Tatar that the Yevsektsiya, the so-called Jewish section of the Soviet Communist Party, had destroyed the synagogue, *mikveh*, and Jewish cemetery in the 1920s or 1930s. In the decades before the Second World War, the Yevsektsiya systematically obliterated, at lightning speed, all traces of the Jewish faith, including imprisoning and murdering rabbis and *shokhtim* and those who taught Judaism to minors. Such destruction occurred particularly in smaller Jewish communities such as Bakhchisaray where the Yevsektsiya wielded absolute power (Gershuni, 1961). In his autobiography, Chazan (1990:16–174) provides a detailed description of the ruthless tactics used by the Yevsektsiya to eradicate traditional Jewish communal life and its institutions in his native Krasnostav, Ukraine, and the Soviet Union in general.

Part III

ADDENDUM

My Life in *Erets-Isruel*

This description of my life in *Erets-Isruel* is an addendum to the third part of my life story. Here I recount what I endured during the World War in general, particularly during my exile to Kfar-Saba, Hadera, and Haifa, until my return home to Petakh-Tikva, and the miracles that God bestowed upon me. With this addendum, I conclude the story of my life, which is related with gratitude to God for all the goodness that He has done for me. "Blessed be His Name forever, Amen and Amen."[1]

---

1 *Psalms* 89:53.

CHAPTER 30

The World War and the Death of My Second Wife, 1913–1916

Taking Along an Orphaned Niece • Buying a House in Petakh-Tikva • A Visit to Jerusalem, the Western Wall, Rachel's Tomb, Hebron, and the Cave of Machpelah • An Arab Snatches a Purse and Its Money • The World War • The Locust • Letters Stopped Arriving • Money is Removed from the Letters • Working as the *Shoykhet* for a Short Time • My Wife Becomes Ill and Dies

When I arrived in *Erets-Isruel,* I thought that from then on I would be able to live my life calmly and serve God and no longer endure any evil or suffering. I thought that my last few years, however many were destined for me to live, would be spent in peace. So I had hoped, but it was not my fate to live calmly, which you will learn from the following recounting of my life in Palestine from the time of my arrival until this very day.

***

You have already known for a long time that I came to *Erets-Isruel* with my small family: my wife, her elderly stepmother whom we called *Mime,*[1] and also a young, orphaned female relative named Reyzl, whom we had taken along out

1 *Mime* literally means "aunt" in Yiddish. A stepmother is usually called an "aunt" in Yiddish.

FIGURE 24. Right to left: Pinkhes-Dov Goldenshteyn's second wife, Feyge (ca. 1854–1916), her daughter-in-law, Klara Kreyzberg; and her stepmother, Udye Yudelevitsh. Taken in Feodosiya, Crimea, in the early 1910s. Note that Feyge's garments cover her fully and that she is wearing a *sheytl,* as married religious Jewish women do as a sign of modesty. The hair of her stepmother, who was the widow of a religious *maskil,* is partially covered with a loosely knitted kerchief. The hair of her daughter-in-law, who was minimally observant, appears to be completely uncovered. For more about Feyge and her family, see Appendix A4 (pp. 730–732). (Courtesy of Shifra Bernfeld of Petakh-Tikva.)

of pity.[2] We thought that life would be good for us here and that we would be able to marry her off to a young colonist.[3]

We arrived at Jaffa precisely on *Rosh-Khoydesh Kislev* 5674.[4] We suffered a great deal between the time we disembarked until an Arab brought us to a hotel. Some eight days after arriving in Jaffa, we decided to travel to Petakh-Tikva, which we did.[5]

We were overjoyed upon arriving in Petakh-Tikva because we found the colony to be in a fine state. To our eyes, everything shone. Wherever we looked, everything was Jewish—our own houses, orchards, fields, and vineyards. Law and order in the colony was in the hands of the Jews themselves, as though there was no other government.[6] Everything lay in the hands of the Jews. We encountered neither police nor drunks in the streets, and all was calm and quiet. When we came to the *shul*, we found constant study and prayer. When it was time for *Minkhe* and *Marev*, a new *minyan* began every four or five minutes. *Minkhe* started at 2:00 in the afternoon, and *Marev* at nightfall. Starting at 2:00 in the morning, the worshipers arrived and studied until the first light of day, when *Shakhris* began, with a new *minyan* starting every ten to fifteen minutes and continuing on until 10 a.m. The crowd consisted of all sorts of Jews: *Ashkenazim*, *Sephardim*, and Yemenites. Every *minyan* included four or five people who could not understand each other, but all served one Creator of the Universe. When I saw this, my heart filled with joy. I thought that here I

---

2 Reyzl (1898–1962) was the oldest of five children of Leyzer Hershkovits (ca. 1854–ca. 1912), the brother of the author's first wife Freyde. According to a 2002 interview with her son Yosef "Yoske" Grinberg of Petakh-Tikva, the author and his second wife Feyge were very fond of Reyzl, so when she heard that they were moving to Palestine, she asked to be taken along. They agreed and took care of her as if she was their own child. Since Reyzl was illiterate, the author taught her to read the Hebrew prayers from the *sidur*. Reyzl was later known as Shoshana in Hebrew, both names meaning "rose." In 1923, Reyzl's husband Yankl sent for her mother Elke (ca. 1876–1955) and two younger sisters. See Appendix D4 (pp. 824–825) for a genealogical chart of the Hershkovitsh family.

3 Jewish settlers from Europe who immigrated to Palestine to establish new Jewish agricultural settlements (i.e., colonies) outside of the traditional Jewish settlements of Jerusalem, Tiberias, Safed, were called colonists.

4 November 30, 1913. The author's date of immigration to Palestine is substantiated by a Hebrew-language postcard (see Appendix B3, pp. 777–778) sent to him by his son Isruel from Feodosiya dated the 25th of *Teyves* 5674 (January 23, 1914) complaining that he has not heard from him since his arrival two months earlier.

5 The author settled in Petakh-Tikva apparently because his second wife Feyge's close relatives, Rabbi Zev "Volf" Berenshteyn and his wife Rifke-Nekhame, had settled there in 1908, as research has uncovered. Their son was the painter Salomon Bernstein. See Appendix A6 (pp. 746–750) for more details about them.

6 Palestine was under Ottoman Turkish rule from 1516 until 1832, and again from 1840 until 1917.

would no longer endure any suffering, so much so that by Pesach I had, thank God, bought a house and become a Petakh-Tikva colonist equal to all others.[7] I paid 9,000 francs for the house and my children began to send me money every month for living expenses. I thought that this would be the end of the troubles I had endured until now and that we would finally live a quiet life.

I very much wanted to go to Jerusalem to pray at the Western Wall and other holy places there, as well as Rachel's Tomb and the Cave of Machpelah in Hebron before returning home.[8] Yet I lacked the money for such an expense because I had spent my last sou on the house. So I could not be in Jerusalem for Pesach. But when *Shvues* arrived and I saw that I still could not travel due to lack of funds, I borrowed the money for the trip, and I, my wife, and her elderly step-mother traveled to Jerusalem and remained there over the *Yontef* of *Shvues*.[9] We also traveled to Hebron where we visited the Cave of Machpelah. On the way back from Hebron to Jerusalem, we stopped off at the Tomb of the Matriarch Rachel. I did not go anywhere else because I became unwell in Jerusalem, so after that we went straight home. The journey cost me almost ten napoleons.[10]

Almost 800 foreign visitors from all sorts of countries were in Jerusalem for *Shvues*. I cannot describe to you the great joy I had in encountering masses of Jews in the streets going to and from the Western Wall. With the great crowds at the Western Wall, it was almost impossible to push your way through to find a place to stand and pray. Returning from the Western Wall, you immediately enter dark and narrow little streets where all you can see are various Arabs running around and making a wild commotion in order to lure you into buying their goods. The streets continue like that until you reach Jaffa Gate or Shechem Gate, where the Arabs indulge in preying on passers-by and taking their possessions. As we were leaving the Western Wall, an Arab boy grabbed

---

7 Pesach began on April 11, 1914. According to the author's Hebrew ethical will written in 1920 (see Appendix B2, p. 766), the author bought the house at 64 Rothschild Boulevard from Khaym-Moyshe Slor (1859–1946). Slor was the civil engineer who originally laid out the streets of Petakh-Tikva (Engel, 1973:55; Hashavia, 1998:186; Slor, 2002:1–11; Tidhar, 1947:1:307).

8 According to the Bible, six progenitors of the Jewish people are buried in the Cave of Machpelah: Abraham, Sarah, Isaac, Rebecca, Jacob, and Leah. In addition, Adam and Eve are buried there, according to the *Zohar*.

9 *Shvues* occurred on May 31, 1914.

10 A napoleon was a twenty-franc gold coin which originally featured the portrait of Napoleon I. Although the portraits changed with the political changes in France, the twenty-franc gold coin remained in usage until the First World War. Both napoleons and francs were used widely in the Middle East.

the purse containing a few coins from our *Mime*'s hand.[11] She raised a clamor since the purse was dear to her. Naturally, I ran after the fleeing boy, but good people turned me back saying that I dared not go after him because I might be beaten and robbed! "Go back, my fellow Jew! May your minor loss serve as an atonement,"[12] they said, and I turned back. By the time I returned, my wife's elderly *Mime* had calmed down. She had noticed that the Arab boy had discarded the purse after taking the few coins inside when he saw me in pursuit. She was able to then retrieve her purse. After arriving safely at our lodgings, we discussed the miracles that had occurred on our way back from the Western Wall. We then returned to Petakh-Tikva.

Upon arriving home, we were quite overjoyed to have been in Jerusalem and in Hebron, and we thanked and praised God that we had merited to be there. We also visited the area of Bethlehem and the hamlet of Bnei Brak, where we took a good look at everything.[13] We had much pleasure from our trip.

Letters would constantly arrive from our children in Russia, America, and Paris, and also casual letters from friends.[14] Each letter brought us news, and we always had something to write in reply; we were content. We thought that this was how we would spend our few remaining years. That is what we assumed.

But our contentment in the country lasted only from the month of *Kislev* until the end of *Tamuz*.[15] Starting on *Rosh Khoydesh Av*—the very month during which Jews have continually mourned the destruction of the Holy Temple until today—my life began to change and my family and I began to suffer and endure unexpected troubles that are impossible to describe.[16] But I will relate them to you in brief so that you can appreciate my persistence in writing my life story in spite of enduring so much hardship. Yes, I write, but not with ink; I write with

---

11 Since Jewish law forbids the carrying or use of money on *Shabes* or *Yontef* (*Kitsur Shulkhan Arukh* 88:6, 99:1), this visit to the Western Wall evidently occurred on the day after *Shvues*.

12 This Yiddish expression denotes that aggravations can atone for one's sins.

13 Bethlehem is referring to Rachel's Tomb (mentioned on p. 606 above), which is located on the outskirts of Jerusalem. Since the modern-day city of Bnei Brak was founded only in 1924, the author is evidently referring to the Arab village of Ibn Ibrak (now called al-Khayriyya), which is 4.7 miles east of Jaffa. It would have been of interest to him since Rabbi Akiva famously held a *Seder* there, as recounted in the Pesach *Haggadah*.

14 The author's children Isruel, Nekhame Brakhtman, and Shloyme were in Tsarist Russia. His sons Yosl, Yankl, and Refuel (known as Joseph Goldeen, Jacob Goldeen, and Raphael Goldenstein, respectively) were in America. His daughter Rukhl was in Paris. Shloyme, Refuel, and Rukhl were unmarried.

15 From November 30, 1913 until July 23, 1914.

16 *Rosh-Khoydesh Av* occurred on July 24, 1914. It begins a nine-day mourning period in commemoration of the destruction of the first and second Holy Temples in Jerusalem and other national calamities that occurred to the Jewish people.

the blood that pours from my heart and the tears that flow from my eyes. I would rather not write, but I want my dear children to know what their father endured, so that they can, in turn, tell their children how God always helped their parents out of all their troubles and gave them the strength to prevail and overcome the bad times and to live to see the good times. May they take a lesson from this that one must never lose faith in God. He who trusts in God is always helped. So it is with the Jewish people and with the individual as well, as it states, "He who has faith in God will be enveloped in kindness."[17]

***

On the 6th of *Av* 5674, when the World War broke out, everyone's hearts were broken, and especially mine.[18] Dark clouds were cast over the lives of all in *Erets-Isruel,* especially over the old, weak Jews in this country whose sole source of support was that which their children sent them to live on or which was sent by strangers. For these people, life was suddenly darkened, and I fell into that same lot.

The first blow struck when I stopped receiving letters. I was used to receiving letters every week from all over the world, but letters started arriving only once every month or two, all opened with half of their contents missing.[19] More than once, while standing at the post office waiting to see if a letter had arrived, I would learn that my wait had been in vain. You can just imagine how many tears I shed, but we tried to console ourselves with the thought that perhaps a letter would arrive with the next mail delivery. And so a long time often passed until we finally received a scrap of a censored letter, yet we would be overjoyed that we had at least recognized the handwriting. But not being able to receive any news even once every six months (as you will read further on) was horribly difficult to bear.

After Turkey entered the World War, foreign goods quickly stopped arriving.[20] As is well known, Turkey had no factories of its own and had to import

17 Psalms 32:10.

18 The 6th of *Av* corresponds to July 29, 1914. Actually, June 28, 1914 was the day that Archduke Franz Ferdinand, the heir to the Austro-Hungarian throne, was assassinated in Sarajevo, Bosnia, resulting in the outbreak of the First World War.

19 The Turks frequently cut out large sections of letters as part of their indiscriminate censorship.

20 Based on the next paragraph, the author is apparently referring to August 1914, when the Ottoman Empire joined the Central Powers (Germany, Austria-Hungary, and Bulgaria) with the signing of the Turko-German Alliance. Turkey formerly entered the First World War on October 28, 1914 with its bombing of Russia's Black Sea ports.

everything, both merchandise and food. When produce stopped arriving, we had to pay higher prices, and everyone tried to prepare for the future by storing as much food as possible.

On the 25th of *Tamuz*,[21] two weeks before the war broke out, I received from my sons in America their monthly stipend of $20 (100 francs) which they had agreed to send me to live on. Who could have imagined that this would be the last money that I would receive and that no more money would be forthcoming? I, naturally, lived life as normal, spent the money, and awaited the next month to receive more. Accordingly, during the first two weeks, I spent about sixty francs on living expenses. So when the war broke out two weeks later and everything became expensive and fear gripped everyone, whoever had money began to hoard whatever kind of food he could. I had only fifty francs to my name, so what could I possibly prepare for the future with that amount? You can well imagine the fear that fell upon us. The fifty francs I owned could only last two weeks, so what would we do afterward? One had to live! We were, after all, four souls! But long live hope, for it strengthened us in believing that the war would not last and would end quickly! We also hoped that, since no fresh, new goods could be imported, neither could any be exported, which would cause everything to be cheap. No white flour was arriving, but we had a lot of bread in the country, even if only black bread, but there was enough and it was not expensive. The same was the case with olive oil; if there was no gas, we would use olive oil.[22] Oranges were not being exported, so we would eat bread and oranges. But none of these hopes came to pass, because God sent a plague of locusts throughout the country, and they destroyed all the vineyards and orchards.[23] Not a single blade of green grass escaped them. Even though the locusts had brought calamity upon the richest landowners, despair did not become rooted in our hearts and we continue to live in hope.

Now that two years have passed since then,[24] you must certainly wonder how I was able to manage when all I had at the start of the war was fifty francs, which was only enough to last me two weeks. And where did I obtain money to live on? This you will learn from my subsequent story.

Hard currency began to become scarce in my home and there was also no one from whom I might borrow, partly because we did not know anyone and

21 July 19, 1914.

22 "Gas" is referring to the kerosene used for lamps (Yakobzon, 1986:54).

23 From February to June 1915, a plague of locusts stripped Petakh-Tikva of almost all vegetation. Despite a herculean effort there to protect their valuable orchards, involving large amounts of money, it was to no avail (Ya'ari, 1929:510–512, Trope, 1949:35–36).

24 The author wrote this chapter and the first section of ch. 31 (pp. 616–619) in the summer of 1916, two years into the First World War.

especially because we were not used to running around asking for loans. Also, the locals were used to charging high rates of interest, even in the good times and particularly during such a terrible time, so I certainly went about worried. Nevertheless, I strengthened myself and hoped to God, thinking that He would certainly help me. Meanwhile, I was not receiving any letters from anyone, so I naturally had to resort to borrowing money. For that purpose, God sent me nothing short of a good person who took a liking to me and loaned me some money with the consideration that repayment would wait until I received remittance from my children. Then, finally, little by little, people began to receive money and letters. So I too waited each day and hoped to receive a letter with money.

Suddenly, on the day after *Yom Kippur*,[25] I received a registered letter from my son Yosef in which he wrote that he was taking the risk of enclosing twenty dollars since he knew that the banks did not want to accept the risk of transferring funds to Palestine. If this succeeded (that is, if we received the money), he wrote that he would do it all the time. Of course, the letter arrived, but the money had been removed in transit. The loss of the money drove away both the joy of hearing from my children and knowing that at least they were alive, thank God. The pain was twofold: I would not have any enjoyment from the money, and my children had undergone an unnecessary loss on my behalf. And now, how could I be helped and when might emerge another opportunity to obtain money? My children would not be sending me any more money until they received notice that I had obtained the twenty dollars. When they did receive the news that the twenty dollars had been lost, they would then have to search for more secure methods of transmittal. But when might that happen? Probably three or four months later! What, in the meantime, could we live on, especially since I was already in debt? Ten months later I received fifty dollars from my children and until those fifty dollars arrived, I had to live in the manner described below.[26]

On *Sukes*,[27] the town *shoykhet* developed an eye illness and had to go to Jerusalem for treatment.[28] In his place, they were going to bring a *shoykhet* from Jerusalem or Jaffa. But since some people in the colony knew that I was a *shoykhet*, they discussed with the rabbi the possibility of using me in place of the previous *shoykhet* so that no *shoykhet* would need to be brought from

---

25 The day after Yom Kippur was October 1, 1914.

26 *Tamuz* 5675 (June–July 1915), as noted on p. 611 below.

27 October 5–10, 1914.

28 Shimon-Dov Horvits (1880–1961) began working as the *shoykhet* of Petakh-Tikva in 1912 (Yakobzon, 1986:84; Tidhar, 1947:2:606).

elsewhere.[29] I was called to meet with the rabbi and the heads of the community and they asked me if I wanted to assume the post of the other *shoykhet.* Understandably, I accepted, but they wanted to see my slaughtering knives and how I worked.[30] In short, when the rabbi and the *sh'khita* council saw my knives, they were extremely impressed and surprised, because they had never seen among their *shokhtim* such sharp and smooth knives as mine. They went with me to the slaughterhouse and could not overcome their amazement at my abilities in slaughtering and examining the animals' lungs to ascertain their kosher status. In short, they were very pleased with me, decided not to bring in another *shoykhet,* and wanted me to remain in the position until the *shoykhet* returned. So it was that the other's illness was my cure. In sum, everyone was pleased: the community, the butchers, as well as the *shoykhet* (namely myself) who was certainly pleased. Not that I was receiving any high salary for my services, but it was better than nothing. Though at my age it was difficult for me to work, I nonetheless disregarded my lack of stamina and took the position, rather than resorting to loans or asking for handouts as others in my situation had to do. I was now earning a napoleon a week and had a bit of meat every day at lunch for which I thanked God. I continued to earn money this way for some five to six months. I became well-known in the colony; everyone knew me to be a skilled *shoykhet,* and everyone who knew me did me the favor of loaning me money, without charging interest, which is how I lived through that period of time until I received the fifty dollars from my children, as related earlier.

The *shoykhet* regained his health, and I stopped earning money and went into serious debt. No one pestered me for repayment, but since I did not want to owe anyone any money, I paid off 200 francs in loans from my $50, leaving 50 francs for my expenses.

When God starts to help, He helps in many ways, one after the other. A short time later, I received 250 francs from my children in Russia. Practically the entire amount was also used in paying off loans. Then, at various times, I received 200 francs on three occasions from my children in Russia, and on these we lived and paid off debts.

---

29 The rabbi of Petakh-Tikva was Rabbi Yisrael Aba Tsitron (1881–1927) who served there from 1910 until his death. In 1922, he changed his surname to Kitroni, though most still referred to him as Tsitron. He was the son-in-law of the eminent Torah scholar, Rabbi Yosef Rozin (1858–1936), known as the Rogatshover (Tsitron, 2010:7–136).

30 It was standard practice for a rabbi to ask a *shoykhet* to sharpen his blades for examination; the *shoykhet* had to make sure that the tiniest indentation would not be perceived on its cutting edge (Berman, 1941:84–85).

In the month of *Tamuz* of 5675,[31] help arrived from my children in America: fifty dollars. It had been precisely a year since I had last received any help from them. I was overjoyed to receive this money, but it was not sufficient to pay back all the debt that I had incurred until then. Still, my cares became lighter to bear. I began to hope that I would soon be free of all debt. So I had figured, but my calculations turned out badly.

Six months later, I received not fifty but twenty-five dollars, and I had to exchange them for francs, so I lost several francs. Even so, I was happy and hoped that God would bring more help later.

Suddenly, a brand-new calamity befell me which was completely unexpected. One day, my dear Feyge reported that she felt that something in her throat was choking and suffocating her when she swallowed, and, when coughing, she felt that a bit of phlegm remained caught in her throat and could not be brought up without great struggle, after which she felt better. Suddenly, a small lump appeared under the skin of her neck, near her throat. At first, I made nothing of it, saying that it had always been that way but that she had not noticed it until now. But she said that it had certainly never been there before. While we were speaking about it, I noticed that she was deeply afraid and in much pain. I calmed her and told her to visit the doctor and ask him about it, which she decided to do. When she visited the local doctor, he told her that she must travel to Jaffa since she might need an operation.[32] She arrived home from the doctor frightened. The next morning, I sent her to Jaffa. Upon returning from Jaffa, she brought a note from that doctor to the local doctor and both confirmed that an immediate operation was required because the growth was still new and small and they feared that it might be the beginning of something cancerous. You can imagine the suffering that the opinions of the doctors brought us, because how could one allow an operation on one's throat?! So it was decided that she would travel again to see greater doctors, which is what she did. This second time, she now returned happily from the doctor, since the greatest doctor, a German non-Jew, told her it was not cancer and gave her medications and salves to apply. Other expert doctors also confirmed that it was not cancer. In short, she put aside the medication from the first doctors and took the medications of the other doctors. Still, we noticed that the growth was growing larger and moving closer to her throat. I decided that she

---

31 June–July 1915.

32 By that time, both of Petakh-Tikva's physicians, Dr. Eliyahu-Eliezer Kohen and Dr. Gershon-Yitskhak Krishevsky, had been conscripted into the Turkish army. In their absence, several unidentified doctors came to assume their duties (Hashavia, 1998:103; Levy & Levy, 2008:213,338).

should travel to Jerusalem to see the doctors there. She met with Dr. Walach and the surgeon, Grussendorf, who both assured her that it was neither cancer nor dangerous and that she could return home rest assured.[33] Of course, she came home calm and happy.

Yes, my dear readers, she came home calm and happy from Jerusalem, but her illness did not recede. The growth on her neck grew larger and larger. Our only consolation was that it was not cancer but a benign tumor, which was not dangerous and could dissolve with time. And thus the months of *Elul, Tishre,* and *Heshvan* passed.[34] Noticing that she was becoming thinner from day to day, I began to grow fearful and to think that perhaps it might be cancer after all. In short, I decided that I should accompany her to Jerusalem, although she objected to my traveling with her because of the added expense. I raised the money I needed for the trip, and, in the middle of the month of *Kislev,* she and I traveled to Jerusalem where we remained until after *Hanukah.*[35] I went with her to all the most famous doctors and almost all of them assured us that this was not cancer. Only one doctor (from Beirut) told me, out of her earshot, that we should not spend any money in treating it as nothing would help. So we returned home, hoping only to God that she would soon be cured.

On the 22nd day of *Teyves,*[36] she took to her bed and did not leave it until the 17th of *Shvut,*[37] which is the day that she returned the soul entrusted to her back to the Master of all souls, thereby freeing her of the terrible pain that she suffered.

She had continually pleaded with God to remove her soul from her, for how long could she be tortured in this way?! She would ask me to say *Vidui* with her,[38] and she requested that after her death I should say *Kaddish* and study

33 The legendary Dr. Moritz (Moyshe) Walach (1866–1957), an Orthodox Jew, came from Germany to Jerusalem in 1890 to build a clinic run according to Torah values. In 1896, work began on the Sha'are Tsedek Hospital, which became known as "Walach's Hospital." Dr. Theodor Grussendorf was born in 1873 in Clauen, Germany, and served as the senior physician of the German Deaconess Hospital in Jerusalem from 1902 until his departure at the end of 1917 (Hübner, 2006:251; Schwake, 2008:108–109).

34 Mid-August until early October 1915.

35 The author and his wife traveled to Jerusalem in late October 1915 and remained there until Hanukah, which lasted until December 9, 1915.

36 December 29, 1915.

37 January 22, 1916.

38 *Vidui* are the Hebrew confessional prayers said before departing from this world to evoke God's mercy and bring great atonement upon oneself (*Kitsur Shulkhan Arukh* 193:14).

the Mishna for her.[39] She also requested that her elderly stepmother continue to remain with me, and that her clothes should be given to the orphan and that I should make sure that the orphan was married off. She discussed everything with me, with clarity of thought and a sound mind. Until her final moments, she could speak and feel, and she knew that she would and must die.

She died on *Shobes* at noon. Her dying lasted two minutes because she simply choked to death. That night she was buried in an honorable grave, as she deserved. Though it took place at night, it was a large funeral. The tragedy that struck me cannot be understood by anyone, and nothing at all can console me. The catastrophe threw me off my feet, but one must calm oneself and go on with life. I say *Kaddish*, study the Mishna, and constantly grieve for her, because such a precious Feyge, being so religious and such a kosher soul, appears very rarely on this earth. "May her soul be bound up in the bonds of eternal life."[40] May she now be a good intercessor in the next world for me so that I should yet merit to live to see my children and grandchildren and the intended spouses of my children Refuel, Rukhl, and Shloyme, who need to now marry. And may she be a good intercessor for her children,[41] for my children, and for all our relatives and close friends. May her soul live on in the World to Come, and may her memory be for a blessing.

Feyge-Rashe, the Daughter of Reb Yitskhok-Dovid
"May her soul be bound up in the bond of eternal life."

39 It is common practice to study the Mishna in memory of those who have departed. The Mishna is the part of the Oral Torah that was codified and written down in around 200 CE. The Talmud is the rabbinical elucidation of the Mishna, which was compiled between 200–500 CE.

40 Samuel I 25:29.

41 The Hebrew inscription on Feyge's tombstone indicates that she died at sixty-two years of age. The author personally engraved Feyge's and her stepmother Udye's tombstones, as related by his granddaughter Aliza Bernfeld in 2001. "Her children" refers to Feyge's only child Duvid Kreyzberg and his wife Klara, who, at that time were either living in Feodosiya or had just moved to Yekaterinoslav.

FIGURE 25. The tombstone of Pinkhes-Dov Goldenshteyn's second wife, Feyge (ca. 1854–1916), which he engraved with his own hands, as he had done for the Karaites in the Crimea. The inscription states: "The honorable woman Mrs. Feyge-Rashe daughter of Yitskhok-Dovid, who immigrated to the Holy Land with her husband P. D. Goldenshteyn, *shoykhet* of the town of Bakhchisaray in the Crimean Peninsula. Her [step-]mother also immigrated with them. They came to P. T. [Petakh-Tikva] in the year 5674 [1913], and here a distressing illness afflicted her. She was sixty-two years of age when she died on the holy Sabbath, 17 *Shvat* of the year 5676 [January 22, 1916]. 'May her soul be bound up in the bond of eternal life.'"

CHAPTER 31

Marrying Off My Niece and Writing a Torah Scroll, 1916–1917

Exchanging Money into Turkish Liras • My Gratitude to My Children • Foreigners Compelled to Become Turkish Subjects • Those Aged Seventeen to Fifty Must Report for Conscription • The Turks' Awful Treatment of the Jews • The Diseases • *Mime* Yudelevitsh Falls Ill and Dies • Marrying Off the Orphan and Fulfilling My Obligations to Her • Falling Ill Before the Wedding • Being Denied Board on the Eve of *Shobes* • Becoming Ill and Ending My Board Arrangement • Renting Out the House and Buying Parchment • Beginning to Write the Torah Scroll

After beginning to calm down after my great tragedy, I began to consider my current standing in the world. I was even further in debt than before. I needed to support a household of three souls, there was not even a sou to be had, and there was no one from whom I could borrow money or obtain a loan. Since inflation was increasing by the day, everyone's situation was very bleak and the general state of the country was very bad. No one earned anything, and everyone lived on funds sent from overseas by children, relatives, and so on. And now, the entire country was shut in from all sides, so it was very rare for any money to reach anyone. If money did arrive, it quickly disappeared since it had to be exchanged for paper currency, which had no value here.[1] In other words,

1 In his memoirs of Petakh-Tikva during the First World War, Yakobzon (1986:64) mentions that funds from the United States had to be sent to Henry Morgenthau, Sr., the US ambassador to the Ottoman Empire in Constantinople. Morgenthau was obligated to exchange the

in place of the gold or dollars that were sent from abroad, the post office only dispensed Turkish liras, calculated on the basis of forty-three *bishliks* (or twenty-three francs) per Turkish lira, though the street value was only thirty *bishliks* per Turkish lira.[2] And the value of this paper money kept falling. As the value of money fell, the price of goods rose ten times as much, so that they became unobtainable. Hunger grew worse from day to day, and people were falling in the streets from hunger. You could see all of this, and nothing could be done to help. Once-wealthy owners of vineyards and orchards also died of hunger, so you can imagine what my life was like. Here I thank you, dear children, for the devotion you showed me by attempting to frequently send me small amounts of money. I often did not receive any letters, but money did arrive. Of what help (you may ask) was the little money I was left with after being compelled to lose so much in exchanging it for liras, but however much was left made it better for me than for those who unfortunately received nothing.

Until Pesach I was happy.[3] I would receive letters from Refuel almost every week, and he would intersperse greetings from my other children. After Pesach, not a single letter arrived from America, so you can imagine the anguish I had.

Though I'll keep it short, I now must describe to you what everyone here in general had to endure. They endured nearly all the curses mentioned in the Biblical rebuke.[4] Even "all the ills and all the plagues not written in this book of the Torah" were inflicted upon them by God.[5] We are so sinful that we must endure all types of punishment and afflictions until God will have compassion on us and redeem us, may it come speedily in our days. Amen.[6]

You know, of course, that all foreigners had to become Turkish subjects. Afterward, the first thing that the Turkish government did was to take control of everyone's possessions. One day they came to take away the horses, the next day the cows, and the day after that they simply took away people to work for them without pay, naturally. And everything was done very fiercely. As a result, another general tragedy occurred, namely that entire families were made miserable and totally impoverished. For example, an announcement was made that

---

dollars for liras in the Turkish bank, which exchanged them for less than ten percent of their actual value.

2 *Palestine During the War* (1921:35) notes that seven Turkish *bishliks* were equivalent to one Turkish pound (lira).

3 April 18–24, 1916.

4 Deuteronomy 28:15–58.

5 Deuteronomy 28:51.

6 This is a reference to the ultimate redemption through the Messiah, which is one of Judaism's fundamental beliefs.

all those who had become Turkish subjects had to report for conscription! You might think that those who were conscripted had a specified term of military service? No! There was no term of service here; rather, all those between the ages of seventeen and fifty had to serve. The doctors did not examine the conscripts to determine if they were healthy or ill. Perhaps you think that each soldier was given a rifle, weapons, clothes, food, and barracks, and was then placed in regiments and sent into battle, and so on? Should you think so, you would be in error! The Jews were neither placed in regiments nor sent into battle but were rather dispatched to do ordinary manual labor, that is, on the railroad, road repair, digging, hauling, and chopping wood. They slept outdoors and were fed next to nothing. Sometimes it would happen that there was not even water to drink. They had to languish for months like this among half-naked Arabs. This type of military life was worse than death for the Jews, God protect us. Since there was a law permitting recruits to buy their way out of military service, which the Turkish government preferred over dispatching them to work, every Jew sold all he owned to ransom himself, regardless of the fact that he and his family were left penniless. Rather than going into service to die there, he preferred to be at home and die among his family. Nonetheless, the local government had a short memory; after collecting the ransom money from someone, it forgot that it had taken it and demanded it again a month later. In other words, paying ransom once did not exempt a recruit from conscription, rather he had to pay it two or three times until he became thoroughly distraught.[7] Aside from this anguish, all sorts of infectious diseases were spreading and they included typhus, malaria, skin diseases, cholera, and so on. Everyone was ill, and everyone had to pay for doctors and medicine and felt weaker and weaker from day to day.

It was already, thank God, after Pesach of 5676.[8] A great heat wave started and lasted for four days. It was impossible to endure, and many fell dead of sunstroke even though they were accustomed to the heat. But we were consoled that the tremendous heat had rescued us from all the horrible parasites which it had wiped off the face of the earth. If not for that, we would have been subject to serious diseases, God forbid. After that consolation, we still suffered from all kinds of diseases. But who knows? Perhaps it would have been much worse if the heat had not killed off the parasites. Thank God, I safely made it through all of this too.

---

7 In his *Arabic Elements in Palestinian Yiddish: The Old Ashkenazic Jewish Community in Palestine, Its History and Its Language*, Kosover (1966:2020) cites this section in his explanation of the Turkish military tax.

8 Pesach ended in the Land of Israel on April 24, 1916.

But starting in the month of *Sivan*,[9] the girl Reyzl and I began to suffer from fevers, so that there were two sick people in the house. Naturally, the girl shook off her fever quicker than I did. I began to feel weaker and weaker from day to day. I suffered bouts of heat and cold and spoke deliriously. My temperature reached higher than forty degrees and someone had to spend the night with me to watch over me. I was given up for dead.[10]

Suddenly our elderly *Mime* Udye Yudelevitsh fell ill and, though sick myself, I crawled out of bed to see how she was doing. In short, she was also feverish; she shivered from cold, then became very hot. I was by then, thank God, somewhat better and was beginning to grow stronger, so I could care for the elderly woman. Seeing that she was not doing well, I hired a Jewish woman to care for her. Since Reyzl was busy with running the house, caring for me, running for the doctor, and going to the pharmacy, I had to hire this other Jewish woman to devote her time exclusively to our *Mime*. After all, she was seriously ill, besides being 85 years old. It started as a fever, but it ended in her death. After lying in bed for seventeen or eighteen days (from the middle of *Tamuz* until the second day of *Av*) she died.[11] I met with the burial society, and she was buried in accordance with Jewish law near Feyge's grave. I built a fence around the two graves, so that they could now rest together just as they had lived together,[12] as it states, "Beloved and pleasant in their lifetime, and in their deaths they were not separated."[13]

Now I was left forlorn, and my orphaned niece remained with me. All my days were spent worrying, thinking, missing, remembering, and, primarily, ailing. I could barely drag myself to *shul* to pray and to say *Kaddish* for my devoted wife. What would become of me, I did not know. Meanwhile, things were not looking well for me! Perhaps God would have compassion by improving my health, giving me the strength to endure this bad period of time, and granting me the privilege of arranging for the girl's wedding while I was yet alive. Since she suffered plenty right along with us, and looked after me in every way until today, I prayed to God to grant me the privilege of living long enough to arrange her wedding, as I had undertaken to do. I also prayed that God

---

9 June 1916.

10 Equivalent to 104 °F.

11 Hence, Udye Yudelevitsh lay in bed from the middle of July until August 1, 1916, when she died.

12 Feyge and her stepmother Udye are buried in the Segula Cemetery in Petakh-Tikva. On her tombstone, the author engraved that Udye before dying asked to be buried next to her "daughter," i.e., her stepdaughter Feyge. By 2002, there was no longer a fence around their graves, probably for many years.

13 Samuel II 1:23.

would grant me the privilege of at least hearing that my unmarried children had married.[14]

***

[Late 1916:] Now I will describe what happened to me and the situation of the Jews in *Erets-Isruel* in general.

Starting on *Rosh-Khoydesh Menakhem Av,*[15] many people began to die of the same illnesses that I had suffered. The number of dead was so great that in the month of *Elul* there were fifty-six victims in Petakh-Tikva,[16] and in the month of *Tishre* there were as many as thirty-eight.[17] God protect us. That was besides the many who were still bedridden. The reason for this was that everyone was exhausted and suffering in need and want. Now, my dear children, you can see how kind God was in keeping your father alive, thank God. My health improved greatly when I stopped suffering from so much deprivation because, thank God, during the past four months of *Tamuz, Av, Elul,* and *Tishre,*[18] I received money every month, sometimes at the beginning of the month and sometimes at mid-month.

Now I will relate what happened in my home. I was still seeking a match for the orphaned girl with a decent, religious young man. Since I would be marrying her off to someone whom I deemed appropriate, I decided that I would take her and her husband into my house after the wedding so that we would all live together. I would pay them a fixed monthly amount so that I would not need to be concerned with the details of household expenses. My mind would then be free so that I might calmly study Torah, pray, and implore God on behalf of all of you, my dear children. And perhaps God would then grant me the merit to carry out the plan which I had long harbored: to write a Torah scroll with my own hand. Then I would know that God had not let me live in vain, but that I might carry out the good thoughts I had nurtured for so long. When God would help me marry off the orphan girl, I would then begin to deal with the matter of the Torah scroll. Perhaps God would show me compassion this way. Anything is possible for God.

---

14 The author is referring to his children Refuel, Rukhl, and Shloyme.

15 July 31, 1916. The Hebrew month of *Av* is often called *Menakhem Av.*

16 September 1916.

17 October 1916.

18 July–October 1916.

The time came and I am involved in finalizing a match with a very fine young man with whom I would certainly be able to live as I had hoped.[19] When the match will be concluded, with God's help, I will put off the wedding but only for a month at the most, since everything was already prepared: her clothes left to her by Feyge and by her elderly stepmother; they simply need to be altered somewhat.

***

[The 20th of *Shvat* 5677[20]]: Thank God, the match was concluded, and I married her off. As a dowry, I gave her fifty napoleons, that is, 1,000 francs, to be paid after the conclusion of the war when I would be able to obtain the funds from my children. I gave the groom a promissory note to that effect, basically using my house as collateral. Apart from the dowry, I undertook to let the young couple live rent-free in my home; in other words, they would live together with me. But if we proved to be incompatible with one another, they would have to move out of my house and I would pay for four years of rent for them somewhere else, which would amount to some fifty napoleons.[21] In addition, I gave her all the clothes that had been left by my wife and her elderly stepmother and had everything altered for her. I also gave her good bedding in addition to all kinds of furniture. I made her into a complete housewife as though of twenty years' standing. May she use it all in good health, and may she remember me for it for the good.

I arranged a beautiful wedding, but it seemed to be decreed that I would not live to see it, just as my good wife Feyge, may she rest in peace, did not live to see it. I do not know whose merit stood by me, but the heavenly decree was at least partially annulled. I remained alive to delight in the *mitzvah* of marrying off my niece, but I felt the taste of death that day and was not able to attend the wedding.

---

19 Reyzl married Yankl Grinberg (ca. 1887–1979) who was born in Pinsk, Belarus, under the surname Kukhlik. At three or four years of age, his parents left by wagon to the Land of Israel via Turkey, which took three months. To leave Tsarist Russia, his father acquired a false passport under the name of Grinberg and kept that name. In 2002, Yankl's only surviving children, Dvora Ben-Ya'akov and Yosef ("Yoske") Grinberg, granted permission to include their father's surname in this translation.

20 February 12, 1917. The date is actually indicated on p. 622, footnote 24 below.

21 As clarified in ch. 34, p. 664, Reyzl and Yankl married on *Rosh-Khoydesh Shvat* 5677 (January 24, 1917), and the author promised them that either they could live with him rent-free for four years or he would rent them separate quarters for four years.

It happened as follows: In the middle of preparing everything for the wedding ceremony, including the marriage contract, and while all the guests were beginning to arrive for the reception, I suddenly fell ill with a temperature of more than forty-one degrees.[22] Once I was put to bed and a doctor was called, I could not remember and could not understand what was happening to me, so the wedding took place without me. They celebrated almost all night and had a very nice time, while I never saw the honored guests. But thank God, who treats me only with compassion, my health was restored so that on the *Shobes* after the wedding I sat at the table and rejoiced with all the guests and took part in the *Sheve-Brokhes*.[23] I viewed this as an explicit sign that God's compassion for me and His granting me my life was because He wanted to help me carry out all my good thoughts and my plan of writing a Torah scroll. So I decided that as soon as I paid off the debts of the wedding and obtained some money, I would buy parchment in Jerusalem. I would then start writing, and God would help me to complete the task at an auspicious time.

Today is Tuesday, the 20th of *Shvat* 5677,[24] and I give thanks to God that I am still alive and able to continue my narrative with the joy of having had the privilege to marry off the orphan, thank God. I thought that afterward I would be able to live calmly with them and carry out my desire to write a Torah scroll, but ultimately my body and soul were quickly and unexpectedly ravaged. Only two weeks after their wedding (and after the start of my arrangement with them where I was deliberately paying the sizable amount of fifty francs a month for my meals), they unexpectedly refused the fifty francs a month with the excuse that it was too little! They decided that I must certainly pay at least eighty francs per month! You, dear children, can imagine how depressed I became from this rejection of our board arrangement. This happened on a Thursday, no less—the eve of *Shobes*. But what could be done on the eve of *Shobes*? How do you go to a stranger right before *Shobes*? It would be a public shaming, and I did not want to be the butt of public laughter.[25] What then did I do? I grieved, cried, and bemoaned my troubles; I had lived through and endured so much.

On Friday, I was eating my heart out, and on *Shobes* I had to eat at the table with them, not eating but downing tears. For me it was not *Shobes* but *Tisha*

---

22 Equivalent to 105.8 °F. In ch. 34, p. 661, he recalls this incident and notes that he had a temperature of 40 °C (104 °F).

23 *Sheve-Brokhes* (literally meaning "seven blessings") refers to the seven Hebrew blessings recited at the end of the meals held in honor of the bride and groom every day of the week following the wedding.

24 February 12, 1917.

25 The author's eating elsewhere on *Shabes* would have made it obvious to all that there was a problem in his household.

B'Av. I cried continually throughout *Shobes*. How could it be that I would grieve so much and allow myself to disturb the *Shobes*, which is so holy? It was truly a grave error on my part! But my pain was so great. Consider the fact that I had just spent so much money on them, paid for their wedding, and provided them with such wealth and furniture, only for my meal arrangement to be undone two weeks after the wedding thereby frustrating my entire plan! My heart had already been filled with pain and soaked in agony and torment from every direction, so to have my meal arrangement completely undone crushed me. Now you can understand why my pain was so unbearably great that I could not hold back my tears though I knew it was *Shobes* when it is forbidden to be sad.[26] I recited the entire Book of Psalms, accompanied by rivers of tears. Given the situation, what would I do now? Marry? Death would be better and easier! Not marry? How would I live? By cooking for myself or going to a hotel for meals? That was no plan either! Now how could I even think about writing a Torah scroll in such circumstances? In short, whichever way my thoughts turned, the outcome was not good.

What bothered me most of all was the hard-heartedness of the young couple and their disloyalty to me. It was only two weeks after their wedding, and they were already treating me like this! How did such cruelty come to such young people?! I did and still wanted to do good things for them and considered them my children, and I figured that they would want to treat me as children do an aged father, especially when their father pays them a good price for his food. Though inflation was raging, I did not cost them any more than forty francs a month! And even if I cost them the entire fifty francs, they would still not be losing any money on my account! In any case, they should not want to profit from me! So how did it occur to a young couple to say that I was costing them money and to demand a payment of eighty francs a month?!

To make the story short, I survived that *Shobes*. After *Shobes* ended, I had a discussion with him. "How can this be? How can you say that you're losing money on my account, especially after only two weeks? Even if you had waited until the end of the month and then shown me the figures proving that you are losing money, it still would not make any sense. After all, I gave you the barley, lentils, coal, salt, and more that I had prepared for the entire winter until Pesach, so how can you be losing money on my account? Go ahead," I said, "total up everything!" In the end, he conceded somewhat that he had not done right by me and said, "Let the amount stay as it was. I regret the pain that I've caused

---

26 *Kitsur Shulkhan Arukh* (72:3).

you." I calmed down somewhat and convinced myself that nothing else would happen between us, especially since he had expressed his regret over the unnecessary pain he had caused me. And our arrangement stayed as it was, and I was back receiving meals, but it did not last long.

***

By the end of the month,[27] Yankl refused the fifty francs a month I was paying and said that if I would not pay eighty francs then I should at least pay seventy, otherwise it was not worthwhile for him.[28] In addition, I must produce the money at once, since he could not wait. At this, I lost my patience and said to him, "If so, you must leave my residence at once. I do not want you in my house. I'll pay your rent, but you must not remain here in the house. If you do not keep your word, then I won't keep mine either! Leave everything in the house and off you go!" At this, he realized that he had dug himself into a hole. He had thought that I had lost my senses, but in the end he saw that his old uncle still had good sense! I then told him that from now on, I would eat on my own. I would buy bread and something to eat it with at the market. If his wife wanted to cook lunch for me, fine; if not, I would have to struggle along on my own. Apart from that, I confided what was happening to a few trusted individuals, all of whom were stirred by my story. They reproached him, and he became quite embarrassed by the episode. In short, he again regretted his actions, but this time I did not let myself become convinced and said to him that I wanted him out of my house. I would eat on my own and did not need a meal arrangement with him. At this point he engaged people to make peace between us because, after all, he could not afford to leave my house. What's more, he was also not losing money on the fifty francs a month that I was paying him for meals, and he was losing respect in the community. So he brought over two fine and respectable townsmen who decided that he was not allowed to charge me more than fifty francs per month and that he must allow up to three months for payment because I had no ready money. In the end, he apologized to me in front of the others and promised that nothing like this would happen again.

Eight days after the agreement, I received a sizeable sum of money: twenty-five dollars from my Refuel, and sixty-three dollars from Duvid Kreyzberg.[29]

27 Referring to the end of the month of *Shvat* 5677 (February 29, 1917).

28 Referring to Yankl Grinberg, the husband of the author's niece Reyzl.

29 Duvid Kreyzberg, who then resided in Feodosiya, was the son of the author's second wife Feyge from her first marriage. See Appendix A4 (pp. 730–732) for more details.

I immediately paid off the full amount that was due my niece and her husband. I thought that things would go calmly for me now and that they would treat me properly, but I was woefully wrong about them. It was true that they provided me with meals for the fifty francs I was giving them, but only enough to keep my body and soul together. Every day I was aggravated at seeing how little respect they gave me. All that interested them was the fifty francs but feeding me was unnecessary. "Does he have to live, too? He's lived long enough! It was better if he would already . . . We would then be his heirs!" The aggravation caused me to develop jaundice, God protect us. The doctor ordered me to eat nothing except milk and a bit of bread. Understandably, I needed five containers of milk per day, but they only gave me two. Even those two seemed to be a lot for them, because he muttered, "I don't have enough money to buy them for him!" not considering the fifty francs he was taking from me every month while I ate nothing else. And so, I was ill for three weeks and suffered greatly. I barely survived and was given little chance to live. But God heard my prayer and allowed me to live, though I had no strength left. Normally after such a bout of illness, a person would need good nutrition including a good bowl of soup and a bit of chicken or fish, but where was I to get that? The young couple was disinterested in strengthening my health. They were disappointed in the fact that I was still alive and wanted to continue living. So I determined once and for all to do with out their board and to live life on my own.

***

You know of course that when we were still living in Russia, in Bakhchisaray, my wife, her elderly stepmother Yudelevitsh, and I spoke about my writing a Torah scroll.[30] But since I was always so involved in earning an income, I was unable to accomplish it there. So we agreed that when God would bring us to the Holy Land, we would do it then. I say "we" because my wife and the elderly Yudelevitsh also wanted to have a share in it. When we were about to leave for *Erets-Isruel,* I wanted to take along parchment, but I was dissuaded because the customs duty would be so high and, besides, parchment in Jerusalem would be better and less expensive than in Russia. So as our bad luck would have it, we came without parchment to the Holy Land. Upon arriving, we hardly had a chance to look for it before the World War broke out. So you yourself can understand that it was impossible to think about buying parchment, especially

30 This section was apparently written in late 1917 or early 1918.

as I was constantly faced with terrible new developments, such as the illnesses which befell us all, the death of my dear wife, the illness and death of our elderly *Mime* Yudelevitsh, my falling ill, and then the aggravation regarding the girl Reyzl. Thank God, I survived all of this and persevered, particularly in such trying times when no money was to be had. So I ask you, could one think about carrying out the sacred idea of writing a Torah scroll at such a time? Certainly not! But it plagued me day and night: When might I have the merit to write a Torah scroll myself? Since God had allowed me to live, He surely wanted to afford me the opportunity to fulfill my sacred idea! But the question was: How? And with what? Was now the time for it? With nothing on which to live and survive through the day, I desired—of all things—to write a Torah scroll and purchase parchment.

Finally, God helped me, and I bought enough parchment on which to write the entire Torah scroll. But do not think that this came as easily to me as I am mentioning it. No, my dear ones, it was very difficult! Only through tremendous self-sacrifice did I obtain the parchment. I then understood that one who performs a *mitzvah* with self-sacrifice is helped by God, and then divine providence causes everything to be as he had hoped—and even better than he had hoped.

Now I will describe for you the self-sacrifice I had in carrying out my sacred idea. You can also learn a lesson from your father, namely that one must give of oneself to perform a *mitzvah* and then God will help! Imagine, beloved children, that I did not have enough money to make it through the day. Even if I managed to borrow a napoleon, I had to write a promissory note to repay three napoleons. When traveling to Jerusalem, my lodging would cost a napoleon and the cost of the parchment I needed would add up to another eight napoleons. One might ask where I could obtain such a sum of money! I could not take a loan against the house since I was already in so much debt. Secondly, in order to borrow ten napoleons I would have to provide a promissory note for thirty napoleons. Even if I were to agree to do that, there was no cash to be had, even at high rates of interest, simply because no one had any ready money. Now ask yourselves, how did I manage to buy the parchment? Certainly you are interested in knowing, and you will learn about it through the following account.

Rosh-Khoydesh Tamuz here in Petakh-Tikva marks the start of annual leases.[31] Whoever needs to rent or let out a dwelling does so from *Rosh-Khoydesh Tamuz* to the *Rosh-Khoydesh Tamuz* of the following year. This is the system used throughout *Erets-Isruel*, the only difference between one town and another being the start date of the lease. For example, in Jaffa the leases start

31 The month of *Tamuz* usually occurs in June or July.

on *Rosh-Khoydesh Kislev,*[32] in Jerusalem on *Rosh-Khoydesh Heshvan,*[33] and here in Petakh-Tikva on *Rosh-Khoydesh Tamuz.* Understandably, both the landlord and the tenant make arrangements some two months before the lease period begins, so that it is already settled between the tenant and the landlord by the time the lease begins. I am explaining this so that you will be familiar with the local lease periods and thereby fully understand what I write below.

I have a house that includes four rooms, a kitchen, and a large terrace, with sheds for firewood and even for cows. I used to lease all of this to a tenant and would charge him an annual rent of thirty napoleons.[34] But during the war, rents became much cheaper, and my tenant became the landlord—meaning that he paid when he wanted and if he did not want to pay, he did not. So a year elapsed without his paying any rent at all. I then had a tenant who was a good person, meaning that he paid his rent on time, and I charged him only eighteen napoleons a year. Right before the start of the annual leases, the colony became filled with refugees from Jaffa, thereby causing housing prices to greatly rise.[35] I could have charged thirty napoleons for my house, but my tenant did not want to move out. Since I had nothing against him, I did not consider it proper to raise his rent. The Jews from Jaffa (the refugees) were creating a rent boom, but the panic would only be temporary; when it was over, everything would be as before. Realizing that this was the time to carry out my sacred idea, I said to him as follows, "Of course, you've seen what's happening in the colony since *Rosh-Khoydesh Sivan.*[36] I don't want to raise your rent. I ask only that you pay me a half-year's rent in advance, meaning nine napoleons." I also told him what I wanted to do with the money. My tenant pleaded that he could not pay that much at one time. But I understood that now was the right time for me to carry out my idea, so I told him again to give me the nine napoleons for the first half-year and the rest at the end of the year. To make a long story short, he agreed and gave me the nine napoleons on the eve of *Rosh-Khoydesh Tamuz.*[37] That very night, I immediately left for Jerusalem. Understandably, upon arriving in Jerusalem, I

---

32 The month of *Kislev* usually occurs in November or December.

33 The month of *Heshvan* usually occurs in October or November.

34 On the lot which the author purchased were two houses connected by a two-story wooden structure with a staircase, as specified in the author's Hebrew ethical will (see Appendix B2, p. 766). He resided in the smaller house, which consisted of three rooms, and rented out the larger house, which consisted of four rooms.

35 In April 1917, about 9,000 Jewish residents evacuated Jaffa, with the majority being directed to Petakh-Tikva (Hashavia, 1998:137–138).

36 May 22, 1917, a month before *Rosh-Khoydesh Tamuz,* when the annual leases began in Petakh-Tikva.

37 June 19, 1917.

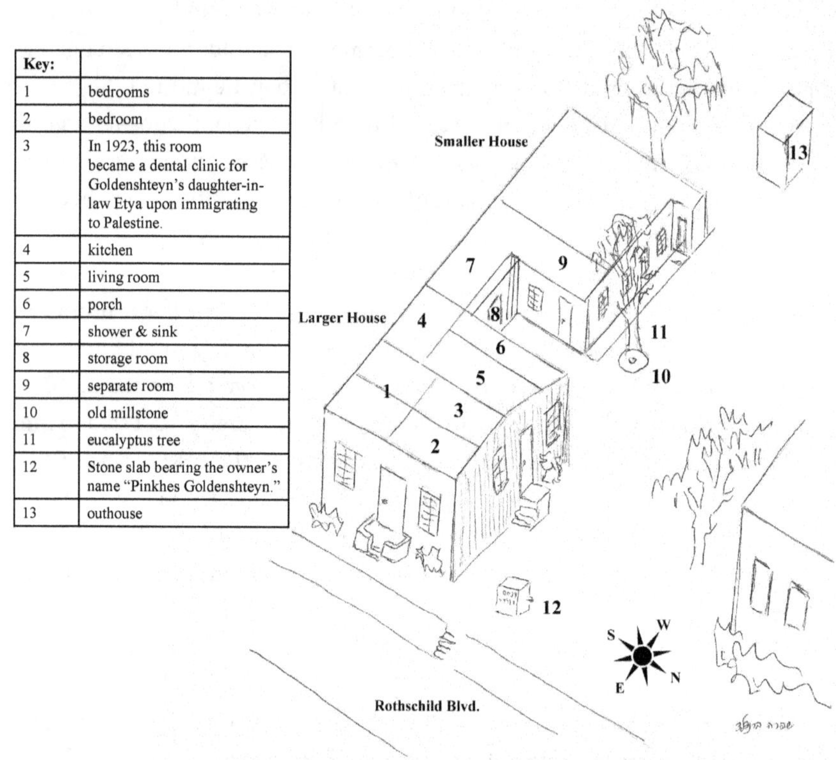

FIGURE 26. Pinkhes-Dov Goldenshteyn's two houses at 64 Rothschild Blvd. in Petakh-Tikva, which he purchased upon his arrival in 1913. For details, see Appendix A1, pp. 677–681. (Illustration by Shifra Bernfeld of Petakh-Tikva, 2023.)

immediately began to search for parchment. But this, too, was not as easy for me as I had expected. No ready parchment was to be had since everyone had become impoverished by the war. Many Torah scribes had fled Jerusalem so that only a small number of the Council of Torah Scribes remained. I had to place an order for them to prepare parchment on my behalf, and this would require several weeks. Accordingly, I left the money in the hands of a reliable person, so that he might pay for the parchment upon delivery to his home. For his efforts, I paid him twenty-five francs, that is, a British pound in gold.[38]

During the time I spent in Jerusalem, I went to the Western Wall, the tomb of Shimon *ha-Tsadik*,[39] and the Tombs of the Sanhedrin.[40] I visited the Mount of Olives three times, seeking to buy two tombstones for the graves of my wife and of her elderly *Mime*.[41] But because there were no hewn stones available, I traveled home without parchment and without the tombstones. I was not too concerned about the tombstones for now because I had fully surrounded the graves with a rock hedge. But the parchment cost me much health.

On the 10th of *Elul* at a propitious hour, I finally received all the parchment from Jerusalem.[42] The parchment was beautiful and clean, and the ink was also good. You yourself can well imagine the joy I felt upon receiving the parchment and upon reaching, thank God, the moment when I could begin the sacred work of writing a Torah scroll with my own hand. As soon as the parchment arrived, I could no longer rest but began to prepare myself to begin writing. I had, thank God, the merit to start on Tuesday, the 17th of *Elul* 5677.[43] In honor of its commencement, I invited a *minyan* of elderly, pious Jews and the brilliant rabbi of the town,[44] and they blessed me and wished me to have the merit to write the Torah scroll from beginning to end. That day was a *Yontef* for me; everyone drank and ate well, and I began writing it as they watched. We parted in peace, with trust in God, and with great hope.

---

38 This British coin is commonly called a "sovereign."

39 The ancient tomb of Shimon *ha-Tsadik* (Simon the Righteous) in Jerusalem is traditionally held to be the burial site of Shimon, a Jewish High Priest, and his students, who lived during the period of the second Temple.

40 Jewish tradition claims that at this burial site lie members of the Sanhedrin, the ancient high court of the Jewish people. It is located in Jerusalem's Sanhedriya neighborhood.

41 The Mount of Olives is the site of an ancient Jewish cemetery on a mountain ridge east of Jerusalem's Old City. The author was seeking to purchase blank (uninscribed) tombstones which he could then engrave himself.

42 August 28, 1917.

43 September 4, 1917. The author writes in his Hebrew ethical will (see Appendix B2, p. 770) that he started writing the Torah scroll on *Rosh-Khodesh Elul* 5677, i.e., August 18–19, 1917.

44 Referring to Rabbi Yisrael Aba Tsitron, who is also mentioned in ch. 30 (p. 611) and ch. 34 (p. 660).

For my part, I did not rest from that day forward. I thought only of writing more and more and did not let a single day go by without writing. Other than *Shobes* and *Yontef*, nothing held me back from writing.[45] Though I wrote from eight in the morning until about five or six in the evening, I did not feel tired—on the contrary, my strength and joy increased the more I wrote. Naturally, my writing went more slowly around the High Holy Days and *Sukes*, but afterward I worked diligently and ignored the fact that there was no improvement at home. I also received no letters from my dear children, yet I continued to write on and on until that dark day arrived that further blackened my life and interfered with my writing.

Since my wish is for you to know everything about your father's struggle during his last years and everything that he endured here in the Holy Land, which did not deter him from continuing his sacred desire of writing a Torah scroll, I am therefore writing a separate chapter about all of this, which will be called "Exile in Kfar-Saba."

45 Jews are forbidden from writing on *Shabes* and *Yontef*.

CHAPTER 32

Exile to Kfar-Saba, 1917–1918

The War in Petakh-Tikva • Orchards and Vineyards Cut Down for Heating Fuel • Bullets Do Not Deter the Writing of the Torah Scroll • Driven from Petakh-Tikva to Kalkilya • The Soup Kitchen in Kfar-Saba • The Hospital • The Guests at the Soup Kitchen • The Refugees Die

Kfar-Saba, Sunday of the Torah Portion of *Tetsave*,[1] 5th of *Adar* 5678[2]

How did I come to be in Kfar-Saba? This question will be addressed later, but meanwhile all you need to know is that I went to Kfar-Saba. It is a small colony not far from Petakh-Tikva, approximately seven *versts* away.

As you may remember, when the Turkish government expelled the Jews from Jaffa, most of them settled in Petakh-Tikva while a smaller portion were scattered about the Galilee.[3] Those in Petakh-Tikva remained there peacefully up until the month of *Tamuz*.[4] Realizing that the Jews of Jaffa had not suffered enough from the exile they had already endured, the government suddenly issued a new decree that all the Jaffa refugees had to leave Petakh-Tikva. They could go wherever they wished, but under no circumstances could they remain in Petakh-Tikva. Understandably, they were very frightened and suffered much anguish. Each family member exerted every effort to bribe the officials in order to be able to remain in Petakh-Tikva, but many families did not have sufficient means and were forced to leave Petakh-Tikva and immigrate to other places. Most of them found it best to immigrate to Kfar-Saba, a small colony nearby. Some left for Hadera, Samarin, and so on.[5]

---

1 Exodus 27:20 to 30:10.
2 February 17, 1918.
3 In April 1917, as mentioned in ch. 31, p. 627.
4 June–July 1917.
5 Samarin, aka Zamrin, was the Arabic name for the site of Zikhron-Ya'akov.

Those who went to Kfar-Saba were convinced that it was a better place than all others, though Kfar-Saba was populated by fifteen colonists who were living in damp, musty dwellings; their small, two-room houses were unplastered and lacked floors. Yet the Jews from Jaffa preferred Kfar-Saba because of its close proximity to both Petakh-Tikva and Jaffa; they hoped to be saved from their dire circumstances at the first opportunity by being allowed to return to their homes, especially since they all were poor and dependent on others for support. The Council of Displaced Persons saw to it that huts were set up for them. Two or three families were placed in each hut and as much aid as possible was provided. They remained like this in Kfar-Saba for a total of nine months.

During those nine months, additional refugees, inhabitants of Petakh-Tikva, arrived. Beginning in the month of *Heshvan* 5678,[6] the government began to empty Petakh-Tikva of all of its Jews, just as they had done in Jaffa. But in Petakh-Tikva, they did not have the opportunity to cause total destruction, though they did cause damage in the value of millions of francs. Though they had planned to completely destroy everything—both Petakh-Tikva's property and its population—God was merciful and did not permit them to cause total wreckage. In the end, the Turks only managed to destroy property.[7] There was only a small number of human victims, and most families were spared. Among the few people who were victims, you can include me, your father, who endured more suffering and pain here than I had ever experienced in my entire life. No human strength can withstand and overcome such pain. But God is, after all, the "Giver of strength to the weary,"[8] and He gave me the strength to overcome it all. Since I want you, my children, to understand what your father endured in Kfar-Saba in his old age, I will describe for you from beginning to end how my how my exile in Kfar-Saba proceeded, how I suffered there, the misery I saw around me, and the fear of death which loomed every day before my eyes. Yet I live with the hope that I will soon find help, that I will be able to converse with you—at least through letters—and that I will be able to continue with my sacred idea of writing the Torah scroll, which I have not been able to do until now.

You know, of course, that I began to write the Torah scroll right after *Sukes* and continued my writing while shells flew over my head.[9] Starting in *Heshvan*,[10]

---

6 October–November 1917.

7 The author explains on p. 633 below that the Turks planned to completely destroy Petakh-Tikva by making it a battleground, though they did not succeed.

8 From the morning blessings printed in traditional prayer books.

9 In ch. 31, p. 629, the author writes that he began writing the Torah scroll on the 17th of Elul, 5677 (September 4, 1917) but was slowed down due to the High Holy Days and *Sukes*. Hence, he began writing earnestly only after *Sukes*, which ended on October 8, 1917.

10 October–November 1917.

the British took Jaffa and began to do battle with the Turks in Petakh-Tikva, a key position for the Turks.[11] The Turks wanted to prevent the British from seizing Petakh-Tikva, because making Petakh-Tikva a battleground would give the Turks an opportunity to destroy the finest Jewish colony in *Erets-Isruel*. After all, Petakh-Tikva was the largest and most beautiful of all the Jewish colonies. By making Petakh-Tikva a battleground, the Turks would be able to avenge themselves on the Jews, whom they regarded as enemies, while appearing justified before the world.[12] Since no one would know that their vengeance had led them to wage war right in Petakh-Tikva, people would think that it was simply an unfortunate consequence of the war strategy. If perhaps you think that Petakh-Tikva includes great hills and valleys or is surrounded by fortifications or a river, I will tell you that not even one of these is to be found in Petakh-Tikva. It is a colony that possesses many orchards and vineyards; they are its riches and the fruit of the settlers' thirty-year labor of blood, sweat, and self-sacrifice.[13] They had just barely begun to enjoy the fruits of their sweat-soaked, hard-earned toil, when along came the Turks, who in their vengeance against the Jews found it necessary to bring the war to Petakh-Tikva. They fortified themselves there strongly and drove the townsmen from their homes, thereby becoming the masters of the town. They dug trenches and cut down fruit trees in the orchards and vineyards and used them as heating fuel in place of common firewood. They placed their cannons next to the houses—one such cannon stood not far from my home—intending to turn the houses into targets. But the British apparently understood the Turkish government's intent and made sure that the colony would not be damaged. Only rarely was a house struck accidentally due to some unpredictable circumstance. Throughout the entire day, the only thing that could be heard was cannon fire. I became so accustomed to it that nothing frightened me or caused me to stop writing the Torah scroll. The cannonballs flew over the roof of my house and the noise deafened me, but I did not care and wrote every day from dawn to dusk. Everyone was amazed at my dedication to

11 During the First World War (1914–1918), the Central Powers, including the Ottoman Empire and the German Empire, were at war with Allied Powers, including Great Britain, France, and Imperial Russia. In 1917, the United States entered the war as an "associated power" rather than a formal ally of Great Britain and France. The Ottoman Turks had ruled over the territory of Greater Syria, which included Palestine, since 1516. With the British in control of Egypt since 1882, Field Marshall Edmond Allenby commanded the British military forces in Egypt northward in the conquest of Palestine and Syria in 1917 and 1918.

12 After uncovering a pro-British spy ring among the Jewish population under Turkish rule in September 1917, the Turks perceived all Jews as enemies and traitors.

13 Petakh-Tikva was founded in 1878, and the first orchards were planted there in 1887 (Trope, 1949:28).

my work. And so I wrote from the beginning of Genesis to the end of the weekly Torah portion of *Shmos*.[14]

According to my calculations, I would complete the Books of Exodus and Leviticus by Pesach, because I had completed writing the Book of Genesis before Hanukah.[15] By Tuesday of the Torah portion of *Mikets*,[16] I had written the Torah portion of *Shmos* up until Pharaoh issued his decree,[17] at which point I was forced to desist from writing due to my being exiled to Kfar-Saba.[18]

I know, dear children, that you will be interested in knowing the reason why I came to be exiled in Kfar-Saba, so I will tell it to you in detail. You know, of course, from my earlier description, that the government had driven the Jews of Jaffa from Petakh-Tikva and that, for the most part, they were resettled in Kfar-Saba. Afterward, the rest of the Jews of Petakh-Tikva were frightened, thinking that a similar fate awaited us all. Well, our fears were not unwarranted, for the government began to drive out all the Jews of Petakh-Tikva. They began to arrest Jews claiming that they were sinful spies, operatives, and traitors; they tied them up and sent them either to Jerusalem or to Damascus to stand trial. All of this was done without any evidence at all, based only on the inferences and opinions of the military commanders. The purpose, of course, was to obtain bribes!

Suddenly the government issued a decree that within a few days not a single person could remain in Petakh-Tikva. Can you imagine the panic and the turmoil? Everyone moaned and cried, "Where shall we run? Where shall we go?" It is easier to withstand the pains of expulsion in a populated country where there are cities, villages, trains, and the like, where one can ride or walk in the hope that there will be food and drink. But here, when you step outside the colony, all is desolate and barren, which made it painful for all the families to leave their homes and belongings. Once the first wave of panic passed, the

---

14 The Torah portion of *Shmos* is Exodus 1:1 to 6:1.

15 Pesach began on March 28, 1918, and Hanukah began on December 10, 1917.

16 In other words, the author finished writing the Book of Genesis before Hanukah (December 9, 1917). He then started writing the Torah portion of *Shmos* (Exodus 1:1 to 6:1) on Sunday, December 9, 1917, which was the beginning of the week of the Torah reading of *Mikets*, and finished writing it by Tuesday, December 11, 1917.

17 At the end of the Torah portion of *Shmos* (Exodus 5:6–18), Pharaoh decrees that his Hebrew slaves are no longer to be given any straw to make bricks but have to gather their own straw and still deliver the same quota of bricks as before.

18 In the original Yiddish, *Mikets* is mistakenly printed instead of *Shmos* and vice versa. The author was certainly exiled on Tuesday of the Torah portion of *Mikets* (December 11, 1917) and not in the week of the Torah portion of *Shmos* (January 1, 1918) since Ya'ari (1929:535) confirms that the expulsion of Petakh-Tikva's Jews began on December 11th. In addition, the author could not have been exiled by the Turks as late as January 1, 1918, since the British entered Petakh-Tikva on December 22, 1917 (Ya'ari, 1929:546).

Turks began to calm the public; the old and the sick would, in fact, be permitted to remain in the colony. So I was hopeful that I might be able to stay and not be driven out after all. Since Reyzl, who was pregnant, was nearing her due date and pregnant women were exempt from the expulsion, I was encouraged in my adamant resolve to stay.[19] In any event I was determined, on pain of death, not to leave my home. After all, I preferred to die in my own home! And, despite the panic, I continued to write the Torah scroll.

On Monday of the Torah portion of *Mikets*,[20] I was still writing the Torah scroll and decided that I would not let myself be led into exile. Early Tuesday morning of that same week, I went to services in *shul* and recited *Slikhes*, *Hoyshanes*, and other prayers to the One above.[21] I then returned home and wanted to continue with my writing, but ultimately God directed me elsewhere. Suddenly, in ran Shloyme, the brother-in-law of Reyzele's husband Yankev.[22] Shloyme was then living in my house with his wife and five little children because the soldiers had robbed them of their home at the end of the colony and had smashed it and burned its doors and windows. Whatever they could save was brought to my house since it was located in the center of the colony. At any rate, he entered with a tremendous shout, "You're still sitting around here? You have to go ahead and flee! The government is providing carts for transporting people to Kfar-Saba only today. Tomorrow they will no longer be sending people to Kfar-Saba but to farther places. And those who refuse to leave will be beaten to death by the government! No one will remain here! Reyzele's husband has already arranged for her transportation: she's already on a cart. He can't go yet because his boss won't let him leave the business until his boss also leaves; only then will he go. As long as his boss doesn't leave, Yankev can't leave." That was what Yankl's brother-in-law fired off sharply. Out of fear and panic, I did not have the opportunity to consider all that he had told me. I was also confused

---

19 Reyzl Grinberg's oldest child, Dvora, was born in early 1918. Dvora later married Arye Ben-Ya'akov.

20 December 10, 1917.

21 Though it was Hanukah, *Slikhes* (normally recited on fast days and during the High Holiday season) and *Hoyshanes* (recited only during *Sukes*) were recited due to the threat of exile and the approaching war front. Ya'ari (1929:534) cites an anonymous diarist from Petakh-Tikva of that period who remembers *Hoyshanes* being recited in the synagogue on Monday, December 10, 1917, the previous day, though he fails to comment on the prayers said in the synagogue on December 11. Perhaps only *Hoyshanes* were said on December 10, and, as the situation became more desperate, *Slikhes* were added on December 11.

22 Shloyme is referring to Avróm-Shloyme Perlkvort (ca. 1880, Jerusalem–1918, Kfar-Saba) who was married to Ester-Rokhl, the sister of Yankl Grinberg. She was generally known as Rokhl (ca. 1884, Pinsk, Belarus–1969, Petakh-Tikva). See Appendix D4 (pp. 824–825) for a genealogical chart of the extended Hershkovitsh family.

by the news that Reyzl was already on a cart. How could I possibly let her go alone at such a time, especially when her husband was not at her side? And then a second messenger arrived and told me that, since Yankev could not ride with her, I had to accompany her! As a father, I was concerned with her being alone.

I did not take the time to consider the tragic step I was then taking, and I left right away on one of the government-provided carts which Shloyme had brought. I took the Torah scroll and whatever else I managed to bring along and rode off with the first exiles, thinking that we were being taken to Kfar-Saba. In the end, we were detoured to an Arab village named Kalkilya and thrown into a house that looked like a hole in the ground. Though the soldiers driving the wagons could have arranged for us to arrive there by day, they deliberately delayed until nighttime so that they could rob us and steal our belongings. I lost my *talis*, *tefillin*, and other things, but I mourned the loss of the *talis* and *tefillin* most of all.[23] In short, I had fallen into a deep state of exile. I foresaw that a new world with new troubles was opening up before me. So that you may know how I arrived in Kfar-Saba and what I endured, I will now describe a bit of my life there.

Upon arriving in Kalkilya, we were placed in a hovel. All thirty families were placed there together, each one with their own meager possessions. During the night more unfortunate refugees from Petakh-Tikva arrived and were placed in the same overcrowded hovel. But, thank God, we survived the night. In the morning, we came out to see where we were. We saw narrow alleys and Arab houses with their windowless walls built right up to the street. The Arabs were standing near their houses laughing at us. We awaited some sort of aid, but a rumor spread that the government wanted to send us by train deep into the interior. Meanwhile, we saw people from Kfar-Saba coming to Kalkilya to take their friends and acquaintances back there. This opened a ray of hope for us that our relatives in Kfar-Saba would also come here and take us to Kfar-Saba, especially since Shloyme, Reyzl's brother-in-law, had left for Kfar-Saba earlier the previous evening.

The next morning Shloyme and his father brought a cart and hastily loaded our things onto it, and we rode off to Kfar-Saba, which was only a half-hour

23 On every day except *Shabes* and Jewish holidays, Jewish males aged thirteen and older are obligated by Jewish law to don *tefillin* which is normally done during morning services, and married Jewish men wear a *talis* every day during the morning service. Hence, these items are of utmost importance to the author. Certainly, the lack of these articles did not prevent the author from fulfilling these *mitzvahs*; he unquestionably borrowed someone else's until he was able to purchase new ones.

away.[24] Upon arriving in Kfar-Saba, I felt good and was quite pleased by my new location. I encountered acquaintances from Petakh-Tikva, close friends, and many others, and I felt at home. But do not think that things were good in Kfar-Saba, though it seemed good if you compared it to Kalkilya.

Yankl's brother-in-law Shloyme was the main factor in my being in Kfar-Saba. He had parents, a sister, and a brother here, all among the first refugees from Jaffa.[25] Shloyme's sister was a cook in the soup kitchen in Kfar-Saba, and his father, who brought us over, was the *kashres* supervisor there.[26] That is how we wound up in the soup kitchen. You might think that it was called a soup kitchen because food was cooked there for distribution to the poor. If so, you are badly mistaken! The soup kitchen was not simply a place where the poor could eat for free but rather a place that served so many communal functions that the masses of needy people there turned it into a living hell.

The entrance to the soup kitchen was through a dirty passageway with small alcoves on both sides. Each alcove housed two or three families. These alcoves were exceedingly small. There were no doors; rather a dirty sack covered the doorway to each alcove. In short, this was the entranceway to the soup kitchen, and it was there that I was given lodging. Can you imagine how we lived there? But considering the living quarters of the other hapless refugees, I realized that my accommodations at the soup kitchen were much better than theirs, which were huts made of tree branches and covered with overgrown grass. The wind kept blowing off their makeshift roofs while casting sand into the huts. And when it rained, everything became soaked. They lay on the ground with their children and suffered from the cold. Two or three families lived in each shack. Some quarreled among themselves since they came from various countries and could not communicate with each other, especially since everyone was so embittered and sad. Many in each hut were sick, both children and adults, and there were neither doctors nor medicine nor anything

---

24 Shloyme Perlkvort's father Khaym-Moyshe (1859–1918) was born in Jerusalem and had settled in Jaffa. He was known as "Khaym [the] *shames*." See the article about him in Tidhar (1947:2:904). Shloyme's mother, Khane (ca. 1860, Hungary-1937/8, Tel-Aviv), had immigrated to the Land of Israel in about 1865. Her brothers, named Raab (aka Ben-Ezer), were among the founders of Petakh-Tikva.

25 See the previous and subsequent footnotes for details regarding Shloyme Perlkvort's parents and sister. His brother's name was Yitskhok (Tidhar, 1947:2:904). After being exiled from Jaffa, they moved to Petakh-Tikva where they lived until being exiled to Kfar-Saba.

26 Shloyme Perlkvort's sister was Ester-Beyle "Beylke" Zusman (1882, Jerusalem–1924, Tel-Aviv), the widow of Arye-Leyb (ha-Kohen) Zusman (1877–1909). Arye-Leyb's widow and children changed their surname to Kohen after the First World War (Tidhar, 1947:2:979). A *kashres* supervisor inspects and supervises the *kashres* (kosher status) of a kosher eating establishment such as a soup kitchen, restaurant, etc.

with which to sustain the victims. I pitied their wretched circumstances. Upon seeing this, I was content with being in the soup kitchen.

Since you are now familiar with the soup kitchen, I will describe the hospital that was under the same roof and was separated from the soup kitchen only by a single, thin wall. It was a large room, which was previously used to house horses and oxen, though no troughs were present. Apparently, for the sake of the soup kitchen, all the troughs for feed and water had been cleared out of the hospital and set up in the soup kitchen, where they were used as tables and benches. Here in the hospital were as many as thirty sick people at one time. All of the patients, poor souls, lay on the ground on the few rags they had, with neither cots nor nightstands. One would be moaning, another would be shouting, while a third, poor soul, would be begging for a little water. The noises they made could be heard all night long, but no one attended to them; there was apparently not a single person to care for the sick, because everyone in Kfar-Saba was ill, so there was no help to be had. By the second night, the man who had been crying out for water was dead. At that point, some merciful people were on hand to take him away and bury him. And that was the fate of all the new arrivals in the hospital. Whoever entered did not emerge alive. For how could a sick person survive the uncleanliness there? While they lay on the ground there, pests easily crawled from one person to another; one could scoop up the lice in one's hands. Should you think I am exaggerating, you will be convinced that I am not by the following story.

A woman named Mashe Skibin, a daughter of Orlov of Petakh-Tikva,[27] saw that an unfortunate young girl in the hospital was pleading for someone to take pity on her since she was being eaten alive by the third plague.[28] So this warm-hearted woman had compassion on her and cut off her hair. While she was carrying the shorn hair in a dish to bury it, I saw it too. The third plague had covered it over so much that it was impossible to determine if it was hair or a creeping animal. The clump moved by itself as though it were some kind of a machine. Though the woman who had cut off the clump was not able to extricate herself from the creeping things for a while, she had thereby saved a human being from certain death.

---

27 For more about Mashe Skibin (1887–1961), see *Kfar Saba* (Engel, 1973:37) and her husband's autobiography, which describes her efforts to help rid the refugees of lice in order to stem the spread of typhus (Skibin, 1947:137–138). Her father, Refuel Orlov, died in 1924 in Petakh-Tikva. Some details about him are included in an article about her sister, Miriam Etan, in Tidhar (1958:9:3273).

28 A Biblical reference to lice (Exodus 8:12–15).

When I looked around and saw where I was, I realized that Reyzl could in no way give birth to her baby here because there was no midwife and no place for her to have her child. She would die, God forbid, if she were to have her child here. So I sent her husband instructions that he had to come take her home or at least had to be with her and not depend on me since I could barely walk about! In brief, he obtained a cart, arrived at night, and took her home. I also wanted to ride home, but the pony was unable to pull us all, so he promised that he would send for me later.

I was so pleased that I had rescued Reyzl that I forgot about myself, and I relied on his promise and waited for him to send for me. I forgot that they were not as devoted to me as I, with body and soul, was to them. I waited a few more days and it was now the eve of *Shobes*, so I thought to myself that they would certainly send for me right after *Shobes*. On Sunday, I saw that there was absolutely no word from them, so I decided to pay as much money as it would cost to leave *Keyver-Saba*. I called it *Keyver-Saba* because whoever was unlucky enough to end up there was buried there.[29] But God had other plans for me. That very *Shobes*, the British entered Petakh-Tikva and passage on the road was cut off.[30] So I had to remain in Kfar-Saba and hope from one day to the next that I would be liberated, meaning that the British would enter Kfar-Saba and we would be saved.

[The week of April 20-26, 1918:] A total of seventeen weeks has now passed since Reyzl went home.[31] Who knew how long it would take until our redemption arrived and who knew whether I would be able to endure the miseries and survive this exile? I will now describe for you, if only briefly, what I lived through in Kfar-Saba since Reyzele's departure, how the exile to Hadera came about, what I did in Hadera, and how I live now. I will describe everything in brief as my strength does not suffice and my mind does not work well; similarly, neither do my eyes, hands, and all my limbs in general. So, you will make do with the little that I can write.

At the soup kitchen, I made space where I could lie down on my few possessions and guard Reyzele's things that she had left behind, but it was impossible to guard it all. A *gabbai* who was a communal worker—but, in my opinion, a real scoundrel—used to come in and turn over everything. He would say he did not like this and he did not like that, and he left everything topsy-turvy. For

---

29 Kfar-Saba means "grandfather's village," while *Keyver-Saba* means "grandfather's grave."

30 Saturday, December 22, 1917. See also Ya'ari (1929:546).

31 Though the original Yiddish states "seventeen months" had passed, it should have stated "seventeen weeks." Seventeen months would have been May 1919, a year after the author left Kfar-Saba (ch. 33, p. 645).

hours on end, I searched to find all my possessions, and many of Reyzl's things remained missing, but I watched carefully the basket containing her clothes. I constantly made sure that the key to the basket's lock had not broken, and the basket, together with my own belongings, went along with me wherever I went.

Suddenly I had guests in my wonderful lodging in the soup kitchen. This was Reb Moyshe Regensberg and his wife. In Petakh-Tikva he was called "The American."[32] They had been placed in a house with the *Rebetsn,* Refoel Rabinovits's mother, but had just fled their lodgings since cannons had been placed right next to the house and it was now surrounded by soldiers.[33] Having no possessions, Reb Moyshe Regensberg grabbed his wife and rushed off to me in the soup kitchen; naturally, one could not remain in such a house under such conditions. The *Rebetsn,* though, remained in the house and did not want to leave because all her son's possessions were there. I took them in as guests and gave them some things with which to cover themselves. But, unfortunately, there was no place to lie down so we sat and huddled next to each other and suffered through the nights like this.

The end of our stay in the soup kitchen was not a good one since Rokhl began to feel ill and so too her children.[34] The people in the huts fell ill and began to die. From day to day, their illnesses grew worse, and the number of deaths increased. Not a day passed without a death or two, or even more.[35] The daylight hours were not long enough to bury all the dead, and some were

---

32 No record of a Moyshe Regensberg in Petakh-Tikva has been found. Several residents of Petakh-Tikva at that time had once lived in the United States, which is a subject deserving separate treatment.

33 Rebetsn Feyge-Mine (Khazan) Rabinovits was the widow of the prominent Rabbi Elyahu David Rabinovits-Teomim (1843–1905), who is commonly known as the Aderet, the Hebrew acronym of his name. He was the rabbi of Ponevezh (Panevezys, Lithuania) and then of Mir, Belarus. In 1901, he immigrated to Jerusalem. He was the father-in-law of Rabbi Abraham Isaac Kook (1865–1935), who was the first Ashkenazi chief rabbi of British Mandatory Palestine. In 2009, Avshalom Aderet of Kiryat Ono, Israel confirmed her and her son Refoel's identities by relating that his grandfather Refoel-Leyvi Rabinovits (1881–1958) left Petakh-Tikva with his wife, children, and mother during the First World War for Kfar-Saba, where his mother, Rebetsn Feyge-Mine, died on January 29, 1918 (16th of *Shvat*).

34 Rokhl was Yankl Grinberg's sister and the wife of Shloyme Perlkvort.

35 In a personal interview in 2001 with the author's granddaughter Aliza Bernfeld, she related that she heard from a number of people who had been in exile in Kfar-Saba as children that the author used to raise the spirits of the children during those horrendous times there by gathering them together and playing and singing with them. Rokhl (Grinberg) Perlvort's two daughters Hadassah Levitt (1904–2005) and Zipporah Sheiner Same (1907–2009) related being in Kfar-Saba with the author, whom they called "*Feter* Pinkhes" (Uncle Pinkhes in Yiddish), with his flowing white beard, and his love of children. (As recalled in correspondence in 2003 with Abraham Solomon "Sol" Levitt after interviewing his mother Hadassah and aunt Zipporah, both of Perth, Australia.)

not buried until the next day.[36] Horrible! It was simply a horrible sight to see. Suddenly the *shames*, Reb Khaym, fell ill.[37] He had been busy every minute with burying the dead. His son Shloyme also fell ill, as did Shloyme's wife Rokhl, his brother Yitskhok, and his sister Beylke—almost all of Reyzl's family.[38] Thus, when I counted the sick in her family, there were fifteen souls, and they were all lying down in the soup kitchen.[39] When I saw this I began seeking a way of escaping from the soup kitchen, which I managed to do. Do you know where I went? To Reb Leyb Khaymovitsh, who had a room as small as could be.[40] A *minyan* convened in that room, and it was there that he fulfilled the *mitzvah* of providing free lodging for guests. He would put his guests on cots and on boards while he himself slept on the ground. It turned out that five guests, one after the other, died in this Khaymovitsh's room.

During the month of *Shvat*, Reyzele's mother-in-law died.[41] Also among the dead were Rokhl's father-in-law, Reb Khaym the *shames*, and husband Shloyme, who left her a poor, sick widow with five young orphans.[42]

---

36 More than 1,500 Jews were exiled to Kfar-Saba, and between 240 and 248 of them died there. Jewish law prescribes that Jews make every possible effort to bury their dead on the day of their deaths (*Kitsur Shulkhan Arukh* 198:3–4).

37 Reb Khaym was Shloyme Perlvort's father. See p. 637, footnote 24 above for details.

38 Yitskhok-Yekhezkel Perlkvort (1893, Jaffa–1959, Tel-Aviv) played an important role in the Council of Displaced Persons which aided the Jaffa refugees (Tidhar, 1961, 11:3735–3736). Beylke is referring to Ester-Beyle (Perlkvort) Zusman (later changed to Kohen).

39 Shloyme Perlkvort's daughter, Hadassah Levitt (1904–2005), contracted malaria at that time and later recovered with quinine therapy in Zikhron-Ya'akov. (Correspondence in 2003 with Hadassah's son Abraham Solomon "Sol" Levitt of Yokine, Australia.)

40 For more about Yehude-Arye "Leyb" Khaymovitsh (1862–1944) and his house, see Engel (1973:54,96).

41 Refering to Yankl Grinberg's mother Sheyne-Khaye, who died in on January 12, 1918 (28th of *Teyves*) in Kfar-Saba. Her granddaughter Zipporah (Perlkvort) Sheiner Same (1907–2009) related that Sheyne-Khaye died of typhus. (As related in correspondence in 2003 with Abraham Solomon "Sol" Levitt of Yokine, Australia, after interviewing his aunt Zipporah.)

42 Rokhl's husband, Shloyme Perlkvort, died on January 22, 1918 (9th of *Shvat*), likely from one of the diseases that were rife in Kfar-Saba at the time, namely typhoid fever, typhus, or malaria. During *shivah*, Shloyme's father Khaym said that he could not live without his son; he became progressively weaker and died shortly afterward on February 1, 1918 (19th of *Shvat*). In addition, Shloyme's nine-year-old niece Reyzl Zusman died on January 30, 1918 (17th of *Shvat*) in Kfar-Saba; she was the daughter of Shloyme's sister Beylke Zusman (later changed to Kohen). (Correspondence in 2003 with Abraham Solomon "Sol" Levitt of Yokine, Australia, after interviewing his mother Hadassah [Perlkvort] Levitt [1904–2005].)

CHAPTER 33

Suffering in Exile and Returning to Petakh-Tikva, 1918

Suffering • Afflicted with the Third Plague[1] • Looking for Water Saves My Life • Exile in Hadera and Haifa • Liberation • Coming to Jaffa by Sailboat • Returning Home to Petakh-Tikva

My inner life at Khaymovitsh's is indescribable and impossible to be expressed. I cannot convey all I was forced to endure, both from the place of lodging itself and from its owner, my host, Mr. Khaymovitsh. He did everything for his own personal gain, yet constantly insisted that whatever he did was completely for the sake of a *mitzvah*. I have encountered all sorts of wicked people, but I had not yet met one who was such an ignoramus. He was in a class of his own. I will discuss him later at length.[2] Meanwhile, I will tell you what I had to endure, in addition to the "wonderful" guesthouse and its owner, my "benefactor."

Do not forget that while I was staying at the soup kitchen, I contracted Pharaoh's plague, that is, lice. It grew much more virulent here at Khaymovitsh's. I do not know how I managed to bear it. Several times a day I would go behind the houses to rid myself of the worms—I called them worms—that were eating me alive. There were so many that I would brush off hundreds of them with my hands. There were all sorts of lice: runners, crawlers, round ones, long and thin ones, and very tiny ones the size of pinheads whose bites were the worst of all. There were black ones, white ones, and yellow ones, and all of them bit me at once. After extricating myself from them, I would find more of them an hour later. That is how rapidly and quickly they multiply. God's plague of lice was such a severe affliction that it had to be caused by "the finger of God."[3] And apart from

1 The third plague was lice, as mentioned in Exodus 8:16–19.

2 See ch. 34, pp. 652–654.

3 Exodus 8:19.

the great pains I endured from the plague itself, which are impossible to describe, I was also assaulted in bed at night by fleas, bedbugs, and mosquitoes, all of which bit me. I became seriously ill, and no one looked after me while I was sick. When they wanted to take me to that wonderful, infamous hospital, I refused to go.

Hearing the word hospital, I shivered in fear and shouted in bitterness, "Doctor! What? You're ordering me to the hospital? No! I won't go! Do you want to put an end to me so soon? No! God will help me without your hospital!" And so I remained there in bed until God helped me out of danger and I began to improve, even though I did not have any milk, soup, or meat to strengthen me.

You must certainly be wondering how I was able to support myself since I was not receiving any financial assistance. Regarding this, I can tell you that Dr. Slor and Khaymovitsh gave me interest-free loans when I was hard-pressed for money.[4] Slor also gave me food for *Shobes*, which saved me a few *bishliks* each week.[5] The butcher Yosefzon also paid me ten to twelve *bishliks* a week for slaughtering, in addition to giving me a few ounces of meat and bit of liver throughout the week, which saved my life. I used to give the meat to Rokhl, and she used to prepare it for me and for herself as well.[6] This was my source of income, and I lived like this in Kfar-Saba for about six months—until I was forced to move to Hadera.

After *Purim*,[7] the Council of Displaced Persons told the refugees to travel to the colonies further north, e.g., Hadera and Samarin.[8] Nobody wanted to leave Kfar-Saba since they thought that their salvation would arrive momentarily. But their refusal to leave did not help them in the slightest. The Council just stopped providing them with support, particularly *matses* for the upcoming

---

4 Tsvi-Arye Slor (1875–1959) was born in Jerusalem, and was the younger brother of Khaym-Moyshe, mentioned in ch. 30, p. 606, footnote 7. Tsvi-Arye lived a colorful life in several countries and was married several times, including to two different nieces named Shoshana Slor. He studied medicine in Germany and later became the doctor to the sultan of Morocco. Upon returning to Palestine in 1901, he practiced medicine in Petakh-Tikva and then moved to Kfar-Saba in 1911, where he opened a medical clinic and a pharmacy. During the First World War, he treated, free of charge, the numerous refugees who arrived in Kfar-Saba (Slor, 2002).

5 A *bishlik* was a monetary unit in Ottoman Turkey, worth an eighth of a *mejid*, i.e., a Turkish pound (lira).

6 As related in ch. 32, p. 641, Rokhl Perlkvort was the recently widowed sister-in-law of Reyzl (Hershkovits) Grinberg, who was the author's niece. See Appendix D4 (pp. 824–825) for a genealogical chart of the extended Hershkovitsh family.

7 February 26, 1918.

8 The Council wanted the refugees to move northward away from the fighting (Engel, 1973:117). Samarin, aka Zamrin, was the Arabic name for the site of Zikhron-Ya'akov.

Pesach, so a few of the refugees gave in and left for Samarin or Hadera before Pesach.[9] After Pesach, almost all of the refugees made a rush toward Hadera or Samarin, because they saw that they had to obey the Council.[10] Six weeks [*sic*] after they left Kfar-Saba for Zikhron, I took over the hut in which Rokhl had lived and resumed writing my Torah scroll there.[11] After all, it had been four months that I had not been able to take a quill in hand because our quarters were jam-packed with no place for me to write. But as people began leaving, I found that Rokhl's dwelling was a good place for me to continue my writing, and I remained in Kfar-Saba, though I went a bit hungry. Yosefzon the butcher and also Mr. Brande had left for Zikhron, so I no longer had earnings from *sh'khita*. I survived strictly on loans that I received from Dr. Slor or Khaymovitsh.[12]

I was so intent on writing the Torah scroll that I ignored the cannonballs flying over my head in all directions. I sat in that hut writing the Torah scroll as if the bombings had absolutely no bearing on me. With a strong will, I continued writing from the Torah portion of *Shmos* and onward.[13] I was up to writing the Torah portion of *Bo*,[14] which describes the plague of hail falling on the Egyptians, while here in Kfar-Saba a hailstorm of cannonballs was thundering.

Once, I walked out of the hut to eat and look for a bit of water to drink, and I left a sheet of freshly written parchment spread out on the table since the letters were still wet. Upon my return an hour later, I found that a bomb had fallen and had completely destroyed the roof. I was barely able to find the sheet of

---

9 A small amount of *matse* was obtained with difficulty, evidently from other sources (Engel, 1973:117). Pesach was from March 28 to April 4, 1918.

10 Most of the refugees left Kfar-Saba immediately after the severe bombing of the night of April 27, 1918, and the residents of Kfar-Saba left a few days later (Engel, 1973:117).

11 The author could not have taken over Rokhl's hut "six weeks" after almost all had left Kfar-Saba right after Pesach, which ended on April 4, 1918, because that would have been May 16, 1918, the day that the author left Kfar-Saba (see p. 645, footnote 19 below). "Six days" likely should have been printed instead of "six weeks." The author clearly continued to lodge at Khaymovitsh's and used Rokhl's former hut only for writing his Torah scroll.

After leaving for Zikhron-Ya'akov (also simply called Zikhron), Yankl Grinberg's father Osher-Yoyne (born ca. 1865) died there on June 22, 1918 (12th of *Tamuz*).

12 Zev "Volf" Brande (1848–1918) immigrated to Palestine in 1882 and was one of the early settlers of Petakh-Tikva. There he devoted his energy to communal activities and in helping the poor. During the First World War, he founded an inexpensive soup kitchen for the poor in Petakh-Tikva. He was exiled to Kfar-Saba. From the author's account, Brande apparently was involved with providing meat to the poor there as well. Brande then left for Zikhron-Ya'akov, where he died in July 1918, shortly before he would have been allowed to return home (Tidhar, 1947:1:128–129).

13 In ch. 32, p. 634, the author writes that he wrote up to the verses describing Pharaoh's issue of his decree, which appears at the end of the Torah portion of *Shmos* (Exodus 5:6–18).

14 The plague of hail appears at the end of the preceding Torah portion, *Va'era* (Exodus 9:13-34).

parchment which was buried under a mound of dirt. I cleaned it off and saw that it was severely damaged. Thank God that I was spared. I *bentsht goyml* for the miracle of my having been out of the hut at the exact moment the cannonball exploded.[15] God not only saved me then, but divine providence saved me constantly. Bombs landed near me many times, but I was not injured, God forbid; I only suffered a bit of a scare.

One night while at my lodgings at Khaymovitsh's, the firing and thundering of cannons was terrifying. I arose and squeezed myself under a bed, where I lay in fear. Everyone there covered themselves with dirt.[16] That night was frightful to endure. In the morning, all was quiet. Only then did I realize the miracle that God had performed by allowing us to live.

***

We suffered greatly from the bombings.[17] Finally we also left Kfar-Saba. Dr. Slor, Khaymovitsh and his family, and I were the last ones to remain. We kept hoping that the British would arrive momentarily and would save us. We only left when we saw that no one else remained, the houses were almost all destroyed, and the Turkish soldiers were pillaging and destroying the rest. We left [for Hadera] right on the eve of *Shvues*.[18]

In Hadera, I ran into many people from Petakh-Tikva as well as those who had left Kfar-Saba earlier.[19] All were my fellow brothers and sisters in exile, and all greeted me warmly and explained to me that it was better here than in Kfar-Saba. Within a short time, I realized that they were correct. It did not take long before I found myself a place to eat, and the Council set up a separate hut for me not far from *shul* where I resumed writing my Torah scroll on a daily basis.[20] I wrote eight to nine hours a day, apart from lunchtime. My writing was

---

15 To *bentsh goymel* means to make the Hebrew blessing of deliverance from danger (*Kitsur Shulkhan Arukh* 61:1–2). For more details regarding this episode, see Appendix E (p. 832).

16 Everyone covered themselves with dirt, apparently, to protect themselves from shrapnel. In those days, many houses had dirt floors.

17 Though this chapter until this point and the next chapter were written in 1919, this section on Hadera was written 1929. In a letter from *Nisan* or *Iyar* 5689 (April 1929), the author states that his period in Hadera was still unwritten (see Appendix B3, p. 794).

18 May 16, 1918. See also Engel (1973, 117).

19 After the war, Hadera became something of an attraction for tourists (including such personages as US Supreme Court Justice, Louis D. Brandeis) in that it had been completely leveled during the war (Engel, 1973:121).

20 Naturally, the author did not write on *Shabes* and *Yontef*, which is forbidden according to Jewish law.

so precious and holy to me that I did not waste a minute. I wanted to complete the Torah scroll as soon as possible, while my hands and eyes still served me.

Hadera rejuvenated me a bit. Here I met Tsipoyre Levin, the widow of the late *shoykhet*.[21] She cooked wholesome meals for others and did not overcharge. In general, she was a good soul who sympathized with others' difficulties. She told me, "Eat lunch here every day. If you're able to pay me, then fine. If not, I trust that your payment won't be delayed for long. Pay me when you have the money." Her words strengthened and consoled me. In short, I began to eat my daily lunch at her home; she gave me meat and soup, and she also gave me tea every morning and evening. And I continued eating at Slor's on *Shobes*. The Council agreed to give me a loan of twenty *bishliks* per week, and they also hired me to be present at the *sh'khita*. Since the *shoykhet* was young and had little experience, the Council asked me to be present while he inspected the cow's lungs, from which I earned ten *bishliks* a week.[22] With these thirty *bishliks*, I survived and was able to pay Tsipoyre Levin, though she was not pressing me for payment. But when I had additional expenditures, such as washing laundry or shoe repairs, those thirty *bishliks* would not suffice and I would remain slightly in debt to her.

During my last few weeks in Hadera, Slor was no longer able to give me any food for *Shobes* because his family had left Hadera. So I began to eat also on *Shobes* at Tsipoyre Levin's, which naturally caused my debt to her to gradually increase to the sizable sum of eighty *bishliks*. Another contributing factor to my mounting debt was that the Council of Displaced Persons was then only able to give me ten *bishliks* a week. To encourage the refugees to travel further north, the Council stopped giving stipends to many of the refugees so that they should not remain there in the shacks during the winter. They did not want a repeat of what had occurred in Kfar-Saba.[23] The Council of Displaced Persons began to concern itself with the problem in advance and sent the refugees to stay in rented apartments in Haifa. In sum, I had accumulated a debt of eighty *bishliks* to Tsipoyre Levin. I had to move on once again so that, first of all, I would not incur even more debt, and secondly, so that I could obtain better living quarters in Haifa.

In Hadera, I led the Rosh Hashanah services.[24] On the first day of Rosh Hashanah, I led *Shakhris*, and on the second day I led *Musaf*. Thank God,

---

21 Tsipoyre was the second wife of the recently deceased *shoykhet* of Hadera, Shloyme-Avigder Levin (1866–1917), whose first wife Ester-Khane died in 1908 (Tidhar, 1947:1:338–339).

22 Checking the lungs of slaughtered livestock for lesions is required by Jewish law. See *Shulkhan Arukh* (*Yoreh Deah* 39:1).

23 During the previous winter in Kfar-Saba, disease was widespread and resulted in a great number of deaths, as described at the end of ch. 32, pp. 640–641.

24 September 7–8, 1918.

I arrived in Haifa on the eve of *Shobes Tshive*.[25] On Yom Kippur, I led *Musaf* and fasted easily.[26]

In Haifa, I rented a clean room, and I was now able to rest peacefully at night, thank God. In a *shul* not far from my lodgings, I was able to resume the writing of my Torah scroll once again, thank God. The Council lent me twelve banknotes, which I exchanged for ten *mejids*, so for the time being I had enough to cover my expenses.[27] I had to eat dry foods because I did not have anyone to cook for me and was not able to afford the meals at the hotels. But this suited me fine since I was in exile.

On the fifth day of the intermediate days of *Sukes* of 5679, a "voice of the herald which brings good tidings" arrived.[28] I thanked God that I had lived to see our salvation and could now hope to soon be home in Petakh-Tikva because on that day I heard that the British had entered Hadera and Samarin and all the refugees there were now liberated. I regretted having left Hadera only a few days before its liberation, but I comforted myself that the British would be here shortly. I was sure that now that the British had begun to advance they would not stay put as they had done for ten months outside of Kfar-Saba. The British advance caused the Turkish military in Haifa to panic. By the intermediate days of *Sukes*, you could see Turkish and German soldiers beginning to flee.[29] It was obvious that the British troops were swiftly approaching. While praying in *shul* on *Hoyshane-Rabe*, people were terrified and joyous at the same time. They were terrified of the cannon fire being shot by the Turks from Mt. Carmel; they feared that the town would be destroyed. If the Turks were to realize how badly they were faring, they might bomb the town from the mountain to demolish it. That would actually have occurred had the British not moved straight toward the Turks and their cannons on the mountain, surrounded them, and captured their entire military, including their cannons.

The invading British soldiers were as numerous as the sand on the seashore. Soon the town was filled with all manner of British military personnel,

---

25 September 14, 1918. *Shobes Tshive* (*Shabat Tshuva* in Modern Hebrew) literally means the "Sabbath of Repentance" and occurs between Rosh Hashanah and Yom Kippur.

26 September 16, 1918.

27 The Council would have loaned funds to the author in Turkish lira (pound) banknotes (*Palestine During the War*, 1921: 35). One Turkish gold *mejid* (pronounced *mezhid*) was equivalent to one Turkish lira (pound).

28 The fifth day of the intermediate days of *Sukes* is called *Hoyshane-Rabe* and occurred on September 27, 1918. The author cites a verse from the end of the special prayers of the day, called *Hoyshanes*, to refer to the news of the British victory.

29 Germany and the Ottoman Empire were allies during the First World War, with Germany sending military advisors and machine gunners to Palestine to help the Ottoman Turks fight the British.

foot soldiers, and cavalrymen, and the streets were replete with unlimited numbers of cannons, horses, camels, and mules. Naturally, we were overjoyed to be rid of the Turks and the Germans. Particularly we, the refugees, rejoiced and danced on *Simchas Torah* with true happiness over the news of our salvation.[30] But we were not yet able to travel home, because, firstly, there were no wagons to be had and, secondly, the roads were filled with British military personnel, and it was dangerous to travel. We were eager to go home, but we had to be patient. But even eight days after *Sukes*, the military was still making a commotion with their constant comings and goings. Even after the commotion had died down somewhat, and one was able to travel, it was very expensive, so I had still had to wait.

I waited until the fourth day of *Heshvan*,[31] when I heard that it was possible to travel via sailboat to Jaffa for twenty *bishliks* a person. We put together a group of seventy people and rented a boat. We departed from Haifa in apprehension but arrived in Jaffa joyfully on the very same day. I was more nervous than everyone else to travel in such a vessel on the sea because I was afraid of my Torah scroll becoming wet from the waves beating against the ship. But God, who guarded me until now, also protected me on the sea. As the prophet says in God's name, "When you pass through water I am with you, and the rivers shall not flow over you; when you go amidst fire you shall not be burned."[32] And that is what happened to me. The bullets and cannonballs that rained and flew above my head did not scathe me and the waves of the sea did not douse me. The sea remained calm, and the boat sailed quickly because the Torah scroll protected it from water damage. But behind our boat were two other vessels whose passengers did suffer a fright and were thoroughly drenched after being immersed in the water. Barely alive, they arrived in Jaffa at night, so they had to sleep on the boat. Unfortunate souls, they suffered greatly. We, however, arrived in Jaffa two hours before nightfall, immediately disembarked, and went into town, each to his own destination. We had to leave our belongings on the boat as demanded by the authorities.

The next morning, upon arriving at the shore, I found many of my fellow passengers. We were all waiting for the high official and the Zionist Council, who needed to ascertain which refugees needed assistance in traveling further. Also, the doctors of Hadassah came to assist those who needed attention.[33]

30 *Simchas Torah* started on Friday night, September 28, 1918, and lasted until the next evening.

31 Thursday, October 10, 1918.

32 Isaiah 43:2. For more details regarding the voyage, see Appendix E, pp. 834.

33 Hadassah is an American Jewish volunteer women's organization which was founded in New York City in 1912. In 1918, it established in Palestine the American Zionist Medical Unit manned by 45 medical health professionals.

This was how we spent that day on the seashore until three in the afternoon, by which time all had received their belongings.

As soon as I arrived in Jaffa, I sent letters to my children in Paris and Russia and informed them that I was alive and that I was in need of funds to repay my debts.[34]

I remained in Jaffa for three days because there were no wagons. With so many exiled families returning, there were not enough wagons for everyone. The price of a wagon was steeper than usual, and you had to wait. When I realized that I would be waiting a long while, I left my possessions with a friend and went on foot to Petakh-Tikva, though I could barely walk. As soon as I left the town, the wagons caught up with me. Upon seeing a hapless old Jew staggering along, they had pity on me and told me to get on and be seated. When they heard that I wanted to pay, they arranged a particularly good place for me and I arrived right at my door in three hours. Upon seeing my house and again upon entering my house, I gave thanks to the Living God for bestowing me with so many kindnesses, allowing me to remain alive and return home. Out of tremendous joy, I cried. With tears, I met my local children, meaning my niece Reyzl and her husband Yankl. Upon seeing me, they were overjoyed because they had been impatiently awaiting my arrival. In summation, all my neighbors were happy to see me return. Upon seeing me, some made the blessing "Blessed are You who revives the dead," as they had thought that I had died in Kfar-Saba. Others made the blessing "Blessed are You who releases the bound," and still others made the blessing of *Shehekhiyonu*.[35] In short, there was a great to-do over me. Everyone acknowledged that God had performed miracles on my behalf—namely that an elderly man had merited returning home, while many strong, healthy, young men were gone for eternity.

---

34 At that time, the author's daughter Rukhl was in France and his sons Isruel-Burekh and Shloyme were in the Ukraine.

35 A Jewish person who has not seen his friend for a year is required to make the Hebrew blessings of "Blessed are You who revives the dead," according to *Shulkhan Arukh* (*Orakh Khayim* 225:1). Someone who has not seen his friend for 30 days is required to make the blessing of *Shehekhiyonu*, praising God "who has granted us life, sustained us, and enabled us to reach this occasion." Nonetheless, these blessings are rarely recited in their full form (that is, mentioning God's holy names) but are said informally as good wishes. Apparently, the author is referring to their informal forms because "Blessed are You who releases the bound" is in fact a blessing recited each morning upon arising, thanking God for the ability to move one's limbs. It would be very unlikely to have been recited in full under the circumstances described in the text.

CHAPTER 34

Completing the Torah Scroll, the Arab Attack, and My Children Join Me in Palestine, 1919–1929

Khaymovitsh's Doings • Receiving a Letter and Money from My Children • Completing the Writing of the Torah Scroll • Celebrating the Escorting of the Torah Scroll to the *Shul* • Falling Ill as the Torah Scroll was Being Brought to the *Shul* • The Calmness is Disturbed • Finding Another Life's Partner • My Niece and Her Husband Leave the House • The Arabs Attack • Four Casualties • Salvation Comes Through the British Government • The End of the Narrative of My Life's Story

Now that I am back home and well rested, I can begin to hope to see some joy in life. After all, since God helped me so much, I can assume my prayers were accepted. I had constantly prayed to God that I should not die in exile. Death itself did not frighten me; dying in exile did, because a person who dies in exile is buried without a shroud, without honor—he is buried like a dog. In exile, the members of the burial society were street toughs who were only looking to earn a few *bishliks*.[1] It made no difference to them whether they were carrying a heavy sack or a dead body, which is why I was terrified of dying in exile. When I was ill, the doctor in Kfar-Saba had given up on me. They whispered to each other, questioning whether I would last until the morning. Because I had such a

1 In normal circumstances, membership in a Jewish burial society is an honor, and prominent members of the community are involved in what is considered to be holy work.

FIGURE 27. Pinkhes-Dov Goldenshteyn, age eighty, sitting in the yard of his house in Petakh-Tikva in 1928. He is sitting under a eucalyptus tree with an old millstone behind it. The photographer was facing east, so one can see the back of the larger of Goldenshteyn's two houses in the background, where his son Shloyme's wife, Etya, and daughter, Dvora, can be seen. (Courtesy of Shifra Bernfeld of Petakh-Tikva.)

high fever, may God protect us, they thought that I did not hear and understand them. But I was fully conscious, and I prayed that God would not let me die a lonely forsaken death.

I heard the whispering among the doctors and my "benefactor" by the name of Khaymovitsh, who was looking forward to getting rid of me as quickly as possible so as to "inherit" my possessions, as he had "inherited" the possessions of the five others who had died in his house.[2] You will learn from my narrative below what I endured from him and, in general, what kind of ignoramus he was.

Upon my arrival in Kfar-Saba, I thought that he was a righteous person. I was sure that he would merit a fine portion in the World to Come for his kindness to the refugees; he encouraged them, helped them financially, and was extremely hospitable. He welcomed them into his home, though it was small and cramped, and he made room for them. He also held a *minyan* at his home so that everyone could pray together. For the first few days after my arrival in Kfar-Saba, I—and everyone else—was deceived by him. But after a very short while I realized that I had to distance myself as far as possible from him and not let myself be persuaded to stay with him, even though it was dark and horrible at the soup kitchen, as you already know. I refused to stay with him because I understood that his motivation was not purely to perform a *mitzvah*. I saw that it was coming from his self-interest.

I would only pray with the *minyan* at his house. I saw how domineering he was. He yelled at everyone and found fault with them. He showed off his Torah scholarship to everyone. He would argue with Torah scholars over a ruling in *The Code of Jewish Law* or regarding a quotation from the Talmud.[3] You would think that he knew a bit of Talmud or had once known something of it. No! He never knew how to study the Talmud, and certainly could not do it now! So what did he argue about? About everything and anything—for no good reason at all! After all, he was the most influential person there! He was the helpful townsman and everyone's benefactor, while we were the Jews in exile, the refugees, and what did refugees know? I once told him that this was the first time I had seen someone who understood everything by himself better than Torah scholars who had studied the subject matter in depth. He replied, "Of course I understand!"

---

2 As mentioned in ch. 32, p. 641.

3 *The Code of Jewish Law* was originally compiled by Rabbi Yosef Caro in the sixteenth century. Together with its commentaries, it is the most widely accepted compilation of Jewish law ever written.

Khaymovitsh was also a *gabbai* of the burial society and earned a profit from every person who died by selling boards and poles to their families.[4] In addition, he would also bring home a *talis*, *tefillin*, or various objects like clothes, a pillow, and laundry from the deceased. Obviously, he did the same with the possessions of the five people who died at his home; they had certainly left many things which he took for himself with the justification that they had owed him money. In order to be perceived as a pious Jew, he claimed that everything he did was only for the sake of the *mitzvah*, but, in reality, everything he did was for his personal gain. For example, among the refugees from Petakh-Tikva were merchants who brought along many types of wares—olive oil, honey, wine, dried grapes,[5] wheat, and household goods—which they deposited with Mr. Khaymovitsh because he was, after all, the trustworthy person there. The merchants then raced from Kfar-Saba back to their homes in Petakh-Tikva, trying to make it in time to save and bring back some more of their merchandise to Kfar-Saba. But they ended up stuck in Petakh-Tikva, because the British had already taken it over, preventing them from returning to Kfar-Saba.[6] So everything remained with their "benefactor" Khaymovitsh, who took their wares and began to sell them, with the excuse that he was taking care of their property. He opened the cans of olive oil and honey in front of my eyes and weighed them, ostensibly writing down the amounts so that he would know what he owed their owners. Obviously, he marked the prices low, and when people heard about the low prices they began to come to make purchases. He, for his part, would sell at a reasonable price for one day only. The next day, he would claim to have run out of merchandise. When people inquired if he had anything available, he would pretend that he was doing them a great favor and sell them merchandise for a steep price. Claiming that he was doing it "for the sake of the *mitzvah*" and for others to have some basic necessities, he charged exorbitant prices, which resulted in the sale lasting an entire month.

I had never met such a merchant in my entire life. Every worthless item that had been thrown out became a commodity by which to make money and earn *mitzvahs*. Everything was merchandise for him including old laundry which had been lying in the streets on piles of garbage, rags left over from the dead, and

---

4 Probably referring to the wooden boards on which the deceased are placed during the end of the purification process of the body before burial (*Kitsur Shulkhan Arukh* 197:2–9). Afterward, the boards served as covers for the wooden coffins. Perhaps the poles were used to carry the coffins.

5 In the original Yiddish, געפרעגלטע טרויבן ("fried grapes") is mistakenly printed instead of געטריגטע טרויבן ("dried grapes") which were used for culinary purposes or to make wine.

6 The merchants thought that the Turks would drive all the Jews from Petakh-Tikva or that it would be destroyed (see p. xx), so they wanted to bring along their merchandise.

taleysim. Toward the end of our exile, when they began to transport the refugees to Zikhron, Haifa, and Hadera, every refugee who could not drag his possessions along would bring them to Khaymovitsh for safekeeping until he would be able to return for them in the future. My host naturally never refused; he allowed everything to be placed under his watch and made place for everything. Since his neighbors had abandoned their houses, he placed and kept all sorts of items in their houses, disregarding the fact that his neighbors' possessions were still there. He was soon selling their possession to other people as well. Settlers from other colonies who came with wagons to transport the refugees also purchased merchandise from him.

When Khaymovitsh himself finally had to leave Kfar-Saba, he picked out the best items and packed them separately, marking them as his own, while he packed up the leftover worthless items and marked them with their owners' names. After that, he left Kfar-Saba for Hadera where he sold everything for a good sum of money. When the former refugees demanded their items back, he claimed that the Turks had taken his things too. Upon learning that he was selling their merchandise, some wanted to file a suit against him with the Council, and he wanted me to serve as his witness. I warned him not to use me as a witness because I would ruin him by disclosing the complete truth. He then stayed clear of me and left Hadera for Zikhron. After the war, he moved from Zikhron to Petakh-Tikva, where many of the former refugees sued him. He was disgraced by them, and I do not know exactly how he settled matters with them. Nonetheless, he continued to do favors and provide interest-free loans to everyone.

It is now time to return to my homecoming and talk about my current life after exile. When the commotion surrounding my return passed and once I had calmed down, I began to examine my house, which had been bombed and had sustained extensive damage on the day the British entered Petakh-Tikva. Upon examining everything, I thanked God for the kindness that He showed me by detaining me in Kfar-Saba so that my niece, her husband, and I would remain alive, because I was supposed to return home that *Shobes*, as I have already described.[7] If I had returned home then, we would have all been killed. And who knows how many others would have been in my house had I been there, and they too would have been injured. So first of all, I praised the Almighty for the

7 The British entered Petakh-Tikva on Saturday, December 22, 1917 (ch. 32, p. 639). When Yankl Grinberg brought his wife Reyzl back to Petakh-Tikva, they did not stay in the author's house. If the author would have returned with them, all would have been killed in the bombing of his house. Upon his return, the author found his house packed with British soldiers (see Appendix E, p. 834).

miracle that He had performed for us. Secondly, I looked around to see which items were lacking. The fact that items were missing did not surprise me. After all, with no homeowner around, everything became ownerless, and anyone entering would have walked away with something. But I was surprised at what was left: two or three beds, bed linen, a table, and chairs.

I then began to yearn for my children. After all, it had already been two years since I last received a letter from my children in America,[8] and it had been four years since I had heard from my children in Russia. Now my sole concern was to hear from my children—to have the privilege of receiving letters from them, to find out where they were, and what their children were doing. In short, I could not live calmly. Nonetheless, I could thank God for not abandoning me because letters quickly started to arrive from my children. The first letter that I received was from my dear daughter Rukhele in Paris, who wrote me that she was healthy, thank God, and was wiring me 200 francs. She was very happy to have heard from me and to find out that I was healthy. A short while later, another letter came from Rukhele in which she let me know how her brothers in America were doing; they had received my letters and had also sent money and letters. Two weeks later, letters and money arrived from my Refuel and Yankev. In short, I was alive, thank God, and had much satisfaction and pleasure from their letters in which they wrote that they and their children were healthy. They wrote the same about Yosef, though he himself was not writing, so they were writing for him.[9] They also wrote that they had not received any letters from my children in Russia for over a year and did not know how they were. But they knew, based on letters they had received in the past, that my son Shloyme was married and already had a child and that Isruel and Nekhame's children were in school and were all healthy, thank God.[10] Thank God that I merited to hear this bit of news, and God will certainly also continue to help.

[May 1919:] Thank God, seven months have already passed since I returned home from exile. I reside in my own home, thank God, together with my niece Reyzl, whom I married off here in Palestine. Now that I received $225

8 The author had apparently not heard from his children in America for two and a half years—since the letter he received from Refuel in April 1916 (ch. 31, p. 617).

9 At that time, Refuel was living in Tacoma, Washington; Yankl (Jacob Goldeen) was in Vancouver, Washington; and Yosl (Joseph Goldeen) was in Anaconda, Montana.

10 While studying pharmacy in Yekaterinoslav, Shloyme used to visit his stepbrother Duvid Kreyzberg, the son of his stepmother Feyge. At Duvid's house, he became acquainted with the younger sister of Duvid's wife Klara, Ester "Etya" Zlatopolsky, whom he married in 1917. On October 18, 1917, Etya gave birth to a daughter Fani, named after his recently departed stepmother Feyge, but the child died in October 1918 at one year of age because medication for dysentery was unavailable during war time.

from my children, I gave $200 of it to her and her husband as payment of the dowry of 1,000 francs which I had obligated myself to give.[11] I kept only $25 of the $225 for myself, so I had that and the 200 francs that I received from my daughter Rukhele for my living expenses.

Meanwhile, my niece Reyzl, whom we are discussing here, gave birth to two beautiful little children, a girl and a boy, and I live together with them.[12] I gave them the best two rooms in the house; one has to walk through my room to reach their rooms. Naturally, I cannot live peacefully but I can do no better because, according to my commitment, I still have to suffer another year and a half.[13] Their children make noise and create quite a commotion; my nerves are weak and it is really important for me to stay calm, but there is nothing I can do, for obviously God wants me to live like this.

Upon returning from exile, I noticed that Reyzl and her husband Yankl's attitude toward me had changed completely for the better. As I began to contemplate the causes that led toward their previous attitude toward me, I realized that Reyzl had been responsible for my having been treated poorly. After all, she had been an unlearned and imprudent young woman and did not know how to live with a husband. Whatever I instructed her, she would tell her husband along with her own embellishments. And when he would then say something against me, she was quick to agree with him; by doing so she hoped to find favor with her husband. But now things are very different; he now knows me well and he knows Reyzl . . . and Reyzl also became smarter. During my period of exile, she began to realize how they should treat me.

***

It is now the 18th of *Heshvan* 5680,[14] and I am once again continuing my life story after a break of six or seven months. First of all, I will relate how I, thank God, merited to finish writing my Torah scroll and to celebrate its completion. Thank God, I am privileged that they regularly read from my Torah scroll in Petakh-Tikva's Great Synagogue and it is considered the most beautiful Torah scroll there.[15]

---

11 See ch. 31, p. 621.

12 Reyzl Grinberg gave birth to Dvora in 1918 and Asher in 1919.

13 When Reyzl and Yankl Grinberg married in late 1916, the author obligated himself to provide them with living quarters for four years, as mentioned in ch. 31, p. 621.

14 November 11, 1919.

15 Petakh-Tikva's Great Synagogue is located on Khovavei Tsion St. in the center of Petakh-Tikva. With the opening in 1927 of the Nakhalat Yisrael Synagogue at 3 Khovevei Tsion St.,

In returning now to the Torah scroll which I was writing, I want to let you know that I had by then written up to the end of the Torah portion of *Shoyftim.*[16] In other words, I only had twenty more columns to write, a total of five sheets of parchment.[17] But my not having those five last sheets was keeping me from completing my holy work. I would have been able to complete the Torah scroll before *Pesach* if I had had them.[18] On *Rosh-Khoydesh Shvat,*[19] I began to negotiate with the Torah scribes in Jerusalem by offering them three times the price for those few sheets of parchment, but "we heard nothing and no one was responding."[20] The suffering I endured was indescribable. After all, I wanted to finish while my hands could still serve me and my eyes could still see. In short, I decided to travel to Jerusalem where I would plead and beg the scribes; they would then be forced to give me the sheets I needed. After all, the entire rest of the Torah scroll was already sewn together and checked for errors.[21] As of the 4th of *Iyar* 5679,[22] only the last five sheets of parchment were lacking, and they needed to be finished in order to celebrate the completion of the Torah scroll.

Finally, with God's help, I received the parchment three weeks before *Shvues.*[23] I started to work immediately and, in the middle of the month of *Sivan,*[24] I finished writing up until the verse, "And Joshua son of Nun was filled with a spirit of wisdom,"[25] meaning that only a few verses were left until the end of the Torah. I did not write the last few verses because I thought I would sell the privilege of writing them, as is customary, and use the money I raised for some charitable purpose. Later I changed my mind, as you will learn. Though I had basically completed the Torah scroll, I still had to check over my work on the last five sheets of parchment for accuracy and sew them onto the end of the Torah scroll. I then had to affix a patch over each seam on the back of the Torah

---

a quarter mile from the author's house, the author moved his Torah scroll, where it remains until today.

16 Deuteronomy 16:18–21:9.

17 The text of a Torah scroll is written in columns, in this case four columns per sheet of parchment.

18 Pesach began the night of April 14, 1919.

19 January 31–February 1, 1919.

20 Kings I 18:26.

21 See Spiegel (1996:74–76) for more regarding the obligation of checking a Torah scroll for errors.

22 May 4, 1919.

23 Approximately May 14, 1919, three weeks before *Shvues*, which occurred on June 4, 1919.

24 Mid-July 1919.

25 Deuteronomy 34:9. The author had three more verses to write to complete the Torah scroll.

FIGURE 28. Pinkhes-Dov Goldenshteyn wrote a Torah scroll and carved the following Hebrew inscription on the top of one the wooden rollers (see p. 659 below): "I, the elderly Pinkhes-Dov, *shoykhet*, Goldenshteyn, the son of Y. R, of blessed memory." On the other roller (not pictured) are the words, "I myself wrote this Torah scroll in the year 5679 [i.e., 1919], Petakh-Tikva." The scroll is housed and regularly used in the Nakhalat Yisrael synagogue in Petakh-Tikva.

scroll from the first Torah portion until the last.[26] (These patches are short strips of parchment affixed over each seam to prevent them from ripping when the Torah scroll is scrolled from one Torah portion to the other.) I affixed three such patches over every seam.[27] I did all of this work myself, thank God, and this caused the parchment to become smudged in a few places, which I cleaned and brightened. It was a joy to look at the Torah scroll. All this work took time, until the middle of the month of *Tamuz*,[28] because I also had a cover sewn for the Torah scroll. On the cover, I had embroidered the name of your *Mime* Feyge,[29] may she rest in peace, because the cover was made from her short, velvet cape. Though she did not merit seeing me start it, she had been in agreement with me that I should write a Torah scroll, so I wanted there to be at least a remembrance for her on the Torah for the sake of her soul.

In short, practically everything was finally completed, except for the wooden Torah rollers.[30] I had to travel to Jerusalem personally to obtain them;

26 A seam is formed when two sheets of parchment are sewn together.

27 The affixing of such patches is a common practice used on all Torah scrolls. Three patches are placed over each seam on the back of a Torah scroll: one at the top of the parchment, one in the middle, and one at the bottom.

28 Mid-August 1919.

29 Referring to the author's second wife who was called *Mime*, meaning "aunt" in Yiddish, by her stepchildren.

30 The two ends of the Torah scroll are affixed to two interlocking rollers, each of which has two handles used for scrolling the text.

they cost me two British pounds. My travel expenses also cost me two British pounds. I brought them home, and I carved the Hebrew inscriptions on them as an eternal remembrance.[31] On one I carved, "I, the elderly Pinkhes-Dov, *shoykhet*, Goldenshteyn, the son of I.R, of blessed memory."[32] And on the other I carved, "I myself wrote this Torah scroll in the year 5679, Petakh-Tikva."[33]

Before everything was completed, the Nine Days arrived, during which no celebrations can be made.[34] So I postponed the celebration until the 15th of *Menakhem Av*,[35] meaning on the Monday of the week in which the Torah portion of *Eykev* is read.[36] I invited all of my friends whom I met in exile by printing an invitation in the newspaper, *Khadashot*, which is published in Jerusalem.[37] I invited all the residents of Petakh-Tikva through a specially-hired messenger, and everyone was interested in taking part in my celebration. I also had guests coming from Jaffa and from Jerusalem. Some guests arrived uninvited, coming out of curiosity. No one in Petakh-Tikva remained in their homes; everyone waited near their houses for the procession with the Torah to pass by. The Torah was carried under a *huppah* with great festivity. All the men were dancing and holding lit candles in their hands while they led the Torah throughout all the streets until arriving at the *shul*. All the town's residents, including women and children, honored the Torah by kissing it as it passed by. Many of those watching the parade joined the passing stream of people. At some houses, the procession with the Torah was stopped and the family members danced with the Torah. Everyone took part in the celebration by carrying the Torah for a bit or at least by touching it. Naturally, all of this took a lot of time until the Torah finally arrived at Petakh-Tikva's Great Synagogue.

---

31 On the top and bottom of each roller are wooden plates, or disks. The author carved these inscriptions on the top two plates.

32 "I.R." are the initials of the author's father's name, Itskhok-Refuel.

33 The Hebrew year of 5679 corresponds to 1918–1919. The translation here is based on the actual inscription on the rollers, which differs slightly from the text noted in the book.

34 The Nine Days (July 28 to August 5, 1919) refer to the first nine days of the Hebrew month of *Av*, which is a period of Jewish national mourning culminating with *Tisha B'Av*.

35 August 11, 1919.

36 *Eykev* is the name of the Torah portion in Deuteronomy 7:12–11:25.

37 *Khadashot ha-Arets*, August 6, 1919 (v. 1, no. 42, p. 1). It was a four-page daily newspaper at the time. The following is a translation of the announcement: "I am hereby honored to inform and request all my brethren in suffering who were with me during the expulsion to Kfar-Saba, Hadera, and Haifa to please come celebrate with me the occasion of the completion of the Torah scroll, which will occur on Monday of the Torah portion of *Eykev*, on the 15th of *Av* [i.e., August 11, 1919], at my house in Petakh-Tikvah. With appreciation and respect, Pinkhes-Dov (*shoykhet*) Goldenshteyn."

Here I must stop and relate what went on at my house before the Torah scroll was carried out of the house. At 4 p.m., a crowd began to gather in my courtyard. The courtyard filled up with people, and of course the houses did too. I had prepared large quantities of liquor and food. Women were appointed to provide for the women, and men were appointed to provide for the men. Even children were not to be deprived of their share, because all are equal when it comes to rejoicing with the *Torah*: rich and poor, young and old, men and women.

Everyone agreed that I should not allow others to write the final letters of the Torah. Since I had written the Torah with such self-sacrifice, in hunger and thirst, and while bombs were flying overhead, they felt that I should not let anyone write any of the letters—not even one. They thought that only I should write all the letters until the end, until the very last words of the Torah, "before the eyes of all Israel,"[38] even though many were interested in writing a letter and a lot of money could have been made from such a large crowd (*kenehore*).[39] But that is what was decided. So I personally finished writing the letters until the final words of the Torah, "before the eyes of all Israel."[40] And everyone wished me *mazel tov*, drank, ate, and became truly joyous.

As we were preparing to take the Torah outside to the *huppah*, I was called to be the first to carry it. But due to the great excitement and overwhelming emotions, my nerves became agitated and I suddenly began to feel ill, so much so that I could barely stay on my feet. When I took the Torah scroll into the courtyard and stood under the *huppah*, I did not even have the strength to lift my feet to dance with the Torah. So I held it while I walked slowly under the *huppah* until we reached the street, where I handed it to the rabbi.[41] The rabbi noticed that I did not seem to be my usual self, and he told me not to continue

---

38 Deuteronomy 34:12.

39 Participating in completing the writing of the last verses of a Torah scroll is considered an honor and is the standard custom at most celebrations of the completion of a Torah scroll.

40 Deuteronomy 34:12.

41 Referring to Rabbi Yisrael Aba Tsitron, who is also mentioned in ch. 30 (p. 611) and ch. 31 (p. 629). Yankl Grinberg's two nieces, Hadassah (Perlkvort) Levitt (1904–2005) and Zipporah (Perlkvort) Sheiner Same (1907–2009) both recalled this celebration as being a notable event. They remembered the Torah scroll being carried to the *shul*, accompanied by a large crowd, music, and singing. Hadassah recalled that some time beforehand, "*Feter* Pinkhes" (Uncle Pinkhes) took his Torah scroll to Rabbi Tsitron to make sure it was kosher since it had been severely damaged while he was in exile in Kfar-Saba (ch. 33, p. 644). There was slight damage to the edge of the parchment, but no letters were damaged. Rabbi Tsitron examined it carefully and found it to be kosher. (As related in correspondence in 2003 with Abraham Solomon "Sol" Levitt after interviewing his mother Hadassah and aunt Zipporah, both of Perth, Australia.)

walking with everyone else but to go directly to the *shul* where I should wait until everyone arrived with the Torah scroll. Since I did not feel that I had the strength to make it there by myself, good people were found who led me to *shul* by supporting me on their arms and then they went to rejoin all the others. May our rabbi live a long life for giving me that bit of advice, because three hours passed before I had the privilege of seeing the Torah arrive at the *shul*. When the sounds of the approaching crowd were heard, the *shul* was illuminated and the Torahs were removed from the Ark and carried toward the approaching new Torah. The new Torah was encircled by all the other Torahs, and then they were all brought into the *shul* to be placed inside the Ark. Even though I had rested for quite some time, my nerves, which had been agitated due to the excitement, had not calmed down, and I could barely stand. With great difficulty I walked to the center of the circle which was surrounded by those carrying all the Torahs. Others danced; not I. Others were joyous but not I. Everyone was concerned about me, especially the rabbi (may he live long) who recalled that the same thing had happened to me at Reyzl's wedding. Right when it was time to lead her to the *huppah*, I became ill with a temperature of forty degrees.[42] While everyone was rejoicing, I lay in bed with a high temperature. Now, though, I did not have a fever, thank God, and I was standing on my feet and seeing with my own eyes how everything was proceeding well and beautifully. So I still have to be thankful to God for that recent kindness that He did for me.

With much strain, I placed my Torah in the Ark, and the cantor of the *shul* made a *Mishebeyrakh*. The crowd stayed on a bit for *Marev* and then all went home. For several days afterward, I was left without any strength, and it took time until my nerves settled. My Torah was used for the first time that *Shobes*,[43] when the Torah portion of *Eykev* was read. I was called up for an *aliya*, and I let them make a *Mishebeyrakh* in which they mentioned by name all of my children and grandchildren, may they live long, and I pledged charity on behalf of their health and wellbeing. I also made a *Mishebeyrakh* on behalf of the rabbi, the *gabbaim* of the *shul*, and the entire community. To the *Kiddush* I invited important people who were not able to come to the celebration earlier that week. I began to feel well only that *Shobes*, and I was finally able to rejoice. Thank God for granting me good health and for granting me the privilege of celebrating the completion of my Torah scroll.[44]

---

42 Equivalent to 104°F. In describing Reyzl's wedding in ch. 31, p. 622, the author writes that he had a temperature of more than 41°C (105.8°F).

43 August 16, 1919.

44 In 1926, upon the opening of the nearby Hasidic-oriented synagogue called Nakhalat Yisrael, at 3 Khovevei Tsion Street in Petakh-Tikva, the author transferred his Torah scroll there and

FIGURE 29. A 1922 photograph of Pinkhes-Dov "Pinye-Ber" Goldenshteyn in Petakh-Tikva, standing in the foreground with his white beard parted in the middle. On the steps (from left to right) are Rabbi Yisrael Aba Tsitron (1881–1927), the rabbi of Petakh-Tikva (and the son-in-law of the renowned Rogatshover Gaon [Genius], Rabbi Yosef Rozin), and Rabbi Yisrael Arye Sapir (1890–1961), the head of the rabbinical court and a rabbinical judge in Petakh-Tikva. On the far right is Petakh-Tikva's first mailman. Standing in the doorway in the background, with the white beard, is Menakhem Yehuda Shtampfer (1864–1940), who was one of the founders of Petakh-Tikva and who served as the treasurer of its municipal pharmacy. The photograph was taken by Pinye-Ber's son, Refuel (Raphael), on a visit from America.

The house was that of Khaym-Moyshe Slor (1859–1946), the first Jewish surveyor in Palestine and a leading citizen of Petakh-Tikva, on 9 Herzl St. (corner of Montefiore St.), from whom Pinye-Ber purchased his own house. After Slor's death, a German Jew named Dr. Moshe Auerbach lived there. In about 1976, the house was taken down. Slor donated the neighboring plot (7 Herzl St.) for the building of the Lomza Yeshiva, which was completed in 1929. (Courtesy of Shifra Bernfeld of Petakh-Tikva.)

---

prayed there regularly. Though no living member of the Goldenshteyn family had seen the Torah scroll in some seventy years and no member of the Nakhalat Yisrael Synagogue knew of its existence, the translator, with the help of synagogue member Shmuel Friedman, were able to locate it there in 2002. The Torah scroll was then sent to be scanned and computer checked, which it passed with excellent results; there were no missing or extra letters. Since then, the congregation uses the author's Torah scroll regularly, particularly since the Torah readers enjoy the relatively large size of its letters in comparison with writing in the other Torah scrolls they have.

I then prayed to God to allow me to hear from my children in Russia that they were alive, please God. I was certain and trusted in God that He would fulfill my request. Just like He had never rejected any of my prayers, God forbid, similarly now He showed me His goodness by accepting my prayers, because I soon began to receive greetings from my children telling me that they were alive, thank God. I first received a letter from my Rukhl in Paris telling me that my youngest son, Shloymele, is alive and living in Yekaterinoslav. A short while later, I received a letter from my Refuel in America that he received a letter from his brother Isruel in Feodosiya, who wrote him that their sister Nekhame and her family are well. A few weeks later, I received a letter from my daughter Nekhamele from Feodosiya in her own handwriting saying that she and her husband and children, along with her brother Isruel, his wife, and children, and her brother Shloyme and his wife are all healthy, and that their children are studying in institutions of higher education.[45] I also received news from Duvid Kreyzberg, my stepson, that he and his family were healthy.[46] In short, I have already had the privilege of hearing from all of my children that they are all healthy, thank God.

Since God helped me to such an extent, I prayed to God to grant me the privilege of hearing soon that Refuel and Rukhl have married.

I am satisfied with my current life, and my health is good. Every month, my children send me financial support which is sufficient to cover my expenses. I am only lacking one thing, and that is peace and quiet. I have no rest at night or during the day. At night, I cannot sleep, and during the day I cannot study. The lack of quiet is due to my living with Reyzl. Her children are constantly screaming and crying throughout the day, and the noise is ear-piercing. When Reyzl puts them to sleep, she deafens me with her lullabies. When they wake up, they scream, and their mother screams at them. Their father comes along and yells at her for not treating them nicely. He then starts to show them his affection and begins to dance, sing, and jump with them, until he leaves. Then the mother quiets them down with gentle words, and if that does not help, she becomes tough. Either way it's constant noise—nonstop. And then his sister arrives with her children, and the commotion starts up all over again with everyone in the house shrieking together.[47] At times it is so bad that I have to leave the house.

45 Nekhame was apparently referring to her brother Isruel's children Frida and Avrum who were studying medicine in Simferopol (see Appendix A2, p. 689).

46 Duvid Kreyzberg of Feodosiya was the son of the author's second wife Feyge from her first marriage. See Appendix A4, pp. 731–723, for details.

47 Yankl Grinberg's sister was Rokhl Perlkvort (ca. 1888–1969), who had five children born between 1904 and 1914.

Rosh-Khoydesh Shvat will be three years since they married, and another year remains for us to live together.[48] Considering that in all probability they will have another child this year, and Yankl's brother will be coming for a visit and another brother will be returning home upon completing his military service—and obviously they will both be staying with me—how will I be able to bear such noise and commotion?[49] And how can I rid myself of the commotion and still have someone around to attend to me? There is a way to be rid of it—by our living apart from each other, meaning that I would give them money to cover the final year of room and board that was due them and they would move out. But then who would attend to me?

People and friends advised me to remarry, and then the issue would be resolved. But who knows if I can find a pious woman who would want to devotedly attend to me and be loyal to me so that I could study with peace of mind? With such a life's companion, I could hope to live a long and healthy life. I am waiting for such a partner in marriage, and then I would be helped, with thanks to God. I trust greatly in God that He will help me and will guide me along the right path.

Meanwhile, I live from the great satisfaction that I derive from my children, a blessing which not everyone is privileged to have. This itself provides me with encouragement to live. I pray to God that I should not lose either my wits or my good sense and that, in general, my entire body should remain sound, as was the case with my grandfather who lived to the age of 105 and died with his intellect and his complete wits about him, and was not ailing.[50] No one lives forever, but anyone can wish to live to such an old age, particularly his dear grandchild, the son of his beloved only daughter, Ester-Khaye. Being Ester-Khaye's son, I was raised by my grandfather; when I became orphaned, my grandfather took me in. The first part of my narrative describes both my grandfather and myself at that time. Until the day he died, he never turned to his children for help, but I must turn to my children, may they be blessed forever for not forgetting me. Apart from the money that they continue to send to sustain me, they also sent me hundreds of dollars so that I could repay my debts to the bloodsuckers, the moneylenders, to whom my needs forced me to turn during the war.

---

48 January 21, 1920. Upon Reyzl and Yankl Grinberg's marriage on January 24, 1917, the author promised to allow them to live with him for four years, as mentioned in ch. 31, p. 621.

49 Yankl Grinberg had three brothers: Simkhe (ca. 1889–ca. 1947), Mikhoel (1898–1973), and Yitskhok (born ca. 1899). Simkhe served in the Turkish army and later moved to South Africa, as related by Yankl's son Yosef ("Yoske") Grinberg of Petakh-Tikva in a personal interview in 2002.

50 Regarding the age of the author's grandfather Yankev Gredenitsky, see ch. 6, p. 147, footnote 2.

I hope that the peace agreement will be completely ratified and that the world will be back to normal.[51] Then, my beloved children will certainly be unable to refrain from paying a visit to their elderly father in the land of our forefathers, and the verse, "That He may turn the heart of the fathers back through the children, and the heart of the children back through their fathers,"[52] will become a reality. May it come true, and may God help me merit seeing the Messianic era! Let us hope. Yes, with regard to hope, one can hope that the Redemption will speedily come for all Jews and that the Jews in *Erets-Isruel* will receive autonomy and a Jewish national home, which appears to be not too far away for us. Already "the blossoms have appeared in the land," referring to the sprouting of the Redemption which is now apparent here in *Erets-Isruel*.[53] All the time, new, important guests are coming here to declare to the Jews in the name of every country that *Erets-Isruel* is for the Jews. Primarily, the British government strongly supports the Jews, and agrees to remain the guardian over Jewish autonomy, so that the Jews can be certain that no one will disturb the resurgence of their home. At this pivotal point in time, I want to keep on living and live to see this unfold. One only has to hope and live with hope and trust in God. Let us hope and trust in God because He is the source of salvation.

Afterward, I did not write for five or six years.

***

Sunday, the 2nd of *Iyar* 5685,[54] the seventeenth day of the Counting of the *Omer*[55]: "Blessed is He who has granted us life, sustained us, and enabled us to reach this occasion."[56] Thank God, a span of five or six years has passed since I stopped writing the continuation of my life's story. Understandably, I endured much over this period of time. But I am alive, thank God, and I can now write you everything that occurred during this period.

---

51 Though Germany formally surrendered on November 11, 1918, the British Empire ceased its war with Germany, Austria, and Bulgaria in 1920 and the United States officially ended its involvement in the war in 1921. A final peace treaty between the Allied Powers and Turkey was not signed until 1923.

52 Malachi 3:24.

53 Songs of Songs 2:12.

54 April 26, 1925.

55 Jews are obligated to count the *Omer* (also called *Sefira*), which involves a daily, verbal counting of each of the 49 days between Pesach and *Shvues*, as stated in Leviticus 23:15–16 (*Kitsur Shulkhan Arukh* 120:1–11).

56 The words of the *Shehekhiyonu* blessing, which is recited to offer thanks for new and unusual experiences.

If you remember, in *Heshvan* 5680 I had not yet decided if I should remarry, because I was afraid of falling into a problematic relationship.[57] Now I can write you, dear children, that God had compassion on me, accepted my prayers, and predestined for me a good partner, who is a prominent and respectable elderly woman in Petakh-Tikva.[58] She is the daughter of a Talmudic scholar and was the wife of a pious master of rabbinic learning. She has no children and is a good-hearted woman. She loves to do *mitzvahs* and is involved in performing *mitzvahs*, as much as her strength permits. I married this woman on the 20th of *Teyves* 5680.[59] Now that it has been six years since she became my companion in marriage, I can certainly say that God did not abandon me and that my prayer was answered. She is a quiet, calm woman, and devoted, but her age often prevents her from tending to me. Poor thing, she wants to, but she is an elderly woman of seventy-five and her strength no longer suffices. I hold nothing against her, God forbid. I do not ask her to do more than her strength permits. Since there is good will between us, I am devoted to her. I have hired someone to come in to help her in the house in order to reduce her workload. As the lady of the house, she supervises everything. We lead a quiet life without noise or commotion—when not interrupted by unexpected events. You may ask when is something unexpected not occurring to me? After all, whenever things are going well, it is only for a short while.

Now I want to describe for you how things were with my nieces and nephews, meaning my Reyzl, her husband, and their children. After all, according to my commitment, they still had another year to live with me in the house. The problem was, how could I become free of them?! They did not want to leave, and I did not want to be a liar by not fulfilling my obligation. But I certainly could no longer continue living with them because I now had a wife. Reyzl's family occupied the best two rooms, meaning the bedroom and the parlor. I resided where I had earlier, in the first room near the entrance, while they would constantly walk in and out through my room and did not want to give us the bedroom. You can understand how pleasant it was for me and my wife. Yet

57 See p. 664 which was written on the 18th of *Heshvan* 5680 (November 11, 1919).

58 The author's third wife was Basye-Dvoyre Yirme (ca. 1848–1934), who was commonly known as Bashe. See Appendix A5 (pp. 733–745) for more details. The author does not mention her by name here or in his Hebrew ethical will (see Appendix B2, pp. 762–773). Vilf (2017:282) and Katsovitsh (1919:367) also remarried in their later years and do not mention their second wives' names in their autobiographies. Similarly, Bashe's tombstone does not mention the name Goldenshteyn but only the surname of her first husband, Yirme. It is common for a woman's tombstone to only mention her first husband's surname if she remarried later in life.

59 January 11, 1920.

we agreed to live such an anguished life and with such a commotion until God would have compassion on us and give these people the good sense to move out, which is what happened.

Reyzl's husband found an apartment and rented it at my expense, meaning that I would pay the rent for the remaining year I still owed them.[60] In this way, I was rid of the noise and commotion. Thank God, it is now quiet at home, and I have begun to breathe freely and live again. Thank God, I walk to *shul* in the morning and evening. I write letters to my children, who are spread out over all the ends of the world, and I receive letters and financial support from them. With God's help, I would love this tranquility to last long. Master of the universe, oh how I wish so! May this come to be.

But with my luck, my life did not remain tranquil for long. Only two months later, in *Adar*,[61] I became ill, but I recovered by Pesach, with God's help.[62] Yet in the colony of Petakh-Tikva, panic began to spread; the Jews were fearful of being attacked. The Arabs desired to take revenge on the Palestinian Jews who had received the Balfour Declaration, which states that the Jews can establish *Erets-Isruel* as their national home and that it would be under British protection for twenty years.[63] Afterward, the Jews would be independent in their own land, in their own country, which would be returned to them once an agreement would be made by all the countries involved and the League of Nations. Naturally, this enraged the Arabs, and since the Jews have many enemies in the world, their enemies incited the Arabs by letting them know that they could not permit the Jews to have an independent home, for the Jews would then drive the Arabs from their country and seize their property. In this way did our European enemies provoke the Arabs with such talk, and in addition they gave the Arabs financial support. The Arabs became enraged to the point of wanting to attack, pillage, and murder the Jews. This would cause the remaining Jews to flee elsewhere, thereby ridding the Arabs of both the Jews and their dreams of an independent home for themselves, the Jewish people. The Jews learned all this before Pesach and were terrified of the approaching Muslim holiday of Nebi Musa. (The Arabs had at one time decided to come up with a new holiday by this name and decided that it should occur on the Jewish holiday of Pesach.[64]) The Jews were frightened because many

60 Yankl and Reyzl moved to 9 Volfson St. in Petakh-Tikva, where their son, Yosef "Yoske" Grinberg, lived until at least 2002.

61 February-March 1920.

62 Pesach started the night of April 21, 1920.

63 The Balfour Declaration was published in the press on November 9, 1917.

64 Nebi Musa means "the Prophet Moses" in Arabic and is a seven-day long Muslim holiday centered on a collective pilgrimage from Jerusalem to a place near Jericho which local

Arabs from the region planned to come into the towns that year to celebrate Nebi Musa. The town-dwelling Arabs, their leaders, and the arriving Arabs would then form an enemy force consisting of thousands. They planned to go to the grave of Nebi Musa, which was not far from Jericho, because their tradition maintains that Moses is buried there. At that point, only one fiery speech would be needed to set off that wild horde which would spread out and attack the Jews by doing whatever they wanted to do and whatever they were commanded to do. You can understand the panic the Jews were in before Pesach. Of course, the fear was greater in the colonies since the British government and military were located in Jerusalem. The only security in the Jewish agricultural colonies was to trust in God that He, and only He, would continue to protect His people as He had done in the past and would guard them as He had done until now, as it states, "And God seeks the pursued."[65] And who is more persecuted than His people, Israel? In short, Pesach came, thank God. The first days and the intermediate days of Pesach passed peacefully.[66] We thanked God for that, and we lived with the hope that no attacks would occur in the future.

On the seventh day of Pesach,[67] a horrible attack on the Jews took place in Jerusalem.[68] Our fear had not been unfounded. Several Jews were killed in the attack, and others were wounded. You can just imagine our fear in the colonies where there was no military. The fear was indescribable, but God helped, and things quieted down. There was an attack on the Jews in Jaffa in May of 5680 (1920), and on the 27th of *Sivan* a horrible attack occurred in Petakh-Tikva where there were four Jewish casualties.[69] I am writing only about the fright and the suffering that I endured and saw, but the details can be learned from writers who thoroughly covered the attacks. God performed a miracle for us and the

---

Arab folklore claims is Moses's burial site. The site of Nebi Musa was originally a point from which Jerusalem Muslims making pilgrimage to Mecca could look across the Jordan Valley to see Mt. Nebo; Christians and some Muslims believe that Moses is buried there (though Deuteronomy 34:6 states that his place of burial is unknown). This lookout point gradually became confused with Moses's gravesite. In the early nineteenth century, the Ottoman-Turks promoted a festive pilgrimage to Nebi Musa that would always coincide with the Christian celebration of Easter (Friedland & Hecht, 1996).

65 Ecclesiastes 3:15. This verse means that God is on the side of the one being pursued.

66 April 3–4, and April 5–8, 1920, respectively.

67 April 9, 1920.

68 This attack on the Jews in and around Jerusalem was the first Arab riot of the British Mandate period, which took place in Jerusalem on April 4–7, 1920. Five Jews were murdered and hundreds were injured.

69 June 13, 1920.

entire Jewish settlement in *Erets-Isruel*, particularly Petakh-Tikva. I will describe the portion of the miracle involving Petakh-Tikva.

The attack on Petakh-Tikva was clandestinely planned. Thirty-six Arab villages agreed to suddenly attack Petakh-Tikva, destroy it, and murder everyone. The first lot was drawn by a certain sheikh, so he was the first to furtively approach Petakh-Tikva along with 100 Arabs. It had been decided earlier among them that additional forces should constantly be joining them from the surrounding area. They were convinced that they would succeed and be able to destroy the entire Jewish population of *Erets-Isruel*, and they brought along camels and canisters of gas to burn all the orchards and houses. But God performed a great miracle for us, and we were saved. Upon learning of the secretly planned attack on Petakh-Tikva, young Jewish men went out to meet up with the enemy forces outside of Petakh-Tikva, engage them in battle, and prevent them from entering Petakh-Tikva. A colonist by the name of Paskal ran to Jaffa to alert the British authorities.[70] Another colonist named Dovid Novik risked his life by racing on horseback to Jaffa, where the headquarters of the British military were located, and alerted the military.[71] The military arrived and found a battle raging between Jews and Arabs near Petakh-Tikva, and they quickly drove away the Arabs. Petakh-Tikva suffered only four casualties, and the Arabs did not have a chance to destroy it since the battle occurred outside of the colony. The British military headquarters in Jaffa also sent airplanes, which spotted hundreds of Arabs ready to attack Petakh-Tikva on its other sides. These Arabs were approaching with camels and donkeys to carry away all the spoils, but the airplanes dispersed them, and many wounded Arabs were left behind on the roads. That was the miracle that God performed for us, but the spine-chilling fright that we experienced is indescribable.

Thank God, everything has been peaceful ever since that attack. I can now close this matter with praise and acknowledgement to God for all that He has done for us.

Now I will briefly relate what happened to me afterward. On *Shushan Purim* of 5681,[72] an important guest came to visit me, and he stayed in *Erets-*

---

70 For more about Perets Paskal (1871–1947), see Ya'ari (1929:590–591) and Tidhar (1947:1:457–458).

71 For more about Dovid Novik (1862–1925), see Ya'ari (1929:591–592) and Tidhar (1947:2:580).

72 February 23, 1921. *Shushan Purim* is the day that Purim is celebrated in Jerusalem. That year was a Jewish leap year, and Purim was celebrated on March 24, 1921. The identity of this guest is unknown. Oddly, the author fails to mention that his son Refuel (Raphael) visited him from America in 1922.

Isruel until after Pesach.[73] After he left, I had the privilege of welcoming my daughter Nekhame, her husband, two sons, and daughter.[74] They lived in my house with me for three years. Unfortunately, her children worked very hard and barely subsisted. But my son-in-law's brother would often send them support, and his good heart led him ultimately to send them visas and boat tickets to travel to America.[75] But before they were able to travel, a great tragedy happened to them; their daughter Ete, who was not yet married, became very ill and left this world at such a young age on Wednesday, the 7th of *Menakhem Av* 5684.[76] "May her soul be bound up in the bond of eternal life."[77]

Afterward, Nekhame and her family could not go to America, since the quota had been filled. So her husband's brother sent them 600 pounds,[78]and they used it to build a house in Tel-Aviv in the neighborhood of Tel-Nordau, where they remained without money and without a means of earning a living.[79] Her children worked hard but were unable to earn much, since things were very difficult in Tel-Aviv at that time. To make a long story short, their names were drawn, and they were able to travel using their prior visas. So Nekhame and her two sons left while her husband remained in Tel-Aviv.[80] A year later, he joined

---

73 Pesach ended there on April 29, 1921.

74 Nekhame, her husband Mendl Brakhtman, and three of their five children (Victor, Mark, and Ester) arrived in Palestine in 1921. Nekhame's oldest child Frida remained in the Soviet Union. Nekhame's second child Moyshe left Tsarist Russia back in 1914 and settled in Portland, Oregon, where he went by the name of Martin Brockman.

75 Referring to Mendl Brakhtman's brother, Gershon, who went by the name Harry Kessler (1873–1960). For details about him, see Appendix A2, pp. 697–699.

76 Ete's proper name was Ester; she was called Esfir in Russian and nicknamed Fira. She died on August 7, 1924 at the age of twenty-three, from the measles. The author personally engraved her tombstone, as he had done for his second wife Feyge and her stepmother Udye, as related by his granddaughter Aliza Bernfeld in 2001. All three are buried in the Segula Cemetery in Petakh-Tikva.

77 Samuel I 25:29.

78 Pounds refers to the Egyptian pound, which circulated in British-Mandated Palestine alongside the Ottoman lira from 1920 until 1927, when the Palestinian pound was introduced. At the outbreak of the First World War, the Egyptian pound was pegged to the British pound at a slightly lesser value, being that Egypt was under British rule from 1882 until 1956.

79 Tel-Nordau was a neighborhood in Tel-Aviv founded in 1926 on the northwestern fringes of the city at the time. That area is now found at the center of Tel-Aviv.

80 Nekhame and her two sons traveled by boat from Jaffa to Alexandria, Egypt, where they boarded the steamship *Sinaia* on March 2, 1926. They arrived in the port of Providence, Rhode Island, on April 5, 1926.

FIGURE 30. Pinkhes-Dov Goldenshteyn's daughter Nekhame Brakhtman (1877–1955) and her husband Mendl (ca. 1867–1932) and sons in 1926 in Palestine, shortly before immigrating to America, where they changed their name to Brockman. Their son Victor (1904–1985) is on the left and the elder son Mark (1902–1990) is on the right. (Courtesy of Lisa Unterberg Delafontaine of Rye Brook, New York.)

them.[81] They now live in America, in Brooklyn. I derive much satisfaction from them, thank God, and they are making a good living, thank God.

Thank God, I am at the end of my narrative. I can write you that my younger son, Shloyme, his wife, and their two small children, arrived in *Erets-Isruel* in 5685 [*sic*].[82] She works as a dentist, and he works in a drugstore as a pharmacist. Thank God, they make a good living. My son is a comfort to me in my old age. Being a devoted son, he watches over me, and I do not feel alone.

---

81 Listed on the ship manifest as "Mendel Brachtman," he arrived in New York City on February 9, 1927 on the steamship *Olympic*, which departed from Cherbourg, France.

82 Shloyme (called Shlomo in modern Hebrew), his wife Etya, and their two daughters, Dvora and Frida (whose name was changed to Aliza in Palestine) did not arrive in 5685 (1924–1925) as the author writes but on December 9, 1923 in Jaffa according to the ship manifest of the *Sardinia*. For more details about Shloyme and his family, see Appendix A2, pp. 720–725.

***

It is now *Iyar* of 5689,[83] which is when I am bringing the story of my life to a close. The printing will be finished in the month of *Sivan*.[84] Being thankful to God for everything, I live quietly and no longer suffer from unexpected events, but I no longer have any strength. My eyes no longer serve me and my feet no longer support my body, but no one is to blame except my age. Yet God can provide one with strength.

My last request is for God to at least allow me the privilege of hearing that Refuel and Rukhl have married and of seeing my dear son Isruel-Burekh and his wife Gitl on a visit to *Erets-Isruel*.[85] Nothing is too difficult for God to do. Then my joy will be complete, and I would know that God is listening to my last request. I would then be able to die in peace with praise to the Almighty for all of the good He has done for me and with the hope that my autobiography will affect my children and grandchildren by strengthening their trust in God so that they will go on along the right path and believe in God and divine providence, as their aged father has in his life. I also hope that through my book even people unknown to me will come to know how to believe in God's providence and live with trust in Him. That is my entire wish, and with this expression of hope I end the story of my life.

Petakh-Tikva, Tuesday of the Torah portion of *Bamidbar*,[86] the 24th of *Iyar* 5689.[87]

83 May–June 1929.

84 The author is referring to the printing of the Addendum to part III (chs. 30–34), which was printed in June-July 1929. See Appendix A7, pp. 751–752, for more details.

85 The author's wish was partially fulfilled. He lived to hear that Refuel, at the age of forty-four, had married on November 12, 1930, in Los Angeles. The author died some three weeks afterward on December 4, 1930. Rukhl married a non-Jew, Vladimir Oulianoff, on November 19, 1929 in Paris; it is likely that the author was not informed of this. As to Isruel and Gitl, his children arranged for them to immigrate to France in 1935. See Appendix A2, pp. 689–725, for more information about the author's children.

86 Numbers 1:1 to 4:20.

87 June 3, 1929.

FIGURE 31. Avrum Goldenshteyn (1898–ca. 1977), the grandson of Pinkhes-Dov Goldenshteyn and the son of Isruel, with his wife, Pola, on their wedding day in 1925 in Feodosiya, Crimea. Pola and their daughter, Ala, were Pinkhes-Dov Goldenshteyn's only descendants to perish in the Holocaust. (Courtesy of Virginia "Ginny" Starr of Grass Valley, California.)

Appendices

Appendix A: The Author and his Relatives

Appendix A1: The Author's Final Years in Petakh-Tikva

His Houses, His Properties, and the Local Synagogues

In 1913, Pinye-Ber arrived in Petakh-Tikva with a combined family unit in which no one shared a blood connection: he traveled with his second wife Feyge (with whom he had no children), her step-mother Udye, and his first wife's niece Reyzl.[1] Pinye-Ber chose to live in Petakh-Tikva primarily because it had many synagogues and a rich religious Jewish life.[2] In addition, his wife Feyge had relatives there, Rivka-Nekhama Berenshteyn and her husband, the parents of the painter Salomon Bernstein.[3]

In Petakh-Tikva, Pinye-Ber purchased the lot at 64 Rothschild Blvd from Khaym-Moyshe Slor (1859–1946), one of the founders of Petakh-Tikva.[4] On the lot were two houses connected by a small two-story wooden structure with a staircase: upstairs was a shower and a sink, and downstairs was a storage room.[5] Pinye-Ber lived with his extended family in the smaller house towards the back of the lot, which had three rooms. It had a very large but simple kitchen, with no sink at all; water flowed from a pipe that came out of the southern wall and a large bucket collected the water. The dishes

---

1 See Appendix D4, pp. 824–825, for a genealogical chart of the extended Hershkovitshes, the family of the author's first wife Freyde.

2 Personal interview in 2001 with Aliza (Goldenshteyn) Bernfeld of Petakh-Tikva, as heard from her father Shloyme, the son of the author.

3 See Appendix A6 (pp. 746–750) for more details.

4 Under the Ottoman-Turkish Empire, the Jews in Palestine were forbidden to erect new permanent structures, so builders like Slor would erect a large tent, under which they built a small house. Upon the house's completion, the tent was removed. Once the building was completed, the Turks would let it be.

5 See ch. 20, p. 360, figure 10.

were washed in a bowl on the kitchen table. The two houses were practically shacks, the walls made from two outer boards with the gaps filled with *kurkar* (porous calcareous sandstone found on the Levantine coast of the Mediterranean Sea).[6] Pinye-Ber rented out the larger house which was situated towards the front of the lot and had four rooms.[7] The two houses had red-tile roofs, and the wide roof overhang of the smaller, rear house provided shading in the yard. In the back of the yard was an outhouse. At first, there were eleven eucalyptus trees on the lot, but by the mid-1920s only seven remained, some of which were so large that it took three people to encircle their trunks.[8] Under the tree that shaded the porch was a large millstone, which had been left by a previous owner or tenant. In front of the yard was a wooden fence including a gate and a small porch with a few steps to enter the house. Rothschild Boulevard was narrow and was paved with stones; there were no cars yet to raise dust, emit exhaust, and make noise. At the entrance to the yard, near the street, stood a large rectangular stone slab with the owner's name, Pinkhes Goldenshteyn (פנחס גאלדענשטיין), engraved on it in Yiddish, likely by Pinye-Ber himself.[9]

In 1916, Pinye-Ber's second wife, Feyge, passed away, followed a few months later by the death of her stepmother, Udye. Pinye-Ber married off his niece Reyzl to Yankl Grinberg in January 1917, and the young couple lived with him in the smaller house. In December 1917, Pinye-Ber was exiled by the Ottoman Turks from Petakh-Tikva and was only able to return in October 1918. He married his third wife, Bashe, in January 1920, and Reyzl and her family moved out shortly afterward.

In 1921, Pinye-Ber's daughter Nekhame Brakhtman and her husband and three children immigrated from Feodosiya to Palestine. Upon their arrival, Nekhame and her family moved into the larger house while Pinye-Ber and Bashe continued to live in the smaller house. At the front of the yard, towards the east, Nekhame's children planted a garden. In 1922, his son Refuel (called Raphael Goldenstein in English) visited from America. In December 1923, his son Shloyme, his wife Etya, and their two daughters

---

6 Personal interview in 2002 with the author's great-granddaughter Shifra Bernfeld of Petakh-Tikva.

7 The two houses are described in the author's Hebrew ethical will. See Appendix B2, p. 766, for a translation.

8 In a personal interview in 2001, Aliza Bernfeld mentioned that years later her husband Nakhman Bernfeld had all the trees, except for one, taken down because their roots were pushing up the floorboards of the house.

9 Photographs of houses and street scenes of Petakh-Tikva from the 1920s and 1930s in various archives do not show such stones in front of other houses.

emigrated to Palestine. Shloyme and his family moved in with Pinye-Ber and Bashe into the smaller house, and Nekhame had to give up the nicest room in the larger house because Pinye-Ber had promised Etya a private room to use as a dental clinic if she emigrated to Palestine. Etya divided the room with a partition; one half was used for dental treatment and the other half as a waiting room. Etya was one of the first female health care practitioners in Petakh-Tikva.

Nekhame's daughter Ester died from the measles in August 1924, and Nekhame and her family moved to Tel-Aviv in 1925. With the larger house now empty, Shloyme and his family moved there, later dividing the large room into two, and Pinye-Ber and Bashe remained in the smaller house, which was no longer so overcrowded. Nekhame and her two sons immigrated to the United States in 1926, and her husband Mendl followed the next year. Shloyme was now Pinye-Ber's only child to remain in the Holy Land and was of tremendous comfort to him in his old age. After Pinye-Ber's death in 1930, Shloyme supported his stepmother Bashe, who continued to reside in the smaller house until her death in 1934. Afterwards, Shloyme rented out the smaller house.

Upon first arriving in Petakh-Tikva in 1913, Pinye-Ber prayed daily at Petakh-Tikva's Great Synagogue. When he completed writing his Torah scroll in 1919, he initially kept it there. In 1925, the printer Reuven Kritsman (ca. 1880–1966) donated the plot at 3 Khovevei Tsion St. for the building of a Hasidic synagogue, which would be close to Pinye-Ber's home. Kritsman, a Stoliner Hasid, named the planned synagogue Nakhalat Yisrael (Inheritance of Israel) after the Stoliner Rebbe, Rabbi Yisrael Perlow (1868–1921). The cornerstone laying occurred on August 3, 1925 (13 *Av* 5685), which was attended by the Stoliner Rebbe's son, Rabbi Avraham Elimelekh Perlow (1891–1942), known as the Karliner Rebbe, who was visiting Palestine.[10] Shloyme's daughter Aliza, almost four at the time, remembered the joyous celebration.[11] With the opening of the synagogue on Rosh Hashanah of 1926, Pinye-Ber moved his Torah scroll to this synagogue and prayed there daily.

---

10 The laying of the synagogue's cornerstone is recorded in the five-page ledger printed by Reuven Kritsman entitled *Beit ha-midrash Nakhalat-Yisrael be-rekhov Khovevei-Tsion, Petakh-Tikvah* (Petakh-Tikva, 1926) which is held in the Nakhalat-Yisrael synagogue. The synagogue is officially known as Nakhalat Yisrael (Kritsman). The ledger states that the synagogue was designated for Hasidim, though not specifically Stoliner Hasidim. For many decades now, it has simply been an Orthodox synagogue. The plot of land donated for the synagogue was next door to Kritsman's two-story building, which housed his business on the first floor and his residence on the second.

11 Personal interview in 2002 with Aliza (Goldenshteyn) Bernfeld of Petakh-Tikva.

Nonetheless, he continued to pray at Petakh-Tikva's Great Synagogue on *Shabes* and the major Jewish holidays, where he sat in the last row (the row closest to the entrance at the back) in the seat closest to the windows on the right. His adoring young granddaughters, Dvora and Aliza, would sit on the wide wooden windowsill near him. (Later, Pinye-Ber had his autobiography printed at Kritsman's printing house, which was next door to the Nakhalat Yisrael synagogue.)

In 1928, a special body appointed by the municipal council of Petakh-Tikva divided 1085 dunams (268 acres) of swampland among 106 of its residents who were artisans, small-time merchants, teachers, and laborers, with each person receiving ten dunams (two and a half acres). Pinye-Ber was one of those individuals, and he gave this swampland to his son Shloyme ("Petakh-Tikva," 1928; Tidhar:1:332–333).

Pinye-Ber passed away in 1930 (details on p. 685 below), and his son Raphael died in 1933 in Portland, Oregon. Only some years later did Pinye-Ber's children address the matter of Pinye-Ber's will, in which he bequeathed his property in equal shares among his seven children.[12] His surviving children, who lived outside of Palestine, except for Raphael's widow Claire, gave up their shares on behalf of their brother Shloyme, since the economic conditions in Palestine were so difficult. Having become estranged from Raphael's siblings, Claire hired a lawyer to claim her share of the inheritance of the property. She was under the mistaken impression that her late father-in-law had gone to the trouble of drawing up a will because the value of his property had been so substantial. Shloyme wrote Claire that his impression of his father's will was that he had merely been trying to encourage his children to immigrate to the Holy Land where his children and grandchildren were more likely to remain Jews. Nonetheless, Claire did not give up her claim.

The swampland was drained in the mid-1930s, and Shloyme and the others who had been allotted the land decided to unite and develop the area. They irrigated the land and had roads paved to reach each plot. Shloyme planted an orchard of Valencia oranges.[13] After being repeatedly cheated by

---

12 See Appendix B2 (pp. 762–773) for a translation of the author's Hebrew ethical will.

13 Most types of oranges ripen in the winter, but Valencia oranges ripen in the spring, thereby enabling them to be sold in the off-season. Nowadays, oranges are available all year round, but before the advent of modern refrigeration, selling in the off-season commanded higher prices.

the man he hired to manage the orchard, Shloyme brought in a merchant who estimated the value of the unripe fruit on the trees and paid Shloyme a down payment, which Shloyme used to help cover some of the costs of marrying off his daughter Aliza in March 1942. After the former manager clandestinely stole all the fruit, Shloyme sold the ten dunams of land to repay his debt to the merchant who had advanced him the down payment. Shloyme gave a great deal of his profits from the sale of the land to his daughter Aliza and her husband Nakhman "Nicu" Bernfeld, who were living in Haifa and were not able to earn enough to live on, being that it was wartime. With those funds, Aliza and her husband opened a stationery shop, which they sold in 1947 at a profit, enabling them to repay her father. While Nakhman served in the Israeli army during the War of Independence, Aliza and her two daughters returned to Petakh-Tikva to live with her parents at 64 Rothschild Blvd. In 1950 Aliza and Nakhman, who by then had three daughters, moved to a new house elsewhere in Petakh-Tikva.

Shloyme continued to live at his house on 64 Rothschild Blvd. until 1956, when he sold it to real estate developers, since the house was old, falling apart, and leaked in numerous places every time it rained. The house was demolished, and a three-story building containing seven apartments was built in its place. It was renumbered 60 Rothschild Blvd. In exchange for the lot, Shloyme was given two of the apartments along with some financial compensation. Through her lawyer, Shloyme's sister-in-law, Claire, obtained a seventh of the estate, a relatively modest amount of money which was deposited into a bank account. A few years later, when her son Henry, nicknamed Hank, was in university, he used this money to travel to Israel and immediately felt at home with his uncle Shloyme and his cousins. Afterwards, Claire visited the family in Israel three times.

Shloyme enjoyed living in the new building for some six years until his death in 1962. Afterwards, his widow Etya and two daughters sold them. Etya and Aliza used their portions to move to a more spacious condominium.

Memories From Those Who Knew Him

In Tsarist Russia, and later in Palestine, Pinye-Ber's extended family would seek out and listen to his counsel, being that he was a Talmudic scholar and a respected *shoykhet.*[14] When his niece Reyzl Grinberg, whom he had brought with him to Palestine, gave birth to her third child in about 1921, she had him named Eliezer after her father Eliezer Hershkovitsh, but the baby died at eleven months of age.[15] Shortly afterward, she gave birth to another boy. Still wanting a son named after her father, she had her newborn son also named Eliezer, but the baby died when only a week old. When her next child, also a boy, was born in about 1925, she again wanted to name him Eliezer, but Pinye-Ber advised against using the name, even as a middle name.[16] He suggested that she rather name the new baby Menakhem, meaning "comfort" in Hebrew, since he was born in the Hebrew month of *Menakhem Av*. The child was named Menakhem, and he lived.[17]

In 2003, Hadassah (Perlkvort) Levitt and her sister Zipporah (Perlkvort) Sheiner Same, both in their late 90s and living in Perth, Australia, recalled that their family had been very close with "*Feter* Pinkhes" (Uncle Pinkhes in Yiddish) in Petakh-Tikva and saw him regularly. (He was their aunt Reyzl Grinberg's uncle.[18]) The entire Perlkvort family of seven had even lived with him for a while in 1917.[19] They remembered his very warm personality, his flowing white beard, and his love for children, particularly during their exile together in Kfar-Saba. During the First World War, the Ottoman Turks exiled 1,500 Jews from their homes in Petakh-Tikva to shacks in Kfar-Saba, which were on the front line between the fighting Ottoman and British forces. In exile, the girls' father, three grandparents, and other close relatives died from diseases rampant at that time. Hadassah also contracted malaria but later recovered with quinine therapy.[20] It was during those horrendous times of cold, hunger, suffering, and death from typhoid fever, typhus, and malaria that Pinye-Ber would try to raise the spirits of the many children in exile there by gathering them together, playing with them, and singing with them.[21]

---

14 Personal interview in the late 1980s with Rose (Chaplick) Carmel (1899–1998) by her grandson Michael Budiansky.

15 See Appendix D4 (pp. 824–825) for a genealogical chart of Hershkovitsh family.

16 For a collection of some of the numerous Jewish laws and customs regarding the naming of children, see Rabbi Y. Z. Wilhelm's *What's in a Name?* (1998).

17 Personal interview in 2002 with Reyzl's son Yosef "Yoske" Grinberg of Petakh-Tikva.

18 See Appendix D4 (pp. 824–825) for a genealogical chart of the extended Hershkovitsh family.

19 See ch. 32, p. 635.

20 Correspondence in 2003 with Abraham Solomon "Sol" Levitt of Yokine, Australia, after interviewing his mother Hadassah Perlkvort Levitt (1904–2005) and his aunt Zipporah (Perlkvort) Sheiner Same (1907–2009).

21 Personal interview in 2001 with Pinye-Ber's granddaughter Aliza Bernfeld of Petakh-Tikva, as heard after Pinye-Ber's death from a number of individuals who had been in exile in Kfar-Saba and Zikhron Ya'akov.

When Hadassah became engaged in 1922 or 1923, Pinye-Ber told her that he could not miss her wedding. Despite his advanced age, he travelled to the Tel-Aviv neighborhood of Neveh Shalom for her wedding. Before the celebration ended, Pinye-Ber became tired, found a room with a bed, and went to sleep. When it was time for all to retire, it was discovered that Pinye-Ber had gone to sleep in the room prepared for the bridal couple. The bride's mother Rokhl (Grinberg) Perlkvort said that *Feter* Pinkhes was not to be disturbed, so some haphazard sleeping arrangements were made for the newly married couple, who were, nevertheless, happy to honor their venerated *Feter* Pinkhes.[22]

Pinye-Ber's grandson Victor Brockman (Brakhtman) used to mention that back in the Crimea, when his grandfather would visit them in Feodosiya, he and his friends would all run over to sit down with Pinye-Ber to hear him sing and regale them with inspirational stories. Victor considered those visits from Pinye-Ber to be some of the highlights of his youth.[23] During his years in Palestine from 1921 until 1926, Victor was reunited with his beloved grandfather. To Victor, Pinye-Ber looked as he imagined Moses had looked—he had a long, flowing white beard, had a dignified and majestic bearing, was well-dressed, and was was well over six feet tall, which was uncommon for Eastern European Jews at that time.[24] He dressed well thanks to his children in America who sent him new clothes regularly.[25]

After Pinye-Ber's son Shloyme and his family arrived in Palestine at the end of 1923, Pinye-Ber used to take care of their two daughters Dvora and Aliza while their parents were working. In his courtyard, he had a swing hung from a wooden beam lodged between two large eucalyptus trees, and all the neighborhood kids would also come to swing on it. Sometimes Pinye-Ber would play with his granddaughters in the yard, and their friends would come over to join in. Pinye-Ber had a cane with which he would playfully draw the children close

---

22 Correspondence in 2003 with Abraham Solomon "Sol" Levitt of Yokine, Australia, after interviewing his mother Hadassah Perlkvort Levitt (1904–2005) of Perth, Australia. Hadassah was married to Paul (Pinkhas) Levitt (1900–1973).

23 Pinye-Ber's visits to Feodosiya lasted until he left for Palestine in 1913, when Victor Brackhtman (later changed to Brockman) was nine.

24 Personal interview in 2001 with Cynthia Unterberg of Westbury, New York, as heard from her father Victor Brockman (formerly Brakhtman). Pinye-Ber's grandson Henry "Hank" Starr (1932–2020), son of his son Refuel, was 6'2".

25 Personal interview in 2001 with Aliza (Goldenshteyn) Bernfeld of Petakh-Tikva. See also Appendix B3, pp. 794 and 795.

to him and then hand them sweets. The neighborhood children believed Pinye-Ber to be Elijah the Prophet.[26]

In Petakh-Tikva, Dvora remembered her grandfather Pinye-Ber as follows:

> He was a wonderful man. He was tall, walked with a straight back, and had a long beard—the very image of how I pictured Elijah the Prophet to have been. He was very religious but liberal in his views and never demanded others to follow him in religious matters. He fulfilled every minor mitzvah but respected the opinions of others including his daughter-in-law and his grandchildren who lived in the same courtyard. He studied a lot of Torah, but also would look at a newspaper. . . . He had an artistic sense and golden hands. He made beautiful paper cutouts for decorating the *sukah* and other decorations. For Hanukah, he poured tin into wooden castings to make menorahs and *dreydlekh.* With a chisel, he carved wooden spoons with decorative handles, the tops of wooden walking sticks in the shapes of whimsical animal heads, and the like. He celebrated the Jewish holidays enthusiastically—with much singing and delight. Many people visited his house to discuss all types of matters, whether holy or mundane. . . . Grandfather was strong and healthy. . . . He would go for walks with us along the streets, fields, and vineyards of Petakh-Tikva. (Gavrieli, 1999)

Pinye-Ber set aside a corner of the yard where he kept animals, such as chickens, lizards, praying mantises, and tortoises for his granddaughters' enjoyment.[27] Dvora recalled, "We learned a lot from Grandfather regarding how to treat every animal with affection and respect. We learned how and how much to feed them and when to let them go if we failed to take care of them properly. The neighboring children were also active in the animal corner . . ." (Gavrieli, 1999).

For *Sukes*, part of the roof of the front of the house would be removed to make a *sukah*. Pinye-Ber would use sheets as canvas to paint beautiful sceneries, flowers, and Hebrew verses in calligraphy, such as "*ve-hayitah akh same'akh.*"[28] The sheets would then be affixed to the walls of the *sukah* to decorate it. He

26 Personal interview in 2001 with Aliza (Goldenshteyn) Bernfeld of Petakh-Tikva.

27 Ibid.

28 Deuteronomy 16:15. The quotation translates to mean "and you will only be happy" and refers to the Jewish holiday of *Sukes*.

made *dreydlekh* for his grandchildren for Hanukah, some carved out of wood and others forged from copper. He also forged a holder for a *Havdalah* candle. He made miniature furniture out of bronze and iron as toys for his granddaughters' dolls, and carved dice out of wood.[29]

In addition to his woodcarving and metal forging abilities, he had become a skilled tombstone engraver back in the Crimea for the Karaites. In Petakh-Tikva, he used this skill to carve the tombstones of his second wife Feyge and of her stepmother Udye Yudelevitsh, both of whom died in 1916 in Petakh-Tikva. They are buried next to each other, and their tombstones lie horizontally, as do many tombstones in the Holy Land. Pinye-Ber carved a pomegranate-branch design around the joint base of the tombstones. When his granddaughter Etl Brakhtman died in 1924 in Petakh-Tikva, he also carved her tombstone, bearing a floral design.[30]

In mid-August 1929, Pinye-Ber became quite ill. His situation was so serious that on August 24, 1929 his son Shloyme took his wife and two daughters, Dvora and Aliza, for their first visit to Jerusalem since their arrival six years earlier to pray at the Western Wall. Due to their struggle to earn a living in a new land, they had not been able to travel there earlier. Upon arriving in Jerusalem, they went straight to the Western Wall, the holiest Jewish site. Unlike today, the area in front of the Western Wall was very narrow. Shloyme instructed his daughters, as many are accustomed to do, to write down their prayers on a piece of paper, fold it up, and place it in one of the crevices of the Wall. Dvora remembered writing, "I want my grandfather to be healthy and live many, many more years." While there, they saw hundreds of Arabs shouting. Shloyme was told that they should leave the area and return to Petakh-Tikva because Jews had just been massacred in Hebron and Safed, and the violence was spreading all over Palestine. They arrived home safely, and their prayers had evidently helped since Pinye-Ber's health improved shortly afterward.

His Demise

Pinye-Ber died on the 14th of Kislev 5681 (October 5, 1930) at the age of eighty-two.[31] His granddaughter Aliza, aged nine at the time, remembered waking up

29 Personal interview in 2001 with Aliza (Goldenshteyn) Bernfeld of Petakh-Tikva.

30 All three are buried in the Segulah Cemetery in Petakh-Tikva.

31 The author's *yortsayt*, the 14th of *Kislev*, is a significant date in the calendar of Lubavitcher Hasidim for it is the wedding anniversary of the Lubavitcher Rebbe, Rabbi Menachem

early that morning before dawn. She and her sister Dvora, aged eleven, were woken up by their parents' voices in the other room. They both decided to get up and see what was going on. By the time they walked out of their bedroom, their parents had left the house. They decided to open the shutters to watch the sunrise and were astonished to see the most brilliant red sunrise that Aliza had ever seen in her life—absolutely indescribable. Their mother, Etya, then walked in and told them that their grandfather had just passed away. Aliza remembered thinking to herself that certainly the Heavens themselves were expressing their extreme joy with a brilliant sunrise in anticipation of welcoming her grandfather's lofty soul.

A huge number of people attended his funeral. His granddaughter Dvora wrote: "The entire colony walked behind his coffin, including my teacher and my entire class, who walked in an orderly line." The author's granddaughter Aliza remembered never having seen a larger funeral, which was fitting since Pinye-Ber had been well known and venerated in Petakh-Tikva. After all, he had been a temporary *shoykhet* in Petakh-Tikva during the First World War, had celebrated the completion of writing his own Torah scroll there, and had published his autobiography there, including the portions about his life in Petakh-Tikva.

After his funeral, Aliza remembered school children coming to her house to relate what their teacher had told them—i.e., that one of the thirty-six *tsadikim* who sustain the world had just died and that his name was Goldenshteyn.[32] Such was Pinye-Ber's reputation in Petakh-Tikva.

His Chabad Legacy

In 1926, Rabbi Avraham Pariz (1899–1968) and his family arrived in Petakh-Tikva from the Soviet Union. He was one of the most devoted Hasidim of the Lubavitcher Rebbe, Rabbi Yosef Yitzchok Schneersohn (1880–1950), and he later accompanied the Rebbe during his ten-day historic visit to the Holy Land in August 1929.[33] The Goldenshteyns knew the Parizes since their arrival in

Mendel Schneerson (1902–1994), who married the daughter of his predecessor, Rabbi Yosef Yitzchok Schneersohn (1880–1950), on the 14th of *Kislev* 5689 (November 27, 1928) in Warsaw, Poland.

32 The concept of thirty-six *tsadikim* (righteous individuals) sustaining the world is mentioned in the Talmud (Sukah 45b; Sanhedrin 97b).

33 During the Lubavitcher Rebbe's 1929 visit, he briefly visited Petakh-Tikva on August 20, 1929 (the 14th of *Av* 5689). Unfortunately, Pinye-Ber was very ill at that time (see p. 685) and could not participate in the gathering held for the Rebbe in Petakh-Tikva's Great

Petakh-Tikva.[34] After Pinye-Ber's death in 1930, Rabbi Pariz's wife, Beyle-Rivka, came to the house to speak with Pinye-Ber's daughter-in-law Etya where she strongly praised Pinye-Ber's autobiography.[35]

Pinye-Ber's granddaughter, Aliza Bernfeld of Petakh-Tikva, had three daughters, the oldest being Tsviya. In 1975–1976, Tsviya, a divorcee with a young son named Shlomo Zilbershtein, began to produce paintings inspired by Jewish motifs. At that time, Tsviya visited her relative Rakhel Likhtenshtein in Bnei-Brak bringing Shlomo's outgrown clothes for her young children.[36] In discussing Tsviya's art, Rakhel invited Tsviya to attend some Torah lectures, which began to influence her to become observant. Shortly afterward, Aliza told Tsviya that her grandfather, Pinye-Ber, had been a Chabadnik, which inspired Tsviya to contact Chabad rabbis and attend their classes. Over time, she became an avid Chabadnik. In support of their daughter, Aliza and her husband Nakhman began to observe *Shabes* and keep a kosher kitchen, which they did not consider difficult since they were vegetarians. In about 1982, Tsviya married Eliyahu Yosef Gelbshtein, a direct descendant of the first Rebbe of Chabad, Rabbi Shneur Zalman of Lyadi.[37] Sadly, Tsviya died suddenly in 1990 at the age of forty-seven when her only child, Shlomo Zilbershtein, was studying in the Central Yeshiva Tomchei

---

Synagogue, which was attended by the town's most prestigious rabbinical and municipal personages (Rotenberg: 1999:201, 203; Wolf, 2001:38). For more regarding the author's connection with his fellow Chabadniks in Petakh-Tikva, see Appendix E, pp. 826–836.

34 Telephone interview in 2002 with Chaya Lerer (1919–2023) of Bnei-Brak, Israel, the daughter of Rabbi Avraham Pariz.

35 Personal interview in 2001 with Aliza Bernfeld of Petakh-Tikva. A Chabad synagogue on Gutman Street in Petakh-Tikva was established in 1919–1920, but Aliza Bernfeld did not remember if her grandfather periodically went there.

36 Rakhel Likhtenshtein's father was Eliezer (ca. 1907–1984), the son of Mordkhe Gershkovits. Mordkhe was a brother to Freyde (née Hershkovits), Pinye-Ber's first wife. (Gershkovits is the Russian pronunciation of Hershkovits.) In a personal interview in 2002 with Yosef "Yoske" Grinberg of Petakh-Tikva, he related that Eliezer was an orphan and was raised in part by his aunt Elke Hershkovits, who was Yoske's grandmother. Eliezer and his wife Shoshana had three children: Yitskhak Gershkovits, Rakhel Likhtenshtein, and Mordechai "Moti" Omer (1941–2011). Moti was an art historian and director and chief curator of the Tel-Aviv Museum of Art from 1995 until his death. See Appendix D4 (pp. 824–825) for a genealogical chart of the Hershkovits family.

37 Tsviya and her husband Eliyahu Yosef Gelbshtein are listed in *Sefer ha-tse'etsa'im* by Rabbi Shmuel Elazar Heilprin (1980:397), which is a genealogical work documenting many of the descendants of the first Rebbe of Chabad, Rabbi Shneur Zalman of Lyadi. See also Appendix A7, p. 757.

Tmimim Lubavitch at 770 Eastern Parkway in the Crown Heights section of Brooklyn.[38]

38 In 1982, seventeen-year-old Shlomo Zilbershtein traveled to Crown Heights to spend the High Holidays and *Sukes* in the Central Lubavitch Synagogue at 770 Eastern Parkway, known as "770," with the Lubavitcher Rebbe, Rabbi Menachem Mendel Schneerson (1902–1994). Meanwhile, his grandmother Aliza Bernfeld had written to her first cousin Victor Brockman of Brooklyn that Shlomo would be spending a month in Brooklyn. Victor and his brother Mark went to "770" but could not find Shlomo among the thousands of visiting Hasidim and guests coming to be with the Rebbe from all over the world. In the age before cellphones, Shlomo had no telephone number at which he could be reached. Undiscouraged, Victor and Mark returned once more. This time, Shlomo, who had by now heard that his grandmother had written Victor, noticed two elderly, clean-shaven men wandering around "770" in search of someone. He approached them, and they turned out to be his relatives. Shlomo was able to communicate with Victor and Mark in Hebrew which they remembered from the five years they spent in Palestine in the 1920s. At that point, the Rebbe had just returned to his office in "770" from praying at the gravesite of his father-in-law in Queens, and he would soon be coming down from his office into the large synagogue for the afternoon prayers. As the Rebbe entered the synagogue, the huge crowd split to make a path for the Rebbe to walk to the front of the synagogue. Since Shlomo had placed Victor and Mark at the beginning of the human corridor, close to the Rebbe's office, the Rebbe made a deep, encouraging, sweeping motion with his hand to Victor, who smiled broadly in response. Of course, Victor knew that his grandfather, Pinye-Ber, had been a Chabadnik and was pleased to have renewed the connection.

Starting in the late 1990s, Victor's daughter Cynthia Unterberg began attending classes at Chabad of Midtown Manhattan, without initially knowing that her great-grandfather had been a Chabadnik. There she became particularly close to Rabbi Shneur Zalman Paris, a great-grandson of Rabbi Avraham Pariz (mentioned on p. 686 above), who went on to found Chabad of Tribeca/SoHo.

Appendix A2: The Author's Children[1]

His Son Isruel (aka Israel Goldenstein 1873–1946)[2]

In 1894, Isruel married Gitl of Feodosiya in the Crimea, where they settled and raised their four children: Freyde (called Frida in Russian), Avrum (called Avraam in Russian), Moyshe (called Mosya in Russian, and later Morris in French), and Mordekhai "Motl" (called Mark in Russian and nicknamed Mara). Isruel served as one of Feodosiya's *shokhtim,* in addition to being a *moyel* and a cantor, like his father. Avrum and Frida both studied in medical school in Simferopol.

During the famine of 1921–1923 in the Ukraine, Isruel and his family suffered greatly. In about 1922, Isruel's son Mosya (1900–1984) and some friends fled the country on a boat to Constantinople (now Istanbul), where thousands of Jews were fleeing. When the Turkish boatmen tried to rob them and throw them overboard into the Black Sea, Mosya managed, with his considerable charm, to convince them to spare them since they were spiritual brothers, being that they were all circumcised. After reaching and settling in Constantinople, Mosya's siblings Frida and Mark joined him there. Isruel, Gitl, and their oldest son Avrum remained in the Soviet Union.

With his accounting background, Mosya became the main breadwinner and was able to support his two siblings. In 1923, Isruel's brother Shloyme with his wife and two daughters arrived in Constantinople and left for Palestine by the end of the year. In Constantinople, Mosya met his future wife Frida Barski, and they were married in 1924. Mosya's sister Frida also met her future husband, a Jewish chemical engineer named Dr. Joseph Pozwolski, nicknamed Osya, who proposed marriage to her. An expert in his profession, he was waiting for a visa to enter France. Joseph's marriage proposal appealed to Frida, especially since he promised to also send for her two brothers and sister-in-law once he arrived in France, where they became engaged. Joseph left for France, and

1 This appendix contains details about the lives of Pinye-Ber's children, particularly after they left their father's house, and some of his grandchildren. See Appendix D3 (pp. 822–823) for a genealogical chart of Pinye-Ber's children and grandchildren.

2 This section, unless otherwise indicated, is based on personal correspondence in 2002 with Isruel's granddaughter Myriam (Pozwolski) Cronin of London.

Mosya was the first of the siblings to arrive in Paris in 1924, with the others following later that year. They did have family in France, namely their father's sister Rukhl (Raya) and a relative, Simkha Apatchevsky.[3] Frida and Joseph were married in Paris in about 1926.

In Paris, Mosya obtained an accounting position. The three siblings felt great concern and overwhelming guilt for having left their parents Isruel and Gitl behind in the Soviet Union. Mosya led the effort to bring their parents out, but all of them saved up money to enable their parents to leave the Soviet Union. Mosya also sent parcels to his parents who were not given rations because they were observant Jews. In 1928, the Yevsektsiya (the so-called Jewish section of the Soviet Communist Party in charge of destroying all vestiges of traditional Jewish life) closed Feodosiya's large choral synagogue, which could seat 1,000 people, and turned it into a sports club.[4] Afterward, Feodosiya's Ashkenazi Jews, including Isruel and Gitl, attended its ancient synagogue, the oldest in Russia, which had an inscription testifying to its construction in the year 909; by 1970, it had been destroyed, either by the Nazis or by the Soviets.[5] At one point, Isruel was arrested, likely by the Yevsektsiya for his work as a *shoykhet* and a *moyel*, and remained in jail during Rosh Hashanah and Yom Kippur.[6] After great effort on their children's part in France, Isruel and Gitl were finally permitted to immigrate to France in 1935. Once in Paris, Isruel became the cantor in a local synagogue and was known locally for his beautiful baritone.

Isruel's youngest son Mark became a chemical engineer and was employed by a French metallurgic company to work in a molybdenum mine in Mazatlán, Mexico from February 1937 until October 1938. By the end of 1938, he returned

---

3 Personal correspondence in 2007 with Simkha's son Pierre Pachet (1937–2016) of Paris, who was a writer and essayist in France. Simkha (1895–1965) was the son of Ersh (who died during the Second World War under unknown circumstances), who was the son of Ester-Khaye Teplitsky Apatshevsky, the daughter of Pinye-Ber's sister Ite. Simkha immigrated to France in 1912–1913. When the Germans invaded France in 1940, Simkha decided not to declare his family as Jews and enrolled his children in a Catholic school, thereby enabling Pierre and his sister Helene (1935–2001) to survive the Holocaust.

4 See ch. 13, p. 207, footnote 15, for more about choral synagogues. For more about the Yevsektsiya, see ch. 29, p. 599, footnote 74. After the Second World War, the choral synagogue was turned into an Officers House of the Russian Navy.

5 When Catherine the Great, Empress of Russia, visited Feodosiya in 1787, she heard that an ancient synagogue had been uncovered during an excavation and ordered it to be renovated. Once the renovations were completed, a dedication ceremony was held in 1788 (Farfel, 1912; Keren, 1912:50,113,211,324). Isruel and Gitl Goldenshteyn may have attended Feodosiya's ancient synagogue even before 1928.

6 See Isruel's letter dated August 28, 1939 in Appendix B3, p. 523.

to his wife Lucie and young daughter Nelly-Jean who had stayed in Paris. In February 1939, Mark's company, La Société Minière Française du Mercure, sent him to French Algeria, then a French colony, as the local manager of the mercury mines in Ras El Ma. Once again, he left his wife and daughter behind in Paris. On September 1, 1939, the Nazis invaded Poland, and two days later France and Great Britain declared war on Germany. All the young French men were mobilized by the army. Being that mercury was needed for the preparation of mercury fulminate, used in ammunition primers and detonators, Mark was immediately ordered to continue managing the Ras El Ma mines. In October 1939, Mark was granted permission to bring his wife and daughter to Algeria, but traveling there during war time was another matter. In the summer of 1940, Lucie and Nelly made the perilous journey from Paris to Marseille during the terrible exodus of eight to ten million refugees who were fleeing their homes to escape the Nazi invasion. In November 1940, Lucie and Nelly barely managed to catch the last civilian boat leaving Marseille for Algeria. Mark and Lucie's son Jean-Pierre was born in Ras El Ma in February 1945. They were able to return to Paris in the summer of 1946.[7]

When Germany invaded France in May 1940, Frida's husband Joseph Pozwolski, a representative of the French firm René Weil, was on a business trip to Yugoslavia. At that time, Italy closed its borders, thereby preventing him from returning to France. During the winter of 1940–1941, Joseph met with a German mining engineer named Dr. Georg Ufer in Belgrade, Yugoslavia concerning the acquisition of a mining site there. The negotiations were broken off when Ufer was unexpectedly recalled to Germany. On April 6, 1941, German, Italian, and Hungarian forces invaded Yugoslavia. The German Air Force (Luftwaffe) bombed Belgrade and other major Yugoslav cities. When Ufer subsequently returned to Belgrade, he found Joseph wearing the Nazi-imposed Jewish badge and working as a slave laborer in the grave-digging unit that was forced to dig up the remains of those who had been buried underneath the rubble resulting from the German bombardments. Ufer, by then a uniformed Wehrmacht major, had Joseph reassigned to his own unit in Skopje, Yugoslavia, as an indispensable technical laborer, which freed Joseph for a while from the obligation of wearing the Jewish badge. With the onset of the deportation of the Jews of Yugoslavia to concentration camps, Ufer realized that he would no longer be able to shield Joseph and, at great risk to himself, transported him across the border to Macedonia. There, Joseph was arrested by the Italians,

7 Personal correspondence in January 2023 from Jean-Pierre and his wife Catherine Goldenstein of Paris to Lisa (Unterberg) Delafontaine of Port Chester, New York.

placed in various camps, but escaped and was able to survive the war by joining the Albanian partisans. Only in 1945 was Joseph located by his family. Ufer was questioned twice by the Security Police concerning persistent rumors that he had smuggled a Jew across the border, but he denied any knowledge of the affair. On May 11, 1980, Yad Vashem recognized Dr. Georg Ufer (1900–1989) as Righteous Among the Nations. Joseph died in 1969 in France at age seventy-seven.

During the war, the rest of the family moved to a small village in the center of France called Saint-Gervais d'Auvergne, which is about fifty kilometers (thirty miles) from Vichy, France. The family members living there were Isruel and Gitl, who were then in their seventies; their son Mosya, his wife Frida, and their daughter Julia (who had a heart condition); and their daughter Frida Pozwolski and her three children Alexandre, Maurice, and Myriam. There they were not compelled to wear the Nazi-imposed Jewish badge. Nearby in the woods was a place where Frida could purchase live chickens, which Isruel, a *shoykhet,* would slaughter, thereby providing kosher meat for his family and other Jewish refugees as well. While walking in the woods one day to buy chickens, Frida came across some French non-Jews who warned her that there were Nazis in the direction in which she was walking, thereby saving her life. Another time, in 1941, there was a knock at the kitchen door, and Frida's daughter Myriam opened it. There stood a man with dark eyes and a dark moustache. Her heart sank for she thought that he was Hitler coming to arrest them. The man turned out to be a very nice Polish Jewish refugee coming to meet Isruel.

Isruel could speak a little French and would go shopping in the market. People thought he was a retired Russian general as he had such deportment—he was tall with a straight back. Gitl helped her daughter, Frida, cook and mind the grandchildren. Despite the rationing of food, the family did not suffer from hunger since, being in the country, they were able to grow vegetables and also received food parcels from both Isruel's and Gitl's relatives in America. Frida also traveled to the farm of Isruel's sister Raya, where she was able to purchase a great variety of produce.

Frida Pozwolski sent her sons Alexandre and Maurice to a far-away preventorium for boys for health reasons. Alex's lungs had become burned by breathing in chlorine gas which he had manufactured himself; he was always conducting chemical experiments. Frida sent her daughter, Myriam, to a Catholic boarding school in Riom, where they treated her superbly and never pressured her to convert. Only one person used to look at her pointedly while saying that unbaptized children do not go to heaven; Myriam hated her. Nonetheless, it was still quite risky there too. One evening in January 1944, a man with a gun entered the boarding school; he was preceded by the head mistress and all the available teachers. Eleven-year-old Myriam was terrified. He was looking for a student who was a participant in the French Resistance. Strangely, he asked a five-year old girl her age, as if she could have been that student. Being a French Nazi sympathizer, he was later caught and shot. In their letters to each other, Myriam and her mother Frida came up with the code-phrase "*la tante est folle*" ("Auntie is crazy") to indicate when the situation was particularly dangerous.

Isruel and Gitl remained in Saint-Gervais with their daughter Frida and son Mosya, along with Mosya's wife Frida and daughter Julia. On December 25, 1943, Isruel, Gitl, and Frida had to leave their home and, for their safety, spent the night in the snow which was two or three feet high. Eventually, Myriam's primary school teacher, Mrs. Vallenet, rescued them by bringing them to her home. Later that night they had another scare when some people banged violently on her door, but it turned out just to be some revelers. Eventually, the six of them had to go into hiding (the count was seven when Myriam was able to return home from boarding school). A farmer's daughter named Lily Laroche hid them during dangerous periods in a two-room structure she owned near her farm. It was without water or sanitation. Lily brought them food, water, and supplies, and she cooked food and emptied the slops, all at her own risk and peril. On several occasions, they stayed there for many months. At one point, they had to be moved and were sheltered by another savior, a farmer called Gauvin, known as "*le pere* Gauvin," whose farm was some distance from the village. He had them stay in a barn which was, unfortunately, rat-infested. Since life was rather difficult for six people crammed into two small rooms, Frida returned at one point to the house in Saint-Gervais, while the other five members of the family remained in hiding. Once, Lily LaRoche came to the house in Saint-Gervais to warn Frida that the Germans were coming. Frida ran to knock at the door of some other Jewish refugees to warn them, but they had already left without notifying anyone. Frida barely made it out of the village when she saw the Germans entering. Later, she saw that they had broken down the doors to her flat and Mosya's flat and found out that they had beaten up a Frenchman who also lived in the house, thinking that he was Mosya.

At the end of the war, Mosya, his wife, and their daughter returned to Paris, and then Isruel and Gitl joined them there for about a year. In April 1946, Isruel and Gitl returned to Saint-Gervais to spend Pesach with their daughter Frida, who was still residing there, but Isruel died there two days before Pesach on April 14 at the age of seventy-three. He was temporarily buried in Saint-Gervais, until his body was exhumed and transported to Paris where Mosya had bought a family plot. Myriam remembers her grandfather Isruel fondly: "He was a very affectionate man. I have lovely memories of the religious feasts at home, even during the war. Though he was a trained *shoykhet*, he was a sensitive man who did not enjoy slaughtering animals." Gitl died in March 1968 at her home in Paris at approximately ninety-three years of age, still of sound mind until the last few days of her illness.[8] Myriam remembers her as "a lovely, devoted mother and grandmother."

In 1939, France had approximately 330,000 Jews, half of whom were foreigners from Eastern Europe who had arrived in the 1930s. Though less than a quarter (72,500) of French Jews were murdered, seventy percent of those murdered were foreigners (Authers and Wolffe, 2002:159). The Goldensteins in France were fortunate that righteous gentiles had risked their lives to help them hide and conceal their identities, but their close family in the Soviet Union was not so fortunate.

Isruel's son, Avrum, had become a physician in the Soviet Union. During the Second World War, he was a colonel in the Soviet army and the head of a military hospital. His wife Pola and daughter Alla wanted to travel to join him, but he told them not to, for he feared for their safety. Pola and Alla were murdered by the Germans; apparently, they were shot. After the war, Avrum did not remarry but lived in Leningrad with his late wife's niece, Maya, whose story was parallel to his; she had lost her husband and child under similar circumstances. In 1970, his sister Frida and her daughter Myriam traveled to Leningrad to visit him. They had not seen each other for almost fifty years. Frida found that Avrum was quite ill with myasthenia gravis, but he was being well looked after by Maya. His brothers Mosya and Mark also visited him. Avrum died in approximately 1977.

His Daughter Nekhame Brakhtman (Noami "Nadya" Brockman, 1877–1955)[9]

In 1897, Nekhame married Mendl Brakhtman, who was born in about 1867 in Snitkov, Ukraine.[10] His parents, Moyshe-Hersh and Ester "Etl" (née Faynyud)

---

8 In French, Gitl's name was spelled officially as Guitel Aguinskaya Goldenstein.

9 The April 5, 1932 death certificate (#7892) of "Mendel Brachtman" indicates that his mother's maiden name was Faynyud, which was also pronounced as Fonyud.

10 The 1875 revision list (poll-tax census) of Soroka, Ukraine, as indexed on the JewishGen Ukraine Database (https://www.jewishgen.org/databases/ukraine), lists Mendl and his brothers in nearby Ataky and states that they were originally from Snitkov (now Snitkiv, Ukraine). After their mother's death in about 1874, their father apparently left the children

Brakhtman,[11] had six children before his mother died when he was about seven. Afterwards, his father remarried and moved his family to Odessa, where he died in the late 1880s. The Brakhtmans claimed to have been related to Baron Horace Günzburg (1833–1909), the Russian-Jewish philanthropist.[12] Upon being conscripted into the Russian military, Mendl served in the cavalry. There he befriended a fellow Jewish cavalryman whose father, N. B. Ratgauz, was a major exporter of grain in the port city of Feodosiya (Keren, 1981:110). After completing his service, Mendl went to Feodosiya where his friend's father hired him as the manager in charge of shipping. In about 1894, new harbor works made Feodosiya a convenient port for grain ships coming out of the Sea of Azov, which brought prosperity to the city and caused Ratgauz's business to flourish. It was in Feodosiya that Nekhame and Mendl were introduced to each other.

Nekhame and Mendl led a comfortable life in Feodosiya with a nice home and servants. They had two daughters and three sons, who grew up relatively carefree in a Russian-speaking home. Nekhame, who was tall and stout, was called Nadya in Russian, and Mendl, who was shorter and thin, was called Mikhail. Nekhame was more religiously observant than Mendl; the enormous difficulties in observing even the most basic precepts of Judaism in the Russian military had weakened Mendl's piety. Jewish communal life in Feodosiya was temporarily marred in October 1905 by a pogrom that killed more than twenty Jews (Keren, 1981:115–120; Merenbach, 1977:17–19).

Nekhame and Mendl's oldest son, Moyshe (1899–1984), was called Moisei in Russian and nicknamed Mosya. After not being admitted into the *gimnaziia* because of its Jewish quotas, he no longer desired to remain in such a prejudiced

---

temporarily with relatives in Ataky. The revision list states that Mendl was eight years old (born ca. 1867), in contrast to documents from the 1920s and 1930s—such as the passenger manifest of the steamship *Olympia* arriving in New York City on February 9, 1927—which indicate that "Mendel Brachtman" was born in 1873. In historical research, generally the earlier a document appears in a person's life, the more reliable is the person's reported age.

11 Mendl's mother's maiden name of Faynyud (also pronounced as Fonyud) is noted on his death certificate (#7892) where his name is indicated as "Mendel Brachtman." He died on April 5, 1932, in Brooklyn.

12 Personal interview in 2006 with Roman S. Brackman of Manhattan. Roman was the son of Yakov (1895–1979) who was the son of Isak Brakhtman (ca. 1865–1943), the brother of Mendl. Roman no longer remembers his family's exact relationship to the Günzburgs. Born in 1931 in Moscow, Roman was sentenced in 1949 to ten years in the Norilsk Gulag penal labor camp for unsuccessfully attempting to escape from the Soviet Union. While there, he participated in a Norilsk prisoner uprising in the summer of 1953, the first major revolt within the Gulag system. In 1962, his relative, David M. Brackman of Boston (see p. 697, footnote 17 below), arranged to bring him to the United States, where Roman Americanized his surname to Brackman. Roman has written multiple works regarding Joseph Stalin and the history, politics, and economics of the Soviet Union and Russia.

country. He ran away from home and hopped on a ship to America. His parents ran after him and retrieved him from the ship, but he ran away again. After his second attempt, he cried so much that they finally gave him permission and he left in 1914. He made his way to his mother's brothers Yosl and Yankl (now known as Joseph and Jacob Goldeen) in Portland, Oregon, where he went by the name Martin Brachtman. He lived with Joseph at first but worked for Jacob. In fact, Martin followed Jacob in his moves to Woodburn, Oregon in 1916 and then to Vancouver, Washington, in 1918. In 1919, Martin Americanized his surname to Brockman and later that year married a non-Jew, which was very distressing for the family. In 1920, he followed Jacob back to Portland, where Martin continued to reside for the rest of his life.

Nekhame and Mendl's youngest child, Victor (1904–1985), showed scholarly qualities; his high marks on the entrance exams gained him entry into the *gimnaziia*, unlike his two older brothers. He was recognized as being the brightest student in his class.

With the start of the Russian Civil War (1917–1922), the life of the Brakhtmans changed dramatically. The country was in such disarray that food supplies became non-existent even though Ukraine had beforehand been the breadbasket of Europe. The Russian Civil War was also fought in Feodosiya where, at times, bullets were flying. During the 1921–1923 famine in Ukraine, the Brakhtmans had to sell their piano for food. Soon Mendl could not obtain food, even though he was the manager of a major exporter of grain. Some of the starving people in Feodosiya even resorted to eating the bark off the trees.

Though only nineteen years old in 1921, the Brakhtman's son, Mark (1902–1990), held a position at the port of Feodosiya which enabled him to obtain passports for his parents, three siblings, and himself, and they made plans to leave the country. On the appointed date of their departure, the Brakhtmans boarded the ship, but daughter Frida was somehow held up. They asked the ship's captain to delay the ship, but after some time the ship was compelled to leave before she arrived. Frida remained in the Soviet Union for the rest of her life. At some point during their voyage, the five of them—Nekhame, Mendl, and their three children Etl, Mark, and Victor—were compelled to change ships, but the captain of the new vessel refused to allow them on board. With her knowledge of Crimean-Tatar, which is similar to Turkish, Nekhame approached the captain, a Turk, and was able to communicate with him and convince him to allow them to board. Upon finally reaching Constantinople, they continued on to Palestine, where they arrived in the late spring or early summer of 1921. In Petakh-Tikva, they moved into the larger of the two houses on Pinye-Ber's property. The Brakhtmans were greatly impressed with Pinye-Ber's third wife Bashe, whom he had just married that January, for she had been a pioneering settler there, enduring so much hardship.[13]

In Palestine, Mendl became a building contractor, Mark worked as a locksmith, and Victor worked as a mason. Here Mark and Victor learned Hebrew and were called by their Hebrew names Mordekhai and Avigdor, respectively. Victor used to walk to and from Petakh-Tikva to Tel-Aviv to work which would take him about two and a half hours each way. They worked very hard but were barely subsisting.

Out of the blue, Mendl received a letter from someone he had not heard from in decades—his younger brother Gershon. Decades earlier, Gershon had immigrated to the United States where he had assumed the name Harry Kessler (1873–1960).[14] Early in his career, he lived for a few years in Argentina where he owned restaurants. During Prohibition, when it was illegal to sell alcoholic beverages in the United States from 1920 to 1933, he made a lot of money selling liquor illegally. He would frequent speakeasies, was friends with New York City's flamboyant mayor, Jimmy Walker, and knew the Bronfmans of Seagram's. Harry was very generous and gave everyone expensive presents.[15] In the course of his business exploits, he traveled the world. His US passport testifies that his travel destinations in the 1930s included Austria, Hungary, Poland, the Soviet Union, and Shanghai.[16] While on a business trip to Boston in 1924, Harry went to a barber shop to have his hair cut. The barber asked him, "What are you doing here, Mr. Brackman? I just cut your hair this morning." Harry quickly realized that the barber had mistaken him for his brother Nathan Brackman, whom he had not seen in years.[17] During Harry and Nathan's reunion, Nathan

---

13 See Appendix A5 (pp. 733–745) for more details about Bashe.

14 The 1875 revision list of Soroka, Ukraine (see p. 694, footnote 10 above), refers to Harry as Gershon. The Hebrew inscription on his tombstone in the Mt. Hebron Cemetery in Queens incorrectly states that his Jewish name was Herts. He is buried next to Mendl and Nekhame and their son Victor and his wife Miriam.

15 Though Harry made a fortune during his lifetime, he did not die a rich man. He was said to have loaned money to people while never seeking to be repaid. He had no progeny of his own.

16 Harry's expired US passport (no. 167216), issued on February 25, 1935, is in the possession of his grand-niece Cynthia (Brockman) Unterberg of Westbury, New York.

17 In about 1891, Nathan (ca. 1869–1925), originally named Nakhman, and Harry left Tsarist Russia together by stowing away on a ship. They first went to Greece, then Turkey, from where they made their way to New York City, according to a personal interview in 2006 with Roman Brackman (see p. 695, footnote 12 above). Nathan originally went by the surname Brachtman but Americanized his surname to Brackman upon moving to Boston in 1901. He was in the millinery business and owned an interest in two movie theatres. He sometimes used the name Carl Martin for business purposes, and two of his eight children later legally

told him that their brother Mendl was in Palestine and was having a difficult time there. Being kind and generous, Harry contacted Mendl to find out how he could help.

After hearing back from Mendl, Harry sent visas and steamship tickets to Mendl and his family to travel to America. But shortly before they were to leave, their twenty-three-year-old daughter Etl contracted measles and died on August 7, 1924. Pinye-Ber personally carved her tombstone, being an experienced tombstone engraver in the Crimea.[18] With their trip delayed, Mendl and his family were not permitted afterwards to immigrate to America since the quotas, just established in May of that year by the Immigration Act of 1924, had been filled. The Immigration Act had been passed specifically to restrict Jewish and Catholic immigration to the United States. Harry then sent Mendl 600 Palestine pounds, which he used to build a house in the Tel-Nordau neighborhood of Tel-Aviv in 1925. The Brakhtmans worked hard but were unable to earn much since the economic conditions in Palestine were very difficult at that time. The next year, they received permission to immigrate to the United States using their prior visas.

Mendl and Nekhame decided that she and their two sons, Mark and Victor, would go to America while Mendl would remain in Tel-Aviv until he sold their house. The three of them traveled to Beirut, Lebanon, where they boarded the steamship *Sinaia* on March 5, 1926. Since Harry had sent them either first- or second-class tickets, they were spared the misery of traveling in steerage as most immigrants to America did. On its way to the United States, the ship stopped in Le Havre, France, where Nekhame's brother Isruel's children Frida, Mosya, and Mark and their spouses came to see them from Paris. The Brakhtmans arrived in Providence, Rhode Island on April 4, 1926. They first went to Boston, where they stayed with the family of Mendl's late brother Nathan Brackman. They then went to New York City, where they met with Nekhame's relatives

---

changed their surname to Martin. One of Nathan's sons was David M. Brackman (1900–1982) who started off as a page in the Massachusetts State Senate in 1919 when President Calvin Coolidge was governor. While there, David became impressed with the Republicans rather than the Democrats, since most of the Democrats were caught up in Boston's corrupt political machine. Despite his being a Republican, he was elected three times to the Massachusetts State Senate by an Irish Democratic constituency, which testifies to his character. (This is based on a telephone interview in 2008 with David's son Joseph L. Brackman of Randolph, Massachusetts.)

18 Personal interview in 2001 with Aliza (Goldenshteyn) Bernfeld of Petakh-Tikva.

Sophie Grover and Rose (Chaplick) Budiansky and Mendl's nephew Morris Brachtman.[19]

By June 1926, Nekhame, Victor, and Mark had arrived in California where her brothers Yosl and Yankl (now known as Joseph and Jacob Goldeen) lived. Nekhame and her sons lived in an apartment in Oakland, California, where her brother James lived and worked; he was the manager of the Oakland branch of the United Manufacturing Company, which manufactured mattresses. Victor and Mark worked in his factory as mattress machine operators, filling the mattresses with stuffing. They had to travel some three hours each way to work. Pinye-Ber wrote to Victor and Mark in Oakland that he was sending them the *Ha-Aretz* newspaper, published in Tel-Aviv, each week—"a present from your grandfather"—so that "you will be able to read and to know what is going on in this country and so that you won't become cut off from Hebrew, because I still hope that you will return to the Holy Land with successful businesses."[20] Nekhame's son, Martin, came to visit them from Portland. In that same letter, Pinye-Ber inquired about Nekhame's son Martin (Moyshe), "I send regards to . . . your Moyshe—does he still remember his grandfather? Does he remember how he used to sing *Yismakh Moyshe* with his grandfather at the *Shobes* table"?[21] In his uncle's factory, Victor could not bear the tremendous dust generated by the stuffing machine, so he quit and moved to New York City around August 1926. In January 1927, Nekhame and Mark followed, for Mark was also affected by the dust.[22] Harry Kessler set them up in an apartment in the Williamsburg neighborhood of Brooklyn in one of the apartment buildings he owned. Almost a year after his wife and sons had left Palestine, Mendl left on January 20, 1927,[23] and arrived in New York City on February 9, 1927 on the steamship *Olympus*. In

19 See Appendix B3 (pp. 776–777) for more details regarding the Grovers and Chaplicks. Morris (Moyshe) Brachtman (1890–1968) was Mendl's nephew, the son of his brother Leon. According to Roman Brackman (see p. 695, footnote 12 above), Leon (Leybl) Brakhtman had been the mayor of Simferopol, Crimea before the First World War and used to ride in a four-horse carriage. During the Russian Civil War, Leon fled to Constantinople but afterwards returned to the Crimea, dying in Yevpatoriya. Morris immigrated to the United States in 1923 and moved to Portland, Oregon in the 1930s. He was married twice but had no progeny.

20 For the complete letter dated July 3, 1926, see Appendix B3, pp. 783–787.

21 *Yismakh Moyshe* (i.e., "Moses will be happy" in Hebrew) is a song with a Yiddish refrain. It is likely that Pinye-Ber chose to sing this particular song with Moyshe because it mentions his name.

22 See Pinye-Ber's letter dated January 27, 1927 in Appendix B3, p. 790.

23 Mendl's date of departure is indicated in the author's letter of January 27, 1927 in Appendix B3, p. 789.

October 1928, Nekhame's brother Raphael also settled in Brooklyn after returning from a trip to Europe, and he remained there for almost a year and a half.

Having been a union member in Palestine enabled Victor to easily join the Bricklayers, Masons, and Plasterers International Union of America. At that point, Harry lent his assistance once again by helping his nephew obtain a position in the construction business as a bricklayer, building apartment houses in Brooklyn and the Bronx. Construction was one of the few industries that remained strong throughout the Great Depression. Mark found employment with his relative Herman Grover (1894–1975) who was in the wholesale paper business; Mark worked for him for quite a few years. In the late 1920s, Victor, Mark, and Nekhame changed their surname to Brockman, as Martin had done.

When Victor became engaged in October 1930, Pinye-Ber was thrilled and showered him with blessings in Hebrew in a letter.[24] Pinye-Ber died on December 4, 1930, and twenty days later Victor and his fiancée Miriam "Mae" Barotz were married. Victor's father-in-law, Louis Barotz, immediately welcomed him into his business, Star Imports (later called Seabord Imports), which imported cultured pearls from Japan and manufactured and imported costume jewelry. Having grown up in the Crimea, which was not as traditional as other parts of Tsarist Russia, Victor had been raised speaking Russian—not Yiddish. But he quickly learned Yiddish from Mae's family who had come from the Ukraine in 1922. Nekhame and Mark continued to live together until Mark married Gertrude in 1936. Unable to have children, Mark and Gertrude adopted a daughter in 1941 whom they named Eileen.

Mendl died on April 5, 1932 from bronchopneumonia at approximately sixty-five years of age. In May 1933, Nekhame returned to Palestine to remarry, though she did not find a suitable mate. She stayed in a rented apartment in Tel-Aviv near the sea. In honor of her father's third *yortsayt* on December 2, 1933, she ordered a tombstone for her father's grave. She regularly visited her brother Shloyme, his wife Etya, and their two daughters in Petakh-Tikva. Nekhame was not satisfied with certain aspects of her sister-in-law Etya's household management. Etya was a working woman who was busy with her dental practice from morning until night. She would stop her work, put something together for a meal for her husband and daughters, and then return to work. Being an expert cook and even a better baker, Nekhame told Etya that she had to cook real meals for her family. Nekhame also criticized Etya for not teaching her daughters how to knit, to which Etya replied that they were too young. But Nekhame, who believed that the younger, the better, took Dvora and Aliza for lessons at a knit-

24 See Pinye-Ber's letter dated October 30, 1930 in Appendix B3, pp. 803–804.

ting school in Tel-Aviv. After almost a year in Palestine, Nekhame decided to return to Brooklyn; after all, Victor now had two little girls Cynthia and Muriel. On April 18, 1934, Nekhame was accompanied by Shloyme and his family to the port of Haifa, where she departed on the steamship *Roma*. The ship stopped briefly in France, where her brother Isruel's three children Frida, Mosya, and Mark and their families came to meet her. Nekhame arrived in New York City on May 4, 1934.[25]

Victor always made sure that Nekhame lived in an apartment close to his home. She had a marvelous relationship with her daughter-in-law, Mae, who was almost like a daughter to her. Mae filled the void of her prematurely deceased daughter Etl and her daughter Frida, who was left behind in the Soviet Union. Over time, Victor and Mae had two more children, Sanford (named Shloyme-Ber after Pinye-Ber) and Rhea. Though Nekhame was not able to speak English well, she understood it; her grandchildren understood Yiddish but could not speak it. Nekhame was close by at most family functions and helped raise Victor and Mae's children. As a little boy, grandson Sanford, nicknamed Sonny, developed a fear of dogs so intense that he would become hysterical upon seeing one even a few blocks away. Nekhame said that the only way that he was going to overcome this phobia was for the family to buy a dog, though Jews do not traditionally own dogs. Her advice was heeded, and Sonny was soon cured. Nekhame's hands were never idle; she was always knitting baby and children's sweaters or crocheting beautiful tablecloths, doilies, aprons, etc. Her granddaughter Muriel Casper remembers Nekhame as a "clever, wonderful, ever-smiling woman" who, like her father Pinye-Ber, was an avid correspondent and kept abreast of the family that was spread out on three continents. Her granddaughter Cynthia Unterberg remembers Nekhame as always having a holy Jewish book in her hands, whether it was a Hebrew Book of Psalms or a *Tsene-rene*. Unlike her brothers in America, Nekhame remained Sabbath observant. She died on September 29, 1955 at the age of seventy-eight.

Nekhame's oldest child, Frida, remained in the Soviet Union. In the 1920s, she studied opera in Moscow, where she met her husband, a Jewish journalist named Sosnovsky. They had a daughter named Elvira in 1927 and a son named Roald, called Adya, in 1929.[26] In the early 1930s, her brothers Victor

25 Personal interview in 2001 with the author's granddaughter Aliza (Goldenshteyn) Bernfeld of Petakh-Tikva. Nekhame traveled under the name "Nechama Brockman." Later she used the name Naomi for official purpose, though relatives and friends called her Nekhame or Nadya.

26 In Pinye-Ber's July 3, 1926 letter (see Appendix B3, p. 786), he notes that Joseph Pozwolski of Paris, the son-in-law of his son Isruel, had recently been in Moscow and he mentions the relatives he met. Since Frida Sosnovsky is not mentioned, she was likely not living in

and Mark obtained visas for Frida and her family to come to America, but circumstances in the Soviet Union prevented her from receiving them. In the late 1930s, Frida's husband was shot to death, evidently in Stalin's purges where anyone suspected of being a threat was executed. During the Cold War, it was difficult for Victor and Mark in the United States to maintain contact with Frida in the Soviet Union. The husband of Frida's daughter Elvira held a high position in the Soviet military, and Frida's son, Roald, had become a nuclear physicist. Because of their sensitive positions, Frida was afraid to have contact with her relatives in the United States, including her own mother. In order for Victor and Mark to send her letters, they had to forward them to their relatives Mosya and Mark Goldenstein in Paris, who then sent their letters to a contact in Poland, who then forwarded them to the Soviet Union.

In 1968, Victor and his wife Mae Brockman traveled to the Soviet Union to visit his sister Frida, whom he had not seen in forty-seven years. They first flew to Israel to visit his cousins Dvora Gavrieli and Aliza Bernfeld and then flew to Turkey, where they caught a plane to Moscow. Because of the high military position of Frida's son-in-law, she was afraid to meet Victor and Mae in her apartment or even to have him telephone her, so they agreed in advance to meet through Musya and Basya Kreyzberg, the unmarried nieces of Victor's uncle Shloyme Goldenstein who lived together in Moscow.[27] Upon arriving in Moscow, Victor realized that the Kreyzbergs' telephone number he had was no longer valid. He quickly cabled his cousins Mosya and Mark Goldenstein in France, who cabled their brother Avrum in Leningrad, who found out the Kreyzbergs' new telephone number and cabled it to relatives in France, who in turn cabled it to Victor in Moscow. Victor called the Kreyzbergs and asked them to tell Frida to meet him at his hotel. On the day of their meeting, there was a huge rainstorm. Frida arrived at Victor's hotel, but she was not allowed inside since it was restricted to foreigners, and the storm prevented them from talking outside. Since Victor and Mae were scheduled to return to New York the next day, they quickly agreed to meet at the Kreyzbergs' apartment the next morning before they left. Upon arriving there, the Kreyzberg sisters made Victor swear never to divulge their telephone number to their first cousins, Dvora Gavrieli and Aliza Bernfeld in Israel, out of fear of reprisals from Soviet authorities for having contact with relatives in Israel; Victor kept his word.[28] In August 1970,

---

Moscow at the time. In 1933, Frida was living in Moscow, as indicated on the U.S. Petition for Citizenship (#176698) at the Eastern District Court of New York in Brooklyn of her mother Nekhame (referred to as Nechama Brockman), dated January 27, 1933.

27 See Appendix A4, pp. 730–732, for details regarding the Kreyzbergs.

28 Personal interview in 2001 with Aliza Bernfeld of Petakh-Tikva.

Victor and Mae once again visited Frida and were able to meet her son Roald. This time, they were accompanied by Victor's brother Mark and his wife Gertie. Frida died in 1983.

As his daughter Muriel Casper writes, "When Victor left Palestine to become an American citizen, his heart and head were still profoundly devoted to the cause of the Jewish homeland." In one of his letters, Pinye-Ber writes to his daughter, Nekhame, about his grandson Victor, "He loves *Yidishkayt*[29] very much, as you know."[30] Victor, and particularly Mae, were very concerned about the Jewish people and staunch supporters of the Jewish community in Palestine and later of Israel. Mae was a diligent worker for over thirty-five years for the Hadassah Women's Zionist Organization of America, Hadassah Medical Center in Jerusalem, and Youth Aliyah, an organization which rescued thousands of Jewish children from the Nazis during the Third Reich. Mae opened her home countless times for fundraising events for Israel Bonds and Hadassah. Over the years, she collected over a million dollars for the State of Israel. Apart from receiving many awards and plaques, she received letters of commendation for her outstanding service to Israel signed by Israel's first president, Chaim Weizmann, and its first prime minister, David Ben-Gurion. When Mae died unexpectedly in 1975 at the age of 68, she was the president of a Hadassah region which included twelve chapters. In tribute to her decades of work, Hadassah gave her a slew of honors. Muriel recalls her mother Mae as leaving a beautiful legacy and of being a "caring role model who radiated love to all, friend and family."

Cynthia recalls her parents, Victor and Mae, as being "very good people whose desire was to be good for the world and their children." Apart from being loving and supportive parents, Victor and Mae were traditional, kept a kosher kitchen, and were active members of their Orthodox synagogue, the Manhattan Beach Jewish Center, where Mae was president of the sisterhood. Mae and Victor kept an open house, and, until today, people still talk about their *Seders* and Hanukah parties. Victor and Mae's home was a necessary destination for all relatives from California, Oregon, or Israel who were either visiting New York City or just passing through. In 1978, Victor had a family tree printed that listed Pinye-Ber's numerous descendants, which he circulated among the family. Victor would often mention his beloved grandfather Pinye-Ber to his children and grandchildren, and he treasured his copy of Pinye-Ber's autobiography, which he kept in an honored place in the living room. Victor's granddaughter Lisa (Unterberg) Delafontaine was inspired by him to give her second son Alex

29 *Yidishkayt* means "Judaism."

30 Excerpted from Pinye-Ber's letter dated October 10, 1926 (Appendix B3, p. 788).

the Hebrew name of Yeshayahu Pinkhas after Pinkhes-Dov, his great-great-great-grandfather.[31]

His Son Itskhok-Yosef "Yosl" (Joseph Edward "Joe" Goldeen, 1880–1954)[32]

Yosl was conscripted into the Russian army in late 1901 and served as an infantry soldier. Eight months before his military service was to end, the Russo-Japanese War broke out in February 1904 and Yosl was ordered to march to the front with the 129th infantry (*Oregonian*, August 20, 1911, sec. 1, p. 11). During their march, he fled, and the military police began looking for him. Yosl raced to Feodosiya where his brother-in-law Mendl Brakhtman supervised shipping for a major exporter of grain. As the military police were chasing him, Yosl ran onto a freight ship with a cargo of grain, where Mendl hid him in a huge coil of rope.[33] Yosl made his way to Liverpool, England where he caught a ship to Boston, arriving on February 24, 1905, and becoming the first of four siblings to immigrate to the United States.[34]

Yosl first stayed with his relatives Sophie and Ephraim Grover, who lived on the Lower East Side of Manhattan.[35] At the Grover's home, Yosl was shown a photograph of Edith (Ite), the daughter of his cousin Itsl (known in English as Isaac Goldstein) of Portland, Oregon, so he decided to go there to marry her. In Portland, he assumed Itsl's surname and became known as Joseph Edward Goldstein. Joseph and Edith married on August 27, 1905.[36] Their wedding, with 300 guests in attendance, was reported in a local newspaper with accompanying photographs of the bride and groom. It describes the wedding

---

31 Shortly before the bar mitzvah of Ian Niederhoffer, the son of Victor's granddaughter Kara Unterberg, it was determined that his Hebrew birthdate was the 14th of *Kislev*, which is Pinye-Ber's *yortsayt*.

32 Unless otherwise indicated, this section is based on a five-page typewritten letter from 1979 from Joseph's daughter Floriene (Goldeen) Merenbach (1912–2000) of San Francisco in response to an inquiry about family history from her first cousin William Glikbarg (1924–2013) of Santa Monica, California.

33 Personal interview in 2002 with Yosl's grandniece Cynthia (Brockman) Unterberg of Westbury, New York. See also Merenbach (1977:106).

34 The manifest of the steamship *Ivernia*, which embarked from Liverpool, lists him as "Joseph Goldenstein." He arrived in Boston on February 24, 1905. He is listed as a resident of Liverpool, indicating that he lived in Liverpool for a short period of time before traveling on to Boston.

35 For details regarding the Grovers, see Appendix B3, pp. 776–777.

36 For more about Isaac (Itsl) Goldstein, see Appendix A3, pp. 726–729.

ceremony as follows, "[T]he full ceremonials of the Jewish Orthodox church were employed. The quaint and curious customs of the maids and women relatives bearing candles, the canopy under which the ceremony is solemnized, the profuse floral and other decorations lent an unusual charm to the occasion" ("Goldstein-Goldstein," 1905).

At first, Joseph was employed as a cabinetmaker for I. Gevurtz & Sons Furniture Company, for which he initially received a salary of $12 a week. Over time, he was promoted to shipping clerk. Once, when Joseph was on vacation, he went up on the roof of his home to make some repairs. Mr. Gevurtz passed by and was furious, saying that he paid Joseph to rest on his vacation, not to work, and he docked his salary. In 1910, Joseph opened his own furniture store.

When Joseph's brother Refuel arrived in Portland from Tsarist Russia in February 1906, Edith was expecting her first child. Her running down the stairs to open the door for him and overexcitement probably resulted in her giving birth within several days to a stillborn boy on February 27, 1906. Refuel, who became known as Raphael Goldstein, lived with them until he left Portland in 1911, and Joseph paid for his schooling. Joseph and Edith later had two girls and then two boys. In August 1906, Joseph's brother Yankl and his wife Fanya (soon known as Jacob and Fannie) arrived and lived with them as well for a while. After Edith's father, Isaac, died in 1907, Joseph and Edith took in her three orphaned siblings, Jennie, Bertha (called Betty), and Sam. Upon being naturalized as a US citizen in 1911, Joseph changed his name from Goldstein to Goldeen. The surname Goldeen was Joseph's own creation, which he thought sounded high class and better for business.[37] His brother Jacob and Edith's siblings Bertha and Sam also changed their names to Goldeen, while Raphael reverted to the name Goldenstein. In 1914, Joseph's nephew Moyshe Brakhtman arrived from Feodosiya and stayed with him for a few months; he later become known as Martin Brockman.

In 1916, Joseph decided to move to Anaconda, Montana, which he thought would develop into a big growth area. Anaconda was essentially a company town dominated by the Anaconda Copper Mining Company, which boasted "The Largest Smokestack in the World." Joseph operated a furniture store there and rented a small house. Edith and the children did not like living there, as his daughter Floriene commented, "I have never been able to figure out why our

37 Telephone interview in 2002 with Samuel S. Goldeen, Jr. (1927–2017), of Monterey, California, who was Joseph's grandnephew.

father took us to such a God-forsaken place as Anaconda, with its six Jewish families." She added that perhaps it was fate, since Edith's sister Jennie met her husband Ben Shapiro (later changed to Sherwood) in Anaconda. Compared to their life in Portland, Anaconda seemed like the American frontier of old. Edith had to bake her own bread in a wood and coal stove, which was kept alight day and night because of the freezing cold, and she chopped the firewood herself. The snowdrifts in the winter were so high that one could not see over them. Edith used to say that their first October in Anaconda was so cold that the blankets froze to the walls. After hanging the laundry out to dry in the backyard, Edith often had to let it thaw before she could fold it. One winter, her hands froze.

In October 1920, Joseph decided to sell his stock of furniture in Anaconda and move to Los Angeles, but they first returned to Portland for an extended visit, where they stayed with Edith's sister Jennie and her husband Ben Shapiro in their small apartment. Joseph decided to take a train to Los Angeles and get settled there before sending for the rest of his family. On the way, the train stopped in San Jose, which is some fifty miles south of San Francisco. He stayed in a hotel that night, expecting to continue his journey the next day. In the morning, he had some time before the train left, so he took a walk and decided that he liked it there. Like Anaconda, he predicted that San Jose would become a big growth area, but this time he was right. Though San Jose would become the largest city in Northern California, with a population of over a million, at the time it only had some 40,000 residents. A second-hand furniture store was for sale, so Joseph decided to make an offer, which was accepted. He called it Goldeen's Furniture Company. He rented a house, and his family joined him there in April 1921. With only sixty Jewish families, San Jose had only one Jewish congregation, a Reform synagogue, which they joined. Joseph was its president for many years.

In 1928, Joseph bought a house in San Jose just a year before the stock market crash. That purchase saved him during the Great Depression, because his money was invested in the house rather than in the stock market. Even so, he was able to pay only the interest on the home and none of the principal, but he managed to hang on to it at a time when so many other people lost everything. Eventually, his business expanded to include three or four stores, which he turned over to his sons Don and Ralph. The stores remained in operation until the mid-1980s.

In 1945, Joseph's daughter Floriene visited her Uncle Jacob (now called James) and Aunt Fanny Goldeen in Portland. Fanny had a niece named Jean (Edelson) White (1905–1992), who was originally from Feodosiya. It was in her home in Portland that Floriene met another native of Feodosiya, Nathan Merenbach (1895–1983), who had been recently widowed and was also visiting from California.[38] They married in 1945 in San Jose and settled in San Francisco.

Like his father Pinye-Ber, Joseph was talented with his hands. He had a workshop in the back of his house in San Jose, and after his retirement he spent time there making furniture and antique reproductions. His grandniece Cynthia (Brockman) Unterberg remembers Joseph and his brother James as being very Americanized, personable, and good conversationalists. Edith died on May 31, 1953, at age sixty-five of a heart condition, and Joseph died a year later, on June 28, 1954, at age seventy-four in his beach house in Rio del Mar, near Los Gatos, California.

His Son Yankev "Yankl" (aka Jacob "James" Goldeen, 1882–1948)

As teenager, Yankl began to be called Yasha, the Russian nickname for Yakov, also by his siblings and his father. In January 1906 in Feodosiya, he married Khine, known as Fanya in Russian, who was the oldest of seven children born to Duvid Tarlo (ca. 1860–ca.1917) and Sure (née Asherov) (ca. 1864–1926).

A few months after their marriage, Yankl and Fanya left Tsarist Russia and made their way to Liverpool, England on the steamship *Umbria*, arriving in New York City on August 5, 1906.[39] They first stayed with Yankl's relative, Sophie Grover, in Manhattan,[40] as his brother Yosl had done, and then went to Portland, Oregon to join his brothers Yosl and Refuel, who were now known as Joseph and Raphael Goldstein. In America, Yankl became known as Jacob Goldstein and Fanya as Fannie. In Portland, Jacob tried his hand at several occupations. At first, he sold cigars, then became a grocer, and then finally went into the furniture business like his brother Joseph. After Joseph changed his surname from Goldstein to Goldeen in 1911, Jacob followed suit the following year.

---

38 Floriene's cousin, Freda Goldeen (1908–1973), was married to Ralph Silver, whose sister Amalia (1906–1945) was Nathan Merenbach's first wife. In his autobiography, Nathan Merenbach (1977:26, 106) writes that he knew members of his wife Floriene's family back in Feodosiya, namely her uncle Isruel Goldenshteyn, a *shoykhet* in Feodosiya, and her uncle James Goldeen's father-in-law Duvid Tarlo, who was a close friend of Nathan's father. See Appendix B, p. 779, footnote 15 for more about the Tarlo family (called Tarlow in America).

39 Yankl and his wife are listed on the passenger manifest as "Jacob and Chiene Goldenstein," residents of Simferopol in the Crimea.

40 For more regarding the Grovers, see Appendix B3, p. 776-777.

In 1916, Jacob moved his family to Woodburn, Oregon, some thirty miles southwest of Portland, where he opened the Goldeen Furniture Company.[41] In 1918, Jacob and the family relocated to Vancouver, Washington, which is in the Portland metropolitan area, and in 1920 they returned to Portland. In about 1925, Jacob moved to Oakland, California, which was forty miles from his brother Joseph in San Jose. There Jacob managed the Oakland branch of the United Manufacturing Co., a Portland-based company that produced mattresses. In the late 1920s, Jacob started using the name "James," though he never officially changed his name.

In 1934, Jacob moved back to Portland, though some of his children remained in California. He worked for his brother-in-law, Milton Tarlow, in his mattress business, Superbilt Manufacturing Company. Fannie died on November 5, 1942, at age fifty-seven, and Jacob died on December 2, 1948, at the age of sixty-six.

Jacob and Fannie had three boys and three girls. In 1932, their son Edwin changed his surname from Goldeen to Golden and soon became one of the country's top life insurance underwriters. Besides lecturing and writing books on insurance selling, he was also active in Jewish charities and organizations ("Edwin Tarlow Golden," 1966). In 1976, while walking one night near his home in San Francisco, he was gunned down and robbed. Jacob and Fannie's youngest child, David (1922–2011), entered the United States Army in October 1942 and rose to the rank of captain. He fought the Nazis in Belgium and was in the Battle of the Bulge, where he was seriously wounded. He was sent to Paris for recovery, where he fully recuperated and remained until the end of the War.

His Son Refuel (aka Raphael Goldenstein, 1885–1933)

Upon arriving in New York City in February 1906, Refuel traveled to Portland, Oregon,[42] where his brother Yosl (now called Joseph Goldstein) resided. There

41 Jacob and Fannie's daughter, Dorothy Nathan (1913–1966), became an author of books for young people. Her autobiographic novel entitled *The Shy One* describes her struggle to overcome her bashfulness as a child. The episodes in the book take place in 1921 in Woodburn, though the author lived in Woodburn from 1916–18. The protagonist, also named Dorothy, describes the arrival of her mother's mother and her mother's youngest brother from Russia to Woodburn.

42 Refuel is listed on the passenger manifest of the steamship *Majestic* as "Raphael Goldstein," with the occupation of preacher. The ship arrived in New York City on February 15, 1906, having left from Liverpool, England. He is listed as being accompanied by his fourteen-year-old female "cousin" (who was actually not related) named "Schon [Sheyne?] Daube," and

he assumed Joseph's surname, becoming known as Raphael Goldstein. Later that same year, their brother Yankl and his wife Fanya arrived in Portland, where they became known as Jacob and Fannie Goldstein. Raphael lived with Joseph and his family from his arrival until he left Portland in 1911, with Joseph paying for his education.

Raphael, who had red hair like his father and blue eyes, first worked as a clerk in a store.[43] To attain proficiency in English, he attended a night school twice weekly at the Neighborhood House, which was founded by the National Council of Jewish Women—Portland Section. Run by a Miss Myers, the night school began operating in 1906 and Raphael was one of its first pupils. A full-page newspaper article about the school describes Raphael and contains his photograph ("A School for Poor Foreigners," 1907):

> It is a privilege to talk with one of her oldest pupils. He is a young man of pleasing manner, ready address and a winning smile; a temperamental face, and expressive of more than ordinary intelligence and responsiveness. Raphael Goldstein is quite ready to talk of Miss Myer's school and its usefulness—and why not?[44] For it has meant to him the means of transition from the heavy drudgery of labor as roustabout to the position of trusted employee; from being the butt of ridicule and scapegoat for the delinquencies of others who scorned him because he could not talk [*sic*] and was at their mercy. It has made him able to converse with ease and to keep himself informed on the news of the day. So Raphael is enthusiastic, and justly so. And how long did it take to accomplish this change? Less than a year—almost incredible, is it not?

From 1909 to 1911, Raphael attended the Allen Preparatory School, which was founded in 1901 by Margaret V. Allen (1855–1927) to prepare students for college.[45] His first published work in English was a translation of Leo Tolstoy's

---

their contact in New York City was her uncle Prof. Joshua A. Joffe (1862–1935), a Talmud instructor at the Jewish Theological Seminary in Manhattan.

43 US Passport Application for "Raphael Goldenstein," dated March 15, 1921.

44 Referring to Caroline "Carrie" Myers (1865–1930), who later became the manager of the Portland Remedial Loan Association and who married Emanuel Herrman in 1914.

45 Raphael's papers include a letter from Margaret V. Allen of San Diego, California, from 1916 or 1917. Allen closed the school in 1912 due to health reasons and moved to San Diego, but she returned to Portland in 1919 and reopened the academy, which she ran until her death

short 1891 essay defending the Jews, entitled "What is a Jew?" which was published in *The Oregonian*, the local newspaper, several months after Tolstoy's death (Tolstoy, 1911). Raphael's translation has been widely reprinted, often without giving credit to its translator.

While Raphael lived in Portland, two rabbis in the Reform movement who later achieved prominence served there early in their careers. Upon Raphael's arrival, Stephen S. Wise (1874–1949) was serving as the rabbi of Temple Beth Israel. He later became a prominent US Jewish leader. Though Wise left Portland in October 1906, only ten months after Raphael's arrival, they had quickly become friends and continued to correspond with each other. Stephen S. Wise was replaced by Jonah B. Wise (1881–1955), though they were not related. Jonah was the son of Isaac Mayer Wise (1819–1900), the founder of both the Reform movement in the United Sates and the Reform rabbinic seminary, Hebrew Union College (HUC) in Cincinnati. In 1925, Jonah moved to New York City where he became a leader of the Reform movement and the founder of the United Jewish Appeal. These two rabbis were influential in Raphael's decision to attend HUC.[46]

In September 1911, Raphael simultaneously enrolled in HUC and the University of Cincinnati, where he majored in philosophy and minored in German. Earlier that year, his brother Joseph had changed his name from Goldstein to Goldeen and his brother James followed suit, but Raphael reverted to Goldenstein, which was the name under which he enrolled in these two educational institutions. Raphael obtained a Bachelor of Arts in June 1915 and was conferred with a rabbinical degree in June 1916. His 1916 thesis at HUC was entitled *The Krimchaks: Their Life and Origin in the Crimea*,[47] which he dedicated to his father: "To my dear old father Phinehas Dov Goldenstein, one of the noblest of the Crimean Jews, this thesis is most affectionately dedicated." In 1915–1916, he volunteered as a government censor in the US Post Office in Chicago during the First World War and did post-graduate work at the University of Chicago.

("Margaret V. Allen Died at Portland," 1927). Raphael's papers are held by his daughter-in-law Virginia "Ginny" Starr of Grass Valley, California.

46 Raphael's papers (see previous footnote) contain four letters from Stephen S. Wise from 1919 and 1920 and two letters from Jonah Wise from 1920. Raphael's correspondence also includes three letters, written in 1917, from Jonah's mother, Selma Wise (1843–1934) of Cincinnati. Copies of these letters have been forwarded to HUC.

47 For details regarding the Krymchaks, see ch. 23, p. 458, footnote 34. In 1945 Raphael's niece Floriene, the daughter of his brother Joseph Goldeen, married Nathan Merenbach, a native of Feodosiya whose maternal grandmother was a Krymchak (Merenbach, 1977:11–12).

In July 1916, Raphael obtained his first position as a rabbi, which was at the Reform congregation Temple Anshe-Emeth in Pine Bluff, Arkansas. In 1917, he compiled and published a history of the congregation in honor of its fiftieth anniversary. He also enlisted in the United States army where he served as a chaplain with the rank of first lieutenant at Camp Pike, which was located near Little Rock, Arkansas. He often went to Little Rock to hold lectures on a variety of Jewish topics. He was also active in all war efforts.

In September 1919, Temple Beth Israel of Tacoma, Washington hired Raphael as its first permanent rabbi. It is likely that his relatives there, Jennie (Goldeen) and her husband Ben Shapiro (later changed to Sherwood), were involved in bringing him there.[48] Until his arrival, services had been held only on Jewish holidays.

In August 1920, vicious rumors found their way into print accusing Raphael of improprieties. Wishing to relieve the congregation of any embarrassment, Raphael voluntarily resigned from his position on August 16, 1920. To the public, he immediately announced that he was resigning in order to travel to Palestine, as reported in a local newspaper article, "Tacoma Rabbi to Visit Father in Palestine: Raphael Goldenstein Hears of Freedom of Parent from Turks" (1920):

> Rabbi Raphael Goldenstein, for the past year head of the Beth Israel congregation here, last night tendered his resignation to the board of trustees of the local congregation to take effect immediately. The action came, he announced, due to a determination to visit his father in Jaffa,[49] Palestine, and because of a contemplated trip to the Holy Land which under other conditions would be impossible.
>
> Until a short time ago Rabbi Goldenstein had been unable to communicate with his father for a period extending over four years due to the fact that his father had been a captive of the Turks.[50] On learning of his whereabouts and his safety at Jaffa,

48 Jennie was not only Raphael's cousin, she was also the sister of Joseph's wife Edith. See Appendix A3 (pp. 726–729) for details.

49 Pinye-Ber lived in Petakh-Tikva—not in Jaffa. Newspapers used to often avoid mentioning obscure towns—as Petakh-Tikva was in those years—and would mention in their stead more widely known nearby cities or towns.

50 Raphael was unable to communicate with Pinye-Ber for two and a half years, from April 1916 until October 1918, as Pinye-Ber writes in ch. 34 (p. 655) not "over four years" as printed in the article. Pinye-Ber was unable to communicate with his children in the Ukraine and Crimea for over four years.

> Rabbi Goldenstein at once planned to visit him. During his captivity among the Turks, the rabbi's father experienced many hardships and his stories of the atrocities and cruelty indulged in by his captors are astounding, declared Rabbi Goldenstein.

Meanwhile, the synagogue board of trustees completed its investigation of Raphael's conduct and issued a statement on August 28, 1920 that that they had determined that "the rumors maligning the name and character of Rabbi Goldenstein are absolutely false and without foundation" and that he was leaving completely voluntarily ("Exonerate Rabbi of Any Misconduct," 1920). Yet after considering the Arab disturbances in Palestine in April of that year and their threats of more violence, Raphael decided to delay his trip. In September 1920, he accepted the position of rabbi at the Reform congregation of Mt. Sinai Temple in Sioux City, Iowa.

By May of 1921, the situation in Palestine had quieted down, and Raphael gave notice to Mt. Sinai Temple that he would be resigning that coming September. On February 4, 1922, he boarded the steamship *Lapland* which was headed to Europe, and from there he traveled to Palestine. Once in Petakh-Tikva, he was reunited with his father and his sister Nekhame, her husband Mendl, and their two sons, Mark and Victor, whom he had not seen in sixteen years. Raphael remained in Palestine for almost three months, where he traveled the length and breadth of the country to gather material for a series of lectures entitled "The Modern Palestine" to be delivered upon his return to the United States. He also visited the principal cities of Central Europe to examine the conditions of the Jews affected by the First World War. Before leaving Europe, he stopped in France to visit with his sister Rukhl (Raya) and her nine-year-old son Boris Blondin. He arrived back in New York City on the steamship *Majestic* on July 25, 1922 ("Rabbi Off for Palestine," 1921; "Rabbi Goldenstein Returns from Tour," 1922).

Raphael quickly obtained a new position as the rabbi of Congregation Albert in Albuquerque, New Mexico. After a year, he moved on to be the first rabbi of Temple B'nai Israel in Pasadena, California where he also stayed for only a year. In September 1924, he obtained the position of rabbi at Temple Sinai Congregation in Lake Charles, Louisiana, which he left in June 1925. At some point in his career, he went to speak at a pulpit in the South where he spoke out against Jews treating the Blacks poorly; he had to be escorted out of town by a protective group.[51]

51 Claire V. Goldenstein Silver letter, June 27, 1972, SC-4028, American Jewish Archives, Cincinnati, Ohio.

In July 1925, he became the rabbi of Congregation Shaarai Shomayim in Lancaster, Pennsylvania at $4,000 per year. He was described as being "reticent, and soft spoken, yet firm and organized." He started to publish the synagogue bulletin again, and had all the bulletins, community yearbooks, and other written materials bound, for otherwise they would have been lost. One of his bulletins includes the tombstone inscription of Joseph Solomon (1710–1777), an early Lancaster Jew and shopkeeper; today, the stone is no longer legible. In another one of his bulletins, he advised, "Never make the terrible mistake of giving parties on Friday nights. Refrain from accepting invitations for Friday evening no matter how important. Remember that Friday nights belong to the Temple and the Home, devoted to Prayer, instructions, religion and the joy of friendship." He reinstated services on Saturday morning, which had been terminated by his predecessor. In the nineteenth century, a Sunday-Sabbath movement had begun among the assimilationist element in the Reform movement where prayer services were moved from Saturday to Sunday. "Rabbi Goldenstein was truly dedicated and stressed the importance of religion and the synagogue . . ." (Brener, 1979:127, 140).

After only a short time, Raphael began to involve himself with the greater Jewish community of Lancaster. He became the president of the re-organized Jewish Welfare Association (JWA), whose income of $410 in 1926 was used to aid local charity cases. He had the unique honor of being elected an honorary member of all five local Jewish communal organizations. In addressing the Council of Jewish Juniors on the subject of intermarriage, he "won the undivided attention of his listeners and his sincere plea was unanimously and enthusiastically received." Nonetheless, a board member, who had served the congregation as its rabbi in the 1910s continued to meddle in the affairs of the congregation, which evidently contributed to each of its three subsequent rabbis—Raphael being the third—staying no more than a couple of years. Raphael left in June 1927, after two years, the longest he would spend as a rabbi in any position (Brener, 1979:123, 127–128).

In October 1927, Raphael was elected to a term of three years as the rabbi of Temple Beth El at Lynn, Massachusetts, which had just finished erecting a $100,000 synagogue with a seating capacity of 600. He was hired at an annual salary of $4200. In January 1928, after three months there, Raphael was discharged without cause. Raphael returned to Lancaster, and in March he filed a breach of contract suit for $4030 in the federal court at Boston, which was widely reported at the time. He stated in his bill of complaints that he had performed all duties required of him. ("Rabbi Brings Suit against Temple Beth-El," 1928). The matter was evidently settled out-of-court, because shortly afterward Raphael went on another trip to Europe. In fact, Raphael was not employed for the next four years.[52]

No longer having the responsibilities of leading a congregation, Raphael now had the time to devote himself to a project that had long been near and dear to his heart—the publishing of his father's autobiography. Pinye-Ber had not believed that his autobiography would be published in his lifetime. He had specified in his Hebrew ethical will, written in 1920, that the manuscript would be left to Raphael who had promised that he would print it. But, by divine providence, Raphael now had the time to devote to bring his father's dream to fruition. He obtained the crucial initial funding needed to print the book from his brothers Joseph and Jacob in California.[53] The funds were then forwarded to their brother Shloyme in Petakh-Tikva, where presumably the publishing costs were less expensive.

With the publishing of the autobiography underway, Raphael traveled in July of 1928 to Europe on the steamship *Île de France*. While there, he visited the Soviet Union. When the new communist state was established, he had hoped that it would be a utopia. But upon his arrival, he was sadly disillusioned and outraged by man's inhumanity to man.[54] From Le Havre, France, Raphael also returned on the *Île de France*, arriving in New York City on October 16, 1928. He settled in Brooklyn, where his sister Nekhame Brakhtman and her two sons Mark and Victor lived. After all the parts of the autobiography were printed and shipped to Brooklyn, Raphael had them hardbound into a single volume, at his own expense, in early 1930.[55] With considerable effort, he arranged for them to be marketed, distributed, and sold.

By July 1930, Raphael had met his wife-to-be, Claire Silber, who had immigrated in 1923 from Montreal to New York City where she was working as a

---

52 Neither city directories nor newspapers indicate that Raphael was gainfully employed from January 1928 until he accepted a position in Los Angeles in the fall of 1930. In fact, his father Pinye-Ber explicitly mentions that Raphael was without work in his letter of July 15, 1930 (see Appendix B3, p. 801). Though the Bronx marriage certificate (#7670) of Morris Brachtman, dated November 28, 1928, indicates that "Raphael of "Temple Beth-El" officiated, Raphael was clearly referring to his last position as the rabbi at Temple Beth El in Lynn, Massachusetts. Raphael simply wrote the name of his last employer where the form requested the officiating rabbi to list his synagogue affiliation. (Morris Brachtman was the nephew of Raphael's brother-in-law Mendl Brakhtman.)

53 Personal interview in 2001 with Aliza (Goldenshteyn) Bernfeld. See Appendix A7 (pp. 751–757) for more details regarding the printing of Pinye-Ber's autobiography.

54 Claire V. Goldenstein Silver letter, June 27, 1972, SC-4028, American Jewish Archives, Cincinnati, Ohio.

55 See the author's letter from July 15, 1930 in Appendix B3, p. 801.

bookkeeper.[56] By September or October, the books had all been either sold or given to a distributor. Being engaged to marry, Raphael moved to Los Angeles to be closer to his brothers and to hopefully find a position as a rabbi. He and Claire married there on November 12, 1930; he was forty-five and she was twenty. Perhaps Raphael finally met his intended one in the merit of his having just fulfilled his aged father's great desire to have his autobiography published. Some three weeks after their wedding, Pinye-Ber passed away on December 4, 1930. In May 1931, Raphael applied for the position of rabbi at Temple Beth Israel located in Fresno, California and went there as a guest speaker, but he was not offered the position ("Rabbi Goldenstein To Speak At Beth Israel Friday," 1931). On February 6, 1932, Claire gave birth to a son in Los Angeles, whom they named Henry Phillip and nicknamed Hank. Hank was given the Hebrew name of Pinkhas after his grandfather.

Shortly after Hank's birth, Raphael was hired as the rabbi of Congregation Ahavai Sholom in Portland, Oregon, back where he had begun his life in America. Tragically, only some five months after being hired, Raphael suffered a severe case of appendicitis which was not treated quickly enough. He underwent an operation but died in the hospital less than two weeks later on July 3, 1933 at the age of 47. Pinye-Ber had been orphaned at the age of seven, his son Raphael had lost his mother at the age of ten, and now Hank was barely seven teen months old when his father Raphael died.

Raphael's entry in *Who's Who in American Jewry, 1926* states that he did social service work in charitable institutions, hospitals, colleges, and prisons, and organized Zionist societies, Hebrew-speaking clubs, B'nai Brith Lodges, and literary circles. He published books, articles, and poems in Hebrew, Yiddish, and English. Raphael's article in Hebrew about the renowned Rabbi Khayim Khizkiyahu Medini (1834–1904) of the Crimea, known as the Sdei Khemed, was printed in the prestigious journal *Ha-Toren* in 1926. Virtually every book or article published since then about the Sdei Khemed quotes Raphael's article.[57]

The daughter of his brother Joseph, Floriene Merenbach recalled that "Uncle Ralph," as Raphael was called by his nephews and nieces on the West Coast, used to spend the summers with their family, "He would spin marvelous

56 See Pinye-Ber's letter of July 15, 1930 in Appendix B3, pp. 801–802.

57 For excerpts from this article, see Appendix C2, pp. 811–813.

stories, and I never tired of them. He also taught me how to make little boats to sail in the creek using a block of wood, some nails, and some string."[58]

Reminiscing about her late husband, Claire wrote:

> Most of us have so little to give but by his quiet and gentle strength he brought comfort and hope where he went. . . . He was extremely honest and had a natural tact. He felt a great reluctance to 'give advice' unless honestly sought after. I remember asking him why he did not offer advice to members of his congregation who seemed bewildered and were destroying themselves. He answered, "I am not God's trapsha [*sic*] (appointed by God).[59] If and when they sincerely seek my help I will give it but I do not want to mix into other people's lives merely because I may recognize their confusion." He loved his work but mostly he loved working with children, and they loved him. Whenever they would see him they would cling to his trouser legs and follow him everywhere. . . . He spoke about seven or eight languages and was very fluent in Hebrew, and, as you know, Hebrew in his time was considered a dead language."[60]

After her husband's death, Claire moved from Portland back to Los Angeles. She wanted Raphael's brother Joseph to adopt Hank, to which Joseph agreed on the condition that Hank change his name from Goldenstein to his name Goldeen. But Hank did not want to be adopted by Joseph for he felt that he was too much of a disciplinarian.[61] Afterwards, Claire ceased having contact with Raphael's relatives. Hank (Starr, 2002) wrote about his childhood as follows:

> My father, who was a rabbi, died when I was an infant, leaving my young mother penniless and destitute. I was raised in orphanages and foster homes in southeast Los Angeles. Living in that fashion, I hardly knew what being Jewish meant, but I knew what it meant to be a Jew. It was during the Second World War; people from Oklahoma and Arkansas were flowing into

58 Private letter from Floriene Merenbach (1912–2000) of San Francisco, in 1979, to her first cousin William Glikbarg (1924–2013) of Santa Monica, California.

59 Referring to the Aramaic word *apitropos* meaning an appointed guardian or trustee.

60 Claire V. Goldenstein Silver letter, 27 June 1972. SC-4028. American Jewish Archives, Cincinnati, Ohio.

61 Personal interview in 2001 with Aliza (Goldenshteyn) Bernfeld of Petakh-Tikva.

> Southern California to work in the defense plants, and they apparently had taught their children that Jews were evil. As a little guy, I was called names, sworn at, and picked on almost every day of my life. It was only as I grew to be the biggest boy in my class, and a pretty good fighter from all the fights I had been subjected to, that I was finally left alone. But it didn't end there. In a thousand subtle ways, as I grew up, I was ostracized for no other reason than that my parents were Jewish. I found that there were areas where Jews were forbidden to live. (It was not until 1961 that such deed restrictions were made unenforceable in California.) From time to time, I came upon signs saying, "No Jews or Dogs Allowed." It was made very clear that Jews were not welcome in certain organizations, groups and places. Private schools, universities and medical schools maintained strict quotas on the number of Jews they would admit. When I graduated law school, although I was at the top of my class and an award winner, there were certain law firms that would employ me and others that would not.

By 1950, Hank was back living with his mother in Los Angeles, and in about 1955 he changed his surname from Goldenstein to Starr. (For a short time after Raphael's death, Claire had used the name of Starr, a variant of her mother's maiden name Stareselsky. She could not find a job which would enable her to support her and her son with the name Goldenstein, because it sounded too Jewish.[62]) In the late 1950s, Hank, and then Claire, who had remarried a builder named Louis R. Silver in 1956, traveled to Israel and established a warm relationship with her brother-in-law Shloyme Goldenshteyn and his family.

In 1972, Claire responded as follows to Dr. Jacob R. Marcus, the founder of the American Jewish Archives at HUC in Cincinnati, who had written her in 1967 seeking biographical information about her late husband:

> You said that you have a microfilm copy of his father's book "Mein Lebengeschichte" (by Phinchas Dov Goldenstein). What would be necessary to be done and how much do you estimate it would cost to have it translated into English? When Rabbi Joseph Jasin was alive we had intended to work together to translate the book but now I don't know anyone I could turn to. I

62 Personal interview in 2004 in Manhattan with Henry "Hank" Starr of Grass Valley, California.

> would especially like for my son to read the book. Aside from its value as a manuscript he does portray, rather well, the life of the Jews in Russia and his immigration to early Israel. The nuance of the writing would be most revealing to my son and perhaps help his own identification. . . . He is a very fine young man, a very good attorney, but there is so much need as to Yiddishkeit[63] and I would very much like him to understand better the life of a Jew and it touches us more when we can identify that life with a member of our family and Phinchas Dov Goldenstein was his paternal grandfather.[64]

His Daughter Rukhl (aka Raissa "Raya" Goldinstein Oulianoff, 1887–1966)

Pinye-Ber writes that his wife Freyde said before she died in 1896, "Only one thing frightens me—the welfare of our Rukhl. If Rukhele will end up with a stepmother . . ." (chapter 27, p. 548). Her mother's intuition proved to be correct, for her life was the least conventional of her siblings'. Perhaps one of the reasons that her mother was frightened for Rukhl's future was because Rukhl was exceptionally brilliant.[65] In Tsarist Russia, Rukhl assumed the Russian name Raissa and was called by the nickname Raya.[66]

Raya went to Paris in 1909 and attended law school at the University of Paris. In Paris, she met a non-Jewish young man named Pierre Blondin (1891–1948), who was a proofreader. She became pregnant, and they wanted to marry, but Pierre's parents, Emile (1868–1948) and Anne Marie Victoria Blondin (1868–1966), refused to allow him to marry a Jew.[67] Raya gave birth to a son on August 21, 1911, whom she named Boris Blondin. She completed only three

---

63 *Yiddishkeit* means "Judaism."

64 Claire V. Goldenstein Silver letter, June 27, 1972, SC-4028, American Jewish Archives, Cincinnati, Ohio.

65 Personal interview in the late 1980s with Rose (Chaplick) Carmel (1899–1998) by her grandson Michael Budiansky. See Appendix D2 (pp. 820–821) for a genealogical chart indicating Rose's relationship to the Goldenshteyns.

66 Rukhl is listed on her son Boris Blondin's 1911 birth record as Rouklia Goldinstein, a variant of Rukhlya, which was probably the spelling of her name on Russian documents. On her 1929 marriage record (see p. 719), she is listed as Raissa Goldinstein.

67 In 1921, Pierre Blondin (1891–1948) married Germaine Ragoulleau (1887–1965), a French writer and poet. They had one child, Antoine Blondin (1922–1991), who was a French novelist and journalist. Antoine had little contact with his half-brother Boris, according to

years of law school and never graduated. At first, Raya worked at a bank.[68] She knew bookkeeping well and eventually finished business school.[69] Nonetheless, Pinye-Ber continued to pray that she would marry a Jewish man and move away from France, which he saw as being the source of her problems. He wanted her to be closer to family, near her brothers in California.[70]

In July 1922, Raya's brother Refuel (aka Raphael Goldenstein) visited her and Boris from America and apparently once again on his 1928 visit to Europe. On November 19, 1929, Raya married a Russian non-Jew named Vladimir Oulianoff in Paris.[71] They had no progeny together. It is unlikely that her aged father, Pinye-Ber, who died in 1930, was informed of the marriage.

With the German invasion of France in May 1940, Raya obtained false papers to hide her Jewishness, thereby becoming Olga. Pierre Blondin, her son Boris's father, helped Raya and Vladimir find a farm on the Causse Noir plateau where they could pose as ethnic-Russian farmers, since farming was a rare occupation for a Jew. Even after the war, they continued to maintain the farm for some years. Raya also continued to be known as Olga, though her family still called her Raya.[72]

Raya's brother, Joseph Goldeen (1880–1954) of San Jose, California used to send her money every year so that she could take an annual vacation.[73] Raya and Vladimir lived their last years in Toulouse, France, and she died in December 1966 at almost seventy-nine years of age.[74] Vladimir died in about 1970 at approximately the age of eighty.

As a young man, Boris joined the French Foreign Legion and served in Algeria and then in Morocco, which were French colonies at the time. At least from the early 1940s, he lived in Morocco's capital Rabat and worked for the police department of Salé, which lies opposite Rabat on the other side of the

---

personal correspondence in 2017 with Boris's granddaughter Agnés Louvrier of Pontarlier, France, the daughter of Edith (Blondin) Montelle.

68 Personal correspondence in 2017 with Boris's granddaughter Agnés Louvrier of Pontarlier, France.

69 According to Pinye-Ber's letter from October 10, 1926 (see Appendix B3, p. 787). According to her grandnephew Jean-Pierre Goldenstein of Le Mans, France, Raya completed a degree in agronomy, evidently at the Institut National Agronomique in Paris.

70 See Pinye-Ber's letters of July 3, 1926 and October 10, 1926 in Appendix B3, p. 786 and p. 787.

71 Vladimir Oulianoff was not related to Vladimir Lenin (1870–1924), the first leader of the Soviet Union, whose original surname was also Ulyanov.

72 Personal correspondence in 2017 with Agnés (Montelle) Louvrier of Pontarlier, France.

73 Personal correspondence in 2002 with Nancy (Merenbach) Petrilla Zuniga, as heard from her mother Floriene Merenbach, daughter of Joseph Goldeen.

74 In 2017, her great-granddaughter Agnes Louvrier was unable to locate a death certificate for her in Toulouse. It is unknown where in France Raya died.

Bou Regreg River. When Morocco gained its independence from France in 1956, Boris returned to France and became a journalist and wrote in major French-language periodicals. He married three times, was widowed once, divorced twice, and had nine children, three of whom died in his lifetime. Later, he had a farm near Paris, but he moved toward the end of his life to a village in northern France called Wasquehal where he died on February 14, 2000 at the age of eighty-eight.

His Son Shloyme Goldenshteyn (Shlomo, 1889–1962)[75]

In 1912, Shloyme (called Solomon in Russian) was working as an assistant pharmacist in Simferopol.[76] The following year, he moved to Sevastopol where he held the same type of position.[77] Shortly before the First World War, Shloyme wanted to study pharmacy in a university in the Crimea. But since many more Jews were applying than were permitted by the Jewish quotas, Shloyme decided to apply to the university in Yekaterinoslav where there were fewer Jewish applicants. He was accepted and moved to Yekaterinoslav, where his newly married stepbrother Duvid Kreyzberg and his wife Klara lived.[78]

At the Kreyzberg's home, Shloyme met Klara's younger sister Ester Zlatopolsky, commonly called Etya. She came from a wealthy family and was one of eleven children, though only seven survived childhood. Her parents, Binyumin (son of Mordekhai) and Shifra (née Shaporinsky) Zlatopolsky, were the owners of a flour mill over which they lived, though her father had died

75 This section is based on personal interviews in 2001 with Shloyme's daughters, Dvora Gavrieli (1919–2017) of kibbutz Givat Khayim Meukhad and Aliza Bernfeld (1921–2008) of Petakh-Tikva, unless otherwise indicated. Also consulted was Dvora's twenty-one-page typewritten Hebrew-language memoir, which she wrote in 1999.

76 In a postcard postmarked October 20, 1912 in Sevastopol, Shloyme writes to his brother Refuel in Cincinnati that he was still working in the pharmacy. (This postcard is among Raphael's papers held by his daughter-in-law Virginia "Ginny" Starr of Grass Valley, California.)

77 Two Russian-language postcards, postmarked January 29, 1913 and November 24, 1913, from Shloyme to his brother Refuel (Raphael) in Cincinnati indicate that Shloyme was living in Simferopol. These postcards are among Raphael's papers held by his daughter-in-law Virginia "Ginny" Starr of Grass Valley, California. See ch. 28, p. 567, for more about the positions that Shloyme held before entering pharmacy school.

78 Duvid Kreyzberg was the son of Feyge, Shloyme's stepmother. For details regarding the Kreyzbergs, see Appendix A4, pp. 730–732.

on a buying trip to Harbin, Manchuria, when Etya was young. Coming from a *maskilic* family, Etya was raised speaking Russian instead of Yiddish.

With the outbreak of the First World War in 1914, Shloyme was conscripted into the Tsarist Russian army while in the middle of his studies, so he asked Etya to wait for him. Being a pharmacy student, Shloyme served as a paramedic in the army. Once, during a battle, he worked tremendously hard attending to the wounded and ill and was unable to lie down to rest for days. Finally, he sat down, the battlefront before him, and slept for three entire days without hearing a sound. Upon awakening, he attempted to find his regiment, but they had been annihilated, leaving him as its sole survivor. Afterward, Shloyme was awarded a medal for heroism, which, he used to quip, was given to him for sleeping.[79]

In 1916, when the leaders of the Russian Empire saw no end to the war after two years of fierce fighting, they temporarily sent home the men who had fiancées so that they could marry and have offspring because they feared there would not be a next generation. Shloyme was among those soldiers sent home. He returned to Yekaterinoslav, where he and Etya married on January 22, 1917. After nine months, their daughter Fani was born; she was named after his recently departed stepmother Feyge, who had raised him since the age of eight. Sadly, Fani died at the age of one because of the lack of medication for dysentery during war time.

Shloyme returned to his battalion and only returned home in 1918. Though he had entered the war as a tall, blond and blue-eyed young man full of cheerfulness and optimism, he returned beaten, sick, and difficult to associate with. Etya's sisters, who were doctors and hospital administrators, rallied together and helped him recover and return to civilian life.

In addition to the war with Germany (1914–1918) that destroyed cities and towns, the Russian Civil War (1917–1922) also resulted in a huge number of human casualties and destroyed the economy. Shloyme received packages of food and warm clothes from his brothers in the United States, which was of great help. Shloyme and Etya worked in their professions in large clinics organized by the new regime. Etya had received a professional certificate in dentistry, but Shloyme had not finished his studies. Since the institutions for holding exams and issuing certifications were temporarily closed, Shloyme never received his certification, which caused him difficulties later. Meanwhile, though, Shloyme was able to become the manager of three pharmacies in Yekaterinoslav. Dvora

79 The medal, which bears the image of Tsar Nicholas II, is in the possession of Shloyme's granddaughter Shifra Bernfeld of Petakh-Tikva.

was born in 1919, and Freyde (Frida in Russian), named after Shloyme's mother, was born in 1921.

As a child, Dvora suffered from very serious illnesses such as ophthalmitis, typhoid fever, etc. The doctors thought that if Shloyme and Etya did not take her to a healthy environment, she would not be able to survive. Greatly alarmed, they took their two daughters and their few remaining possessions after the tremendous looting which occurred during the war and the revolution, and moved back to the Crimea, specifically to Feodosiya where Shloyme's brother Isruel and sister Nekhame Brakhtman lived. The Crimea's warm climate combined with the many vegetables and fruits that grew there succeeded in curing Dvora. They spent a year there, until Pinye-Ber, with the help of his three sons in the United States, managed to arrange for Shloyme and his family to leave the country.

At the end of 1922, Shloyme and his family left Feodosiya for Odessa, where they had to wait a few months until they were able to travel by ship to Constantinople, Turkey. They booked passage on a commercial ship, which was much cheaper than a passenger vessel since Shloyme had very little money to fall back on after the rise of communism. Upon arriving in Constantinople, they were reunited with his brother Isruel's children Frida, Mark, and Mosya, who had also recently arrived from Feodosiya and were trying to immigrate to France. In the meantime, Shloyme and his family were awaiting entry permits from the British Mandatory authorities in Palestine. Pinye-Ber had filed the necessary paperwork stating that he would be responsible for Shloyme and his family, but bureaucracies move slowly. Once they finally received their entry permits, they had to wait several months until they were eventually able to book passage on a cargo ship named the *Sardinia*, which was bound for Jaffa.[80] The voyage lasted three months because the ship would stop for several days at every port to unload and load the cargo it was transporting. The Mediterranean was often stormy, the weather was freezing cold, and they were starving from lack of sufficient food. They finally arrived in Jaffa on December 9, 1923, where they were greeted by two relatives: Pinye-Ber and Etya's first cousin Yehoshua Khankin.[81] Apart from Shloyme and his family being together again with Pinye-Ber, they were reunited with Shloyme's sister Nekhame Brakhtman, her husband, and three grown children, who had arrived in Petakh-Tikva from

80 "Israel, reshimot olim," accessed June 15, 2023, www.myheritage.com/research/collection-11018/israel-immigration-lists.

81 Yehoshua Khankin (1864–1945) was a Zionist activist responsible for most of the major land purchases of the Zionist Organization in Ottoman Palestine and Mandatory Palestine. After their arrival in Palestine, Shloyme and his family never met Khankin again.

Feodosiya in 1921. They were also meeting Pinye-Ber's third wife, Bashe, for the first time.

Pinye-Ber's lot had two houses on it. Shloyme and his family moved into the smaller house with Pinye-Ber and Bashe. And Nekhame and her family continued to live in the larger house, except that Pinye-Ber asked her to vacate the large room at the front of the house which he had promised to Etya for her to use as a dental clinic if she would move to Palestine. Having lived only in large cities, Shloyme's daughters were surprised to find that most of their neighbors in Petakh-Tikva owned their own cows and donkeys and that a Jewish herder would come take all the cows to pasture every day. When Nekhame and her family moved to Tel-Aviv in 1925, Shloyme and his family moved into the larger house, while Pinye-Ber and Bashe remained in the smaller house. After Nekhame and her two sons left for America in 1926, Shloyme remained Pinye-Ber's only child in Palestine and was of great comfort to him in his old age.[82] As Pinye-Ber writes in one of his letters, "Thank God that I have Shloyme near me. He is truly faithful to me and is devoted to me. With God's help, he practically saved me from death. Praise God that I merited to have near me such a beloved child."[83]

Never having completed his studies in pharmacy, Shloyme (called Shlomo in modern Hebrew) was unable to find work as a pharmacist in Petakh-Tikva, so he decided to rent a plot of land and grow tobacco. He obtained a donkey to transport the tobacco from the field. The large tobacco leaves were hung to dry over wires before being packed and sent to the factory. Because he had no experience with farming, Shloyme's venture was short-lived. Luckily, he found a job as a pharmacist's assistant in the local municipal pharmacy. He integrated very well into the pharmacy team and quickly gained the doctors' trust.[84]

Etya opened her dental practice with the poor equipment that she had brought with her from the Ukraine, including a straw treatment chair and a foot-powered dental drill. In any case, Palestine, as a whole, did not yet have electricity. The first time that Etya saw an electric drill was in 1933–1934 when

82 See Appendix A1 (pp. 683–685) for Dvora Gavrieli's and Aliza Bernfeld's memories of their grandfather Pinye-Ber.

83 See Pinye-Ber's letter from October 30, 1930 in Appendix B3, p. 723.

84 Hashavia (1998:100) includes an impressive photograph of the inside of Petakh-Tikva's municipal pharmacy; Shloyme is standing on the far left. Trope (1949:101) shows a picture of the outside of the same pharmacy. Though the faces are unclear, Shloyme is apparently standing in the middle, to the right of Menakhem Yehuda Shtampfer (1864–1940) who served as the treasurer of the pharmacy. Shtampfer can be seen, though faintly, in a photograph with the author in ch. 34, p. 662, figure 29.

a Jewish refugee, a dentist named Yankelevitsh, arrived from Nazi Germany. Yankelevitsh brought with him a lot of beautiful and luxurious electrical equipment. Though the Nazis were still permitting Jews who were fleeing Germany to take furniture and equipment with them at that time, they confiscated all professional certificates, which prevented Yankelevich from opening his own dental practice in Palestine. Acquaintances put Etya in touch with Yankelevitsh, and they were able to help each other; she provided him with an area to set up his practice on half of the porch, and, in return, he gave her an electric drill, a modern treatment chair, and other equipment, including strong electric lighting. The dental clinic flourished and provided a good income for both families.

In their first years in Palestine, Shloyme and Etya were busy earning a living and treating everyone with loyalty, devotion, and warm and compassionate hearts, which endeared them to all with whom they came in contact. Shloyme was tall and kind-hearted and welcomed everybody. He was the destination for neighbors and acquaintances seeking all types of medical aid. He would dress wounds, treat sprained limbs, provide medicine for common ailments, etc.—all free of charge. During the Great Depression (1929–1939), when life was particularly trying for so many, Etya would invite a hungry stranger to the dinner table. People who could not pay for dental care were given discounts or full exemptions as well as a meal and sometimes clothing for their children. As their daughter Dvora remembered, "People like my parents never became rich. They felt fortunate to have jobs. Grandfather said that mother was an angel."

When Shloyme's youngest daughter Frida first went to school, her teacher gave her the Hebrew name of Simkha, since her original Yiddish name of Freyde and Simkha both mean "joy." In their zeal for Hebrew, the teachers there replaced Yiddish names with Hebrew names. When taking attendance, the teacher called out the name Simkha, and Frida was shocked to see a boy stand up as well. Having now learned that Simkha was also a name used for boys, Frida refused to return to that school because she did not want to be called by a boy's name. Her parents then sent her to a different school where the teacher gave her the Hebrew name of Aliza, which also means "joy."

During the Second World War, Palestine was at risk of being bombed by German airplanes. Between July 1940 and September 1942, raids carried out by German, Italian, and French aircraft against targets in Palestine killed over 200 civilians (Arieli, 2010). To minimize outdoor light to prevent crews of enemy aircraft from being able to identify their targets by sight, a blackout was enforced. Citizens were required to remain in their homes at night and either close their wooden shutters or use dark blue shades. During the nights when they were sequestered at home, Shloyme would read his father's autobiography to his family line by line from the Yiddish, and translate it into Hebrew. In this manner, Aliza learned how to speak and read Yiddish fluently. In Palestine, Shloyme learned Hebrew well, but Etya could not read it at all. Surprisingly, Shloyme learned Arabic faster than Hebrew because he was not embarrassed to make mistakes in speaking Arabic as he was in Hebrew.

Shloyme was traditional and throughout his life attended his father's synagogue, the Nakhlat Yisrael Synagogue, on *Shabes*, except for the one Saturday a month when he was required to work in the pharmacy. Until the end of their lives, Shloyme and Etya were held in high esteem by the older residents of Petakh-Tikva, who were grateful for the help and warm treatment they had received from them over the years. Shloyme died on August 22, 1962 at age seventy-two, and Etya on February 7, 1965 at age seventy-seven. Afterward, the home of Aliza Bernfeld (1921–2008) became the focal point for relatives visiting Israel from France and from all over America. In one of his letters, Pinye-Ber describes his young granddaughter Aliza as "bright as the day, beautiful as the moon, and shining as the sun."[85] Aliza loved family, was an avid correspondent with its many far-flung branches, and was a treasure house of family history.

85 See the letter dated April 1929 in Appendix B3, p. 725.

Appendix A3: His Nephew Itsl (Isaac Goldstein, 1862–1907)[1]

Pinye-Ber's nephew Itsl Goldstein, his sister Ite's son, was the earliest known member of his extended family to immigrate to the United States.[2] Itsl, his wife Khaye (née Baranovsky), and their two young children, Avrum (Abe in English) and Itele (Edith in English), left Tiraspol and arrived in New York City on the steamship *Gellert* on December 24, 1889.[3] They traveled to St. Paul, Minnesota, where they joined Khaye's cousin Louis Baranov, who had shortened his name from Baranovsky.[4] There, Itsl, known in English as Isaac, ran a kosher meat market (*R.L. Polk*, 1890:577). In St. Paul, Khaye (called Ida in English) lost two children who died in infancy and then had two more daughters, Jennie and Bertha, born in 1893 and 1894, respectively.

In 1894–1895, Itsl moved his family to San Francisco, where Ida's aunt Anna (née Baranovsky) and her husband Philip (Fishl) Nudelman resided.[5]

---

1 Unless otherwise indicated, this section is based on a five-page typewritten letter composed in 1979 by Floriene (Goldeen) Merenbach (1912–2000) of San Francisco in response to inquiry about family history from her first cousin, William Glikbarg (1924–2013) of Santa Monica, California. Floriene was the daughter of Edith, who was Itsl's oldest child.

2 See Appendix D1 (pp. 818–819) for a genealogical chart of the author's siblings and their offspring.

3 Khaye's father's name was Eliyahu, as indicated on the Hebrew inscription on her tombstone at Neveh Zedek Cemetery in Portland, Oregon. Since the Hebrew inscriptions on her and her husband's tombstones are now illegible, the cemetery was kind enough to provide rubbings of both tombstones. Khaye's tombstone refers to her in English as Ida Goldstein and she died on January 2, 1903. Her maiden name of Baranovsky is indicated on the St. Paul birth certificates of her two daughters: Jennie, born January 3, 1893, and Bertha, born January 1, 1894.

4 Private correspondence in 2002 with Isaac's grandson, William Glikbarg (1924–2013) of Santa Monica, California. Louis Baranov moved from St. Paul to Chicago in the late 1890s. According to the Hebrew inscription on the tombstone of Louis Baranov (1861–1928) in Waldheim Cemetery (Gate 53, Lot 708), his Jewish name was Yehuda-Leyb, son of Tsvi.

5 Anna's Jewish name was Nekhame, daughter of Avrum, as indicated in the Hebrew inscription on her tombstone (which lists her in English as Neoma) at the Neveh Zedek Cemetery in Portland. Anna's maiden name of Baranovsky is indicated on the birth certificate of her daughter Myrtle (under the spelling "Myrtel"), who was born April 23, 1899 in Portland.

The lives of Anna and her husband Philip (Fishl) Nudelman (ca. 1859–1931) were intertwined with that of his brother Joseph Nudelman (1844–1935) who immigrated to the United States in 1882 where he led various efforts to start Jewish collective farms.

Itsl ran a kosher meat market together with Rev. Henry N. (Khaym-Nosn) Schoenfeld (*Crocker-Langley*, 1896:680).[6] In 1895, Ida gave birth to her fifth and last child, Shloyme, who was called Samuel in English. By 1898, Itsl had left the kosher meat business and moved to Cloverdale, a town north of San Francisco, where he was the proprietor of a variety store. In 1900, Itsl and Ida again followed her aunt Anna Nudelman, this time to Portland, Oregon, where he become the proprietor of a secondhand store.

In July 1901, Itsl relocated his family to Vancouver, Washington, which is part of the Portland metropolitan area, where he decided to try his hand at another business. Their oldest child Abie, as the family called him, was then seventeen and had grown to be tall and thin, but he was sickly. A few weeks after moving to Vancouver, a group of five non-Jewish peers invited Abie to tag along on a hunting and camping trip to Mount St. Helens, Washington, which is some sixty-five miles north of Vancouver. Thinking that the fresh air and exercise would do Abie good, Ida encouraged him to go along. On Sunday, July 17, 1901, after walking for about a mile and a half, Abie was said to have complained of feeling unwell and headed back alone to their camp at the base of the mountain. Only upon returning to the campsite that evening did the others notice his absence. The next day, a search party, including Itsl, set out looking for Abie but could not locate him. A mountaineer said that he had traced Abie's footprints to the brink of a glacier on the mountain and presumed that he had fallen over the precipice. The family was uncertain what to believe and could not rule out the possibility that he had been accidentally shot and his body hidden. His body was never found ("A Tragic Death," 1901; "Lost in the Wilderness," 1901).

In 1883, he led a group of nine families, including his brother Philip and his family, to file claims for homesteads in the Jewish farming settlement called the Painted Woods Colony, twenty-five miles north of Bismarck, Dakota Territory (later North Dakota). Due to the severe winter weather, the rugged lifestyle, and poor crops, all eventually left the settlement except for Joseph, who joined some of those who had gone to Portland, Oregon in 1892. Almost a year later, Joseph, along with his brothers Philip and Israel, decided to take up farming near Porterville, California. In about 1894, Joseph found a new place to farm close to Folsom, California. Meanwhile, his brothers Philip and Israel and their families moved to San Francisco and then to Portland. In 1896, Joseph established a Jewish farming settlement in Wellington, Nevada, forty-five miles south of Carson City. Nonetheless, most of the 100 settlers had left by 1899 due to difficulties in earning a living there and relocated to Portland, with Joseph following in 1902. That brought an end to Joseph's attempts to establish Jewish farming settlements, and he then ran a kosher meat market in Portland (Marschall, 2002; Nudelman, 1969).

6 Until the middle of the nineteenth century, in English-speaking countries, *shokhtim* often affixed the title Reverend before their names.

After this tragedy, Itsl moved the family back to Portland where he opened a dry goods store but later opened a clothing store with a partner. Sadly, Ida remained overwhelmed with guilt for having encouraged her son to go on the trip which had led to his disappearance. Out of desperation, she turned to clairvoyants and explored other means to try to locate her son, but to no avail. She became so inconsolable that she made herself ill. Forgetting her four remaining children, she pined away. Ida was eventually hospitalized and underwent some sort of surgery from which she did not recover, dying on January 2, 1903, at the age of thirty-nine. Her oldest child Edith, age fourteen, had a vision of Ida and Abie embracing each other, only to find out later that the vision had occurred at the moment her mother had passed away. Edith now had to take over the household duties and the care of her younger sisters and brother. In any case, her schooling had ended shortly beforehand with her completion of the seventh grade. She did not know much about cooking, so her great-aunt, Anna Nudelman, gave her some lessons. At times, Edith would cry in front of her mother's portrait, and, somehow, the recipe would come to her, and so she managed.

In 1905, Itsl's first cousin Yosl Goldenshteyn, the son of his uncle Pinye-Ber, joined him in Portland, where he assumed Itsl's surname and became known as Joseph Goldstein. Upon first arriving in New York City, Yosl had stayed with his relative Sophie (Sose) Grover, where he was shown Edith's photograph. He promptly decided to travel to Portland to marry her. Joseph and Edith married later that year; Edith was only seventeen and Joseph was eight years her senior.[7] Edith married at such a young age because she needed someone to help her take care of her younger sisters and brother. Sadly, Itsl died on April 7, 1907, at the age of forty-four. After the deaths of Ida and Itsl, their three daughters made sure that their brother Sam said *Kaddish* for the full eleven months for each of their parents.[8] To make matters even worse, Itsl's business partner took the entire business away from his children and gave them nothing. With their father now also gone, Edith and Joseph took in her three younger siblings and put them through school. In 1911, Joseph changed his name from Goldstein to Goldeen, and Edith's siblings, Jennie and Sam, followed suit. Jennie and Bertha ended up staying with Joseph and Edith until they married. Bertha married Manuel M. Glikbarg in November 1914 in Portland and then settled in Salinas, California.

---

7 For more about Edith's married life, see Appendix A2, pp. 704–707.

8 Personal correspondence in 2002 with Nancy (Merenbach) Petrilla Zuniga, as heard from her mother Floriene (Goldeen) Merenbach, daughter of Joseph.

In 1916, when Joseph and his family moved to Anaconda, Montana, Edith's siblings Jennie and Sam moved with them. Jennie worked as a bookkeeper in Joseph's furniture store, where she met her husband Benjamin Shapiro when he walked into the store. They married in 1917 and settled in Tacoma, Washington. Jennie and Benjamin returned to Portland ca. 1919 and moved to Los Angeles in about 1922. The couple changed their surname from Shapiro to Sherwood in the 1940s or 1950s.

Upon leaving high school, Sam worked as a clerk at Joseph's furniture store. Eventually, Joseph set up a branch of his furniture store in a little town in Oregon, which Sam ran for a short while. When Joseph moved the family to Anaconda, Montana, they closed that branch of the store and Sam moved with them.

Sam Goldeen enlisted in the army during the First World War. After the war, he returned to Anaconda, where he obtained a job at the Anaconda Copper Mining Company. He was not a miner but was an ore sampler. Sam used to describe his job as follows: when enough ore for the week had been brought up from the mine via the seemingly endless conveyer belt, Sam was to shove the conveyer belt off its pulleys. It would take about a week to put the conveyer belt back again, by which time they conveniently needed more ore. In 1921, Joseph moved the family to San Jose, California, and shortly afterwards Sam moved to Lincoln, California, where he opened a men's clothing store. In Lincoln, Sam married his wife Doris Levin, who was originally from Portland. They named their oldest son John (1925–2006) and their second son Samuel Solis Goldeen, Jr. (1927–2017). When Joseph heard of Sam's blatant break with the Ashkenazi Jewish tradition of not naming after the living, he was extremely upset. In a slight gesture of deference to Joseph, Sam changed his son's middle name from Solis to Edwin. (When Sam Jr., signed up for the draft at age eighteen in 1945, he changed his name back to Samuel Solis Goldeen, Jr.) In 1933, Sam, Sr. moved to Berkeley, California, where he operated a men's clothing store until 1971. Sam and Doris both passed away in 1984 in Berkeley.[9]

9 Telephone interview in 2002 with Samuel S. Goldeen, Jr. (1927–2017), of Monterey, California.

Appendix A4: His Second Wife Feyge (ca. 1854–1916)

Pinye-Ber married Feyge-Rashe, his second wife, in 1897 in Odessa (chapter 28, p. 551). He writes that Feyge, as she was commonly called, "was beautiful in her acts of loving kindness and was good natured. . . . I firmly decided to only marry for the children's welfare and not my own. . . . I can say that a stepmother like her is a rarity" (chapter 28, p. 552). Feyge was called *Mime* Feyge (meaning Aunt Feyge in Yiddish) by the author's older children, which is the common appellation for a stepmother in Yiddish, and simply *Mame* (Mama) by his younger children, the youngest of whom was eight years old when Feyge joined the family.[1] In a postcard from 1913 sent from Pinye-Ber's son Shloyme to his brother Refuel (Raphael), he refers to their father Pinye-Ber and stepmother Feyge as "our parents."[2] After her death, Pinye-Ber writes that "such a precious Feyge, being so religious and such a kosher soul, appears very rarely on this earth" (chapter 30, p. 614).

Feyge was born about 1854 in Lithuania.[3] Apparently, her mother died when she was a child. By 1865, her father Yitskhok-Dovid Yudelevitsh had left Feyge with relatives in Lithuania while he moved to Odessa, a center of the Haskalah in Tsarist Russia, to which he was drawn ("Al derekh," 1865). There he remarried a woman named Hadassah, nicknamed Udye, with whom he had more children.[4] In Odessa, Yitskhok-Dovid was a member of the Mekitse Nirdamim (Rousers of Those Who Slumber) Society which was dedicated to the publication of medieval Hebrew manuscripts; was the subscription agent in Odessa for the Hebrew newspaper *Ha-Magid*; and was very active in the

---

1 Personal interview in 2001 with the author's granddaughter, Aliza (Goldenshteyn) Bernfeld.

2 This Russian-language postcard, postmarked November 24, 1913, was sent by Shloyme in Simferopol to his brother Refuel (Raphael) in Cincinnati. It is among Raphael's papers held by his daughter-in-law, Virginia "Ginny" Starr of Grass Valley, California.

3 Feyge's tombstone states that she was sixty-two years old at the time of her death, i.e., she was born ca. 1854. An extract of the 1875 revision list (see details on p. 731, footnote 5 below) of Vilna appearing on the website of the Lithuanian-Jewish Special Interest Group, www.litvaksig.org, states that she was twenty years old, i.e., she was born ca. 1855, and her first husband Moyshe-Avrom Kreyzberg was twenty-two years old.

4 Udye was originally from Starokonstantinov, Ukraine, as noted in her 1895 divorce record in Odessa from Moyshe Kirbas (see p. 731, footnote 8 below).

Alliance Israelite Universelle in Paris which was noted for establishing French-language schools for Jewish children throughout Northern Africa, Iran, and the former Ottoman Empire. He died in 1874 at approximately forty-eight years of age. A lengthy obituary for him appeared in *Ha-Magid* which notes that he left a widow, namely Udye, and small children (Feldman, 1874).

In about 1873, Feyge married Moyshe-Avrom Krezberg who was from Vilna, where they made their home.[5] In 1875, Feyge and her husband moved to Odessa, perhaps to help her recently widowed stepmother, Udye, take care of her young half-siblings. In Odessa, they became known as the Kreyzbergs.[6] Their only child, Duvid, was born in Odessa in 1875. Tragically, Moyshe-Avrom died in 1884 at about thirty-two years of age from some sort of bone malady.[7] In the 1880s, Feyge's stepmother, Udye, remarried a man named Moyshe Kirbas, but they divorced in 1895.[8] In 1913, Feyge and her husband Pinye-Ber, accompanied by Udye, immigrated to Palestine. Feyge died on January 22, 1916, followed several months later by the death of Udye on August 1, 1916. Being an experienced tombstone engraver, Pinye-Ber personally carved both of their tombstones.[9]

Feyge's son Duvid Kreyzberg (known in Russian as David) moved to Yekaterinoslav in January 1913,[10] where he met and married Klara (Khaye) Zlatopolsky, a widow with a son named Grisha.[11] David and Klara had two daughters of their own, Basya and Musya, born in approximately 1914 and 1916, respectively. When Pinye-Ber's son Shloyme studied pharmacy in

---

5 Feyge and her first husband Moyshe-Avróm Kreyzberg are listed as Movsha and Feiga (daughter of Itsko-David) Krezberg in an extract of the 1875 revision list (poll-tax census) of Vilna (now Vilnius, Lithuania) appearing on the website of the Lithuanian-Jewish Special Interest Group, www.litvaksig.org. Moyshe-Avrom's parents were Yitskhok-Hirsh (ca. 1821–1900) and Sore (born ca. 1823).

6 Pinye-Ber's granddaughters Dvora Gavrieli and Aliza Bernfeld pronounced their maternal uncle Duvid's surname as Kresberg.

7 Duvid Kreyzberg's birth record (#688) indicates that he was born on August 8, 1875 (Old Style dating) and misspells his surname as Kraizberg. His father Moyshe-Avrom's death record (#43) indicates that he died on January 15, 1884 (Old Style dating). Both records are held in the State Archives of Odessa Oblast (DOAA).

8 Udye's divorce record (#99), dated July 12, 1895 (Old Style dating), is held in the State Archives of Odessa Oblast (DOAA). It refers to her as Gudya in Russian and states that she was 57 (born ca. 1838), which is more reliable than the age of 85 on her tombstone (born ca. 1831).

9 Personal interview in 2001 with Aliza Bernfeld.

10 A Russian-language postcard, postmarked January 29, 1913, sent by Pinye-Ber's son Shloyme Goldenshteyn to his brother Refuel (Raphael) in Cincinnati, mentions that Duvid Kreyzberg had come a few days earlier and had settled down, presumably in Yekaterinoslav.

11 Grisha's surname is unknown. He married and lived in Leningrad and had no progeny, according to a personal interview in 2001 with Aliza (Goldenshteyn) Bernfeld.

Yekaterinoslav before the First World War, he frequented his stepbrother David's home where he met Klara's sister Etya. Shloyme and Etya were later married in 1917. By 1917, David and his family had moved to Feodosiya, where he was the director of the local branch of the Azov-Don Bank and became the chief activist for the Zionist movement there (Keren, 1981:218, 223, 229). Even after his mother Feyge's death in 1916, he continued to generously send funds to his stepfather Pinye-Ber in Petakh-Tikva (chapter 31, p. 624). By 1921, the Azov-Don Bank, along with other private banks, had been nationalized and had become part of Gosbank, the State Bank of the Soviet Union. In the 1920s, David and Klara returned to Yekaterinoslav. In 1926, Pinye-Ber's grandson-in-law, Joseph Pozwolski (son-in-law of Isruel), visited Moscow, and Klara traveled there to visit him; she "impressed him as being quite an educated, refined, and smart person."[12] Tragically, Klara was killed when struck by a truck in 1935. Musya and Basya never married and were last known to be living together in Moscow in 1970.[13]

12 See the author's July 3, 1926 letter in Appendix B3, p. 786.

13 Personal interview in 2001 with Aliza (Goldenshteyn) Bernfeld of Petakh-Tikva.

Appendix A5: Bashe's *Tsores*[1]—The Story of the Author's Third Wife

Bashe's Background

Basye-Dvoyre, commonly called Bashe, was born in approximately 1849 in Bialystok to Elkhonen-Yitskhok "Khonl" Yirme (ca. 1829–1900) and his wife Rokhl (ca. 1835–1905).[2] Khonl was a Torah scholar who derived practically "no benefit from the physical world," meaning that he was a spiritual person who

1 *Tsores* (plural of *tsarah*, as pronounced in Modern Hebrew) has two definitions: trouble and a co-wife in a polygamous marriage.

2 The 1922 British Mandate Census (available at the website of the Israel Genealogical Society, http://www.isragen.org.il) states that Bashe was seventy-five years old (i.e., born ca. 1847). In ch. 34 (p. 666) of his autobiography, Pinkhes-Dov Goldenshteyn states, in a section dated 1925, that Bashe was seventy-five years old (i.e., born ca. 1850), and her 1934 Petakh-Tikva death record states that she was eighty-five (i.e., born ca. 1849). Hence, she was born ca. 1849. The name of Bashe's mother was obtained from the 1862 birth record in Bialystok of Bashe's brother "Refail Irmi," who apparently died in infancy or early childhood.

Though Bialystok is currently in Poland, the Jews in northeastern Poland were *Litvaks* (Lithuanian Jews) and spoke the Northeastern (Lithuanian) Yiddish dialect. In this Yiddish dialect, Hebrew-given names such as Yirmye (Jeremiah) and Yisroel (Israel) were pronounced as Irmye and Isroel. Hence, the Yirme surname, which derives from the given name Yirmye, was originally pronounced and sometimes spelled as Irme (אירמע). By the early twentieth century, the surname began to be pronounced as Yirme. In Palestine, dialectal pronunciations diminished as Hebrew pronunciation became more regulated in the wake of Yiddish speakers from all over Eastern Europe. Bashe's full name of Basye-Dvoyre is engraved on her tombstone (see p. 745, footnote 36 below). Though Bashe can be a Yiddish name unto itself, in Lithuania and northeastern Poland it was almost always a nickname for Basye (pronounced Batya in modern Hebrew).

was not interested in worldly pleasures.[3] He was a successful goldsmith, as had been his own father Nisan (ca. 1806–1886).[4]

In about 1867, Bashe married her first cousin, Reb Avrem-Shimen Yirme, who was about three years her senior and whose father, Shloyme-Zalmen, had died when he was a boy.[5] Avrem-Shimen was very learned in Torah and received rabbinical ordination. Though his brother became a rabbi in Hungary, Reb Avrem-Shimen never wanted to become a rabbi, for he used to say that he wanted to heed the words of the Mishna (Avot 4:5), "Do not make the Torah . . . a spade with which to dig," i.e., a means by which to earn a living. Avrem-Shimen's occupation as a merchant compelled him to travel considerably, and, over time, he became one of the wealthier Jews in Bialystok. As was common in Yiddish, Bashe was referred to by her husband's name—Bashe-Avrem-Shimens. Reb Avrem-Shimen and Bashe were very happily married and loved each other greatly. The only factor that marred their happiness was not being blessed with children. Although Jewish law permits couples to divorce after ten years of marriage without children, they decided to remain married.[6] The custom among many rabbinical authorities is to encourage such couples to remain together.

---

3 Pinkhes-Dov Goldenshteyn writes in his autobiography (ch. 34, p. 666) that Bashe's father was a Torah scholar, and Elkhonen-Yitskhok's 1901 tombstone in the Segulah Cemetery in Petakh-Tikva notes that he had practically no benefit from the physical world. Bashe's father's full name was Elkhonen-Yitskhok, as noted in three places: his tombstone; his daughter Leye Mortkovitz's 1926 tombstone in the same cemetery; and the plaque in the Shone Halakhot synagogue in Petakh-Tikva in honor of Leye (see p. 743 below).

Bashe's tombstone, also in the Segulah Cemetery, mistakenly states that her father's name was Yitskhok-Elkhonen. The Segulah Cemetery is Petakh-Tikva's oldest cemetery and is the burial place of all those mentioned in this article who died in Petakh-Tikva. Her mother Rokhl's 1905 tombstone states that her father's name was Hirsh-Leyb.

4 In a private interview in 2002, Shoshana (Yirme) Kaplan of Petakh-Tikva related that Bashe told her that her father had been wealthy. The 1862 birth record in Bialystok of Bashe's brother Refoel "Irmi" states that his father was a goldsmith. In a list dating from the 1880s or 1890s of the early settlers of Petakh-Tikva, Bashe's father is referred to as "Elkhonen *tsoref*," meaning "goldsmith" (Ya'ari, 1929:207). Yellin (1899:2) refers to Bashe's brother Hirsh-Leyb (see pp. 736–737 below) also as a goldsmith. The 1861 death record in Bialystok of Bashe's paternal grandmother Gute "Irmia" states that her husband, Nisan, was a professional goldsmith. Nisan Irmia's 1886 death record from Bialystok states that he died at the age of eighty.

5 Shoshana (Yirme) Kaplan (see p. 740 below) said that Reb Avrem-Shimen was eighty-four when he died in 1923, i.e., born ca. 1839. But the 1922 British Mandate Census (available at the website of the Israel Genealogical Society, http://www.isragen.org.il) states that he was seventy-six years of age, i.e., born ca. 1846. Reb Avrem-Shimen's mother may have been named Khaye-Rokhl, which was his oldest daughter's name. In Yiddish, the name Avróm (Avraham in modern Hebrew) is pronounced as Avrem when the bearer is called by two given names and Avrem comes first.

6 Personal interview in 2002 with Shoshana (Yirme) Kaplan of Petakh-Tikva.

FIGURE 32. Bashe's first husband, Reb Avrem-Shimen Yirme (ca. 1846–1922), who is shown holding his newly printed book *Ishei Hashem* in 1906. Bashe was Pinkhes-Dov Goldenshteyn's third wife. (Courtesy of his grandson Moshe Perry of Petakh-Tikva.)

In 1883, after being married for over fifteen years without having any children, Reb Avrem-Shimen and Bashe decided to move to the town of Petakh-Tikva in Palestine.[7] Over the course of that year, some forty families (sixty individuals) from in and near Bialystok moved to Petakh-Tikva (Ya'ari, 1929:244), including the town's first rabbi, Rabbi Aharon Orlansky (1854–1910). Within a few years, Bashe's parents joined them, and eventually her only brother, Hirsh-Leyb, her only sister Leye, and her aunt and other relatives moved to Petakh-Tikva as well.[8] As they settled into their new home, Reb Avrem-Shimen had enough money to live on but was not as wealthy as many people presumed. As one of his relatives said, "You did not come to Petakh-Tikva in those years to make money. You came to bury money,"[9] because of the lack of opportunity and the poor economic conditions. Reb Avrem-Shimen did

---

7 The year of Reb Avrem-Shimen's immigration is found on the inscription on his tombstone. Perhaps by moving to the Holy Land they had hoped to merit the blessing of children. See Braver (1966:16) and Yellin (1924:7) for accounts of childless couples who moved to the Holy Land for just such reasons.

8 In an article about Bashe's brother Hirsh-Leyb, his parents are noted as having been early settlers of Petakh-Tikva (Min ha-Modi'im, 1899:3).

9 Personal interview in 2002 with Shoshana (Yirme) Kaplan.

not accept any money from Baron Edmond de Rothschild (1845–1934), who helped sustain many of the early settlers. The lack of great wealth meant that Bashe would eventually need to contribute to the household's financial welfare.

In late 1890 or 1891, Reb Avrem-Shimen opened Petakh-Tikva's first store, which was located on Baron Hirsch St. and sold food staples (Trofe, 1949:125, Ya'ari, 1929:673). Bashe did most of the work in the store, thereby allowing her husband to spend his time in Talmudic study. And after a few years, when other stores opened, it was primarily Bashe who would fearlessly take the horse and wagon alone, without a driver, once a week to Jaffa to buy produce. The road from Petakh-Tikva to Jaffa was sometimes frequented by Arab robbers, and she once returned quite shaken after an encounter with some of them, though she somehow came away unscathed.[10]

After opening his store, Reb Avrem-Shimen planted vineyards and started making his own wine, which he did not do for the income.[11] In his house, one room was devoted to winemaking and the wine was kept in barrels in the cellar. Another room in his house served as a small synagogue, a *shilkhl*. Though not the official rabbi of Petakh-Tikva, Reb Avrem-Shimen was constantly asked questions regarding Jewish law. In 1906, he published a book entitled *Ishei Hashem*, a collection of the laws of separating *ma'aser* translated into Yiddish.[12] It includes an approbation by Rabbi Abraham Isaac Kook, who was at that time the rabbi of Jaffa and the surrounding agricultural colonies.[13]

In 1899, tragedy struck Bashe and her family. Bashe's only brother, Hirsh-Leyb Yirme, was helping Reb Avrem-Shimen acquire fertilizer for the settlers of Petakh-Tikva. Hirsh-Leyb used to travel with an Arab wagon driver to the Arab village of Mir (also known as Al-Mirr) to purchase the fertilizer from Bedouins. At dusk, on 29 *Tishrei* 5660 (October 3, 1899), the wagon driver returned to Petakh-Tikva only to inform Reb Avrem-Shimen that he was unable to locate Hirsh-Leyb in Mir that afternoon, despite having searched for him everywhere. It was eventually discovered that Bashe's brother had been murdered by

---

10 Personal interview in 2002 with Moshe Perry of Petakh-Tikva.

11 Personal interview in 2002 with Shoshana (Yirme) Kaplan.

12 Jewish law requires the separation of *ma'aser* (tithing) from produce grown in the Land of Israel. When the Holy Temple was extant in Jerusalem, these separated portions were distributed in a specified manner to the *kohanim* (priests), *Levi'im* (Levites), and the poor, or eaten in Jerusalem. While *ma'aser* is no longer distributed or eaten in Jerusalem, the requirement to separate and designate it is still in effect.

13 Reb Avrem-Shimen's grandson, Moshe Perry, related that after his grandfather's death, his widow, Hinde, donated his entire library, including all the unsold copies of his book, to the Hebron yeshiva. In 1929, Arabs massacred almost seventy Jews there, seriously injured scores of others, and pillaged and ransacked their synagogues and homes, including those unsold copies of his book. Hence, few copies of the book exist.

someone in Mir for the few coins that were left in his pocket (Ya'ari, 1929:377, Idelshtein, 1939:1:68–70). Avraham Shapira (1870–1965), a colorful figure and head of the *shomrim* (guardsmen) in Petakh-Tikva, located the body and tracked down the murderer. This first murder of a Jew in Petakh-Tikva caused the whole town to be in turmoil.[14]

A Novel Plan

Now we come to an episode in Bashe's story that highlights the difference between our notions of spousal duty and one woman's notions in the late nineteenth century. Bashe strongly felt her husband's pain over not having any progeny, especially a son who would be able to recite the *Kaddish* prayer during the eleven months after his death. She suggested to her husband that perhaps he could marry a second wife.[15] After all, they no longer lived in Europe where Ashkenazi Jewish men are forbidden to marry more than one wife; they now lived under the Turks where some Sephardic Jews did marry more than one wife at a time. Bashe was quite willing to remain married to him while he took another wife who would, God willing, bear him children.

This plan, although proposed by Bashe out of love, ended up creating a fair amount of controversy in Petakh-Tikva. There was a longstanding *kherem* (ban) against polygamy instituted among the Jewish communities of France and Germany, often attributed to the great medieval Talmudic scholar Rabbi Gershom, the son of Yehuda (ca. 960–1028). Some authorities maintain that the *kherem* was not meant to absolve a man from the Biblical obligation to procreate and he could marry a second wife if his first wife was barren. Other authorities held that a *heter me'ah rabanim* (the permission of 100 rabbis in at least three different countries) could, under certain circumstances, release a man from this ban.[16] Wanting to fulfill all rabbinic opinions, Reb Avrem-Shimen

---

14 Hirsh-Leyb Yirme did not leave behind a family; his wife had died some two years earlier, and they had no children (Min ha-Modi'im, 1899:3). In Beirut, the murderer was sentenced to five years of hard labor in prison (Carmon, 2020:29–30).

15 Both Abu-Elbanat (1935) and Yakobzon (1986:55) report that Bashe, and not Reb Avrem-Shimen, first brought up the idea of his taking a second wife.

16 This ban, often called the *kherem* of Rabenu Gershom, was accepted by virtually all Ashkenazic communities. Nonetheless, in a case such as Reb Avrem-Shimen's, where the wife had not had children for ten years or more, there is a difference of opinion among rabbinical authorities whether the *kherem* of Rabenu Gershom even applies. A *heter me'ah rabanim* is a special provision made for extraordinary situations where the rabbis see a particular need to allow a man to marry a second wife, such as if the first wife is insane and cannot accept a writ of divorce made in accordance with Jewish law. In such a case, the husband must secure a letter

undertook a journey around a great part of the Middle East collecting the signatures of 100 rabbis.[17] Meanwhile, Bashe was seeking out an appropriate woman who would agree to become her husband's second wife, and she found the right candidate in a relative named Khane-Reyzl.[18] Upon his return from his travels, Reb Avrem-Shimen and Khane-Reyzl were married in the late 1890s.[19] Though they did not broadcast their actions, the residents of Petakh-Tikva eventually came to realize that the new member of the Yirme household was not merely a relative who had moved in with them but was, in fact, Reb Avrem-Shimen's second wife.

It was at this point that the public controversy began. In his memoirs of Petakh-Tikva, Khayim Yakobzon (1986:55–56) describes the community split caused by the second marriage.[20] On one side were the Torah scholars who supported the decision to take a second wife. Khayim Yakobzon relates the way that his father spoke about the situation to these supporters:

> The new, young wife would give birth to children on the lap, so to speak, of the barren Bashe. The children would practically be adopted by Bashe. And after her death, they would recite the mourner's *Kaddish* for Bashe at her gravesite. Throughout the rest of her life, Bashe would still be supported by her husband, the Torah scholar, and be able to hear *Kiddush* and *Havdalah*

---

signed by 100 rabbis (which includes Torah scholars) who reside in three different countries (or communities) and who are all knowledgeable and proficient in Jewish law, which then allows the husband to remarry ("Kherem de-Rabenu Gershom," 1987:411–414).

17 Personal interview in 2002 with Moshe Perry of Petakh-Tikva, as told to him by Simkha Shnaider (ca. 1903–1969) of Petakh-Tikva, who was married to Elisheva (ca. 1904–1984), the daughter of Zalman Yirme. Zalman (ca. 1876–1948), who originally bore the last name of Rubin, was Reb Avrem-Shimen's sister's son. In about 1892, Reb Avrem-Shimen sent for Zalman, who was having a difficult time studying in a *yeshiva*, and helped Zalman establish himself. Zalman became like a son to Reb Avrem-Shimen and adopted his uncle's surname of Yirme. Later, Zalman's parents, Avrem-Yitskhok (son of Zorakh) Rubin (died 1905) of Gonyonds (Goniądz in Polish) and Sheyne-Rive (ca. 1848–1926), immigrated to Petakh-Tikva, where they died and are buried.

18 Interview with Moshe Perry, as heard from his relative Simkha Shnaider. Khane-Reyzl was Reb Avrem-Shimen's relative; it is unknown if she was also Bashe's blood relative, being that Reb Avrem-Shimen and Bashe were first cousins.

19 Abu-Elbanat (January 16, 1935) states that their marriage occurred over thirty-five years beforehand. While the outcry over the incident occurred in late 1900, according to "Misaviv ha-moshavot" (1900), Moshe Perry related that it only occurred when some time had passed after Reb Avrem-Shimen and Khane-Reyzl's marriage.

20 These events occurred before the birth of Khayim Yakobzon (1904–1993), as noted in the previous footnote.

> and fulfill all the Jewish precepts, without having to constantly turn to others for favors.

It seems clear from this that Reb Avrem-Shimen saw the prospect of children as benefiting Bashe as much as himself. Yet, on the other side were those in Petakh-Tikva who opposed the plan. They mainly consisted of the younger generation, including the intellectual, less religious women, as well as Avraham Shapira, the man who had tracked down the killer of Bashe's brother. Mr. Shapira argued,

> How can something like this happen? Should Petakh-Tikva become like the Arabic village of Yehudiya? If so, then Petakh-Tikva will no longer serve as an example to the Muslim bigamists of Kafr Ana. There must be strict adherence to the rules, with no compromises, flexibility, or mercy.

Shapira and others appear to have believed that the polygamous household would undo a quality that made Petakh-Tikva distinctively Jewish amidst its Arab neighbors. One bright day, a group of women, led by Shapira, went out and demonstrated outside of Reb Avrem-Shimen's house. They yelled and threw stones, breaking windows. The incident was even reported at the time in the Hebrew press ("Misaviv ha-moshavot," 1900):

> In Petakh-Tikva, they were also looking for sins and it is obvious that the most blatant sin they found was in the house of Avrem-Shimen, the man with two wives. They shattered windows and broke and destroyed whatever possible. The persecuted [Avrem-Shimen] brought his case to the Seraya House.[21]

Reb Avrem-Shimen turned to the rabbi of Petakh-Tikva, Rabbi Orlansky, for a ruling. By the time the uproar had occurred, some time had already passed and Khane-Reyzl had not become pregnant. Faced with an extraordinary case, Rabbi Orlansky decided that, for the sake of peace in the community, it would be best for Reb Avrem-Shimen to divorce both wives.[22] After some thirty-five years

21 The Seraya House was the municipal administration building in Jaffa where the Turkish-Ottoman government was located. In the original article, the Hebrew for "the most [blatant sin]" was misprinted as "היתר" instead of "היותר."

22 Interview with Moshe Perry, as heard in the early 1960s from his relative Simkhe Shnaider. Simkhe also related then that Khane-Reyzl had never remarried and was still alive and living in Tel-Aviv.

of marriage, Reb Avrem-Shimen and Bashe divorced. As Yakobzon (1986:56) writes, "Everything returned to its peaceful state. The barren Bashe spent many years alone and miserable and needed to resort to the kindness of others to hear *Kiddush* and *zmires* and celebrate the Pesach *Seder*. . . ."

Bashe's Continued Efforts

So great was Bashe's love and devotion to Reb Avrem-Shimen that after their divorce she began to seek out yet another woman for him to marry and to provide him with progeny. She went to Jerusalem to find a suitable bride, and she found Hinde-Gitl Ayzenman (ca. 1888–1960). When she was about ten years old, Hinde had immigrated to Jerusalem with her parents Beynish and Tsine Ayzenman from Kamenits-Litovsk (now Kamyanyets, Belarus), which was less than sixty miles from Bialystok. Reb Avrem-Shimen and Hinde were married about 1908 when she was about twenty; he was almost fifty years her senior.[23] Apparently, Reb Avrem-Shimen's appeal to Hinde was that he was a Torah scholar and financially secure. Hinde gave birth to a daughter, Khaya-Rakhel, in 1909, and then another daughter, Shoshana, in 1912.[24] Shoshana was born when her father was some seventy-three years of age, and she died in 2004 at the age of ninety-two. She was the last surviving child of any of the early settlers of Petakh-Tikva.

Bashe remained a close member of Reb Avrem-Shimen's family; she became a friend to Hinde and a mother-figure to his daughters who took part in

23 Personal interview in 2002 with Moshe Perry.

24 Five sources mention Reb Avrem-Shimen having been married to two wives simultaneously: 1) a newspaper article entitled "Misaviv ha-moshavot" (1900); 2) a list of the early settlers of Petakh-Tikva until 1900 compiled by Ben-Ezer (2012:5) in 1958; 3) a lengthy obituary for Bashe written by Abu-Elbanat (1935); 4) the memoirs of Yakobzon (1986); and 5) Carmon (2018). Only the last three sources attempt to summarize the circumstances involved in the incident, yet all three mistakenly state that Reb Avrem-Shimen was married to Bashe and Hinde (the mother of his two daughters) at the same time, even though he only married Hinde after divorcing both Bashe and his second wife Khane-Reyzl in the early 1900s. Born ca. 1888, Hinde could not have been Reb Avrem-Shimen's second wife since she was only twelve years old at the time. Carmon (2018) states that he had contact with Reb Avrem-Shimen's grandson Moshe Perry through his son Dan, but Moshe's health and memory had been failing for a few years by then and he was evidently not able to remember as many details as he had in our personal meeting in 2002. Reb Avrem-Shimen's marriage history is complex; in fact, when I related the story to a friend, the very next day I heard that friend retell the story while completely omitting his second wife, Khane-Reyzl.

Figure 33. The daughters of Reb Avrem-Shimen Yirme (ca. 1846–1922) and his third wife, Hinde, posing with Bashe, who was Reb Avrem-Shimen's first wife and Pinkhes-Dov Goldenshteyn's third wife. The daughters (left to right) are Khaya Freidenberg (1909–1963) and Shoshana Kaplan (1912–2004). Note that Bashe is dressed very modestly and is wearing a *sheytl*, as married religious Jewish women do as a sign of modesty. The photograph was taken in the early 1920s in Petakh-Tikva. (Courtesy of Khaya's son, Moshe Perry, of Petakh-Tikva.)

raising the children.[25] Shoshana remembered walking as a girl with her mother through the fields to Bashe's home near the *moshav* (cooperative farm) Ein-Ganim. Shoshana remembered Bashe being almost like a second mother to her and her sister. But Bashe was better than a mother for she did not discipline them: "She loved us more than a mother–she spoiled us. Bashe loved Hinde as well," said Shoshana. "When I think about how well my father, his former wife Bashe, and my mother all got along with each other, I'm amazed." Her parents never mentioned her father's having once been married to Bashe and Khane-Reyzl at the same time, with the exception of a vague reference once, which she only understood years later. The daughters only heard about that episode from others, though they knew that their father and Bashe had once been married but later divorced because they had no children. Shoshana noticed that her father and Bashe still had great admiration for each other. She also knew that her father and mother had little in common, which was due not only to the large age gap between them but also because Hinde was uneducated and from a simple family, while Reb Avrem-Shimen was a Torah scholar and an intellectual who knew French, the international language at the time.

Reb Avrem-Shimen continued to be a respected figure in Petakh-Tikva, and many people preferred to ask him their *shayles* (questions regarding

25 According to Shoshana (Yirme) Kaplan, after the divorce, Bashe lived in Petakh-Tikva near Ein-Ganim and not with her former husband Reb Avrem-Shimon, as Abu-Elbanat (1935) presumes.

Jewish law which constantly arise in the course of daily life) rather than consult the rabbi of Petakh-Tikva, Rabbi Yisrael Aba Tsitron (1881–1927), since Reb Avrem-Shimen was lenient, and his door was always open. His daughter Shoshana remembered people constantly coming to their house to ask her father *shayles.*

Bashe's Sister Leye

The life of Bashe's younger and only sister Leye (ca. 1861–1926) and her family was closely connected with Bashe's. Leye's only child was a son named Avraham-Yehoshua. She was widowed early by the death of her husband, Akiva Mortkovitz.[26] In Petakh-Tikva, she lived in a small, neglected house, which she owned. By March 1915, her son had moved to Cairo, Egypt, which had been under British rule since 1882. In Cairo, he Anglicized his name to Abraham Dykes and worked for the Egyptian State Railways, which was under British management. He advanced quickly through the ranks, and, in September 1918, he was appointed the Assistant Mamur Zapt (Head of Cairo's Secret Police under British Rule) on behalf of the Supplies Control Board, where he was to assist in combating illicit trading in oil and in enforcing the tariff. Abraham was also responsible for a sum of money belonging to the Board from which he made payments to the secret agents working under him. He had an office at the Cairo Governorate ("Letter from Cairo," *Near East* 14, no. 385 [September 20, 1918]: 759).

Back in the early 1900s, when Bashe and Reb Avrem-Shimen had divorced, Reb Avrem-Shimen had given Bashe 11.026 dunams (2.7 acres) of vineyards. In August 1918, Bashe transferred her vineyards to her nephew, Abraham, since he was her only nephew. During a visit to his mother in January 1919, Abraham met with the rabbi of Petakh-Tikva, Rabbi Yisrael Aba Tsitron (1881–1927) to formalize the transfer.[27]

---

26 Akiva Mortkovitz's first name is known from his son Abraham's probate record and from a 1919 document from the Petakh-Tikva archives (see the next footnote). He is not buried in Petakh-Tikva; he likely died in Europe. British documents generally referred to Leye as "Leah Mortkovitz," though her name is occasionally spelled in Yiddish as מורדכוויץ. The British Mandate Census of 1922 lists Leye as being sixty years of age (i.e., born ca. 1862), while her 1926 death record states that she was sixty-five (i.e., born ca. 1860).

27 A copy of this document (file #13, document 63), dated 16 *Shvat* 5679 (January 17, 1919), was obtained in 2013 from the Oded Yarkoni Historical Archives of Petakh-Tikva (www.ptarchive.co.il). The document, signed by Bashe, notes that she gives her 11.026 dunams (2.7 acres) of land to Abraham Dykes, the son of her sister, Leye Mortkovitz. In 2001,

Shortly after Abraham's return to Egypt, the Egyptian Revolution of 1919 broke out against the British occupation of Egypt and Sudan. Approximately seventy-five Britons were killed or injured that spring and summer, including Abraham. On April 3, 1919, Abraham was shot twice and killed in Abdin Square, thirty yards from the barracks of the Egyptian Army. He was evidently targeted because of his high rank. As Abraham's beneficiary, Leye received an allowance from the British government on which she was able to survive (Mak, 2011:224; Probate: Abraham Dykes, 1919; Yakobzon, 1986:83).

With the murder of her son, Leye sunk even further into depression and despair. In 1924, now bereft of any heirs, she formalized the donation of the lot on which her house stood toward the building of a synagogue after her death. After she died in 1926, her house was leveled, and a synagogue named Shone Halakhot was built on the lot. It is an active synagogue in the center of Petakh-Tikva.[28] Yakobzon (1986:83) writes in his memoirs, "I remember how Leye, the bereaved widow, would sit together with her sister, the barren Bashe, and [they would] recount their sorrows to each other."

Bashe and her Marriage to Pinkhes-Dov Goldenshteyn

Towards the end of his life, Reb Avrem-Shimen became very weak and likely could no longer support Bashe. His daughter Shoshana (Yirme) Kaplan believed that this was the economic impetus that spurred Bashe to remarry. Bashe would not consider selling the gold that she had inherited from her father or her vineyards in order to support herself since Jews at that time tried to leave an inheritance for their younger relatives.

On January 11, 1920 (the 20th of *Teyves* 5680), Bashe married Pinkhes-Dov Goldenshteyn, as he notes in his autobiography (chapter 34, p. 666). Noting Bashe's devotion to him, he wrote, "Since there is good will between us, I am devoted to her." Apparently, Bashe's welfare prompted Pinye-Ber to write a Hebrew ethical will six months after their marriage, on June 22, 1920 (6 Tamuz,

---

Shoshana (Yirme) Kaplan related that after Dykes's death, Bashe's friends (not members of the Goldenshteyn family) convinced her to donate the land to the municipality.

28 The street address of the Shone Halakhot synagogue is 42 Khoveve-Tsion St. A plaque in the synagogue and the inscription on her tombstone testify to Leye's having donated the land upon which the synagogue was built. The wording on the plaque is printed in Grayevski (1929:22). In a letter dated January 27, 1927 (24 *Shvat* 5687), Pinkhes-Dov Goldenshteyn writes to his daughter Nekhame Brockman in California that he is sending her a very good prayer book, which was left over from Leye's estate.

5680).[29] In section 13 of his will, he stipulated that Bashe was to be provided with economic support from his five sons and would be allowed to reside in his house for the duration of her life.

Even after her marriage to Pinye-Ber, Bashe was still referred to as Bashe-Avrem-Shimens. Her former husband, Reb Avrem-Shimen, died on November 19, 1923 (28 *Heshvan* 5684).[30] After his death, his widow, Hinde, kept running the store, though on a much smaller scale.

In 1921, Pinye-Ber's daughter, Nekhame Brakhtman, her husband, and their three teenage children arrived in Petakh-Tikva from the Soviet Union. The Brakhtman children greatly admired Bashe for all the challenges and hardship she had endured as one of the early settlers of Petakh-Tikva.[31] Pinye-Ber's son Shloyme, his wife, and their two little girls, Dvora and Aliza, arrived from Constantinople in 1923, and they moved in with Pinye-Ber and Bashe, though Bashe did find the noise of the children trying at times.[32]

When Pinye-Ber died in 1930, the law in Palestine under the British Mandate was that only one-fourth of all property went to the surviving spouse. Bashe wanted to arrange for a synagogue to be built on her quarter of Pinye-Ber's property, just like her sister, Leye, had done with the lot on which her house had stood. Although Shloyme resisted the idea, Bashe was quite adamant about this desire of hers, and her relative, Tsvi Zabludovitsh (1853–1948), was called in to help settle the matter with Pinye-Ber's son Shloyme, who lived in the rest of the house with his family.[33] Eventually, an agreement was reached that Bashe would give up her share of the inheritance, and, in turn, Shloyme would support and provide for her for the rest of her life. Pinye-Ber had continued to receive some support from his sons in America but that had stopped with his death. So Shloyme rented out the other two rooms of the house in the back of the courtyard, which added to his income and made it easier to support Bashe. Shloyme's wife, Etya, would cook meals for Bashe who was very weak in her final years, and Shloyme would go to her room to make *Kiddush* for her on *Shabes* and *Yontef*.

---

29 See Appendix B2 (pp. 762–773) for a translation of his Hebrew ethical will.

30 In about 1987, Reb Avrem-Shimen's daughter, Shoshana Kaplan, completed all the paperwork necessary to have a street in Petakh-Tikva named after her father. At that time, there were still people who remembered Reb Avrem-Shimen, and the municipality approved her application and honored him with a small street in his name.

31 Interview with Cynthia Unterberg, as heard from her father Victor Brockman (Brakhtman), the son of Nekhame.

32 Personal interview in 2001 with Pinye-Ber's granddaughter Aliza (Goldenshteyn) Bernfeld.

33 For more regarding Zabludovitsh, see Tidhar (1947:2:644).

Bashe was already too weak to come to Shoshana's wedding in 1932. When Hinde's oldest daughter, Khaya, became engaged to Binyamin Freidenberg, Khaya took her fiancé to meet Bashe, and he was very impressed with her, describing her as an aristocratic lady.[34] But Bashe did not live to see them married.

When Bashe lay in bed dying in November 1934, Hinde and her daughter Shoshana came to visit. Bashe turned to Hinde and said, "Hinde-Gitl" (Hinde was almost never called by her full name), "*Vest kumen af mayn khasene*?" ("Will you come to my wedding?"), "wedding" being a euphemism for a funeral.[35] Bashe died on the 17th of *Kislev* 5695 (November 24, 1934) at approximately eighty-five years of age. There was a large turnout at her funeral (Abu-Elbanat, 1935).[36]

As Yakobzon (1986:56) writes, "I knew Bashe and her virtues and righteousness. According to my humble opinion, this noble woman deserved a happier life." An obituary for Bashe states, "Bashe had received a generous sum of money from Reb Avrem-Shimen upon their divorce, which she would distribute to charity and used for good deeds. She was always walking with a basket full of goodies in her hand for the poor, both those openly in need and those concealing their impoverishment. Until her last day, Bashe was and remained an upright and righteous woman. Among the very women of Petakh Tikva who had once condemned and dishonored her, Bashe's name came to be used as a blessing" (Abu-Elbanat, 1935).

---

34 Personal interview in 2002 with Moshe Perry, the son of Khaya and Binyamin Freidenberg.

35 Personal interview in 2002 with Shoshana (Yirme) Kaplan.

36 In his obituary for Bashe, Abu-Elbanat (1935) bemoans the fact that Reb Avrem-Shimen's two daughters, Khaya and Shoshana, who were born as a result of her tremendous self-sacrifice, did not even attend her funeral. Upon finding this obituary in 2011 and sending it to Khaya's son, Moshe Perry, he related that his father Binyamin had heard about Bashe's death in time to tell Khaya but did not tell her because he did not want to cause her any grief, since he knew how much she loved Bashe. In 2002, Shoshana related that she could not attend the funeral because she had to take care of her one-year-old-son, Avraham. Bashe's tombstone only bears the surname Yirme and not Goldenshteyn. It is quite common for a woman who remarried late in life to have only her first husband's surname on her tombstone.

Appendix A6: Salomon (Shlomo) Bernstein, Relative and Portraitist of the Author

Salomon Bernstein, a relative of Feyge, the second wife of Pinkhes-Dov "Pinye-Ber" Goldenshteyn, was a successful painter who studied art in Odessa and Paris, taught painting in Jerusalem, and presented his work at numerous art exhibitions in Paris, Tel-Aviv, and Jerusalem. In the late 1920s or early 1930s, he painted two portraits of Pinye-Ber, both evidently based on the photograph taken of him in 1927 (see p. 84). One depicts Pinye-Ber at age seventy-eight, as in the photograph, and the other depicts him years earlier when his beard was still red. (Reproductions of the portraits appear on p. 393 and p. 747)

Although we know that Bernstein was a relative of Feyge, specifying the precise family relation between them is difficult.[1] Bernstein was born on February 11, 1886 in Uzda, Belarus, Russia, and was originally named Shlomo-Moshe Berenshteyn (Cornfeld, 1947:37; "Ta'arukhat," 1927).[2] His father, Rabbi Z'ev "Volf" (the son of Yitskhak-Mordekhai) Berenshteyn, was born in 1841 in Uzda, where he served as the head of the yeshiva and as a rabbinical judge (Krol & Leinman, 1940:54).[3] His mother, Rifke-Nekhame, was the daughter

---

1 In a personal interview in 2001, Aliza Bernfeld related that she heard from her father, Shloyme Goldenshteyn, son of the author, that Feyge was Salomon Bernstein's aunt. But she could not have been Bernstein's aunt since his parents' and grandfathers' names (see the next paragraph) do not correspond with Feyge's father's name, Yitskhok-Dovid Yudelevitsh, or with the parents' names of Feyge's first husband Moyshe-Avrom (son of Yitskhok-Hirsh and Sore) Kreyzberg. Feyge also could not have been Salomon's half-aunt since her father was born ca. 1828, as is known from his obituary, making him too young to be the father of either of Salomon's parents who were both born ca. 1841. And Feyge's first husband Moyshe-Avrom Kreyzberg also could not have been Salomon's half-uncle since his parents were married in 1838 in Vilna at ages seventeen and fifteen, respectively, likewise making them too young to have been married previously with children. Evidently, Feyge was a relative of one of Salomon's parents and was merely called an aunt. For details regarding Feyge's family, see Appendix A4, p. 730.

2 Upon moving to France in 1901, he was known as Salomon Bernstein. Sometimes he spelled his first name as Schlomo.

3 The name of Salomon's father was obtained from his tombstone in the historic Trumpeldor Cemetery on Trumpeldor Street in Tel-Aviv, also known as the Old Cemetery. His father is also buried there.

Figure 34. A portrait of a middle-aged Pinkhes-Dov Goldenshteyn by the painter Salomon Bernstein. At the beginning of this volume appears another portrait he painted of Goldenshteyn in his later years. (Courtesy of Kara Unterberg of New York City)

of Moyshe, who was also a rabbi.[4] From early childhood, Bernstein would draw pictures all over the walls of his home. His father opposed his interest in art, and he suffered much in his youth because of his penchant for drawing. In 1897, Bernstein was accepted as a student in the yeshiva in Mir, Belarus, but a short time later the head of the yeshiva wrote his father that it would be better for him to study a trade since he would never be a rabbi. Only with difficulty did he receive permission from his father to travel to Vilna (now Vilnius, Lithuania) to study drawing and painting ("Ta'arukhat," 1927).

In 1901, at age fifteen, he traveled to Odessa, where he studied at the Odessa Drawing School for some four years under Kyriak Konstantynovych Kostandi (1852–1921), Ladizhensky, and Popov, who was the dean of the institute ("Ta'arukhat," 1927; Talphir, 1971:27).[5] At that time, Arnold Borisovich

4 Salomon's mother lies in the Segulah Cemetery in Petakh-Tikva. Her tombstone specifies that she was the wife of Rabbi Z'ev Berenshteyn from Uzda. Her surname is spelled ברינשטיין on her tombstone and indicates that she was 73 years old when she died on 23 *Heshvan* 5675 (November 12, 1914).

5 The Odessa Drawing School was renamed the Grekov Odesa Art School in 1965. Though Feyge (Yudelevitsh) Goldenshteyn had moved away from Odessa in 1897 upon her marriage to Pinkhes-Dov Goldenshteyn, Bernstein may still have had relatives living in Odessa, namely Feyge's step-mother Udye and her younger half-siblings. They would have been Bernstein's relatives if he was related to Feyge through her father.

Lakhovsky (1880–1937), Isaak Izrailevich Brodsky (1884–1930), and Arie Orland (1887–1954) were studying there as well. After the end of the Russo-Japanese War in September 1905, Bernstein traveled to Paris with the financing of his relative Pinkhes-Dov Goldenshteyn.[6] Bernstein studied at the École Nationale Supérieure des Beaux-Arts, where entry was almost impossible for foreigners because they were required to take grueling examinations in French. The painter Leon Bonnat (1833–1922), who was appointed director of the École Nationale Supérieure des Beaux-Arts in 1905, became his patron and assisted him in receiving a grant sponsored by Baron Edmond de Rothschild (1845–1934). He studied under Jules-Joseph Lefebvre (1836–1911), who had previously taught the internationally celebrated Henri Matisse (1869–1954) (Talphir, 1971:27). Bernstein also studied at the Académie Julian, where he received several awards. He also studied under Tony Robert-Fleury (1837–1912), Francois Flameng (1856–1923), and Adolphe Déchenaud (1868–1929) (Bénézit & Busse, 1999:195).

In 1914, Bernstein relocated to Petakh-Tikva, where his parents had moved in 1908 (Krol & Leinman, 1940:54; "Ta'arukhat," 1927). There, his father served as a rabbi and gave Torah lectures (Krol & Leinman, 1940:54). Bernstein's relatives, Feyge and Pinye-Ber, had left Tsarist Russia and settled in Petakh-Tikva the year before. Shortly after Bernstein's arrival there, his mother died in November 1914. With the advance of British forces towards Palestine in 1917, the Ottoman Turks exiled 6,000 Russian citizens who resided in Jaffa and Tel-Aviv to Alexandria, Egypt, and Bernstein was among them (Cornfeld, 1947:37). He supported himself there by lecturing and portraiture. During the First World War, his father relocated to Tel-Aviv, where he died in 1923 (Krol & Leinman, 1940:54).

Bernstein returned to Palestine in 1919 to teach at the Bezalel Art School in Jerusalem, which he did until 1920. He presented the country's first solo art exhibition, which was held at the Herzliya Hebrew Gymnasium in Tel-Aviv where one hundred of his paintings were displayed. This exhibition enjoyed the country's first art review, which was written by the journalist Y. Koplewitz, later known as Yeshurun Keshet (Ofrat, 1999:37). Bernstein was counted among the founders of the Hebrew Art Association. In 1921, he became engaged to Tilly Farbridge, who was born in Tsarist Russia and had immigrated to Manchester, England in the 1890s, before immigrating to Palestine ("Meorasim," 1927). They subsequently married, but, to their sorrow, had no

6 In 1909, Pinye-Ber's daughter, Rukhl, moved to Paris to study law (see ch. 28, p. 564). Bernstein helped her settle down in France, according to a personal interview in 2001 with Aliza Bernfeld as heard from her father, Shloyme Goldenshteyn, the son of Pinye-Ber.

progeny. He participated in the 1924 art exhibition held at the Tower of David in Jerusalem. In 1927, he had a one-man exhibition at Bet Sefer Le-Banim (School for Boys) in Tel-Aviv, and Baron James de Rothschild (1878–1957) purchased one of his paintings on display. One of his pictures, "War (A Fantasy)," was acquired by Vicomte d'Aumale, the French Consul General in Palestine, who presented it to the Tel-Aviv Museum of Art (Cornfeld, 1947:37).

In 1928, he returned to France, where he exhibited at the Salon d'Automne of 1928 and at the Salon des Indepéndants of 1930 (Bénézit & Busse, 1999:195). He painted portraits of many prominent people, including Justin Godart (1871–1956), the Minister of Health of France in 1930.[7] In 1931, he participated in an exhibition of Jewish artists at Henri Brandley's gallery, with Waldemar George writing the preface to the exhibition's catalog.[8] In the years 1929, 1930, and 1931, he participated in the Salon de la Société des Artistes Français (The Salon of the Society of French Artists). He had a one-man exhibition at the Bernheim-Jeune gallery in Paris, and the French sculptor, Naum Lvovich Aronson (1872–1943), and the Belgian historian, Gustave Cohen (1879–1958) wrote the introduction to the catalog. Upon his return to Palestine in 1932, he was appointed art instructor at the Bet Midrash Le-Morim (Teachers Institute) in Jerusalem, which was associated with Mizrachi, the religious Zionist organization, and periodically held exhibitions (Talphir, 1971:27).

Bernstein and Pinye-Ber, his relative, were fond of each other. Pinye-Ber funded his young relative's sojourn to study art in Paris. Bernstein was enamored with Pinye-Ber and would say that Pinye-Ber, who was over six feet tall, had such a presence that when he entered a room one almost felt that Moses himself had arrived. Though Bernstein asked Pinye-Ber to sit for him so that he could paint his portrait, he refused.[9] Bernstein's desire to capture his relative in paint was strong, however, and in the late 1920s or early 1930s, as discussed above, he appears to have relied on a photograph to paint two portraits of Pinye-Ber. Upon his return to Jerusalem in 1932, after four years in Paris, Bernstein sent his portrait of Goldenshteyn at age seventy-eight as a gift to his son Shloyme

7 Godart was not only the author of a large number of important works on political and social subjects, but was honorary president of the National Jewish Fund in the 1930s.

8 Waldemar George was the pseudonym of the French Jewish art critic, George Jarocinski (born 1893).

9 Personal interview with Goldenshteyn's great-granddaughter, Cynthia Unterberg of Westbury, New York, as heard from her father Victor Brockman.

in Petakh-Tikva.[10] When Pinye-Ber's daughter Nekhame Brockman visited Palestine that same year, she heard from her brother Shloyme about Bernstein's second portrait and made a special trip to Jerusalem to purchase it from him. Upon Nekhame's arrival at his home, Bernstein went to a back room to retrieve it and returned holding the portrait in front of his face. Nekhame shrieked, "*Tate*!" ("*Father*!" in Yiddish) for the painting was so realistic that it appeared to her that her father was walking towards her.[11]

Bernstein spent decades on the sidelines without mingling with the artistic community in Israel. After his wife Tilly died in 1962, he became even more isolated (Talphir, 1971:28). Nonetheless, it is important to note that he was a person of refined taste with a pleasant disposition. Remarkably, he remained an Orthodox Jew throughout his life, which was unusual for a painter with his training. He died on March 17, 1968, in a home for the aged in Holon, Israel. His funeral was arranged by Zalman Shachor (1900–1981), chairman of Mizrachi in Tel-Aviv.[12]

Bernstein's drawings show much ability and are captivating. In his inviting paintings, which include landscapes and still lifes of Jerusalem and the environs of Tel-Aviv, one recognizes a delightful impressionistic undertone that reveals his sensitivity to the application of paint on canvas. These works vividly reveal an aesthetic temperament and an artistic perception. Indeed, they have a lyrical thread to them, which emerges from his soothing use of a diverse range of hues, generally consisting of warm yet subtle tones (Talphir, 1971:28).

---

10 Personal interview in 2001 with Aliza (Goldenshteyn) Bernfeld. This portrait is in the possession of Aliza's daughter, Shifra Bernfeld of Petakh-Tikva. (A reproduction of the photograph of Goldenshteyn taken in January–February 1927 appears in vol. 1, p. 84.)

11 Interview with Nekhame's granddaughter, Cynthia (Brockman) Unterberg of Westbury, New York. This portrait is now in the possession of Cynthia Unterberg's daughter, Kara Unterberg.

12 Personal correspondence in 2002 with the Chevra Kadisha (Jewish burial society) of Tel-Aviv/Jaffa. In 2011, a Facebook page was made in tribute to Bernstein and his work (https://www.facebook.com/people/Salomon-Bernstein-Artist-Painter/100071757386063).

Appendix A7: The Printing of the Autobiography

Pinye-Ber apparently started writing his autobiography in the early 1900s.[1] By 1909, he had written up to chapter 23, which comprises most of his work. Shortly after arriving in Petakh-Tikva in November 1913, he had written up to chapter 29 out of 34 chapters. Afterward, he continued to add accounts of his experiences in Palestine in 1918, 1919, 1925, and 1929.

As late as 1920, Pinye-Ber did not think that his autobiography would be printed in his lifetime, as implied in his Hebrew ethical will written that year: "I am also giving to Refuel, my son, my autobiography, which is in manuscript form with me, in five parts, and he will have it printed, as he has already promised me. . . ." Nonetheless, by March 1929 he was insistent that it be in three parts with an addendum, as opposed to the contents of the addendum being a fourth part.[2]

In October 1927, Refuel (called Raphael Goldenstein in English) was elected to a term of three years as the Reform rabbi of Temple Beth El in Lynn, Massachusetts, at an annual salary of $4200. In January 1928, after serving there three months, he was discharged without cause. Raphael filed a breach of contract suit for $4030 in the federal court at Boston, which apparently resulted in an out-of-court settlement. Now without the responsibilities of leading a congregation, Raphael seized the moment to arrange for his father's autobiography to be published.[3] The crucial initial financing came from his brothers Yosl (Joseph Goldeen) and Yankl (Jacob "James" Goldeen) in California.[4] Nonetheless, Pinye-Ber writes in a letter from March 14, 1929 to his daughter Nekhame in Brooklyn, "I think that you should ask at least three shillings for each book, that means not quite an entire dollar. I must have money to pay for its printing."[5]

---

1 See the Introduction, p. 12.
2 See the author's letter from March 14, 1929 in Appendix B3, p. 793.
3 See Appendix A2, pp. 710–718, for more details regarding Raphael's employment history.
4 Personal interview in 2001 with the author's granddaughter Aliza (Goldenshteyn) Bernfeld of Petakh-Tikva.
5 See Appendix B3, pp. 791–793, for the entire letter.

It was decided that the book would be printed in Palestine, because it was less expensive. In fact, Pinye-Ber was well acquainted with a local printer. Since 1926, Pinye-Ber had attended a synagogue near his home called Nakhalat Yisrael.[6] The land on which it was built had been donated by Reuven Kritsman (ca. 1880–1966), who had established Petakh-Tikva's first printing house, Ha-Tekhiya, after immigrating to Palestine in 1920. Ha-Tekhiyah (The Renaissance) was a name used by a number of establishments publishing works in Modern Hebrew, which was then experiencing a renaissance as a spoken language.[7] Of the fourteen titles published in Kritsman's press, printed between 1921 and 1942, all were in Hebrew except for Pinye-Ber's Yiddish-language autobiography and one title in Judeo-Arabic. In his review of the author's autobiography, Niger (see p. 753 below) points out the irony of a book being published in Yiddish in Petakh-Tikva, which was part of the New Yishuv, the largely non-religious Zionist settlements of Palestine known for their rejection of Yiddish and adoption of modern Hebrew.

Part I was printed in August or September 1928,[8] part II in March 1929,[9] and part III and the addendum in June–July 1929.[10] The title of the original Yiddish version is *Mayn lebens-geshikhte: farshidenartige pasirung'n un epizod'n fun a yosem* (My life story: various events and episodes of an orphan). Pinye-Ber's granddaughter Aliza, who was eight years old at the time, remembered the boxes of books stacked up in their home. By that time, Pinye-Ber was old, weak, and did not walk around very much. Besides having been an opportune time for Raphael to arrange for the publishing of the book, it was completed not a moment too soon; the Great Depression began only a few months later, in August 1929, after which his brothers Yosl and Yankl would not have been able to provide the necessary funds.

Five hundred copies of each of the three parts and the addendum were printed; 400 copies were sent to Brooklyn while 100 copies remained in Palestine.[11] The books were shipped to Pinye-Ber's daughter Nekhame's home

---

6 See Appendix A1, p. 679, for more details regarding the Nakhalat Yisrael synagogue.

7 Publishing houses named Ha-Tekhiyah existed in Jerusalem, Tel-Aviv, Odessa, Kharkov, and Philadelphia.

8 The author's "In Lieu of a Preface" (p. 85), which was written shortly before the printing of part I, is dated *Rosh Khodesh Elul* 5688 (August 16–17, 1928).

9 The author writes in his letter from March 14, 1929, "Yesterday, I sent you and Refuel the second part . . ." See Appendix B3 (pp. 791–793) for the entire letter.

10 The last few paragraphs of the author's autobiography are dated the 24th of *Iyar* 5689 (June 3, 1929). There he writes that the printing will be finished in the month of Sivan (June–July 1929).

11 Personal interview in 2001 with the author's granddaughter Aliza (Goldenshteyn) Bernfeld of Petakh-Tikva.

in Brooklyn, since Raphael was away from his Brooklyn apartment on a visit to his brothers in California, and the books arrived in November 1929.[12] Upon his return, the books were moved to Raphael's apartment, since he was handling their marketing, distribution, and sale in America.

In early January 1930, Raphael approached Shmuel Niger, the foremost Yiddish literary critic of his day, and presented him with a copy of the autobiography. He asked him to write a review in his newspaper column, to which Niger agreed. Some three weeks later, on February 11, 1930, Raphael wrote Niger a letter in Yiddish asking him, "I would very much like to know the reason why you are not keeping your word to me and my father. Are you still thinking about writing about it? Did you not like the book? Please answer me right away."[13]

In Palestine, each of the three parts and the addendum had been individually staple bound with off-white paper covers. In January or February 1930, Raphael had the parts hardbound in a single volume with a navy-blue cover at his own expense.[14] He also had a page printed bearing the author's photograph taken in 1927 (see p. 84), which was inserted before the title page.[15]

On March 2, 1930, Niger's lengthy review appeared in the Sunday issue of the New York Yiddish daily, *Der Tog*.[16] The very fact that Niger reviewed a relatively unknown work at such length and found such significance in it, indicates its importance. After all, a privately printed book, particularly a work written by an unknown author, would rarely draw the attention of a leading literary critic.

On March 5, Raphael sent Niger a letter in Yiddish expressing profuse gratitude for his review:

---

12 See the author's letter from November 21, 1929 in Appendix B3, p. 795.

13 Archives of YIVO Institute for Jewish Research in New York City, S. Niger Collection (RG 360, box 75, folder 1634).

14 Raphael had the books hardbound in January or February 1930, since he offered Niger a hardbound copy in his letter of March 5, 1930. A hardbound copy was not yet available when Raphael visited Niger in early January. The author's letter from July 15, 1930 (Appendix B3, p. 801) mentions Raphael's spending his own money on the books.

15 The title and author's surname are embossed in small gold lettering only on the spine, with no lettering on the navy-blue cover. In binding the parts together, the original paper covers were discarded. Since the name of the press, Ha-Tekhiyah, was printed only on the back paper cover of part I, which was discarded, American catalogers were unable to identify the printer. (Nonetheless, "Ha-Tekhiya, R. Kritsman" was printed on the title pages of parts II and III.) Though found in libraries throughout the United States, few libraries in Israel possess copies since the original paper covers and stapling quickly deteriorated.

16 See the Introduction (pp. 2, 6–8, 10–11, 18–20, 66) where various parts of Niger's review are discussed.

> I cannot express my joy and thanks in words for your article. . . . You are a writer of substance and a good person with a warm Jewish heart and very refined feelings. I am very happy that I had the opportunity to meet you and elicit from your pen such a precious pearl, which itself is a contribution to our people's literature . . .[17] The Yiddish language can consider itself lucky to have such a critic as you in America. Your language is beautiful, smooth, and unpretentiously fluid like a wide river quietly flowing under the shade of thick, green trees. You certainly deserve more tangible compensation than this letter, but now is unfortunately not the best of times for me. Nonetheless, I hope that in the future you will be rewarded according to your worth, efforts, and amicability. If you could advise me as to how I could sell the book as quickly as possible, I would be most appreciative. . . . If you would like a hardbound volume for your personal library, I would be happy to send you one.[18]

Niger's review evidently made waves in Warsaw. The April 1930 issue of *Ortodoksishe Yugnd Bleter* (Orthodox Youth Newspaper), published by Agudath Israel, reported that Pinye-Ber's book "has generated much interest."

In a letter from June 22, 1930, Pinye-Ber writes that his son Joseph Goldeen of San Jose, California, had sent a shipment of books to the Soviet Union to be distributed to family and residents of Bakhchisaray but they "were lost because they did not let them into Russia."[19] In his "In Lieu of a Preface" (p. 85), Pinye-Ber writes, "I also want those who plagued and tormented me and are currently in Russia to read this in order to learn the moral lesson that there is a God in the world who protects the harassed and oppressed and repays everyone according to his deeds." The religious nature of the books was likely the reason why they were confiscated and no doubt destroyed.

On August 8, 1930, Abraham I. Shinedling (1897–1982), a Reform rabbi, writer, and editor, wrote the following concise overview of the autobiography, which appeared in an unknown periodical. Perhaps Raphael had asked him to write it to promote the book; both of them were graduates of Hebrew Union College in Cincinnati, Raphael in 1916 and Shinedling in 1920:

---

17 This ellipsis appears in Raphael's original letter.

18 Archives of YIVO Institute for Jewish Research in New York City, S. Niger Collection (RG 360, box 75, folder 1634).

19 See Appendix B3, pp. 797–800, for the entire letter.

Life In Russia and Palestine

> *Mein Lebensgeschichte,* by P.D. Goldenstein. Pethach-Tikvah, Palestine. $1.75. (Rabbi Raphael Goldenstein. 374 South 2nd St., Brooklyn, N.Y.).
>
> This autobiography of a plain and simple "Shohet," a man now ninety-two years old, is a fascinating and moving life-story. In a fine flowing Yiddish in which Hebrew and Russian phrases are pleasingly commingled the author tells of his parents' early struggles in Russia; his own struggles ever since he was five years old, when he was left an orphan; how he became a Shohet, or ritual slaughterer, and his trials as such for more than forty years; intimate details as to his family life and children; finally, his experiences in Palestine as an old retired "Yosheb Eretz Yisrael"[20] before the World War and after, up to 1928. He describes in [an] unforgettable manner the various kinds of Hasidim in Russia and their mode of life; the "Kest" system of marrying off daughters to Yeshiva students and of supporting the young couple often for years; petty politics and chicanery in small congregations; the "financial" method whereby Shohets secure positions in small Russian towns; the method of naming persons according to place of origin, wife's name, or physical defects; "arranged marriages" and their results; the precarious economic life and situation of millions of Eastern European Jews from the 1840's to today; finally, England's conquest of Palestine. The work is a valuable historical and folkloristic document, and should be translated into English.

By September or October 1930, Raphael had either sold the books or given them to a distributor. Having recently become engaged to be married, he decided to move to Los Angeles to be closer to his brothers and to hopefully find a position as a rabbi.

Pinye-Ber died on December 4, 1930. Shortly afterwards, Raphael made contact with Bloch Publishing in New York City which, in 1929, had begun issuing a bi-monthly sales bulletin called *Bloch's Book Bulletin.* For many years, it was the most reliable listing of Jewish books in print, whether in English,

20 Resident of the Land of Israel.

Hebrew, or Yiddish. The January 1931 issue (no. 12, p. [2]) of *Bloch's Book Bulletin* includes a two-sentence description of Pinye-Ber's autobiography, stating that the author had died, that his autobiography "contains very interesting material of Jewish life in Russia and Palestine," and that it costs $2.00. Perhaps this notice was responsible for Pinye-Ber's autobiography being held in over thirty libraries throughout the United States.

In the 1930s, Shloyme wanted to reprint his father's autobiography, but his cousin Yankl Grinberg threatened to take him to court for defamation of character if he did so. Though Yankl's surname is not mentioned in the book, enough people in Petakh-Tikva knew Pinye-Ber and would have been able to identify his nephew, Yankl. Naturally, Shloyme did not have it reprinted. Nonetheless, the Goldenshteyns and Grinbergs remained close.[21]

In the January–April 1943 issue (3, nos. 2–1) of *Yidishe Shprakh* (The Yiddish language), the renowned Yiddish scholar, Yudl Mark, under the pseudonym M. Rekhtman, wrote a lengthy linguistic review of Pinye-Ber's work, which brought it to the attention of Yiddish scholars.[22] In his review, he writes, "Understandably, it is difficult to say whether all was taken 'as is' from his environs or whether there are his own creations here. Some words sound quite modern, like neologisms." Some Yiddish linguists and lexicographers have used this statement as cause to doubt the authenticity of Pinye-Ber's language. Yet they failed to notice a letter to the editor by Yankev-Ber Verlin which Mark, as the editor of the journal, printed in the July-December 1943 issue to dispel this very statement. Verlin, a native of the Ukraine, writes that in the numerous quotations from Pinye-Ber's autobiography mentioned in Mark's article, he saw no neologisms and thought that Pinye-Ber used "a thoroughly pure idiomatic Yiddish commonly spoken in our region."[23]

In the late 1950s or early 1960s, Pinye-Ber's son, Shloyme, went to Kfar-Chabad, the Chabad village founded in 1949 in the center of Israel, to see if

---

21 In 2002, Yankl's only surviving children, Dvora Ben-Ya'akov and Yosef "Yoske" Grinberg, granted permission to include their father's surname in this translation. Yoske said that his father, Yankl, was an exemplary person beyond reproach and that any complaints against him could only have been due to misunderstandings. Yoske related that his father was so pious and well regarded that the renowned Rabbi Avraham Yeshaya Karelitz (1878–1953) of Bnei-Brak, known as the Khazon Ish after his magnum opus, wrote in a letter at one point that he would only purchase wine produced by Yankl Grinberg of Petakh-Tikva. See Finkelman (1989:61) for more details.

22 See the Introduction (pp. 71–73) for a summary and discussion of Mark's review, which can be accssed online at https://www.hebrewbooks.org/43597.

23 See the Introduction (p. 72) for a more complete citation of the letter to the editor written by Yankev-Ber Verlin (Jacob B. Werlin, 1877–1945).

they were interested in reprinting his father's work, since they published books there. After all, Pinye-Ber was a Chabadnik and wrote about his visits to Lubavitch. They were unable to accommodate his request.

In 1986, Shloyme's granddaughter Tsviya (Bernfeld) Gelbshtein, along with her husband and son, spent a *Shabes* at the home of Rabbi Ya'akov Yehoshua Laufer, a prominent Chabadnik of Bnei-Brak. There she related that she had been inspired to become a Chabadnik by her great-grandfather, Pinye-Ber, who had written his autobiography.[24] Rabbi Laufer's son Mordechai Menashe Laufer (who later became a researcher and a prolific writer) was home from yeshiva that *Shabes*, and he later told the outstanding Chabad historian Yehoshua Mondshine about Pinye-Ber's book.[25] Mondshine promptly located it in the National Library of Israel, where he worked, and later that year included a chapter about it in the first volume of his three-volume work entitled *Kerem Khabad*. In that chapter, Mondshine summarized Pinye-Ber's autobiography and translated into Hebrew the sections describing his two visits to Lubavitch, thereby brining Pinye-Ber's work to the attention of Lubavitcher Hasidim at large.[26] Since then, virtually every article or book about Rabbi Menakhem-Mendl Schneerson (1789–1866), the third Rebbe of Chabad, has included Pinye-Ber's account of visiting his court in 1865 (chapter 16).

Over the years, various efforts have been made by Pinye-Ber's descendants to translate the book. In 1972, Dorothy (Cheslaw) Bengelsdorf (1907–1992), a first cousin of Ralph Goldeen's wife Freda, prepared a 39-page typed translation into English of the first seven chapters.[27] In the early 1980s, Pinye-Ber's granddaughter Dvora (Goldenshteyn) Gavrieli of kibbutz Givat Khayim Meukhad worked with a friend who knew Yiddish to prepare a 131-page typewritten Hebrew shortened translation which was circulated among the family in Israel. In 2003, Blaise Goldenstein of France had the autobiography translated into French; the 112-page translation was circulated among the family in France.[28]

The Shochet: A Memoir of Jewish Life in Ukraine and Crimea is the first complete translation of Pinye-Ber's autobiography into English. Volume 1, which was published in September 2023, has been favorably received in academic circles as well as by the Jewish community at large.

---

24 For more details regarding Tsviya Gelbshtein, see Appendix A1, p. 687.

25 Private correspondance in 2024 with Tsviya's sister Shifra Bernefeld of Petakh-Tikva.

26 The translator also first learned of Pinye-Ber's autobiography from *Kerem Khabad*, as mentioned on p. xvii.

27 Ralph N. Goldeen (1914–1984) was a son of Yosl (Joseph Goldeen), the author's son.

28 Blaise Goldenstein is the son of Jean-Pierre Goldenstein, the grandson of Mark Goldenstein, and the great-grandson of Isruel, the author's son.

Appendix B: Translations of Documents Written by the Author

Appendix B1: Hebrew Engagement Contract for His Daughter Nekhame (1897)

Handwritten by Pinkhes-Dov Goldenshteyn in Hebrew, the following tenaim *(engagement contract) formalized the wedding engagement between the author's daughter Nekhame and Menakhem-Mendl Brakhtman.*

Tenaim, *which literally means "conditions" in Hebrew, is an engagement contract that sets out the terms of the marriage, which include the commitment of marriage, the date of the wedding, the resources each side will bring to the marriage (e.g., the bedding, which was a major expense and was usually mentioned), the financial responsibility of each family to the other (e.g., the dowry, the wedding clothes, the wedding meal, etc.), and the penalties to be paid if either side breaks off the engagement. The reading and signing of the* tenaim *are a joyous occasion involving refreshments and the inviting of family and friends.*[1]

May it [i.e., their marriage] come up and sprout forth like a luscious garden and may the benevolent God approve of this match. "He who finds a wife finds great good."[2]

May the One Who determines the ultimate from the outset bestow a good name and lastingness to the obligations and conditions which were discussed and stipulated to by the two parties, that is, from one side, the

1 Many Orthodox rabbis today encourage that the writing of the *tenaim* take place immediately before the wedding, if at all, out of concern that if the engagement is broken, its binding effect under Jewish law would require a *get* (Jewish writ of divorce).

2 Proverbs 18:22.

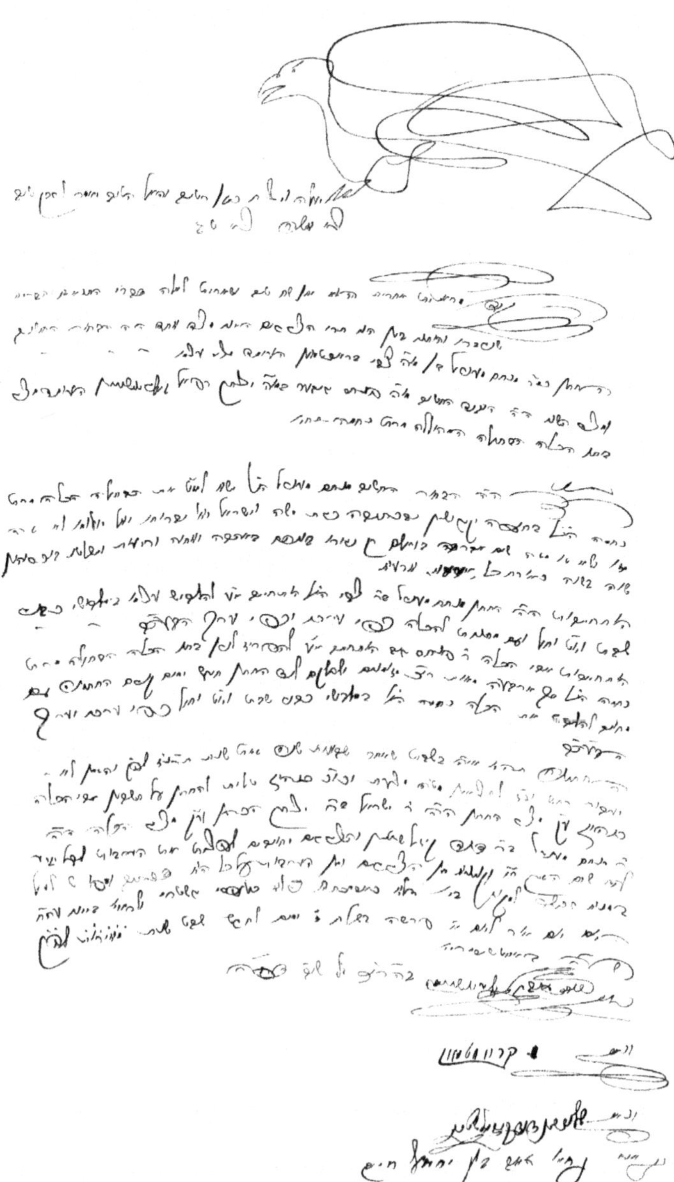

FIGURE 35. The Hebrew-language engagement contract written by Pinkhes-Dov Goldenshteyn on the occasion of his daughter Nekhame's engagement to Menakhem-Mendl Brakhtman in 1897. Goldenshteyn begins the document by extending the first letter into a drawing of a bird. In Scharfstein's *The Heder in the Life of the Jewish People* (1943:117) is reproduced a Hebrew-language letter decorated with a fantastically elaborate bird and a fish; he comments that many used to make such adornments at the beginnings of their letters. (Courtesy of Cynthia Brockman Unterberg of Westbury, New York.)

respectable young man, the groom Mr. Menakhem-Mendl son of the honorable Tsvi Brakhtman[3] who is representing himself, and from the second side the respectable, noble, and honorable Pinkhes-Dov-Ber[4] son of the honorable Yitskhok-Refuel Goldenshteyn who represents the praiseworthy maiden Miss Nekhame, may she live long.

Our bridegroom, namely the respectable young man, the above-mentioned Menakhem-Mendl, will marry, at an auspicious time, the maiden bride, the above-mentioned Miss Nekhame, with a *huppah* [i.e., wedding canopy], betrothal, and marriage contract, in accordance with the laws of Moses and Israel [i.e., the Jewish people]. They shall not avoid [their obligation] nor conceal [any of their possessions], neither he from her nor she from him, [nor] avoid [their obligation] in any conceivable manner, but they will finalize [all] with love, comradeship, and friendship, and they will share their possessions equally as done in each and every land.

The obligations of the above-mentioned bridegroom Menakhem-Mendl son of Reb Tsvi [include] attiring himself in honorable clothing for *Shobes, Yontef,* and weekdays, according to his means and the standards of his community. The obligation of the bride's father Reb Pinkhes-Dov [include] obligating himself to provide a generous dowry for his daughter, the above-mentioned maiden bride Miss Nekhame, in the amount of 400 silver rubles in cash to be given over to the hand of the bridegroom five days before the wedding. He also obligates himself to attire his daughter, the above-mentioned bride Nekhame, with honorable clothing for *Shobes, Yontef,* and weekdays, according to their means and the standards of their community.[5]

---

3 Though the engagement contract states that the name of Mendl's father was Tsvi, his complete name was Moyshe-Tsvi, as noted in the *ksube* (marriage contract) and elsewhere. Such details are not important in an engagement contract but are crucial in a *ksube*. Here, his father is given the honorific title of *morenu ha-rav* indicated by the abbreviation מו"ה, which literally means "our teacher, our rabbi," though he was not a rabbi. Many communities were accustomed to use this title in written documents for most married men, while actual rabbis were indicated using other terms.

4 The author writes his name here as פנחס דובער. The name דובער is not pronounced as Duber (as it would appear to be pronounced in Yiddish) but as Dov-Ber, being that it a variant manner of writing the names Dov (דוב) and Ber (בער) together. Dov is the Hebrew calque of the Yiddish name Ber, both meaning "bear."

5 In his autobiography (ch. 27, p. 550), the author writes that his daughter's clothing cost him 600 silver rubles, and the wedding (including the wedding meal) cost him 200 silver rubles.

God willing, the wedding will take place on the *Shobes*[6] following *Shvues* of this year 5657 and not past that time.[7] The fees for the officiating rabbi, cantor [at the *huppah*], and *shoykhet* [who will slaughter the animals used for the wedding feast], and musicians will be shared equally. The bed set, quilts, and pillows [will be provided] as is customary.[8] The bridegroom's *talis* will be paid for by the bride's father.[9] The guarantor for the bridegroom's party is Yisruel, the son of Yitskhok *Ha-Kohen.*[10] The guarantor for the bride's party is Menakhem-Mendl, the son of Duvid Kizelshteyn. Both parties are responsible for compensating the guarantors that no loss, God forbid, should befall them. Both parties and guarantors made a binding agreement explicitly on all the above in a valid matter and neither as a halfhearted agreement nor as a meaningless transaction. As proof, we have signed today, Saturday night, the 7th of the month of *Shvat* 5657.[11]

Here in Bakhchisaray.

Signed: Pinkhes-Dov Goldenshteyn, son of Reb Y. R., of blessed memory, the local *shoykhet*

Signed: M. Brakhtman

Signed: Shulem, son of Duvid Kizelshteyn

Signed: Nekhemye-Z'ev, son of Yekhiel-Khaym[12]

---

6 In Tsarist Russia and other parts of Eastern Europe, most Jewish weddings were celebrated on Fridays before the onset of *Shabes*. The Friday night *Shabes* meal doubled as the wedding feast. Nonetheless, it was common practice to write in the *tenaim* that the wedding was occurring on *Shabes* itself.

7 Friday, the 11th of *Sivan* 5657 (June 11, 1897). The wedding did not take place then but a month later, on Sunday, the 4th of *Tamuz* (July 4, 1897), as indicated in the *ksube*, i.e., the marriage contract. Both the original *tenaim* and the *ksube* are in the possession of Nekhame's granddaughter, Cynthia (Brockman) Unterberg.

8 Traditionally, the bride's family supplied these items.

9 Traditionally, the bride's family purchased the bridegroom's *talis*. Eastern European Jewish men (and their descendants) traditionally begin wearing a *talis* upon marrying.

10 *Ha-Kohen* (i.e., the *Kohen*) is not a surname but denotes that he was a member of the priestly subdivision of Jews, who have certain additional obligations in Judaism.

11 January 10, 1897.

12 This witness also signed the *ksube*.

Appendix B2: Hebrew Ethical Will (1920)

Goldenshteyn wrote an ethical will in June 1920, which was likely motivated by three recent events in his life: First, having completed writing a Torah scroll in August 1919, he attempted to entice his children to move to the Holy Land by promising that whoever moved there would inherit the Torah scroll. No doubt, he was trying to encourage their move to the Holy Land because he saw that there they had a better chance of remaining connected to Judaism and having their children marry Jews, particularly since his grandson, Martin Brockman, had just married a non-Jew in November 1919 in Portland, Oregon. Secondly, he had just finished writing his autobiography in January 1920; he added only a few final pages in 1925 and 1929. Not believing that his autobiography would be printed in his lifetime, he specified in his will that he was leaving the manuscript to his son Refuel (Raphael Goldenstein) who had promised to have it printed. Finally, he married for a third time in January 1920; hence, article 12 of the will provides for his third wife, Bashe.

Additionally, a contributing factor motivating his writing his ethical will was likely his mistaken belief that he was almost eighty years old, when he was only seventy-one.[1] *With none of his children nearby, Goldenshteyn stresses his fear of dying alone and his desire to have his children, most of whom had strayed from Jewish observance, follow in his ways.*

It is unknown whether the author distributed copies of his will to his children, but if he did, then perhaps it succeeded in influencing them to move or visit him in Palestine. His daughter, Nekhame Brakhtman, her husband, and their three children moved there in 1921 (where they remained until 1926–1927), his son Refuel visited him in 1922 from America, and his son Shloyme and his family permanently immigrated to Palestine in 1923.

Though the original handwritten document no longer exists, a typewritten version, signed by Nekhame but unsigned by Goldenshteyn, was graciously furnished by Shloyme's granddaughter Shifra Bernfeld of Petakh-Tikva, from which this translation was made. Upon being shown a copy of the Hebrew will in 2005, Gershon Nof (1939–2024), the compiler of a collection of Hebrew ethical wills entitled Tsivita tsedek: tsavaot shel gedole Yisrael, *commented that he was impressed by*

1 For details, see the Introduction, pp. 67–70.

its complete originality, since so many ethical wills were largely copied from earlier such works or from didactic Jewish ethical literature. He was also impressed by the warmth with which Goldenshteyn wrote it as well as the great care that he took in ensuring that his widow would be provided for:

Your compassion, God, is great. In Your justice may You let me live long and good years to serve You and to forever cause pleasure before Your holy throne.

A person, being only human, is subject to all kinds of accidents and unfortunate mishaps, etc., which may result in death . . . And how much more so, a person such as myself at present, who has already reached the age of "strength,"[2] having already achieved the age of seventy-eight, close to the age of "strength," with God's help. Most certainly, an old and weak person like myself, for whom one day does not pass in which he does not feel some sort of a weakness or feebleness in his body and whose strength wanes from day to day—a person like this is obligated to remember that he will not live forever. Perhaps his end is very near, and death lurks behind him. Perhaps an accident will occur to me that will bring on sudden death and thereby not afford me the opportunity to leave over my directives to my remaining family, as mandated by Jewish tradition from time immemorial. And my sudden death is so much more probable today, during this time of upheaval, world war, and mêlée that has descended upon the world and that is liable to bring a holocaust and total destruction in a moment on a nation and on the individual together. One does not know what tomorrow will bring, particularly for an elderly and weak person oppressed with pain who suffers, such as I currently do. Being bereft of all his dear, beloved children, may they live long, who are spread in every direction, even in the far West, their elderly father thinks about them from the East. He is abandoned and left alone the entire day by all of his sons, daughters, grandsons, granddaughters, sons-in-law, daughters-in-law, and, in general, from all members of his esteemed family. He sits alone all day locked in the settlement of Petakh-Tikva, afflicted with various illnesses under a yoke of affliction, poverty, and distress that is too great to bear. Someone like me must definitely act quickly in order not to miss the opportunity, God forbid, to remember to direct his family while he is still alive and healthy, thank God, to fulfill that which is written in the verse, "For I have singled him [Abraham] out, that he may instruct his children and his

2 The Mishna (Avot 5:21) states that the age of strength is eighty. As mentioned on p. 762 above, the author was actually seventy-one years old. For details, see the Introduction, pp. 67–70.

posterity... to perform righteousness and justice..."[3] Hence, I decided today to take my pen in hand and this sheet of paper upon which to record my thoughts, my desires, and the will of my heart for my surviving sons and daughters. This should serve as a directive to teach them the path that they should follow after my death and the manner in which they should conduct themselves and to inform them of the inheritance that they should be bequeathed. I feel that it is best to write these words down now while I am still alive; while my body, all of my limbs, and my physical capabilities are still healthy; and while my mental faculties are still sound, i.e., while my intellect is still clear, pure, and precise as it was yesterday, the day before, and all the preceding days that I have lived on this earth. Being of sound mind, I approach this task of my own free will, independently, and without any pressure, provocation, or outside incitement. Therefore, I am writing these words of my own free will, as mentioned above, to direct my surviving sons and daughters through all that I am writing here on these pages [that they will hold] in front of them. I hereby direct my heirs not to alter my directives, will, desires, or any part of any details discussed herein. Know, my sons and daughters, that your abiding by my directives will be a comfort to my soul, the soul of your father. Whoever alters this will be held liable, and I will not forgive them in any manner...

Article 1: With the kindness of God above, I was privileged to beget and raise five sons and two daughters, may they live long. Altogether, they are seven in number. The eldest of the male children is Isruel-Burikh, a *shoykhet* in Feodosiya, and cantor and *moyel* there in the province of Taurida, Crimea. My next son is Itskhok-Yosef Goldeen who lives in the city of Anaconda and is a businessman who owns a store that sells furniture and home furnishings.[4] My next son is Yankev Goldeen,[5] who also resides in America, in the city of Portland, Oregon, and has a store that sells furniture and home furnishings, like his brother. My next son is the intellectual, the wise, and the accomplished Refuel, who obtained the honorable position of rabbi in the community of Tacoma, Washington, in America. He is known as Rabbi Raphael Goldenstein. My next son, the youngest of the brothers, the son of my old age, is Shloyme, who resides in Russia, in Yekaterinoslav. He is a pharmacist (*provizor* in Russian) by profession, and is erudite and well known. And these are the names of my daughters, may they live long: the eldest one's name is Nekhame, the wife of Menakhem-Mendl Brakhtman, in the city of Feodosiya, in the province of Taurida, Crimea; and the youngest one's name is Rukhl Goldenshteyn, who is erudite and an

3 Genesis 18:19.

4 Known as Joseph Goldeen, he lived at the time in Anaconda, Montana.

5 Yankev was known as Jacob Goldeen.

intellectual who completed her study of law, which is called jurisprudence.[6] Her place of residence is Paris, France. These are my seven dear children, fruit of my loins, the inheritors of my estate and all that is mine and under my possession. They are the ones mentioned above by name and place. Upon my death, they and their agents will be the legal inheritors of their father's estate, as per Jewish law.

Article 2: Now, after all that was mentioned above, I am turning to you, my children, my inheritors, my sons, my daughters, my grandsons, my granddaughters, that you should accept these directives and fulfill my will and desires.

A. You should always remember the rock from which you were hewn, be proud of the righteousness of your ancestors, and to go in their ways.

B. Remember to always seek righteousness and to be just, good, and proper in God's eyes. Bestow kindness, both materially and monetarily, upon every person. Be compassionate to the poor, the oppressed, orphans, the bereft, and wretched, with all types of generosity and compassion. You should involve yourselves with them and reach out to them with help at the time of their pain as you saw with your own eyes in your parents' home.

C. Just as I taught you to do only good, even to those who are not of the Jewish faith, so you should teach your children not to divert from this good and fine way all of their lives.

D. Observe very carefully the laws of *Shobes* and the Jewish holidays in order that they should not be desecrated, God forbid, through your actions. In regard to all aspects of the house (in general), you should also conduct yourselves by keeping kosher and observing the Jewish religion just as I taught you from your youth and as you saw in the house of your parents and your prestigious and noble family. So should you and your descendants conduct yourselves all your lives. If you do this and you conduct yourselves as I instruct you, God will grant you success all of your lives, forever, in all of your endeavors. You will be blessed by God wherever you turn. You will be successful and enjoy all manner of good, all the days of your lives. May your days and years be long, including all of your descendants and their families. And your good name will spread forth to all the four corners of the earth, and

6 Rukhl, known as Raissa "Raya" Goldinstein, never completed her law degree. For details, see Appendix A2, pp. 718–719.

your Jewish brethren, the people of your nation and religion, will say, "Lucky are those who begot you." Amen, so may it be His will.

Article 3: These are the details of my estate that I have to bequeath to my sons and daughters mentioned above, with the help of God, blessed be He. In *Kislev* 5674,[7] I merited to come to the Holy Land and settled in Petakh-Tikva with my small family.[8] I acquired for myself a house and a courtyard in the above-mentioned settlement of Petakh-Tikva with the money that I had in cash. I acquired the house and courtyard from my friend, Mr. Moyshe Slor, for 9,000 francs in cash.[9] The layout of the house is as follows: facing the street are four rooms, besides the porch and a large kitchen; on the side of the kitchen is a raised section designated as a washroom, with a tub and a shower, which is called a *tush* in Yiddish; below the raised section is a storage pantry and a closet to place kitchenware and household utensils. In the courtyard, to the west, is built another residential dwelling, which consists of three rooms, a kitchen, and a porch.[10] On the south side of the courtyard are three stables, which are used for horses, domestic animals, and other residential uses. Eucalyptus trees are also present for beauty and for health—to purify the air with them, as is the custom in all the courtyards here in this settlement. Those trees, eleven in number, belong solely to me and no stranger has a part in them. This is the estate, which God, in His great goodness and kindness, has granted me and bequeathed to us in the Holy Land. And now I have the merit, with God's will, to bequeath it to my surviving sons and daughters. Hence, after my death, you should apportion it among you, from the oldest of the brothers to the youngest of the sisters, in seven equal and complete portions. Upon inheriting it, they should divide it equally in order to merit the acquisition of my estate in the Holy Land, in the above-mentioned settlement of Petakh-Tikva, that I bequeath you.

Since I know the generous hearts and good nature of my children, I have confidence that my sons will not be insulted that I gave equal portions in my inheritance to my daughters. And I am confident in the justice of their good hearts that they will certainly relinquish the portion that legally should be theirs and forfeit from their portions to allow their sisters, my daughters, to be

---

7 As mentioned in ch. 30, p. 605, of his autobiography, the exact date of the author's arrival was *Rosh-Khodesh Kislev* 5674, i.e., November 30, 1913.

8 The author arrived with his second wife Feyge, her stepmother Hadassah "Udye" Yudelevitsh, and his first wife's niece, Reyzl Hershkovitsh (later known as Shoshana Grinberg).

9 Khaym-Moyshe Slor (1859–1946) was one of the founders of Petakh-Tikva (Tidhar, 1947:1:307). The address of the author's house was 64 Rothschild Blvd.

10 The two residential dwellings were connected by a two-story wooden structure with a staircase. See Appendix A1, pp. 677–678, for more details and the drawing of the house in ch. 31, p. 628, figure 26.

included in their father's inheritance in the Holy Land so that the sisters should also have a portion in the Holy Land, which is very precious to them.[11] With their good will, they will divide with their sisters, my daughters, equal portions, in accordance with my strong desire in this matter and in accordance with my wishes. They should not change my words to go against my will. Whoever alters this will be held liable.

Article 4: Each and every one of the inheritors or their representatives are able and permitted to give as a present or to forfeit their portion of their father's inheritance, i.e., one-seventh of the entire inheritance, so that each of my seven children, my inheritors, who are mentioned above, is permitted to give his portion of the inheritance which is due him to his second, third, fourth, or fifth brother or also to one of his two sisters, the older or the younger one, according to his good will and the desire of his heart. He can forfeit a portion of his inheritance to give as a present, also for payment, or any other agreement decided among themselves. Since I know that all my children, my inheritors, are all busy and occupied with their businesses in foreign lands and are unable to come to *Erets-Isruel* to settle, perhaps one or two of them will be able to come to *Erets-Isruel* at some future date to settle and dwell in the land of our holy forefathers. Therefore, I have permitted those remaining in foreign lands to give their portion to those who will be settling in *Erets-Isruel* as a present or for payment. But everything should be done with the agreement and will of all the inheritors; they should give their signatures on this agreement as concrete evidence that they were not coerced, then this will be done according to my heart's desire and my will.[12]

Article 5: Even though I permitted and allowed them the ability to forfeit their portions between themselves, from one to the other, whether by means of gift or payment, and even if through this the inheritance will go to only one of the brothers or one of the sisters, even though I permitted them to do this between themselves as mentioned above, nevertheless, I will not permit in any way whatsoever for anyone of them to give his portion or a part of his portion to a stranger who does not number among my descendants or inheritors, who are mentioned individually above by name in Article 1. None of you are allowed or permitted, God forbid, to give from his portion as a gift or for payment through

---

11 According to Jewish laws of inheritance, the firstborn, if a male, receives a double portion, the other sons receive single portions, and the daughters receive no inheritance, unless explicitly stated to the contrary in the will. In the author's case, he was not considered to have a firstborn son since his oldest child was a daughter who died in infancy.

12 See Appendix A1, p. 680, for details as to the division of the author's property among his offspring.

sale to a Jewish stranger who is not from among my inheritors because this will cause controversy and strife between them and will cause them to forget about inheriting their father's portion in the Holy Land, which he gave them as an inheritance. In any case, they have no permission in any way whatsoever to permit themselves to do this. Even if all the inheritors will agree and, God forbid, all the inheritors will stipulate in a legal contract to do the above, even so, I, for my part, refuse and do not give permission to do this in any way, manner, or form, and I will not forgive anyone who will go against my word and will do this. It is against my will to introduce some strange party among my children, my inheritors, and thereby bring division among them and disturb their brotherliness and peace, God forbid. Therefore, I am not able to allow them to do this in any manner whatsoever.

Article 6: If all of them or some of them will not be able to or will not want to come to the Holy Land to settle on the inheritance that I give them, they have permission to rent out the courtyard and the houses for a rental that they will agree upon. The rental of the courtyard and the houses will be divided among them yearly. Each one has permission to dedicate from his portion of the rental, which is due him according to his portion, the money that is due him, to a charitable cause or to one of the charitable societies that are found here in Petakh-Tikva. But he has no permission to donate his portion of the rental outside of *Erets-Isruel*, i.e., that he should not take a part of the rental of the estate and donate it to some charity outside of *Erets-Isruel*. They are only able to donate from the rental of the houses to a charitable cause in Petakh-Tikva, as mentioned above. Also, they have no permission to completely sell the courtyard or the houses to strangers, who are neither my inheritors nor their representatives, even if all the inheritors will agree. The inheritance should not go to any strangers in any manner, as mentioned above.

Article 7: From my entire library that I had in Russia, I brought only a small portion to the Holy Land. I left all my bookcases, which contained the Talmud, *poskim*,[13] Maimonides, *midrashim*,[14] the Hebrew Bible, *Turim*,[15] etc., there in the town in which I dwelled, Bakhchisaray, where I lived for almost thirty-five years and served as cantor, *shoykhet*, and *moyel*. There they begged, pleaded, and beseeched me to leave my books there together with the bookcases as a

13 *Poskim* refers to books of rabbinical decisions.

14 The *midrashim* are the classic collections of the Sages' homiletical teachings on the Torah.

15 The *Turim* is the *Arba'ah Turim*, a monumental Jewish legal code compiled by Rabbi Ya'akov ben Asher (1270–c. 1340).

remembrance of me.[16] I consented to their request and left the books in the *bes-medresh* so that it should be available to them in the synagogue (where I prayed as long as I lived there) for all who would like to consult them or study them, thereby being a holy remembrance of me.[17] Only a very few books remain from those books which I put aside for myself, from those few books that I brought here to Petakh-Tivkah, because most were stolen and robbed from me at the time of the occupation, crisis, and war that took place here. Hence, I am bequeathing to you, my dear ones, the small number of books that remain. You may either divide them equally among yourselves or forfeit your portion to be given to the oldest and most learned among you or to be given entirely or in part as a present to a synagogue, according to your will. So have you permission to do.

Article 8: All the furniture, home furnishings, dressers, chairs, tables, beds, quilts, pillows, blankets, bedspreads, all types of utensils, cups, plates, metal and copper pots and pans, various earthenware, and anything pertaining to the kitchen, everything is an inheritance for you, my dear children. You have permission to sell them, obtain their full value, and then to equally divide the money among you, or to give your portion as a present to someone, a poor person or a friend, even if he is not among my inheritors. You have permission to do any of the above, but without any arguments or hard feelings, God forbid, only with peace, calmness, and goodwill. May you merit all good things, amen.

Article 9: Remaining in my possession from my late wife, Feyge, of blessed memory, are gold earrings inlaid with precious stones, called [in Yiddish] *goldene dimentene oyring*;[18] a fox-fur coat, called *fiksener mantl*; and also one large, good down comforter, called a *pekheve perene*. She requested from me before she passed away that all of these items be given to her offspring: her only son and his family, his wife and his children.[19] I promised her that I would send all of those items to her offspring via the post office. Until now, the borders have not been open, so I have not had the opportunity to send them to the designated individuals. Even now that over four years have passed since her death, all the borders are still closed. Therefore, I am now instructing you, my dear inheritors, that you should do this and send those items, as I promised my late wife, of blessed memory. When I die, if I have not had the opportunity to send them

---

16 With the destruction of Bakhchisaray's synagogue in the 1920s or 1930s by the Soviets, all of these religious Hebrew books would certainly have been destroyed as well.

17 Both *bes-medresh* and synagogue are apparently referring to the same building in Bakhchisaray.

18 Literally, "golden diamond earrings."

19 Feyge's son was Duvid Kreyzberg, who was married to Klara. They had two daughters, Basya and Musya. See Appendix A4, pp. 731–732, for details.

to those individuals, my inheritors after me shall do this. It is a mitzvah to fulfill the words of the deceased and the will of an elderly father who instructs his inheritors. Hence, I am convinced that my children will fulfill the words of their elderly father and will do as I instructed them in order to fulfill the words of the deceased and to send the above-mentioned items to her only child, Mr. Duvid Kreyzberg, who resides in Feodosiya, in the province of Taurida in the Crimea. May God bless you with all that is good and many long years, great enjoyment, satisfaction from your children, peace, serenity, and security forever. Amen, so may it be.

Article 10: My *Megilla*, which was written on high-quality vellum, is very dear to me because it is the fruit of the work of my youth, and I have read from it every Purim in public all the years of my life from the age of twenty-five until the present, when I am seventy-eight.[20] I am leaving it as a remembrance to my dear learned son, the intellectual, Refuel, may he live long, who has been installed as a rabbi in Tacoma, Washington, America. I am giving this *Megillah* to him as a gift, an inheritance. I am also giving to Refuel, my son, my autobiography, which is in manuscript form in my posession, in five parts, and he will have it printed, as he has already promised me, and he will definitely fulfill his promise, if he will only be able to do so. May God give him the merit to be able to do so.[21]

Article 11: Blessed is God above, whose kindness overwhelms me. He gave me the merit to fulfill my oath that I vowed when I still resided in Russia to personally write a Torah scroll. On *Rosh-Khodesh Elul* 5677,[22] I was privileged to begin writing the Torah scroll, and on the 16th of *Menakhem Av* 5679, I merited to finish it and give it to the synagogue here in this settlement.[23] I wrote this Torah with my own hands from the beginning of Genesis to the end of the last verse, "before the eyes of all Israel."[24] Also, with my own hands, I carved and whittled into the Torah rollers my name, my surname, that I wrote it, when it was written, and the name of the settlement.[25] Now I can give thanks to God for all of the goodness and kindness that he did for me. I am now bequeathing the Torah scroll to you as an inheritance. Each one of you has a part in this Torah

---

20 In ch. 14, p. 225, of his autobiography, the author notes that he wrote his *Megilla* in 1865 when he was sixteen. The current whereabouts of the Megillah are unknown.

21 The author's autobiography was printed in 1928–1929 in three parts, including an addendum to part three regarding his years in Palestine.

22 August 18–19, 1917. In ch. 31, p. 629, the author writes that he started writing the Torah scroll on the 17th of *Elul*, i.e., September 4, 1917.

23 August 12, 1919. In ch. 34, p. 659, the author writes that he celebrated its completion on the 15th of *Menakhem Av*, i.e., August 11, 1919.

24 Deuteronomy 34:12.

25 The inscription is described more fully in ch. 34, p. 659.

scroll which was written by your aged father, as mentioned above. None of you has a greater part in this Torah scroll than another and no one has more rights to it than any of the other inheritors, but each one of you has equal rights and one equal portion. But if one of the siblings will come to establish residency in *Erets-Isruel,* then the right to the Torah scroll will be given to him as something that belongs to him himself, if he wants. For example, he could take it out of the synagogue in Petakh-Tikva, and place it in the city or settlement where he lives in the Holy Land. And if his will shall be that the Torah scroll which he inherited from his father should be with him in one place, then he has permission and should do according to his will, because he will then be the inheritor since he merited to settle in the Holy Land.[26] But he has no right or permission to take it entirely out of the Holy Land to a foreign land; not him, nor any of the inheritors, have any permission to remove it from the Holy Land to a foreign land. But in the Holy Land, all the inheritors who will come to settle permanently have the right to take it from place to place in the land itself as mentioned above but not outside of *Erets-Isruel,* God forbid, unless there arises some extraordinary circumstance necessitating it being saved from theft, robbery, or some other disaster or circumstance, God forbid. In such a case, they shall ask a wise person and do as he shall guide them.

Article 12: Approximately six months ago, I married a woman in my old age.[27] She is a modest, generous woman who serves me faithfully with compassion. It is proper and fitting to show your appreciation to her and to reward her accordingly. Therefore, I am instructing you, my beloved sons, that each one of you should give her five Egyptian liras, which is used in *Erets-Isruel.*[28] This will result in her receiving twenty-five Egyptian liras from my sons, my inheritors, as gratuity and payment for the *ksube,* which is due her by rabbinical law.[29] If she would like to dwell in my house, as long as she is a widow, you, my inheritors, shall give her a nice, good room as her dwelling place in my house and courtyard

---

26 Since the author's son, Shloyme, was the only one of his children to permanently settle in Palestine, the Torah scroll became his. Originally, the author kept his Torah scroll at Petakh-Tikva's Great Synagogue on Khovavei Tsion St. With the opening, in 1927, of the Nakhalat Yisrael Synagogue at 3 Khovevei Tsion St. a quarter mile from the author's house, the author moved his Torah scroll there. After the author's death, Shloyme continued attending the Nakhalat Yisrael Synagogue and eventually gave them the Torah scroll, where it remains until today.

27 In ch. 34, p. 666, the author writes that he married his third wife, Basye-Dvoyre "Bashe" Yirme, on the 20th of *Teyves* 5680, i.e., January 11, 1920.

28 Upon the conquest of Palestine by the British in 1918, the Egyptian lira (pound) was made legal tender. Egypt was a British protectorate from 1914 until 1922. The British began to implement Palestinian currency only in 1927.

29 A *ksube* (*ketubah* in Modern Hebrew) is a Jewish wedding contract.

that you inherited. You have no permission to evict her from my house, but she should live in my house in a special room for her sake all of her life or as long as she wants to live in that house.[30]

The portable items, namely pillows and quilts, clothing, utensils, and furniture, which she brought into my house when she joined my household, only she herself shall use and she shall take with her all of the above if she shall leave my house or if she wants to sell them because they belong solely to her. One wardrobe, one table, one bed, and three chairs are hers. And everything that she says is hers, believe her, because I trust her more than 100 witnesses, and she would not lie, God forbid, in order to cheat you out of anything.

Article 13: One more holy obligation that I promised for my sake and for the sake of my soul, I place upon you, my sons: I promised to donate 1,000 francs to charitable institutions here in Petakh-Tikva, to the four associations that I will specify by name: the burial society, the interest-free loan society, the benevolent society for the ill,[31] and the hospitality society. The details of each of these contributions are as follows: to the burial society, a total of 300 francs—200 francs to their treasury and 100 francs for plots, burial needs, shrouds; to the interest-free loan society, 300 francs to their treasury for them to bestow kindness on every unfortunate, needy, hapless, and suffering person; to the benevolent society for the ill, 200 francs to their treasury to support and help the weak and sick, unfortunate and oppressed to find doctors, medication, and all kinds of help for their pain; and 200 francs to the hospitality society. A total of 1,000 francs will be contributed to the four above-mentioned institutions. I am appointing you, my dear inheritors, upon my death to pay those associations without delay the 1,000 francs in cash to each society as is due them.

All of this was made and written with good will, a healthy body and soul, a clear and precise mind and lucid thought, and good and clear reasoning. Hence, this last will and testament shall not be voided, and its power shall not be weakened by any manner of claims or arguments in the world—not by means of any missing or extra letters or words, smudges, erasures, drops of ink,

---

30 After the author's death, she continued to live in the household of his son, Shloyme, until her death in 1934. See Appendix A5 for details.

31 *Linat tsedek* (literally "The righteous bedside" in Hebrew) in the original. Yakobzon (1986:59) describes this society in Petakh-Tikva in the 1910s and 1920s as being, "comprised of male and female volunteers who would feed the sick in their own homes. These volunteers had a number of utensils at their disposal, such as enemas, cups used in cupping therapy, thermometers, etc. When necessary, the volunteers would even take turns spending the night with the ill in their homes and extend any possible assistance to them. Among the righteous women in this organization were those who would go around to all the houses in town to collect funds, clothing, and food for the poor in need." Such organizations were essential in towns like Petakh-Tikva, which did not have hospitals.

or ink bleedings due to the poor quality of the ink. Rather, everything should be judged and interpreted for the benefit of the holders of this will and against any complainants. The strength of this will, like the strength of all wills which are made according to the rules of our rabbis and not like an unintended agreement or a form document, should not be tampered with or altered. Everything is valid and legal. And on this I sign on Tuesday, in which we read the Torah portion including the verse, "From Matanah to Nakhaliel, and from Nakhaliel to Bamot,"[32] the 6th of *Tamuz* 5680,[33] here in the settlement of Petakh-Tikva, near Jaffa, signed Pinkhes-Dov-Ber Goldenshteyn, the son of my teacher, Reb Yitskhok-Refuel, who was the *shoykhet* and a cantor in the city of Bakhchisaray in the Crimea, in the province of Taurida, in the country of Russia, and he settled here in Petakh-Tikva in the year 5674 in the month of *Kislev*.[34]

[Place for the Author's Signature]

I, the undersigned, Nekhame Brakhtman, the daughter of the late Pinkhes-Dov Goldenshteyn, attest with my complete will that I have no objections to the last will and testament of my late father, dated in his hand and signed by him on the 6th of *Tamuz* 5680, in the settlement of Petakh-Tikva. My desire is for this will, with all of its articles, to be executed, and I am requesting the chief rabbis of the area of Jaffa and Tel-Aviv to certify this will and to give it power according to its authority by act of the King and his council in the year 1922.[35]

[Nekhame Brakhtman's signature in Yiddish]

[Undated Stamp in Hebrew and English stating:] Rabbi M.A. Kaplan, Rabbi in Boro Park[36]

---

32 Numbers 21:19. This verse is part of a section discussing the journeys taken by the Jews in the desert under Moses's leadership and is often translated as "The gift went to the valley, and from the valley to the heights." The author uses it here as an allusion to the subject at hand; Matanah denotes a "gift" and Nakhaliel also denotes an "inheritance." This verse is similarly used in Mishna (Avot 6:2).

33 June 22, 1920.

34 December 1913.

35 The two chief rabbis of Tel-Aviv/Jaffa at that time were Rabbi Shlomo Aronson (1863–1935) and Rabbi Bentsion Meir Khai Uziel (1880–1953). The King of England at that time was King George V. Nekhame's statement notes that her father, who died in 1930, was deceased by that time; hence, she must have brought it before the chief rabbis of Tel-Aviv/Jaffa during her almost year-long visit to Palestine in 1933–1934.

36 Nekhame Brakhtman (changed to Brockman in America) lived in Brooklyn from 1926 to her death in 1955. In Brooklyn, she brought her father's will to Rabbi Mordechai Aaron Kaplan (1889–1951), whose stamp is imprinted on the type-written copy. Rabbi Kaplan was a prominent rabbi in the Boro Park section of Brooklyn where he served as the rabbi of Congregation Bnei Yehuda on 5311 Sixteenth Ave from 1926 until his death.

Appendix B3: Family Letters

Below are the translations of twelve letters, including ten from Pinkhes-Dov "Pinye-Ber" Goldenshteyn, from 1926 until 1930, and two from his son Isruel from 1914 and 1939. Almost all were translated from the Yiddish and were addressed to Pinye-Ber's children in America. The two exceptions were his son Isruel's 1914 letter written to his father in Palestine in Hebrew and the section of Pinye-Ber's October 30, 1930 letter addressed to his grandson, Victor Brockman, which was mostly written in Hebrew. An ellipsis in square brackets [. . .] has been used to indicate illegible words or omitted phrases or sentences deemed to be too personal for publication.

The main individuals mentioned in the letters are listed below, along with their places of residence from 1926 until 1930. See also Appendices D2 and D3 for genealogical charts of the family. For more details regarding the author's children, see Appendix A2, pp. 689–725.

- This is the list of Pinye-Ber's children.
    - Isruel-Burekh, usually called Isruel (known as Israel Goldenstein in France), and his wife Gitl (spelled Guitel in French) lived in Feodosiya until immigrating to France in 1935. Their four children were:
        - Freyde, nicknamed Freydl (aka Frida in Russian), her husband Yosef (Joseph "Osya") Pozwolski (1891–1969);
        - Avrum-Duvid "Avrum" (aka Avraam in Russian) and his wife Pola;
        - Moyshe (aka Mosya in Russian) and his wife Frida;
        - Mordekhai "Motl" (aka Mark and nicknamed Mara in Russian), his wife Lucie.
    - Nekhame, nicknamed Nekhamele (aka Nadya in Russian), was married to Menakhem-Mendl "Mendl" Brakhtman. Nekhame and her sons Victor and Mark left Palestine and arrived in Providence, Rhode Island, on April 4, 1926. They first stayed a short while in Boston and then in New York before traveling to California, where her brothers lived. Victor moved to Brooklyn in August 1926, and Nekhame

and Mark followed suit in January 1927. Mendl arrived in America in early 1927. Nekhame and Mendl's oldest son, Moyshe (Martin) had immigrated in 1914 to Portland, Oregon and changed his name from Brachtman to Brockman in 1919. Nekhame and her other two sons also changed their name to Brockman in the late 1920s. Only their sons residing in America are mentioned in the letters:
        - Moyshe (Martin) of Portland, Oregon;
        - Mordekhai (Mark, nicknamed Mara in Russian);
        - Avigdor (Victor, nicknamed Vitya and Vityake).
    - Itskhok-Yosef, generally called Yosef and nicknamed Yosl (aka Joseph Goldeen in English), of San Jose, California, and his wife Itl "Itele" (Edith), who was his cousin (see below).
    - Yankev "Yankl" (aka Jacob "James" Goldeen in English) and his wife Fanya (aka Fannie in English) of Oakland, California. He was called by the Russian nickname of Yasha.
    - Refuel "Refulikl" (Raphael Goldenstein) was a Reform rabbi in Lancaster, Pennsylvania and moved in October 1928 to Brooklyn, New York.
    - Rukhl (Raissa, nicknamed Raya in Russian) Goldinstein of Paris, France.
    - Shloyme (aka Shlomo in Modern Hebrew) of Petakh-Tikva and his wife Etya and their two daughters, Dvora and Aliza.

- Bashe, Pinye-Ber's third wife, whom Pinye-Ber refers to as Aunt Bashe to his children. (Stepmothers are referred to by the title of "Aunt" in Yiddish.)
- Itele (Edith) Goldeen was not only the wife of the author's son Yosef (Joseph) Goldeen but was also the daughter of Itsl (Isaac) Goldstein, Pinye-Ber's nephew. Her siblings are also mentioned in the letters. (For more details, see Appendix A3, pp. 726-729.):
        - Jennie Shapiro (1893–1976) (later changed to Sherwood) of Los Angeles;
        - Bertha Glikbarg (1894–1972) of Salinas, California;
        - Samuel Goldeen (1895–1984) of Lincoln, California.

- Reyzl (née Hershkovitsh) Grinberg (1898–1962), the niece of Pinye-Ber's first wife, Freyde, and her husband Yankl Grinberg (ca. 1887–1979). They are mentioned extensively in the author's autobiography (chapter 30-34). The following are Reyzl's close relatives mentioned in the letters.

- Elke Hershkovitsh (ca. 1870–1955) was Reyzl's mother and the sister-in-law of Freyde, the author's first wife. Elke immigrated from Romania to Palestine in 1923, where she remarried Dov Shof (ca. 1865–1946).
- Freyde (aka Frida), Reyzl's sister. She married (and later divorced) a man named Shof, whose father Dov later married Freyde's mother, Elke.
- Sheyndl "Sheyndele" (aka Yafa in Hebrew) (ca. 1911–2002), Reyzl's sister. She married a man named Yerushalmi.

- Isruel (Israel) Chaplick (1875–1971) of New York City, whose late wife, Feyge, was Pinye-Ber's grandniece.[1] His two daughters are also mentioned in the letters:
  - Reyzl (Rose "Rozele") Budiansky;
  - Dvoyre (Dora), later married to Gershon Asculai.

- Sose "Sosele" (Sophie Grover, ca. 1860–1941), Pinye-Ber's first cousin, the daughter of his maternal uncle Pinkhes Gredenitsky. Her

---

1 Israel Chaplick moved with his family from Tirsapol to Odessa in about 1904, where his daughter Khana died at the age of one. During the famine of 1921–1923 in the Ukraine, his wife Feyge died in April 1922 along with their two sons Monye and Yakov. Israel was then only left with his oldest and youngest children, Rose and Dora. Rose and her husband Louis Budiansky arrived in America in 1921–1922 and went to Murfreesboro, Tennessee, where Rose managed a rooming house. The Budianskys subsequently moved to New York City, where their son Bernard was born in 1925 and Rose worked as a sewing-machine operator. Israel and Dora crossed most of Europe on foot and arrived in 1923–1924 in Quebec City, Canada, where Israel worked for a while at the historic Château Frontenac hotel before moving to Montreal. In 1927, they moved to New York City at Rose's behest since she was now divorced and needed help raising her son. In 1941, Rose remarried her second cousin, David Carmel (originally Berditshevsky). In 1932, Dora married Gershon Asculai, and they moved to Palestine that same year where they had two sons, Ephraim and Samuel. (Based on personal correspondence in 2007 with Ephraim and Samuel Asculai, of Omer, Israel, and Toronto, respectively. Feyge's date of death is indicated on Israel's Petition for Naturalization #339836, dated December 7, 1939, at the United States District Court for the Southern District of New York.)

Bernard Budiansky (1925–1999) became a renowned scholar in the field of applied mechanics. Ephraim is a prominent expert on issues of nuclear and environmental safety and in 1986 went to work for the International Atomic Energy Agency (IAEA) on issues of radiation protection of the public. Samuel has a PhD in microbiology and has invented and developed products such as a topical treatment for a precancerous skin condition commonly called sunspots.

husband was Ephraim Grover (ca. 1859–1934) and two of their six children are mentioned:[2]
  - Khanele (Ann Grover Pansy 1890–1975);
  - Yankl (James A. Grover, born 1886).

- Duvid "Duvidl" (born 1864) of Kishinev (Chişinău, Romania) was the son of Tsipe, the author's sister. Since he was raised by his mother's sister, Sure Vaynberg, he may have gone by the name Vaynberg.
  - Shimen Kanter of New York City was Duvid's half-nephew. Shimen was the son of Reyzl, the daughter of Shloyme-Leyzer and his first wife. Shloyme-Leyzer's second wife was Tsipe, the author's sister. In other words, Shimen was Tsipe's step-grandson.

- Sonya of New York City is likely referring to Sonya Glubman (1902–1973) who had no progeny. She was apparently related to the Hershkovitshes, the family of Pinye-Ber's first wife, Freyde.
- Libe Nutkevitsh (died 1940) of Palestine was a close family friend. She was originally from Yevpatoriya, Crimea.

January 23, 1914—Postcard from the Author's Son Isruel in Feodosiya to Pinye-Ber in Petakh-Tikva

The 25th of *Teyves*, Friday, the Eve of *Shabes*, the Torah Portion of *Vaera*,[3] 5674, here in Feodosiya[4]

Peace and all the best to my dear father, Pinkhes-Dov, may his light shine!

When you see this postcard, I ask you to immediately have pity on me and write the reason for your silence until now. It has been about two months from the day that you wrote me your first letter.[5] Until now, I did not get a response to my letter. What happened? Who's preventing you from writing? It's shocking that you are letting me worry so much. Why are my feelings not precious in your eyes? Why are you demeaning me in front of my friends? Afterall, I am only asking of you something small and puny—that you should send me a

2 The author's grandson, Mark Brockman, worked for many years for another of Sose Grover's sons named Herman Grover (1894–1975), who was in the wholesale paper business.

3 The name of the weekly Torah portion, Exodus 6:2 to 9:35.

4 The postcard is also postmarked January 23, 1914.

5 The author arrived in Palestine on November 30, 1913, and he evidently wrote his son a note shortly after his arrival.

postcard about your health and well-being, which is my sole request. My heart has practically given up hope from so much emotion. I am not used to this. From day to day, I wait to hear interesting news from you about your trip to Jerusalem. What did you see and what did you hear about the Technikum in Haifa?[6] "There was no voice and no one answered."[7]

Thank God, my family and I are alive and well. The children are studying their lessons with diligence, and they are seeing results from their toil. The days are full of rain and dampness. We have not seen the sun in more than a month. We received a postcard from Refuel, who asked us to let him know of any news from you, and I answered him whatever I knew.[8] I have not received any letters from Rukhl.[9] Shloyme is also full of anger at her, so she won't answer him.[10] For God's sake, answer me immediately. Be well.

With the blessings of your son who has been concerned about your wellbeing his entire life,

Isruel-Burekh Even-Zahav[11]

Take a magnifying glass, look at this picture, and you will recognize it.[12]

June 1926—Letter[13] from the Author in Petakh-Tikva to His Children Yankev, Nekhame, and Yosef in California

To My Dear and Important Son, Yankev Goldenshteyn,

---

6 The Technion—Israel Institute of Technology was originally known by the German name Technikum. Though its cornerstone was laid in 1912, its first session of classes was not held until 1924.

7 Kings I 18:26.

8 Refuel, Isruel's brother, was studying at Hebrew Union College in Cincinnati.

9 Rukhl, Isruel's sister, lived in Paris, France.

10 Shloyme, Isruel's brother, was living in Simferopol in November 1913 (see Appendix A2, p. 720), though shortly afterwards he moved to Yekaterinoslav to attend pharmacy school. Perhaps Isruel and Shloyme were angry at Rukhl for having been in a relationship with a non-Jew named Pierre Blondin with whom she had a son, Boris, in 1911. Perhaps Rukhl only told her family about Boris's birth shortly before this letter was written.

11 Even-Zahav is the Hebrew translation of the surname Goldenshteyn, meaning "gold stone."

12 On the front of the postcard on which this note is written appears a photograph of the port of Feodosiya.

13 This undated letter was written shortly after the author's daughter Nekhame Brakhtman (later Brockman) arrived in Oakland, California, where Yankev (Jacob Goldeen) lived. She first arrived with her sons Avigdor (Victor) and Mordekhai (Mark) in Providence, Rhode Island, on April 4, 1926, and then briefly stayed with relatives in Boston and then in New York. The author wrote this letter after *Rosh Khodesh Tamuz* (June 12–13, 1926) since he mentions this date at the end of his letter, and before his next letter which is dated 21 *Tamuz* 5686 (July 3, 1926).

How are you doing, my dear son? Has God by now sent you a complete recovery? Has God already had mercy on you and sent you a complete recovery from Heaven? Certainly, it is already time for you to be cured. I think that by the time this letter reaches you in your home, you will have already completely recovered. And I am very satisfied that particularly at this time, when such precious guests have come to you, you will be able to rejoice with them in good health and completely recuperated. And may the guests also share in your joy, and may you never suffer from your protracted illness again. Each day, I impatiently await your letter with the good news of your recovery [...].

I kiss you endlessly, and so too my dear daughter Fanya and your dear, beautiful children.[14] I kiss you and all your lovely children, and I wish you happiness and health.

Your elderly father who constantly prays to God for your health and happiness.

Your father,

Pinkhes-Dov, *shoykhet*, Goldenshteyn

I send warm regards to your brothers-in-law, sisters-in-law, and elderly Tarlo mother-in-law.[15] My wife sends warm regards to all.

As signed above.[16]

To My Daughter Nekhame,

(This is a continuation of my response to Nekhame's long letter.) I have so much to write, but I am forgetting many matters of interest. I reminded myself that Refuel wrote me again that he will be marrying soon, but I no longer believe him.[17] Write what you know about his getting married. Will it happen one day? Have you been in his city where he serves as a *rabiner*?[18] How does he live there

---

14 Though the author affectionately refers to his daughter-in-law Fanya (aka Fannie) as "my daughter."

15 Fannie's maiden name was originally Tarlo, though the name was changed to Tarlow in America. Fannie had a number of siblings residing in Portland. Since Fannie's mother, Sarah (Asherov) Tarlow, died in Portland in May 1926, this letter was written before the author heard the news of her death. (See Eric A. Kriss's genealogical tree of the Tarlows at www.krissfoundation.org.)

16 Postscripts in Yiddish and Hebrew letters would often close with, "As signed above."

17 Refuel only later did Refuel meet his wife, Claire, in New York. They married in 1930 in Los Angeles.

18 *Rabiner* refers here to a non-Orthodox rabbi; see chapter 23, p. 561, footnote 41, for more details. Refuel was then the reform rabbi of Congregation Shaarai Shomayim in Lancaster, Pennsylvania. Though Nekhame did not visit Refuel in Lancaster, she did see him in New York when he came to visit her shortly after her arrival in the United States ("Passover Services at Duke Street Temple," 1926).

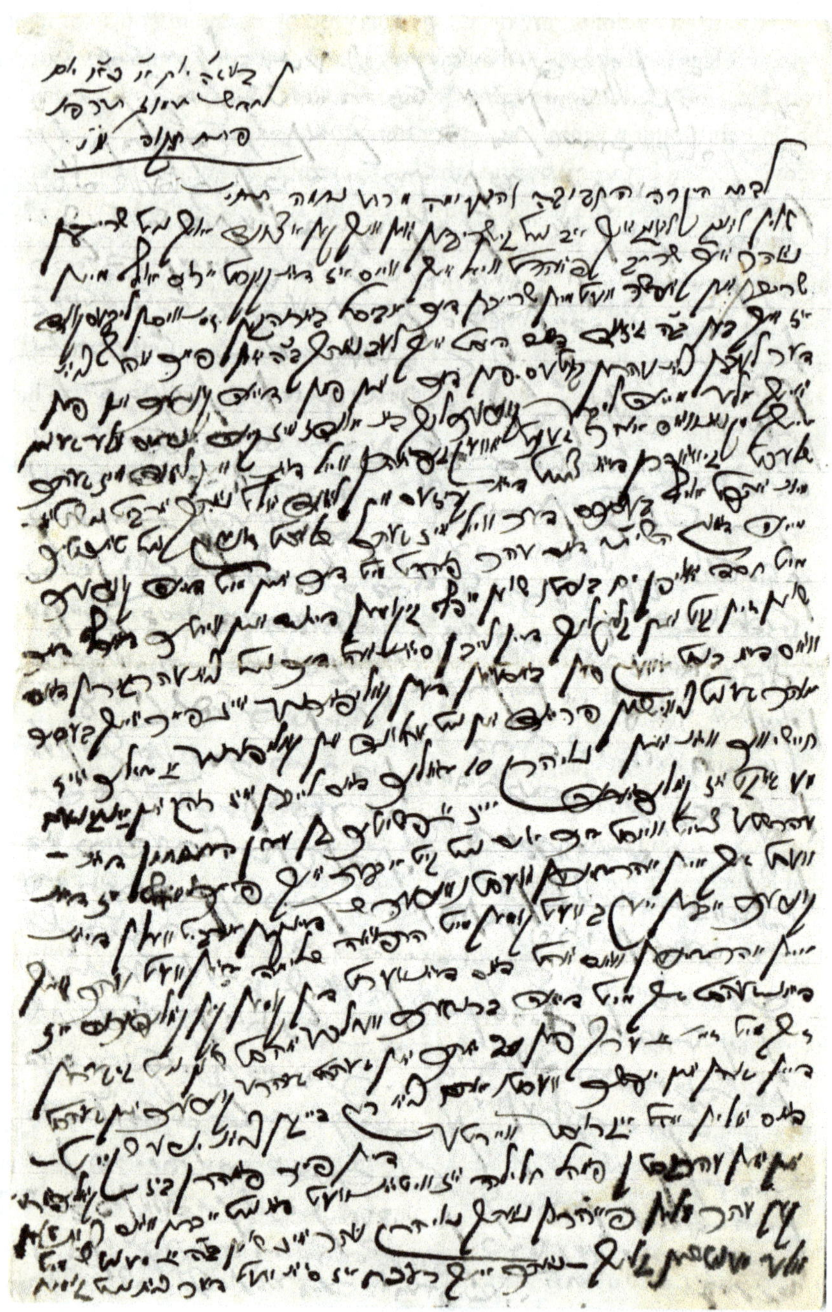

FIGURE 36. The first page of Pinkhes-Dov Goldenshteyn's Yiddish-language letter from July 3, 1926 (21 *Tamuz*, 5686) to his daughter, Nekhame Brakhtman (later Brockman), in Oakland, California. (Courtesy of Cynthia Brockman Unterberg of Westbury, New York.)

and what do they say about him? If he were married, he would be treated much more honorably than as the savage he is treated like now. A rabbi without a wife—a nice appearance he has! [. . .] I am sick over it, and I can't bear that two empty trees are growing in my garden.[19]

Freyde's wedding occurred before Pesach at my house and she is living, thank God, very nicely.[20] Her husband earns five to six schillings a day from dyeing, and they have their own apartment. His father has his own house [. . .].[21] May they grow old together in wealth and in honor and live long.

Similarly, Libe Nutkevitsh also made out well. Her husband is a good and pious man, who sits the entire day in *shul* where he prays and studies. He is devoted to her and considers himself lucky to have found such a good, devoted, and religious wife. He was wealthy in his town of Kuznitse in Poland,[22] and he has respectable children who send him eight pounds a month to live on, apart from packages of clothing and linen. She can certainly praise and thank God for the kindness that He has done for her. And I thank and praise God who granted me the privilege of doing the mitzvah of saving a soul and enabling her to achieve her goal of getting married.[23] She and her husband lived with me for two months from *Rosh-Khoydesh Iyar* until *Rosh-Khoydesh Tamuz*,[24] that means until [. . .] they moved to Gross's where they pay one pound a month. Today she came to visit. She sends her loving regards to you and thanks you for your regards.

Last week, Sheyndele returned from Egypt—a fine young lady [. . .].

Rukhl Shvitko[?] visited me in my house. She is a fine young lady, who is clever and pretty. I am very pleased with her. She is worthy of a fine husband, but where does one find him? But God will certainly provide. She thanks Vitya for his regards and sends you her warm regards.

Reyzl sends her regards along with [her husband] and children. Thank God, they live well and are healthy. Also, Bashe sends her warm regards and

19 The author is referring to his son Refuel in Lancaster, and daughter Rukhl in Paris, both of whom were unmarried.

20 Freyde (Frida) Herskhovitsh, a niece of the author's first wife Freyde, was married to a man named Shof.

21 Shof's father, Dov, later married Freyde's mother Elke.

22 Referring to Kuźnica, Poland, near Grodno (now Hrodna, Belarus).

23 The author was evidently instrumental in introducing the bride and groom to each other.

24 From April 14–15, 1926 until June 12–13, 1926.

thanks you for your regards to her. The nursemaid sends regards to you and is going to write to you a letter.[25]

Now that I remind myself, I forgot to calm you down regarding the empty area which is next to my house and which I had in mind to purchase [. . .]. You should know that the owner of that empty area personally came from America, asked Vilensky to leave, and is about to build a new house there.[26] I don't know now if this happened as a result of my prayers to have a better neighbor—but meanwhile it is better. Such moments of respite are good. God will help in the future. So, for now, you can stay calm. I am not buying it, and I don't currently have plans to buy it. I had spoken and considered buying that area—it was not my own idea, but it was because of the tremendous racket made by Vilensky with his three automobiles, the cows, the calves, the bulls, and the *Khalutsim* who were staying at his house.[27] The *Khalutsim*'s tremendous racket used to make my life loathsome; they didn't let me rest by day nor by night. If I did not own my house, I would have fled, but where does one flee from one's own house? But I have not spoken to the point. Now, my child, be calm. I am also calm now, thank God—no more noise, no more racket, no more automobiles, no more *Khalutsim*, and no more cows and calves. Remain healthy and live happily, which I, your faithful, elderly father, wish you from the depths of my heart.

Your father,

Pinkhes-Dov, as mentioned above.

I know nothing and hear nothing regarding Mendl.[28] He is staying with Zilberman in Jaffa [. . .]. I know nothing more.

To My Dear and Important Son, Itskhok-Yosef Goldenshteyn, May His Light Shine,

Dear son, how is your health? Nekhame writes me that you are suffering from your eyes! How did this happen to you? But you always had strong, healthy eyes. Can't you wear eyeglasses? Aren't there doctors who can treat you and make your eyes better? Don't let your teeth be pulled out, God forbid. Why turn yourself into a sick person. You'll get a bad stomach because one gets a sick stomach without teeth, and who knows if this will help your eye condition.

---

25 The nursemaid apparently worked for Reyzl Grinberg.

26 The owner's name was Y. Goodman (often called Gutman in Hebrew).

27 *Khalutsim* refers to young Jewish settlers who came from abroad in the late nineteenth and early twentieth centuries to establish agricultural settlements in the Land of Israel.

28 Nekhame's husband, Mendl Brakhtman, temporarily remained in Palestine to sell their house, while she and their two sons immigrated to America.

My son, concern yourself with your guests. Everything has its time and now has come the time to see to the welfare of your sister and her two sons. You should strive to ensure that they become established and are able to make a living. You, Yankl, your sons, and Itsl's children can each help them, little by little, to establish themselves: one with a good recommendation, another with some good advice, and another by taking pains on their behalf. Take an interest in them, and then everything will be good.

I am expecting a letter from you. You should write me everything with all the details. Nekhame praises your wife Itele and your children to me very much. Itele is, of course, from our family, from our blood. One's own blood is certainly warmer and more faithful.[29] All the details are in the section of this letter to Nekhame, so I am writing to you little. Be well and live happily and have much pleasure from your children. I kiss you and your wife, my dear daughter Itele,[30] and your children, may they be healthy. Be happy with your dear guests, and don't forget me, your elderly father who prays to God constantly for your health and happiness.

Your father,

Pinkhes-Dov Goldenshteyn

My wife sends her warm regards to you. Reyzl sends her warm regards.

As signed above.

July 3, 1926—Letter from the Author in Petakh-Tikva to His Daughter Nekhame in Oakland, California

With the help of God

Sunday, the 21st of *Tamuz* 5686

Petakh-Tikva, *Erets-Isruel*

To My Dear, Honorable, Sweet Daughter Nekhame, May She Live and Be Well,

I have not written in a long, long time. I also can't write now, but I write anyway because I know that you look forward it and that possibly my writing will calm you down a bit. You should know, my dear child, that I am healthy, thank God. That means that I am still alive, thank God, and I hope to live to hear good news from you, from your children, and from all of you, my dear children. There is no news regarding us. Everyone is envious of you that you

29 The author means that since his son Yosl's wife, Itele (Edith), is also a blood relative, she has been particularly warm to Nekhame and her two sons.

30 The author affectionately refers to his daughter-in-law, Edith, as his daughter.

left because the times are very bad over here. The economic crisis here still continues. There is no work. We hope for better times. Meanwhile, it is very bad. Don't sin, my daughter; thank God that He treats you and your children with kindness.[31] While on the ocean, you suffered your share, but from now on, your life needs to be good and happy. Don't let it bother you that you first had to be in Boston, since California is better for you. There you are among relatives and are not alone. In California, one dollar goes farther than ten dollars in New York. Life is calm and pleasant there. They say that California is simply a terrestrial paradise. At first, nothing will be to your liking, but I hope you will think differently once you have settled down. Your children will have work there. Yankev will have a complete recovery, and he will then arrange your affairs. What is the worth of your having gone to California if you can't see your brothers (whom you haven't seen in about twenty years), their children, and your son. And perhaps you will bring them back to Judaism, which itself would make your stay there have a tremendous worth. In the worst case, God forbid, if Vitya will not find anything to do, he can go to New York alone. He is, thank God, a mature and responsible person now, but I don't think that it will come to that. He will find work with good wages there in California or in Portland. I thank God that you are now in a place close to your brothers, near your son, and near other relatives—Itsl's children, Itele's sisters and brother: Becky [*sic*]; Betty; and Sam,[32] who do not live far from *Ekland*[33] and are well to do. After all, they are family—relatives—and things are already good once one is not alone. Be calm, my child. God will not abandon you.

I just received your letter from New York. Shloyme wrote a reply.[34] I wasn't able to write. I received another letter from you from Oakland, in which you write that you sent out a long letter the day before. But you wrote me that I should save this new letter so that I won't slide into the mud by buying that shack of a house in which Vilensky lives along with the accompanying large piece of land.[35] Shloyme also replied to this new letter, while I awaited the previ-

---

31 The author is instructing Nekhame not to sin by being ungrateful to God for having taken her from Palestine, a land experiencing economic crisis.

32 Itsl (Isaac) Goldstein (died 1907) was the author's nephew. He had four children: the oldest, Edith, who married the author's son Yosef (Joseph Goldeen); Jennie Shapiro (later changed to Sherwood); Bertha Glikbarg; and Sam Goldeen.

33 The author refers to Oakland, California, as *Ekland* (*ek* denotes "end" in Yiddish) because he felt that it was at the end of the earth, both physically on the other side of America and spiritually far removed from traditional Jewish life.

34 The author lived in the same courtyard with his son Shloyme and his family in Petakh-Tikva.

35 The author had been contemplating purchasing his neighbor Vilensky's house because of the noise that he and his tenants caused. For details, see p. 782 above.

ously sent long letter that arrived eight days later. I am personally replying to this long letter now, and I thank you for having written in such detail.

Please write me more often and with detailed descriptions of your brothers' lives and of your Moyshe's life, and whether he is far, far removed . . .[36] And about his wife and children . . .[37] I understand that my children have *treyf* homes there, and that you will also have to eat *treyf* because there is no *shoykhet* and no synagogue.[38] Write me everything in detail. It grieves me—tremendously. Woe to my age that I have lived to see that my children conduct themselves in this manner and that you, my beloved, pious daughter, also must conduct yourself like this. Write about everything and at least let me truthfully know how my children are living. I presume that you will conduct yourself as a Jew there also, and God will assist you in your needs.

In your letter from New York, you wrote that you met there my sister Ite's grandchild named Kanter. You are mistaken. He is my sister Tsipe's [step-] grandson. His first name is Shimen.[39] When I still lived in Russia, I used to correspond with him in New York [. . .]. His father was [. . .] a cantor and a *moyel* in a synagogue. [. . .] His mother was also supposed to have had two daughters. One is named Tsipe, and I don't remember the other one's name. Write me Shimen's address, and I will correspond with him. He is our Duvid's [step-]nephew. [Shimen and his two sisters] are the children of Duvid's [half-]sister [Reyzl], who died so young. She endured suffering continuously from the moment she was born. [. . .] Last week I received a letter [from Duvid in Kishinev]. He, poor thing, writes about the very hard times he is having, but how can I help him? He has, thank God, married children and grandchildren and is tremendously poor. And Beyle, his wife, has a lame hand—a result of one of the pogroms that took place there.[40]

Last week, I received barely a letter from Isruel. This week, I will also reply to him. He writes that they are all healthy, thank God, and asks what news you

---

36 Since Nekhame's son, Moyshe (Martin Brockman), married a non-Jew, the author is likely inquiring whether Martin apostatized to Christianity. In Tsarist Russia, if a Jew wanted to marry a non-Jew, the church required the Jew to apostatize before marrying. Moyshe did not give up his Jewish faith.

37 Martin and his wife Rebecca lived in Portland, Oregon. At that time, they had two children, Donald and Eugene, and later had two more.

38 "My children" refers to his sons, Yankev (Jacob Goldeen) and Yosl (Joseph Goldeen) who lived in California.

39 Referrring to Shimen Kanter.

40 The first Kishinev pogrom took place on April 19–21, 1903. During those days, 49 Jews were killed, more than 500 injured, and 2,000 families were left homeless. A second pogrom took place in Kishinev on October 19–20, 1905, where 19 Jews were killed and 56 were injured.

have written me and thanks you for writing about Peyske and his wife.[41] He also writes that his son-in-law was in Moscow,[42] and that Klara impressed him as being quite an educated, refined, and smart person.[43] And that Isruel's daughter-in-law, Avrum's wife, was also in Moscow because Avrum could not get away before his exams.[44] Freydl's husband was going to look into a business proposition for Avrum. In short, Freydl has lived through a lot, with her husband's enjoyment of traveling. May God help them. May God give Isruel and his wife Gitl great satisfaction from her and from all of their children.

I have received no letters from Rukhl. I wait from day to day and am eager to hear from her. I don't know for certain if she is coming and don't know when she can come.[45] I don't even have an answer as to whether she received the money that I sent her to help her get out of that purgatory, Paris. I don't understand what type of person she is [that she has not written to me]. Write me in your letter what you have heard from her. We must get her out of Paris. She does not want to move to Palestine, so, let her go to America. Just as long as she does not remain in Paris, cut off from her relatives and living so alone.

I received a letter from Refuel this week. He writes that you have gone to a terrestrial paradise, California, and that it was good that you went there.

I suppose that I have written you everything, but you must forgive me for ending now because it is difficult for me to write. I kiss you without end and bless you that God should make you happy wherever you will turn and that you should live to see great satisfaction from your children.

As wished to you by your father, who loves you so much,

Pinkhes-Dov, *shoykhet*, Goldenshteyn

I send regards to Vitya and Mara, my dear, beloved grandchildren. Last week, I sent you both the *Ha-Aretz* so that you would be able to read and to know what is going on in this country and so that you won't become cut off

---

41 Peyske is a nickname for the given name Peysekh (i.e., Pesach). Peyske was evidently Isruel's friend from Feodosiya who had immigrated to America, where Nekhame met him.

42 Referring to Joseph Pozwolski of Paris, the son-in-law of his son Isruel. Joseph had gone on business to Moscow.

43 Klara (Zlatopolsky) Kreyzberg was the wife the wife of David Kreyzberg, who was author's stepson through his second wife Feyge. Klara was also the sister of Etya, the wife of the author's son Shloyme. Apparently, Klara traveled to Moscow to meet Joseph Pozwolski. Since she moved during the 1920s from Feodosiya to Yekaterinoslav, it is unknown in which city she was living at this time.

44 Avrum Goldenshteyn, Isruel's son and the author's grandson, was studying medicine. In the early 1920s, he studied medicine in Simferopol. It is not known whether he was still in Simferopol at this time. His wife's name was Pola. She went to Moscow specifically to see Joseph Pozwolski.

45 Rukhl did not end up visiting her father.

from Hebrew, because I still hope that you will return to the Holy Land with successful businesses.[46] You will continue to get the *Ha-Aretz* from me every week—a present from your grandfather.

I send regards to Yosef, Yankev, and their families and to your Moyshe—does he still remember his grandfather? Does he remember how he used to sing with his grandfather at the *Shobes* table "*Yismakh Moyshe*"?[47] Aunt Bashe sends you regards and thanks you for your regards to her. Libe and her husband send you their warm regards. She did well by marrying him, thank God. Shloyme, Etya, and the children send their warm regards.

The words of your father, as mentioned above.

October 10, 1926—Letter from the Author in Petakh-Tikva to His Daughter Nekhame in Oakland, California

With the Help of God

Sunday, the 2nd of *Heshvan* 5687, Petakh-Tikva, *Erets-Isruel*

To My Dear Daughter Nekhame, May She Live and Be Well,

It has been a long time since I last wrote to you, but you must forgive me, my dear child, that I cannot write when I want to but only when I am able. From before Rosh Hashanah until now I was not able to take a pen in hand.[48] And now that I am already holding a pen in my hand, I am still not sure if I will be able to write everything as I want to and as you would like. But thank God for however long that I will be able to continue my writing. First, you should know that I am still alive, thank God, and hope to live to see more satisfaction from my children, namely, to see my children married off, to hear good news from you and to hear about a good future for my Rukhl, namely, that she is near you and her brothers and not miserable being far away from her family. She should go to America. It would be good for her, and I would live in peace. With her abilities, she would even be able to earn a living by working for our Yosef. She knows bookkeeping well. She finished business school.

You should also know that I received a letter from Vitya in New York. He is happy that he is once again in New York. He says that he feels like he is in the Garden of Eden now that he is once again among Jews, among friendly people.

---

46 The *Ha-Aretz* is a Hebrew-language newspaper printed in Palestine and still published to this day in Israel.

47 *Yismakh Moyshe* (i.e., "Moses will be happy" in Hebrew) is a song with a Yiddish refrain. It is likely that Pinye-Ber chose to sing this particular song with Moyshe because it mentions his name.

48 Rosh Hashanah was September 9–10, 1926.

He loves *Yidishkayt*[49] very much, as you know. He says that in New York there is pure goodness and no *goyishkayt*[50] and that [in California] no one has any friendly feelings for another person.

Secondly, I received a letter from Vitya for his father and found five dollars in the letter. I forwarded the letter, Vitya and Mara's, to Mendl, and I wrote to him that I am keeping the five dollars with me because on Thursday I need to bring one pound to the bank to cover the debt that he owes. Therefore, he should remain calm and not drive himself crazy to find one pound to cover his debt to the bank. Vitya and Mara wrote a very friendly letter [...].

So, it is now time [...] to speak about something important. I would like to know from you if Yankev and Yosef conduct themselves Jewishly, meaning do they have kosher kitchens? Are you able to pray every *Shobes* in a synagogue? Write me everything in detail. Did Yosl [*sic*] have a Jewish *huppah*?[51] Wish him mazel tov and wish the new couple mazel tov from their elderly grandfather, who wishes them happiness, long years, and that their parents should live to see much satisfaction from them. Regards to Yosef and Itl and their beloved children. Regards to your friends whom I thank for their friendship and humanity towards you. Regards to your Moyshe, and very warm regards to the Tarlos.[52] Regards to Vitya—and let him know that when I can, I will answer him separately. Everyone sends their regards and thanks you for your regards to them. Libe and her husband send their regards; they are living quite nicely together. Shloyme wrote to you; about what, I don't know. He probably wrote to you everything that he knows. I received twenty-five dollars from Yosef on Friday, the first day of *Rosh-Khoydesh* Heshvan.[53] Thank him very much. [...]

As your father wishes you and prays to God for you every day and every minute,

The words of your father,
Pinkhes-Dov, *shoykhet,* Goldenshteyn

---

49 *Yidishkayt* means "Judaism."

50 *Goyishkayt* refers to they ways of non-Jews.

51 The author means to ask if his son Yankl (Jacob)—not Yosl (Joseph)—had made a Jewish wedding for his son, Alfred, who was married on September 22, 1926 in Sacramento, California. Alfred later changed his surname from Goldeen to Golden.

52 The Tarlos (changed to Tarlow in America) were the siblings of Fannie, the wife of Yankev (Jacob). They were from Feodosiya.

53 October 9–10, 1926.

January 27, 1927—Yiddish Letter from the Author in Petakh-Tikva to His Daughter Nekhame in Brooklyn

With the Help of God

Thursday, Torah Portion of *Mishpatim*[54]

The 24th of *Shvat* 5687, Petakh-Tikva

[Wishing] peace and happiness, good health, and much satisfaction from your children to my beloved, precious daughter Nekhamele, may she be well and healthy, along with her two dear sons, who are so devoted and beloved, may they be healthy and strong and have happy lives, Amen.

Already a bit of time—quite a bit of time—has elapsed since I wrote to you. I was waiting until Mendl would leave here,[55] and I was also waiting for a reply to my long letter [. . .]. He bade me farewell on Tuesday. He needed to be on the ship on Thursday.[56] Meanwhile, your letter arrived stating that you were leaving Oakland for New York. On Thursday, I sent Shloyme to the ship to tell Mendl that he needs to stop in New York and not continue on to *Ekland*.[57] [. . .] I hope that God will have mercy and will let you be comforted and also reach a good, ripe old age with much joy from your children. It's not so bad, my child. Be calm. Be honest. With trust in God, you will see how God can help when He simply wants to and how He surrounds all those who trust in Him with kindness; He performs acts of kindness for such people from all sides.

With Mendl, I sent you a nice book of *tkhines* from Rabbi Alfasi[58] [*sic*]—*tkhines* for every occasion of the year—and a nice prayer book left over from Aunt Bashe's sister,[59] which Aunt Bashe cannot use because she uses a *Nusakh Ashkenaz* prayer book and that prayer book is *Nusakh Sfard*.[60] This prayer book

---

54 The name of the weekly Torah portion, Exodus 21:1 to 24:18.

55 The author was waiting to write Nekhame until her husband Mendl left Palestine for the United States.

56 Mendl boarded the ship on Thursday, January 20, 1927.

57 As mentioned on p. 784, footnote 33 above, the author sometimes refers to Oakland, California, as *Ekland*. Mendl was not to continue on to Oakland since the author just received word from Nekhame that she and her sons had moved to Brooklyn.

58 *Tkhines* (*tkhinot* in modern Hebrew) are Yiddish prayers primarily recited by women. Rabbi Bentsion Alfes (1850–1940) was a prolific religious writer, mainly in Yiddish. Goldenshteyn evidently gave her Rabbi Alfes' work, *Mekor dimah: shas tkhina khadasha* (Vilna: Rozenkrants ve-Shriftzetser, 1925), a book of *tkhines*.

59 The author's third wife, Bashe, had a sister named Leye Mortkovitz who died in October 1926 in Petakh-Tikva. For details regarding Leye, see Appendix A5, pp. 742–743.

60 A *Nusakh Ashkenaz* prayer book contains the version of prayers used mainly by non-Hasidim, while Nekhame used a *Nusakh Sfard* prayer book, traditionally used by Hasidim and their descendants.

will be very good for you. Use it in good health and pray for everything good for you, for your children.

When I received your letter telling me that you had left *Ekland*, I had not yet received your letter from New York that you are already in your own place, thank God, and are once again the mistress of your own house. Now that I have your address in New York, I am writing to you a response with the fatherly and loyal wish that God should help you to merit living in one place without having to wander from one location to another, God forbid, and that your current residence in that city should be for luck and happiness. May you have much satisfaction from your children and may your children be satisfied with the life you lead. May you now have a [. . .] calm and beautiful life, Amen.

I am overjoyed that you have returned to be among Jews and that you feel at home among your own. It is also good for your children that they remain Jewish and not get stuck . . .[61] I understand that California is a non-Jewish place with little Judaism. Thank God [that you are now in New York]. Whatever way in which God runs things is right. Don't regret anything—don't regret that you were in California. How else would you have been able to see your brothers, get to know their families, and become familiar with their lives? And the same could be said regarding your son, Moyshe, and his family. You would have had to travel there—if not now, then later. And if you would have delayed your trip for later, you wouldn't have any rest until you saw and met with your son and brothers. So, now you have already accomplished this—and how so? Since you've now accomplished this, you can now rest and have peace of mind. Now, in your present life in New York, where *Yidishkayt* is to be found so much in all the streets, thank God, and where Jews have worth, you must thank and praise God for His kindness that he bestows upon you and your children because God will hopefully continue not to forsake you and you will be able to rejoice with good and happy news, as I wish for you.

I believe that, by the time my letter arrives, Mendl will already be together with you [. . .].[62] May God help that my wish becomes fulfilled and that I will be able to live the last bit of my life that God grants me serenely so that I can live as all others. It hurts to hear that Mara's health is unfortunately suffering. See to it that you do not stop tending to his illness. Don't let him work at jobs that are harmful to his health.[63] Let him seek out cleaner work and God certainly will help.

61 The author apparently leaves out the painful words "in an intermarriage."

62 Mendl arrived in New York on February 9, 1927.

63 In Oakland, Nekhame's son Mark ("Mara") worked in the mattress factory managed by his uncle Jacob Goldeen. The dust from the mattress filling affected his health for a short while afterwards.

Regards to my relative [Ephraim] Grover and his wife, Sose, my uncle's daughter, and their children. I remember [their children] Yankl and Khanele. They probably have grandchildren. Regards to all of them. Tell them that I would like to receive a letter from them and that I will respond [. . .].

My regards to Sonya. [. . .]

Everyone sends regards. Reyzl's letter evidently was lost in the mail. Reyzl sends her regards along with those of Yankev and their children. Freydl and her husband are living quite calmly and serenely. They send their warm regards. [. . .] and their children send their warm regards. I have heard nothing from Rukhl. Thank you for writing about her. I often get postcards from Refuel.[64] I received his $100 already a while ago. I am awaiting the $100 this month that he is supposed to send. It will probably arrive in time. Dear child, now that you live close to him, see to it that he marries. How long will he remain a bachelor?

In today's letter, I have written a lot, but there is a lot that I am not remembering to write. It may be that I have not written anything of interest, or perhaps I have actually written something of interest. I offer my apologies, but I am not calm. [. . .] I am ending my letter. Shloyme is writing to you separately.

I send loving regards to Mara and Vitya. My dear children [i.e., grandchildren], see to it that you go in the Jewish way and with Jewish ideas. You yourselves are in New York but your hearts are in the Jewish land. Don't forget this, and God will also not forget you and will bestow good health, blessings, and success in your actions. And wherever you turn, may you have the right ideas. Amen. I kiss you all and bless you with the best of everything.

Your father, your grandfather, who prays to God for you in the Holy Land.

Your Father,

Pinkhes-Dov Goldenshteyn

Aunt Bashe sends warm regards to all of you. Libe and her husband send warm regards. Adieux, adieux, adieux.

As signed above.

March 14, 1929—Letter from the Author in Petakh-Tikva to His Daughter Nekhame in Brooklyn

Thursday, the 2nd of Adar II, 5689, Petakh-Tikva, *Erets-Isruel*

To my honorable daughter, the esteemed Nekhame, may she live and be well,

64 Refuel (Raphael Goldenstein), the author's son, was the reform rabbi of Congregation Shaarai Shomayim in Lancaster, Pennsylvania

You should know, my dear child, that I received your letter. I thank God for the kindness that my dear grandson Vityake has recovered, and that you all are healthy and well.

Though God is a father and will not abandon you, it very much grieves me that you are suffering from your old illness, which had left you and for which you had counted yourself lucky. Now, apparently, it has come up again and once more inflicts pain. Regarding an illness, they say that if it returns, it will be even stronger than before. But what can you do, my dear child, when such is your lot? You must continue to bear it until God will have mercy and deliver you from it in a good manner. God is full of mercy and will certainly have mercy on you, but everything has its own time. When the time comes, you will be helped. How so? Only God Himself knows, but don't lose trust in God and accept everything with love and then you will see that God will help you. Don't let it worry you, my dear child. Be a mother to your children and place your hope in God, and you will then live to see much satisfaction from them. Then you will forget your current troubles and old illness. Amen and Amen.

I thank you very much for the regards and news that Duvidl's nephew is in New York, and that he will send some monetary assistance to Duvidl. I understand that he must be the son of Duvidl's [half]-sister Reyzl. My sister Tsipe married off Reyzl—Reyzl is Shloyme-Leyzer's daughter from his first wife. Reyzl lived in Kishinev. When you receive the second part of my book, you will find out how Reyzl devoted herself to Duvidl and Ester-Khaye, the little orphaned children of Tsipe. Please see him, why don't you, and prevail upon him to allow himself to be regarded as a relative. Write me all the details of your accidental encounter with him. And send my regards. Ask him about his parents. Are they still alive? How are they doing? Where are they and their children? Have him read my work. He will find interesting information about his parents and family.

Yesterday, I sent you and Refuel the second part of my book.[65] I am waiting for a reply from him and from you in order to know what I have to do—whether I should send the books as they are or should I have them hardbound? I think that binding them there in Brooklyn will be less expensive and that the binding here and shipping from here will be expensive. Whatever you tell me, I will do.[66]

Darling daughter, I think that you should ask at least three shillings for each book, that means not quite an entire dollar. I must have money to pay for its printing. The rest of my book will be ready after Pesach [. . .], and there will

---

65 Refuel (Raphael), the author's son, was living in Brooklyn.

66 In Palestine, each part of the autobiography was staple bound and had paper covers. Out of the 500 copies printed, 400 were sent to Refuel in Brooklyn. There he had the parts hardbound in a single volume in February 1930. See Appendix A7, p. 752, for details.

be a second section to part III, because I want the entire book to be in three parts, including the part about Kfar-Saba.[67] May God help me that I should live and merit to complete this while I am alive. Then I will be able to go to my eternal resting place . . . Then I will know that I have left an inheritance for my darling children for generations . . .

Darling daughter, I thank you very much for what you have in mind to do for Sheyndl.[68] See to it, my child, that you collect as much as you can, little by little, from whomever you can—just those things that can be used by a bride for a wedding. She is a [. . .] healthy and fine young lady but very poor and has practically nothing. She is staying with Reyzl and earns barely £1 a month. Her small earnings are used up quickly, and nothing remains for savings. Certainly, it is a great mitzvah to help her start her life. In the merit of all of this, may God help you and grant you great satisfaction from your children and contentment forever, and save you from all types of distress, and allow you to be well established. Amen.

I must end my writing. Be healthy, have trust in God, and don't worry. Follow my advice and you will see how God will help you. I kiss you endlessly and pray to God for you and for you all.

Your father, who is very concerned about you,

Pinkhes-Dov Goldenshteyn

Bashe sends you her loving regards and thanks you for the regards from the Ginzbergs.[69] [. . .] Shloyme sends regards to all of you. He is writing to you separately. All your relatives here send their warm regards. I kiss my darling grandchildren, Mara and Vitya. I wish you good health and happiness forever.

April 1929[70] Letter from the Author in Petakh-Tikva to His Daughter Nekhame in Brooklyn

Nekhame,

I am sending you a note that I received from Galatz, Romania from Aunt Leye's daughter, Khayele.[71] Yosef must remember her from when he stayed

---

67 The author wanted the entire book to be in three parts—as opposed to the contents of the addendum being a fourth part. Hence, the second part of part III was called an addendum (chs. 30–34), which includes his experience in Kfar-Saba (ch. 32 and the first half of ch. 33).

68 Nekhame was collecting items for a trousseau for her first cousin, Sheyndl Hershkovitsh.

69 The Ginzbergs lived across the street from the author.

70 This letter was apparently written in April of 1929, since the author mentions here that he has not yet finished writing his autobiography; in his letter from March 14, 1929, he writes that it will be finished after Pesach, which ended on May 4th that year.

71 Galatz is now called Galați, Romania.

with her in Perkon, when he was traveling on furlough on his way home from Kiev.[72] She sends me this note together with a newspaper clipping from which she understood that they were referring to me. Since I know, dear children, that you will also find it interesting to read, I am forwarding it to you together with my letter. It is very difficult for me to write but, for you, nothing is too difficult for me.

My book must be written correctly. It bothers me that so much is still unwritten. My experiences in Hadera are not written. I was also in Hadera and suffered much there, and I continued to write my Torah scroll there.

Here in Palestine, an article about me and my Torah scroll was printed in Hebrew.[73] I imagine that this news item was also reprinted in America because each newspaper takes from the other and rewrites it. When you, my daughter, read it, you will see that they are writing about your father and take note that they think I had a black beard. Hopefully, the writer meant to portray me to the world as being more handsome than I am by making my once-red beard out to be black. But his description of Aunt Bashe with her *tkhines*—how do you like that? I even like the soup that she cooks for my supper because it is more than half mixed with *tkhines* and prayers . . .

How do you like Aunt Leye's age? Poor thing, that such a dear, kosher soul should sadly suffer at such an advanced age. Her son, Velvl, with whom she is staying, is Rukhl's father. [. . .] Blessed is the person who has good children. Blessed are the children who have good parents. I know that God has blessed me that I have, thank God, good, devoted children, may they be well, and may God bless them.

Another time I will describe for you Aunt Leye and her [. . .] children. May God watch over you to live to such an age.

The words of your father,

Pinkhes-Dov Goldenshteyn

Shloyme's children are, thank God, healthy, happy, beautiful, and dear children, may they be well. When the *khalát* arrived, they were overjoyed, thinking that the package was for them.[74] But when they opened it and found out that it was a *khalat* for me, they stopped, poor things, as if they had been spanked. When they calmed down, one said to the other, "Grandfather is older, so they

72 Yosef (Joseph Goldeen), the author's son, served in the Russian military from 1901 until 1904. Leye was clearly a relative of the author's first wife, Freyde, since she lived in Perkon where the author's parents-in-law resided at one time. Perhaps Leye was the widow of Duvid-Leyb Rozyman, the brother of Freyde's mother, Dvoyre Hershkovitsh.

73 For more about this article and the article printed in Romania mentioned above, see Appendix E, pp. 826-836.

74 A *khalat* (pl. *khalatn*) is a man's lightweight silk or woolen robe generally worn by Hasidim at home, especially on the Sabbath and Jewish holidays.

sent him something first. And we, we are little, so they will send us later. But write that our aunt should send us something as quickly as possible . . ." The little one is, *kenehore*, bright as the day, beautiful as the moon, and shining as the sun.[75] They send their regards and speak about you, Aunt Nadya, the entire day. They boast to everyone that they have an Aunt Nadya, and that she will send them beautiful, good, sweet things.

The words of your father, as mentioned above.

November 21, 1929-Yiddish Letter from the Author in Petakh-Tikva to His Daughter Nekhame in Brooklyn

With the Help of God

Thursday, the 18th of *Heshvan* 5690, Petakh-Tikva, *Erets-Isruel*

To My Dear Daughter Nekhame, May She Live and Be Well,

You should know that we are, thank God, healthy and feel very good, thank God. The heat subsided and the air is cool, which is very good for me. I am now writing letters to everyone, though I don't see the little letters that I am writing and can't read them by myself. I think that only good eyes could read them. So, I am writing with the hope that you will be able to read my letter easily, and I ask you to write whether you can read my current handwriting. I reminded myself that I have not yet thanked you for the presents. Thank you, my dear child, my faithful daughter, for the two *khalátn* that you sent. They fit me well. The silken one is even better, longer, and wider than the other one made from simple material, but I wear both of them on *Shobes* and during the week. Also, the slippers that Refuel sent me through you are very good. I wear them and never take them off my feet. I am constantly thanking God that I have such faithful children who make sure their elderly father has everything. May God comfort you with long years and with much happiness and good health.

Dear Nekhame, I received your letter. It makes me sick that I caused you trouble and pain by sending the books to you.[76] But how can I change things now? I only ask you to have patience until Refulikl returns to Brooklyn—then, God willing, everything will be all right.[77] He is a very devoted son to me, may he live and be well. He is my guardian angel. He is now about to rescue me from my creditors and is sending me his yearly stipend a month early so that I can be

75 Referring to Shloyme's daughter Aliza (later Bernfeld).

76 Referring to the shipment of the author's published autobiography.

77 Refuel was visiting his brothers Yosef and Yankl (Joseph and James Goldeen) in California, as mentioned later in the letter.

released earlier from my creditors whom I need to pay on January 1. May he live a long life. With this, he infused me with a new soul. May God give him health and happiness and always make him prosper with success and blessing and with all that is good. He will also probably be involved in the selling of my books and will know what he has to do with them. One only has to have a bit of patience and not be hasty. With time, all will be sold, and you all will send the proceeds to me. That money will then be reserved for me to live on because Refuel's money would have been used, of course, to release me from my debts, as mentioned earlier. You should not have any pain on my behalf. I have enough hope and trust that God will not abandon me, and I have no regret that I published my book. Nothing, but nothing, comes easy for me, and I have cut through everything with effort, strenuous effort, and toil, but I am satisfied that I have, thank God, accomplished this. I await your letter after Refuel's arrival to know where things stand after his return from visiting his brothers.

Warm regards to Mendl and the children. I send you fatherly kisses without number, and wish you everything good.

Your father,

Pinkhes-Dov Goldenshteyn

Regards to my dear relatives, the Grovers, and wish them long lives and years with great satisfaction from their children, delight, blessing, and success. Amen, may it be His will. Regards to Sonya. Tell her that Pava and his wife visited me during the intermediate days of *Sukes* and bought a copy of my book.[78] They were surprised that I had not heard news about any joyous occasions. Landshaft and his family send regards to Sonya and ask her to write and not distance herself.

Aunt Bashe sends her warm regards to all of you. She thanks you for the regards from Anna Ginzberg and asks you to give the Ginzberg family regards from her and me.[79] We are surprised that Khane,[80] Miss Ginzberg, does not send us the photograph that she took of us. I would be interested to see how it turned out.

Rezyl, Yankl, and their children send warm regards, as well as her mother and her sister Freyde. Freyde has a very fine husband, and, thank God, she lives calmly and quietly. Sheyndl is already, thank God, engaged to be married and

78 The identity of Pava is unknown. The male name Pava is usually a nickname for Pavel (Paul). The intermediate days of *Sukes* were on October 20–25, 1929.

79 The Ginzbergs lived across the street from the author in Petakh-Tikva. Evidently, several of them were visiting or had moved to America.

80 Khane is one and the same as Anna Ginzberg, mentioned in the previous sentence.

has found a very fine man from a respectable family. His father was a *shoykhet* in Mariupol in the province of Yekaterinoslav and now lives in Hadera. He works for the government in the radio-telephone department in Be'er-Sheva. He earns a salary of £12 a month, and he is marrying her without a dowry. He likes her, and his family is agreeable, too, because they know her family.[81] Your busy involvement [to help Sheyndl with a trousseau] was not in vain. You did a great mitzvah. May you be protected in merit of this mitzvah. May God protect you from want and need and comfort you with great satisfaction and delight from your children. Amen and Amen.

Regards to Reyzl, her husband, son, and sister Dvoyre.[82] Have them send me their photographs. I want to see how they look now. And regards to their father Isruel Chaplick. Why doesn't he ever write me a letter? Warm regards to Kanter.[83] When you see Kanter, tell him on my behalf that I am asking him to write me. Thirty-six years ago, when I still lived in Russia, he used to write to me. How is his sister doing? Ask him that and write me the answer if he doesn't write. Regards to Duvidl's nephew, Reyzl's son from Kishinev.[84] I saw him as a child in Kishinev. I knew his father. His father had a tobacco store and was in my house more than once in Bakhchisaray. Give them my regards. Make sure they don't forget Duvidl and his impoverished family. I am now ending all my regards and have finished writing.

The words of your elderly father,

Pinkhes-Dov Goldenshteyn, as mentioned above.

June 22, 1930—Letter from the Author in Petakh-Tikva to His Daughter Nekhame in Brooklyn

With the Help of God

The 26th of *Sivan* 5690

Petakh-Tikva, *Erets-Isruel*

Peace and Good Health to My Dear Beloved Daughter Nekhamele and Her Husband and Dear Children, May They Be Healthy and Live Happily with Many Long Years, Amen,

---

81 In other words, Sheyndl's husband's family was agreeable to his marrying her even though she had no dowry.

82 Referring to the author's grandnephew Israel Chaplick's two daughters: Rose (Reyzl) Budiansky and Dora (Dvoyre).

83 Referring to Shimen Kanter was the step-grandson of Tsipe, the author's sister.

84 The author is again referring to Shimen Kanter.

Dear Beloved Daughter,

I received and read your lovely letter. I can calm you down from being distraught over the Jewish people. We have a tremendous God in Heaven. He takes care of his impoverished sheep. Don't be afraid. Our beloved God will not abandon us. He will help us against all our enemies, none of whom will live to see their vengeful plans come to fruition. We will outlive all of them and foil them. May we live to see the complete redemption very soon . . .

Regarding Refuel, I can write to you that he is not to be blamed for anything. He, poor thing, is embittered, has a broken life, and has no enjoyment from life. I am constantly concerned about him, and I pray to God that at least from now on He should keep an eye on him and have mercy on him, that he should now begin to know a wealth of happiness along with everyone else. Don't blame him. Better to bear in mind the little bit of happiness that he has had in his life. Don't ask him to make an accounting. He certainly won't accept mine. He may accept yours sooner or later. He should do as he thinks best. I know that he is devoted to me, but he needs to use his own common sense as to what he thinks is best. Don't anger him. He is a very embittered person and has not tasted a sweet day in his life. May God let me live to see him when God will have mercy on him.[85] And perhaps God allows me to continue to live to hear such good news regarding my dear son Refulikl.

Beloved Daughter, don't become so distraught over me... God will assist me. I am about to be freed from poverty. One has to suffer and suffer. One can somehow get used to suffering and bearing pain. You tear food out of your mouth and send it to me. I don't deserve your good heart. But I know your situation. I know that you are being supported by your children. I ask you not to do this.[86] I kiss your two precious sons and bless them with good health and happiness and that, in due time, they should get married and set up homes for themselves.

I am writing a letter but who knows if you will be able to read it easily for I myself can't read what I have written. I ask you to write to me whether you can read my current handwriting and ask that your letter to me should be written in black ink so that I will be able to read it myself.[87] I have become blinder and deafer and am, in general, going to pieces. I traveled to this distant country

85 The author is referring to when Refuel marries.

86 The author did not want Nekhame to send him any portion of the little bit of money that she received as support from her sons. Her sons only became financially stable later on.

87 If not written in black ink, the author would not been able to read the letter, and he would need to ask others to read it to him.

where the climate apparently causes those who come here to lose their physical senses.

Just imagine, my child, what I have lived through during this 90-year journey to this county from the city of my birth. But as soon as I came to this country my strength immediately weakened, I became deafer and blinder, and I am, in general, going to pieces. There is no one with whom I can communicate, for I can't hear when someone speaks, and others can't hear me when I speak. When I speak to another person, I don't know who it is because I can't see his face. Everyone in this country is sick. Well, that is how we live in such a barren county where we live without strength, without health, without food, without being able to see, and without being able to walk. Even every limb is difficult to move. The longer one stays in this country, the worse one's physical senses become. Such is the climate of this country. This was related to me by those who came to this county before I did, and I also see that it is true because I myself feel the same as they do.

I ask you to hold onto my last letter, for as time continues, I feel that I will stop writing . . . Let it be for you as a memento . . .[88] My dear child, be well and may God help you live to see great satisfaction from your beloved, devoted sons, Mordekhai and Avigdor. May God grant them absolute goodness and abundance as only He is able. They deserve it. And may you have great satisfaction from them and from all their children. Those who live afar and who distanced themselves and fooled themselves, may God have mercy on them and bring them back . . . home . . .[89] I had more to write but I have acquired in my new country the nature to forget. In the middle of praying, I forget where I am up to. In the middle of the *Shiminesre* prayer, I remain stuck and don't know where I am up to, and I have to remain put and can't continue praying. So, it should also come as no news if I leave out a few sentences in my letter.

Give my warm regards to the Grovers. I believe that their daughter is already healthy, thank God. I only know their daughter Khanele. How is she doing? Is she healthy? Give them all my warm regards. Give regards to all my relatives and friends. Give regards to Rozele and Dvoyrele, Chaplick's children. How are things with them? Dvoyrele is a nice-looking girl. Why hasn't she married? How is Chaplick doing, their unlucky father?[90] Give regards to Duvidl's

---

88 The author is apparently asking his daughter Nekhame to hold on to his last letter as a keepsake because he believes that his current letter is barely legible, as he writes above.

89 The author is referring to Nekhame's son, Moyshe (Martin), in Portland, Oregon, who married a non-Jew. He might also be referring to his own two sons, Yosl and Yankl, in California.

90 Regarding the tragedies that befell Israel Chaplick, see Appendix B3, p. 776, footnote 1.

relative.[91] Do you hear from Duvidl? I hear nothing from him. Write me what you know about him. Refuel wrote me that he sent him a copy of my book. Did he receive it? Write me if you know that he received it, for it would make me happy. Do you remember that I sent him one, but he didn't get it? Yosef's books were lost because they did not let them into Russia.[92]

Write me. I love your letters.

I kiss you endlessly and bless you with a good and happy life with much satisfaction from your children. And I wish that you should yet get to come to *Erets-Isruel* under happy circumstances.

According to the wishes of your father, who loves you very much and prays to God for you and for you all,

Your elderly father,

Pinkhes-Dov Goldenshteyn

Aunt Bashe sends you and everyone her regards. Reyzl, Yankl, and their children send you their regards. Freyde and Sheyndl and their mother Elke send you their warm regards. There's no news in Petakh-Tikva. The Feldmans and their children send you their warm regards.[93] They are all healthy, thank God. How are your Moyshe and his children doing? How are things going with him? Shloyme is writing to you separately. He has two children who are gems, thank God. They are beautiful, clever, and bright, may they live and be well. They send their regards to "*Tyotya* Nadya."[94] All the neighbors and those acquainted with you send you their regards and are constantly asking about you. Write me how all those from Bakhchisaray are doing in New York. What do they write—those back in Bakhchisaray? Send my warm regards to everyone.

As signed above.

July 15, 1930—Letter from the Author in Petakh-Tikva to His Daughter Nekhame in Brooklyn

With the Help of God

Tuesday, the 19th of *Tamuz* 5690, Petakh-Tikva, *Erets-Isruel*

To My Dear and Good Daughter, Nekhame, May She Live and Be Well,

---

91 "Duvid's relative" refers to Duvid's half-nephew, Shimen Kanter of New York.

92 The author's son, Yosef (Joseph Goldeen) tried unsuccessfully to send a shipment of books to realtives in the Soviet Union. See Appendix A7, p. 754, for more details.

93 The Feldmans were friends who lived in Tel-Aviv. Their daughter, Adina, a comedienne and a writer, was married to the Israeli comedian Yankele Ben-Sira (1927–2016).

94 Shloyme's daughters referred to Nekhame as *Tyotya* Nadya, meaning Aunt Nadya in Russian.

I received your letter in good form. I also received the five dollars that you enclosed in the letter. But it is risky to do so. The money and the letter could have been lost because the postal workers could have taken it. It would be better to send such painstakingly saved-up money through the postal service rather than risking it. You don't have any money yourself, yet you take the food from your mouth to send to your father in order to make his life easier, yet you risk losing such carefully saved-up money, God forbid. Such foolishness succeeded only once, but one mustn't risk it a second time. The five dollars were very useful for me, and I thank you very much for it, but my heart aches for you, my child, for you need it yourself. In merit of this, may God fulfill your prayers with a full hand for the new year, and may He give you a good year and inscribe and seal you and your children for all the best with health, success, blessing, and a long, good, happy year with everything that is good. Amen and Amen.

Today I sent a letter to Yosef and Yankev. I asked Yosef to help me out with a bit of money so that I can live out my weak old years in peace. I also asked Itele to help out by asking her sisters and brother, Itsl's children, for a present for my sake. And they should take copies of my book, which speaks about their father and his family, as a keepsake. I know that Yankev is undergoing hard times, so I asked him at least to make sure to send me his monthly support on time, thereby saving me from worry and want. Now I will see how my letters affect these American businessmen.[95] Perhaps it will touch them and remind them how much their father did and suffered for them. I told them to read my book so that they should see how much effort and energy their father had put in for them. Though poor and also surrounded by enemies who hindered his ability to earn a livelihood, their father found a means of doing so by going to Chufut-Kale to engrave tombstones just to earn a livelihood for the sake of his children and to support them.[96] I think that my current letter to them will have the desired impact and that they will do something on my behalf.

I have no complaints with Refulikl. I think quite well of him. He, poor thing, is without a livelihood, and he has already given me his due a long time ago. So how can I add on to his obligations, particularly when he works so much on my behalf with the books and lays out his own money? He needs to recover his expenses.[97] I save whatever he sends me. Bless him! I hope to hear at this time some good news. And so it seems from his letters [that he will be engaged

---

95 Referring to the author's sons, Joseph and James Goldeen.

96 For more regarding the author's engraving tomstones in Chufut-Kale, see ch. 25, pp. 509–510

97 Refuel (Raphael) had the parts of his father's autobiography hardbound into a single volume. See Appendix A7, p. 753, for details.

shortly].[98] Write me what is going on over there with the prospective matches that people are suggesting to him and what he thinks about them . . . I only know from him that he hopes to write me shortly with some happy, good news regarding his future. May it only be, Master of the Universe, that this should happen, as I wish and hope to God. [. . .] My dear child, I send you fatherly kisses and wish you blessing, success, and a long, good, and happy life.

The words of your elderly father,

Pinkhes-Dov Goldenshteyn

I kiss my grandchildren, Mordekhai and Avigdor. May God send them good wives, according to their worth, and may He bless them with blessings, success, with all that is good, and with lengthy days and years. Amen, may it be His will. Aunt Bashe sends her regards to all of you. Reyzl, her mother, and her sisters send you all regards. I send very warm regards to all my relatives and friends. Shloyme and Etya and their children send very warm regards. The Feldmans also send their very warm regards.[99]

As signed above.

October 30, 1930—Letter from the Author in Petakh-Tikva to His Daughter Nekhame and Grandson Avigdor (Victor) Brockman in Brooklyn

With the Help of God

Thursday, the 8th of *Heshvan* 5691, Petakh-Tikva, *Erets-Isruel*

Wishing peace and everything good to my dear daughter, Nekhamele, may she live and be well, and her good children and their households, may they live and be well,

Mazel tov, mazel tov, my beloved daughter. I can't express my joy in writing.[100] In this distant land that I have come to live in, I am steadily going to pieces. I practically can't see anything, and my head is no longer a head—it no longer has in it any brains, any thoughts, and can no longer remember anything. So, I am satisfied, my beloved child, with your knowing from my writing to you that I am still alive, thank God, and that I have merited to hear such a precious mazel tov and that I know that God gives you great satisfaction from your children. The match is a salvation for you. Now you will live with Avigdor and his

98 Refuel had already met his wife-to-be, Claire Silber, whom he married on November 12, 1930 in Los Angeles.

99 See p. 800, footnote 93 above.

100 Nekhame's son, Avigdor (Victor) Brockman, became engaged.

wife.[101] And because they will be occupied with their business and will not be able to run a house, they will have you run the house, because they won't be able to find anyone else more faithful.[102] It will be good for both of you, and it will not cost them more—and Mara will also be able to find a match and live apart and run a home according to his means. In this manner, you will have great satisfaction from both of your sons, God willing, and you yourself will also have a life. In short, however God runs things is good. If one has trust in God, then He will help. Have trust in God, and He will help you even better than you wished yourself. I can't write anymore. I don't have any more strength and my eyes don't see, so I am ending this letter. Shloyme probably wrote to you everything. Thank God that I have Shloyme near me. He is truly faithful to me and is devoted to me. With God's help, he practically saved me from death. Praise God that I merited to have near me such a beloved child. May God bless him with health, a livelihood, and great satisfaction from his children, and with a long life. I similarly also wish you all, my beloved children, because you are all devoted to me and assist me so completely with your financial support. May God support you, may you not know any want, and may you have a life of rich, honorable years, Amen, may it be His will.

As I, your father, wish you from the depths of my heart,

Pinkhes-Dov, *shoykhet*, Goldenshteyn

I forgot to ask you to give my regards to the Grovers. Give regards to all of them. I am quite overjoyed that you are friendly and acquainted with my grandfather Reb Yankev Gredenítsers's grandchildren and great-grandchildren and that you meet them together [...] in America. Regarding this Reb Yankev—you Nekhame are Reb Yankev Gredenítser's great-grandchild, and Sosele is also a great-grandchild [*sic*]. All of your children are great-great-grandchildren, and the family is staying connected as friends. You need not be ashamed of your ancestor Reb Yankev, may he rest in peace. He died at the age of 105.[103] May his merit protect us all. He was God fearing, a tremendous Torah scholar, and his memory evokes blessing and brings to mind his good name.

To My Dear and Esteemed Grandson, Avigdor Brakhtman, may he live and be well,

---

101 Nekhame did not live with Victor, but Victor always arranged for her to live in an apartment close by to his home.

102 Victor's future father-in-law, Louis Barotz, took him into his business.

103 For more regarding the Yankev Gredenitser's age, see chapter 6, p. 147, footnote 2.

Shloyme already wrote congratulations on my behalf, but I can't rest [until I write to you myself]. I can no longer write, but I must write at least a bit. I am unable to express my joy, so you must understand and excuse me [for not writing at length]. Mazel tov, mazel tov. May your marriage come up and sprout forth like a luscious garden and may the benevolent God approve of this match. "He who finds a wife has found good,"[104] May God help that your wedding should be only good, beautiful and pleasant, and at an auspicious time with blessing and success. May riches and honor be granted on your right, and lengthy days and years on your left. May great satisfaction from your children be ahead for you, may much joy follow you, and may God illuminate your path before you and bring you success at every turn, and may you not be in want of anything for all time. Amen and Amen. Send my regards to your in-laws, the bride, and all my blessings should apply to them as well because that was included in my intentions. Please let me know which city [in Europe] they are from and their surname.[105] I hope that God will grant me life so that I will merit to bless the couple with blessings in honor of their upcoming wedding, God willing. And then I will give thanks to God for all the good that He does for me.[106] With this short blessing, I bid you goodbye.[107]

The words of your grandfather, who kisses you and blesses you with all that is good,

Pinkhes-Dov Goldenshteyn

August 28, 1939—Letter from Isruel and His Wife Gitl Goldenstein in Saint-Gervais, France, to his Sister Nekhame in Brooklyn

The 13th of *Elul* 5699/August 28, 1939[108]

Dear Sister Nekhame,

---

104 Proverbs 18:22.

105 Avigdor (Victor) Brockman's bride was Miriam "Mae" Barotz. She was born in Petshere (now Pechora, Ukraine), and her original surname was Tkatsh.

106 The author died on December 4, 1930, twenty days before Victor's wedding, which was held in Brooklyn.

107 This paragraph was translated from the Hebrew. Like most Jews of his generation in the Crimea, Avigdor (Victor) was raised speaking Russian, not Yiddish. He learned Yiddish only later from his wife's family, but he knew Hebrew from having lived in Palestine for several years.

108 World War II started three days later on September 1, 1939. The Germans invaded France on May 10, 1940. See Appendix A2, pp. 689–694, for more details regarding Isruel and his children's lives in France.

If you are angry with me for my long silence and are therefore punishing me with the same and are starving me from everything by your also not writing, then I deserve it. I have to say to you that apart from that, I see in myself that I have changed in many ways, so I have probably changed in the area of writing as well. But as I understand it, the greatest blame for the overall occurrences of change happening over the world is a result of that infamous Haman, Hitler, who has disturbed and upset everyone, especially all of Europe.

On a daily basis, we are on edge and in terror. Certainly you also know about the latest news regarding the pact made between Russia and Germany over which there has now occurred a mobilization of forces in France, England, Belgium, etc.[109] And we foreigners now find ourselves living in unoccupied dwellings among provincial French farmers.[110] With God's help, we must see to it that we settle down here so that God will protect us from evil, being that this is far from the borders.[111] They sent us a packed crate with winter clothes (that I prepared in advance). You understand that this is taking its toll on my heart. Moyshe's wife and their child are also here. And Motl's child will be with French people [i.e., non-Jews] who are keeping her to educate her. They travel often to Brittany and will take her with them. Motl will certainly be taken [into the French army] but will not be sent to the front. And Moyshe will also not be sent to the front. But even such a life in the military is also not very sweet. Now, where do I get the courage to write?

It has now also been a good few months since Yasha has written. And hearing from Itskhok-Yosef is already long out of the question. Poor thing, he is very sick, and no members of his family are replying to my letters. From my dear son in Russia, we have to try every possibility and wait months to write to him a postcard with a few words on it.[112] Well, how is that for a free world in which everyone strives for a free life?

---

109 On August 23, 1939, Germany and the Soviet Union signed a non-aggression agreement known as the Molotov-Ribbentrop Pact.

110 Since Isruel and Gitl immigrated from the Soviet Union to France in 1935, they were considered foreigners. Seventy percent of France's Jews who were murdered in Nazi concentration camps and death camps were foreigners who came to France in the 1930s (Authers and Wolffe, 2002:159).

111 At that time, Isruel, his wife Gitl, and daughter Freyde (Frida) Pozwolski and her children were living in a small village in the center of France, Saint-Gervais d'Auvergne, about thirty miles from Vichy, France. When the war broke out on September 1, 1939, they remained in that village until the end of the war.

112 Isruel's son, Avrum, was the only one of his children to remain in the Soviet Union. Apparently, Isruel's family was able to send him a postcard only every few months by special means. Avrum's wife, Pola and daughter, Ala were the only members of Isruel's family to perish in the Holocaust.

I believe that you will not be astonished for long by the news that I am about to write to you. It won't surprise you to find out that Freyde's husband, Yosef, is has now been back here for several weeks, that he was in New York for two days, was extremely busy with his business affairs, and did not see anyone from the family.[113] So what do we do regarding such a subject matter? Even more, he is now completely without a job.[114] He says that he doesn't want to remain in his prior position (they asked him strongly to return). He has other offers, but he wants something better. One can't get any details out of him, as some wives are able to do. [. . .] May we not suffer from want, God forbid. Regarding the money for expenses that, *kenehore,* such a family needs to have during such inflation, particularly since the children [. . .] were given everything until recently (may it be God's will that the situation never becomes worse), they say that they have a lot of savings. Let us hope that it will suffice for a year. Perhaps he has some money hidden somewhere—we don't know. We only see that this time he did not bring back [from New York] any presents for anyone. Now he is in Paris. He had a discussion with his boss regarding financial matters. He is asking for three knowledgeable individuals to determine the proper salary that he is due. We have little hope regarding this because the rich always prevail since they can spend lavishly on lawyers. Meanwhile, we let Freyde leave so that she could go heal her nerves and her inability to sleep. You yourself can now understand that this is not an easy situation for us to be in with such indulged children. But what can we do? We have to help her as long as it is possible and to make her life easier so that she can continue to raise her children who very much need her help. Certainly, you understand our disappointment in our son-in-law for not seeing any of our relatives [in New York]. But we do not reprimand him because how would it help?! Sister, now you know about everything that is happening to us.

When I see the difficulties involved with traveling now, it will turn out that I will be here all alone on Rosh Hashanah and Yom Kippur—just like when they arrested me (may it never happen to anyone).[115] And I will have to write

---

113 Referring to Isruel's son-in-law Joseph Pozwolski.

114 In correspondence from 2002, Joseph Pozwolski's daughter, Myriam Cronin, commented on this passage that she did not think that her father was really without a job, "If he was, he may have left after an argument but was very sought after because he was extremely clever and would not have been unemployed for long!" In any case, at the outbreak of the Second World War, Joseph was in Yugoslavia on a business trip when Italy closed its borders, and he could not return to France. He miraculously survived the Second World War and was only united with his family in 1945. See Appendix A1, pp. 691–692, for details.

115 In other words, Isruel prayed alone, without a *minyan*, on the High Holy Days. The exact circumstances of his arrest are unknown, though he was likely arrested by the Yevsektsiya (the

and cancel my plans to lead the services in the *minyan* where I was hired [back in Paris]. It is already too dangerous to remain there. Whoever can leave is dispersing to wherever they can. I don't mind the loss,[116] as long as things change towards peace. You can imagine how disturbed and upset the High Holidays will be this year. The World Jewish Congress was also sufficiently disturbed; they did everything quickly and then went their separate ways.[117]

Today is actually the 13th of *Elul*, when my parents and I went and stood in Meyer Rogalsky's wedding hall under the *huppah* with my intended wife, Gitl, and her family and heard the blessings and the good wishes that everyone didn't spare from sharing.[118] I remember all the details just as if it occurred today—though then it flew by like a dream. Oh, shivers and quakes come over me when I recollect the difference between then and now. If one would earnestly calculate how much we have lived—deducting when we slept, when we were sick, and the emotional pains when we were in pain—the bottom line would be that we have lived very little. So, to live just as long once again would only be harmful, but perhaps we would be able to get in a slightly larger amount of living the second time around. My desire just revealed itself in its entirety in the form of hope—that we still want to live to see the old promised Jewish land, given by that old, well-known eternal Creator, where Jews in every corner of the world want to gather together and live in peace. Sister, I wish for you to be signed and sealed for good for the new Jewish year of 5700 along with all Jews and along with your children and grandchildren.

With all the best wishes which your own flesh-and-blood brother can wish,

Yours,

Isruel-Burekh

Moyshe and his wife and children, Freyde and her children, Motl and his wife and child, and Avrum-Duvid with his wife and child, all ask me to wish you along with your children, relatives, and old friends a good, sweet year filled with a good life and for peace in the entire world.

---

so-called Jewish section of the Soviet Communist Party in charge of destroying all vestiges of traditional Jewish life) for his work as a *shoykhet* and a *moyel*. For more about the Yevsektsiya, see ch. 29, p. 599, footnote 74. Isruel and his wife, Gitl, left the Soviet Union in 1935.

116 Isruel is apparently referring to the fees he lost from his inability be in Paris to lead the services during the High Holidays.

117 The World Jewish Congress was established in Geneva, Switzerland in August 1936 in reaction to the rise of Nazism. With the outbreak of the Second World War in September 1939, their headquarters moved from Paris to Geneva.

118 Slutsky (1981:113) refers to Rogalsky by his Russian name, Miron Rogalsky.

I wish all of you a good year. I have little to write. You must understand what my heart is bearing now. I worry a lot about my children. May it be God's will that we should not suffer any sorrow and have a year of peace.

Gitl

Appendix C: Translations of Additional Documents

Appendix C1: Hebrew Letter from Rabbi Medini (Sdei Khemed) Regarding the Author (1879)

The original 1879 letter written by Rabbi Khayim Khizkiyahu Medini (1834–1904) was donated to the Klau Library—Hebrew Union College-Jewish Institute of Religion in Cincinnati (Acc 477, 12v–13r) by either Pinkhes-Dov Goldenshteyn's son Refuel (Raphael Goldenstein, 1885–1933), a graduate of Hebrew Union College, or his widow Claire Silver (1910–1994). A microfilm copy is housed at the Institute of Microfilmed Hebrew Manuscripts at the National Library of Israel. A Hebrew transcription of this letter was printed, with a few minor transcription errors, in the published collection of Rabbi Medini's letters, Igrot Sdei Khemed *(2006, 1:11).*

Rabbi Medini's letter is an important outside source which corroborates Goldenshteyn's account of the unwarranted persecution that he suffered at the hands of the community leaders of Bakhchisaray. It also confirms his date of arrival there as March 1879 (chapter 23, p. 468). Goldenshteyn does not mention this letter in his autobiography, but he does mention a more severe letter of reproach from Rabbi Medini sent to the community leaders of Bakhchisaray in February 1880 (chapter 24, p. 483).

With the help of God, Sunday of the Torah Portion of *Khayey-Sora*,[1] 5640,[2] peace unto Israel.

Abundant peace and grand salvation to the Holy Nation, the remnants whom God calls the holy of Israel; men of valor, who have the fear of God near to their souls; men of strength, who fulfill His words and hearken to the call of the living God, the God of Israel; wealthy nobles, officers, leaders, and appointees, shepherds of Israel; a pure people chosen and exceptional; brothers of the house of Israel; the treasured individuals of the worthy city of Bakhchisaray, May God be with you and grant you long life, Amen.

After wishing life and peace to all your most honorable persons, I will allow my quill to speak of the worries concerning the unpleasant rumors which have reached my ears. The worries relating to the turmoil which has developed in your camp regarding the learned *shoykhet*, Pinkhes-Dov, the son of Reb Y. R. It is some eight months since he was accepted, willingly and by the entire community, to serve as *shoykhet* in your camp, and now, due to dissension and conflict which has arisen between you, some of you are trying to drive him from his position. Fear and trembling have gripped me. How can I see a holy Jewish community commit so terrible an act? As the Torah states, "The remnant of Israel shall not commit injustice."[3]

My dear friends and brothers, how can you even contemplate dismissing him from his holy position? "In matters of holiness, demotion is not acceptable."[4] He is a man with whom no fault can be found. Were it not for the fact that I heard it from others, I would have found it difficult to believe or suspect that faithful Jews could do such a despicable thing. This type of action is contrary to decent human behavior. Who ever heard of a community accepting a *shoykhet*, having him travel with his wife and children from a distant land, pulling up his stakes from his native home, from a place where he was well established, and then sending him away on some slight pretense? Even this is accompanied by a prohibition which is based on the ruling of our holy Torah. I am not aware of anyone among you who is sufficiently knowledgeable in the Talmud and the Jewish legal codes. I am not aware that any of you are capable of debating him in matters of Jewish law regarding the prohibitions [of the laws of *sh'khita*].

Any *shoykhet* that will move into your holy community at the present time will be transgressing the prohibition of, "Do not move the boundaries . . . set

1 Genesis 23:1 to 25:18.
2 Referring to the 16th of *Heshvan* 5680 (November 2, 1879).
3 Zephaniah 3:13.
4 Babylonian Talmud (Brakhot 28a).

by those who came before you."[5] And as it states in the codes, this transgression is compounded in a case such as this. I already warned the *shoykhet* Reb Shmuel, who was prepared to accept the position in your community, that he is not allowed to practice as *shoykhet* in the place of the above-mentioned Reb Pinkhes-Dov. If he does accept the position, bitter will be his end.

If, God forbid, there actually is some slight stain to be found in the character of the *shoykhet,* Reb Pinkhes, and that is the reason they desire to have him removed, perhaps [you are justified]. But how can you take such a step on your own? "For Israel is not widowed,"[6] since God has left us remnants [i.e., Torah scholars], and there are many great rabbis even in our generation. Rabbis who despise wealth and seek truth, can be sought, and you can present your grievances in a straightforward and honest manner before them. They will pronounce a verdict, for they are qualified, and you will be clear of any and all iniquity.

Therefore, I am expressing myself before you, I am appealing to you from the depths of my heart, I am calling upon you: listen and your souls will blossom. For the sake of the honor of our Torah, draw close those who are near and do not release the above-mentioned *shoykhet,* Reb Pinkhes, from your hands. Hold on to him, because, according to that which we heard he is a fine and good person. Do not be a partner in harming innocent blood, God forbid. He should remain in his position serving his brothers, and no stranger should encroach upon his territory.

May the Blessed God satisfy you, your children, and all whom you hold dear, with all manner of good. May God be with you and bless you that you shall hear of no calamities or misfortune in your midst. You who cleave to God will all merit life. Amen, so may it be.

The writer, who signs with blessings of peace and intense love,

Behold here are my words, humbly yours, Khayim Khizkiyahu Medini, may God protect me and save me, here in Karasubazar, may God protect it. Amen.

---

5 Deuteronomy 19:14. This prohibition includes unfair business practices.

6 Jeremiah 51:5.

Appendix C2: Episodes Related by the Author about Rabbi Medini (*Sdei Khemed*)

Raphael Goldenstein, *The Krimchaks: Their Life and Origin in the Crimea* (graduation thesis for rabbinical degree at Hebrew Union College, Cincinnati, 1916), 77–78.

> [In 1899, Rabbi Medini's] heart's desire was fulfilled, and he returned to Jerusalem. The Krimchaks tried their very best to keep him, at least persuade him to stay a few more years with them, but without avail. He was determined to leave the Crimea, although not without a sense of deep regret, because he was very much attached to his community who saw in his departure the loss of a great leader, the equal of whom they never had and perhaps shall never have again. The feeling of regret and sorrow of his departure was therefore mutual. I am sure no Jewish leader was ever given a warmer send-off than the Haham in 1889 [*sic*].[1] Men, women and children marched after him, upon leaving the city of Karasubazar, with sad drooping heads and gloomy faces, as though the father of the community was leaving them orphaned, without any one to help them in their difficulties and comfort them in their sorrows. People from all parts of the Crimea turned out in large numbers to meet him at the station as he passed by and thousands went as far as Sebastopel [*sic*][2] to see him for the last time, when he sailed on [a] steamer to Constantinople.[3] My father, who was one of his great admirers and who too went to Sebastopel [*sic*] to bid him good-bye, told me he never saw a more touching scene in his life.[4]

---

1 Haham (or *Khakham*) literally means "wise man" in Hebrew and is used as a title for rabbis among the Sephardic Jews. Rabbi Medini went to the Holy Land in 1899.

2 Sevastopol.

3 A steamer is another name for a steamship.

4 "My father" refers to Pinkhes-Dov Goldenshteyn.

Raphael Goldenstein, "R. Khayim Khizkiyahu Medini" [Hebrew], *Ha-Toren* [New York] 11, no. 6 (September 1925): 15–16, 18. (*Ha-Toren*, "The mast," was a prestigious Hebrew-language journal published in New York between 1913 and 1925, which dealt with current issues and literary topics.)

> [Rabbi Medini] was incomparable in his hate for bribery. As an illustration of this, my father related the following anecdote. On one occasion in 5649 [1888–1889] in Sevastopol a tremendous halakhic issue arose regarding a butcher who had sold eight feet from one ox. . . . Understandably he had somehow mixed non-kosher feet with kosher ones. This disgrace became known, and a tremendous conflict arose. The city was in turmoil because of this vile incident. The community and the other kosher butchers wanted to dispose of him. So they sent for the *Khakham* of Karasubazar to quiet the unrest, and the *Khakham* spent two days in Sevastopol. They gave the *Khakham* fifty rubles as compensation for his time which he adamantly refused to accept. And he said to them, 'I've heard that you have a *mikveh* that isn't adequate; therefore, it would be much more appropriate to expend the fifty rubles towards the repair of the *mikveh*.' Immediately upon hearing his words, they raised an additional 300 rubles among themselves and built a new, beautiful *mikveh* according to the latest style.
>
> In addition, to understand the great character of this great man and to realize how noble he was and to the extent he disapproved of bribery, my father recounted that every time the *Khakham* traveled to Sevastopol, the expenses of his trip—which generally amounted to twenty-five rubles—were paid by the community. Upon returning home once, he made an exact accounting of all his expenses and had two and half rubles remaining. One clear day, the community of Sevastopol received in the mail the two and a half rubles along with a short note giving the exact accounting and explaining that two and half rubles was all that remained. . . .
>
> After thirty-three years of working with the community of Krimchaks in Karazubazar, the Rabbi Khayim-Khizkiyahu Medini hoped to return to his homeland – Hebron. In 1889 [*sic*]

he returned to the Land of Israel. Separating from his community was as difficult for him as the parting of the Red Sea since it was stressful for the faithful shepherd to leave his flock, and it was difficult for the flock to be separated from their shepherd, their teacher, and the crown of their heads, whose soul was tied to theirs. Many asked and pleaded with him not to leave and implored him to remain at least another few years, but, once he had announced his plans, he would not retract them. Therefore, on Tuesday of the Torah portion of *Shlakh* in 1889 [*sic*] the *tsadik* left Karasubazar.[5] With his leaving, radiance departed, glory departed, splendor departed, and the city was in despair. In seeing him off, everyone—men, women, and children—followed him. On his departure from Russia for the Holy Land, members of his own community as well as residents from all over the Crimea showed him great honor. My father, a dear friend of the *Khakham* and a strong admirer of his, also traveled to Sevastopol with the intention of seeing him off. He wanted to see him one last time and to bless him with a good journey. He told me that he had never seen such a beautiful departure as this one—hundreds, even thousands, came to the seashore and stood in place until the ship disappeared on the waters of the Black Sea.[6]

---

5 *Shlakh* is the name of the Torah portion found in Numbers 13:1 to 15:41. Since Rabbi Medini left the Crimea in 1899, Tuesday of *Parashat Shlakh* corresponds to the 21st of *Sivan* (May 30, 1899).

6 This depiction in *Ha-Toren* of Rabbi Medini's departure in 1899 for the Holy Land is cited in practically every biographical work and article about him.

Appendix C3: Two Certificates in *Sh'khita* Obtained by the Author's Son Refuel (1904 and 1906)

The original certificates in sh'khita *were donated to the Klau Library—Hebrew Union College-Jewish Institute of Religion in Cincinnati (Acc 477, 12v–13r) by either Pinkhes-Dov Goldenshteyn's son Refuel (Raphael Goldenstein, 1885–1933), a graduate of Hebrew Union College, or his widow Claire Silver (1910–1994).*

בא לפני המוכ"ז האברך הרבני המופלג י"א מו"ה רפאל ב"ר פנחס דוב גאלדנשטיין שו"ב מעיר באחציסריי הסמוכה לפה ובקש ממנו לתהות על קנקנו בדיני שו"ב ושאלתי אותו בכמה הלכות בדיני שו"ב וראיתי כי למד ושנה הרבה בדיני שו"ב בשמ"ח [בשמלה חדשה] ואחרונים ויודע ובקי בהלכות שו"ב. וגם העיד לפני השו"ב דפה ובכתב אשר נתן על ידו כי יש לו הרגשת פגומה דמה"ד [דקה מן הדקה] ומומחא הוא להעמיד סכין של שחיטה חד וחלק וכי גם יראת שדי על פניו ע"כ ראוי הוא להיות שו"ב בכל תפוצות ישראל כי בטח יחזור על למודו בכל חדש כדת גם לא ישיג גבול רעהו ומותר לכל ישראל לאכל מזביחתו ובטוח אני שלא יצא ח"ו דבר שאינו מתוקן כל צרכו מת"י [מתחת ידו] ומי יתן וירבו כמותו שובי"ם ביראת ד' ומדות טובות וחפץ ד' בידו יצליח יאכלו ענוים וישבעו.

באתי עה"ח אור ליום ועש"ק כד כסלו שנת התרסה לפ"ק סעוואסטאפאל

נאום שמואל ירוחם יונאוויטש רדפ"ק [רב דפה קהילתנו]

The bearer of this letter, namely the young God-fearing, exceptional rabbinic scholar, our master, Reb Refúel, the son of Reb Pinkhes-Dov Goldenshteyn, the *shoykhet* of Bakhchisaray, which is in our vicinity, requested that I test him on the laws of *sh'khita*, and I tested him regarding many of the laws of *sh'khita*. I have seen that he has studied and reviewed many of these laws as found in *Simla Khadasha*[1] and in the works of other later authorities and is well versed in them.

1 *Simla Khadasha* is a fundamental work on the laws of *sh'khita* written by Rabbi Aleksander-Sender Shor (1673–1737) and first published in 1733.

Also, the local *shoykhet*[2] testified before me and wrote in a written statement that Reb Refuel can detect even a very slight nick in a slaughtering knife, can sharpen a slaughtering knife to the point that it is sharp and smooth, and the fear of God is upon him. Hence, he is fit to be a *shoykhet* in any Jewish community for he will certainly be reviewing his studies on a monthly basis as is required by Jewish law and will not encroach on the rights of his fellow *shoykhet*. It is permissible for any Jew to partake of meat that he has slaughtered. I am confident that he will never, God forbid, allow anything that is not completely kosher to reach the consumer. I only wish that there were many more God-fearing and refined *shokhtim* of his caliber. May he be successful in fulfilling God's desires. The humble may eat [meat slaughtered by him] and be satisfied.

Signed the eve of Friday, the 24th of *Kislev* 5665,[3] Sevastopol
Shmuel-Yerukhem Yunovitsh, Rabbi of the Local Jewish Community

---

בא לפני האברך המשכיל המפואר הבחור מר רפאל בן השו"ב פ"ד אבן-זהב עם תעודותיו מהשובי"ם והרבנים הנודעים לי, וביקש ממנו שחפצו לעמוד בכור המבחן גם לפני. ועתה אחרי עבדו בכל יום בלי הפוגות זה כמה שבועות וירחים בהשחזת סכינים לשחיטה ובבדיקת הריאות פנים וחוץ ובנסיונות דיני שו"ב ובכל חילוקי דיעותיהם. מצאתי לי און להגיד ישרו בפני כל, ולהעיד עליו, כי אומן גדול הנהו הן בהשחזת סכינים גדולים וקטנים להעמידם חו"ח [חד וחלק] כדת בלי שום פגומה דמה"ד [דקה מן הדקה]. והן בשחיטת כל דבר הצריך שחיטה. גם הוא בקי בהריעותות הנמצאים בריאה פנימי וחצון. כאחד השובי"ם הישישים העומדים על משמרתם זה כמה עשרות שנים. ועל כולם י"א בלבו, והשכלה טהורה מצאה קן אצלו. ולכן ידי תכון עמו לסעדו ולהעיד עליו כי מותר לאכול משחיטתו ובדיקתו בלי שום מחשבה ורעיון זר, כי לא יוציא ח"ו דבר שאינו מתוקן. ולהעדה שתפול בגורלה שו"ב הגון כזה שרוח הבריאות נוחה הימנו, גם רוח המקום נוחה הימנו.
באתי על החתום ביום מלאת לי שלשים וארבעה שנים לחיי, וי"ז שנים בעבודתי במלאכת השו"ב יום ו' ערש"ק פ' ויגש ח' טבת שנת תרס"ו לפ"ק פה ק"ק פעאדאסיע פלך טבריא מדינת קרים נאום הכותב באמת
ישראל ברוך גאלדענשטיין שו"ב

The single young man Refuel, the son of the *shoykhet* P. D. Even-Zahav,[4] a wonderful intelligent young man, appeared before me with his certificates

---

2 Among the list of donors who contributed to the publication of Rabbi Khayim-Khizkiyahu Medini's *Sde Khemed* (1896:[5]) are mentioned the rabbi of Sevastopol, Rabbi Shmuel-Yerukhem Yunovitsh, and its two *shokhtim*, Shloyme Kahn and Mikhl Kheyfets.

3 December 2, 1904.

4 Isruel writes their surname of Goldenshteyn, which means "gold stone," in Hebrew translation as Even-Zahav.

from certain *shokhtim* and rabbis who are known to me. He requested that I should also test his knowledge of the laws of *sh'khita*. After now having worked here tirelessly on a daily basis for a number of weeks and months sharpening slaughtering knives to make them fit for *sh'khita*, inspecting animal lungs inside and out to assure that they are free of lesions, and being constantly tested on all the finer points of the laws of *sh'khita*, I feel confident in proclaiming his integrity before one and all. I can testify that he is a talented craftsman and can sharpen large and small slaughtering knives until they are sharp and smooth without even the slightest nick, as required by Jewish law, and he performs the *sh'khita* of all livestock professionally. He is as proficient in the various flaws that can be found on the inside and outside of the lungs as an experienced *shoykhet* who has plied his trade for many decades.

Above all he is God fearing in his heart, and pure wisdom has found its place in him. Therefore, my hand will vouch for him. I will testify without the slightest hesitation that it is permitted to eat from the livestock that he slaughters and inspects. He would never allow, God forbid, anything that is not fully kosher to pass as kosher. And [fortunate will be] the community that merits to have such a fine *shoykhet* to fall to its lot, someone who is pleasant with all people and the spirit of God will also be pleased by him.

Signed today on my thirty-fourth birthday[5] and seventeen years since I began my work as a *shoykhet*, Friday, the Eve of the Holy *Shabes* of the Torah portion of *Vayigash*, the 8th of *Teyves* 5606,[6] here in Feodosiya, province of Taurida, Crimean Peninsula.

Signed by one who writes in truth,
Isruel-Burekh Goldenshteyn, *shoykhet*

---

5 In ch. 21, p. 381, Isruel's birthday is noted as being the 8th of *Teyves* 5633 (January 7, 1873). Hence, he was actually thirty-three years old and not thirty-four as he writes here.

6 December 25, 1906.

Appendix D

D1. The Author's

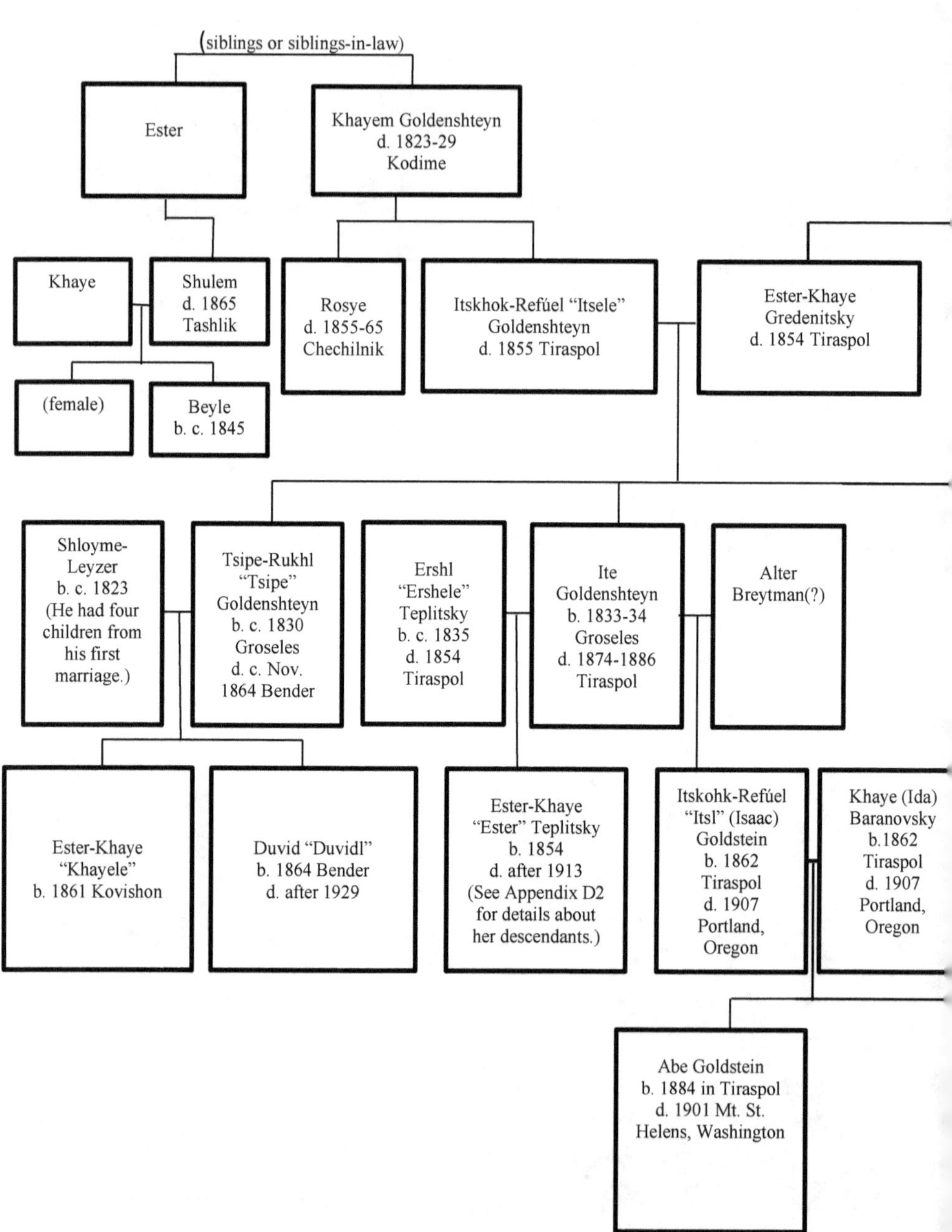

Genealogical Charts

Ancestors and Siblings

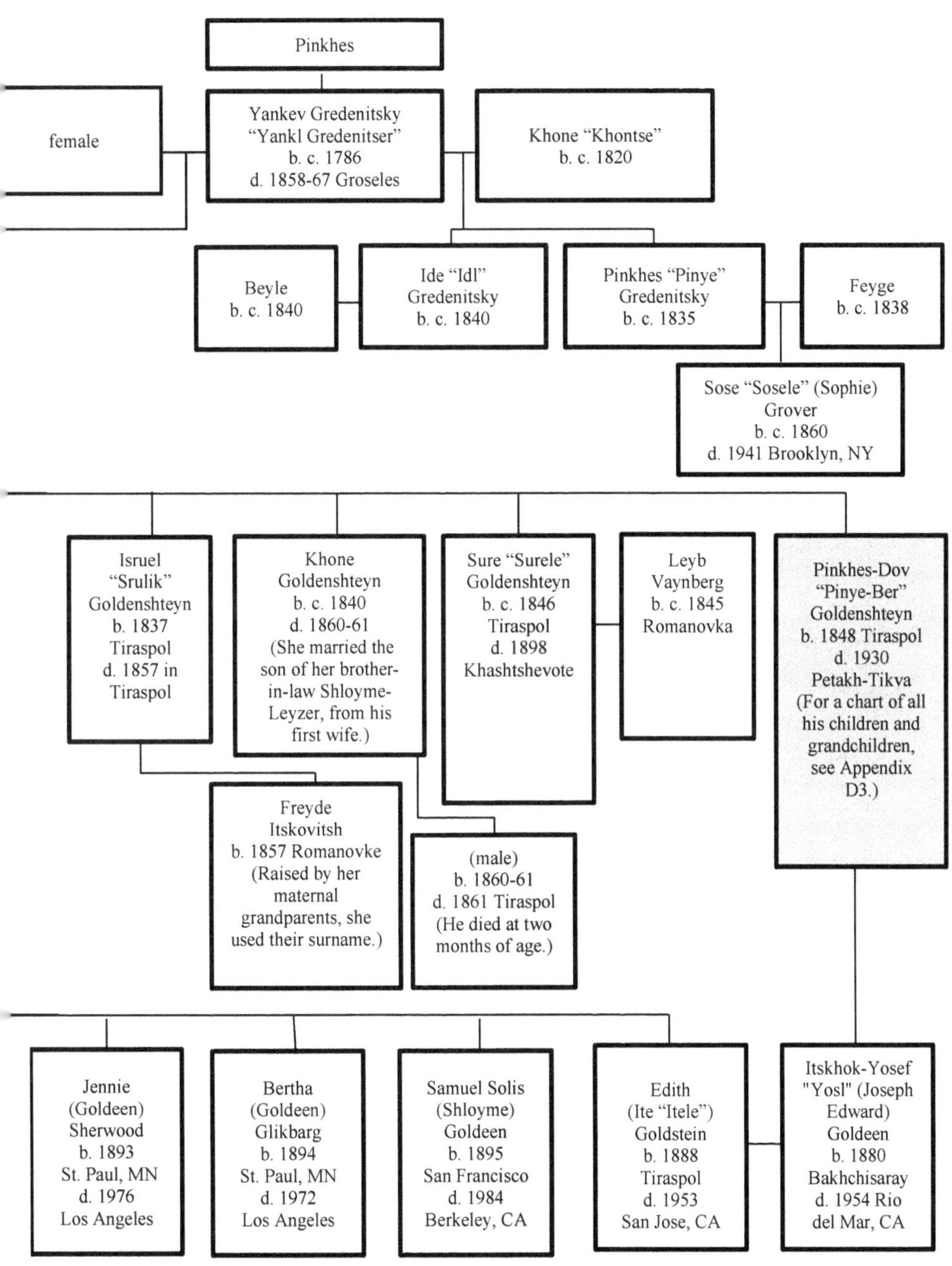

D2. The Extended Family of Ersh

(Shaded boxes indicate those individuals mentioned, sometimes n

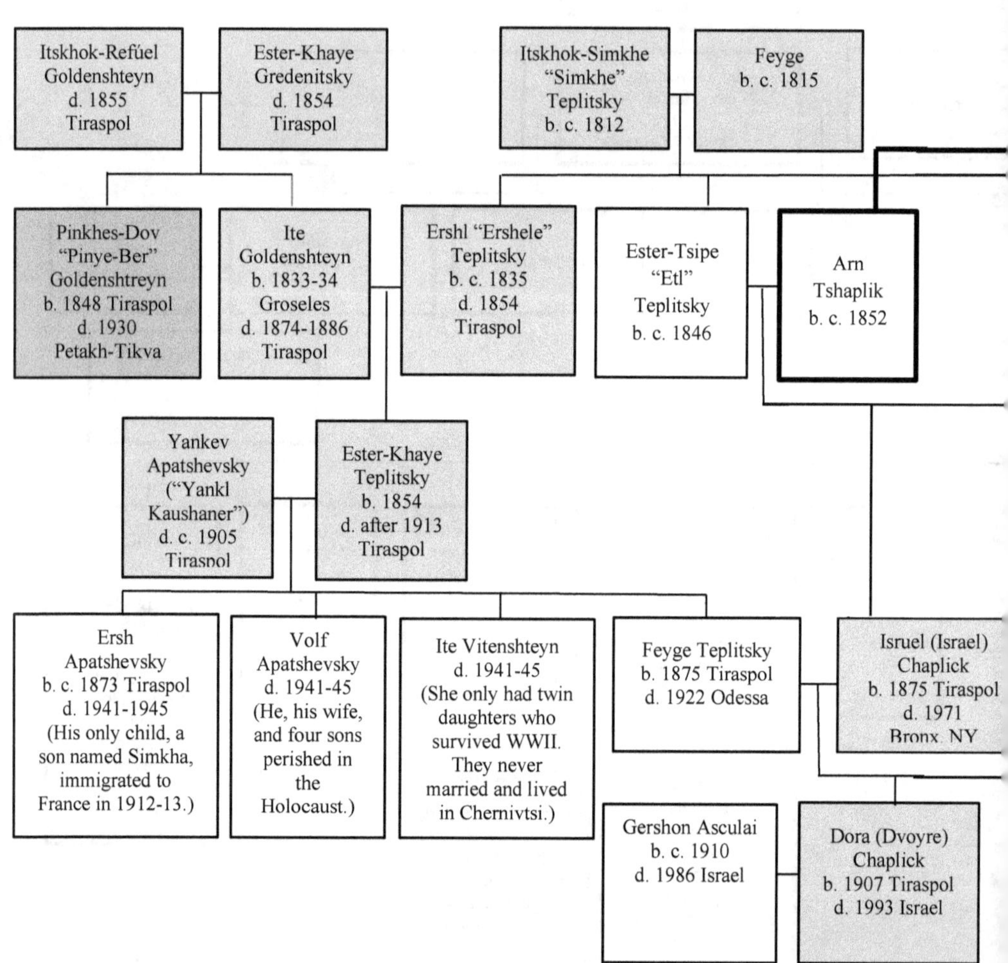

1 This chart is primarily based on information found in Pinye-Ber Goldenshteyn's autobiography, the 1858 additional revision list (poll-tax census) of the Jews of Tiraspol, and, most notably, the genealogical chart made by Bernard Budiansky (1929–1999) and his son Michael based on an interview with Bernard's grandfather Israel Chaplick in the mid-1960s, who was said to have a photographic memory. Not necessarily all known children for any given couple are shown or mentioned.

Teplitsky, the Author's Brother-in-Law

name, in the text of the book or in the author's letters.)

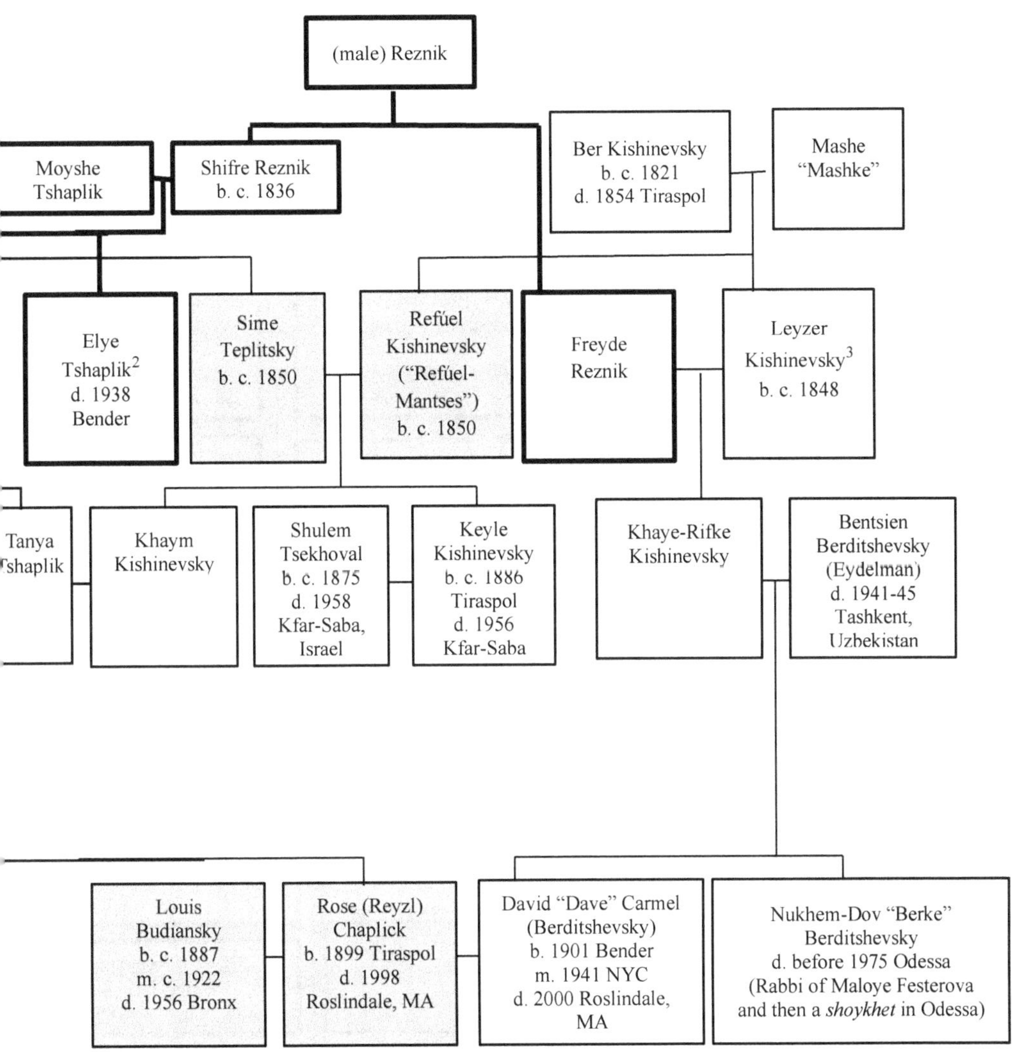

2 Elye Tshaplik, a *shoykhet* in Bender, is mentioned at some length in Tamari (1975:242–245, 418, 441–442). Tamari (1975:xx,418) mentions that Elye's granddaughter Ne'ila Glick married Rabbi Shlomo Carlebach (1925–1994) in 1972.

3 In his article about the Jewish community of Bendér in *Kehllat Benderi*, David Carmel (1975:263,265,269) mentions his grandfather Leyzer Kishinevsky, father, father-in-law (and second cousin) Israel Chaplick, and great-uncle Refúel Kishinevsky and their relationships with tbe Bendérer *Rebbes*. See also Tamari (1975:212,321,377,xix-xx) for information regarding Carmel, his father, and siblings.

D3. The Author's Children

(The boxes of Pinye-Ber ar

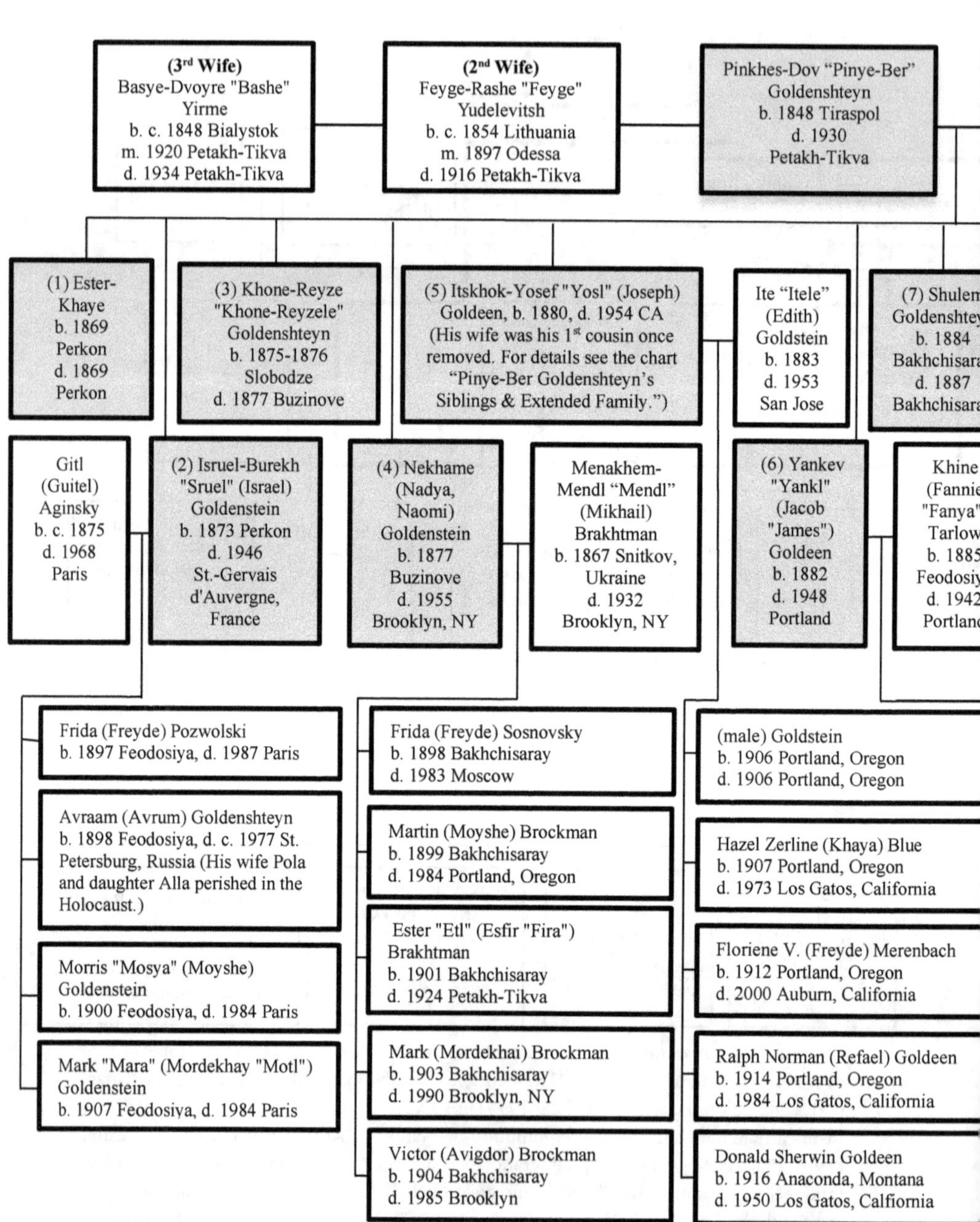

and Grandchildren

his 13 children are shaded.)

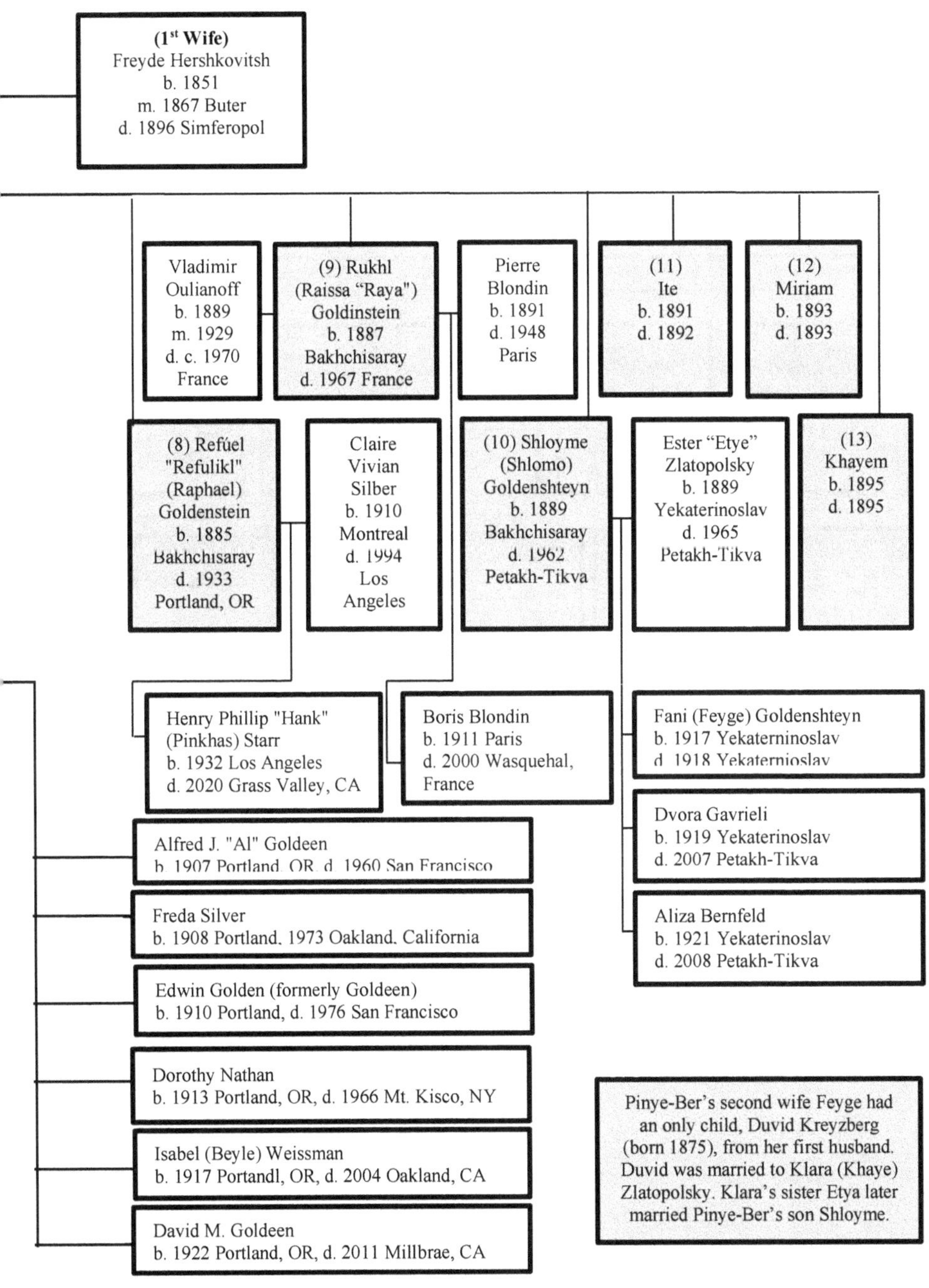

D4. The Extended Hershkovitsh Family

(Including the Grinbergs and Perlkvorts who suffered in exile from Petakh-Tik

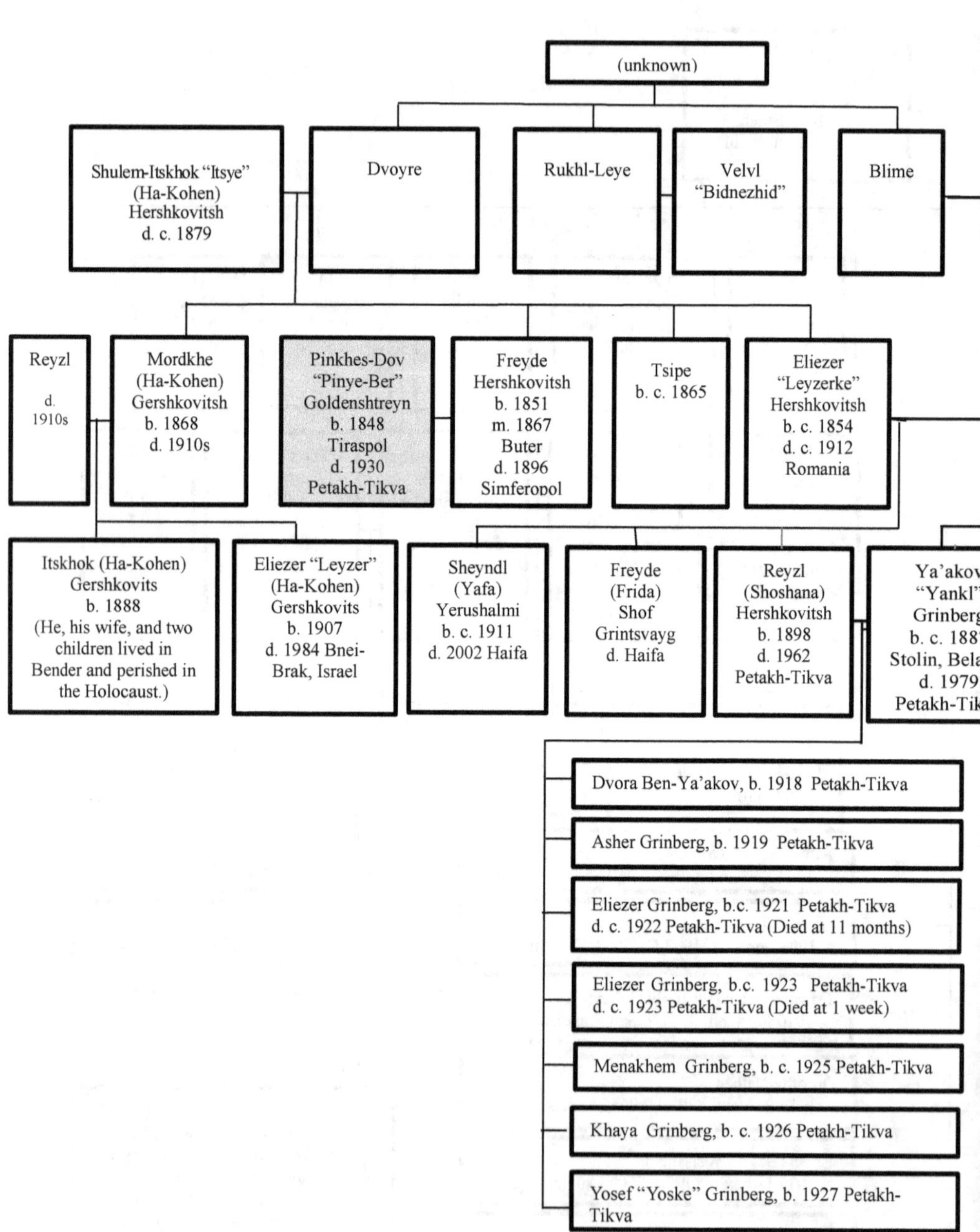

the Family of the Author's Wife Freyde

together with the author in 1918, as described in chs. 32 and 33.)

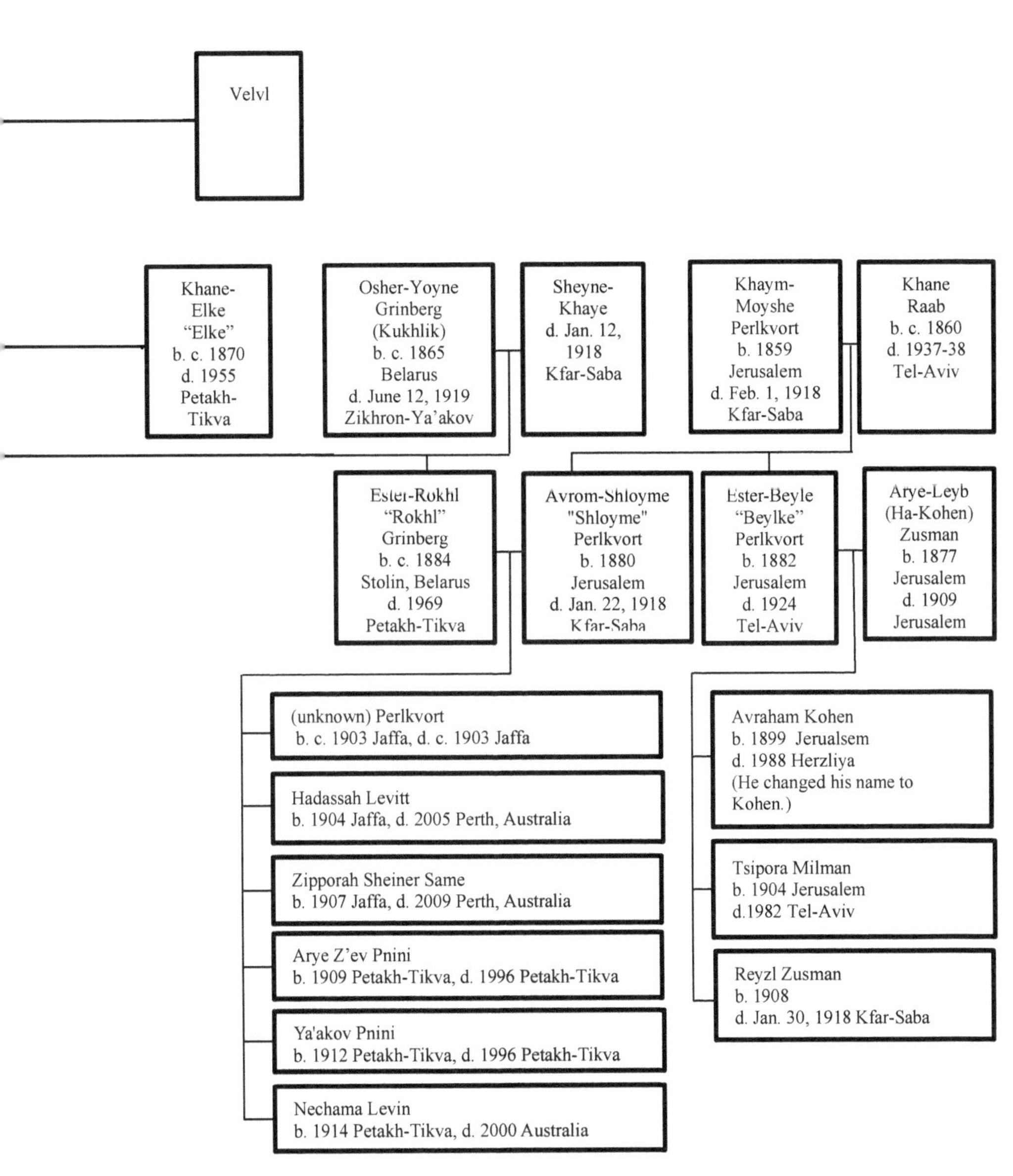

Appendix E: Pinye-Ber, His Torah Scroll, and the Chabadniks of Petakh-Tikva—A 1926 Kishinev Newspaper Article

A 1926 Yiddish-language article about Pinkhes-Dov Goldenshteyn was located only a few weeks before the publication of this volume.[1] Although the article does not mention Goldenshteyn by name, it is clearly about him, the former *shoykhet* of Bakhchisaray who moved to Petakh-Tikva and wrote a Torah scroll. In an April 1929 letter, Goldenshteyn mentions having read two articles about himself, one in a Romanian newspaper and the other in a Hebrew one printed in Palestine (Appendix B3, 794). From the two details that he mentions about the Hebrew article, it is clear that he read a version of the 1926 article.[2]

The article was written by the secular author and journalist Rokhl Feygenberg (1885-1972), who began her prolific career writing in Yiddish and then transitioned to Hebrew, often using the pseudonym of Rakhel Imri. The article was first published in 1926 in a Yiddish newspaper in Chişinău (formerly Kishinev), Romania (now in Moldova), where she had lived in 1921. Most of the article can be corroborated by Goldenshteyn's autobiography. While adding some important details, it also includes numerous inaccuracies, as noted in the footnotes to the English translation.

In 1942, Feygenberg's Hebrew version of the article was reprinted in the Hebrew daily newspaper *Hegeh* (Rudder).[3] Overall, it is a

---

1 Thanks to Menachem Nemanov, an enthusiastic reader of *The Shochet*, for bringing the 1942 Hebrew version of this article to my attention (see below). Its discovery was instrumental in locating the original 1926 version on the website of the Historical Jewish Press (www.nli.org.il/en/newspapers). The exact article that Goldenshteyn saw in 1929 has not been located.

2 The two points about the article that Goldenshteyn mentions are its description of him as having had a black beard when he was younger (his beard had actually been red) and his wife's reciting many *tkhines*.

3 "Ha-sofer sta"m: mi-parashat khayav shel Yehudi Erets-Yisraeli" (The Scribe of Torah Scrolls, Tefillin, and Mezuzahs: From the Life Story of a Jew of the Land of Israel), *Hegeh*,

straightforward translation of the original Yiddish, though the Hebrew version incorrectly portrays Goldenshteyn as a strong proponent of secular education and as an ardent Zionist, when he was virtually uninvolved politically. She also adds the following opening sentence, “I chanced upon his house one autumn night in the year 5685 [fall of 1924], and I was impressed by its owner who came out to greet me,” which testifies to her having personally conversed with Goldenshteyn, rather than having heard his story secondhand.[4]

Feygenberg's article, which appeared before the publication of Goldenshteyn's original Yiddish-language autobiography in 1928-1929, is significant because we know that Goldenshteyn read it and commented on only two details, indicating that he had little criticism of its content as a whole. The article provides a completely independent and contemporaneous impression of Goldenshteyn, whereas the interviews conducted by the translator with Goldenshteyn's elderly relatives took place more than seventy years after his passing. In addition to confirming the image portrayed by his relatives of Goldenshteyn as a cheerful person, the article highlights his Hasidic fervor and the great efforts he took to serve God with joy, without worry or fear. This might belie the impression some readers are left with upon reading his often harrowing autobiography.[5] The article also indicates that Goldenshteyn's entire career in the Crimea may have been even more distressing than his depiction of it in his autobiography, for the article reveals that he came to hate being a *shoykhet*, a profession that he carried out faithfully for so many decades. Other hardships are mentioned in the article which he does not include in the book.

March 17, 1942, p. 1 and March 18, 1942, p. 2. A *sofer* is a specially trained scribe who writes the Hebrew text of Torah scrolls, tefillin, or mezuzas on parchment using the traditional form of calligraphy.

4 Nonetheless, when meeting and conversing with Feygenberg, Goldenshteyn apparently did not realize that she was a journalist who would be writing an article about him, for he refers to the author of the article in his 1929 letter as “he.” Apparently, the version that Goldenshteyn read in 1929 either abbreviated her name or omitted it altogether. Of course, Feygenberg might not have intended to write a story about Goldenshteyn when she first spoke with him.

5 See also the Introduction, 59.

The article is also the first known evidence that Goldenshteyn had been in contact in the early 1900s with the Lubavitcher Rebbe, Rabbi Shalom Dov-Ber Schneerson (1860-1920),[6] and had extensive contact with his fellow Chabadniks in Petakh-Tikva. In his autobiography, Goldenshteyn never mentions Lubavitch, or Chabad for that matter, after his second trip there in 1873 (ch. 21).[7]

This translation follows the 1926 Yiddish version. However, the 1942 Hebrew version was consulted when the Yiddish was unclear or when the Hebrew version was more elaborate. The Hebrew version concludes on a different note than the Yiddish, and a translation of it has been included in a footnote.

---

6 Rabbi Shalom Dov-Ber Schneerson, known as the Rebbe Rashab (an acronym of his name), was the fifth Rebbe of Chabad and the son of his predecessor, Rabbi Shmuel Schneerson (1834-1882), whom Goldenshteyn traveled to see in Lubavitch, as described in ch. 21 (pp. 375-380).

7 In a private interview in 2001 with Aliza (Goldenshteyn) Bernfeld, of Petakh-Tikva, she recalled her grandfather Pinkhes-Dov Goldenshteyn telling her that he was a Chabadnik. Before hearing this, the translator did not know whether Goldenshteyn continued to consider himself to be a Lubavitcher throughout his life. Aliza (born in October 1921) and her older sister Dvora Gavrieli (born in September 1919) did not know whether their grandfather ever attended the Chabad synagogue in Petakh-Tikva, called the Beit ha-Knesset Tsemakh Tsedek on 24 Gutman St. They only remember him attending Petakh-Tikva's Great Synagogue on *Shabes*, and they knew that in his final years he attended the Nakhalat Yisrael synagogue which opened in 1926 and which was close to his house. The Torah scroll was moved from Petakh-Tikva's Great Synagogue at that time. (See Appendix A1, 679-680.)

"The Old Nest"[8]

by Rokhl Feygenberg

Unzer Tsayt (Our Times), Chişinău (Kishinev) October 1, 1926 (*Simchas Torah* 5787), No. 1227, p. 3

Though nearly eighty years old, the venerable Jew before me stands tall and strong. He carries his gray head proudly on his broad shoulders, and from under his thick eyebrows he looks out onto God's world with a wise and intense gaze indicating that he has still not finished drinking from the goblet of life's joy. He is the oldest Hasid in the Chabad *minyan* in Petakh-Tikva, and in his youth he traveled on foot from his *shtetl* on the Dniester to Lubavitch in order to hear Torah from Reb Mendele and partake of his *Shabes* and *Yontef tishn.*[9]

All his years he was a *shoykhet* and cantor for the coarse Jewish community of the city of Bakhchisaray in the Crimea. There, both Jew and non-Jew considered him to be their great Torah scholar and a very important person, and the coarse community prided itself on his towering build and handsome black beard.[10] They loved him for his pleasant voice and witticisms, and he acquired a fine reputation among the Karaites in the area for his talent in engraving Hebrew inscriptions on their tombstones. This expertise provided him with a large income, which led him to believe that he had become a *shoykhet* in error; he should not be slaughtering cattle and calves with his refined hands but should rather be writing Torah scrolls.

This idea sunk into his head, and he came to hate the profession of *sh'khita*. At the same time, he became a fervent Lover of Zion and began to dream of throwing away his *klingl* ["little blade" in Yiddish], as he refers to his *sh'khita* knife to this very day, traveling to the Land of Israel, and occupying himself with agriculture. But it was difficult to move at that time for his wife was a gentle

---

8 "The Old Nest" refers to Goldenshteyn's yearnings to be back with his rebbe in Lubavitch.

9 Referring to the Lubavitcher Rebbe, Rabbi Menakhem-Mendl Schneerson (1789-1866), known as the Tsemakh Tsedek. *Tishn* is plural of *tish* (meaning a table in Yiddish); a *tish* is a Hasidic gathering led by a rebbe. For the author's description of a Hasidic gathering led by the Tsemakh Tsedek, see ch. 16, pp. 247-248. The 1942 Hebrew version omits mentioning that Goldenshteyn was originally from a *shtetl* on the Dniester, a fact which would have been of interest to the readership of the Yiddish version printed in Romania since that river runs through the Romanian border of that time.

10 In his 1929 letter, Goldenshteyn comments, "When you, my daughter, read it [i.e., the article], you will see that they are writing about your father and take note that they think I had a black beard. Hopefully, the writer meant to portray me to the world as being more handsome than I am by making my once-red beard out to be black" (Appendix B3, p. 794).

soul with a weak constitution, his six young children were barely out of diapers, and he had little savings. So, for thirty-five years he was compelled to serve as *shoykhet* and cantor for that coarse Jewish community of Bakhchisaray and raise his children in that Russified environment. He knocked on all the non-Jewish doors to provide his children with some education, and he and his wife sent them to study in different cities in Europe.[11] During the first years of unrest in Tsarist Russia before the war, he had to bail them out of all sorts of trouble.[12] At the same time, he sent *pidyoynes* and *kvitlekh* to Lubavitch,[13] engraved Hebrew inscriptions on Karaite tombstones in their cemetery in Chufut-Kale near Bakhchisaray, and remained a fervent Lover of Zion. Personally, he still cherished the idea of throwing away his *klingl* once and for all and moving to the Land of Israel, if not to be involved with agriculture, then at least to buy a little house for himself in his later years where he could write a Torah scroll with his own hand.

And God helped him. He lived to see a time when his children, who were scattered across the seven seas, no longer needed him, and his well-to-do sons in America promised to send him a monthly stipend.[14] Then he took his elderly wife, along with his few possessions, and traveled off to the Land of Israel.[15]

He settled in Petakh-Tikva. There, among the Jewish orchards and gardens, he bought a nice house in which he would be able to write his Torah scroll with true contentment. But at that time, war broke out and his plans were disrupted.[16] He could not have imagined that here in the Holy Land something

---

11 Goldenshteyn opposed his daughter Rukhl's efforts to graduate from a *gimnaziia*. Also, he would have preferred if she had not moved to France and studied at a university. It is also clear that he would have been happier had his son Refuel remained studying in yeshiva and not immigrated to America to attend college and university. The only child whom Goldenshteyn did assist in obtaining a secular education was his son Shloyme, since he had been a sickly child and could not be apprenticed to an artisan (ch. 28, pp. 558-566).

12 This passage is evidently referring to Goldenshteyn encouraging and helping his son Yankl and his wife in 1906 to leave Sevastopol, a site of considerable revolutionary unrest, and immigrate to America. He gave them three hundred rubles towards their expenses (ch. 28, pp. 555-556). "The war" refers to the First World War (1914-1919).

13 The Lubavitcher Rebbe at that time was Rabbi Shalom Dov-Ber Schneerson (see footnote 6 above). *Pidyoynes* (literally "redemptions" in Hebrew) is a term used by Hasidim to refer to monetary donations given to a rebbe to redeem one's soul. The donation is accompanied by a petitionary note known as a *kvitl* (see ch. 16, p. 251, footnote 27).

14 Goldenshteyn's two well-to-do sons in America, Yosl and Yankl, agreed to send him monthly stipends (ch. 30, p. 609).

15 Goldenshteyn's first wife, Freyde, the mother of his children, died in 1896. He immigrated to the Land of Israel in 1913 with his second wife Feyge.

16 The war referred to is the First World War.

would disrupt him from accomplishing his holy plans. Clearly this was the work of Satan himself.

How many times in the past had he desired to purchase parchment and begin writing, but it never came about. Each time he would comfort himself by thinking that the delay would be for his benefit and he would begin writing once he moved to the Land of Israel. And since he had decided that he would write the Torah scroll in the Land of Israel, what would be the purpose of buying parchment in the Crimea to bring it there?[17] But now that he was in the Land of Israel, would he have to delay his plans again? Not only was he not working the land, but he would not even be writing a Torah scroll. No, that would not be happening. He gathered all his strength and, with fists raised, challenged himself: "Because you don't want to, I want nothing less than to do it! And I want to do it precisely because there's a war! It's easy to sit peacefully here in the Land of Israel among Jewish orchards and write a Torah scroll when it is tranquil. I want to write it precisely because there is a war!" And stubbornly he grabbed the few napoleons which he had saved to sustain him and his wife and went to Jerusalem for the explicit purpose of buying parchment.[18]

Upon his return to Petakh-Tikva, a few of the Hasidim from the Chabad *minyan* in the colony came over to look at the parchment he had obtained in Jerusalem, at a time when the world was being devastated by war. They simply wanted to see what he was up to because none of them believed that he was of sound mind. With great joy, he showed them the expensive parchment that was prepared for him to write on, and the crowd was shocked that he had actually purchased it. With looks of sorrow, they wished him that he should live to complete it, but at the same time added that since the world was now being devastated by war everyone should safeguard the bit of money that they had for difficult times to come when it might be needed to buy a dry piece of bread so they should not die of hunger. He listened to them, but then said that he had managed to find some liquor in Jerusalem and had them drink *le'khaym* in honor of his beginning this undertaking. As for what the future would bring, he had trust in the Master of the Universe.

---

17 Goldenshteyn's autobiography states, "When we were about to leave for Erets-Isruel, I wanted to take along parchment, but I was dissuaded because the customs duty would be so high and, besides, parchment in Jerusalem would be better and less expensive than in Russia" (ch. 31, p. 625).

18 In his autobiography, Goldenshteyn discusses how he remarkably raised the funds and was able to obtain the parchment when hardly any was to be found (ch. 31, pp. 626-629).

He had not written very much of his Torah scroll, only three Torah portions,[19] when he was interrupted by the British forces' drove further north into Palestine, which caused the retreating Turks to exile many of the inhabitants of Petakh-Tikva to Kfar-Saba, a small Jewish settlement surrounded by the Turkish army. Our old-timer fled there with his parchment in hand and without a sou to his name. Each month his American sons sent remittances of money orders via the post office, but he was not allowed to collect the funds. So he went hungry, and, in addition, his elderly wife had no strength and died quietly and calmly just as she had lived.[20] Nonetheless, the obstinate elder continued his work of writing the Torah scroll among the filth, squalor, and lice, in the midst of the fever-ridden and those dying of hunger. He continued writing one Torah portion after the other in this dire situation.

Once, when sitting next to a window in a dark, dilapidated clay house at work on his Torah scroll, horrible pains of hunger afflicted him greatly, and he decided to look for some water to at least wet his lips. But as soon as he stepped outside, an airplane dropped a bomb directly on the roof of the clay structure in which he had just been sitting, and it exploded, reducing everything to a mound of dust and dirt. He stood frozen and completely stunned. He was shocked by the miracle which left him alive in such a remarkable manner, but the miserable luck of his Torah scroll crushed him like a worm trodden into the ground. Nonetheless, he quickly came round and with his last bit of energy threw himself onto the mound of ash where the house had stood, digging with his hands in the dust. Incensed and upset, he dug for a long time with both hands in the clay and dust until he was able to pull out his holy parchment. It had remained whole. The writing had not been damaged. Only some of the shimmer of the blank reverse side of the parchment had been rubbed out.[21] The overjoyed scribe *bentsht goyml*,[22] and wrote on the backside of the parchment that the Torah scroll was damaged by a bomb which fell on the Turkish army encamped in Kfar-Saba.[23] He then resumed his work in a grimy corner of his

---

19 Goldenshteyn was in the middle of writing the Torah portion of *Shmos*, the thirteenth Torah portion—not the third—when he was exiled to Kfar-Saba in December 1917 (ch. 32, p. 634). For details regarding napoleons, see ch. 30, 606 footnote 10.

20 Goldenshteyn's second wife, Feyge, died in January 1916 in Petakh-Tikva before the Turks drove the Jews out in December of 1917.

21 In his autobiography, Goldenshteyn describes the damage caused to his Torah scroll in ch. 33, pp. 644-645; see also ch. 34, 660, footnote 41.

22 *Bentsh goyml* denotes reciting the Hebrew blessing of deliverance from danger (*Kitsur Shulkhan Arukh* 61:1–2).

23 After this newspaper article was found, Shmuel Friedman of the Nakhalat Yisrael synagogue in Petakh-Tikva, where Goldenshteyn's Torah scroll is housed, was contacted and asked to examine the back of the Torah scroll to see if he could find Goldenshteyn's note. And,

FIGURE 37.

היריעה הזאת נפצעה במלחמה בכפר סבא

"This sheet of parchment was damaged during the war in Kfar-Saba." (Note the signs of damage in the photograph above the writing.)

During the First World War, Goldenshteyn was trapped in the village of Kfar-Saba between the Turkish and British forces battling in Palestine. At that time, he was in the midst of writing his Torah scroll. He had reached the verses which describe "the plague of hail falling on the Egyptians" just when "in Kfar-Saba [as] a hailstorm of cannonballs was thundering" (ch. 33, p. 644). At one point, Goldenshteyn stepped away, only to return to find that the hut in which he had been writing the Torah scroll had been bombed. A recently discovered newspaper article notes that Goldenshteyn wrote on the back of that particular sheet of parchment that it had been damaged by cannon fire (see p. 832, footnote 22 above). And, indeed, Shmuel Friedman of the Nakhalat Yisrael synagogue in Petakh-Tikva, where the Torah scroll is housed, found that Goldenshteyn had written, apparently in pencil, the wording above. The word נפצעה literally means "wounded" and is an odd choice of word to denote damage to an inanimate object. In describing the damaged Torah scroll in his original Yiddish-language autobiography, Goldenshteyn uses the obscure Yiddish word *geranyet* which also means "wounded" (p. 487). Evidently, a Torah scroll is considered so sacred that it is described as if it were a living being.

filthy tent above which bombs dropped and bullets flew.[24] He wrote under such conditions in Kfar-Saba, and he wrote under such conditions in Haifa when the Turks drove the Petakh-Tivka refugees into the Carmel Mountain region after the British forces advanced.[25]

The last trial which he and his Torah scroll withstood was when the refugees from the colony returned home via small ships from Haifa to Jaffa. But this time, too, he was lucky. During the seventeen hours which he traveled on the ship, he held his Torah scroll high on his shoulders wrapped in a blanket, and the stormy waves from the shores of the Land of Israel did not harm it.[26]

Upon returning home, he found his house a scene of destruction. The walls and beams had been shot to pieces, windows and doors were broken, pieces of the wooden furniture lay strewn about, and all the rooms were packed with British soldiers. Nonetheless, they made room for the elderly owner and gave him a bed to sleep in, and he continued his work. He once again sat himself next to a window to write his Torah scroll. That is how he sat for days and weeks. He forgot to eat and drink. He did not remember the days of the week and did not hear what was said to him. The British soldiers regarded him with great respect and were pleased to serve him with humility as one would serve a holy person.[27]

---

indeed, he found the writing on the back of the sheet of parchment containing the section from Exodus 7:1 until the middle of Exodus 9:29 in the Torah portion of *Va'era*. See Figure 37 on p. 833.

24 Though Goldenshteyn in his autobiography fails to mention that he had stepped out because he was starving (ch. 33, p. 644), he does mention later that he had "written the Torah with such self-sacrifice, in hunger and thirst, and while bombs were flying overhead" (ch. 34, p. 659). We learn from Feygenberg's account that Goldenshteyn stayed in a tent in Kfar-Saba after the bomb fell. There are several discrepancies between Feygenberg's version of this episode and Goldenshteyn's. Feygenberg mentions that a bomb fell from an airplane, whereas Goldenshteyn writes that it was a cannonball fired from a cannon. Feygenberg writes that he was knocked down by the blast, but according to Goldenshteyn's description he was nowhere near the explosion. Feygenberg writes that the blank backsides of the parchment were barely damaged, while according to Goldenshteyn's account it seems that the parchment was severely damaged.

25 The Turks did not drive the refugees to Haifa, rather the Council of Displaced Persons sent the refugees from Hadera to rented apartments in Haifa (ch. 33, pp. 646-647).

26 Goldenshteyn writes in his autobiography that the trip from Haifa to Jaffa took a few hours, but the two ships which left afterwards arrived at night and the passengers were forced by the authorities to spend the night on their ships (ch. 33, p. 648). Apparently Goldenshteyn told Feygenberg that the passengers of the other two ships—not his—spent seventeen hours on board.

27 Feygenberg's description of Goldenshteyn's damaged house is more detailed than the description in Goldenshteyn's autobiography where he merely mentions that it had been "bombed and had sustained extensive damage" (ch. 34, p. 654). His autobiography leaves out any mention of British soldiers occupying his house, although it is highly plausible that they did and is unlikely to be an embellishment by Feygenberg.

Finally, the joyous time came when he finished his Torah scroll. His house was now free of soldiers. Finally, he received the money orders from his sons in America, which had lain in the post office for years, and he was able to fix up his house. He then called together his fellow Chabad Hasidim from the colony to celebrate the completion of the writing of the Torah scroll. The Chabad *minyan* joined the meal with joy and song, and he himself drank a lot and danced with his guests. But he did not allow anyone to buy a letter in the Torah scroll, regardless of the amount they offered, for each and every letter had more value in his eyes.[28]

Having danced through the celebration with the Torah scroll in the synagogue,[29] the elderly Jew remained without any work, and he became sad. His large, beautiful house was now empty, and he felt alone like someone lost in the desert.[30] At that point, a friend from his Chabad synagogue advised him to remarry. His household would then become re-established with a housewife and happy *Shabosim* and Jewish holidays. He followed that advice and married a fine, honorable Jewish lady with a prestigious lineage, from the old generation of settlers in the colony.[31] But she did not make his life happier. She prayed too much and recited too many *tkhines*.[32] She thought too much about the next

---

28 Feygenberg implies that only Chabad Hasidim participated in the celebration, but Goldenshteyn's autobiography states that all of Petakh-Tikva was invited and that everyone took part in the celebration by carrying the Torah for a while or at least by touching it (ch. 34, p. 659). Though Feygenberg writes that Goldenshteyn danced and drank at the celebration, Goldenshteyn writes in his autobiography that his nerves became agitated due to the excitement and that he could barely stand, let alone dance (ch. 34, pp. 660-661); Goldenshteyn mentions several times in his autobiography that he abstained from drinking alcohol. Feygenberg states that Goldenshteyn did not want to sell off any of the letters, but Goldenshteyn's account does not seem to corroborate this point (ch. 34, pp. 659-660). For more about the custom of selling letters, see ch. 34, 660, footnote 39.

29 Referring to Petakh-Tikva's Great Synagogue. It is possible that Goldenshteyn's Torah scroll was kept in Petakh-Tikva's Great Synagogue because at that time the Chabad synagogue, Beit ha-Knesset Tsemakh Tsedek, was not yet built (Wolf 2001: 38).

30 In actuality, Goldenshteyn's house was not totally empty since his niece Reyzl Grinberg and her family lived with him (ch. 34, p. 655).

31 In January of 1920, Goldenshteyn married Bashe Yirme, his third wife (see Appendix A5, pp. 733-745).

32 *Tkhines* are Yiddish prayers primarily recited by women. In his April 1929 letter regarding a Hebrew version of this article (Appendix B3, p. 794), Goldenshteyn comments about this section of the article about his wife Bashe's *tkhines*, "But his [*sic*] description of Aunt Bashe with her *tkhines*—how do you like that? I even like the soup that she cooks for my supper because it is more than half mixed with *tkhines* and prayers." It is difficult to know if he is disagreeing with the writer or being whimsical.

world and about suffering later in purgatory. So, he went to seek comfort in the Chabad synagogue where he spent his days and evenings.

But the Chabadniks in Petakh-Tikva were not fervent Hasidim; they did not appreciate the true soul of the *Tanya*,[33] and none merited experiencing the special atmosphere of the Lubavitcher Rebbe's *Shabes* or *Yontef tishn*. If only he could transport himself over the sea and set off on foot there—to Lubavitch as in the past—to hear Torah from the Rebbe, Reb Mendele himself. As in the past.[34]

---

33 The *Tanya* by Rabbi Shneur Zalman (1745–1812) of Lyadi is the seminal work of Chabad Hasidism.

34 The 1942 Hebrew version replaces this final paragraph with the following:
Day after day he sat in the Chabad *minyan* of the colony where he enjoyed spending the long winter evenings. But the Chabadniks there were sensible, so they caringly appealed to him to begin writing another Torah scroll since his eyesight had not yet diminished, but they warned him to be wary of the evil eye. Hasidim who have lost their fire are fearful by nature and apparently lacking in their trust in God. But he did not know what fear was. With his own eyes he had seen bombs falling in the midst of battle, landing at their designated addresses. From his many tribulations during the war, he knew that no bomb falls until its address below has been determined. And if that address is not your address, you can sit and relax under the open sky and you won't be harmed, even as a torrent of fire descends upon you. This was how he tried to prove his point to those fearful Chabadniks in the colony, but they were not convinced, and no response would satisfy them. They do not trust in God and are drowning in sadness. And his simple wife does not stop crying out of her great fear of punishment in the afterlife. Her tears flow onto the *tkhines* she recites. His wife lives in a physical world full of light and pleasure that could delight the heart, yet her soul trembles at every moment out of fear of the torments of purgatory that may one day be inflicted upon her. But he must save himself from his fretful friends. So, he needs to go back to writing a Torah scroll, writing by day and night—only this time he will write like one possessed. The old man shrugs and begins to prepare himself for his new undertaking.
NB: His fellow Chabadniks were warning him that the jealousy caused by his still being able to write a Torah scroll at his age could cause him physical harm. Goldenshteyn clearly did not give credence to such matters. If Goldenshteyn began writing a second Torah scroll, then he certainly did not write much of it, for his granddaughters Dvora Gavrieli and Aliza Goldenshteyn who lived with him during the last years of his life, from 1923-1930, apparently were unaware of such an undertaking.

Bibliography

Abelson, Yehoshua, and Yitskhak Ya'akov Abelson (eds.). *Ets khayim: she'elot u-teshuvot khidu-she Torah ve-khikre halahkah mi-toratam shel 3 dorot le-veit Abelson*. Hadera, Israel: Y. & Y.Y. Abelson, 1985.

Abrahams, Bernard. *Mayne zibetsik yor*. Johannesburg, South Africa: Kayor Publishing House, 1953.

Abu-Elbanat [pseudonym]. "Demuyot ve-Tipusim Petakh-Tikvatiyim: Basheh Avraham Shimon's." *Doar ha-Yom*, January 16, 1935, 5.

Adat tsadikim. Lemberg: I. M. Stand, 1865.

Agnon, Shmuel Yosef. "Be-levav yamim." In idem, *Elu ve-elu*. Jerusalem, Israel: Shoken, 1969.

"Al derekh Khevrat Mekitse Nirdamim." *Ha-Magid*, December 27, 1865, 2.

Apple, Max. *I Love Gootie: My Grandmother's Story*. New York: Warner Books, 1998.

Arieli, Nir. "'Haifa is Still Burning': Italian, German and French Air Raids on Palestine during the Second World War." *Middle Eastern Studies* 46, no. 3 (May 2010): 331–347.

Aronson, Chaim. *A Jewish Life under the Tsars: The Autobiography of Chaim Aronson, 1825–1888*. Translated by Norman Marsden. Totowa, New Jersey: Allanheld, Osmun & Co., 1983.

Asaf, Simkha. *Beoholei Ya'akov: Essays on the Cultural Life of the Jews in the Middle Ages*. Jerusalem, Israel: Mosad ha-Rav Kuk, 1943.

Assaf, David. *Derekh ha-malkhut: R. Yisrael me-Ruzin u-mekomo be-toldot he-khasidut*. Jerusalem, Israel: The Zalman Shazar Center for Jewish History, 1997.

———. *Hetsits ve-nifga: anatomyah shel makhlokket khasidit* [Beguiled by knowledge: Anatomy of a Hasidic controversy]. Haifa: University of Haifa, 2012.

Authers, John, and Richard Wolffe. *The Victim's Fortune: Inside the Epic Battle over the Debts of the Holocaust*. New York: HarperCollins Publishers, 2002.

Avrutin, Eugene M. *Jews and the Imperial State: Identification Politics in Tsarist Russia*. Ithaca, NY: Cornell University Press, 2010.

Avtzon, Meir. *Orot be-afelah*. Brooklyn: n.p., 1988.

Bar-Levav, Avriel. "'When I was Alive': Jewish Ethical Wills as Egodocuments." In *Egodocuments and History: Autobiographical Writing in its Social Context since the Middle Ages*, edited by Rudolf Dekker, 45–59. Hilversum: Verloren Publishers, 2002.

Beider, Alexander. *A Dictionary of Ashkenazi Given Names: Their Origins, Structure, Pronunciation, and Migrations*. Bergenfield, NJ: Avotaynu, Inc., 2001.

———. *A Dictionary of Jewish Surnames from the Russian Empire: Revised Edition*. Bergenfield, NJ: Avotaynu, Inc., 2008.

Beinfeld, Solon, and Harry Bochner. *Comprehensive Yiddish-English Dictionary*, Bloomington, IN: Indiana University Press, 2013.

Ben-Ezer (Raab), Barukh. *Reshimat ha-rishonim she-ani zokher ad le-shenat 1900 ba-moshava Petakh Tikvah.* Tel-Aviv, Israel, 2012. Accessed February 27, 2023. https://library.osu.edu/projects/hebrew-lexicon/hbe/01356002.pdf.

Bénézit, E., and Jacques Busse. *Dictionnaire Critique et Documentaire des Peintres, Sculpteurs, Dessinateurs, et Graveurs de Tous les Temps et de Tous les Pays . . . .*, Paris: Jacques Gründ, 1999.

Berlin (Bar-Ilan), Meir (Rabbi). *Fun Volozin biz Yerusholayim: epizoden.* New York: Oriom, 1933.

Berman, Jeremiah J. (Rabbi). *Shehitah: A Study in the Cultural and Social Life of the Jewish People.* New York: Bloch Publishing Co., 1941.

Berman, Shlomo. "Mishpekhot kehilah kedoshah Shklov." *Kovets al yad, sidrah khadasha* [Khevrat Mekitse Nirdamim, Jerusalem, Israel] 1, no. 11 (1936): 142–187.

Blady, Ken. *Jewish Communities in Exotic Places.* Northvale, NJ: Jason Aronson Inc., 2000.

Bloy, Amram. "Sha'are avodat ha-lev: yeme khayav shel ha-rav ha-kodesh Rabi Aharon ha-Levi Horovits mi-Shtrasheli." *Heikhal ha-Besht* [Monsey, NY] 24 (2008): 122–154.

———. *Bnei ha-Tsemakh Tsedek.* Jerusalem, Israel: Mayanotekha, 2020.

Botoshansky, Jacobo. *Di Lebnsgeshikhte fun a Yidishn zhurnalist: memuarn.* Buenos Aires: Komitet aroystsugebn di memuarn fun Y. Botoshansky, 1942.

Bonchek (Bontshek), Samuel. *Vi es gedenkt zikh.* New York: Schulsinger Brothers, 1955.

Braver, Mikhael, and Avraham Ya'akov Braver. *Zikhronot av u-beno.* Jerusalem, Israel: Mosad ha-Rav Kuk, 1966.

Brener, David. *The Jews of Lancaster, Pennsylvania: A Story with Two Beginnings.* Lancaster, PA: Congregation Shaarai Shomayim, 1979.

Brook (Bruk), Khayim Shaul (Rabbi). "Ashkavta de-rabi: histalkut kevod kedushat admor ha-Tsemakh Tsedek." *Kerem Khabad* [Kfar Chabad, Israel] 2 (1987): 66–69.

Bruder, Khayim Yitskhak Meir. *Kuntres toldot ha-Ri"m.* Pietrekov (now Piotrków Trybunalski), Poland: Defus H. Folman, 193–?.

Burbank, Jane. *Russian Peasants Go to Court: Legal Culture in the Countryside, 1905–1917.* Bloomington, IN: Indiana University Press, 2004.

"Butor." In *Localitățile Republicii Moldova,* vol. 2, 527–533. Chişinău: Agenția Națională de Presă "Moldpres," 2000.

Cahan, J. L. (ed.). *Jewish Folklore* [Yiddish]. Wilno (Vilnius): Yiddish Scientific Institute-YIVO, 1938.

Carlebach, Eliyahu Chaim (Rabbi) (ed.). *Shivkhei ha-Baal Shem Tov.* Jerusalem, Israel: Mekhon Zekher Naftali, 1990.

Carmel, David. "Undzer shtot." In *Kehilat Benderi: sefer zikaron,* 262–271. Tel-Aviv, Israel: Va'ad yotse Benderi be-Yisrael ube-Artsot ha-Brit, 1975.

Carmon, Micha. *Hirsh Leyb B"R Elkhanan mi-Petakh-Tikvah: retakh be-Yarkon—1899.* 2018. Accessed February 27, 2023. http://carmonia.net/files/hirsch-leib.pdf.

Chazan, Aaron. *Deep in the Russian Night.* New York: CIS Publishers, 1990.

Cherednichenko, Anatolii Pavlovich (ed.). *Odesskaia oblast'.* Kyiv, Ukraine: Ukrainskaia Sovetskaia Entsiklopediia, 1978.

Chitrik [Khitrik], Yehuda (Rabbi). *Reshimot devarim.* Part 2. Brooklyn: n.p., 1985.

Code of Jewish Law. See Glossary 1, p. 859.

Corliss, William R. *Remarkable Luminous Phenomena in Nature.* Glen Arm, MD: Sourcebook Project, 2001.

Cornfeld, Peretz (ed.). *Palestine Personalia 1947.* Tel-Aviv, Israel: Palestine Personalia, 1947.

Crocker-Langley San Francisco Directory for Year Commencing April 1896. . . . San Francisco: H. S. Crocker Company, 1896.

Deinard, Ephraim. "Selah ha-Yehudim." *Ha-Magid,* June 11, 1873, 3.

———. *Masa ba-khatsi ha-i Krim.* Warsaw: Aleksander Ginz, 1879/1880.

Deutsch, Simon. *Sefer hen goalti.* Brooklyn: n.p., 1972.

Domnitch, Larry. *The Cantonists: The Jewish Children's Army of the Tsar.* Jerusalem, Israel: Devora Publishing, 2003.

Draper, Mordekhai. "Ha-Mikvaot be-Ashkenaz mi-yeme ha-rishonim ad he-khurban ha-shoah." *Yerushatenu* [Bnei Brak, Israel] 9 (5776 [2016]): 231–280.

Dubnow, Simon. *History of the Jews in Russia and Poland: From Earliest Times Until the Present Day.* Translated by I. Friedlander. Philadelphia: Jewish Publication Society of America, 1918.

"Edwin Tarlow Golden." In *History of the Greater San Francisco Bay Region: Family and Personal History,* vol. 2, 211. New York: Jewish Historical Publishing Company, 1966.

Ehrmann, Naftoli Hertz. *The Baal Shem of Michelstadt.* Translated by Manfred F. Kuttner. Jerusalem, Israel: Feldheim Publishers, 1973.

——— [Judaeus]. *Der Baalschem von Michelstadt: Kulturgeschhichtliche Ehrzälung.* Frankfurt am Main, Germany: Israelit, 1907.

Eisenstadt, Benzion (Rabbi). *Dor rabanav ve-sofrav. . . .* Book 3. Vilnius, Lithuania: A. G. Katsenelenbogen, 1901.

———. *Dor rabanav ve-sofrav. . . .* Book 4. Vilnius, Lithuania: Shraga Fayvel Garber, 1902.

Elset (Avida), Jehuda. *Melokhes un bale-melokhes: folstimlikhe redensarten, glaykhvertlekh un anekdoten.* Warsaw, Poland: Levin-Epshtein, 1920.

Engel, Shlomo (ed.). *Kfar Saba: 70 shanah le-yisud Kfar-Saba.* Kfar-Saba, Israel: Iriyat Kfar-Saba, 1973.

Errera, Leo. *The Russian Jews: Extermination or Emancipation?* London: David Nutt, 1894.

Etkes, Imanuel, and Shlomo Tikochinski (eds.). *Memoirs of the Lithuanian Yeshiva* [Hebrew]. Jerusalem, Israel: The Zalman Shazar Center for Jewish History, 2004.

Evans, Richard J. "Epidemics and Revolutions: Cholera in Nineteenth-Century Europe." *Past & Present* 120, no. 1 (1988): 123–146.

Even, Isaac. *Fun'm Rebin's hoyf: zikhryones un mayses.* Brooklyn: n.p., 1922.

"Exonerate Rabbi of Any Misconduct." *News Tribune* [Tacoma, Washington], August 28, 1920, 1.

"Expulsion of Foreign Jews in Russia." *Jewish Chronicle* [London], January 2, 1885, 12.

Farfel, Eliyahu. *Bet ha-keneset ha-atik ha-nimtsa be-ir Feodosiya mi-zeman ha-Kuzarim.* Piotrków Trybunalski, Poland: n.p., 1912.

Feldman, Aba. "Emek ha-bakha." *Ha-Magid,* September 16, 1874, 5.

Felshin, Uri (Rabbi). *Sefer zikaron le-Rabi Uri Felshin.* Rekhovot, Israel: n.p., 1974.

Fedorchuk, Artyom (Eldad) and Dan D. Y. Shapira. "The Tombstone Inscriptions NN 1–326 from the Book *Avnei Zikkaron* by Avraham Firkowicz, according to Their Authentic Texts and with Their Real Dates: A Preliminary Publication" [Hebrew]. In *Eastern European Karaites in the Last Generations*, edited by Dan D. Y. Shapira and Daniel J. Lasker, 36–82. Jerusalem, Israel: Ben-Zvi Institute for the Study of Jewish Communities in the East of Yad Izhak Ben-Zvi and the Hebrew University of Jerusalem, 2011.

Feilberg, H. F. "Ghostly Lights." *Folklore* 6, no. 3 (September 1895): 288–300.

Feinstein, Moshe (Rabbi). *Igrot Moshe: khoshen mishpat.* Vol. 4. New York: n.p., 1963.

Feldman, Marc D., Jacqueline M. Feldman, and Roxenne Smith. *Stranger than Fiction: When Our Minds Betray Us.* Washington, D.C.: American Psychiatric Press, 1998.

Finkelman, Shimon (Rabbi). *The Chazon Ish; The Life and Ideals of Rabbi Avraham Yeshaya Karelitz.* Brooklyn: Mesorah Publications, 1989.

Fishman, Joshua A. *Ideology, Society & Language: The Odyssey of Nathan Birnbaum.* Ann Arbor: Karoma Publishers, Inc., 1987.

Freeze, ChaeRan Y. "Following the Paper Trail: Genealogical Resources in the Ukrainian and Moldovan Archives." In *Jewish Roots in Ukraine and Moldova: Pages from the Past and Archival Inventories*, edited by Miriam Weiner, 7–17. Secaucus, NJ: The Miriam Weiner Routes to Roots Foundation / New York: YIVO Institute for Jewish Research, 1999.

———. *Jewish Marriage and Divorce in Imperial Russia.* Hanover, NH: University Press of New England, 2001.

Friedland, Roger, and Richard Hecht. "The Nebi Musa Pilgrimage and the Origins of Palestinian Nationalism" [Hebrew]. In *Pilgrims and Travelers to the Holy Land*, edited by Bryan F. Le Beau and Menachem Mor, 89–118. Omaha, NE: Creighton University Press, 1996.

Friedlander, Alex E. "New Sources for Jewish Genealogists in Polish Archives." *Avotaynu: The International Review of Jewish Genealogy* 29, no. 2 (2013): 11–20.

Frumkin (Rodkinson), Michael Levi. *Adat tsadikim.* Lviv, Ukraine: n.p., 1869.

Furman, Israel. *Yidishe shprikhverter un rednsartn.* Tel-Aviv, Israel: Hamenora Publishing House, 1968.

Gammer, Moshe. "A Report by Solomon Beym to the French Authorities." In *Eastern European Karaites in the Last Generations*, edited by Dan D. Y. Shapira and Daniel J. Lasker, 68–122. Jerusalem: Ben-Zvi Institute for the Study of Jewish Communities in the East of Yad Izhak Ben-Zvi and the Hebrew University of Jerusalem, 2011.

Ganzfried, Shlomo (Rabbi). *Keset ha-sofer.* Ofen, Hungary: Königl. ungr. Universitäts-Buchdruckerei, 1835.

Gavrieli Goldenshteyn, Dvora. *Shorashim.* Unpublished manuscript, typescript. Kibbutz Givat Khayim Meukhad, Israel, September 12, 1999.

Gellman, Uriel. "The Heder in Eastern Europe: An Annotated Bibliography." In *The Heder: Studies, Documents, Literature and Memoirs*, edited by David Assaf and Immanuel Etkes, 68–122. Tel-Aviv, Israel: Tel-Aviv University, 2010, 68–122.

Gershuni (Romanov), Aharon Eliyahu. *Yahadut be-Rusiyah ha-Sovyetit: le-korot redifot ha-dat* [Judaism in Soviet Russia: The History of Religious Persecution]. Jerusalem, Israel: Mosad ha-Rav Kuk, 1960.

Ginsburg, Saul M. *Historical Works* [Yiddish]. New York: S. M. Ginsburg Testimonial Committee, 1937.

———. *The Drama of Slavuta*. Translated by Ephraim H. Prombau. Lanham, MD: University Press of America, 1991.

Glicman [Glikman], Levi (Rabbi). *Zikhronot bet Levi*. Chişinău, Moldova: Tehnic, 1934.

Glitsenshtein, Avraham Khanokh (Rabbi). *Rabenu ha-Tsemakh Tsedek*. Brooklyn: Otsar ha-Khasidim, 1967.

———. *Rabbi Shmuel Shneursohn me-Lyubavitsh, admor Maharash*. Brooklyn: Kehot Publication Society, 1986.

Goldenstein (Goldenshteyn), Raphael. *The Krimchaks: Their Life and Origin in the Crimea*. Unpublished thesis for a rabbinical degree, Hebrew Union College, Cincinnati, 1916.

———. *History and Activities of Congregation Anshe-Emeth, Pine Bluff, Arkansas: 1867–1917: Compiled and Edited in Commemoration of its Fiftieth Anniversary*. [Pine Bluff]: n.p., 1917.

———. "R. Khayim Khizkiyahu Medini." *Ha-Toren* [New York] 11, no. 6 (September 1925): 13–20.

"Goldenstein, Raphael." In *Who's Who in American Jewry, 1926*, 207. New York: Jewish Biographical Bureau, 1927.

"Goldstein-Goldstein." *Sunday Oregonian* [Portland], September 3, 1905, 27.

Golovinskii, N. *Putevoditel' po Krymu*. Odesa, Ukraine: n.p., 1894.

Gotlib, Shmuel Noakh. *Ohole shem*. Pinsk, Belarus: M. M. Glouberman, 1912.

Grayevski, Pinkhas Mordekhai. *Avne-zikaron....* Vol. 5. Jerusalem: n.p., 1929.

Greenwald, Leopold (Yekutiel Yehuda) (Rabbi). *Toyznt yor Idish lebn in Ungarn*. Brooklyn: Parish Press, 1945.

———. *Ha-Shokhet veha-shekhitah ba-sifrut ha-rabanut*. New York: Philipp Feldheim, Inc., 1955.

Grodner, A. "Nicknames Used in Grodno" [Yiddish]. *Yidishe Shprakh* [Yiddish Scientific Institute-YIVO, New York] 11 (1951): 58–60.

Grosman, Levi. *Shem ve-she'erit*. Jerusalem, Israel: Betsalel, 1989.

Gurwitz [Hurvits], Aleksander-Ziskind. *Seyfer zikhroynes fun tsvey doyres*. Part 2. New York: n.p., 1935.

Gutman, Matitiyahu Yekhezkel. *Mi-gibore he-Hasidut: Rabi Dov me-Liovah*. Tel-Aviv, Israel: Sifriyat Netsakh, 1952.

Hager, Yosef Yerukham Fishl, "Ha-Rav ha-kadosh Rabi Shlomoh mi-Savran-Tshitshilnik," *Heikhal ha-Besht*, Monsey, NY, no. 9 (2002): 111–128; no. 12 (2006): 85–94.

Harkavy, Alexander. *Yiddish-English-Hebrew Dictionary*. New York: Hebrew Pub. Co., 1928.

Harshav, Benjamin. *The Meaning of Yiddish*. Berkeley: University of California Press, 1990.

Hashavia [Khashaviyah], Arye. *Em ve-ir: 120 ha-shanim ha-rishonot*. Petakh-Tikva, Israel: Iriyat Petakh-Tikva, 1998.

Haspelmath, Martin, and Uri Tadmor, Uri (eds.). *Loanwords in the World's Languages: A Comparative Handbook*. Berlin: De Gruyter Mouton, 2009.

Heilman, Khayim Meir. *Beit Rebbi*. Berdychiv, Ukraine: H. Y. Sheftil, 1902.

Heilperin, Shmuel Elazar. *Sefer ha-tse'etsaim: ilan yukhasin le-tse'atsae... Rabi Shneur Zalman me-Liadi*. Jerusalem: n.p., 1980.

Heller, Marvin J. "He should be Called Sama'el: Michael Levi Rodkinson—The Life and Literary Career of a Jewish Scoundrel Revisited." *Jewish Culture and History* 7, no. 3 (Winter 2004): 77–92.

Heschel, Abraham Joshua. *The Earth is the Lord's: The Inner World of the Jew in Eastern Europe.* New York: Farrar, Straus, Giroux, 1978.

Hindes, Leyb. *Mayne kinder-yorn af di Pyaskes: zikhroynes fun mayn heym-shtot Byalistok fun di yorn 1882–1905.* Boston: L. Hindes bukh-komitet, 1963.

Hirschbein, Peretz. *Shvartsbukh: tsen khadoshim mit di Yidishe ibervandere in Ratnfarband: Agay, Krim 1928–1929.* Vilnius, Lithuania: B. Kletskin, 1930.

Hirshler, Shimon. *Or ha-khamah: masekhet khayav, halikhotav, u-ketsot darkav shel . . . Rabi Khayim Khizkiyahu Medini.* Tel-Aviv, Israel: Shem Olam, 2001.

Huberman, N. "Ha-Admor R. Refael mi-Bershed." *He-Avar* 1 (1952): 102–109.

Hübner, Ulrich. *Palaestina Exploranda: Studien zur Erforschung Palästinas im 19. und 20.* Wiesbaden, Germany: Harassowitz, 2006.

Idelshtein, Yehudah. *Avraham Shapira: Sheikh Ibrahim Mikhah: be-shene kerakhim.* Tel-Aviv, Israel: Yedidim, 1939.

"India." In *Localitățile Republicii Moldova*, vol. 7, 459–460. Chişinău, Moldova: Agenția Națională de Presă "Moldpres," 2007.

"Inyane ha-Yehudim." *Ha-Zeman* [Vilna] 18 (April 20, 1914): 3.

Isaac, Erich. "The Citron in the Mediterranean: A Study in Religious Influences." *Economic Geology* 35, no. 1 (January 1959): 71–78.

Jacobs, Neil G. *Yiddish: A Linguistic Introduction.* Cambridge: Cambridge University Press, 2005.

Jaffe, Zalmon, *My Encounter with the Rebbe.* Vol. 1. Brooklyn: PCL Publishing, 2002.

Jerusalem Talmud. See *Talmud* in Glossary 1, p. 863

Kahan [Ha-Kohen], Refael Nakhman. *Shmuot ve-sipurim me-rabotenu ha-kedoshim.* Brooklyn: n.p., 1990.

Kahana, Yitskhak Z'ev. *Mekhkarim be-sifrut ha-teshuvot.* Jerusalem, Israel: Mosad ha-Rav Kuk, 1973.

Kaplan, Arye (Rabbi). *Made in Heaven: A Jewish Wedding Guide.* New York: Moznaim Publishing Corporation, 1983.

Kasdai, Tsvi. "Ketae zikhronot." *Reshumot* [Tel-Aviv, Israel] 4 (1926): 216–230.

Katsovitsh [Kasovich], Yisrael Iser [Israel]. *Zekhtsig yohr leben.* New York: M. N. Mayzel, 1924.

Keren (Rogalsky), Yekhezkel. *Yahadut Krim me-kadmutah ve-ad ha-shoah.* Jerusalem, Israel: Rubin Mass House, 1981.

"Khazaka." In *Talmudic Encyclopedia*, vol. 13, 553–760. Jerusalem, Israel: Talmudic Encyclopedia Institute, 1998.

Khazanov, Anatoly. *The Krymchaks: A Vanishing Group in the Soviet Union.* Jerusalem, Israel: The Hebrew University of Jerusalem, The Marjorie Mayrock Center for Soviet and East European Research, 1989.

"Kherem de-Rabenu Gershom." In *Entsiklopediyah Talmudit*, vol. 17, 318–454. Jerusalem, Israel: Talmudic Encyclopedia Institute, 1983.

Kitov, Eliyahu (Rabbi). *The Book of Our Heritage*. Translated by Nathan Bulman. Jerusalem, Israel: Feldheim Publishers, 1978.

Kitsur Shulkhan Arukh. See Glossary 1, p. 865.

Kofman, Shmuel. *Zikhronot*. Tel-Aviv, Israel: n.p., 1955.

Kopeloff [Kopelov], Isadore. *Amol iz geven*. New York: M. N. Mayzel, 1926.

Kosover, Mordecai. *Arabic Elements in Palestinian Yiddish: The Old Ashkenazic Jewish Community in Palestine, Its History and Its Language*. Jerusalem, Israel: Rubin Mass, 1966.

Kotik, Yekhezkel. *Journey to a Nineteenth-Century Shtetl: The Memoirs of Yekhezkel Kotik*. Edited by David Assaf. Detroit Wayne State University Press, 2002.

Kraus, Shmuel. *Zikaron Shmuel*. Brooklyn: n.p., 1989.

Krol, Tsvi, and Tsadok Leinman. *Bet ha-kevarot ha-yashan be-Tel-Aviv*. Tel-Aviv, Israel: n.p., 1940.

Kunstlicher, M. A. Z., and S. J. Spitzer. *The History of the Jewish Community of Zelem (Deutschkreutz) and Its Sages*. Bnei Brak, Israel: Machon Zikaron, 1989.

Kubijovyč, Volodymyr. *Encyclopedia of Ukraine*. Toronto, Canada: University of Toronto Press, 1984.

Lestschinsky, Jacob. *Dos Yidishe folk in tsifern*. Berlin, Germany: Klal Verlag, 1922.

Levin, Vladimir. "Reform or Consensus? Choral Synagogues in the Russian Empire." *Arts* 9, no. 2 (June 2020). Accessed February 27, 2023. https://doi.org/10.3390/arts9020072.

Levine, Sholom-DovBer (Rabbi). *Toldot Khabad be-erets ha-kodesh. . . .* Brooklyn: Kehot Publication Society, 1988.

———. *Sifriyat Lyubavitsh*. Brooklyn: Kehot Publication Society, 1993.

Levy, Nissim, and Yael Levy. *The Physicians of the Holy Land, 1799–1948* [Hebrew]. Zikhron-Ya'akov, Israel: Itay Bahur Publishing, 2008.

Liberman, Haim. "Der badkhonishn repertuar." In idem, *Ohel Rakhel*, part 2, 307–313. Brooklyn: n.p., 1980.

Lifshits [Lipschutz], Shabtai. *Sefer likutei segulot Yisrael: Yisrael li-segulato*. Jerusalem, Israel: Feldheim, 5768 [2008].

"Lost in the Wilderness." *Morning Oregonian* [Portland], July 19, 1901, 4.

Lubecki (Lubetski), Menachem Mendel Zusil. *Kovets Toldot R' Menakhem Mendel* [Shneerson, 1867–1942]. 2008. Accessed March 16, 2024. http://www.teshura.com/teshurapdf/Lubeztki%20-%206%20Adar%202,%205768.pdf.

Luria, Ilia. *The Habbad Movement in Czarist Russia, 1828–1882* [Hebrew]. Jerusalem, Israel: The Hebrew University and Magnes Press, 2006.

———. "Education and Ideology: The Beginnings of the HaBaD Yeshivah" [Hebrew]. In *Let the Old Make Way for the New*, vol. 1: *Hasidism and the Musar Movement*, edited by David Assaf and Ada Rapoport-Albert, 185–222. Jerusalem, Israel: The Zalman Shazar Center for Jewish History, 2009.

Mak, Lanver. *The British in Egypt: Community, Crime, and Crises, 1882–1922*. London: I. B. Tauris, 2011.

"Margaret V. Allen Died at Portland." *True Republican* [Sycamore, Illinois], February 2, 1927, 1.

Marmor, Kalman. *Mayn lebns-geshikht*. Vol. 1. New York: Yiddisher Kultur Farband (YKUF), 1959.

Marschall, John P. "Jewish Agricultural Experiment, Wellington, Nevada, 1896–1902." *Agricultural History* 76, no. 2 (2002): 244–259.

Matthews, Mervyn. *The Passport Society: Controlling Movement in Russia and the USSR*. Boulder, CO: Westview Press, 1993.

Masliansky, H. *Masliansky's Memoirs: Forty Years of Life and Struggle* [Yiddish]. New York: Zerubabel, 1924.

Medini, Khayim Khizkiyahu (Rabbi). *Sdei Khemed*. Part 2: *Ma'arekhet khamets u-matsah*. Warsaw, Poland: n.p., 1896.

———. *Sdei Khemed*. Part 10: *Kuntres ha-klalim*. Warsaw, Poland: n.p., 1901.

———. *Igrot Sdei Khemed*. Edited by Shimon Hirshler. Bnei Brak, Israel: Makhon Shem Olam, 2006.

Meir, Natan M. *Kiev, Jewish Metropolis: A History, 1859–1914*. Bloomington: Indiana University Press, 2010.

Meir, Yonatan. *Literary Hasidism: The Life and Works of Michael Levi Rodkinson*. Translated by Jeffrey G. Amshalem. Syracuse, NY: Syracuse University Press, 2016.

Meiselman, Shulamith. *The Soloveitchik Heritage: A Daughter's Memoir*. Hoboken, NJ: KTAV, 1995.

Mekler, David L. *Fun Rebns hoyf: Talne*. New York: The Jewish Book Publishing Company, 1931.

Melamed, Avraham-Shlomo. *Khayim kemo she-hem: avtobiografiya mefaretet. . . .* Part 1. Kushta [Istanbul, Turkey]: L. Babuk u-vanav, 1922.

Mendelevich, Yosef. *Ha-Kantonistim: ne'arim Yehudim be-mosdot ha-tsava ha-Rusi, 1827–1856*. Jerusalem, Israel: Erez, 2011.

"Meorasim" [Engaged]. *Doar ha-yom* [Jerusalem], October 27, 1921, 1.

Merenbach, Nathan. *Grampa: The Autobiography of Nathan Merenbach*. San Francisco: n.p., 1977.

"Misaviv ha-moshavot" [Around the Colonies]. *Ha-Tsvi* [Jerusalem], November 23, 1900, 1.

Milch [Milkh], Yaakov. *Oytobiografishe skitsn*. New York: Yiddisher Cultur Farband, 1946.

Min ha-Modi'im [David Yellin]. "Mikhtavim mi-Yerushalayim." *Ha-Melits*, October 29, 1899, 2–3.

Minkovsky, Pinkhas. "Mi-sefer khayai." *Reshumot* [Tel-Aviv, Israel] 1 (1918): 97–122; 2 (1922): 125–158; 4 (1926): 123–144; 5 (1927): 145–160; 6 (1930): 71–100.

Mirsky, Samuel K. (Rabbi). *Jewish Institutions of Higher Learning in Europe: Their Development and Destruction* [Hebrew]. New York: Ogen, 1956.

Mishna. See Glossary 1, p. 869.

Mondshine, Yehoshua. *Migdal oz*. Kfar Khabad, Israel: Mekhon Lubavitsh, 1980.

———. "Ekhad be-ekhad yigashu." *Kerem Khabad* 1 (Tishre 5747 [1986]): 60–66.

———. *Otsar minhage Khabad: Elul-Tishre*. Jerusalem, Israel: Heikhal Menakhem, 1995.

———. "Ka-asher anshe Vilna ve-Dvinsk khabru 'la'asot tsarot.'" *Kfar Khabad* 933 (2000): 28–35.

———. *Ha-Masa ha-akharon: matayim shana le-masao shel ha-admor Rabi Shneur Zalman ba'al ha-Tanya be-itsumah shel milkhemet Napoleon. . . .* Jerusalem, Israel: Knizhniki, 2012.

Nathan, Dorothy. *The Shy One*. New York: Random House, 1966.

Nigal, Gedalyah. *Magic, Mysticism, and Hasidism: The Supernatural in Jewish Thought*. Translated by Edward Levin. Northvale, NJ: Jason Aronson, Inc., 1994.

Nissenbaum, Yitskhak (Rabbi). *Ale kheldi: 5629–5689*. Warsaw, Poland: n.p., 1929.

Nof, Gershon (comp.). *Tsivita tsedek: tsavaot shel gedole Yisrael*. Brooklyn: Mesilah, 2002.

Nudelman, Eugene Ross, Sr. *The Family of Joseph Nudelman*. Unpublished manuscript. Portland, OR, 1969.

Oberlander, Boruch (Rabbi), and Elkana Shmotkin. *Shanim rishonot: shenotav ha-rishonot shel ha-Rabi mi-Liubavitsh . . . 1902–1929*. Brooklyn: Jewish Educational Media, Inc., and Kehot Publication Society, 2021.

Ofrat, Gideon, *One Hundred Years of Art in Israel*. Boulder, CO: Westview Press, 1998.

Olidort, David. "Mi-Sipure Rabi Khayim Avraham Dukhman ha-Levi, a.h., al badkhano shel ha-Tsemakh Tsedek." *Heikhal ha-Besht* [Monsey, NY] 35 (2013): 155–156.

Olson, James S. *An Ethnohistorical Dictionary of the Russian and Soviet Empires*. Westport, CT: Greenwood Press, 1994.

Palestine during the War: Being a Record of the Preservation of the Jewish Settlements in Palestine. London: Zionist Organization, 1921.

Paperna [Papirno], Avraham Ya'akov. *Zikhroynes*. Translated by P. Ra—ski. Warsaw: Farlag "Tsentral," 1923.

"Parkany." In *Słownik geograficzny Królestwa Polskiego i innych krajów słowiańskich*, vol. 7, 866. Warszawa, Poland: Filip Sulimierski i Władysław Walewski, 1886.

"Passover Services at Duke Street Temple." *Lancaster New Era*, April 3, 1926, 5.

Perlov, Khayim Mordekhai (Rabbi). *Likutei sipurim*. Brooklyn: n.p., 1992.

Petrovsky-Shtern, Yohanan. "Military Service in Russia." *YIVO Encyclopedia of Jews in Eastern Europe*. Accessed March 16, 2024. http://www.yivoencyclopedia.org/article.aspx/Military_Service_in_Russia.

Polishchuk, Mikhail L. *Evrei Odessy i Novorossii: Sotsial'no-politicheskaia istoriia evreev Odessy i drugikh gorodov Novorossii, 1881–1904*. Moscow, Russia: Mosty Kultury, 2002.

Polonsky, Antony. *The Jews in Poland and Russia*. Vol. 1: *1350 to 1881*. Oxford and Portland, OR: The Littman Library of Jewish Civilization, 2010.

Probate: Abraham Dykes (1919). The National Archives of the UK (TNA), FO 841/182/52.

"Rabbi Brings Suit Against Temple Beth-El." *Daily Item* [Lynn, MA], March 20, 1928, 1.

"Rabbi Goldenstein Returns from Touro." *Sioux City Journal*, August 18, 1922, 11.

"Rabbi Goldenstein to Speak at Temple Beth Israel Friday." *The Fresno Morning Republican*, May 20, 1931, 5.

"Rabbi Off for Palestine." *Sioux City Journal*, February 3, 1921, 11.

R.L. Polk & Co's St. Paul City 1890–91. St. Paul, MN: R.L. Polk & Co., 1890.

Rotenberg, David-Z'ev. *Masa ha-Rabi be-Erets-ha-Kodesh*. Kfar Chabad, Israel: Sifriyat Eshel–Kfar-Chabad, 1999.

Rabinovits, Y. L. "Bakhchisaray." *Ha-Tsefirah*, August 20, 1900, 3.

Rekhtman, M. [Yudl Mark]. "The Language of the Memoirist P. Goldenshtain" [Yiddish]. *Yidishe Shprakh* [Yiddish Scientific Institute-YIVO, New York] 3 (1943): 32–43.

Refael, Yitskhak. *Al hasidut ve-hasidim*. Jerusalem, Israel: Mosad ha-Rav Kuk, 1991.

Reisman, Yisroel. *The Laws of Ribis: The Laws of Interest and Their Application to Everyday Life and Business*. Brooklyn: Mesorah Publications, Ltd., 1995.

Reiss, C. (ed.). *Generations: The Mikvah through the Ages.* Brooklyn: Mikvah Yisroel of Flatbush, 1995.

Report of the Commissioner of Patents for the Year 1855: Agriculture. Washington, D.C.: C. Wendell, 1856.

Rivkind, Isaac. *Jewish Money: In Folkways, Cultural History, and Folklore: A Lexicological Study* [Yiddish]. New York: American Academy for Jewish Research, 1959.

Rolnick, Joseph. *Zikhroynes.* New York: n.p., 1954.

Rosenthal, Herman. "Kuna." In *Jewish Encyclopedia,* vol. 7, 583. New York: Funk and Wagnalls, 1906.

Rosman, Moshe. *Founder of Hasidism: A Quest for the Historical Ba'al Shem Tov.* Berkeley: University of California Press, 1996.

Rozhanski, Shmuel. *Rumenish, antologye.* Buenos Aires: Literatur-gezelshaft baym YIVO in Argentine, 1981.

Rubin, Eli. "Rabbi Shmuel Schneersohn of Lubavitch ("Maharash," 1834–1882) and the False Twilight of Chabad Hasidism." *AJS Review* 45, no. 2 (November 2021): 348–381.

Sacks [Zaks], Chaim. *S'iz geven a mol*. . . Johannesburg, South Africa: Dorem Afrike, 1969.

Sadan, Dov. *Kheyn-gribelekh: tsu biografye fun vort un vertl.* Buenos Aires: Alveltlekher Yidisher Kultur-Kongres, 1971.

Schaechter, Mordkhe. *Laytish mame-loshn.* New York: League for Yiddish, 1986.

———. *Pregnancy, Childbirth and Early Childhood: An English-Yiddish Dictionary.* New York: League for Yiddish, 1991.

———. *Yiddish II: An Intermediate and Advanced Textbook.* New York: Yiddish Language Research Center, 2005.

Scharfstein, Zevi. *The Heder in the Life of the Jewish People* [Hebrew]. New York: Shilo Publishing House, 1943.

Schneersohn, Isaac. *Lebn un kamf fun Yidn in Tsarishn Rusland, 1905–1917.* Paris: Les Editions Polyglottes, 1968.

Schneersohn, Yosef Yitzchok (Rabbi). *Igrot-Kodesh.* Brooklyn: Kehot Publication Society, 1982–2011.

———. *Likkutei Dibburim: An Anthology of Talks by Rabbi Yosef Yitzchak Schneersohn of Lubavitch.* Translated by Uri Kaploun. Brooklyn: Kehot Publication Society, 1987–2000.

Schneerson, Barukh Shneur. *Reshimot ha-Rabash.* Brooklyn: Kehot Publication Society, 2001.

Schneerson, Menachem Mendel (Rabbi) (1789–1866). *Tsemakh Tsedek: orakh khayim.* Brooklyn: Kehot Publication Society, 1946.

———. *Or ha-Torah: Devarim.* Brooklyn: Kehot Publication Society, 1994.

Schneerson, Menachem Mendel (Rabbi) (1902–1994). *Likutei Sikhot.* Vol. 22. Brooklyn: Kehot Publication Society, 1983.

———. *Sikhot kodesh.* Brooklyn: Kehot Publication Society, 1986.

———. *Torat Menakhem: reshimat ha-yoman.* Brooklyn: Kehot Publication Society, 2006.

Schneerson, Shmuel (Rabbi). *Likutei Torah—Torat Shmuel*. . . *5633.* Brooklyn: Kehot Publication Society, 1994.

———. *Likutei Torah—Torat Shmuel: sefer drushe khatuna.* Brooklyn: Kehot Publication Society, 2003.

Schochet, Jacob Immanuel (Rabbi). *Mystical Concepts in Chassidism: An Introduction to Kabbalistic Concepts and Doctrine.* Brooklyn: Kehot Publication Society, 1988.

Schoenfeld [Sheynfeld], Samuel. *Memoirs of a Compositor* [Yiddish]. New York: Yiddish Scientific Institute-YIVO, 1946.

"A School for Poor Foreigners." *Oregon Daily Journal* [Portland], June 9, 1907, 34.

Schwake, Norbert. *Deutsche Soldatengräber in Israel: der Einsazt deutscher Soldaten an der Palästinafront im Ersten Weltkrieg und das Schicksal ihrer Grabstätten.* Münster, Germany: Aschendorff Verlag, 2008.

Shapira, Aharon. *Sefer yeme zikaron.* Bnei Brak, Israel: n.p., 1990–2001.

Shapiro, Malkah. *The Rebbe's Daughter: Memoirs of a Hasidic Childhood.* Translated by Nehemia Polen. Philadelphia: The Jewish Publication Society of America, 2002.

Shapiro, Pinkhas (Rabbi). *Sefer imre Pinkhas ha-shalem.* Bnei Brak, Israel: Y. Sh. Frankel, 2003.

Sharot, Stephen. "Hasidism and the Routinization of Charisma." *Journal for the Scientific Study of Religion* 19, no. 4 (December 1980): 325–336.

Shmuel, B. *Meore Yisrael.* Jerusalem, Israel: Mekhon Ohale Yosef, 5754 [1994].

Shochat, Azriel. *The Crown Rabbinate in Russia: A Chapter in the Cultural Struggle between Orthodox Jews and "Maskilim"* [Hebrew]. Haifa: University of Haifa, 1975.

Shor, Aleksander Sender (Rabbi). *Simlah Khadashah: al hilkhot sh'khitah ve-trefot. . . .* Zolkove [Zhovkva, Ukraine]: Defus ha-akhim Aharon ve-Gershon benei Khayim David Segal, 1733.

Shtern, Yekhiel. *Kheyder and Beys-Medrash.* New York: Yiddish Scientific Institute-YIVO, 1950.

Shulkhan Arukh. See entry for Code of Jewish Law in Glossary 1, p. 859.

Shvartsburg, A. L. *Der khurbn fun mayn shtetl un ire kedoyshim.* New York: Seliber un Zaliner untershtitsungs fareyn, 1934.

Skibin, Dov. *Zikhronot ish Kfar-Saba.* [Ramat Gan], Israel: Masadah, 1947.

Slor, Efrayim. *Yoter le'at bevakashah: mishpakhat Slor be-ikvot ha-neder.* S.l. [Israel]: n.p., 2002.

Slutsky, Yehuda (ed.). *Bobruisk: sefer-zikaron li-kehilat Bobruisk u-venoteha.* Tel-Aviv, Israel: Tarbut ve-khinukh, 1967.

Slutsky, Yehuda. "Caucasus." In *Encyclopaedia Judaica,* vol. 5, 257–259. Jerusalem, Israel: Keter Publishing House, 1972.

———. "The Russian Military Service Act (1874) and the Jews" [Hebrew]. *He-Avar* 21 (June 1975): 3–19.

Slutsky, Yehuda, and Eliyahu Feldman. "Bakhchisarai." In *Encyclopaedia Judaica,* vol. 4, 116. Jerusalem, Israel: Keter Publishing House, 1972.

Spector, Mordecai. *Mayn lebn.* Part 1: *Kinderyorn.* Warsaw, Poland: Akhisefer, 1927.

Spiegel, Yaakov Shmuel. *Chapters in the History of the Jewish Book: Scholars and Their Annotations* [Hebrew]. Ramat-Gan, Israel: Bar-Ilan University Press, 1996.

Stanislawski, Michael. "Jewish Apostasy in Russia: A Tentative Typology." In *Jewish Apostasy in the Modern World,* edited by Todd M. Endelman, 189–205. New York: Holmes & Meier, 1987.

Starr, Hank. "Waging the Israeli/Arab War in Nevada County." *Union* [Grass Valley, CA], May 18, 2002. Accessed February 2, 2023. www.theunion.com/opinion/waging-israeliarab-war-in-nevada-county.

"The Steppes of Southern Russia. No. I." *Asiatic Journal and Monthly Register for British and Foreign India, China, and Australia* [William H. Allen & Co., London], new series, 36 (September-December 1841): 133–142.

Subtelny, Orest. *Ukraine: A History*. Toronto: University of Toronto Press in association with the Canadian Institute of Ukrainian Studies, 1988.

"Ta'arukhat ha-tsayar Sh. Bernshtein" [Exhibition of the Painter S. Bernstein]. *Doar ha-Yom* [Jerusalem], September 19, 1927, 1.

"Tacoma Rabbi to Visit Father in Palestine." *Tacoma Daily Ledger*, August 17, 1920, 1.

Talmud. See Glossary 1, p. 878.

Talphir, Gavriel. *100 Artists in Israel* [Hebrew]. Tel-Aviv, Israel: Gazith Art Publishing, 1971.

Tamari, M. (ed.). *Kehilat Benderi: sefer zikaron*. Tel-Aviv, Israel: Va'ad yotse Benderi be-Yisrael ube-artsot ha-brit, 1975.

Tehilim im ma'amadot. Zhytomyr, Ukraine: Arye Leyb Shapiro, 1866.

Tidhar, David. *Entsiklopediyah le-khalutse ha-yishuv u-vonav*. Tel-Aviv, Israel: Sifriyat rishonim (David Tidhar), 1947–1971.

"Tiraspol." In *Słownik geograficzny Królestwa Polskiego i innych krajów słowiańskich*, vol. 12, 718–719. Warszawa, Poland: Filip Sulimierski i Władysław Walewski, 1892.

Tolstoy, Leo. "What Is a Jew? Count Tolstoi Makes Answer." Translated by Raphael Goldenstein. *Oregonian*, January 15, 1911, sec. 5, 9.

Toyber, Khayim (Rabbi). *Totsaot Khayim*. Pressburg [Bratislava, Slovakia]: n.p., 1835.

Trope, Elazar. *Yesodot le-toldot Petakh-Tikvah*. Petakh-Tikva: n.p., 1949.

"A Tragic Death." *Seattle Daily Times*, July 18, 1901, 3.

Tsitron, Yisrael Aba (Rabbi). *Hidushe ha-Rav Tsitron-Katroni: Rabah shel Petakh-Tikvah [5]670–[5]687*. Petakh-Tikva: Kolel Retson Yehuda, 2010.

Urussov, Serge Dmitriyevich. *Memoirs of a Russian Governor*. Translated by Herman Rosenthal. London: Harper & Brothers Publishers, 1908.

Valershtein, DovBer. "Tekufat Mohlev be-khaye Rabenu. . . ." In *Ha-Rav: Rabenu admor ha-zaken Rabi Shneur Zalman mi-Liadi . . .*, edited by Nochum Grunwald, 653–658. Lakewood, NY: Mekhon ha-Rav, 2015.

Vilf, Refael. *Netivot Refael: pirke yoman ve-sipurim mi-tokh ketavav shel he-khasid R' Refael Vilf . . . mi-Yerushalayim*. Jerusalem, Israel: 2017.

Vsia Rossiia: Russkaia kniga promyshlennosti, torgovli, sel'skago khoziaistva i administratsii. St. Petersburg, Russia: Izd. A. S. Suvorina, 1895.

Weinreich, Uriel. *Modern English-Yiddish/Yiddish-English Dictionary*. New York: YIVO Institute for Jewish Research, 1968.

Walhouse, M. J. "Ghostly Lights." *Folklore* 5, no. 4 (December 1894): 293–299.

Wertheim, Aaron (Rabbi). "Zikhroynes fun Benderer Rabinat." In *Kehilat Benderi: sefer zikaron*, 298–301. Tel-Aviv, Israel: Va'ad yotse Benderi be-Yisrael ube-artsot ha-brit, 1975.

———. *Law and Custom in Hasidism*. Translated by Shmuel Himelstein. Hoboken, NJ: KTAV, 1992.

Wiener, Moshe. *Hadras Ponim—Zokon: The Cutting and Growth of the Beard in Halachic Perspective*. New York: n.p., 2006.

Wilensky, Mordecai. *Hasidim and Mitnaggedim* [Hebrew]. Jerusalem, Israel: Bialik Institute, 1970.

Wilhelm, Y.Z. (Rabbi). *What's in a Name? = Ziv ha-shemot: Laws and Customs regarding the Naming of Children and Related Topics.* Translated by Shimon Neubort. Brooklyn: S.I.E. Publications, 1998.

Wolf, Eliyahu. *Ekhad hayah Avraham: ha-rav he-khasid Rav Avraham Pariz.* Kfar Chabad, Israel: Sifriyat Eshel–Kfar-Chabad, 2001.

Wormser, Seckel Loeb (Rabbi). *Ba'al Shem mi-Mikhelshtat: khidot u-teshuvot. . . .* Jerusalem, Israel: Sifriyat Artur Hubert, 1983.

Ya'ari, Y. *Sefer ha-yovel: li-melot khamishim shana le-yisud Petakh-Tikvah, 638–688 [1878–1928].* Tel-Aviv, Israel: Va'adat sefer ha-yovel she-al yad ha-mo'etsah ha-mekomit, 1929.

Yakobzon, Khayim. *Petakh-Tikvah be-reshit ha-meah.* Petakh-Tikva, Israel: n.p., 1986.

Yashar, Mosheh Meir (Rabbi). *Ha-Gaon Malbim.* Jerusalem, Israel: Hod Publishers, 1976.

Yellin, Yehoshua. *Zikhronot le-ven-Yerushalayim, 694–678.* Jerusalem, Israel: Ariel, 1924.

Yirme, Avrem-Shimen (Rabbi). *Ishei Hashem.* Jerusalem, Israel: Defus Frumkin, 1906.

Zaionchkovsky, Peter A. *The Abolition of Serfdom in Russia.* Translated by Susan Wobst. Gulf Breeze, FL: Academic International Press, 1978.

Zinner, Gavriel (Rabbi). *Nite Gavriel: hilkhot nesuin.* Brooklyn: Cong. Nitei Gavriel, 1998.

———. *Nite Gavriel: hilkhot yikhud.* Brooklyn: Cong. Nitei Gavriel, 2001.

———. *Nite Gavriel: halakhot ve-halikhot bar mitsvah.* Brooklyn: Cong. Nitei Gavriel, 2002.

Zipperstein, Steven J. *The Jews of Odessa: A Cultural History 1794–1881.* Palo Alto, CA: Stanford University Press, 1985.

Zunser [Tsunzer], Eliakim. *Tsunzer's biografye: geshriben fun im aleyn.* New York: Zunser Jubilee Committee, 1905.

Glossaries

Introduction to the Glossaries and the Romanization/ Transliteration Schemes

This glossary lists non-English words and phrases used in this translation. Most entries are from the Yiddish, but it also includes words in Hebrew, Aramaic, Russian, and Turkish. Apart from their listings in the glossary, most words or phrases are defined in a footnote the first time they appear in the text, though generally not when it first appears in the chapter summaries at the beginning of each chapter. The definition in the footnotes can be more elaborate than the definition in the glossary, or vice versa. Some common words are only defined in the glossary and not in the footnotes. Words and phrases have generally been translated only as used in this work. Most non-English words and phrases mentioned in the footnotes have also been included in the glossary. Non-English words and phrases mentioned only in the footnotes are often not listed in the glossary. Similarly, Non-English words and phrases mentioned only once in the appendices are defined in the footnotes and are not generally listed in the glossary.

Most foreign words are italicized in the text. Yiddish words have generally been romanized following Uriel Weinreich's system in his *Modern English-Yiddish/Yiddish-English Dictionary* (1968). Although based on the Northeastern Yiddish dialect, his system provides a uniform manner of romanizing Yiddish words in any Yiddish dialect (see Schaechter, 1995:443–446). Some minor variations have been made, such as the spelling of surnames ending in *–sky* (instead of *–ski*), as was commonly done by pre-World War I immigrants from Tsarist Russia to English-speaking lands. Similarly, Hebrew and Aramaic components of Yiddish have often been romanized according to the Ashkenazi-Hebrew pronunciation (e.g., *kheyder* instead of *heder*), following the same system. Though Yiddish and Hebrew have only one case of letters, words that would be capitalized in English (e.g., proper nouns, names of prayers, adjectives derived from proper nouns, etc.) are generally capitalized.

When Hebrew words have been transliterated according to the Modern Hebrew (MH) pronunciation, a modified form of the Library of Congress

Hebrew transliteration system has generally been used, which includes the absence of diacritical marks, the omission of the letter "h" corresponding to a final *heh* (ה), and the transliteration of both the letters *khaf* (כ) and *khet* (ח) as *kh*. (When no Modern Hebrew pronunciation is listed in the glossary, it is an indication that the word does not originate from Hebrew.)

When foreign terms have accepted spellings or academic spellings, those spellings have generally been used (e.g., Pesach instead of *Peysekh*; Hasid instead of *Khusid* or *Khosid*; *Simchas Torah* instead of *Simkhes-Toyre*, Chabad instead of Khabad; Lubavitch instead of Lubavitsh, and Schneerson instead of Shneyerson). The exceptions are when these accepted spellings differ considerably from the Yiddish (e.g., *Teyves* instead of *Tevet*). Though foreign terms with accepted English spellings often do not appear in italics, they are generally defined in both the footnotes and the glossary.

Russian words are also generally romanized according to the Library of Congress system. The grammatical variations of Slavic words have been avoided.

The Glossary of Words and Phrases has been set up along the lines of the glossary in Joshua A. Fishman's *Ideology, Society & Language: The Odyssey of Nathan Birnbaum* (1987), in which multiple pronunciations are indicated. Appearing directly after each word in the glossary are initials in parenthesis that indicate the dialect used for that entry. In general, words have been romanized according to the Yiddish dialect (which includes the corresponding Ashkenazi pronunciations of the Hebrew and Aramaic components in Yiddish) used by the person speaking. Not all the nuances in each dialect are indicated, though there was an emphasis to capture the nuances of the author's dialect, spoken in the southernmost part of the region where Southeastern Yiddish (SPSEY). In Lubavitch and Shklov in Belarus and later in Petakh-Tikva, which was predominantly settled by Jews who spoke the Northeastern Yiddish (NEY) dialect, the NEY dialect has been used. In the Crimea, the Southeastern Yiddish (SEY) dialect has been used since it was primarily settled by Jews from the Ukraine. For an overview of Yiddish dialects, see Schaechter (2005:443–446). Note that these abbreviations refer to the dialect in which the word or phrase is romanized and not to the language of the entry. Sometimes a word is listed with more than one symbol, (e.g., Y, MH), which indicates that the word is pronounced similarly in Yiddish and Modern Hebrew, though the stress is usually on different syllables. Each entry in glossary is followed by one of the abbreviations below in parenthesis, which indicate the dialect being used. Afterward appear their pronunciations in the other dialects, each separated by a semicolon.

In Yiddish (including the Ashkenazic pronunciation of Hebrew words), the stress tends to be on the penultimate syllable while in Modern Hebrew the stress is generally on the last syllable. For Yiddish words, personal names, and geographic names in which the accent does not lie on the penultimate syllable, the stressed syllable is indicated by an accent mark directly over the stressed vowel (e.g., Avrúm [Abraham]), as done by Schaechter (2005). In the glossary of geographic places, when the last syllable is stressed and consists of an "i", the statement "(stress on the last syllable)" has been noted since an "i" with an accent mark is not readily discerned. Note that sometimes the traditional pronunciations of Yiddish words (particularly for the Hebrew elements in Yiddish) differ from the manner in which they are pronounced by most of today's Yiddish speakers.

The following abbreviations are used in the glossaries:

SEY: Southeastern Yiddish (so-called "Ukrainian" Yiddish). This dialect was spoken in most of pre-Second World War Ukraine, pre-Second World War Romania (Bessarabia, Moldavia, Bukovina), and the easternmost part of Galicia.[1] In terms of pronunciation, Southeastern Yiddish can be considered to occupy an intermediate position between the two other major Yiddish dialects, Northeastern ("Lithuanian") Yiddish and Central ("Polish") Yiddish. The major differences between the three dialects are in their systems of vowels. The Southeastern dialect has, for example, *luzn* (let), *kikn* (to look), *koyfn* (buy), and *fan* (fine), while the Northeastern dialect has *lozn, kukn, keyfn,* and *fayn,* and the Central dialect (Polish type) uses *luzn, kikn, koyfn,* and *fan.* Note that only two of the three major dialects are reflected in this work, Southeastern Yiddish and Northeastern Yiddish, but not Central Yiddish, since Goldenshteyn never lived in the areas where it was spoken. Central Yiddish was spoken in pre-Second World War

1 A result of the early deterioration of traditional Judaism in the Ukraine is that there are no traditional Jewish communities today that speak the Southeastern (Ukrainian) dialect of Yiddish, though there are Jewish communities that speak Northeastern (Lithuanian) Yiddish and Central Yiddish (spoken in Poland, Hungary, and Galicia). Even among the Skverer Hasidim (originating in Skvira, Ukraine) of New Square, New York, almost no one is a descendant of Skverer Hasidim who lived in the Ukraine; most descend from Hungarian Jews. Nonetheless, in keeping with the Skverer tradition, the Hasidim recite their Hebrew prayers according to the Southeastern Yiddish pronunciation scheme.

Central and Western Poland, Eastern Slovakia, Northern and Eastern Hungary, Maramures, and Transylvania.

SPSEY: Southernmost part of the region where SEY was spoken. This subdialect of SEY was spoken in the Tsarist Russian provinces of Bessarabia, southern Podolia, southern Kiev, western Kherson (now in the contemporary nations Ukraine and Moldova), and the Romanian region of Moldovia. This was the dialect spoken by the author. It is colloquially called *tote-mome lushn* (i.e., *tote-mome* language) since its most distinguishing feature is the pronunciation of "a" as an "o" in most cases. Hence, *tate* (father) is pronounced as *tote; mame* (mother) as *mome;* Kaddish as *Kodesh; Shabes* as *Shobes;* the name Zalmen as Zolmen; and even Chabad as *Khabod.* Another characteristic of SPSEY, though not an exclusive feature, is its lack of the "h" consonant. Hence, the name Hershl is pronounced as Ershl. In order to add some local color, some easily recognized words are romanized using this dialect, as indicated above. In this dialect (as well as in some other Yiddish dialects), words starting with "yi" are pronounced as "i," e.g., Isruel (Israel) instead of Yisruel. Recordings of a native of Bendér, which is close to the author's hometown of Tiraspol, can be heard on the website of the Language and Culture Atlas of Ashkenazi Jewry at: http://www.eydes.de/index/li/li-019.html.

NEY: Northeastern Yiddish (so-called "Lithuanian" Yiddish). This dialect was spoken in Lithuania, Belarus, northeastern Poland, northern Ukraine, Latvia, and Estonia. This dialectal pronunciation is provided when the SEY pronunciation would not be easily recognizable (e.g., *Sukes* instead of *Sikes; Shvues* instead of *Shvies*). Instead of using a purely ethnic NEY in this work, I have used the modern Standard Yiddish dialect which is based on NEY and is used in Uriel Weinreich's *Modern English-Yiddish/Yiddish-English Dictionary* (1968). NEY is also used in the bibliography in romanizing the titles of Yiddish books.

Y: Yiddish. Referenced when both the Southeastern Yiddish (SEY) and the Northeastern Yiddish (NEY) dialects pronounce the entry similarly.

MH: Modern Hebrew. This pronunciation is only relevant to the Hebrew components of Yiddish. This pronunciation is provided when even the NEY pronunciation would not be easily recognizable, e.g., *gabbai* instead of *gabe.*

pl.: indicates the plural form of the entry in the relevant dialect. Often the plural form is simply indicated in parentheses without "pl.," e.g., *shteytl(ekh)*, demonstrating that the plural of *shteytl* is *shteytlekh*.

E: English. This is only used in the Glossary 2 when listing English equivalents of personal names.

Glossary 1: Words and Phrases

Adar (MH) (SEY: *Uder*; NEY: *Oder*): the month of the Hebrew calendar which usually corresponds to parts of February and March. In leap years, it is preceded by a thirty-day month called *Adar* I and then it itself is called *Adar* II. The holiday of *Purim* is generally celebrated on the 14th of *Adar*.

Adon Olam (MH) (Y: *Adoyn Oylom*): the initial words (meaning "Eternal Lord") of a prayer recited at the beginning of morning services.

aguna (MH) (SEY: *agine*; NEY: *agune*): a married woman who became separated from her husband and cannot remarry, either because she cannot obtain a Jewish divorce (i.e., *get*) from him or because it is unknown whether he is still alive.

aliya (MH) (Y: *alie*): the honor of being called up to the reading of the Torah scroll which is read on Mondays, Thursdays, Saturday (*Shabes*), and Jewish holidays. The honoree recites a Hebrew blessing before and after a designated reader reads a portion of the Torah for the congregation.

A gite vokh (SEY) (NEY: *A gute vokh*): at the conclusion of the Sabbath, at nightfall on Saturday, it is customary for people to wish each other "*A gite vokh*," meaning "a good week."

Alter Rebbe (Y) (SPSEY: *Olter Rebbe*): referring to Rabbi Shneur Zalman of Lyadi (1745–1812) and meaning "Old Rebbe" in Yiddish.

Anim Zmires (Y) (MH: *Anim Zmirot*): meaning "I will sweetly sing songs" in Hebrew, it is part of the liturgy recited at the end of morning services on the Sabbath (*Shabes*) and, in some communities, on Jewish holidays.

arman(es) (Y): threshing floor(s). See ch. 20, p. 362, footnote 36.

Ashkenazi, pl. *Ashkenazim* (Y, MH): 1) a Jew of central or eastern European origin, descended originally from the Jews of France and Germany; 2) pertaining to such Jews.

Asher Yotser (NEY) (SEY: *Asher Yutser*; MH: *Asher Yatsar*): the Hebrew blessing thanking God for a functioning body which is recited after relieving oneself.

Askinu Seudoso (NEY) (SEY: *Askini Se'idusu*; MH: *Atkinu Seudata*): meaning "I shall arrange the meal" in Aramaic, this liturgical poem is chanted or sung prior to the Friday evening Sabbath meal and is found in most traditional prayer books.

atore (MH) (SEY: *ature*; NEY: *atore*; MH: *atara*): a band of cloth made of silver thread and sewn onto the edge of the *talis* that is draped over the head.

Av (MH) (SEY: *Uv*; NEY: *Ov*): the eleventh month of the Hebrew calendar which usually corresponds to parts of July and August. Also called *Menakhem Av*.

Baal Shem Tov: referring to Rabbi Israel Baal Shem Tov (ca. 1700–1760), the founder of Hasidism. (Hasidic speakers of Southeastern and Northeastern Yiddish pronounce his name as *Bal Shemtev*, while Hasidic speakers of Central Yiddish pronounce it as *Bal Shemtov*.)

badkhn, also ***batkhn***, pl. ***badkhonim*** (Y) (SPSEY: *bodkhen, botkhn*; MH: *badkhan[im]*): a traditional Jewish performer specializing in humorous and semi-improvised rhymes.

bal-takse (Y) (SPSEY: *bal-tokse*): kosher meat-tax farmer. See ch. 23, p. 470, footnote 56.

Bamidbar (MH) (Y: *Bamidber, Bamidbor*): the name of the weekly Torah portion comprising Numbers 1:1 to 4:20. See also Torah portion.

belfer(s) (Y): an assistant to a *dardeke melamed*.

bentsh goyml (Y): literally meaning "make (the blessing of) *goyml*." *Goyml* (*gomel* in Modern Hebrew) means "causes" in Hebrew and refers to the full blessing of, "Blessed are You, oh Lord, our God, King of the universe who causes great acts of kindness for His nation Israel." This blessing is said after being delivered from danger. See *Kitsur Shulkhan Arukh* (ch. 61) for details. (It also appears in the text is the third person singular form, *bentsht goyml*.)

bes-medresh (Y), pl. *bute-medrushim* (SEY) (MH: *bét-midrash*, pl. *baté-midrashim*): used to denote a Torah study hall where no formal instruction took place but where students studied independently and prayers services were also held, as opposed to a *shul* (synagogue) which was established solely for prayer services. Today the *bes-medresh* and *shul* have merged together.

bes-médreshnik (Y): someone who studies Torah full time in a *bes-médresh*.

bidke (Y): a two-wheeled cart.

Bidne Zhid: "miserable Jew." See also *Zhid*.

bimah (MH) (Y: *bime*): the elevated platform traditionally in the center of a synagogue where the Torah reading takes place.

bishlik (Turkish): a monetary unit in Ottoman Turkey. Seven Turkish bishliks were equivalent to one Turkish pound (lira).

Bney Odom, also *Bney Odem* (NEY) (SEY: *Bney Udem*; MH: *Bne Adam*): a prayer recited during *kapores*.

Bo (MH) (Y: *Boy*): the name of the weekly Torah portion comprising Exodus 10:1 to 13:16. See also Torah portion.

bodgelt (NEY) (SEY: *budgelt*): the silver coins for the midwife, which used to be thrown into the bathtub in which a child is bathed shortly after birth.

Boi ve'shulem (SEY) (NEY: *Boi ve'sholem*; MH: *Boi ve-shalom*): the opening words (literally "Come in peace") to the last stanza of the Friday-night Hebrew prayer *Lekho doydi* (i.e., "Come my Beloved"), which ushers in the Sabbath.

Borukh hu uvorukh shmoy (NEY) (SEY: *Burekh hi uvurekh shmoy*; MH: *Barukh hu u-varukh shmo*): these Hebrew words, meaning "Blessed is He and blessed is His Name," are recited upon hearing the leader of prayers invoke God's name in reciting a blessing, of which there are many in the Jewish prayer services.

boydek (Y) (MH: *bodek*): literally "examiner" in Hebrew and denotes an examiner of the lungs of a slaughtered animal. Jewish law necessitates the checking of the lungs of slaughtered cattle, goats, etc. to ensure that no holes or scar tissue have rendered the animal forbidden. Since this is an essential part of the slaughtering process, only the word *shoykhet* is used whenever the author writes "*shoykhet* and *boydek*."

Breyshis (Y) (MH: *Be-reshit*): meaning "In the beginning" and referring to the first of the weekly Torah portions in the annual cycle of reading the Torah, which comprises Genesis 1:1 to 6:8. See also Torah portion.

bris(n) (Y) (MH: *brit*): circumcision of male children at the age of eight days which the Jewish people are commanded to perform in Leviticus 12:2.

britshke (Y): often spelled "britzka" in English, it is generally a type of large four-wheeled carriage with a folding top over the rear seat and a rear-facing front seat, which is pulled by two horses.

buryan(es): the tall, wiry, and often thorny weeds and grasses that grow on the steppe.

bute medrushim (SEY): pl. of *bes-medresh*.

Chabad (NE: *Khabád*; SPSEY: *Khabód*; MH: *Khabád*): acronym derived from the Hebrew words *Chochma, Bina, Da'at,* meaning "wisdom," "understanding," and "knowledge," which refers to the philosophy of mind over emotion developed by the Hasidic Rebbe, Rabbi Shneur-Zalman (1745–1812) of Lyady.

Chabadnik (NEY: *Khabádnik*; SPSEY: *Khabódnik*): a Hasid of one of the Rebbes of Chabad. With the end of the other branches of Chabad Hasidism in Kopust and Lyadi during the early twentieth century, the terms Chabadnik (i.e., Chabad Hasid) and Lubavitcher Hasid have come to be used interchangeably. (In the 1960s or 1970s in Israel, Chabadniks began to be called Chabadskers by some non-Hasidic, ultra-Orthodox Jews. Since then, the term has spread to America and to non-Chabad Hasidic circles. Before the Second World War, this term did not exist; only the adjective form, Chabadske, existed in Yiddish, e.g., a Chabadske *shul.*)

chetvert (pronounced *tshetvert*): an obsolete Russian unit of measurement. It was equivalent to 126.39 lbs.

chumak (pronounced *tshumak*): the historic occupation of wagoners and traders common in the Ukraine, primarily the transportation of salt and salt-cured fish via ox-drawn wagons Sometimes traveling in huge caravans, the *chumaks* prospered until the second half of the nineteenth century, before the advent of railways.

Code of Jewish Law (MH: *Shulkhan Arukh*; SEY: *Shulkhen-Urekh*; NEY: *Shulkhen-Orukh*): compiled by Rabbi Yosef Caro in the sixteenth century, the Code, together with its commentaries, is the most widely accepted compilation of Jewish law ever written.

dardeke melamed (Y) (MH: *melamed dardeki*): a beginning-level *melamed,* who teaches his students the Hebrew alphabet.

desyatin (Y): the Yiddish *desyatin* corresponds to *desiatina,* an obsolete Russian unit of measurement. It was used in measuring farming land. One *desyatin* was equivalent to 3.6 acres.

Detsakh Adash Be'akhav (Y, MH): in the Passover Haggadah, the first letters of the Hebrew names of the ten plagues are divided into these three acronyms.

dikát(n) (Y): ducat(s).

dmei pan (MH, Y): literally meaning "petition money" in Hebrew. Used by Lubavitcher Hasidim to refer to the money accompanying a petitionary note (*pan,* an acronym for *pidyen nefesh*) to their Rebbe when meeting with him. Non-Lubavitcher Hasidim use the word *pidyen.*

dukhn(en) (NEY) (SEY: *dikhn[en]*): the *kohen*'s recital of the priestly blessing (Numbers 6:24–26) in front of the congregation. For Ashkenazi Jews living outside the Land of Israel, it is generally recited as part of the *Musaf* prayer service on *Yontef.*

Elul (MH) (Y: *Elel*): the twelfth month of the Hebrew calendar immediately preceding Rosh Hashanah and usually corresponds to parts of August and September.

Erets-Isruel (SPSEY) (NEY: *Erets-Yisroel*; MH: *Erets-Yisrael*): the Land of Israel.

Erets-Yisroel: see *Erets-Isruel*.

esn teg (NEY) (SEY: *esn teyg*): literally meaning "eating-days" in Yiddish, and denoting the established system in European yeshivas (before the advent of yeshiva kitchens) by which the students were assigned different days to eat their meals at the homes of local residents; hence, the name *esn teg*.

esreg; pl. *esroygim* (Y) (MH: *etrog[im]*): the citron used as part of the *mitzvah* of the four species. Based on the Biblical commandment (Leviticus 23:40), the four species (citron and branches of the palm, willow, and myrtle) are taken by Jews each day of *Sukes* and are traditionally held together and waved in a prescribed manner (*Kitsur Shulkhan Arukh*, 137).

Eykev *(Y) (MH: Ekev):* the name of the Torah portion comprising Deuteronomy 7:12 to 11:25. See also Torah portion.

eymer (SEY) (NEY: *emer*): literally a "pail," referring to a unit of volume used in measuring wine that is roughly equivalent to a gallon.

eynikl (Y): literally meaning "grandchild" in Yiddish, it refers in ch. 3 (p. 120) to a descendant of a Hasidic Rebbe who is considered to be something of a Hasidic Rebbe himself.

Eyshes Khayil (Y) (MH: *Eshet Khayil*): literally meaning "Woman of Valor" in Hebrew, these are the opening words of praise for the virtuous woman contained in Proverbs (31:10–31). It is traditionally sung by the husband (alone or together with the children) on Friday night before Kiddush.

feldsher (Y): a kind of medical assistant who often had obtained some medical knowledge by being a medic in the army.

funt (Y): this obsolete Russian unit of measurement was equal to 409.5 grams, which is slightly less than the current weight of a US pound (453.6 grams).

gabbai; pl. *gabbaim* (MH) (SEY: *gabe*, pl. *gabuem*; SPSEY: *gobe*, pl. *gabuem*; NEY: *gabe*, pl. *gaboyim*): 1) warden of an institution such as a yeshiva or a society, such as a burial society, but especially of a synagogue; 2) a Hasidic Rebbe's administrative assistant.

gabbaim: see *gabbai*.

get (Y, MH): Jewish bill of divorce.

gartl(n) (Y): A cloth belt, often made of silk, worn primarily by Hasidim around their *kapótes* or similar coats, especially during prayers.

gildn (Y) (SPSEY: *giln*): a fifteen-kopek coin.

gimnaziia: Generally referring to a state-run school in Tsarist Russia equivalent to high school or a junior college.

Giter-Yid, pl. *Gite-Yidn* (SEY) (SPSEY: *Giter-Id*; NEY: *Guter-Id*): literally meaning a "Good Jew" in Yiddish but used to denote a Hasidic Rebbe, though this term generally stopped being used after the Second World War. Chabad Hasidim have always refrained from using this term to refer to their own Rebbes.

Gite vokh: see *A gite vokh.*

Gite-Yidishe shtik: pretenses of being a *Giter-Yid*, i.e., a Hasidic Rebbe.

Gite-Yidn: pl. of *Giter-Yid.*

Git Yontef, also "*A git Yontef*" (SEY) (NEY: *Gut Yontef*): meaning "Good holiday" and said on Jewish holidays.

Goles (NEY) (SEY: *Gules*; MH: *Galut*): the Jewish Diaspora, which Judaism views as a period of spiritual as well as physical exile.

goy (Y, MH): non-Jew.

goyish (Y): the non-Jewish vernacular. See ch. 8, p. 170, footnote 7.

goyml: see *bentsh goyml*

groshn (Y): a half-kopek coin.

guberniya (Y: *gubernye*): a province in Tsarist Russia.

Ha-Azinu (NEY, MH) (SEY: *Ha'Azini*): the name of the weekly Torah portion comprising Deuteronomy 32:1–52. See also Torah portion.

Haftorah (Y: *Haftoyre*; MH: *Haftarah*): the selection from the books of Prophets of the Hebrew Bible that is read publicly in the synagogue and thematically linked to the weekly Torah portion. The *Haftorah* reading follows the Torah reading on each Sabbath, Jewish holiday, and fast day.

Haggadah (SEY: *Hagude*; SPSEY: *Agude*): the text that sets forth the order of the Pesach *Seder*. Reading the *Haggadah* at the *Seder* table is a fulfillment of the commandment (Exodus 13:8) for each Jew to "tell your son" about the Jewish liberation from slavery in Egypt.

Hanukah (Y: *Khanike*; SPSEY: *Khonike*; MH: *Khanuka*): the Jewish holiday celebrating the re-dedication of the Temple in Jerusalem after the victory of the Maccabees over Antiochus of Syria in the second century BCE. The holiday lasts eight days, during which a special eight-branched lamp called a *menorah* is lit, beginning with one light and adding an additional light each day.

halakha (MH) (SEY: *halukhe*; SPSEY: *alukhe*; NEY: *halokhe*): the entire body of Jewish law. See also *Code of Jewish Law* and *Kitsur Shulkhan Arukh.*

halakhic: pertaining to *halakhah.*

Hallel (Y: *Halel*; *SPSEY: Olel*): a prayer generally consisting of Psalms 113–118, which are said as a unit on most Jewish holidays.

ha'moytse (Y) (SPSEY: *amoytse*; MH: *ha-motsi*): referring to the Hebrew blessing required to be recited before eating bread (*Kitsur Shulkhan Arukh* 41:1–10).

Hasid (SEY: *Khusid*; NEY: *Khosid*; MH: Khasid): literally meaning "pious" in Hebrew, it refers to a follower of Hasidism and usually of a Hasidic Rebbe. After the death of its founder, Rabbi Israel Baal Shem Tov (ca. 1700–1760), Hasidim branched out into numerous individual rabbinic dynasties; a follower of one of these leaders (i.e., a Hasidic Rebbe) is called a Hasid. Hence, a follower of the Lubavitcher Rebbe is called a Lubavitcher Hasid.

Hasidic: relating to or denoting Hasidism.

Hasidim (Y: *Khsidim*; MH: *Khasidim*): plural of Hasid.

Hasidism: the movement within Judaism founded by Rabbi Israel Baal Shem Tov (c. 1700–1760), which focuses on serving God on a deeply spiritual level, loving one's fellow Jew, and delving into the inner dimensions of Torah.

Haskalah (MH) (SEY: *Haskule*; SPSEY: *Askule*; NEY: *Haskole*): the Jewish Enlightenment Movement was an eighteenth- and nineteenth-century modernization movement critical of traditional Jewish society, particularly Hasidism, and sought to spread knowledge of the secular world among the Jewish masses. Over time, advocates of this movement, called *Maskilim,* and their offspring, tended to become distanced from Judaism.

Havdalah (SEY: *havdule*; SPSEY: *avdule*; NEY: *havdole*): literally meaning "separation" in Hebrew, it is the prayer said over wine, made after nightfall at the conclusion of *Shabes* and Jewish holidays. It marks the end of every holy day and the transition to the regular days of the week.

Heshvan (Y: *Kheshven*; MH: *Kheshvan*): the second month of the Hebrew calendar, which usually corresponds to parts of October and November.

High Holidays: *Rosh Hashanah* and *Yom Kippur.*

hoyf (Y): literally meaning a "courtyard" in Yiddish, this word is also used to refer to a Hasdic Rebbe's residence or to his synagogue.

Hoyshane-Rabe, also *Heshane-Rabe* (Y) (MH: *Hoshana Raba*): literally meaning "Great Supplication," it is the seventh day of the Jewish holiday of *Sukes* and the fifth day of the intermediate days of *Sukes.*

Hoyshanes, also *Heshanes* (Y) (MH: *Hoshanot*): a series of prayers recited each day of *Sukes* following the *Hallel* prayer, where the leader holds the four species and encircles the *bimah* followed by the congregation (*Kitsur Shulkhan Arukh*, 137:11).

huppah (NEY: *khupe*; SEY: *khipe*; MH: *khupa*): a canopy under which a Jewish couple traditionally stands during their wedding ceremony. It can also be used as a canopy of honor under which a newly written Torah scroll is carried when first brought into a synagogue.

interfirers (SEY) (NEY: *unterfirers*): both the bride and the groom each designate a married couple, usually their parents, to act as *interfirers* to lead them to the wedding canopy. Either the groom's *interfirers* lead the groom and the bride's *interfirers* lead the bride to the wedding canopy, or, as done among Hasidim, the two fathers lead the groom and the two mothers lead the bride.

Iyar (MH) (Y: *Iyer*): the eighth month of the Hebrew calendar, which usually corresponds to parts of April and May.

Jerusalem Talmud: see *Talmud*.

Kabules Shobes (SEY) (NEY: *Kaboles Shabes*; MH: *Kabalat Shabat*): literally "Receiving the Sabbath" in Hebrew. It refers to the part of the Friday evening service welcoming the Sabbath, which precedes the regular evening prayer.

Kaddish (MH) (Y: *Kadesh*; SEY: *Kodesh*): 1) the mourning prayer recited during all three daily prayer services for eleven months following a Jewish person's death and in the three daily prayers on the anniversary of their death, often referred to as "saying kaddish"; 2) though not common today, a son used to be referred to in Yiddish as his parents' *kaddish* (or *kaddishl*), since a son's reciting the *Kaddish* prayer for the souls of his departed parents holds great spiritual significance.

kal (Y, MH): light, frivolous. See ch. 22, p. 423, footnote 43.

Kamer, kamer, hoyz (NEY): meaning "chamber, chamber, house," referring to a children's game described in ch. 6, p. 151.

kapores (NEY) (SEY: *kapures*; MH: *kaparot*): a custom carried out by men, women, and children in the early morning of the eve of Yom Kippur or on the preceding days. Each male takes a live rooster, and each female takes a hen. The live chicken is taken in the right hand and moved in a circular motion around the head three times, while reciting certain prayers. The custom is that the chicken is then slaughtered and given to the poor. See *shlogn kapores*.

kapote (Y): a man's long, double-breasted frock coat worn by traditional Jews, particularly in Tsarist Russia.

Karaites: a Jewish sect that broke off from rabbinic Judaism in the eighth century by rejecting the Talmudic-rabbinic tradition.

kashres (Y) (MH: *kashrut*): *kosher* status, e.g., *kashres* inspector, a person who inspects and supervises the *kosher* status of establishments serving *kosher* food.

Kedushah (MH) (SEY: *Kedishe*; NEY: *Kedushe*): literally meaning "holiness" in Hebrew, it is a passage in the public prayer service, with portions recited responsively by the cantor and the congregation.

kénehóre (NEY) (SEY: *kenehure*): *kenehore* is the common Yiddish pronunciation of the words *keyn ayin hore* (MH, literally "no evil eye"). It is customarily added after saying words of praise or commenting on something desirable, thereby expressing the wish that the evil eye should have no effect.

Ken yovdu (NEY) (SEY: *Ken yuvdi*; MH: *Ken yavdu*): a Hebrew expression based on Judges 5:31 and is traditionally said upon hearing of the death of or misfortune befalling a rabid antisemite.

kest (Y): a prearranged agreement to provide a son-in-law with food and board for a specified number of years after marriage so that he could continue his Torah studies in peace.

keyver (Y) (MH: *kever*): grave.

Khakhám: meaning "wise man" in Hebrew, it is a title for rabbis among Sephardic Jews and Jews of the Arab lands.

khalát(n) (Y) (SPSEY: *khalót[n]*): a Jewish man's lightweight silk or woolen robe generally worn by Hasidim at home, especially on the Sabbath and Jewish holidays.

khale (Y) (SPSEY: *khole*; MH: *khala*): a loaf of white egg bread, usually braided and traditionally eaten by Jews on the Sabbath and Jewish holidays.

khapers (Y) (SPSEY: *khopers*): see *khoytfim*.

khazaka (MH) (SEY: *khazuke*; NEY: *khazoke*): referring in this work to the exclusive rights to perpetually practice *sh'khita* (kosher slaughtering) in a town. This privilege is obtained from the previous *shoykhet* or from the community. *Khazaka* is a *halakhic* term referring in general to the rights of possession.

khazn (Y) (SPSEY: *khozn*; MH: *khazan*): cantor.

kherem (MH) (Y: *kheyrem*): rabbinic ban.

kheyder (Y): a one-room, traditional Jewish religious school, usually for boys of a similar academic level in which the teaching is done by a *melamed*.

khimesh (SEY) (NEY: *khumesh*; MH: *khumash*): refers to the Five Books of Moses in Hebrew, which usually also include such classic commentaries as Rashi.

khole-nofel (MH) (Y: *khoyle-noyfl*): epilepsy.

khoytfim (Y) (MH: *khotfim*): meaning "snatchers" in Hebrew, referring to Jews who forcibly seized Jewish men and children to fill military quotas in Tsarist Russia. More commonly referred to by the Yiddish term *khapers*.

khoyzer (Y) (MH: *khozer*): a *Hasid* who memorized the discourses delivered by the Rebbes of Chabad on *Shabes* or *Yontef*, when no writing is permitted.

Khside (Y) (MH: *Khasida*): term for a Hasidic woman only used in writing. See *Khsideste*.

Khsideste (Y): a Hasidic woman. See *Hasid* and *Khside*.

Kiddush (MH) (Y: *Kidesh*): 1) the blessing recited over a goblet of wine (or some other quality drink) after the evening and morning prayer services thereby sanctifying the Sabbath (*Shabes*) and Jewish holidays. Nothing may be eaten or drunk until it is recited; 2) the refreshments following the recital of *Kiddush*.

kine (SEY) (NEY: *kune*): denotes the corporal punishment described in ch. 4, p. 133.

kines (Y) (MH: *kinot*): popularly referring to the collection of elegies recited on Tisha B'Av.

Ki Seytse (Y) (MH: *Ki Tetse*): the weekly Torah portion comprising Deuteronomy 21:10 to 25:19. See also Torah portion.

Kislev (Y, MH): the third month of the Hebrew calendar, which usually corresponds to parts of November and December. *Hanukah* begins on 25 *Kislev*.

kitl (Y): a white robe-like garment worn by the groom at the wedding ceremony and by married men on Yom Kippur (and by some during the Pesach *Seder*).

Kitsur Shulkhan Arukh (MH) (SEY: *Kitser Shilkhen Urekh*; NEY: *Kitser Shulkhen Orekh*): meaning "Abridged Code of Jewish Law." Compiled by Rabbi Shlomo Ganzfried (1804–1886), it is a summary of the *Code of Jewish Law* with reference to later commentaries and was first published in 1874. It has become the classic guide to practical observance among all Orthodox Jews.

klipa (MH) (Y: *klipe*): a Kabbalistic term, literally meaning "peel," used to denote negative and evil forces which conceal the divine presence as a peel conceals fruit.

klipat noga (MH) (YL *klipes noyge*): a Kabbalistic term, literally meaning "bright peel," and generally indicating a type of *klipa* (negative force) containing some good, which has the possibility of being transformed into holiness.

Kloyz (Y) (SPSEY: *kluz*): a *bes-medrash.*

kofeyne(s) (Y): coffee house(s); tavern(s).

Kohanim: pl. of *Kohen.*

Kohen, pl. *Kohanim* (MH) (Y: *Koyen*, pl. *Kehanim*): a patrilineal descendant of the sons of the Biblical Aaron, brother of Moses, who served as priests in the Temple in Jerusalem. Traditionally, they receive special honors in the synagogue, but are also subject to certain restrictions.

Kohen Gadol (MH) (SEY: *Koyen Gudl*; NEY: *Koyen Godl*): the high priest in the Holy Temple in Jerusalem.

Kol Mekadesh (Y, MH): one of the popular songs chanted during the Friday-night Sabbath meal.

Kol Nidre (MH) (Y: *Kol Nidrey*): a declaration recited in the synagogue before the evening service as Yom Kippur begins.

kopek: the smallest denomination of a Russian coin, equivalent to one-hundredth of a ruble.

Korben Minkhe (Y) (MH: *Korban Minkha*): the name of a prayer book (*sidur*) usually used by women. It includes the Yiddish translation of many prayers, Yiddish-language supplications, and instructions in Yiddish for many laws pertaining to a Jewish household that are traditionally overseen by women, including the laws of salting meat, etc.

korobka (Y: *korobke*): box-tax on kosher meat (see ch. 23, p. 470, footnote 56).

kosher (NEY) (SEY: *kusher*; MH: *kasher*): literally meaning "fit" or "permitted" (to be eaten), it refers to food which satisfies the intricate requirements of Jewish law.

krumer (NEY) (SEY: *krimer*): lame, squint-eyed, or crooked.

krupnik (Y): a soup made of potatoes and grains, which could be barley, buckwheat, or any other grain.

Krymchaks (Y: *Krimtshak[es]*; SPSEY: *Krimtshok[es]*): an indigenous Rabbinite Jewish community of the Crimean Peninsula that spoke its own dialect of Crimean Tatar, a Turkic language.

ksube (NEY) (SEY: *ksibe*; MH: *ketubah*): a Jewish wedding contract.

kukeruze (Y): corn.

kvater (Y) (SPSEY: *kvoter*): the man honored with carrying the baby into the room to undergo a *bris.*

kvitl(ekh) (Y): non-Lubavitcher Hasidim use this word to refer to a petitionary note given to a Rebbe, which is accompanied by a donation. Among

Chabad Hasidim, such notes are called a *tsetl*, a *pidyen nefesh* (literally meaning "redemption of one's soul" in Hebrew), or a *pan* (the acronym of *pidyen nefesh*).

Lag BaOmer (Y: *Leg B'Oymer*): the thirty-third day of the counting of the *Omer*, which is counted from the second day of Passover until *Shvues*. On this day, a plague killing 24,000 disciples of Rabbi Akiva ceased (ca. 50–135 CE). It is also the anniversary of the death of one of Rabbi Akiva's most eminent disciples, Rabbi Shimon bar Yokhai. It is a minor festival and a day of rejoicing. See also *Omer* and *Sfira*.

le'khaym (Y) (SPSEY: *le'khaem*; MH: *le-khayim*): meaning "to life" in Hebrew, this expression is traditionally used as a toast. Hence, "drinking *le'khaym*" denotes drinking and offering good wishes.

Lekhó doydi (NEY) (SEY: *Lekhu doydi*; MH: *Lekha dodi*): a Friday-night Hebrew prayer ushering in the Sabbath.

Lite (Y): particularly before the First World War, this term was not used to refer to the boundaries of today's independent Lithuania but refers to the areas in Eastern Europe where the northeastern dialect of Yiddish was traditionally spoken, namely Lithuania, Belarus, northeastern Poland, northern Ukraine, Latvia, and Estonia. See also *Litvak*.

Litvak (Y) (SPSEY: *Litvok*): used particularly before the First World War to refer to a Jew speaking the northern dialect of Yiddish, also known as Lithuanian Yiddish, which was predominantly spoken in Lithuania, Belarus, northeastern Poland, Latvia, Estonia, and northern Ukraine.

Lubavitcher: a follower of the Rebbes of Lubavitch and their Chabad philosophy. Synonymous with Lubavitcher Hasid.

Maftir (MH) (Y: *Mafter*; SPSEY: *Mofter*): the name of the last *aliya* during the reading of the Torah on the Sabbath (*Shabes*), Jewish holidays, and some other occasions. The person called up for *Maftir* also reads the Haftorah (the weekly selection from the Biblical book of Prophets) or has someone read it in his stead. Receiving this *aliyah* is considered a special honor and is reserved for prominent people or those observing a *yortsayt*, bar-mitzvah, wedding, etc.

magid(im) (Y, MH) (SPSEY: *mogid*): a Jewish preacher who speaks about moral and religious issues, often including much social criticism.

magid meyshorim (NEY) (SEY: *magid meyshurim*; SPSEY: *mogid meyshurim*; MH: *magid mesharim*): same as *magid*.

Maharshó (NEY) (SEY: *Maharshú*; MH: *Maharasha*): acronym of the words *Morenu ha-Rav Shmuel Eideles*, i.e., "Our Teacher, Rabbi Shmuel

Edels" (1555–1631), who wrote one of the primary commentaries on the Talmud.

malkhes pletselekh (Y): literally "*royal pletselekh*" (see *pletsl*) and denoting a children's game described in ch. 6, p. 151.

mamaliga (Y: *mámelige*; SPSEY: *momelige*): cornmeal made into a thick, solidified porridge. It was a staple food in Bessarabia (most of which is currently part of Moldova) and Romania.

Marev (SEY) (NEY: *Mayrev*; MH: *Ma'ariv*): evening prayers, the last of the three daily prayers.

Maskil(im) (H) (Y: *Maskl*, pl. *Maskilim*): a follower of the *Haskalah* movement.

matse(s) (Y) (SEY: *motses*; MH: *matsa*): a flat, unleavened bread eaten by Jews on Pesach, when leavened bread and products are forbidden.

Mayim Akhroynim (Y) (SPSEY: *Mayem Akhroynem*; MH: *Mayim Akharonim*): the water used to wash one's fingertips right before reciting the blessings after completing a meal eaten with bread. It literally means "final water" in Hebrew, as opposed to the first water used for washing before a meal (*Kitsur Shulkhan Arukh* 44:1–2).

mayl (Y) (SPSEY: *mal*): corresponds to the obsolete Russian unit of measurement called *milia*, which was equivalent to seven *versts* or 4.64 US miles.

mazel tov (Y: *mazl-tov*; SPSEY: *mozl-tov*; MH: *mazal tov*): 1) wishing of congratulations; 2) a happy occasion.

Megilla (MH) (Y: *Megile*): literally meaning "scroll," it often refers to the Biblical book of Esther handwritten on a scroll of parchment. The *Megilla* is read twice in the course of the holiday of Purim.

mejid: unit of Ottoman Turkish coinage. One gold *mejid* (pronounced *mezhid*) was equivalent to one Turkish pound (Lira).

melamed: see *melomed.*

Melava Malka (MH) (Y: *Mlave-Malke*; SPSEY; *Mlove-Molke*): the meal marking the conclusion of the Jewish Sabbath on Saturday after nightfall. These words literally mean "escorting the queen" in Hebrew, referring to Jews' figuratively escorting the "Sabbath Queen" on her way out as one would escort royalty upon their departure.

melomed, pl. *melomdim* (SPSEY) (Y: *melamed*, pl. *melomdim*; MH: *melamed*; pl. *melamdim*): a teacher in a *kheyder*, a traditional Jewish elementary school.

Menakhem Av (MH) (NEY: *Menakhem Ov*; SPSEY: *Menokhem Uv*): see *Av*.

menorah (MH) (Y: *menoyre*): the special eight-branched lamp lit during Hanukah. On the first night, one light is lit and an additional light is added each day for a total of eight days.

Menoyres ha'Moer (NEY) (SEY: *Menoyres ha'Muer*; MH: *Menorat ha-Maor*): an ethical work, whose title translates as *Lamp of Light*, which was written by the fourteenth-century rabbinic author, Yitskhak Abuhav (Aboab) of Toledo, Spain. First translated into Yiddish in 1701, subsequent Yiddish translations were widely popular among European Jewry, especially among women.

mentsh(n) (Y): a decent, responsible person with character.

meshores (NEY) (SEY: *meshures*; MH: *mesharet*): literally "assistant," referring to a Hasidic Rebbe's attendant.

meshoyrerim (Y) (MH: *meshorerim*): accompanying singers to a cantor.

meshumed (SEY: *meshimed*; MH: *meshumad*): A Jew who has apostatized, i.e., renounced Judaism, for Christianity.

mestl(ekh) (Y): Literally "a small measurement" in Yiddish. The author defines a *mestl* as being an eighth of a *chetvert* in ch. 19, pp. 320–321; hence, it is equivalent to 15.8 lbs.

mezuzah (MH) (SEY: *mezize[s]*; NEY: *mezuze[s]*): a parchment that Jews affix to their doorposts, on which a scribe has hand-written two paragraphs from Deuteronomy, each including the commandment to affix a *mezuzah* on the doorpost. In these paragraphs, God states that great rewards await those who observe this commandment.

Mikets (Y) (MH: *Mi-kets*): the name of the Torah portion comprising Genesis 41:1 to 44:17. See also Torah portion.

mikveh (Y, MH): a specially constructed ritual pool containing at least 200 gallons of water into which Jews immerse for purification.

Mime (SEY) (NEY: *Mume*): aunt.

Minkhe (Y) (MH: *Minkha*): afternoon prayers, one of the three daily prayers.

minyan(im) (MH) (SEY: *minyen*, pl. *minyúnim*; NEY: *minyen*, pl. *minyonim*): 1) the quorum of ten Jewish men necessary for the recitation of certain prayers; 2) the locale where Jewish prayer services are held.

Mishebeyrakh (Y) (MH: *Mi she-berakh*): each person called to the Torah (see *aliya*) is given the opportunity to have blessings (beginning with the words *mishebeyrakh*, literally meaning, "He who blessed . . .") said on his behalf for his family members and friends. Traditionally, each blessing is accompanied by a pledge to donate to the synagogue or some other charitable cause. The reciting of this blessing is called in Yiddish, "making a *Mishebeyrakh*."

Mishna (MH) (Y: Mishne): 1) the first major written redaction of the Jewish oral tradition known as the Oral Torah compiled by Rabbi Yehuda ha-Nasi at the beginning of the third century CE; 2) a single statement of law from this work.

Misnagdic: of, relating to, or characteristic of a *Misnaged*.

Misnaged, pl. *Misnagdim* (Y) (SEY: *Misnoged*, pl. *Misnogdim*; MH: *Mitnaged*, pl. *Mitnagdim*): literally meaning "opponents" (of Hasidism) in Hebrew and generally referring to non-Hasidic Orthodox Jews, particularly from Lithuania and Belarus.

mitzvah (MH) (Y: *mitsve[s]*): 1) literally "commandment," it refers to one of the 613 divine commandments incumbent upon Jews mentioned in the Hebrew Bible; 2) a good deed or religious precept.

mnishke (also *monashke*) (Y): nun.

motuske(le) (NEY) (SEY: *mutiske[le]*): teacher's pet. See ch. 7, p. 161, footnote 14.

Mome (SPSEY) (Y: *Mame*): mother.

monashke: see *mnishke*.

Moyde Ani (Y) (MH: *Mode Ani*): the name of a short prayer said upon first awaking in the morning.

moyel (Y) (MH: *mohél*): a Jewish man specially trained to circumcise Jewish boys according to Jewish law.

Musaf (MH) (SEY: *Misef*; NEY: *Musef*): an additional prayer service recited in the morning directly after the morning prayer service (*shakhris*) on the Sabbath (*Shabes*) and most Jewish holidays.

myertshúk(es): the diminutive of the word *myera* (or *mera*), a pre-metric unit of dry measurement once used in most Slavic lands.

napoleon: a twenty-franc gold coin, which originally featured the portrait of Napoleon I. Although the portraits changed with the political changes in France, the twenty-franc gold coin remained in usage until the First World War. Both napoleons and francs were used widely in the Middle East.

Nine Days (SEY: *di nayne teyg*; NEY: *di nayne teg*): the first nine days of the Hebrew month of *Av*, a period of Jewish national mourning, which culminates with *Tisha B'Av*.

Nisan (MH) (Y: *Nisn*): the month of the Hebrew calendar in which Pesach occurs and which usually corresponds to parts of March and April.

nu (NEY) (SEY: *ni*): a multipurpose interjection often analogous to "Well?" or "Come on!"

Omer (MH) (Y: *Oymer*): see *Sfira*.

Oy (Y): Oh.

Oy-vey (Y): an exclamation indicating dismay or grief.

pan: see *kvitl*.

Pale of Settlement: the westernmost provinces of Tsarist Russia to which permanent residence by Jews was restricted from 1791 to 1917. It included all of Moldova, Belarus, and Lithuania, and most of present-day Ukraine, a part of eastern Latvia, and some parts of western Russia. Though the ten provinces of Congress Poland were not officially part of the Pale, they were included for all practical matters.

Parshes ha'Khoydesh (Y) (MH: *Parashat ha-Khodesh*): the section of the Torah consisting of Exodus 12:1–20, which is the last of the four additional Torah readings connected with the Hebrew months of *Adar* and *Nisan*. It discusses the commandment to maintain a calendar and the commandments associated with Pesach.

Parshes Pore (NEY) (MH: *Parashat Para*): the section of the Torah consisting of consisting of Numbers 19:1–22, which is the third of four additional Torah readings connected with the Hebrew months of *Adar* and *Nisan*.

Pas le'Orkhim (Y) (MH: *Pat le-orakhim*): literally meaning "Bread for Guests," it was the name of a synagogue in Odessa.

Pesach (Y: *Peysekh*; MH: *Pesakh*): the Jewish holiday occurring in the early spring, which celebrates the exodus of the Jewish people from slavery in ancient Egypt. It is observed by avoiding all leavened foods and is highlighted by the *Seder* meals.

peyes (Y) (MH: *peot*): sidelocks grown by Orthodox males in accordance with the Biblical prohibition, "You shall not round the corners of your heads" (Leviticus 19:27). Some ultra-Orthodox Jews grow them particularly long to emphasize this *mitzvah*.

pidyen, pl. *pidyoynes* (Y) (MH: *pidyon[ot]*): literally meaning "redemption" in Hebrew. Non-Lubavitcher Hasidim use it to refer to a monetary donation given to a Hasidic Rebbe to redeem one's soul, which accompanies a petitionary note, which they call a *kvitl*. Lubavitcher Hasidim refer to this money as *moes pan* or *dmei pan*. See also ch. 16, p. 251, footnote 27.

pidyen nefesh (Y) (MH: *pidyon nefesh*): see *kvitl*.

pidyoynes: pl. of *pidyen*.

Piyut (MH) (Y: *Piyet*): the liturgical poetry added to the High Holiday prayers services. Usually referred to today in the plural form, *Piyutim*.

pletsl(ekh) (Y): generally, a flattened roll of bread strewn with poppy seeds, chopped onion, and coarse salt.

Poland: see *Poylisher*.

potshtar: mail keeper.

Poyeley Tsedek (NEY) (SEY: *Poyeley Tseydek*; MH: *Poale Tsedek*): "righteous workers" in Hebrew. A *bes-medresh* or synagogue bearing this name indicated that it was attended by artisans.

Poylisher (Y): Polish Jew. Apart from the Jews of Congress Poland, the Jews in the provinces of Volhynia, Podolia and Kiev (in contemporary Ukraine) were also referred to as Polish Jews by many Jews in Tsarist Russia, since these areas had been part of the Commonwealth of Poland whose sovereignty ended in 1795 with the Third Partition of Poland. Similarly, these provinces were also referred to as *Poyln* (Poland).

prizbe (Y): the foundations of older houses in the Ukraine often used to reach higher than ground level and were wider than the houses built upon it. This ledge-like portion of the foundation surrounding the entire width of the house is called a *prizbe.*

provizor: pharmacist in Russian.

pud: an obsolete Russian unit of measurement equivalent to 36.07 lb (40 *funt*). See also *funt.*

Purim (SEY: *Pirem*; NEY: *Purem*; MH: *Purim*): A joyous Jewish festival commemorating the survival of the Jewish people in the fifth century BCE when they were marked for death by their Persian rulers. The story is related in the Biblical book of Esther. It is generally celebrated every year on the fourteenth day of the Hebrew month of *Adar* (late winter/early spring).

rabbi: see *Ruv* and *rabiner.*

rabiner (Y): a crown rabbi. Beginning in the 1830s, Jewish communities in Tsarist Russia had a double rabbinate consisting of an authentic, traditionally educated rabbi (*Ruv*) who served as the community's spiritual leader, and a state rabbi (*rabiner*) who, as a government official, recorded Jewish vital records and delivered addresses in Russian on various occasions but who had no real religious jurisdiction.

Rashi: in the context of this book, it is referring to Rashi's classic commentary on the Five Books of Moses. Rashi is an acronym for Rabbi Shlomo Yitskhaki (1040–1105) of France.

Reb (Y): An honorific used before a man's first name. It does not denote that the person was a rabbi.

Rebbe (Y): 1) Hasidic Grand Rabbi (capitalized in the text), also known as a *tsadik,* who often leads a Hasidic movement; 2) the term used to address a communal rabbi or a *melamed.*

rébetsn (Y): the wife of a rabbi or a *melomed.* Often rendered into English as Rebbetzin but pronounced in Yiddish as *rebetsn.*

rendlekh (Y): the Yiddish name for ducats, which were used in Romania and other countries.

rendlekh dikatn: see *rendlekh.*

revizskie skazki: Literally meaning "revision lists," this phrase refers to the Russian poll-tax census. In Tsarist Russia, a series of poll-tax censuses were taken between 1772 and 1858 for taxation and conscription purposes. Each census was a revision of the previous one (hence its name). Such census records generally listed all family members and their ages.

Riboyn Kol ha'Oloym (Y) (MH: *Ribon Kol ha-Olam*): literally meaning "Master of the World" in Hebrew, these are the first words of a liturgical poem chanted or sung prior to the Friday evening Sabbath meal, which is found in most traditional prayer books.

Rosh Hashanah (MH) (*Y: Rosheshone*): the Jewish holiday marking the first and second days of the Jewish year and beginning on the first of the month of *Tishre.* It is a day of judgment and coronation of God as king.

Rosh-Khoydesh, also *Resh-Khoydesh* (Y) (MH: *Rosh Khodesh*): the beginning of every Hebrew month, which lasts either one or two days and is observed as a minor holiday in Judaism. For example, *Rosh-Khoydesh Shvat* is the beginning of the month of *Shvat.*

ruble: see *silver ruble.*

Ruv (SEY) (NEY: *Rov*; MH: *Rav*): a traditional, authentic rabbi, as opposed to a *rabiner.*

samovar: widely popular in Tsarist Russia, a *samovar* is a metal urn with a spigot near its base to boil water for tea. It is traditionally heated with coal in a chimney-like tube which runs through the center of the urn.

schlimazel (Y *shlimazl*; SPSEY: *shlimozl*): a misfortunate person.

Seder (MH) (Y: *Seyder*): literally meaning "order" in Hebrew, it is the festive meal of Passover during which the *Haggadah* is recited and symbolic foods representing the exodus of the Jews from Egypt are eaten. It is held on the first two nights (or first night in the Land of Israel) of Passover and celebrates the birth of the Jewish people and the transmission of Jewish identity from generation to generation.

Sephardic: relating to or denoting *Sephardim.*

Sephardim: Jews whose ancestors lived in the Iberian Peninsula during the Middle Ages.

Sfira (MH) (Y: *Sfire*): Jews are obligated to verbally count the forty-nine days between the second day of Pesach (the anniversary of Moses leading the Jews out of Egypt) and *Shvues*, when the Jewish people received the Torah at Mt. Sinai. In Yiddish, it is called *tseyln sfire,* i.e., counting *Sfira,* and is often referred to in English as "counting the *Omer*." On each of these forty-nine days, a special Hebrew blessing is recited, followed by the number of days counted (*Kitsur Shulkhan Arukh*, 120:1–11).

Sha'arei Tsion (MH) (Y: *Sharey Tsiyen*): a book of prayers and meditative passages based on kabbalistic writings. Before the Second World War, it was very popular and underwent dozens of printings, having first been printed in Prague in 1662.

Shabes: see *Shobes*.

Shabosim: see *Shobes*.

Shakhris, also *Shakhres* (Y) (SPSEY: *Shokhres*; MH: *Shakharit*): morning prayers, the first of the three daily prayers.

shalashne shul (Y): a tent-like synagogue. See ch. 13, p. 206, footnote 10.

Sháleshides (SEY) (NEY: *Sháleshúdes*; MH: *Seudat Shlishit*): the third and last meal on the Sabbath (*Shabes*) eaten before dusk on Saturday.

shames: see *shomes*.

Shehekhiyonu (NEY) (SEY: *Shehekhiyuni*; MH: *She-hekhiyanu*): literally "who has granted us life," referring to the Hebrew blessing which thanks God for enabling us to experience a new or special occasion.

Sheve-Brokhes (NEY) (SEY: *Sheyve-Brukhes*; MH: *Sheva Brakhot*): literally meaning "seven blessings," referring to the seven Hebrew blessings recited at the end of the festive meals held in honor of the bride and groom every day of the week following the wedding.

sheyner Yid (Y): a prestigious person (see ch. 7, p. 158, footnote 5).

sheytl (pl. *sheytlekh*) (Y): a wig worn by married religious Jewish women as a sign of modesty.

shil: see *shul*.

Shimenésre (Y) (MH: *Shmona Esre*): the silent Hebrew prayer consisting of nineteen blessings. It is the main prayer of each of the three Jewish daily prayer services.

shirayim (NEY) (SEY: *shiraem*; MH: *shirayim*): literally meaning "leftovers," this word denotes the custom among non-Chabad Hasidim to eat from the leftover food remaining on the platter after the Rebbe has taken his portion. According to Hasidic teachings, the Hasid can become more God-fearing by eating a Rebbe's *shirayim*.

shivah (MH) (Y: *shive*): the seven-day period of mourning that Jews observe after the death of a close relative and is often referred to as "sitting *shivah*."

shkalik: an obsolete Russian unit of measurement equivalent to 2.08 fluid ounces.

sh'khita (MH) (Y: *shkhite*): the slaughtering of animals according to Jewish law. (The word *sh'khita* is also used in this work as a shortened form of "*sh'khita* and *b'dika*," slaughtering and inspection, since the latter is an essential part of the slaughtering process.)

shlogn kapores (NEY) (SEY: *shlugn kapores*): literally meaning "to waive the *kapores*." It involves taking a live chicken in the right hand and moving it in a circular motion around the head three times while reciting certain prayers. See *kapores*.

Shma: the first Hebrew word of the verse, "Hear, O Israel; the Lord is our God, the Lord is One" (Deuteronomy 6:4). It is used to refer to the three sections of the Hebrew Bible (Deuteronomy 6:4–9 and 11:13–21, and Numbers 15:37–41) that are the centerpiece of the morning and evening Jewish prayer services. The *Shma* is a daily declaration of faith and is considered to be the most important prayer in Judaism. Its recitation twice daily is a Biblical commandment incumbent on Jews. The first line of the *Shma* is often recited at times of danger. See also *Shma Yisruel*.

Shma Yisruel (SEY) (NEY: *Shma Yisroel*; MH: *Shma Yisrael*): literally "Hear, O' Israel," these are the first two words of the verse, ""Hear, O Israel; the Lord is our God, the Lord is One" (Deuteronomy 6:4). Since this verse is considered a basic tenant of Judaism, the entire verse is traditionally recited at times of danger. See also *Shma*.

shmalts (Y) (SEY: *shmolts*): animal fat.

Shmini (Y, MH): the name of the Torah portion comprising Leviticus 9:1 to 11:47. See also Torah portion.

Shmini Atseres (NEY) (SEY: *Shmini Atseyres*; MH: *Shmini Atseret*): meaning "Eighth (day) of Assembly," it is the Jewish holiday immediately following the seven days of *Sukes*. Outside of the Land of Israel, *Shmini Atseres* is celebrated for two days, with the second day being called *Simchas Torah*. In the Land of Israel, *Shmini Atseres* is celebrated for one day and coincides with *Simchas Torah*.

shmita (MH) (Y: *shmite*): sabbatical year.

Shmos (Y) (MH: *Shmot*): the first weekly Torah portion in the book of Exodus comprising Exodus 1:1 to 6:1. See also Torah portion.

shmure matses (NEY) (SEY: *shmire matses*; SPSEY: *shmire motses*; MH: *shmura matsot*): literally meaning "guarded *matses*," referring to round handmade *matses* made from grain that has been closely guarded from any contact with moisture from the moment of harvesting. This is done in order to ensure that no fermentation or leavening occurs.

Shobes, pl. *Shabusim* (SPSEY) (NEY: *Shabes*, pl. *Shabosim*; MH: *Shabat[ot]*): the Jewish Sabbath, which starts at sundown on Friday and ends at dusk on Saturday.

shochet: see *shoykhet.*

shofar (MH) (Y: *shoyfer*): a *shofar* is the hollowed-out horn of a kosher animal. Hearing the shofar being blown is the central *mitzvah* of *Rosh Hashanah.*

Shobes ha'Gudl (SEY) (NEY: *Shabes ha'Godl*; MH: *Shabat ha-Gadol*): the *Shabes* immediately preceding Pesach.

Shobes Tshive (SPSEY) (SEY: *Shabes Tshive*; NEY: *Shabes Tshuve*; MH: *Shabat Tshuva*): literally meaning the "Sabbath of Repentance," occuring between Rosh Hashanah and Yom Kippur.

shokhtim: pl. of *shoykhet.*

Sholem Aleykhem (NEY) (SEY: *Shulem Aleykhem*; MH: *Shalom Alekhem*): opening words of a liturgical poem welcoming the Sabbath angels to the home on Friday night. According to the Talmud (Shabat 119b), two angels accompany every Jew home from the synagogue on Friday night, the beginning of the Sabbath.

sholem-aleykhem-gelt (NEY): welcoming money, generally given to children when adults arrived (or returned) from out of town (see ch. 9, p. 166).

shomes (SEY) (NEY: *shames*; MH: *shamash*): 1) the sexton of a synagogue; 2) a Hasidic Rebbe's attendant.

Shoshanat Ya'akov (MH) (Y: *Shoyshanas Yankev*): prayer recited after the reading of the Megilla on Purim.

Shoyftim (Y) (MH: *Shoftim*): the name of the Torah portion comprising Deuteronomy 16:18 to 21:9. See also Torah portion.

Shoykhet, pl. *shokhtim* (Y) (MH: *shokhet*, pl. *shokhatim*): one who slaughters animals in accordance with Jewish law.

shteln tikn: see *tikn.*

shtender (Y): a lectern-like stand used for studying and praying by Orthodox Jews.

shtetl(ekh): see *shteytl(ekh).*

shteytl(ekh) (SEY) (NEY: *shtetl*): Literally meaning a "town" in Yiddish, and generally referring to a market town in pre-First World War Eastern Europe that had a substantial population of Jews.

shtik (Y): tricks, chicanery.

shtrayml (NEY) (SEY: *shtraml*): a fur hat worn by Hasidic Jews on the Sabbath, holidays, and special occasions.

shul (NEY) (SEY: *shil*): synagogue.

Shulkhan Arukh (MH) (SEY: *Shilkhen Urekh*; norther Yiddish: *Shulkhen Orukh*): see *Code of Jewish Law.*

Shushan Purim (MH) (SEY: *Shishn-Pirem*; NEY: *Shushn-Purem*): the day that Purim is celebrated in Jerusalem.

Shvat (Y, MH): the fifth month of the Hebrew calendar which usually corresponds to parts of January and February.

Shvues (NEY) (SEY: *Shvies*; MH: *Shavuot*): the Jewish holiday celebrated fifty days after Pesach and usually occurring in late May or June. It is the anniversary of the day that God gave the Torah to the Jewish people on Mount Sinai. Outside of the Land of Israel, it is celebrated for two days, while in the Land of Israel it is celebrated for one day.

sidur (MH) (Y: *sider*): Jewish prayer book.

silver ruble: the silver ruble coin circulated in Tsarist Russia simultaneously with the paper ruble, which was worth less.

Simchas Torah (Y: *Simkhes-Toyre*; MH: *Simkhat Torah*): outside of the Land of Israel, the second day of the two-day holiday of *Shmini Atseres* is called *Simchas Torah,* meaning "Rejoicing with the Torah," and is an extremely joyous holiday. Inside the Land of Israel, *Shmini Atseres* is celebrated for one day and coincides with *Simchas Torah.*

Sivan (MH) (Y: *Sivn*): The ninth month of the Hebrew calendar which usually corresponds to parts of May and June. The holiday of *Shvues* occurs on the 6th and 7th of *Sivan.*

Slikhes (Y) (MH: *Slikhot*): Literary "pardons" in Hebrew, referring to: 1) special Jewish penitential prayers recited in the period leading up to the High Holidays generally beginning on the Saturday night before Rosh Hashanah; and, by some communities, during the Ten Days of Repentance between Rosh Hashanah and Yom Kippur. They are also recited on fast days; 2) the period of time preceding Rosh Hashanah when *Slikhes* is recited.

soykhenes (NEY) (SEY: *soykheynes*; MH: *sokhenet*): bed warmer (See Rabbi David Altshuler's classic Biblical commentary, *Metsudat Tsion,* on Kings I 1:2.)

starosta sinagogi: a Russian term meaning "synagogue elder," which was used by the city council in Bakhchisaray to refer to a *gabbai* (possibly the main *gabbai*) of the synagogue (see ch. 26, p. 536, footnote 39).

Sukes (NEY) (SEY: *Sikes*; MH: *Sukot*): the seven-day Jewish holiday beginning on the 15th of Tishrei, which is celebrated by dwelling in a *sukah* and taking the four kinds (see *esreg*). *Sukes* is often used to refer to the seven days of *Sukes* and the following two days of *Shimini Atseres/Simchas Torah*. See also *sukah.*

sukah (MH) (SEY: *sike;* NEY: *suke*): during the holiday of *Sukes,* Jews reside in *sukah.* Here families eat their meals, entertain guests, relax, and even sleep.

takse: see *korobka.*

taleysim: pl. of *talis.*

talis, also *tales,* pl. *taleysim* (Y) (SPSEY: *toles;* pl. *taleysim;* MH: *talit[ot]*): A large four-cornered shawl with intricately knotted fringes attached to its corners, as prescribed in the Torah (Numbers 15:38–41), which is worn during *shakhris.* In many areas of Eastern Europe and in many Orthodox circles today, they are worn only by married men.

talis-kutn, also *tales-kutn* (SEY) (SPSEY: *toles-kutn;* NEY: *tales-kotn;* MH: *talit-katan*): A poncho-like, shirt-sized *talis* worn at all times by Orthodox Jewish men and boys. Commonly referred to today as *tsitsis.*

Talmud: the basic compendium of Jewish law and thought; its tractates elucidate the statements of the Mishna. When unspecified, it refers to the edition developed in Babylonia and compiled and edited at the end of the fifth century CE; the Jerusalem Talmud is the edition compiled and edited in the Land of Israel at the end of the fourth century CE.

Talmud Torah (MH) (Y: *Talmed Toyre*): in Eastern Europe, it denoted a traditional Jewish elementary school, but differed from the privately funded *kheyder* in that it consisted of several grades, was financed by the community, and usually served the children of the poor.

Tamuz (MH) (Y: *Tamez*): the tenth month of the Hebrew calendar, which usually corresponds to parts of June and July.

Tanákh (Y, MH): the Hebrew Bible. Its Hebrew name is an acronym of the initial letters of its three traditional subdivisions: *Torah* (also known as the Five Books of Moses), *Nevi'im* ("Prophets"), and *Ketuvim* ("Writings").

Tate: see *Tote.*

Tazriya-Metsora (MH) (Y: *Tazriye-Metsoyre*): two weekly Torah portions often read together on the same Sabbath (*Shabes*) when there is no leap year in the Hebrew calendar. The portions comprise Leviticus 12:1 to 15:33. See also Torah portion.

tefillin (MH) (Y: *tfiln*): two small leather boxes, each containing strips of parchment inscribed with passages from the Five Books of Moses. From the age of bar-mitzvah, Jewish men are commanded in the Torah (Exodus 13:9, Deuteronomy 6:8, and Deuteronomy 11:18) to wear them on their forehead and forearm during weekday morning services.

Teyves (Y) (MH: *Tevet*): the fourth month of the Hebrew calendar, which usually corresponds to parts of December and January.

tikn (Y): "*shteln tikn*" refers to someone providing liquor (often accompanied by food) for the congregants after weekday morning services on the *yortsayt* (i.e., anniversary of death) of a departed relative or Hasidic Rebbe and other special occasions. The *tikn* affords the congregants the opportunity to make a blessing over the liquor (and/or the edibles) in the merit of a departed soul, thereby serving to elevate the soul. (*Tikn,* or *tikun* in modern Hebrew, means "to repair" or "to elevate.")

tish(n) (Y): literally meaning a "table" in Yiddish, a *tish* is Hasidic gathering led by a Rebbe.

Tisha B'Av (MH) (SEY: *Tishe buv*; NEY: *Tishe bov*): literally "the ninth of the month of *Av*," generally occurring in July or August, which commemorates the destruction of both holy Temples in Jerusalem.

Tishre: first month of the Hebrew calendar and the month in which the High Holy Days and *Sukes* occur.

tkhines (Y) (MH: *tkhinot*): Yiddish prayers primarily recited by women.

Tolner kloyz: refers to a *bes-medresh* (Torah study hall) for the Hasidim of the Tolner Rebbe.

Torah (MH) (Y: *Toyre*): when Torah is mentioned in this work in conjunction with the education of children or Rashi's classic commentary, it refers to the Five Books of Moses (see *khimesh*). In phrases such as "Torah scholarship" or "Torah study," it usually refers to the cumulated wealth of all Jewish religious knowledge and texts and primarily the study of the Talmud.

Torah portion: the Five Books of Moses are divided into fifty-two weekly Torah portions, which are read consecutively throughout the year from a Torah scroll. The Hebrew name of each is taken from the first unique Hebrew word(s) of that Torah portion.

Tote (SPSEY) (Y: *Tate*): father.

Toysfes (Y) (MH: *Tosafot*): literally meaning "additions" in Hebrew, referring to the medieval school of Talmudic scholars whose novellae are printed in all standard editions of the Talmud.

treyf (Y): generally referring to something nonkosher, but in Jewish law it refers to an animal that has been slaughtered and discovered to be halakhically unfit for consumption due to certain irregularities in the animal's internal organs.

treyfes (Y) (MH: *treyfot*): animals that have been slaughtered and then discovered to be *treyf,* meaning halakhically unfit for consumption due to certain irregularities in the animal's internal organs.

treyber (Y): the expert removal of certain sinews and fat of cattle, sheep, and goats, which Jewish law prohibits eating. (See *Shulkhan Arukh, Yore Deah* 64–65.) It also appears in the text in the infinitve form, *treybern.*

treybitshkes (Y): the forbidden fats removed from the slaughtered animals through *treybern* (see *treyber*).

tsadéykes *(Y)* (MH: *tsadéket*): an extremely righteous woman.

tsadik(im) (Y) (SEY*: tsodik(em)*; MH: *tsadik[im]*): literally "righteous man," used by Hasidim (except Chabad Hasidim) to refer to Hasidic Rebbes. Since the Second World War, Hasidim generally no longer refer to their Hasidic Rebbe as "the *tsadik,*" as in "We are traveling to the *tsadik.*"

Tsarist Russia: the entire territory of the Tsarist Russian Empire, including the Pale of Settlement and Congress Poland.

Tsene-rene (SEY; Yiddish: *Tsene-rene*; MH: *Tse'ena u-re'ena*): a Yiddish paraphrase with commentary on the Five Books of Moses, the *Haftorahs,* and the Five Scrolls, which was widely used by women in pre-Second World War Europe since they did not know Hebrew. It was written at the end of the sixteenth century by Rabbi Ya'akev Ashkenazi. Its title is taken from Song of Songs (3:11) and literally means, "Come and see." The late Dr. Mordkhe Schaechter noted that it was referred to as *Tsene-verene* in the areas of the Bessarabia, Bukovina, and the Ukraine, instead of the more widespread pronunciation of *Tsene-rene.*

Tsene-verene: see *Tsene-rene.*

tsetl: see *kvitl.*

tseyln sfire: see *Sfira.*

tush (Y): shower.

ufruf (NEY) (SEY: *ifrif*): Literally meaning "calling up" in Yiddish, it refers to the calling up of the groom for an *aliya* on the *Shobes* preceding his wedding.

Vayekhi (Y, MH): the name of the weekly Torah portion comprising Genesis 47:27 to 50:26. See also Torah portion.

Vayigash (Y, MH)*:* the name of the weekly Torah portion comprising Genesis 44:18 to 47:27. See also Torah portion.

Vayshishlakh (Y, MH): the name of the weekly Torah portion comprising Genesis 32:4 to 36:40. See also Torah portion.

verekh: the crown of a hat. Hasidim today, at least those familiar with this Yiddish term, refer to the crown of a *shtrayml* as the *vyerekh.*

verst(s) (Y: *vyorst[n]*): from *versta,* an obsolete Russian unit of length equivalent to 0.6629 mile or 1.067 kilometers.

Vidui (MH) (Y: *Vide*): the Hebrew confessional prayers recited before departing from this world to evoke God's mercy and bring great atonement upon oneself (*Kitsur Shulkhan Arukh* 193:14).

yarmlke (Y) (NEY: *yármulke*): skullcap worn by Jews.

yeshiva (MH) (Y: *yeshive*): Jewish institution of higher learning, where primarily the Talmud is studied at advanced levels.

Yidishkayt (SPSEY: *Ideshkayt*): Judaism.

Yoma (MH) (SEY: *Yime*; NEY: *Yume*): Mishnaic tractate discussing the laws of Yom Kippur.

Yom Kippur (MH) (Y: Yonkiper): literally meaning "Day of Atonement," it is the holiest day in the Jewish calendar year and occurs on the tenth day of *Tishre*. For nearly twenty-six hours, Jews abstain from food and drink and other forbidden actions and spend the day in the synagogue, praying for forgiveness.

Yomtov: see *Yontef.*

Yontef (Y) (MH: *Yomtov*): a major Jewish holiday, such as *Rosh Hashanah, Sukes,* Pesach, or *Shvues,* where all the laws of *Shabes* are observed except that cooking, baking, lighting a fire from a pre existing flame, and carrying in a public domain are permitted.

yortsayt(n): see *yurtsayt(n).*

Yoreh Deah (MH) (Y: *Yoyre-Deye*): one of the four sections of the *Shulkhan Arukh* (*The Code of Jewish Law*), which deals with various prohibited and permitted subjects, such as dietary laws, interest, purity, and mourning.

yurtsayt(n) or ***yurtsat(n)*** (SEY) (NEY: *yortsayt[n]*): the anniversary of a person's death according to the Hebrew calendar.

zal (Y) (SPSEY: *zol*): literally meaning a "hall" in Yiddish and used by Lubavitchers to refer to a study hall (*bes-medresh*).

Ze khalifosi (NEY) (SEY: *Zey khalifusi*; MH: *Ze khalifati*): a prayer recited during the *kapores* ritual on the Eve of Yom Kippur. See ch. 22, p. 436, footnote 74.

zemlyankes: dugout houses

Zhid: in the Russian language, *zhid* is a pejorative term for Jew.

Zhidovchik (pronounced *Zhidovtshik*): an endearing form of *Zhid,* a pejorative term for Jew in Russian and Ukrainian. See the entry for *Zhid.*

Zhidúk: variant of *Zhid.*

zmires (Y) (MH: *zemirot*): the Hebrew songs sung during the *Shobes* meals and at the close of the *Shobes,* which are printed in many prayer books.

Glossary 2: Jewish Personal Names

See the Introduction to the Glossaries (pp. 851–855) for general guidelines regarding the use of this glossary. The entries in both the glossary of Jewish personal names and of geographic names are listed in the sub-dialect of Southeastern Yiddish spoken by the author, referred to here as SPSEY. When the SPSEY pronunciation does not differ from the Southeastern Yiddish (SEY) pronunciation, then the SEY pronunciation is the main entry. When the pronuncaiton in the SEY and the Northeastern Yiddish (NEY) dialects are the same, then Y (Yiddish) is listed for the main entry. When no modern-Hebrew pronunciation is listed, this is an indication that the name does not originate from Hebrew. Only the diminutives found in this work are included in the Glossary of Personal Names. Name orgins are not listed. Hence, Tsipe is not listed as a diminutive of Tsipoyre since in Eastern Europe Tsipe was often a name unto itself. Note that before the twentieth century, Hebrew personal names such as Dov (meaning "bear"), Tsvi ("deer"), and Z'ev ("wolf") were rarely used in vernacular life, except for religious purposes or when written. Instead, their corresponding Yiddish calques, or their diminutives, were used, namely Ber, Hersh, and Volf, respectively. For more about names, see Alexander Beider's *A Dictionary of Ashkenazi Given Names: Their Origins, Structure, Pronunciation, and Migration* (2001).

MALE NAMES:

- Alter (Y): see Olter
- Aron: see Arn
- Arn (Y); MH: Aharon; E: Aaron
- Asher (MH): see Usher
- Avigder (Y); MH: Avigdor
- Avigdor (MH): see Avigder
- Avrem (Y): pronunciation of Avrúm when used in a double name, i.e., Avrem-Shimen
- Avróm (NEY): see Avrúm
- Avrúm (SEY); NEY: Avróm; MH: Avraham; E: Abraham (see also Avrem)
- Azriel (Y, MH)

- Benyúmin (SEY); NEY: Binyomin; MH: Binyamin; E: Benjamin
- Ber, Beyr (SEY), diminutives: Bere, Berl, Bérele, Bérenyu (Dov is the Hebrew calque of Ber)
- Bere (NEY): see Ber
- Bérele (Y): see Ber
- Bérenyu (Y): see Ber
- Betsalel (Y): see Bestolel
- Betsolel (SPSEY); NEY: Betsalel; MH: Betsalel; E: Bezalel
- Beyr (Y): see Ber
- Binyomin (NEY): see Benyumin
- Borukh (NEY): see Burekh
- Boye: possibly a nickname for Burekh
- Burekh (SEY), diminutive: Burekhl; NEY: Borukh, Borekh; MH: Barukh
- Dov: see Ber (See details on p. 883.)
- Dov-Ber: See the foonote in Appendix B1, p. 760, footnote 4.
- Dovid (NEY): see Duvid
- Duvid (SEY), diminutive: Duvidl; NEY: Dovid; MH: David; E: David
- Elieyzer (SEY), diminutives: Leyzer, Léyzerke, Leyzerl; NEY: Eliezer, diminutive Leyzer; MH: Eliezer
- Elimeylekh (SEY), diminutive: Meylekh; NEY: Elimelekh, diminutives: Meylekh, Melekh; MH: Elimelekh
- Eliyahu (MH): see Elye
- Elkhonen (NEY), diminutive: Khonl; SEY: Elkhunen; MH: Elkhanan
- Elye (Y), diminutive of Elyuhi; NEY: Elyohu; MH: Eliyahu; E: Elijah
- Elyuhi (SEY): see Elye
- Ersh (SPSEY), diminutives: Ershl, Ershele; SEY: Hersh; NEY: Hirsh (Tsvi is the Hebrew calque of Ersh)
- Ershele (SPSEY): see Ersh
- Ershl (SPSEY): see Ersh
- Gavriel: see Govriel
- Gedalye (Y): see Gedolye
- Gedolye (SPSEY); SEY: Gedalye; NEY: Gedalye; MH: Gedalya
- Gershon: see Gershn
- Gershn (Y); MH: Gershon
- Govriel (SPSEY); Y: Gavriel; H: Gavriel; E: Gabriel
- Hersh (SEY), diminutives: Hershl, Hershele: see Ersh
- Hershele (SEY): see Hersh
- Hershl (SEY): see Hersh
- Hilel (Y), diminutive: Hilke; Ilke; MH, E: Hillel

- Hillel: see Hilel
- Hirsh (NEY): see Ersh
- Ide (SEY), diminutives: Idl; NEY: Yehude, Yude; MH: Yehuda; E: Judah
- Idl (SEY): see Ide
- Isruel (SPSEY), diminutives: Sruel, Srulik, Srulikl; SEY: Yisruel; NEY: Yisroel; Isroel; MH: Yisrael; E: Israel
- Isroel (NEY): see Isruel
- Itse(le) (Y): see Itskhok
- Itsek (Y): see Itskhok
- Itsikl (Y): see Itskhok
- Itskhok (SPSEY), diminutives: Itse, Itsek, Itsele, Itsikl, Itsl, Itsye; NEY: Yitskhok, Itskhok; MH: Yitskhak; E: Isaac
- Itsl (Y): see Itskhok
- Itsye (Y): see Itskhok
- Isukher (SPSEY), diminutive: Sukher; NEY: Yisokher; Isokher; MH: Yisakhar
- Kelmen (Y): variant of Kolmen
- Khayem (SEY), diminutive: Khayeml; NEY: Khaym; MH: Khayim (See also Khaym)
- Khaym: pronunciation of Khayem in SEY when used in a double name, i.e., Khaym-Shloyme
- Khotskl (SPSEY): see Yekhezkel
- Kolmen (SPSEY), also Kelmen; NEY: Kalmen, Kelmen
- Ksiel (Y): see Yekisiel
- Lebke: diminiutive of Lebe (a variant of Leyb in and around Bessarabia)
- Leyb (Y), diminutive: Leybenyu (Arye is the Hebrew calque of Leyb.)
- Leyvi (Y); MH: Levi; E: Levi
- Leyzer (Y): see Elieyzer
- Léyzerke (Y): see Elieyzer
- Motisyuhi (SPSEY), diminutive: Motes; SEY: Matisyuhi; NEY: Matisyohu; MH: Matityahu
- Melekh (NEY): see Elimeylekh
- Menakhem (NEY): see Menokhem
- Menokhem (SPSEY); (NEY): Menakhem; (MH): Menakhem
- Mendl (Y)
- Meshilem (SEY), diminutive: Shilem; NEY: Meshulem; MH: Meshulam
- Meyer (Y); MH: Meir
- Meylekh (SEY): see Elimeylekh

- Mikhoel (NEY): see Mikhuel
- Mikhuel (SEY); NEY: Mikhoel; MH: Mikhael; E: Michael
- Monis (SEY); Y: Manis
- Mordekhai: see Mordkhe
- Mordkhe (Y), diminutives: Mordkhele; MH: Mordekhai; E: Mordecai
- Moshe: see Moyshe
- Moyshe (Y), diminutives: Moyshele; MH: Moshe; E: Moses
- Nakhmen (Y): see Nokhmen
- Nekhemye (Y); MH: Nekhemya; E: Nehemiah
- Nesonl (SPSEY); Y: Nesanl; MH: Netanel; E: Nathaniel
- Nisan: see Nisn
- Nisn (Y); MH: Nisan
- Nokhmen (SPSEY); Y: Nakhmen; MH: Nakhman
- Nokhum (NEY): see Nukhem
- Nosn: see Nusn
- Noyakh (NEY): see Noyekh
- Noyekh (SEY); NEY: Noyakh, Neyakh; MH: Noakh; E: Noah
- Nukhem (SEY), diminutives: Nukheml, Nukhemtse; NEY: Nokhum, Nokhem; MH: Nakhum
- Nusn (SEY); NEY: Nosn; MH: Natan; E: Nathan
- Nute (SEY); NEY: Note
- Olter (SPSEY); Y: Alter
- Osher (NEY): see Usher
- Perets, Peyrets (SEY): NEY: Perets; MH: Perets
- Peyrets (SEY): see Perets
- Pinele (Y): see Pinkhes
- Pinkhas (MH): see Pinkhes
- Pinkhes (Y), diminutives: Pinye, Pinele; NEY: Pinkhes; MH: Pinkhas; E: Phineas, Pincus
- Pinye (Y): see Pinkhes
- Refoel (NEY): see Refúel
- Refúel (SEY), diminutives: Refulikl, Fulikl; NEY: Refoel; MH: Refael; E: Raphael
- Refulikl (SEY): see Refúel
- Sender (Y)
- Shaye (Y): see Yeshaye
- Shie (Y): see Yeshie
- Shimen (Y); MH: Shimon; E: Simon
- Shimon (MH): see Shimen
- Shimshen (Y); MH: Shimshon; E: Samson

- Shlomo: see Shloyme
- Shloyme (Y), diminutive: Shloymele; MH: Shlomoh: E: Solomon
- Shloymele (Y): see Shloyme
- Shneur (MH): see Shneyer
- Shneyer (Y); NEY: Shneyer, Shneyur (Often spelled Shneur in English.)
- Shoel (Y); MH: Shaul; E: Saul (See also Shoyl.)
- Sholem (NEY): see Shulem
- Shoyl (Y), diminutives: Shoylik, Shoylikl (Shoyl [שויל] is a variant of Shoel [שאול])
- Shoylik(l) (Y): see Shoyl
- Shmiel (SEY); NEY: Shmuel; diminutive: Shmulke; MH: Shmuel; E: Samuel
- Shmulke (NEY): see Shmiel
- Shmuel (NEY): see Shmiel
- Shulem (SEY), diminutive: Shuleml; NEY: Sholem; MH: Shalom
- Simkhe (Y), diminutive: Simkhele; MH: Simkha
- Srul (SEY): see Isruel
- Srulikl (SEY): see Isruel
- Sukher (SEY): see Isukher
- Tsvi: see Ersh (See details on p. 883.)
- Usher (SEY); NEY: Osher; MH: Asher
- Velvl (Y): see Volf (see also Z'ev)
- Volf (Y), diminutive: Velvl (Z'ev is the Hebrew calque of Volf)
- Ya'akov (MH): see Yankev
- Yankev (Y), diminutives: Yankl, Yankele; MH: Ya'akov; E: Jacob
- Yankele (Y): see Yankev
- Yankl (Y): see Yankev
- Yehuda (MH): see Ide
- Yekhezkel (Y), diminutive: Khotskl (SPSEY); NEY diminutive: Khatskl; MH: Yekhezkel; E: Ezekiel
- Yekhiel (Y, MH)
- Yekisiel (SEY), diminutive: Ksiel; NEY: Yekusiel; MH: Yekutiel
- Yerakhmiel (Y): see Yerokhmiel
- Yerokhmiel (SPSEY); Y, MH: Yerakhmiel
- Yerikhem (SEY); NEY: Yerukhem; MH: Yerukham
- Yerukhem (NEY): see Yerikhem
- Yermye (SEY); NEY: Yirmye, Irmye; MH: Yirmya; E: Jeremiah
- Yerikhem (SEY) (NEY: Yerukhem; MH: Yerukham)
- Yerukhem (NEY): see Yerikhem

- Yeshaye (Y), diminutive: Shaye; MH: Yeshaya; E: Isaiah
- Yeshie (Y), diminutive: Shie; MH: Yehoshúa; E: Joshua
- Yide (SEY): see Ide
- Yisroel (NEY): see Isruel
- Yisruel (SEY): see Isruel
- Yitskhok (NEY): see Itskhok
- Yosef (Y), diminutives: Yosefl, Yosl, Yosele; MH: Yosef; E: Joseph
- Yosele (Y): see Yosef
- Yosl (Y): see Yosef
- Yoyl (Y); MH: Yoel; E: Joel
- Yoyne (Y); MH: Yona; E: Jonah
- Yóykhenen (Y); MH: Yokhanan
- Zalman: see Zolmen
- Zalmen (Y): see Zolmen
- Z'ev: see Volf (See details on p. 883.)
- Zolmen (SPSEY); Yiddish: Zalmen
- Zorakh (NEY); SEY: Zurkeh; MH: Zerakh
- Zindl (SEY); NEY: Zundl
- Zundl (NEY): see Zindl

FEMALE NAMES:

- Bashe (Y): can be either a nickname for Basye or a Yiddish name unto itself
- Basye (Y), diminutive: Bashe; SPSEY: Bosye; MH: Batya
- Beyle (Y), diminutive: Beylke
- Beylke (Y): see Beyle
- Dvora (MH): see Dvoyre
- Dvose (Y); SPSEY: Dvosye
- Dvoyre (Y); MH: Dvora; E: Deborah
- Gite (Y); NEY: Gite or Gute
- Gute (NEY): see also Gite
- Ete (Y): often the diminutive of Ester but can also be a name unto itself
- Etye (Y): often the diminutive of Ester but can also be a name unto itself
- Ester (Y), diminutives: Ete, Etye; MH: Ester; E: Esther
- Frime (SEY); NEY: Frume
- Ite (Y), diminutives: Itele, Itye
- Itele: see Ite
- Itye: see Ite
- Khaye (Y), diminutive: Khaykele; MH: Khaya

- Khine (Y)
- Khone (SPSEY), diminutives: Khonele, Khontse; Y: Khane, Khanele; MH: Khana; E: Hannah
- Khonele: see Khone
- Khontse: see Khone
- Leye (Y), diminutive: Leytse; MH, E: Leah
- Leytse: see Leye
- Libe (Y)
- Mants(y)e (Y)
- Mashe (Y), diminutive: Mashke
- Mashke (Y): nickname for Mashe
- Maryem (Y): Yiddish variant of Miriam
- Maryase (Y), diminutive: Maryaske
- Mine (Y)
- Mirke (Y): see Mirye
- Mirye (Y), diminutive: Mirke
- Nekhame (Y), diminutive: Nekhamele: see Nekhome
- Nekhamele (Y): see Nekhame
- Nekhome (SPSEY); Y: Nekhame; MH: Nekhama
- Rashe (Y)
- Reyzl (Y), diminutive: Reyzele
- Reyzele (Y): see Reyzl
- Rifke (Y); MH: Rivka; E: Rebecca
- Rivka: see Rifke
- Rosye (SEY): A Southeastern Yiddish variant of Rashe
- Rukhl (SEY), diminutive: Rukhele; NEY: Rokhl; MH: Rakhel; E: Rachel
- Rukhele (SEY): see Rukhl
- Sime (Y)
- Sluve (SEY); NEY: Slave, Slove
- Sore: see Súre
- Súre (SEY), diminutives: Súrele, Surke; NEY: Sore; MH, E: Sarah
- Súrele (SEY): see Súre
- Surke (SEY): see Súre
- Tsipe (Y): Yiddish name deriving from Tsipoyre.
- Tsipoyre (Y); MH: Tsipora
- Zlote (Y): also pronounced as Zlate

Glossary 3: Geographic Places in Eastern Europe

See the Introduction to the Glossaries (pp. 851–855) for general guidelines regarding the use of this glossary. Practically all place names in Goldenshteyn's autobiography have been identified. This glossary provides each locality's current name, various prior names, and geocoordinates. The left-hand column of the table below generally lists place names as used by the author. When the author refers to a locality by more than one name, the alternate name (or alternative pronunciation) is also provided in parentheses. Though the author mostly uses the Yiddish names of geographic locations, he sometimes uses the Russian names. In the text, the author's versions have generally been used, apart from some well-known cities such as Kiev, Odessa, and Lubavitch, or when the official spelling is very similar to the romanized Yiddish spelling, e.g., Chechelnik instead of Tshetshelnik. Often, the author uses the Yiddish name for a location but not the most authentic Yiddish form, which is sometimes noted here. In his review of this list, Paul (Hershl) Glasser, the former dean of the Max Weinreich Center at YIVO and the compiler of www.yivo.org/Yiddishland, identified such variances as not authentic Yiddish names; as indicated in the footnotes.

Not indicated in the table below is that Bessarabia was part of Romania between 1918 and 1940. Note that the Moldavian Soviet Socialist Republic (SSR) and Ukrainian SSR were two of the fifteen republics of the Soviet Union that existed from 1940 to 1991.

As Written by the Author	Official Pre-WWI Name (name, province, country)	Official Post-WWII Name	Official Post-1991 Name	Lat/Long.
Adés	Odessa, Kherson, Russia	Odessa, Ukrainian SSR	Odesa, Ukraine	46°28'N 30°44'E
Aleshkis[1]	Aleshki/Alyoshki, Taurida, Russia	Tsyurupinsk, Ukrainian SSR	Oleshki, Ukraine	46°37'N 32°43'E
Antshekrák	Anchokrak, Bessarabia, Russia	Tarutino, Ukrainian SSR	Tarutyne, Ukraine	46°12'N 29°09'E
Armyansky Bazar	Armyanskiy Bazar, Taurida, Russia	Armyansk, Ukrainian SSR	Armyansk, Crimea	46°06'N 33°42'E
Bakhchisaray[2]	Bakhchisaray, Taurida, Russia	Bakhchisaray, Ukrainian SSR	Bakhchysaray, Crimea	44°45'N 33°52'E
Baronev	Baranovo, Kherson, Russia	Baranovo, Ukrainian SSR	Baranove, Ukraine	46°56'N 30°24'E
Behúsh (Bush)	Buhuşi, Romania	Buhuşi, Romania	Buhuşi, Romania	46°43'N 26°42'E
Bendér	Bendery,[3] Bessarabia, Russia	Bender, Ukrainian SSR	Bender (aka Tighina), Moldova	46°50'N 29°28'E
Berditshev	Berdichev, Kiev, Russia	Berdichev, Ukrainian SSR	Berdychiv, Ukraine	49°54'N 28°35'E
Bérshed	Bershad, Podolia, Russia	Bershad, Moldavian SSR	Bershad, Ukraine	48°22'N 29°31'E
Beshtemák	Beshtemak, Bessarabia, Russia	Beshtymik, Moldavian SSR	Beştemac, Moldova	46°32'N 28°32'E

1 The author refers to the town of Oleshki as Oleshkis. Speakers of Yiddish sometimes added an "s" to place names including plural words, for example: Novi Mlyny, Ukraine (meaning "new mills") was called Novi-Mlines in Yiddish (Felshin, 1974:4); and a sandy section of Bialystok, Poland called Piaski in Polish (meaning "sands") was called Pyaskes in Yiddish (Hindes, 1963:5). Like the last example, the author may have called it Oleshkis because of the nearby sandy massif called Oleshkivsky Piski (Oleshki Sands).

2 Though the author writes Bakhtshiseray, this slight variation does not indicate an authentic Yiddish name, according to Paul (Hershl) Glasser, former dean of the Max Weinreich Center at YIVO.

3 Between the two world wars, Bender was known as Tighina, Romania.

Bolte	Balta, Podolia, Russia	Balta, Moldavian SSR	Balta, Ukraine	47°56'N 29°37'E
Borshchi (train station)	Stantisya Borshchi, Podolia, Russia	Borshchi, Moldavian SSR	Borshchi, Ukraine	47°52'N 29°30'E
Borshtshi: see Borshchi				
Brod	Brody, Galicia, Austria-Hungary	Brody, Ukrainian SSR	Brody, Ukraine	50°05'N 25°09'E
Bruditshésht	Brădiceşti, Romania	Brădiceşti, Romania	Brădiceşti, Romania	46°51'N 27°54'E
Búter	Butor, Kherson, Russia	Butor, Moldavian SSR	Butor, Moldova	47°02'N 29°24'E
Buzinove (Buzinovke)	Buzinovo Kherson, Russia	Buzinovo, Ukrainian SSR	Buzynove, Ukraine	46°59'N 30°29'E
Buzinovke: see Buzinove				
Chechelnik: see Tshetshelnik				
Chimishliya: see Tshimishlye				
Dniester (Nester) (river)	Dnestr	Dnestr	Dnister	
Dubrovne	Dubvrovno, Mogilev, Russia	Dubrovno, Byelorussian SSR	Dubrouna, Belarus	51°48'N 30°07'E
Dzhankoi	Dzhankoi, Taurida, Russia	Dzhankoi, Ukrainian SSR	Dzhankoi, Crimea	45°43'N, 34°24'E
Feodósiya[4]	Feodosiya, Taurida, Russia	Feodosiya, Ukrainian SSR	Feodosiya, Crimea	45°02'N 35°23'E

4 Though the author writes Feodosye, this slight variation does not indicate an authentic Yiddish name.

Gredinitse	Gredinitsa, Bessarabia, Russia	Gredinitsa, Moldavian SSR	Grădinița, Moldova	46º40'N, 29º37'E
Grigoriopol[5]	Grigoriopol, Kherson, Russia	Grigoriopol, Moldavian SSR	Grigoriopol, Moldova	47° 9'N, 29° 18'E
Grofinye	Grafinya (aka Manzyr), Bessarabia, Russia	Lesnoya, Moldavian SSR	Lisne, Ukraine	46°28'N 29°21'E
Gróseles	Grosulovo, Kherson, Russia	Velikaya Mikhailovka, Ukrainian SSR	Velyka Mykhailivka, Ukraine	47°05'N 29°51'E
Groys Molev: see Molev				
Hish (Ish), Romania	Huşi, Romania	Huşi, Romania	Huşi, Romania	46°41'N 28°04'E
Homlye	Gomel, Mogilev, Russia	Gomel, Byelorussian SSR	Homyel, Belarus	52°27'N 30°59'E
Iassy: see Yos				
Imen ("n" is palatalized)	Uman, Kiev, Russia	Uman, Ukrainian SSR	Uman, Ukraine	48°45'N 30°13'E
Intern-Borg Dorf[6]	Indiya, Kherson, Russia	Indiya, Moldavian SSR	India, Moldavia	47°03'N 29°23'E
Kakhovka[7]	Kakhovka, Taurida, Russia	Kakhovka, Ukrainian SSR	Kakhovka, Ukraine	46°49'N 33°29'E
Kalarásh	Kalarash (aka Tuzora), Bessarabia, Russia	Kalarash, Moldavian SSR	Călăraşi, Moldova	47°15'N 28°18'E
Karasúbazár	Karasubazar, Taurida, Russia	Belogorsk, Ukrainian SSR	Bilohirsk, Crimea	45°03' N 34°36'E

5 Grigoriopol was called Tshorne in Yiddish.
6 This Yiddish nickname means Foot-of-the-Mountain Village.
7 Though the author writes Kekhovke, this slight variation does not indicate an authentic Yiddish name.

Kaushán: see Kovishón				
Katarzhi	Katarzhi, Kherson, Russia	Chervono-Znamenka, Ukrainian SSR	Chervono-Znamyanka, Ukraine	47°01'N 30°18'E
Kazatin	Kazatin, Volhynia, Russia	Kazatin, Ukrainian SSR	Koziatyn, Ukraine	49°43'N 28°50'E
Késhenev	Kishinev, Bessarabia, Russia	Kishinev, Moldavian SSR	Chişinău, Moldova	47°00'N 28°51'E
Kháshtshevóte	Khashchevata, Podolia, Russia	Khoshchevatoye, Ukrainian SSR	Khashchuvate, Ukraine	48°18'N 29°57'E
Khersón	Kherson, Kherson, Russia	Kherson, Ukrainian SSR	Kherson, Ukraine	46°38'N 32°36'E
Khotin[8] (accent on last syllable)	Khotin, Bessarabia, Russia	Khotin, Ukrainian SSR	Khotyn, Ukraine	48°29'N 26°30'E
Kiev	Kiev, Kiev, Russia	Kiev, Ukrainian SSR	Kyiv, Ukraine	50°26'N 30°31'E
Kishinev: see Késhenev				
Kitskón	Kitskany, Bessarabia, Russia	Kitskany, Moldavian SSR	Chiţcani, Moldova	46°47'N 29°36'E
Kodayésht	Codăeşti, Romania	Codăeşti, Romania	Codăeşti, Romania	46°52'N 27°45'E
Kódeme	Kodyma, Podolia, Russia	Kodyma, Ukrainian SSR	Kodyma, Ukraine	48°06'N 29°07'E
Kópenke	Kopanka, Bessarabia, Russia	Kopanka, Moldavian SSR	Copanca, Moldova	46°43'N 29°37'E
Kovishón (Kaushán)	Kavushan, Bessarabia, Russia	Kaushany, Moldavian SSR	Căuşeni, Moldova	46°39'N 29°25'E
Kózelets	Kozelets, Chernigov, Russia	Kozelets, Ukrainian SSR	Kozelets, Ukraine	50°55'N 31°07'E

8 Khotin was called Khetin (accent on the last syllable) in Yiddish.

Kozlov	Kozlovo, Kherson, Russia	Nechayannoye, Ukrainian SSR	Nechayannoye (aka Nechayne), Ukraine	46°57'N 31°33'E
Libavitsh[9]	Lubavich, Mogilev, Russia	Lyubavici, Belorussian SSR	Lyubavichi, Russia	54°11'N 31°43'E
Linoye	Glinoye, Kherson, Russia	Glinoye, Moldavian SSR	Hlinaia, Moldova	46°39'N 29°48'E
Litin	Litin, Podolia, Russia	Litin, Ukrainian SSR	Lityn, Ukraine	49°20'N 28°04'E
Lubavitch: see Libavitsh				
Lyadi (accent on last syllable)	Lyady, Mogilev, Russia	Lyady, Byelorussian SRR	Lyady, Belarus	54°36'N 31°10'E
Lyeve, Romania[10]	Leovo, Bessarabia, Russia	Leovo, Moldavian SSR	Leova, Moldova	46°29'N 28°15'E
Mayak	Mayak, Bessarabia, Russia	Mayak, Moldavian SSR	Maiac, Moldova	47°15'N 29°24'E
Melitopol	Melitopol, Taurida, Russia	Melitopol, Ukrainian SSR	Melitopol, Ukraine	46°50'N 35°22'E
Mogilev: see Molev				
Molayésht	Molayésht, Bessarabia, Russia	Maloyeshty, Moldavian SSR	Mălăieşti, Moldova	47°05'N 29°08'E
Molev (Groys Molev) ("l" is palatalized)	Mogilev, Mogilev, Russia	Mogilev, Belorussian SSR	Mahileu, Belarus	53°55'N 30°20'E
Nikolayev	Nikolayev, Kherson, Russia	Nikolayev, Ukrainian SSR	Mykolayiv, Ukraine	46°58'N 32°00'E
Odessa: see Adés				

9 Regarding the pronciation of Lubavitch as Libavitsh, see chapter 15, p. 241, footnote 15.

10 In 1856, part of southern Bessarabia (including Lyeve) was ceded by the Russian Empire back to the Principality of Moldavia, which in 1862 became the Principality of Romania. In 1878, this area was transferred back to Tsarist Russia.

Olt-Dubesár[11]	Staryye Dubossary, Kherson, Russia	Staryye Dubossary, Moldavian SSR	Dubăsarii Vechi, Moldova	47°08'N 29°12'E
Olt-Konstantin[12]	Starokonstantinov, Volhynia, Russia	Starokonstantinov, Ukrainian SSR	Starokostyantyniv, Ukraine	49°45'N 27°13'E
Orshe	Orsha, Mogilev, Russia	Orsha, Byelorussian SSR	Orsha, Belarus	54°31'N 30°24'E
Perekop	Perekop, Taurida, Russia	Perekop, Ukrainian SSR	Perekop, Crimea	46°10'N 33°42'E
Peresetshine	Peresechina, Bessarabia, Russia	Peresechina, Moldavian SSR	Peresecina, Moldova	47°15'N 28°46'E
Perkón	Parkany, Bessarabia, Russia	Parkany, Moldavian SSR	Porcani, Moldova	46°51'N 29°31'E
Petótsk	Pototskavo, Kherson, Russia	Severinovka, Ukrainian SSR	Severynivka, Ukraine	46°50'N 30°35'E
Petrokva: see Petrovke				
Petrovke	Petrovka, Bessarabia, Russia	Petrovka, Moldavian SSR	Petrovca, Moldova	46°59'N 29°05'E
Plosk	Plosk, Kherson, Russia	Ploskoye (or Bolshoye Ploskoye), Ukrainian SSR	Velykoploske, Ukraine	47°01' N 29°40' E
Rizhin (accent on the last syllable)	Ruzhyn, Kiev, Russia	Ruzhyn, Ukrainian SSR	Ruzhyn, Ukraine	49°43'N 29°14'E
Rómanóvke	Romanovka (aka Romanenko), Bessarabia, Russia	Besarabeaska, Moldavian SSR[13]	Basarabeasca, Moldova	46°20'N 29°01'E
Rozdelnye	Rozdilna, Kherson, Russia	Rozdilna, Ukrainian SSR	Rozdilna, Ukraine	46°51'N 30°05'E

11 *Olt* is a dialectal form for the Yiddish *alt*, meaning "old."

12 See the previous footnote.

13 Romanovka's name was changed to Besarabeaska in 1956.

Sadigór	Sadagora, Bukovina, Austria-Hungary	Sadgora, Ukrainian SSR	Sadhora,[14] Ukraine	48°21’N 25°58’E
Savrán (“n” is palatalized)	Savran, Podolia, Russia	Savran, Ukrainian SSR	Savran, Ukraine	48°08’N 30°05’E
Selts[15]	Selts, Kherson, Russia	Limanskoye, Ukrainian SSR	Limanske, Ukraine	46°67’N 29°97’E
Shishken	Shishkina, Kherson, Russia	Rossiyanovka, Ukrainian SSR	Rosiyanivka, Ukraine	47°14’N 29°42’E
Shklov	Shklov, Mogilev, Russia	Shklov, Byelorussain SSR	Sklou, Belarus	54°13’N 30°18’E
Shtefenésht	Ştefăneşti, Romania	Ştefăneşti, Romania	Ştefăneşti, Romania	47°48’N 27°12’E
Shvarts-Time[16]	Belaya Tserkov, Kiev, Ukraine	Belaya Tserkov, Ukrainian SSR	Bila Tserkva, Ukraine	49°47’N 30°07’E
Simferopol	Simferopol, Taurida, Russia	Simferopol, Ukrainian SSR	Simferopol, Crimea	44°57’ N 34°06’ E
Skulén	Skulyany, Bessarabia, Russia	Skulyany, Moldavian SSR	Sculeni, Moldova	47°19’N 27°38’E
Skvere (Skver)	Skvira, Kiev, Russia	Skvira, Ukrainian SSR	Skvyra, Ukraine	49°44’N 29°40’E
Slobodze	Slobodzeya, Bessarabia, Russia	Slobodzeya, Moldavian SSR	Slobozia, Moldova	46°44’N 29°41’E
Sovitskis[17]				
Speye	Speya, Kherson, Russia	Speya, Moldavian SSR	Speia, Moldova	47°00’N 29°18’E

14 Sadhora is now part of the city of Chernivtsi, Ukraine.

15 The author evidently mistakenly refers to it as Silts in chapter 1, p. 94.

16 Regarding the name Shvarts-Time, see chapter 16, p. 257, footnote 49.

17 Sovitskis is probably referring to either one of two places: Novosavitskaya, Moldova (now Novosavițcaia) which is 10.5 miles ESE of Tiraspol; or Novo-Savitskoye, Ukraine (now Novosavycke) which is 10.7 miles NNE of Tiraspol.

Talmóz	Talmaz, Bessarabia, Russia	Talmaz, Moldavian SSR	Talmaza, Moldova	46°38'N 29°40'E
Tashlik (accent on last syllable)	Tashlyk, Kherson, Russia	Tashlyk, Moldavian SSR	Taşlîc, Moldova	47°04'N 29°24'E
Teplik	Teplik, Podolia, Russia	Teplik, Ukrainian SSR	Teplyk, Ukraine	48°40'N 29°44'E
Ternifke	Ternovka, Kherson, Ukraine	Ternovka, Moldavian SSR	Tirnauca, Moldova	46°49'N 29°33'E
Tiraspol[18]	Tiraspol, Kherson, Russia	Tiraspol, Moldavian SSR	Tiraspol, Moldova	46°50'N 29°39'E
Tolne	Talnoe, Kiev, Russia	Talnoye, Ukrainian SSR	Talne, Ukraine	48°53'N 30°42'E
Topolefke	Topolevka, Podolia, Russia	Topolevka, Ukrainian SSR	Topolivka, Ukraine	48°45' N 29°45' E
Tshetshelnik	Chechelnik, Podolia, Russia	Chechelnik, Ukrainian SSR	Chechelnyk, Ukraine	48°13'N 29°22'E
Tshimishlye	Chimishliya, Bessarabia, Russia	Chimishliya, Moldavian SSR	Cimişlia, Moldova	46°31'N 28°47'E
Tshobritsh	Chobruchi, Bessarabia, Russia	Chobruchi, Moldavian SSR	Cioburciu, Moldova	46°41'N 29°45'E
Tshornitse	Chornitsa (aka Chernitsa), Kherson, Russia	Gyrtop (aka Gartop), Moldavian SSR	Hirtop, Moldova	47°14'N 29°22'E
Tumanov	Tumanovo, Kherson, Russia	Pavlovka, Ukrainian SSR	Pavlivka, Ukraine	47°15'N 29°34'E
Uman: see Imen				
Untsésht	Untseshty, Bessarabia, Russia	Untseshty, Moldavian SSR	Unţeşti, Moldova	47°15'N 27°49'E
Vasluy	Vaslui, Romania	Vaslui, Romania	Vaslui, Romania	46°38'N 27°44'E
Vinitse	Vinnitsa, Podolia, Ukraine	Vinnitsa, Ukrainian SSR	Vinnytsya, Ukraine	49°14'N 28°29'E

18 The authentic Yiddish name of Tiraspol is Treshpil (with a palatalized "l").

Vinnitsa: see Vinitse				
Volontirovke	Volontirovka, Bessarabia, Russia	Volontirovka, Moldavian SSR	Volontiri, Moldova	46°25'N 29°36'E
Yekaterinoslav	Yekaterinoslav, Yekaterinoslav, Russia	Dnepropetrovsk, Ukrainian SSR	Dnipro,[19] Ukraine	48°27'N 34°59'E
Yevpatoriya[20]	Yevpatoriya, Taurida, Russia	Yevpatoriya, Ukrainian SSR	Yevpatoriya, Crimea	45°12'N 33°21'E
Yos (Yas)	Iaşi,[21] Romania	Iaşi, Romania	Iaşi, Romania	47°10'N 27°36'E
Yuzeve: see Yuzevke				
Yuzevke (Yuzeve)	Yuzovka (aka Yuzovo), Yekaterinoslav, Russia	Donetsk,[22] Ukrainian SSR	Donetsk, Ukraine	48°00'N 37°48'E
Zakhárovka: see Zarivke				
Zarivke (Zarifke)	Zakhárovka, Kherson, Russia	Frunzovka, Ukrainian SSR	Zakharivke, Ukraine	47°20'N 29°45'E

19 In 2016, the name was changed from Dnipropetrovsk to Dnipro.

20 The author refers to it as Yevpatorye-Kozlov, meaning that it was called Yevpatoriya and also Kozlov, a Russified version of its Crimean Tartar name, Kezlev. Though the author writes Yevpatorye, this slight variation does not indicate an authentic Yiddish name.

21 Iaşi is often referred to as Iassy or Jassy.

22 Yuzevke was called Stalino from 1924 until 1961, when it was renamed Donetsk.

Indexes of Subjects, Places, and Names for Volumes 1 and 2

Subjects

Places

Names

www.ingramcontent.com/pod-product-compliance
Lightning Source LLC
LaVergne TN
LVHW020501100826
845148LV00003B/686

* 9 7 9 8 8 8 7 1 9 6 1 3 8 *